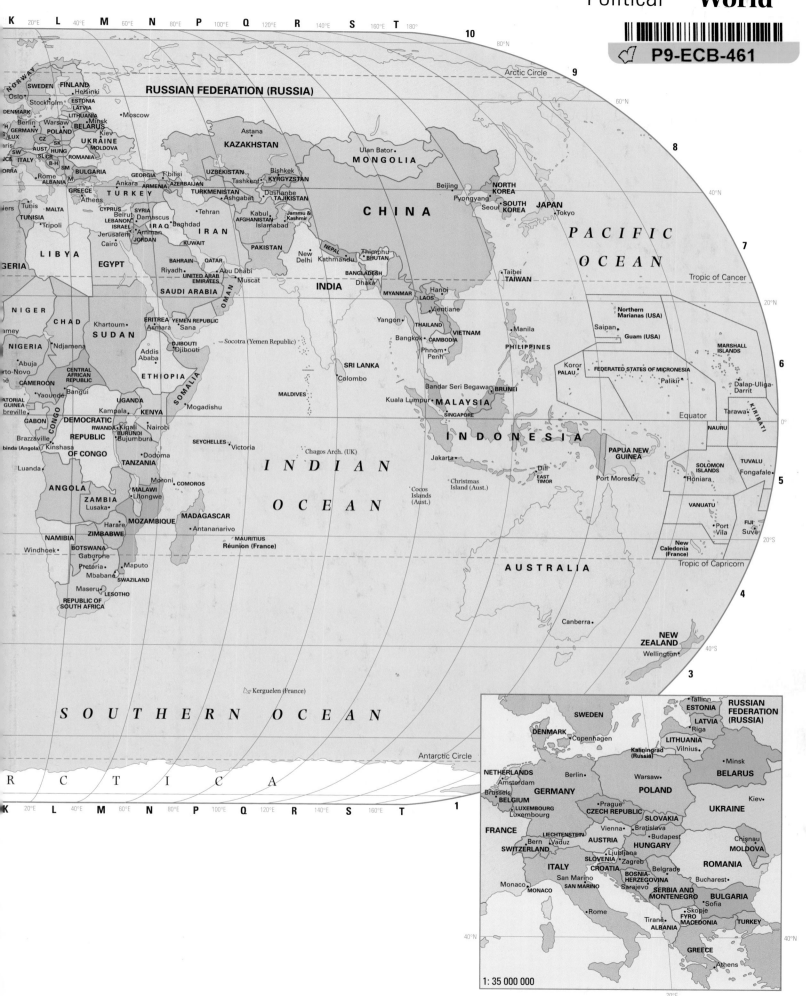

Political **World**

P9-ECB-461

1: 35 000 000

© Oxford University Press   Eckert IV Projection

February 22, 2004.

CANADIAN OXFORD
World Atlas

FIFTH EDITION

Quentin H. Stanford
GENERAL EDITOR

OXFORD
UNIVERSITY PRESS

2 Contents

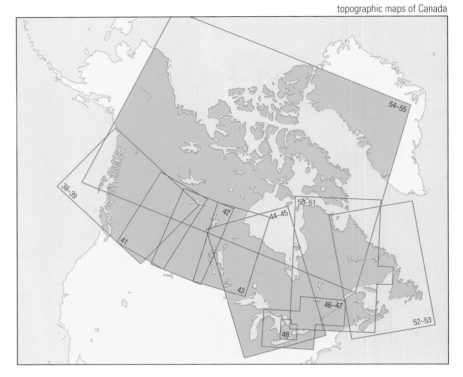
topographic maps of Canada

topographic maps of North America

topographic map of South America

© Oxford University Press

Contents 3

topographic maps of Europe

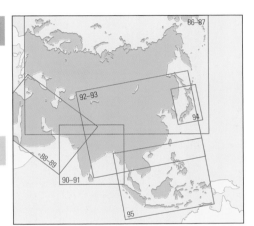
topographic maps of Asia

topographic map of Africa

topographic map of Oceania

topographic maps of the Oceans

Understanding topographic maps

Topographic maps show the main features of the physical landscape as well as settlements, communications, and boundaries. Background colours show the height of the land.

There are small differences in the symbols and colours used for the maps of Canada and those for the rest of the World.

Canadian maps

boundaries
- ━━━━ international
- ──── province/territory
- ----- regional municipality/ district/county
- ──── national/provincial park/sanctuary

communications
- ═══ expressway/other multilane highway
- ──── other highway
- ----- winter road
- ──── railway
- ┼┼┼┼ canal
- ----- ferry
- ⊕ major airport
- ✈ other airport

settlements
- ⬡ built-up area
- ■ over 1 million inhabitants
- ● more than 100 000 inhabitants
- • smaller urban places

physical features
- ～ river, lake
- ～～ marsh
- ⸙⸙ ice cap

Non-Canadian maps

boundaries
- ━━━━ international
- - - - disputed
- ──── internal

communications
- ═══ expressway
- ──── major road
- ──── railway
- - - - canal
- ✈ major airport

settlements
- ⬡ built-up area
- ■ over 1 million inhabitants
- ● more than 100 000 inhabitants
- • smaller cities

physical features
- ～ river, lake
- --- seasonal river
- ～ seasonal lake
- ～～ marsh
- ⬭ salt lake
- ⸙ salt pan
- ⸙ ice cap
- ⸙⸙ sand dunes

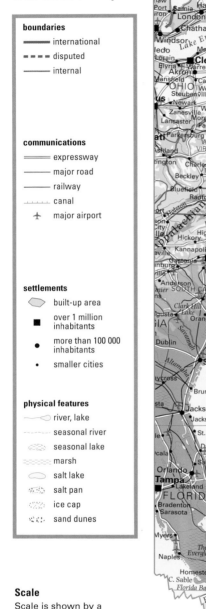

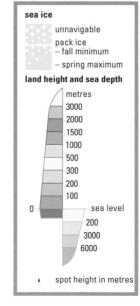

sea ice
- unnavigable
- pack ice – fall minimum
- – spring maximum

land height and sea depth

metres
- 3000
- 2000
- 1500
- 1000
- 500
- 300
- 200
- 100
- 0 — sea level
- 200
- 3000
- 6000

▲ spot height in metres

Scale

Scale is shown by a representative fraction and a scale line.

Scale 1: 5 000 000

0   50   100   150   200   250 km

Sea ice

White stipple patterns over the sea colour show the seasonal extent of sea ice.

Land height and sea depth

Colours on topographic maps refer only to the height of the land or the depth of the sea. They do not give information about land use or other aspects of the environment.

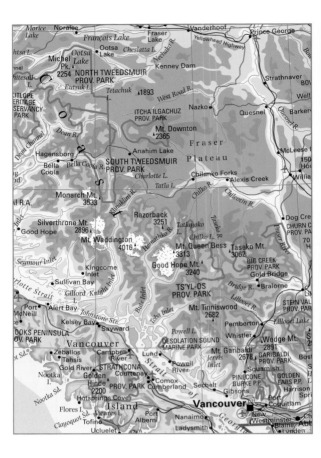

Place names

Anglicised spellings are used. Former names (where places have recently changed their names), and alternative spellings are shown in brackets.

This atlas has been designed for English speaking readers and so all places have been named using the Roman alphabet.

Type style

Contrasting type styles are used to show the difference between physical features, settlements, and administrative areas.

Physical features are separated into two categories, land and water. Land features are shown as roman type:

e.g.   { Coast Mountains }

Water features are shown in italics:

e.g.   { *Hudson Bay (Baie d'Hudson)* }

Peaks are shown in condensed type:

e.g.   { Mt. Logan 5951 }

Settlement names are shown in upper and lower case:

e.g.   { Hamilton }

Administrative areas are shown in capital letters:

e.g.   { ONTARIO }

The importance of places is shown by the size of the type and whether the type face is bold or medium:

e.g.   { **Ottawa** }   { Calgary }   { Louisbourg }

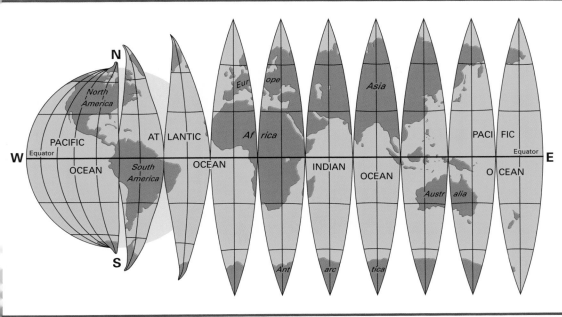

The most accurate way of looking at the earth's land and sea areas is to use a globe. For obvious reasons maps are more convenient to use than globes. One method of changing the surface of the globe into a map is to unpeel strips or gores from the globe's surface, but such a method has obvious drawbacks. Since it is impossible to flatten the curved surface of the earth without stretching or cutting part of it, it is necessary to employ other methods in order to produce an orderly system of parallels and meridians on which a map can be drawn. Such systems are referred to as **map projections**.

There are two main types of projections: **equal area projections**, where the area of any territory is shown in correct size proportion to other areas, and **conformal projections**, where the emphasis is on showing shape correctly. No map can be both equal area and conformal, though some projections are designed to minimize distortions in both area and shape.

The **Oblique Aitoff projection** is equal area. The arrangement of the land masses allows a good view of routes in the northern hemisphere. The position of North America and Asia on either side of the Arctic is shown clearly.

——— major air routes

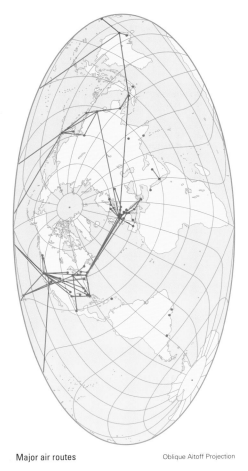

Major air routes   Oblique Aitoff Projection

Mercator's projection is a conformal projection and was initially designed (1569) to be used for navigation. Any straight line on the map is a line of constant compass bearing. Straight lines are not the shortest routes, however. Shape is accurate on a Mercator projection but the size of the land masses is distorted. Land is shown larger the further away it is from the equator. (For example, Alaska is shown four times larger than its actual size).

- - - - - line of constant compass bearing
——— shortest route

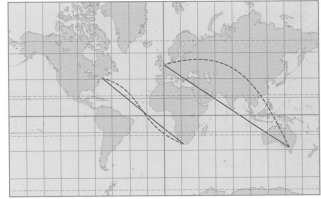

Navigation chart   Mercator's Projection

Eckert IV projection is the fourth map projection designed by the German cartographer Max Eckert (1868–1938). It is an equal area projection, showing the true area of places in relation to each other. This projection is often used in this atlas, the maps permitting fair comparisons to be made between areas of the world.

 tropical forest

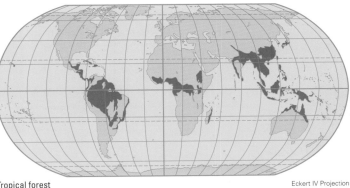

Tropical forest   Eckert IV Projection

Gall's projection compromises between equal area and conformal. A modified version is sometimes used in this atlas as a general world map. This map shows plate boundaries.

——— plate boundaries

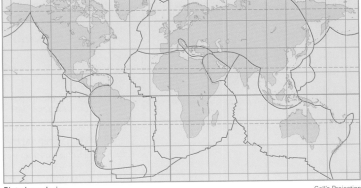

Plate boundaries   Gall's Projection

6 Latitude, longitude, and scale

The Earth is a small, blue planet. Seen from space it has no right way up.

Latitude

Parallels of latitude are concentric circles that diminish in diameter from the Equator to the Poles. They are used to determine locations either north or south in relation to the Equator. North of the Equator parallels are designated north (N), while those south of the Equator are labelled south (S). The Equator is at latitude 0°. The Poles are at latitudes 90°N and 90°S.

Longitude

Meridians of longitude pass through both Poles intersecting all parallels of latitude at right angles. The meridian through Greenwich, England was chosen in 1884 as the Prime Meridian and given the value 0°.

Meridians determine locations east (E) or west (W) of the Prime Meridian. The 180° meridian of longitude was designated the International Date Line and has a special role in the operation of Standard Time.

The Equator divides the Earth into halves: the Northern Hemisphere and the Southern Hemisphere. The Prime Meridian and the 180° meridian together also divide the Earth into halves: the Western Hemisphere and the Eastern Hemisphere.

The Tropics of Cancer (23°26'N) and Capricorn (23°26'S) are parallels of latitude that represent the northern and southern limits of the overhead sun. The Arctic (66°33'N) and Antarctic Circles (66°33'S) are also parallels of latitude. The sun is not visible poleward of these parallels during their respective winter solstices.

An imaginary grid is used to pinpoint the position of any place on Earth.

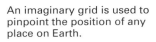

The grid consists of two sets of lines. Those running east and west are called parallels of latitude and those extending north and south are called meridians of longitude. Both are measured in degrees.

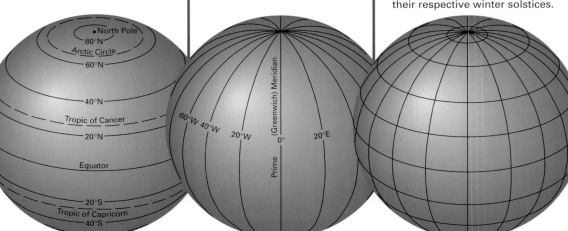

When used together, lines of latitude and longitude form a grid. The position of places on the surface of the Earth can be located accurately using this grid.

To locate places really accurately, each degree of latitude and longitude can be divided into 60 minutes and each minute into 60 seconds. A location specified in degrees, minutes, and seconds (for example, 44° 25' 14" N, 80° 45' 36" W) will describe a location accurately to within a few metres.

Scale

Maps or globes are devices used to represent all or part of the surface of the Earth. Every map has a scale to indicate how much the area on the map has been reduced from its actual size on the Earth's surface. Thus the map scale indicates the proportion (or ratio) between a distance on a map and the corresponding distance on the Earth's surface.

Scale can be shown in three ways :

The scale statement	1 cm to 5 km	which means 1 centimetre on the map represents five kilometres on the Earth's surface.
The representative fraction (RF)	1: 500 000	which means 1 centimetre on the map represents 500 000 centimetres on the Earth's surface, or one of any unit of measurement represents 500 000 of the same units.

The linear scale  which is a measured line divided into units representing distances on the earth.

It is important to understand the **relationship between scale and area**. In this atlas Canada is shown mainly on maps that have a larger scale than the rest of the World.

For example:
All of northern Africa appears on page 100 at a scale of 1: 26 000 000, while British Columbia, on pages 38–39, has a scale of 1: 5 000 000. We know from the scale that the African map shows a greater area, but how much greater?

The table shows that as the scale doubles, the area it represents increases four times. Thus a square centimetre on the Africa map represents an area more than twenty-seven times larger than a square centimetre on the British Columbia map.

Scale	Scale statement	Area of 1 cm²
1: 10 000	1 cm to 0.1 km	0.01 km²
1: 20 000	1 cm to 0.2 km	0.04 km²
1: 100 000	1 cm to 1 km	1 km²
1: 200 000	1 cm to 2 km	4 km²
1: 5 000 000	1 cm to 50 km	2500 km²
1: 10 000 000	1 cm to 100 km	10 000 km²
1: 20 000 000	1 cm to 200 km	40 000 km²

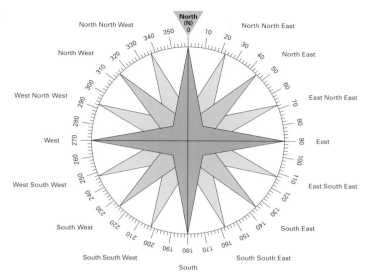

Direction

A direction can be expressed either in terms of north, east, south, and west and various intermediate positions as shown on the diagram of the compass rose, or in degrees as a bearing. Direction by bearing ranges from 0° (north) to 359° (one degree west of north).

The North Pole, where all meridians of longitude converge, is referred to as true or geographic north. Conversely, the South Pole is known as the true or geographic south. By convention, most maps are oriented so that true (geographic) north occurs toward the top of the map. Thus, when we refer to north and south on most maps, we are speaking of these poles.

There is also a magnetic North and South Pole. The north magnetic pole is presently located to the north of Ellef Ringnes Island in the Canadian Arctic *(see pages 10–11)* and is moving about 24 km a year in a north-easterly direction. When using a magnetic compass, the north arrow points to this pole.

In the atlas, the cardinal points (north, east, south, and west) can be determined from the parallels and meridians. Thus all parallels run north and south, and meridians east and west. Intermediate directions require the application of the compass rose or the use of bearings. Direction using bearings can be accomplished using a protractor.

Satellite imagery

Satellite images are found on a number of pages throughout this atlas. These images are taken by satellites orbiting the Earth at high altitudes. For example, most of the images in this atlas were produced by Landsat satellites which orbit the Earth 14.5 times each day at an altitude of approximately 900 km. As a satellite travels, it is continuously scanning an area 185 km wide. In order to be visible, objects on the Earth must be at least 30 m² in size.

Most cameras are sensors that operate only in the "visible" part of the electromagnetic spectrum and thus produce a record of what the eye can see. The images that are normally described as satellite images are produced by instruments that use a multi spectral scanning system to record reflected energy from different parts of the electromagnetic spectrum from microwaves, through infrared, and visible light to the near ultraviolet sections. The scanner sends the radiation received in specifically designated bands to a set of detectors on the satellite. The signal is digitized and then transmitted back to Earth. It is then transformed into images such as the ones shown in this atlas.

The various objects that make up the Earth's surface such as rocks, soil, vegetation, crops, and building materials such as concrete or asphalt absorb and reflect radiation differently (each has its own spectral signature) and so can be easily recognized on satellite images. Even within any surface category there are different spectral signatures; thus, one crop can be distinguished from another and different types of wetland can be recognized. Because these surfaces reflect one part of the electromagnetic spectrum better than others, the colours we see on the images are false colours. For example, green vegetation reflects better in the red than the blue-green, urban areas are blue-grey, and bare soil will show as black to green to white depending on its moisture, and organic content.

Satellite images can also be shown in true colour when false colour images are converted to produce realistic land surface colours. Most of the Canadian satellite images in this atlas are examples.

Satellite image of the area around Winnipeg, Manitoba.

0   15   30 km

Winnipeg

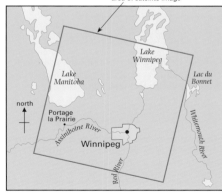

area of satellite image

north

Lake Winnipeg

Lake Manitoba

Lac du Bonnet

Portage la Prairie

Assiniboine River

Winnipeg

Red River

Whitemouth River

The number of uses that have been developed for satellite imagery is very great and beyond the scope of this brief description. Some of the non-military applications include: weather prediction, land-use planning, crop and forest inventories, changes in sea ice, surveillance of fishing fleets, and monitoring air pollution.
New uses are continually being found.

© Oxford University Press
LANDSAT data received by the Canada Centre for Remote Sensing.
Provided courtesy of RADARSAT International.

8 The Earth in Space

The Earth is part of the **solar system**.
This system consists of a group of planets
and moons that orbit the Sun.
The Solar System is part of the **galaxy** known as the **Milky Way**. This is a
huge group of more than 100 billion stars that orbits around a galactic
centre. Tens of billions of galaxies like the Milky Way make up the
Universe, which is so vast that its outer limits are unknown.

All parts of the Universe are in **constant motion**.
The Milky Way rushes through space at a speed of 600 km/s,
or 2 160 000 km/h. Our Sun is actually a medium-sized star.
It moves around a common galactic centre at a speed of
800 000 km/h. The Earth revolves around the Sun at 106 300 km/h.

Light travels at 299 460 km/s or 10 trillion kilometres in one year.
This distance is known as a light year. It takes 8 min 17 s for light
to travel from the Sun to the Earth, and about 5.5 h for light to travel from
the Sun to the farthest extent of our Solar System. The closest star to the
Earth, Proxima Centauri, is 4.22 light years away. The Milky Way is
approximately 100 000 light years in diameter. The farthest known galaxy
from the Earth, called Quasar PKS 2000-330, is 15 billion light years away.

Spiral Galaxy NGC 7742
An image of the spiral galaxy NGC 7742
taken from the Hubble Space Telescope.

Pluto	**Neptune**	**Uranus**	**Saturn**	**Jupiter**	**Mars**	**Earth**	**Venus**	**Mercury**	
mean distance from the Sun, in million km									
5 900	4 497	2 870	1 427	778	228	150	108	58	
time to orbit the Sun, in days									
90 502	60 275	30 660	10 767	4 343	687	365	225	88	
diameter, in km									
3 000	48 400	52 000	120 000	142 800	6 794	12 756	12 104	4 878	
period of rotation, in days									
6.38	0.67	0.45	0.42	0.41	1.02	0.99	243.0	58.67	

Human use of Earth space

Satellites can be placed in
different orbits around the Earth.
For each satellite purpose
there is a preferred orbit.

low orbits: at 300 km from the Earth, these
are the easiest to reach. Space Shuttle and
the Mir Space Station use these orbits.

polar orbits: these cover the whole globe as it turns on
its axis, and are the chosen orbits for survey satellites.

elliptical or eccentric orbits: often used for satellites
designed to study particular areas of the Earth and
needing to spend long periods over a chosen area.

geostationary orbits: at 35 880 km above the Equator,
these are the highest orbits. They enable satellites to
view a large area of the Earth. Each orbit takes 24 h, the
same time that it takes the Earth to rotate on its axis.
So they remain in the same position relative to the Earth.
Communications and weather satellites use these orbits.

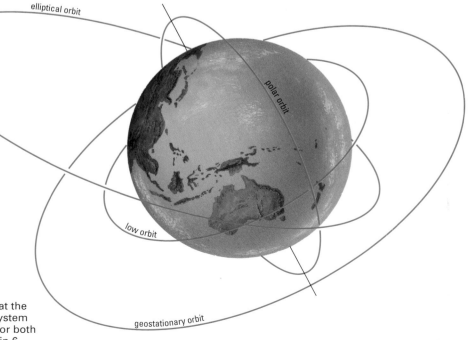

The NAVSTAR Global Positioning System (GPS) is managed at the
Space and Missile Centre, Los Angeles Air Force Base. The system
provides highly accurate navigation and timing information for both
civilian and military users. It consists of 24 satellites orbiting in 6
circular orbits at an altitude of 11 000 nautical miles.

The diagram shows how the Earth **revolves** around the Sun every 365.25 days, while **rotating** on a **tilted axis** of 23.5° every 24h. The Earth's revolution on its tilted axis causes the four seasons, while its rotation causes day and night. The seasons on this diagram apply to the Northern Hemisphere.

The Earth completes one revolution of the Sun every 365.25 days. It follows an elliptical, or slightly egg-shaped, orbit. Thus the distance between the Earth and the Sun varies, from a maximum of 152 million kilometres on July 4th to a minimum of 147 million kilometres on January 3rd. However, this variation has little effect on temperatures on Earth.

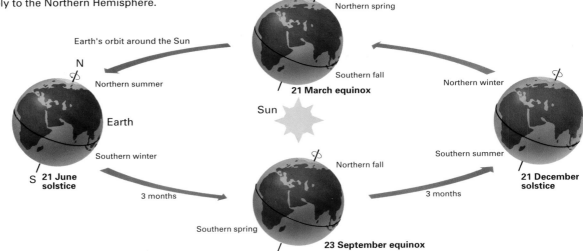

The diagram of the Earth in June and December shows the variations in the length of day and night. In June, the Northern Hemisphere is tilted at 23.5° towards the Sun, as a result it receives more hours of sunshine. The Sun's rays strike the Earth's atmosphere more directly than at other times of the year, resulting in summer, with its warm temperatures.

Six months later the Earth has rotated halfway around the Sun. Now the Southern Hemisphere is tilted at 23.5° towards the Sun. Thus in December it is summer in the Southern Hemisphere, while it is winter in the Northern Hemisphere.

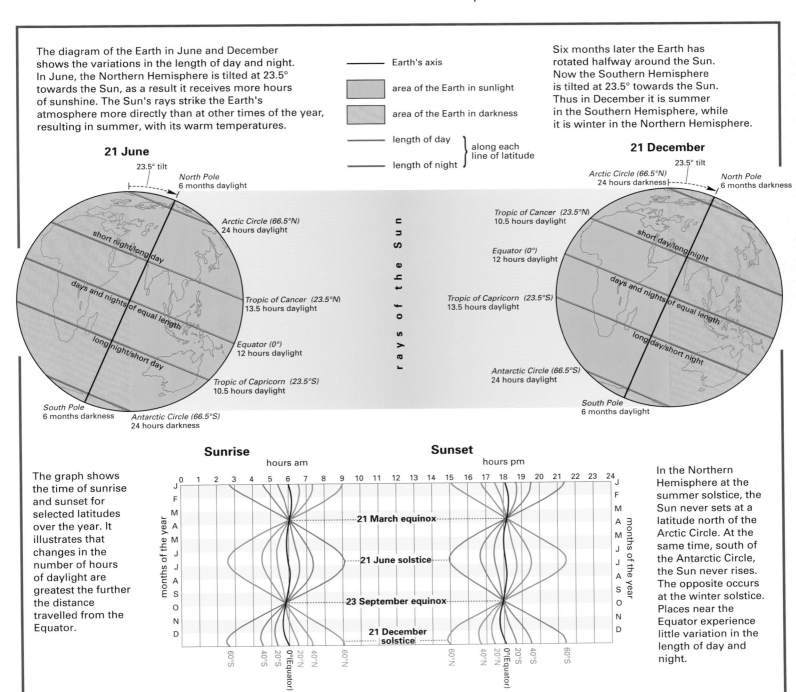

The graph shows the time of sunrise and sunset for selected latitudes over the year. It illustrates that changes in the number of hours of daylight are greatest the further the distance travelled from the Equator.

In the Northern Hemisphere at the summer solstice, the Sun never sets at a latitude north of the Arctic Circle. At the same time, south of the Antarctic Circle, the Sun never rises. The opposite occurs at the winter solstice. Places near the Equator experience little variation in the length of day and night.

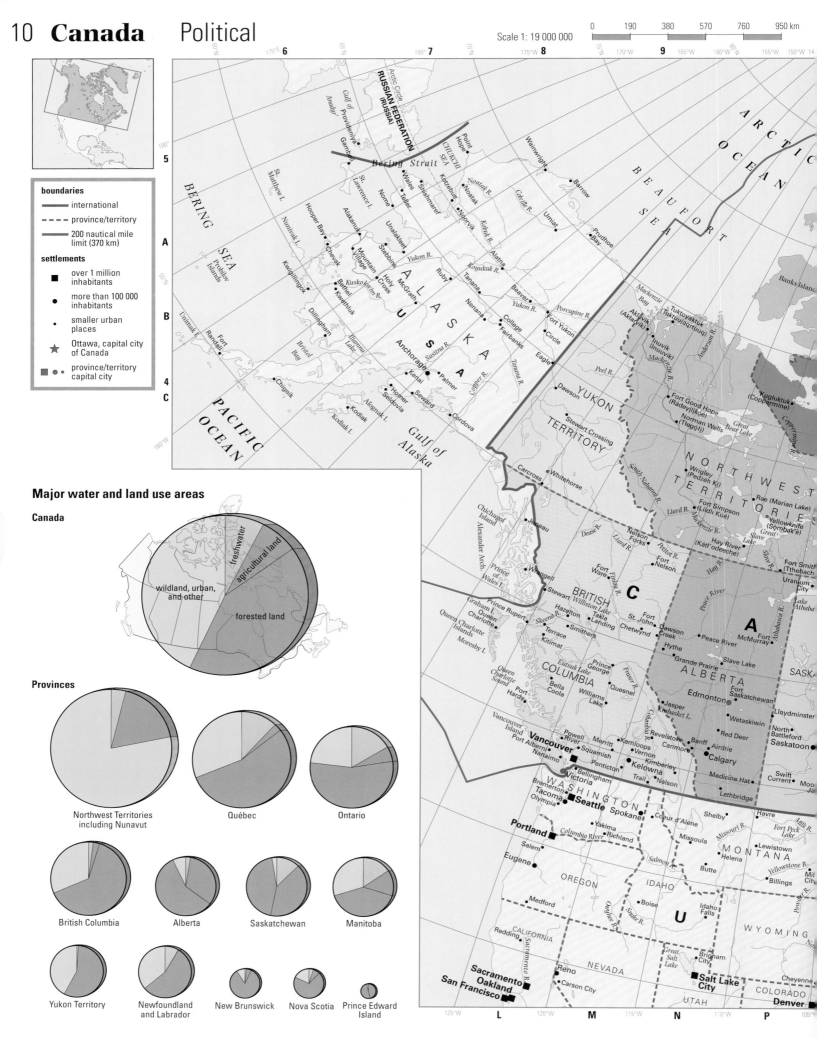

Scale 1: 19 000 000

0 190 380 570 760 950 km

boundaries
— international
--- province/territory
— 200 nautical mile limit (370 km)

settlements
■ over 1 million inhabitants
● more than 100 000 inhabitants
· smaller urban places
★ Ottawa, capital city of Canada
■·● province/territory capital city

Major water and land use areas

Canada

freshwater
agricultural land
wildland, urban, and other
forested land

Provinces

Northwest Territories including Nunavut

Québec

Ontario

British Columbia

Alberta

Saskatchewan

Manitoba

Yukon Territory

Newfoundland and Labrador

New Brunswick

Nova Scotia

Prince Edward Island

Zenithal Equidistant Projection   © Oxford University Press

Canada
Land area: 9 093 507km²
Total area: 9 984 670km²

Census Population

1871	3 689 257
1891	4 833 239
1911	7 206 643
1931	10 376 786
1951	14 009 429
1961	18 238 247
1971	21 568 310
1981	24 343 181
1991	27 296 859
2001	30 007 094
Rural	20.3%
Urban	79.7%

Census Metropolitan Areas, 2001 (over 500 000)

Toronto	4 682 897
Montréal	3 426 350
Vancouver	1 986 965
Ottawa-Hull	1 063 664
Edmonton	937 845
Calgary	951 395
Québec	682 757
Winnipeg	671 274
Hamilton	662 401

Gross Domestic Product
(2001 $939.1)

goods producing	%
Agriculture	1.4
Forestry	0.7
Fishing & Trapping	0.1
Mining	3.9
Manufacturing	17.3
Construction	5.3
other utilities	2.9

service producing	%
Wholesale & Retail	11.5
Transport	4.6
Information	4.7
Finance, Insurance, & Real Estate	19.5
Other services	22.5
Public administration	5.6

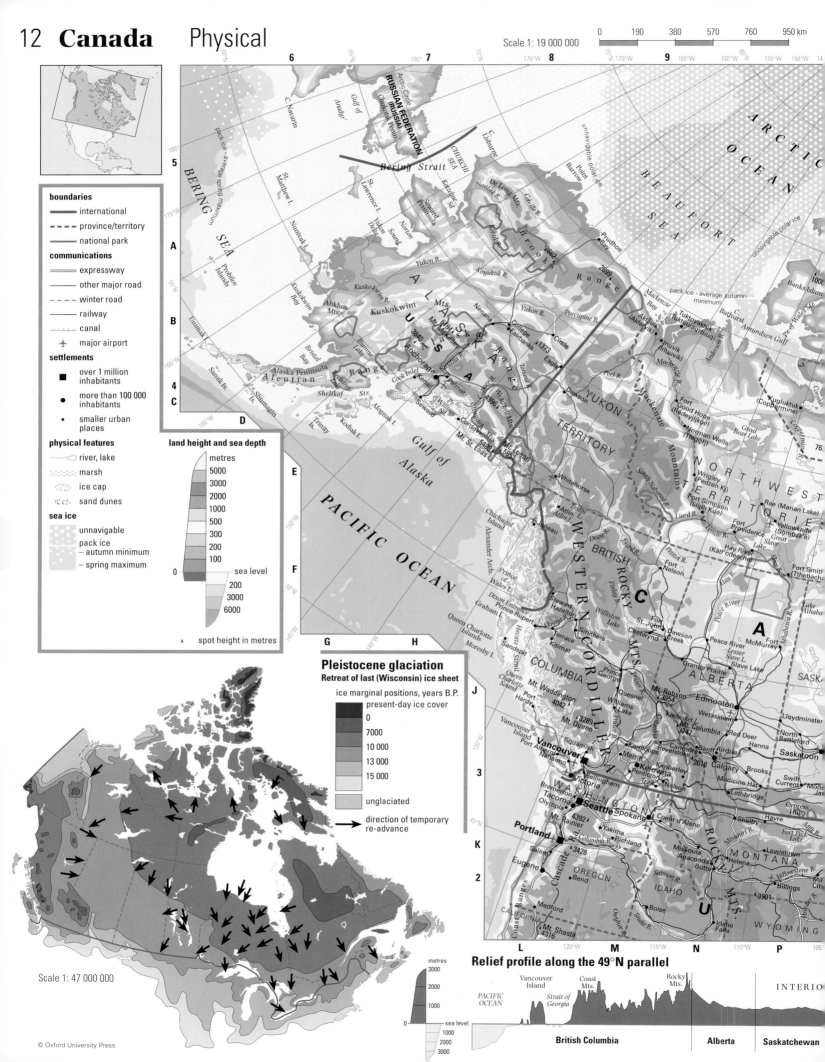

Distance chart official highway distances, in kilometres

	Calgary	Charlottetown	Edmonton	Fredericton	Halifax	Montréal	Ottawa	Québec	Regina	St. John's	Saskatoon	Thunder Bay	Toronto	Vancouver	Victoria	Whitehorse	Winnipeg	Yellowknife	
	•	4917	299	4558	5042	3743	3553	4014	764	6183	620	2050	3434	1057	1123	2385	1336	1811	Calgary
		•	4949	359	232	1184	1374	945	4163	1294	4421	2878	1724	5985	6051	7034	3592	6460	Charlottetown
			•	4598	5082	3764	3574	4035	785	6212	528	2071	3455	1244	1310	2086	1357	1511	Edmonton
				•	346	834	1024	586	3813	1622	4070	2527	1373	5634	5700	6684	3241	6109	Fredericton
					•	1318	1508	912	4297	1349	4554	3011	1857	6119	6185	7168	3726	6593	Halifax
						•	190	270	2979	2448	3236	1693	539	4801	4867	5850	2408	5275	Montréal
							•	460	2789	2638	3046	1503	399	4611	4677	5660	2218	5086	Ottawa
								•	3249	2208	3507	1963	810	5071	5137	6120	2678	5546	Québec
									•	5427	257	1286	2670	1822	1888	2871	571	2297	Regina
										•	5684	4141	2987	7248	7314	8298	4855	7723	St. John's
											•	1543	2927	1677	1743	2614	829	2039	Saskatoon
												•	1384	3108	3174	4157	715	3582	Thunder Bay
													•	4492	4558	5528	2099	4966	Toronto
														•	66	2697	2232	2411	Vancouver
															•	2763	2298	2477	Victoria
																•	3524	2704	Whitehorse
																	•	2868	Winnipeg
																		•	Yellowknife

horizontal scale 1 : 19 000 000

vertical exaggeration (land) x 98

vertical exaggeration (sea) x 49

© Oxford University Press

Zenithal Equidistant Projection

Scale 1 : 24 000 000

0	240	480	720 km

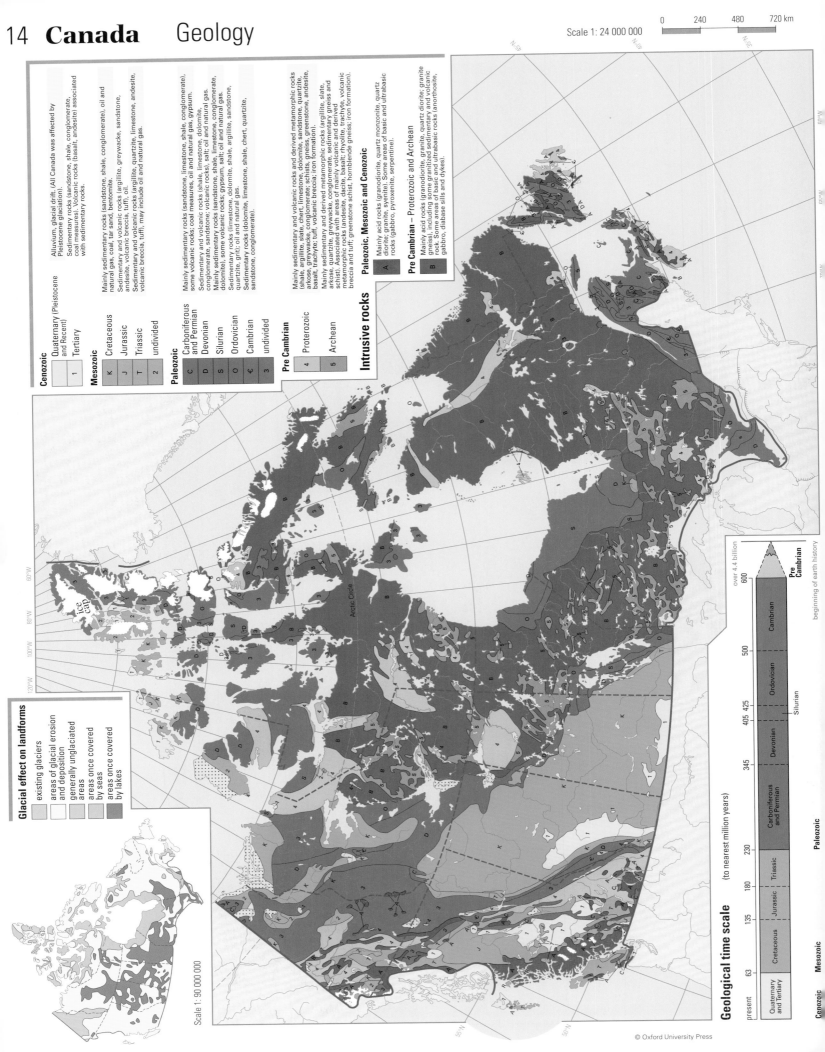

Glacial effect on landforms

- existing glaciers
- areas of glacial erosion and deposition
- generally unglaciated areas
- areas once covered by seas
- areas once covered by lakes

Scale 1 : 90 000 000

Cenozoic

	Quaternary (Pleistocene and Recent)	Alluvium, glacial drift. (All Canada was affected by Pleistocene glaciation).
1	Tertiary	Sedimentary rocks (sandstone, shale, conglomerate, coal measures). Volcanic rocks (basalt, andesite) associated with sedimentary rocks.

Mesozoic

K	Cretaceous	Mainly sedimentary rocks (sandstone, shale, conglomerate), oil and natural gas, coal, tar sand, bentomite.
J	Jurassic	Sedimentary and volcanic rocks (argillite, greywacke, sandstone, andesite, volcanic breccia, tuff), oil.
T	Triassic	Sedimentary and volcanic rocks (argillite, quartzite, limestone, andesite, volcanic breccia, tuff), may include oil and natural gas.
2	undivided	

Paleozoic

C	Carboniferous and Permian	Mainly sedimentary rocks (sandstone, limestone, shale, conglomerate), some volcanic rocks; coal measures, oil and natural gas, gypsum.
D	Devonian	Sedimentary and volcanic rocks (shale, limestone, dolomite, conglomerate, sandstone); volcanic rocks), salt; oil and natural gas.
S	Silurian	Mainly sedimentary rocks (sandstone, shale, limestone, conglomerate, dolomite), some volcanic rocks; gypsum, salt; oil and natural gas.
O	Ordovician	Sedimentary rocks (limestone, dolomite, shale, argillite, sandstone, quartzite, grit); oil and natural gas.
Є	Cambrian	Sedimentary rocks (dolomite, limestone, shale, chert, quartzite, sandstone, conglomerate).
3	undivided	

Pre Cambrian

4	Proterozoic	Mainly sedimentary and volcanic rocks and derived metamorphic rocks (shale, argillite, slate, chert, limestone, dolomite, sandstone, quartzite, arkose, greywacke, conglomerate; schists, gneiss, greenstone, andesite, basalt, trachyte; tuff, volcanic breccia; iron formation).
5	Archean	Mainly sedimentary and derived metamorphic rocks (argillite, slate, arkose, quartzite, greywacke, conglomerate, sedimentary gneiss and schist). Associated with areas of mainly volcanic, volcanic and derived metamorphic rocks (andesite, dacite, basalt; rhyolite, trachyte, volcanic breccia and tuff; greenstone schist, hornblende gneiss; iron formation).

Intrusive rocks

Paleozoic, Mesozoic and Cenozoic

A	Mainly acid rocks (granodiorite, granite, quartz monzonite, quartz diorite; granite, syenite). Some areas of basic and ultrabasic rocks (gabbro, pyroxenite, serpentine).

Pre Cambrian — Proterozoic and Archean

B	Mainly acid rocks (granodiorite, granite, quartz diorite; granite gneiss), including some granitized sedimentary and volcanic rock. Some areas of basic and ultrabasic rocks (anorthosite, gabbro, diabase sills and dykes).

Geological time scale

(to nearest million years)

present	63	135	180	230	345	405	425	500	600	over 4.4 billion

Quaternary and Tertiary	Cretaceous	Jurassic	Triassic	Carboniferous and Permian	Devonian	Silurian	Ordovician	Cambrian	Pre Cambrian
Cenozoic	Mesozoic			Paleozoic					

beginning of earth history

© Oxford University Press

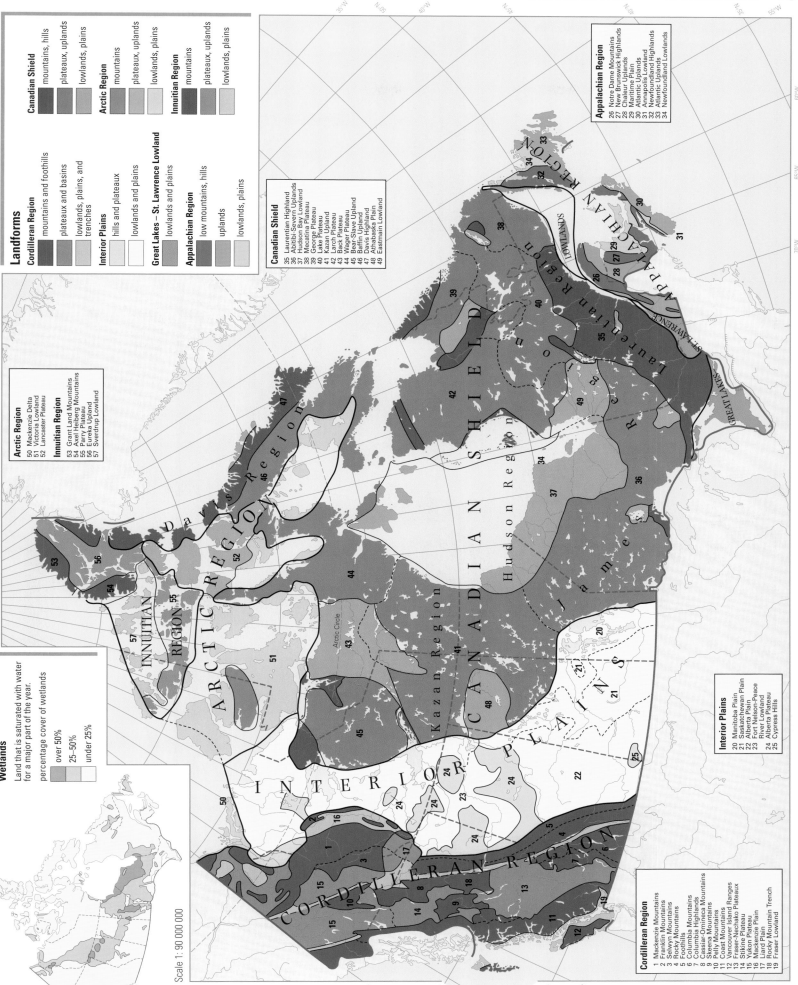

Landforms

Cordilleran Region
- mountains and foothills
- plateaux and basins
- lowlands, plains, and trenches

Interior Plains
- hills and plateaux
- lowlands and plains

Great Lakes – St. Lawrence Lowland
- lowlands and plains

Appalachian Region
- low mountains, hills
- uplands
- lowlands, plains

Canadian Shield
- mountains, hills
- plateaux, uplands
- lowlands, plains

Arctic Region
- mountains
- plateaux, uplands
- lowlands, plains

Innuitian Region
- mountains
- plateaux, uplands
- lowlands, plains

Canadian Shield
35 Laurentian Highland
36 Abitibi-Severn Uplands
37 Hudson Bay Lowland
38 Mecatina Plateau
39 George Plateau
40 Lake Plateau
41 Kazan Upland
42 Larch Plateau
43 Back Plateau
44 Wager Plateau
45 Bear-Slave Upland
46 Baffin Upland
47 Davis Highland
48 Athabaska Plain
49 Eastmain Lowland

Appalachian Region
26 Notre Dame Mountains
27 New Brunswick Highlands
28 Chaleur Uplands
29 Maritime Plain
30 Atlantic Uplands
31 Annapolis Lowland
32 Newfoundland Highlands
33 Atlantic Uplands
34 Newfoundland Lowlands

Arctic Region
50 Mackenzie Delta
51 Victoria Lowland
52 Lancaster Plateau

Innuitian Region
53 Grant Land Mountains
54 Axel Heiberg Mountains
55 Parry Plateau
56 Eureka Upland
57 Sverdrup Lowland

Interior Plains
20 Manitoba Plain
21 Saskatchewan Plain
22 Alberta Plain
23 Fort Nelson-Peace River Lowland
24 Alberta Plateau
25 Cypress Hills

Cordilleran Region
1 Mackenzie Mountains
2 Franklin Mountains
3 Selwyn Mountains
4 Rocky Mountains
5 Foothills
6 Columbia Mountains
7 Columbia Highlands
8 Cassiar-Omineca Mountains
9 Skeena Mountains
10 Pelly Mountains
11 Coast Mountains
12 Vancouver Island Ranges
13 Fraser-Nechako Plateaux
14 Stikine Plateau
15 Yukon Plateau
16 Mackenzie Plain
17 Liard Plain
18 Alberta Plateau
19 Fraser Lowland

Wetlands

Land that is saturated with water for a major part of the year.

percentage cover of wetlands
- over 50%
- 25–50%
- under 25%

Scale 1 : 90 000 000

Zenithal Equidistant Projection

© Oxford University Press

Heating the Earth
The Greenhouse Effect

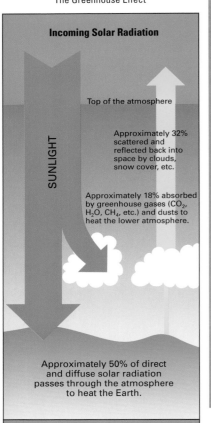

Incoming Solar Radiation

Top of the atmosphere

SUNLIGHT

Approximately 32% scattered and reflected back into space by clouds, snow cover, etc.

Approximately 18% absorbed by greenhouse gases (CO_2, H_2O, CH_4, etc.) and dusts to heat the lower atmosphere.

Approximately 50% of direct and diffuse solar radiation passes through the atmosphere to heat the Earth.

Outgoing Earth Radiation

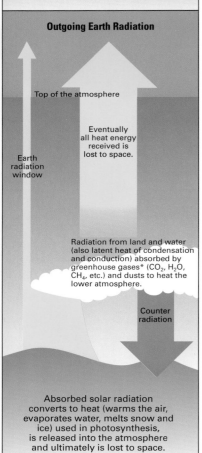

Top of the atmosphere

Eventually all heat energy received is lost to space.

Earth radiation window

Radiation from land and water (also latent heat of condensation and conduction) absorbed by greenhouse gases* (CO_2, H_2O, CH_4, etc.) and dusts to heat the lower atmosphere.

Counter radiation

Absorbed solar radiation converts to heat (warms the air, evaporates water, melts snow and ice) used in photosynthesis, is released into the atmosphere and ultimately is lost to space.

* Global warming is occurring because of additions to greenhouse gases (see page 125) resulting from human activity.

Temperature

Isotherms

°Celsius
20
15
10
5
0
−10
−20
−30
−35

Isotherms join places having the same average monthly temperature.

Isolines, as seen on the other maps on these pages, join places having the same average temperature range, precipitation, etc.

Permafrost

The state of the ground (soil or rock) that remains below 0°C for more than a year.

approximate southern limit of:

⎯⎯⎯ continuous permafrost (90–100% underlain by permafrost)

- - - - discontinuous permafrost (10–90% underlain by permafrost)

Further information on permafrost can be found on page 54.

Scale 1: 45 000 000

Zenithal Equidistant Projection
© Oxford University Press

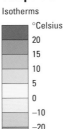

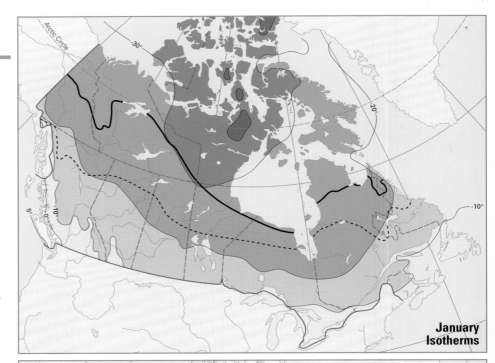

January Isotherms

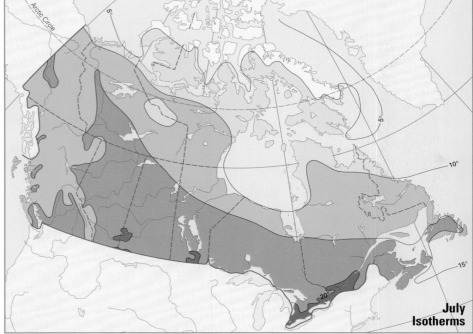

July Isotherms

Temperature range

The difference between the average daily mean temperature in January and July

°Celsius
40
30
20
10
0

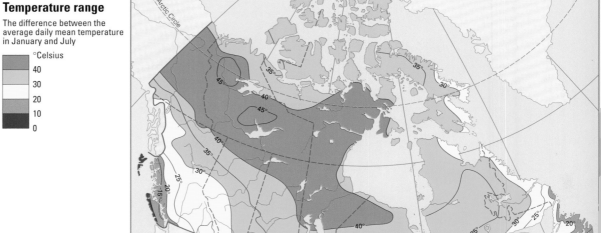

Precipitation

mean annual precipitation

mm
2000
1000
600
400
200
0

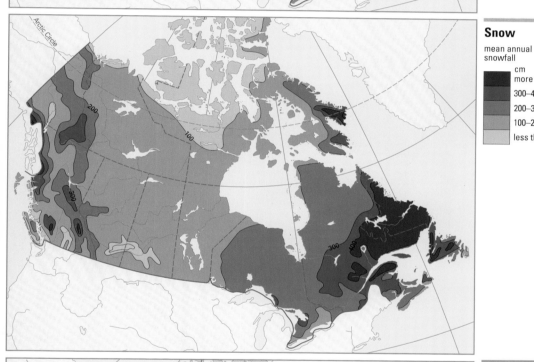

Snow

mean annual snowfall

cm
more than 400
300–400
200–300
100–200
less than 100

Thunderstorms

average annual number of days with thunderstorms

days
20
10
5

Tornadoes

average annual frequency of tornadoes per 10 000 km²

more than 2.0
1.2–2.0
0.8–1.2

Scale 1: 45 000 000

Zenithal Equidistant Projection
© Oxford University Press

Air masses and winds

→ prevailing winds

➤ polar jet stream (average position)

semi-permanent pressure

H high

L low

Scale 1: 108 000 000

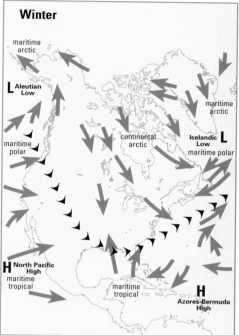

Winter

maritime arctic

L Aleutian Low

maritime polar

maritime arctic

continental arctic

Icelandic Low **L**
maritime polar

H North Pacific High
maritime tropical

maritime tropical

H Azores-Bermuda High

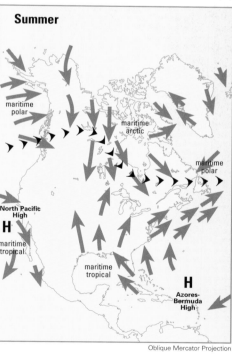

Summer

maritime polar

maritime arctic

maritime polar

H North Pacific High

maritime tropical

maritime tropical

H Azores-Bermuda High

Oblique Mercator Projection

The term **air mass** denotes a mass of air usually several thousands of kilometres in extent, with similar temperature characteristics. Their boundaries are marked by frontal surfaces along which mid latitude cyclonic storms occur.

Jet streams are high altitude streams of rapidly moving air characterized by large stationary or slow moving waves. They circle the Earth and change locations with the seasons. They are associated with the fronts between air masses and thus have a major influence on surface weather.

Humidex

The humidex was developed in Canada in 1965. Its purpose is to combine temperature and humidity into one number to reflect how hot humid weather is perceived by the average person.

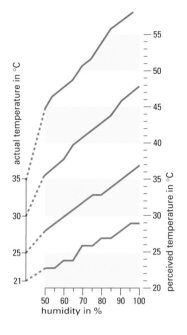

Growing season

average number of days with an average temperature over 5°C

	over 260
	220–260
	180–220
	140–180
	100–140
	60–100
	under 60

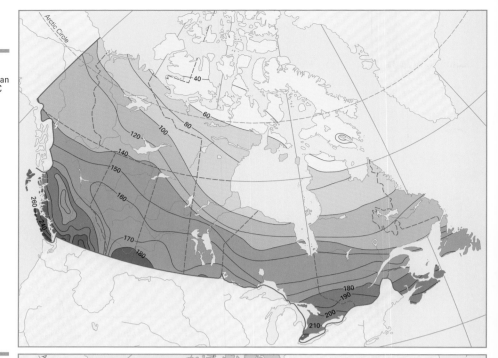

Sunshine

average annual hours

	2000
	1600
	1200

253 number of days with some sun

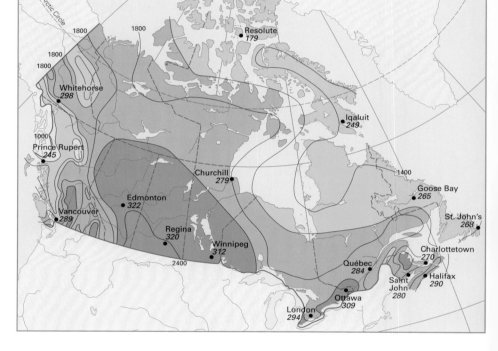

Humidex	Degree of discomfort
over 54	*heat stroke imminent*
45–54	*dangerous*
40–45	*great discomfort*
30–40	*some discomfort*
under 30	*no discomfort*

Scale 1: 45 000 000
Zenithal Equidistant Projection

Canadian weather records

highest air temperature	45°C Midale and Yellow Grass, Sask. *July 5, 1937*
lowest air temperature	-63°C Snag, Y.T. *February 3, 1947*
coldest month	-47.9°C Eureka, N.W.T. *February, 1979*
highest sea-level pressure	107.96 kPa Dawson Y.T. *February 2, 1989*
lowest sea-level pressure	94.02 kPa St. Anthony, Newfoundland *January 20, 1977*
greatest precipitation in 24 hours	489.2 mm Ucluelet Brynnor Mines, B.C. *October 6, 1967*
greatest precipitation in one month	2235.5 mm Swanson Bay, B.C. *November 1917*
greatest precipitation in one year	8122.6 mm Henderson Lake, B.C. *1931*
greatest average annual precipitation	6655 mm Henderson Lake, B.C.
least annual precipitation	12.7 mm Arctic Bay, N.W.T. *1949*
greatest snowfall in one season	2446.5 cm Revelstoke, B.C.
highest average annual number of thunderstorm days	34 days London, Ontario

UV Index

The UV Index (ranges from 0 to 10) is a measure of the intensity of the sun's ultraviolet radiation in the sunburning spectrum. As the index increases, the sun's rays do more harm to skin, eyes, and the immune system, and it becomes necessary to take more precautions to protect exposed skin. In Canada, the UV forecast is issued daily for 48 locations.

The risks from exposure to ultraviolet radiation have increased in recent years due to the thinning of the ozone layer. This thinning has meant that, on average, ultraviolet radiation has increased by about 7 per cent since 1982. *(Environment Canada)*

UV Index	Category	Sunburn time
over 9	Extreme	*less then 15 minutes*
7–9	High	*about 20 minutes*
4–7	Moderate	*about 30 minutes*
0–4	Low	*more than one hour*

Wind chill equivalent temperature

Wind chill is a measure of the wind's cooling effect, as felt on exposed flesh. So as not to confuse it with actual temperature, wind chill is expressed as a temperature-like index, without the degree symbol.

actual air temperature in °C

wind speed at 10 metres in km/h	5	0	-5	-10	-15	-20	-25	-30	-35	-40
5	4	-2	-7	-13	-19	-24	-30	-36	-41	-47
10	3	-3	-9	-15	-21	-27	-33	-39	-45	-51
15	2	-4	-11	-17	-23	-29	-35	-41	-48	-54
20	1	-5	-12	-18	-24	-31	-37	-43	-49	-56
25	1	-6	-12	-19	-25	-32	-38	-45	-51	-57
30	0	-7	-13	-20	-26	-33	-39	-46	-52	-59
35	0	-7	-14	-20	-27	-33	-40	-47	-53	-60
40	-1	-7	-14	-21	-27	-34	-41	-48	-54	-61
45	-1	-8	-15	-21	-28	-35	-42	-48	-55	-62
50	-1	-8	-15	-22	-29	-35	-42	-49	-56	-63
55	-2	-9	-15	-22	-29	-36	-43	-50	-57	-63
60	-2	-9	-16	-23	-30	-37	-43	-50	-57	-64

Scale 1 : 35 000 000

0   350   700   1050 km

Climate graphs

for selected stations

- average rainfall in mm
- average snowfall in mm
- average daily temperature in °C
- growing season*
- asl   above sea level

10mm of snowfall is the water equivalent of 1mm of rainfall

* that part of the year when average daily temperature remains above 5°C

Yellowknife 208m asl

Annual precipitation 267.3mm

Resolute 67m asl

Annual precipitation 139.6mm

Inukjuak 5m asl

Annual precipitation 387.0mm

Iqaluit 21m asl

Annual precipitation 433.0mm

Dawson 320m asl

Annual precipitation 306.0mm

Prince Rupert 34m asl

Annual precipitation 2551.6mm

Climate regions

- mild wet winter and warm summer
- cold winter and cool summer; warmer in valleys
- cold winter and warm summer
- cold winter; precipitation decreasing northwards
- cold winter and hot summer; very dry in the south
- cold and dry throughout the year
- cold throughout the year; light precipitation
- long cold winter and short warm summer
- cold winter and hot summer
- cold winter with heavy snowfalls; hot humid summer
- cold stormy winter with heavy rain and snow; warm summer

Arctic Circle

West Arctic

East Arctic

North Mountain

North Interior

Pacific

South Mountain

Prairie

North Laurentian

South Laurentian

Atlantic

Lower Lakes

Dawson
Resolute
Yellowknife
Iqaluit
Prince Rupert
Prince George
Vancouver
Edmonton
Medicine Hat
Winnipeg
Inukjuak
Schefferville
Kapuskasing
Québec
Halifax
Toronto

Additional climate statistics for 28 Canadian locations can be found on pages 174 and 175, while similar data for 21 other global locations is on page 118.

© Oxford University Press

Vancouver 3m asl

Annual precipitation 1167.4mm

Prince George 676m asl

Annual precipitation 628.0mm

Edmonton 671m asl

Annual precipitation 465.8mm

Schefferville 522m asl

Annual precipitation 769.0mm

Halifax 32m asl

Annual precipitation 1473.5mm

Medicine Hat 721m asl

Annual precipitation 348.0mm

Winnipeg 239m asl

Annual precipitation 504.4mm

Kapuskasing 229m asl

Annual precipitation 872.0mm

Toronto 173m asl

Annual precipitation 818.9mm

Québec 73m asl

Annual precipitation 1207.7mm

Scale 1 : 24 000 000

0   240   480   720 km

Vegetation regions

- Boreal (mainly forest)
- Boreal (forest and barren ground)
- Boreal (forest and grassland)
- Subalpine
- Montane
- Coast
- Columbia
- Deciduous
- Great Lakes-St. Lawrence
- Acadian
- Grassland
- area of commercial forest (more than 50% of the total land area)

Tundra

- Alpine sedges/grasses and shrubs
- Dwarf shrubs/sedges/lichen/heath
- Arctic stony lichen/heath
- Rock desert
- ice cap

Main tree species

- Black Spruce, White Spruce, Balsam Fir, Jack Pine, White Birch, Trembling Aspen
- Black Spruce, White Spruce, Tamarack
- Trembling Aspen, Willow
- Alpine Fir, Engelmann Spruce, Lodgepole Pine
- Douglas Fir, Lodgepole Pine, Ponderosa Pine, Trembling Aspen
- Western Red Cedar, Western Hemlock, Douglas Fir, Sitka Spruce
- Western Red Cedar, Western Hemlock, Western Red Pine
- Beech, Sugar Maple, Black Walnut, Hickory, Red Oak, White Elm, Butternut
- Eastern White Pine, Eastern Hemlock, Red Pine, Yellow Birch, Sugar Maple, Oak
- Red Spruce, Balsam Fir, Maple, Spruce Yellow Birch, Red Pine, White Pine
- Trembling Aspen, Willow, Bur Oak

Forest dependency

percentage of community income dependent upon forest products

- over 90%
- 70–90%
- 50–70%

Further information on this topic is located in the Canada Statistics section which begins on page 147.

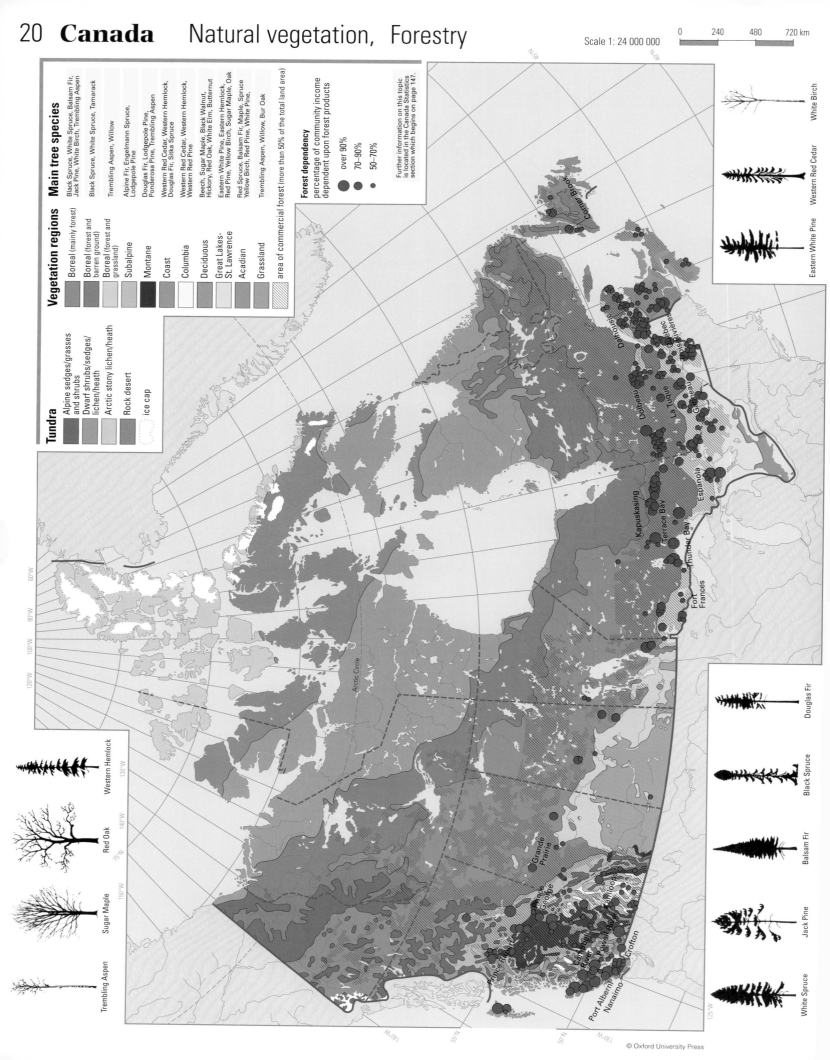

White Birch

Western Red Cedar

Eastern White Pine

Douglas Fir

Black Spruce

Balsam Fir

Jack Pine

White Spruce

Western Hemlock

Red Oak

Sugar Maple

Trembling Aspen

Corner Brook

Dalhousie

Québec

Trois-Rivières

Dolbeau

La Tuque

Gatineau

Kapuskasing

Terrace Bay

Espanola

Thunder Bay

Fort Frances

Grande Prairie

Prince George

Kamloops

Prince Rupert

Quesnel

Williams Lake

Clearwater

Port Alberni

Nanaimo

Crofton

Arctic Circle

© Oxford University Press

Atlantic coast fishing

Flemish Cap

Nose

the Grand Banks of Newfoundland

Grand Bank

Tail

200 nautical mile limit (370km)

Hamilton Bank

Tooker Bank

Burgeo Bank

St. Pierre Bank

Green Bank

Banquereau

Banc de Bradelle

Scotian Shelf Middle

Sable Island Bank

Emerald Bank

Browns Bank

Georges Bank

200 nautical mile limit (370km)

Fishing

pelagic and esturial
fish usually found in shoals near the surface, e.g. herring, sardine, swordfish, salmon

groundfish
fish that live at depths below 50 m as well as on the sea bottom, e.g. cod, haddock, pollock, flounder, sole

molluscs and crustaceans
hard-shelled invertebrates found in shallow waters, e.g. lobster, scallops, oysters, clams

some major salmon spawning rivers

sea depth
0–500 m
more than 500 m

Further information on this topic is located in the Canada Statistics section which begins on page 147.

Ecozones (see Statistics table on page 169)

A large or more or less environmentally homogeneous area in terms of landforms, water, soils, vegetation, climate, wildlife, and various human uses that are ecologically related. Considerable variation may occur within an ecozone and boundaries between them are seldom sharply defined.

Ecozones	Population, 1996 ('000)	Density (person/km²)
	2 549	12.5
	14 840	130.212
	2 895	1.5
	3 979	8.575
	744	1.057
	851	1.737
	2 848	13.372
	32	0.07
	358	0.001
	23	0.039
	36	0.027
	12	0.032
	11	0.014
	18	0.012
	1	0.005

In July 1992, the federal government announced a moratorium on the northern cod fishery to rebuild the stock of this species. Moratoria apply to other groundfish, such as haddock, redfish, and plaice, in certain areas, while the government sets out each year a Total Allowable Catch (TAC) for most other groundfish as well as other species.

Mackenzie

Yukon

Pacific coast fishing

200 nautical mile limit (370 km)

Atlantic coast fishing

Pacific coast fishing

Arctic Cordillera

Northern Arctic

Southern Arctic

Taiga Plains

Taiga Shield

Taiga Cordillera

Boreal Cordillera

Montane Cordillera

Pacific Maritime

Boreal Plains

Prairie

Boreal Shield

Hudson Plain

Taiga Shield

Boreal Shield

Mixed Wood Plain

Atlantic Maritime

Arctic Circle

Scale 1: 35 000 000

0   350   700   1050 km

Soils

Forest soils
- transition black
- grey-brown, dry in summer
- lime rich
- clay belt podzolic
- grey-brown, podzolic
- podzol grey-brown transition
- podzol, leached
- poorly developed in mountains
- peat and iron-rich podzolic
- peat and podzolic

Grassland soils
- brown
- dark brown
- black

Other soils
- bog and subarctic
- alluvial, often poorly drained
- very stony with rocky outcrops
- ice cap
- boundary of the Canadian Shield

Further information on this topic is located in the Canada Statistics section which begins on page 147.

Soil capability

Soil capability refers to the ability of the land to accommodate agriculture. There are seven classes of soil capability, ranging from Class One (the best soils for agriculture) to Class Seven (no ability to sustain agriculture). The map illustrates classes One to Three while the table shows the distribution of classes One to Six. Class One soils have no limitations for agriculture, Class Two have moderate limitations, and Class Three have moderately severe limitations. Class Four soils have marginal capability for the production of field crops. Class Five and Six soils are unsuitable for field crops and are used mainly for pasture and forage production. The factors in determining soil capability include climate, fertility, drainage, stoniness, salinity, and susceptibility to erosion.

Soil capability categories by Province

as a percentage for each category

Province	Classes 1, 2 & 3	Class 4	Classes 5 & 6
Newfoundland & Labrador	1.2	0.23	5.9
Prince Edward Islands	0.85	0.09	0.18
Nova Scotia	2.5	1.7	0.18
New Brunswick	3.1	7.5	3.2
Québec	4.8	10.5	3.0
Ontario	16.1	10.8	5.58
Manitoba	10.8	9.5	7.9
Saskatchewan	35.8	15.8	21.3
Alberta	22.2	36.9	27.4
British Columbia	1.9	6.3	21.8

Agroclimate Resource Index

The agroclimatic resource index illustrates agricultural potential in Canada. The index was based on the number of frost-free days divided by sixty days (the minimum growing period for most crops). The index was then adjusted downward to take into account other climatic factors such as the shortage of moisture in the Southern Prairies and the lack of sufficient summer heat in coastal areas. The higher the value of the index, the greater the climatic potential for agriculture.

Index value
- 3
- 2.5
- 2
- 1

Soil capability
- land area with Classes One, Two, and Three

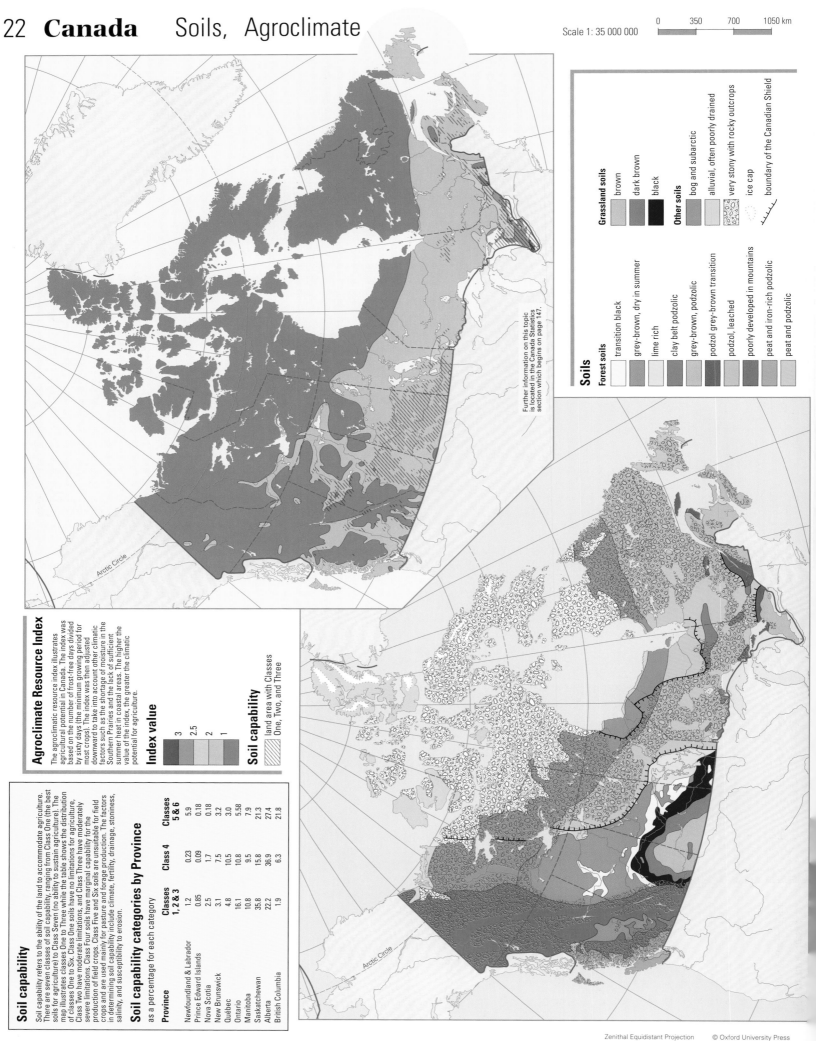

Arctic Circle

Zenithal Equidistant Projection   © Oxford University Press

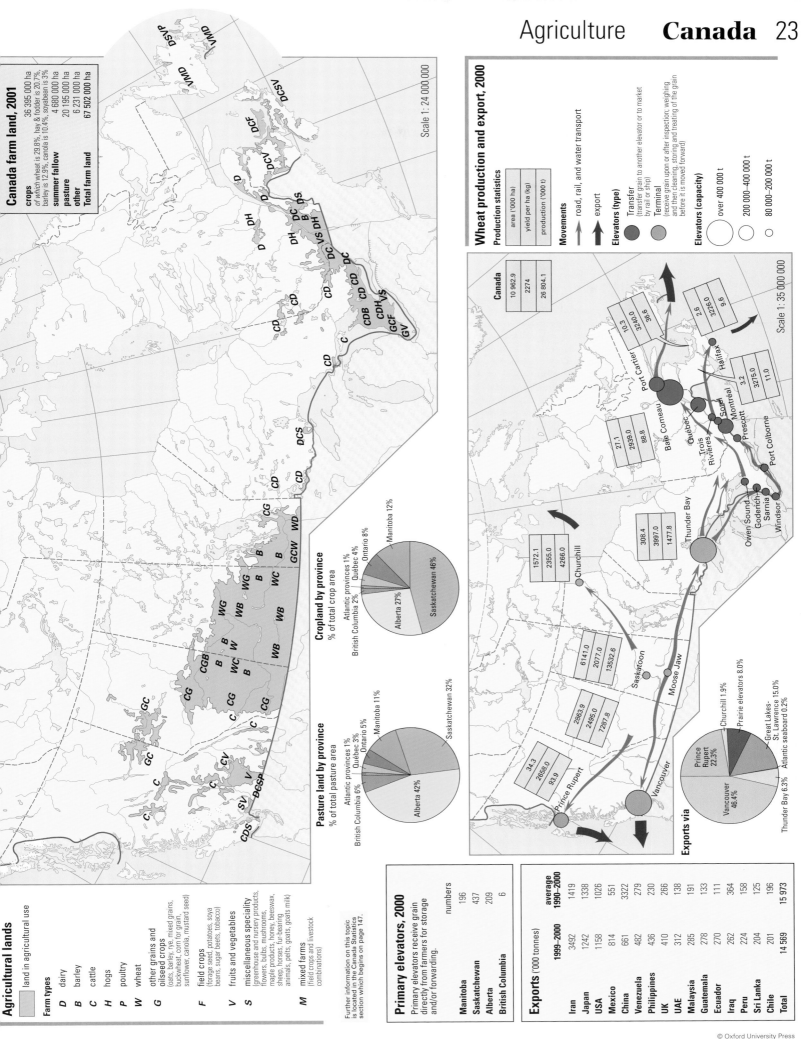

Agricultural lands

land in agricultural use

Farm types

D dairy

B barley

C cattle

H hogs

P poultry

W wheat

G other grains and oilseed crops
(oats, barley, rye, mixed grains, buckwheat, corn for grain, sunflower, canola, mustard seed)

F field crops
(forage seed, potatoes, soya beans, sugar beets, tobacco)

V fruits and vegetables

S miscellaneous speciality
(greenhouse and nursery products, flowers, bulbs, mushrooms, maple products, honey, beeswax, sheep, horses, fur-bearing animals, pelts, goats, goats milk)

M mixed farms
(field crops and livestock combinations)

Canada farm land, 2001

crops	36 395 000 ha
of which wheat is 29.8%, hay & fodder is 20.7%, barley is 12.9%, canola is 10.4%, soyabean is 3%	
summer fallow	4 680 000 ha
pasture	20 195 000 ha
other	6 231 000 ha
Total farm land	**67 502 000 ha**

Scale 1 : 24 000 000

Cropland by province
% of total crop area

- Saskatchewan 46%
- Alberta 27%
- Manitoba 12%
- Ontario 8%
- Québec 4%
- Atlantic provinces 1%
- British Columbia 1%

Pasture land by province
% of total pasture area

- Alberta 42%
- Saskatchewan 32%
- Manitoba 11%
- British Columbia 6%
- Ontario 5%
- Québec 3%
- Atlantic provinces 1%

Primary elevators, 2000

Primary elevators receive grain directly from farmers for storage and/or forwarding.

	numbers
Manitoba	196
Saskatchewan	437
Alberta	209
British Columbia	6

Further information on this topic is located in the Canada Statistics section which begins on page 147.

Exports (000 tonnes)

	1999–2000	average 1990–2000
Iran	3492	1419
Japan	1242	1338
USA	1158	1026
Mexico	814	551
China	661	3322
Venezuela	482	279
Philippines	436	230
UK	410	266
UAE	312	138
Malaysia	285	191
Guatemala	278	133
Ecuador	270	111
Iraq	262	364
Peru	224	158
Sri Lanka	204	125
Chile	201	196
Total	**14 569**	**15 973**

Wheat production and export, 2000

Production statistics

area ('000 ha)	
yield per ha (kg)	
production ('000 t)	

Movements

road, rail, and water transport

export

Elevators (type)

Transfer (transfer grain to another elevator or to market by rail or ship)

Terminal (receive grain upon or after inspection; weighing and then cleaning, storing and treating of the grain before it is moved forward)

Elevators (capacity)

- over 400 000 t
- 200 000–400 000 t
- 80 000–200 000 t

Canada	
	10 962.9
	2274
	26 804.1

Scale 1 : 35 000 000

Exports via

- Vancouver 46.4%
- Prince Rupert 22.3%
- Great Lakes-St. Lawrence 15.0%
- Prairie elevators 8.0%
- Thunder Bay 6.3%
- Churchill 1.9%
- Atlantic seaboard 0.2%

© Oxford University Press

Earthquakes

magnitudes greater than 5.5 on the Richter Scale

- epicentre

Landslides and avalanches

in the 20th Century involving loss of life

+ major landslides and avalanches

Tornadoes

average annual frequency of tornadoes per 10 000 km²

- over 7.5
- 2.5–7.5
- 1.0–2.5

Earthquakes
Earthquakes are caused by the shifting of the earth's plates (see page 123). Canada is one of the least affected countries in the world.

Landslides and avalanches
Landslides and avalanches involve mass movements of rock, soil, and snow and can take many different forms. While particularly common in mountainous regions, they can occur anywhere where the subsurface conditions on sloping lands are unstable.

Tornadoes
Tornadoes are rotating columns of high velocity winds (which can exceed 200 km/h) that reach the ground as funnel-shaped clouds. While their path on the ground is seldom very wide and usually completely unpredictable, almost everything in its path – trees, buildings, and other structures – may be destroyed.

Other natural disasters

Tsunamis
Tsunamis are sea waves produced by earthquakes or volcanic eruptions. They can travel across the open oceans at speeds as high as 450 km/h and reach heights on the shore as great as 30 m. Damaging tsunamis are relatively rare along Canadian coastlines; the last serious one occurred in British Columbia in 1964 causing considerable damage with waves up to 6 m.

Volcanoes
While there has been only one documented volcanic eruption in Canada, there are many dormant volcanoes in western Canada particularly north-western British Columbia.

Drought
Drought is an extended period of below average precipitation. It can result in huge losses of both crops and livestock and severely depleted water supplies. Generally, the lower an area's average annual precipitation, the more vulnerable it is to drought. Global warming is believed to be an important factor in the increased frequency and severity of droughts around the globe. One of the worst droughts in Canada occurred in 1988 when an estimated $1.8 billion in damage resulted in areas stretching from southern Alberta to southern Ontario.

Flooding
- designated flood risk areas

Hail
average annual number of days with hail
- over 3
- 1–3

Fog
visibility less than half a nautical mile in July, measured in percentage frequency
- over 40
- 20–40
- 5–20
- under 5

Freezing rain
Freezing rain can also cause serious damage. An ice storm that occurred in January 1998 moved across Southern Ontario and Southern Québec and parts of New Brunswick resulting in billions of dollars in property damage, damage to forests, and loss of life. Ice storms of this severity are rare (see inset).

Freezing rain
freezing rain accumulations in mm between January 4th and 10th, 1998

mm
100
80
60
40

Scale 1: 19 000 000

Fog
Fog forms when warm humid air is cooled below its dew point. The waters off Canada's eastern coast are particularly vulnerable. Here the warm air associated with the Gulf Stream meets the colder air associated with the southward moving Labrador Current.

Hail
Hail occurs in the warm updrafts of thunderstorms usually between May and October. Hail can strike the earth at 130 km/h and result in severe damage to crops, buildings, and vehicles. One of the costliest natural disasters in Canada was a hailstorm in the Calgary area in September 1991 in which insured damage was estimated at $400 million.

Almost all of Canada except the far north may experience hailstorms. Areas that have hail on average more than one day a year are shown on the map.

Flooding
Flooding is a natural phenomena made worse by human changes to the natural environment, such as the destruction of vegetation cover. Floods most often occur during spring thaw or after heavy rains. Some notable floods: Red River in 1950 and 1997; the Saguenay region in July 1996; and Toronto in 1954 (due to Hurricane Hazel).

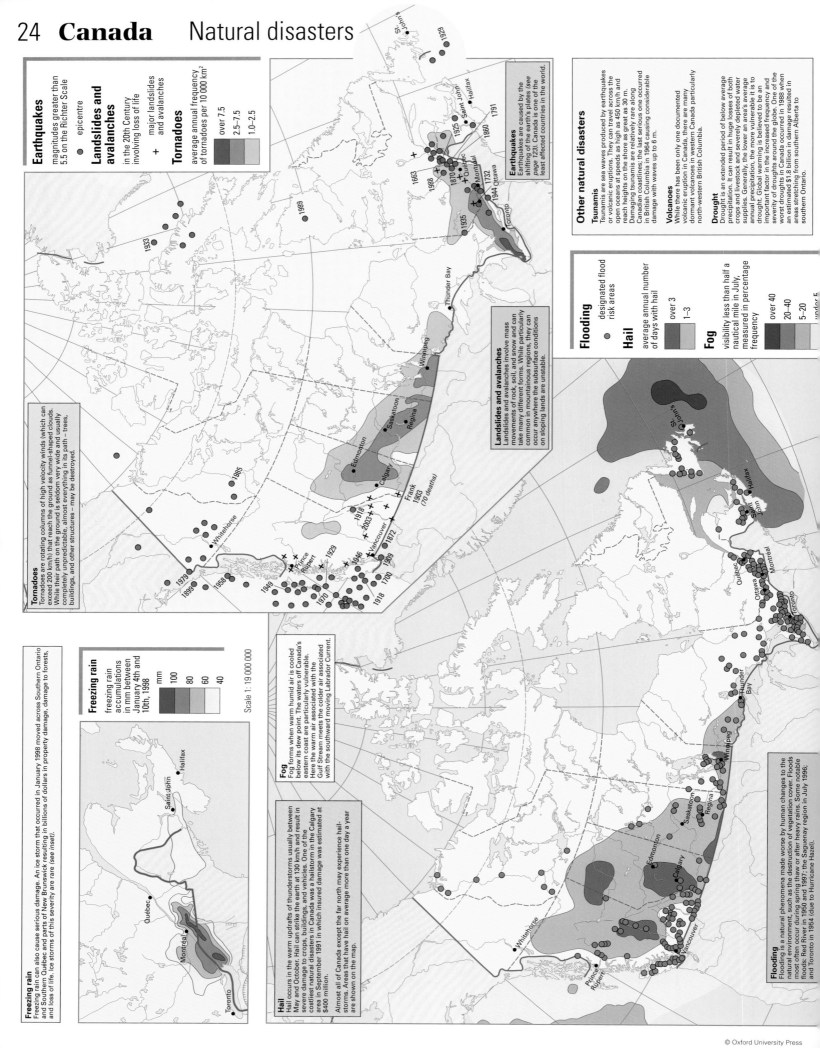

© Oxford University Press

Scale 1 : 35 000 000

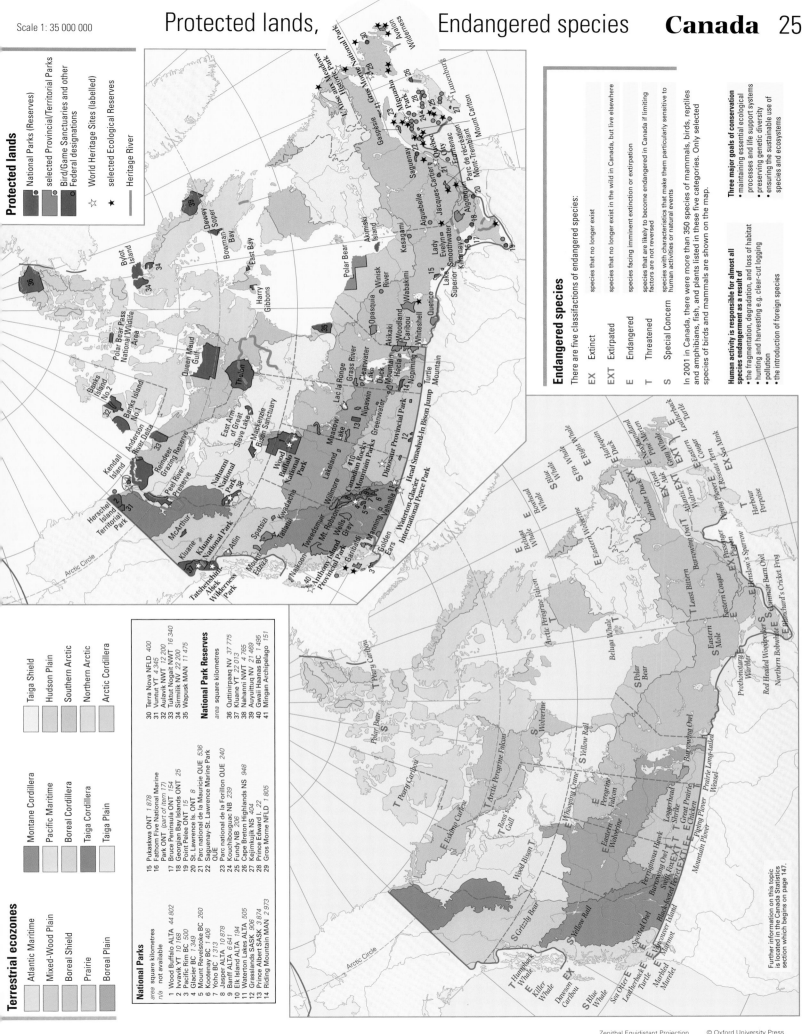

Protected lands

Protected lands

National Parks (Reserves)

selected Provincial/Territorial Parks

Bird/Game Sanctuaries and other Federal designations

☆ World Heritage Sites (labelled)

★ selected Ecological Reserves

—— Heritage River

Terrestrial ecozones

Atlantic Maritime

Mixed-Wood Plain

Boreal Shield

Prairie

Boreal Plain

Montane Cordillera

Pacific Maritime

Boreal Cordillera

Taiga Cordillera

Taiga Plain

Taiga Shield

Hudson Plain

Southern Arctic

Northern Arctic

Arctic Cordillera

National Parks

area square kilometres
n/a not available

1 Wood Buffalo ALTA *44 802*
2 Ivvavik YT *10 168*
3 Pacific Rim BC *500*
4 Glacier BC *1 349*
5 Mount Revelstoke BC *260*
6 Kootenay BC *1 406*
7 Yoho BC *1 313*
8 Jasper ALTA *10 878*
9 Banff ALTA *6 641*
10 Elk Island ALTA *194*
11 Waterton Lakes ALTA *505*
12 Grasslands SASK *906*
13 Prince Albert SASK *3 874*
14 Riding Mountain MAN *2 973*

15 Pukaskwa ONT *1 878*
16 Fathom Five National Marine Park ONT *(part of item 17)*
17 Bruce Peninsula ONT *154*
18 Georgian Bay Islands ONT *25*
19 Point Pelee ONT *15*
20 St. Lawrence Is. ONT *8*
21 Parc national de la Mauricie QUE *536*
22 Saguenay–St. Lawrence Marine Park QUE
23 Parc national de la Forillon QUE *240*
24 Kouchibouguac NB *239*
25 Fundy NB *206*
26 Cape Breton Highlands NS *948*
27 Kejimkujik NS *404*
28 Prince Edward I. *22*
29 Gros Morne NFLD *1 805*

30 Terra Nova NFLD *400*
31 Vuntut YT *4 345*
32 Aulavik NWT *12 200*
33 Tuktut Nogait NWT *16 340*
34 Sirmilik NV *22 200*
35 Wapusk MAN *11 475*

National Park Reserves

area square kilometres

36 Quttinirpaaq NV *37 775*
37 Kluane YT *22 013*
38 Nahanni NWT *4 765*
39 Auyuittuq NV *21 469*
40 Gwaii Haanas BC *1 495*
41 Mingan Archipelago *151*

Endangered species

Endangered species

There are five classifications of endangered species:

EX	Extinct	species that no longer exist
EXT	Extirpated	species that no longer exist in the wild in Canada, but live elsewhere
E	Endangered	species facing imminent extinction or extirpation
T	Threatened	species that are likely to become endangered in Canada if limiting factors are not reversed
S	Special Concern	species with characteristics that make them particularly sensitive to human activities or natural events

In 2001 in Canada, there were more than 350 species of mammals, birds, reptiles and amphibians, fish, and plants listed in these five categories. Only selected species of birds and mammals are shown on the map.

Human activity is responsible for almost all species endangerment as a result of
• the fragmentation, degradation, and loss of habitat
• hunting and harvesting e.g. clear-cut logging
• pollution
• the introduction of foreign species

Three major goals of conservation
• maintaining essential ecological processes and life support systems
• preserving genetic diversity
• ensuring the sustainable use of species and ecosystems

Further information on this topic is located in the Canada Statistics section which begins on page 147.

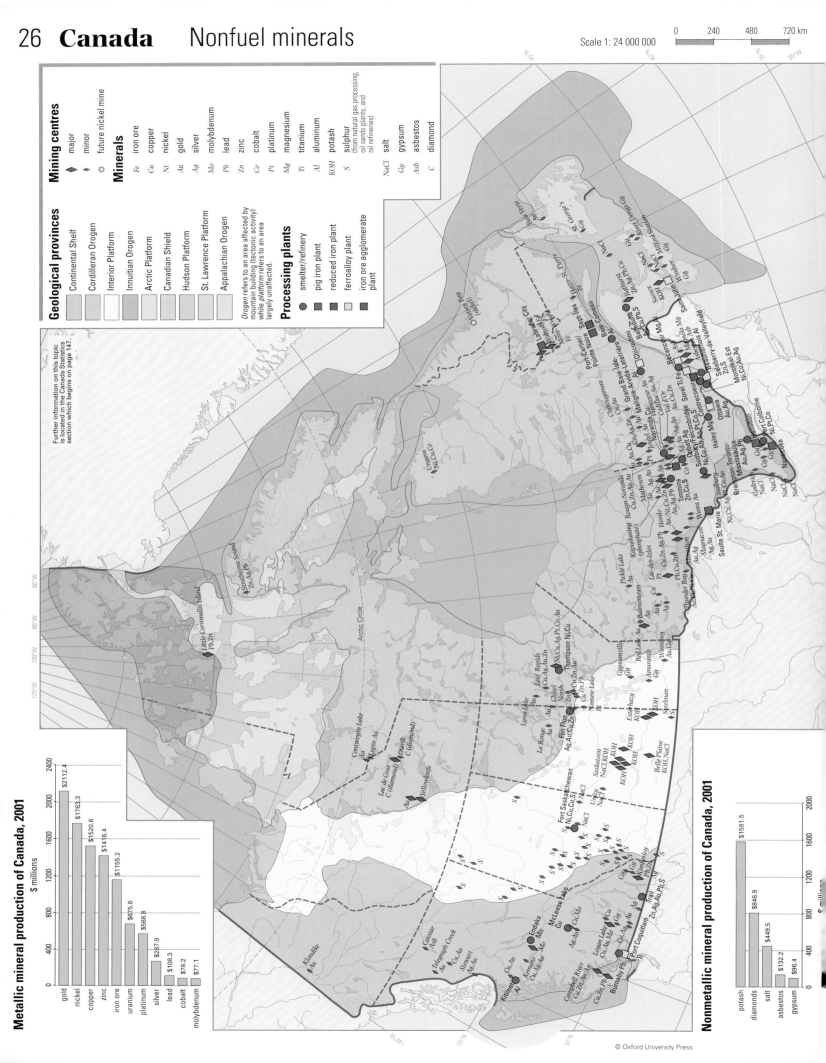

Scale 1 : 24 000 000

Geological provinces
- Continental Shelf
- Cordilleran Orogen
- Interior Platform
- Innuitian Orogen
- Arctic Platform
- Canadian Shield
- Hudson Platform
- St. Lawrence Platform
- Appalachian Orogen

Orogen refers to an area affected by mountain building (tectonic activity) while *platform* refers to an area largely unaffected.

Mining centres
- major
- minor
- future nickel mine

Minerals
- Fe iron ore
- Cu copper
- Ni nickel
- Au gold
- Ag silver
- Mo molybdenum
- Pb lead
- Zn zinc
- Co cobalt
- Pt platinum
- Mg magnesium
- Ti titanium
- Al aluminium
- KOH potash
- S sulphur (from natural gas processing, oil sands plants, and oil refineries)
- NaCl salt
- Gy gypsum
- Asb asbestos
- C diamond

Processing plants
- smelter/refinery
- pig iron plant
- reduced iron plant
- ferroalloy plant
- iron ore agglomerate plant

Further information on this topic is located in the Canada Statistics section which begins on page 147.

Metallic mineral production of Canada, 2001
$ millions
- gold $2112.4
- nickel $1763.3
- copper $1520.6
- zinc $1416.4
- iron ore $1155.2
- uranium $675.6
- platinum $568.8
- silver $267.9
- lead $108.3
- cobalt $78.2
- molybdenum $77.1

Nonmetallic mineral production of Canada, 2001
- potash $1581.5
- diamonds $846.9
- salt $449.5
- asbestos $132.2
- gypsum $96.4

© Oxford University Press

Oil and gas

- oil field
- oil sands deposits (surface and non-surface)
- oil pipeline
- gas field
- gas pipeline

Oil refineries

capacity in barrels per day
- more than 100 000
- 25 000–100 000
- 5000–25 000

Coal

producing mines of over 1 million tonnes per annum
- major
- minor
- coal exports (% of production)
- coal imports

Uranium mines

- major
- other
- processing plant

Geological provinces

- Continental Shelf
- Cordilleran Orogen
- Interior Platform
- Innuitian Orogen
- Arctic Platform
- Canadian Shield
- Hudson Platform
- St. Lawrence Platform
- Appalachian Orogen

Orogen refers to an area affected by mountain building (tectonic activity) while *platform* refers to an area largely unaffected.

Further information on this topic is located in the Canada Statistics section which begins on page 147.

Natural gas transfers, 2000
billion cubic metres per day
- interprovincial
- export

6.2
10.1
16.1
11.9
2.1
14.1
6.9
22.3
20.1
7.6
23.1
10

Crude oil transfers, 2000
thousand cubic metres per day
- interprovincial
- export
- import

1.0
58.0
27.5
57.1
20.3
0.2
10.0
15.9
3.5
37.2
7.2
70.7
44.6
13.5
9.4
13.1
20.4
3.9
8.8

Arctic fields are non-producing

Skate
Cisco
Drake
Hecla

Kobl

Norman Wells

Rainbow Lake
Keg River
Zama
Clarke Lake
Buick Creek
Pejan
Bonduran
Latah
Kaybob
South Brazeau River
Pembina-West Pem
Strachan
Ricinus
Elmworth
Taylor Morlas
Prince George

TRANSMISSION
WESTCOAST
TRANSMOUNTAIN

Prince George
Prince Rupert

coal exports

80% via Vancouver
17% via Prince Rupert

to Japan 42%
Korea 16.5%
USA 5.1%
Brazil 4.6%
Taiwan 4.2%
Italy 3.7%
UK 3.6%
Chile 3.1%
others 17.2%

Vancouver
North Burnaby

Lloydminster (refinery)
Lloydminster (oilfield)
Regina
Moose Jaw
Coleville
Smiley
Kisbey
Oungre
Dollard
Osterton

INTERPROVINCIAL

Estevan
Weyburn
Midale
Tilden

Cluff Lake
McClean Lake
Rabbit Lake
McArthur River
Key Lake

TRANSCANADA

Alberta 0.03%
Manitoba 2.8%

Port Hope
Oakville
Sarnia (3)
Etobicoke
Ontario 73.6%

coal imports

Montréal (2)
St. Romuald
Québec 4.2%
New Brunswick 5.6%
Nova Scotia 12%
Newfoundland 0.4%

Saint John
Dartmouth

Most of imported coal enters Canada via the USA ports of Toledo, Sandusky, Ashtabula and Conneaut

Hibernia
Terra Nova

Come by Chance
North Tranquil

Sept Îles
Rabuliming
Nain

Arctic Circle

© Oxford University Press

Zenithal Equidistant Projection

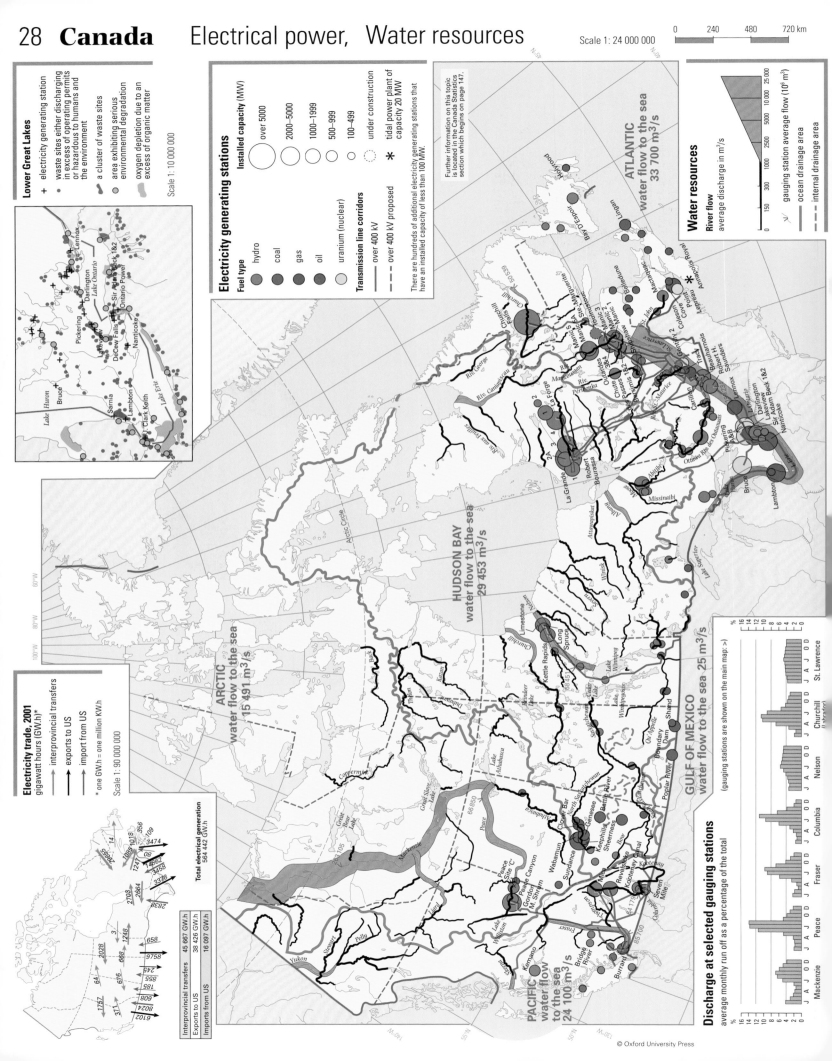

© Oxford University Press

Scale 1: 22 500 000

0 225 450 675 km

Manufacturing industries, 1999

The colour indicates the major industrial group and the numbers indicate important manufacturing subdivisions in some groups.

wood
1 wood industries
2 furniture

paper
3 paper products
4 printing and publishing

food and beverages

textiles and clothing

metals
5 primary metals
6 fabricated metals

machinery
7 machinery
8 transportation equipment
9 electrical equipment

non-metallic minerals

chemicals
10 refined petroleum and coal
11 chemicals

plastics and rubber

computers and electronics

others
including the above industrial groups where the value added is less than 5% of the total or where the information is not available for reasons of confidentiality

$188.3* value added by manufacturing ($000 000)

The value of manufactured goods shipped less the cost of materials and supplies used, including fuel and electricity.

Canada
$202 930 million *
value added by manufacturing

food and beverages
textiles and clothing
wood
paper
metals
1 2 3 4 5 6 7 8 9 10 11
machinery
non-metallic minerals
chemicals
plastics and rubber
computers and electronics
others

Further information on this topic is located in the Canada Statistics section which begins on page 147.

Newfoundland and Labrador $947.1

Prince Edward Island $329.8

Nova Scotia $3 008

New Brunswick $3 094

Québec $53 983

Ontario $106 851

Manitoba $4 218

Saskatchewan $2 086

Alberta $13 415

British Columbia $14 982

Yukon Territory $6.7

Northwest Territories $10.3

Nunavut $0.4

Arctic Circle

Manufacturing centres

These centres include Census Metropolitan Areas (CMAs), Specified Census Agglomerations and selected Municipalities. Manufacturing outside CMAs, towns and cities is not shown.

○ dominant
○ major
○ secondary
• minor

© Oxford University Press   Zenithal Equidistant Projection

Value of exports, 2000

by country of destination

$ million

- over 5 000
- 3 000–5 000
- 1 000–3 000
- 500–1 000
- 200–500
- 50–200
- under 50

All exports exceeding $200 million in value are listed and indicated in bold, with their value in $ millions shown. The others listed have a value between $100 and $200 million. Because of space limitations, all of the exports in the second category are not shown. This is especially true for the United States and Canada's other large trading partners.

The United States dominates Canada's trade, receiving 86.7% of Canada's exports in 2000.

Trade with the United States
Total $334 145

top fifteen exports, 2000

	$ millions
vehicles	83 872
fuels	52 215
machinery	27 546
electrical equipment	25 089
pulp and paper products	16 585
wood products	16 585
plastics	10 117
iron and steel products	8 633
furniture	8 055
aluminum products	6 819
aircraft and parts	6 807
chemicals	4 762
precious metals	4 445
optical equipment	4 284
rubber products	3 571

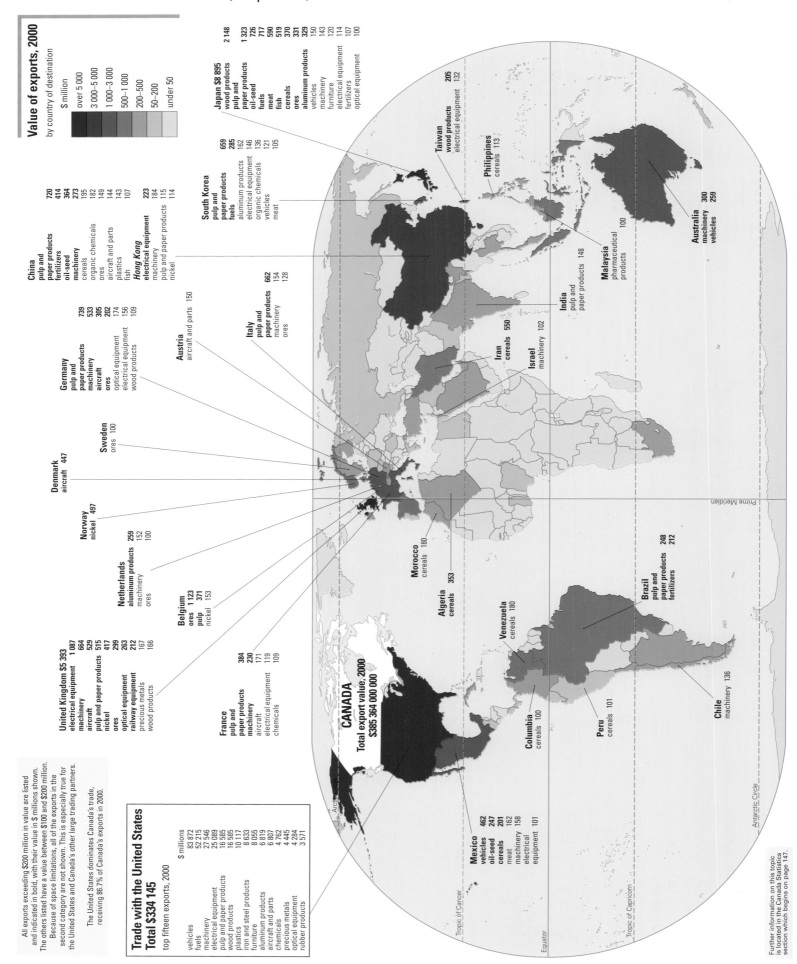

Japan $8 895
wood products	**2 148**
pulp and	
paper products	**1 323**
oil-seed	**726**
fuels	**717**
meat	**590**
fish	**519**
cereals	**370**
ores	**331**
aluminum products	**329**
vehicles	150
machinery	143
furniture	120
electrical equipment	114
fertilizers	107
optical equipment	100

Taiwan
wood products	205
electrical equipment	132

Philippines
cereals	113

South Korea
pulp and	
paper products	**659**
fuels	**285**
aluminum products	162
electrical equipment	146
organic chemicals	136
vehicles	121
meat	105

China
pulp and	
paper products	**720**
fertilizers	**414**
oil-seed	**364**
machinery	**273**
cereals	195
organic chemicals	182
ores	149
aircraft and parts	144
plastics	143
fish	107

Hong Kong
electrical equipment	**223**
machinery	184
pulp and paper products	115
nickel	114

Malaysia
pharmaceutical products	100

Australia
machinery	**300**
vehicles	**259**

India
pulp and	
paper products	148

Iran
cereals	**550**

Israel
machinery	102

Italy
pulp and	
paper products	**662**
machinery	154
ores	128

Austria
aircraft and parts	150

Germany
pulp and	
paper products	**739**
machinery	**533**
aircraft	**305**
ores	**202**
optical equipment	174
electrical equipment	156
wood products	109

United Kingdom $5 393
electrical equipment	**1 087**
machinery	**664**
aircraft	**529**
pulp and paper products	**515**
nickel	**417**
ores	**299**
optical equipment	**263**
railway equipment	**212**
precious metals	167
wood products	166

Sweden
ores	100

Denmark
aircraft	447

Norway
nickel	497

Netherlands
aluminum products	**259**
machinery	152
ores	100

Belgium
ores	**1 123**
pulp	**371**
nickel	153

France
pulp and	
paper products	**384**
machinery	**230**
aircraft	171
electrical equipment	119
chemicals	109

Morocco
cereals	180

Algeria
cereals	**353**

Venezuela
cereals	180

Columbia
cereals	100

Peru
cereals	101

Brazil
pulp and	
paper products	**248**
fertilizers	**212**

Chile
machinery	136

CANADA
Total export value, 2000
$385 364 000 000

Mexico
vehicles	**462**
oil-seed	**247**
cereals	**201**
meat	162
machinery	158
electrical equipment	101

Tropic of Cancer

Equator

Tropic of Capricorn

Antarctic Circle

Prime Meridian

Arctic Circle

Further information on this topic is located in the Canada Statistics section which begins on page 147.

© Oxford University Press

Scale 1: 160 000 000

Value of imports, 2000
by country of origin

$ million

over 5 000
3 000–5 000
1 000–3 000
500–1 000
200–500
50–200
under 50

All imports exceeding $200 million in value are listed and indicated in bold, with their value in $ millions shown. The others listed have a value between $100 and $200 million. Because of space limitations, all of the imports in the second category are not shown. This is especially true for the United States and Canada's other large trading partners.

The United States dominates Canada's trade, sending 64.3% of Canada's imports in 2000.

Trade with the United States
Total $229 330

top fifteen imports, 2000

	$ millions
vehicles	48 947
machinery	45 246
electrical equipment	26 588
plastics	10 028
optical and photo equipment	8 882
iron and steel products	8 328
pulp and paper products	5 948
rubber products	4 023
fuels	3 943
furniture	3 744
aluminum products	3 246
organic chemicals	3 190
pharmaceutical products	3 006
printed material	2 791
wood products	2 603

CANADA
Total import value, 2000
$356 486 000 000

Mexico $12 080
electrical equipment	3 592
vehicles	3 516
machinery	2 082
furniture	495
fuel	397
iron and steel	222
optical equipment	218
clothing	211
vegetables	122
fruit and nuts	113

El Salvador
aircraft and parts 111

Jamaica
chemicals 159

Cuba
ores 362

Venezuela
fuels 1 321

Guyana
metals and precious stones 185

Chile
ores 210
fruit and nuts 145

Brazil
machinery	236
iron and steel	213
rolling stock	153

Republic of Ireland
chemicals	388
pharmaceutical products	372
machinery	262

France
machinery	986
aircraft	619
beverages	386
iron and steel	277
optical equipment	214
pharmaceutical products	180

United Kingdom $13 000
fuel	1 997
electrical equipment	1 333
machinery	1 262
aircraft	1 248
vehicles	770
optical equipment	750
iron and steel	509
beverages	399
	359
	303

Belgium
machinery 153
vehicles 127

Netherlands
machinery 290

Norway
fuels 4 001

Denmark
machinery 184

Sweden
machinery	768
pharmaceutical products	336
vehicles	203

Germany $7 482
machinery	2 422
vehicles	1 461
electrical equipment	624
optical equipment	469
iron and steel	379
chemicals	319
plastics	207
pharmaceutical products	202

Switzerland
machinery	431
pharmaceutical products	281
optical equipment	119

Finland
machinery 190
pulp and paper products 101

Austria
machinery 195

Italy
machinery	1 136
leather products	192
footwear	189
beverages	180
clothing	168
furniture	154
vehicles	151
optical equipment	143
ceramics	109

China $11 281
electrical equipment	1 997
toys and games	1 333
machinery	1 262
textiles and clothing	1 248
footwear	770
furniture	750
leather products	509
plastics	399
iron and steel	359
optical equipment	303

Hong Kong
machinery 512
clothing 420

South Korea $5 160
machinery	2 412
vehicles	763
ships	396
iron and steel	387
clothing	345
rubber	110

Japan $16 600
machinery	7 469
vehicles	5 044
optical equipment	1 098
iron and steel	558
rubber	288
toys and games	285
photo equipment	163
plastics	128

Taiwan
machinery	1 840
electrical equipment	1 263
iron and steel	352
clothing	235
vehicles	181
furniture	135
plastics	118
toys and games	108

Thailand
electrical equipment 472
fish products 272
machinery 202

Philippines
electrical equipment 932
machinery 166

Malaysia
electrical equipment 1 670
machinery 383

New Zealand
meat 1 134
aircraft 119

Indonesia
machinery 170
clothing 132

Australia
chemicals 580
meat 147

Bangladesh
clothing 155

India
clothing 392
iron and steel 151

Singapore
machinery 638
electrical equipment 523

Pakistan
clothing 123

Iraq
fuel 684

Saudi Arabia
fuels 795

Israel
machinery 255
precious stones 125

Russia
fuels 170
iron and steel 102

South Africa
iron and steel 125

Nigeria
fuels 453

Algeria
fuels 1 237

Spain
machinery 140
fuel 132

Prime Meridian

Tropic of Cancer

Equator

Tropic of Capricorn

Arctic Circle

Antarctic Circle

Further information on this topic is located in the Canada Statistics section which begins on page 147.

© Oxford University Press · Eckert IV Projection

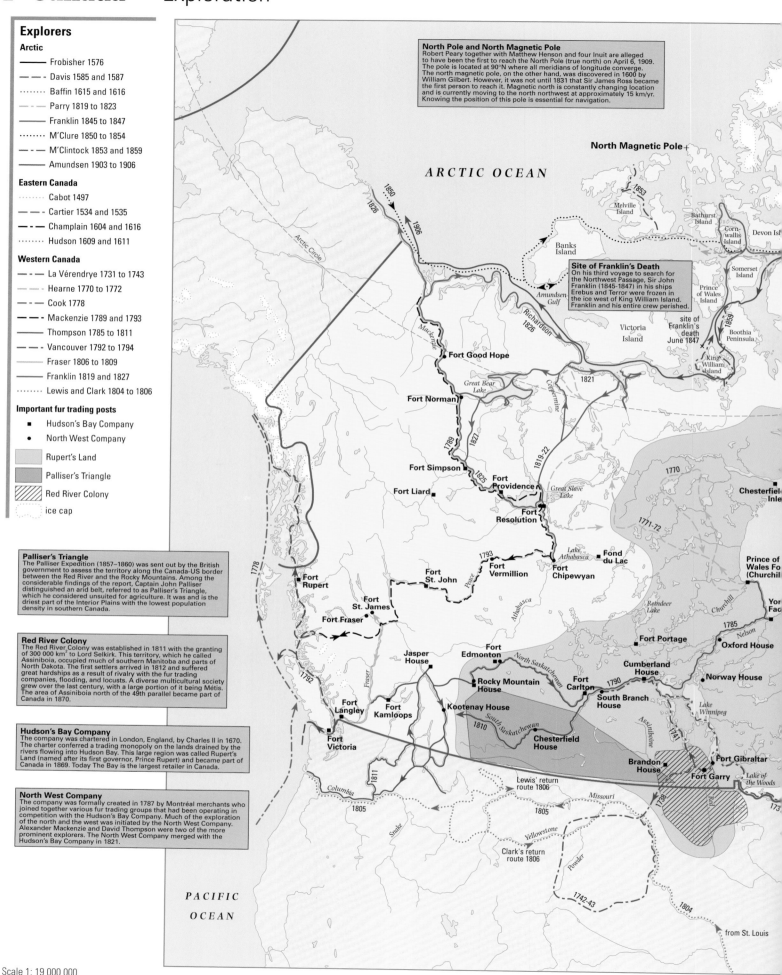

Explorers

Arctic
— Frobisher 1576
– – – Davis 1585 and 1587
······· Baffin 1615 and 1616
–·–·– Parry 1819 to 1823
——— Franklin 1845 to 1847
········ M'Clure 1850 to 1854
–··–··– M'Clintock 1853 and 1859
——— Amundsen 1903 to 1906

Eastern Canada
········ Cabot 1497
– – – Cartier 1534 and 1535
–·–·– Champlain 1604 and 1616
–··–··– Hudson 1609 and 1611

Western Canada
–··–··– La Vérendrye 1731 to 1743
– – – Hearne 1770 to 1772
–·–·– Cook 1778
–··–··– Mackenzie 1789 and 1793
——— Thompson 1785 to 1811
– – – Vancouver 1792 to 1794
——— Fraser 1806 to 1809
——— Franklin 1819 and 1827
········ Lewis and Clark 1804 to 1806

Important fur trading posts
■ Hudson's Bay Company
● North West Company

▨ Rupert's Land

▨ Palliser's Triangle

▨ Red River Colony

▨ ice cap

Palliser's Triangle
The Palliser Expedition (1857–1860) was sent out by the British government to assess the territory along the Canada-US border between the Red River and the Rocky Mountains. Among the considerable findings of the report, Captain John Palliser distinguished an arid belt, referred to as Palliser's Triangle, which he considered unsuited for agriculture. It was and is the driest part of the Interior Plains with the lowest population density in southern Canada.

Red River Colony
The Red River Colony was established in 1811 with the granting of 300 000 km² to Lord Selkirk. This territory, which he called Assiniboia, occupied much of southern Manitoba and parts of North Dakota. The first settlers arrived in 1812 and suffered great hardships as a result of rivalry with the fur trading companies, flooding, and locusts. A diverse multicultural society grew over the last century, with a large portion of it being Métis. The area of Assiniboia north of the 49th parallel became part of Canada in 1870.

Hudson's Bay Company
The company was chartered in London, England, by Charles II in 1670. The charter conferred a trading monopoly on the lands drained by the rivers flowing into Hudson Bay. This large region was called Rupert's Land (named after its first governor, Prince Rupert) and became part of Canada in 1869. Today The Bay is the largest retailer in Canada.

North West Company
The company was formally created in 1787 by Montréal merchants who joined together various fur trading groups that had been operating in competition with the Hudson's Bay Company. Much of the exploration of the north and the west was initiated by the North West Company. Alexander Mackenzie and David Thompson were two of the more prominent explorers. The North West Company merged with the Hudson's Bay Company in 1821.

North Pole and North Magnetic Pole
Robert Peary together with Matthew Henson and four Inuit are alleged to have been the first to reach the North Pole (true north) on April 6, 1909. The pole is located at 90°N where all meridians of longitude converge. The north magnetic pole, on the other hand, was discovered in 1600 by William Gilbert. However, it was not until 1831 that Sir James Ross became the first person to reach it. Magnetic north is constantly changing location and is currently moving to the north northwest at approximately 15 km/yr. Knowing the position of this pole is essential for navigation.

Site of Franklin's Death
On his third voyage to search for the Northwest Passage, Sir John Franklin (1845-1847) in his ships Erebus and Terror were frozen in the ice west of King William Island. Franklin and his entire crew perished.

ARCTIC OCEAN

North Magnetic Pole +

Scale 1: 19 000 000

0 190 380 570 760 950 km

Zenithal Equidistant Projection   © Oxford University Press

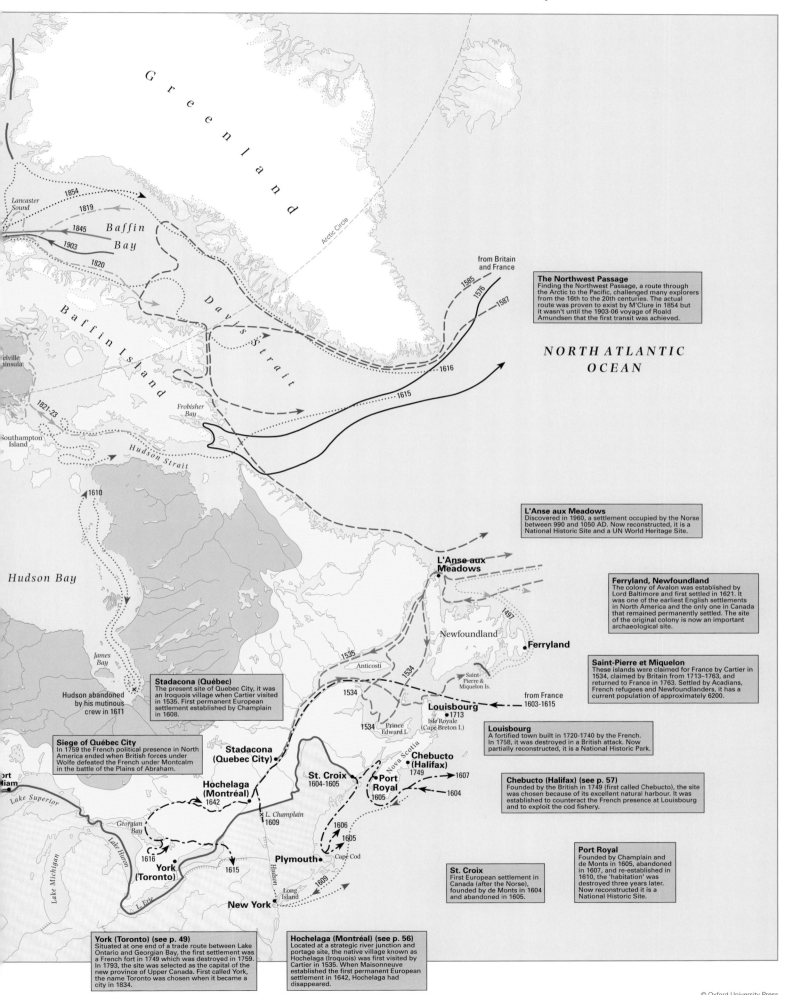

Greenland

Lancaster
Sound
1854

1819

1845
Baffin
Bay
1903

1820

Baffin Island

Davis Strait

Arctic Circle

from Britain
and France

1585
1576
1587

The Northwest Passage
Finding the Northwest Passage, a route through
the Arctic to the Pacific, challenged many explorers
from the 16th to the 20th centuries. The actual
route was proven to exist by M'Clure in 1854 but
it wasn't until the 1903-06 voyage of Roald
Amundsen that the first transit was achieved.

*NORTH ATLANTIC
OCEAN*

1616

1615

Melville
Peninsula

1821-23

Southampton
Island

Hudson Strait

Frobisher
Bay

1610

L'Anse aux Meadows
Discovered in 1960, a settlement occupied by the Norse
between 990 and 1050 AD. Now reconstructed, it is a
National Historic Site and a UN World Heritage Site.

Hudson Bay

James
Bay

Hudson abandoned
by his mutinous
crew in 1611

L'Anse aux
Meadows

1497

Newfoundland

Ferryland

Ferryland, Newfoundland
The colony of Avalon was established by
Lord Baltimore and first settled in 1621. It
was one of the earliest English settlements
in North America and the only one in Canada
that remained permanently settled. The site
of the original colony is now an important
archaeological site.

Stadacona (Québec)
The present site of Quebec City, it was
an Iroquois village when Cartier visited
in 1535. First permanent European
settlement established by Champlain
in 1608.

1535

1534

Anticosti

Saint-
Pierre &
Miquelon Is.

from France
1603-1615

Saint-Pierre et Miquelon
These islands were claimed for France by Cartier in
1534, claimed by Britain from 1713–1763, and
returned to France in 1763. Settled by Acadians,
French refugees and Newfoundlanders, it has a
current population of approximately 6200.

1534

Louisbourg
1713
Isle Royale
(Cape Breton I.)

Louisbourg
A fortified town built in 1720-1740 by the French.
In 1758, it was destroyed in a British attack. Now
partially reconstructed, it is a National Historic Park.

Siege of Québec City
In 1759 the French political presence in North
America ended when British forces under
Wolfe defeated the French under Montcalm
in the battle of the Plains of Abraham.

Stadacona
(Quebec City)

St. Croix
1604-1605

1534   Prince
Edward I.

Nova Scotia

Chebucto
(Halifax)
1749

1607

Port
Royal
1605

1604

Chebucto (Halifax) (see p. 57)
Founded by the British in 1749 (first called Chebucto), the site
was chosen because of its excellent natural harbour. It was
established to counteract the French presence at Louisbourg
and to exploit the cod fishery.

Fort
William

Lake Superior

Georgian
Bay

Lake Huron

Lake Michigan

Hochelaga
(Montréal)
1642

× L. Champlain
1609

1616

York
(Toronto)

1615

L. Erie

Hudson

1606

1605

Plymouth

Cape Cod

1609

Long
Island

New York

Port Royal
Founded by Champlain and
de Monts in 1605, abandoned
in 1607, and re-established in
1610, the 'habitation' was
destroyed three years later.
Now reconstructed it is a
National Historic Site.

St. Croix
First European settlement in
Canada (after the Norse),
founded by de Monts in 1604
and abandoned in 1605.

York (Toronto) (see p. 49)
Situated at one end of a trade route between Lake
Ontario and Georgian Bay, the first settlement was
a French fort in 1749 which was destroyed in 1759.
In 1793, the site was selected as the capital of the
new province of Upper Canada. First called York,
the name Toronto was chosen when it became a
city in 1834.

Hochelaga (Montréal) (see p. 56)
Located at a strategic river junction and
portage site, the native village known as
Hochelaga (Iroquois) was first visited by
Cartier in 1535. When Maisonneuve
established the first permanent European
settlement in 1642, Hochelaga had
disappeared.

Scale 1: 45 000 000

Scale 1: 22 500 000

| 0 | 225 | 450 | 675 km |

Population distribution, 1901

one dot represents 1000 people

Boundaries, 1901

—— international

- - - province/territory

NEWFOUNDLAND

PRINCE EDWARD ISLAND
NOVA SCOTIA
NEW BRUNSWICK

DISTRICT OF UNGAVA

QUÉBEC

ONTARIO

DISTRICT OF KEEWATIN

DISTRICT OF MACKENZIE

DISTRICT OF ATHABASKA

DISTRICT OF SASKATCHEWAN

DISTRICT OF ASSINIBOIA

MANITOBA

DISTRICT OF ALBERTA

BRITISH COLUMBIA

YUKON

2001 Census

Total:	30 007 094	
urban:	23 915 654	(79.7%)
rural:	6 091 440	(20.3%)

Further information on this topic is located in the Canada Statistics section which begins on page 147.

St. John's
Halifax
Saint John
Sherbrooke
Montréal
Chicoutimi-Jonquière
Québec
Kingston
Trois-Rivières
Ottawa
Ottawa-Hull
Toronto-Niagara
St. Catharines
Hamilton
London
Greater Sudbury
Owen Sound
Kitchener
Windsor
Thunder Bay
Winnipeg
Saskatoon
Regina
Edmonton
Calgary
Vancouver
Abbotsford
Victoria

Census Metropolitan Areas

'000 people, census 2001

one small square represents 50 000 people

Toronto	4 683													
Montréal	3 426													
Vancouver	1 987													
Ottawa-Hull	1 064													
Calgary	951		Edmonton	938		Québec	683		Winnipeg	671		Hamilton	662		London 432

Kitchener 414
St. Catharines-Niagara 377
Halifax 359
Victoria 312
Windsor 308
Oshawa 296
Saskatoon 226
Regina 193
St. John's 173
Greater Sudbury 156
Sherbrooke 155
Abbotsford 154
Kingston 147
Trois-Rivières 147
Saint John 122
Thunder Bay 123
Chicoutimi-Jonquière 138

A Census Metropolitan Area (CMA) is an urban-centred region that includes a large urbanised core (with more than 100 000 people) together with adjacent urban and rural fringe areas that have a high degree of economic and social integration with that core.

Population distribution, 2001

settled area (ecumen)

· one red dot represents 1000 people

· one black dot represents 100 people north of latitude 60°N

○ cities with more than 20 000 inhabitants

Regina ◎ cities with more than 100 000 inhabitants, Census Metropolitan Areas (CMAs)

Since the date of this census, Ottawa-Hull has been renamed Ottawa-Gatineau, and Chicoutimi-Jonquière has been renamed Saguenay.

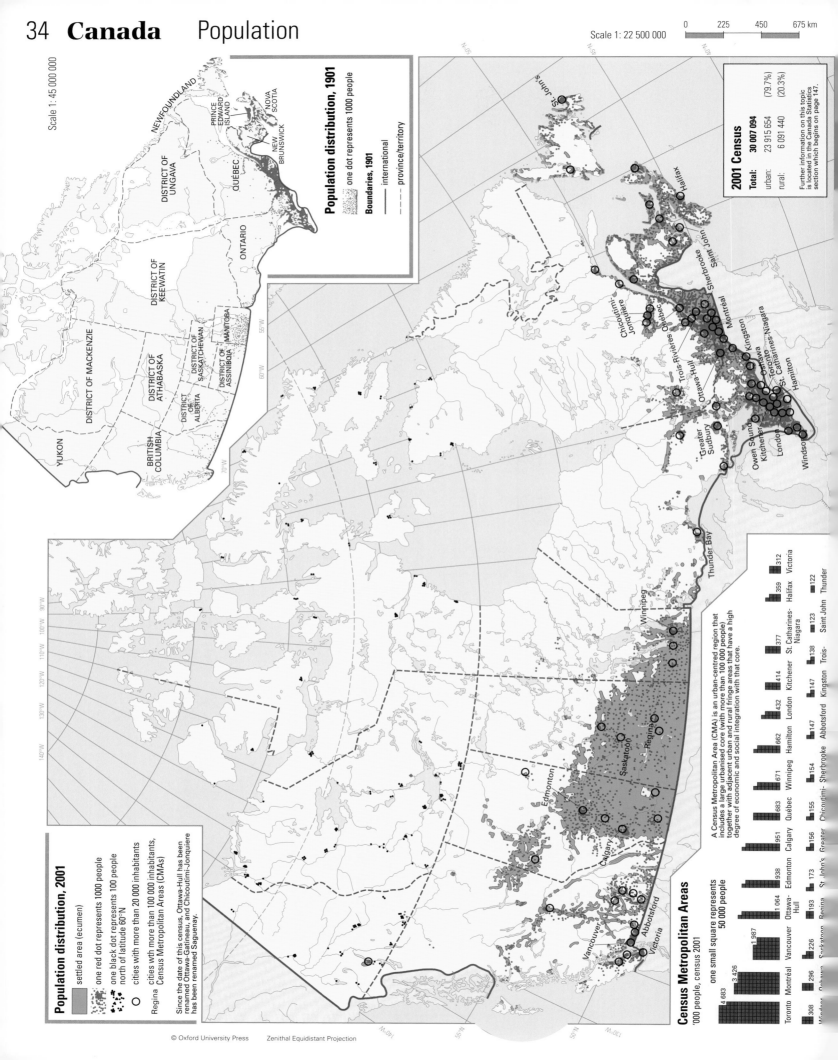

© Oxford University Press   Zenithal Equidistant Projection

Scale 1: 35 000 000

Canada
11.9 33.2 15.7
8.0 17.7 4.4 9.1
59.3 22.9 17.8

94.1 4.3 1.6
5.1 0.3 4.2
2.0
4.0 22.1 62.3

3.8 3.0
93.2 0.9 6.2
8.1 3.7
9.9 17.1 54.1

98.5 0.4 1.1
34.1 51.9
0.5 1.4 5.5
1.2 5.4

65.2 33.2 1.6
0.6 41.4 28.8
4.5 3.9
3.8 17.0

7.9 82.0 10.1
7.6 29.3
52.2 2.0 2.2 5.5 1.2 2.2

71.6 4.4 24.0
7.6 39.0
11.2 20.7 2.7 8.5 10.9

26.3 1.5 72.2
14.7 3.0
85.8

77.9 1.4 20.7
5.4 3.0
14.3 33.7 36.1 17.9 12.5

85.8 1.9 12.3
1.7 1.0
13.8 31.9 39.6 28.1 11.2

78.0 2.7 19.3
12.3 30.7 52.9 8.0 2.7 1.2 10.4

81.8 2.0 16.2
7.3 2.8
6.7 30.3 42.6 19.4 13.8 11.2

87.2 3.2 9.6
2.1 0.9
14.3 20.5 47.7 24.4 13.6

74.0 1.4 24.6
2.2 44.5
5.5 12.8 22.6 16.7 8.5

Arctic Circle

Percentages are based on total population and may exceed 100 since multiple responses are included.

Immigration to Canada by Province, 2001
as a percentage of the total number of immigrants

Total immigration in 2001 was 250 346

0.3 0.2 0.05 0.04 0.03 0.002
ON BC QC AB MB SK NB NS NF PE NT YT N
55 50 20 15 10 5 0

Interprovincial migration, 1996–2001

Net migrants equal the difference between the number of incoming and outgoing migrants. These numbers are for internal migrants only.

−1 275 net migration

Immigrant population, 1996–2001

percentage by place of birth

1mm line width represents 2%

2.1 1996–2001 annual average

(0.4) comparative data for 1971–1980

Scale 1: 45 000 000

Further information on this topic is located in the Canada Statistics section which begins on page 147.

rest of Europe
6.2 (3.1)

Algeria
1.2 (0.08)

Romania
2.1 (0.4)

Russian Federation
2.6 (0.3)

Iran
3.2 (0.4)

UK
2.1 (13.5)

NEWFOUNDLAND AND LABRADOR
−31 865

PRINCE EDWARD IS.
+135

NOVA SCOTIA
−1 275

NEW BRUNSWICK
−8 425

QUÉBEC
−57 315

USA
3.1 (6.7)

ONTARIO
+51 905

NUNAVUT
−330

MANITOBA
−18 560

SASKATCHEWAN
−24 940

NORTHWEST TERRITORIES
−3 170

ALBERTA
+119 420

Mexico and Jamaica
2.5 (4.9)

YUKON
−2 760

BRITISH COLUMBIA
−23 630

Pakistan
4.5 (1.0)

rest of Asia
10.3 (6.1)

India
9.5 (6.8)

Philippines
5.8 (4.8)

Taiwan
3.2 (0.4)

China (including Hong Kong)
16.9 (8.3)

Arctic Circle

Population by language, 2001
one small square represents 1% of the population, by province

English
French
non official

Ethnic origin, 2001
percent of population, by province

British
French
German
Aboriginal
other European
Asian
other

Canada, 2002

females
males
Age
80- 70- 60- 50- 40- 30- 20- 10- 0

percent of total population
5 4 3 2 1 0 1 2 3 4 5

Total population: 31 413 990
Crude Birth Rate per thousand: 11
Crude Death Rate per thousand: 8

Foreign born, 2001
as a percentage of the metropolitan population, for selected cities

50%
40
30
20
10
0

Toronto (Canada)
Miami (USA)
Vancouver (Canada)
Sydney (Australia)
Los Angeles (USA)
New York (USA)
Montréal (Canada)

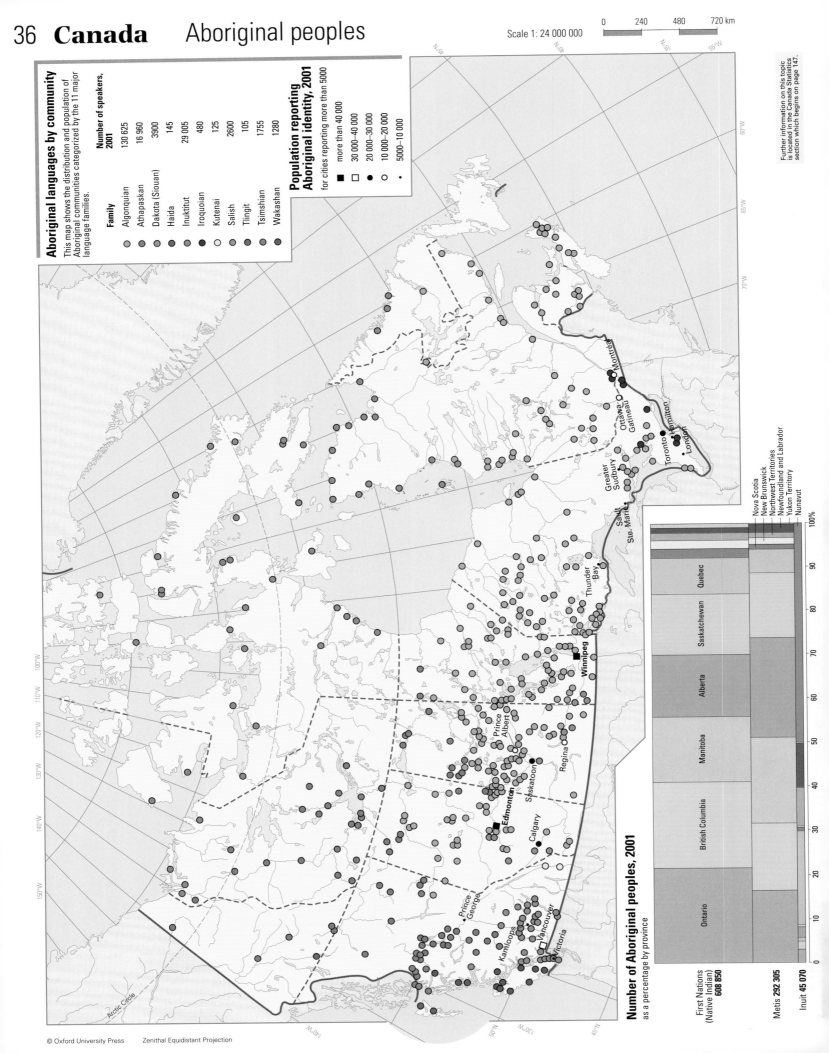

Scale 1: 24 000 000

0 240 480 720 km

Aboriginal languages by community

This map shows the distribution and population of Aboriginal communities categorized by the 11 major language families.

Family	Number of speakers, 2001
Algonquian	130 625
Athapaskan	16 960
Dakota (Siouan)	3900
Haida	145
Inuktitut	29 005
Iroquoian	480
Kutenai	125
Salish	2600
Tlingit	105
Tsimshian	1755
Wakashan	1280

Population reporting Aboriginal identity, 2001

for cities reporting more than 5000

- ■ more than 40 000
- □ 30 000–40 000
- ● 20 000–30 000
- ○ 10 000–20 000
- · 5000–10 000

Further information on this topic is located in the Canada Statistics section which begins on page 147.

Number of Aboriginal peoples, 2001

as a percentage by province

First Nations (Native Indian) **608 850**

Metis **292 305**

Inuit **45 070**

Ontario · British Columbia · Manitoba · Alberta · Saskatchewan · Quebec · Nova Scotia · New Brunswick · Northwest Territories · Newfoundland and Labrador · Yukon Territory · Nunavut

© Oxford University Press   Zenithal Equidistant Projection

The Dominion of Canada was formed in 1867 and included the provinces of Nova Scotia, New Brunswick, Quebec and Ontario. The North-Western Territory, Rupert's Land, and Manitoba were added in 1870; British Columbia in 1871; Prince Edward Island in 1873; and Saskatchewan and Alberta in 1905. On December 6, 2001, Newfoundland's name was officially changed to Newfoundland and Labrador.

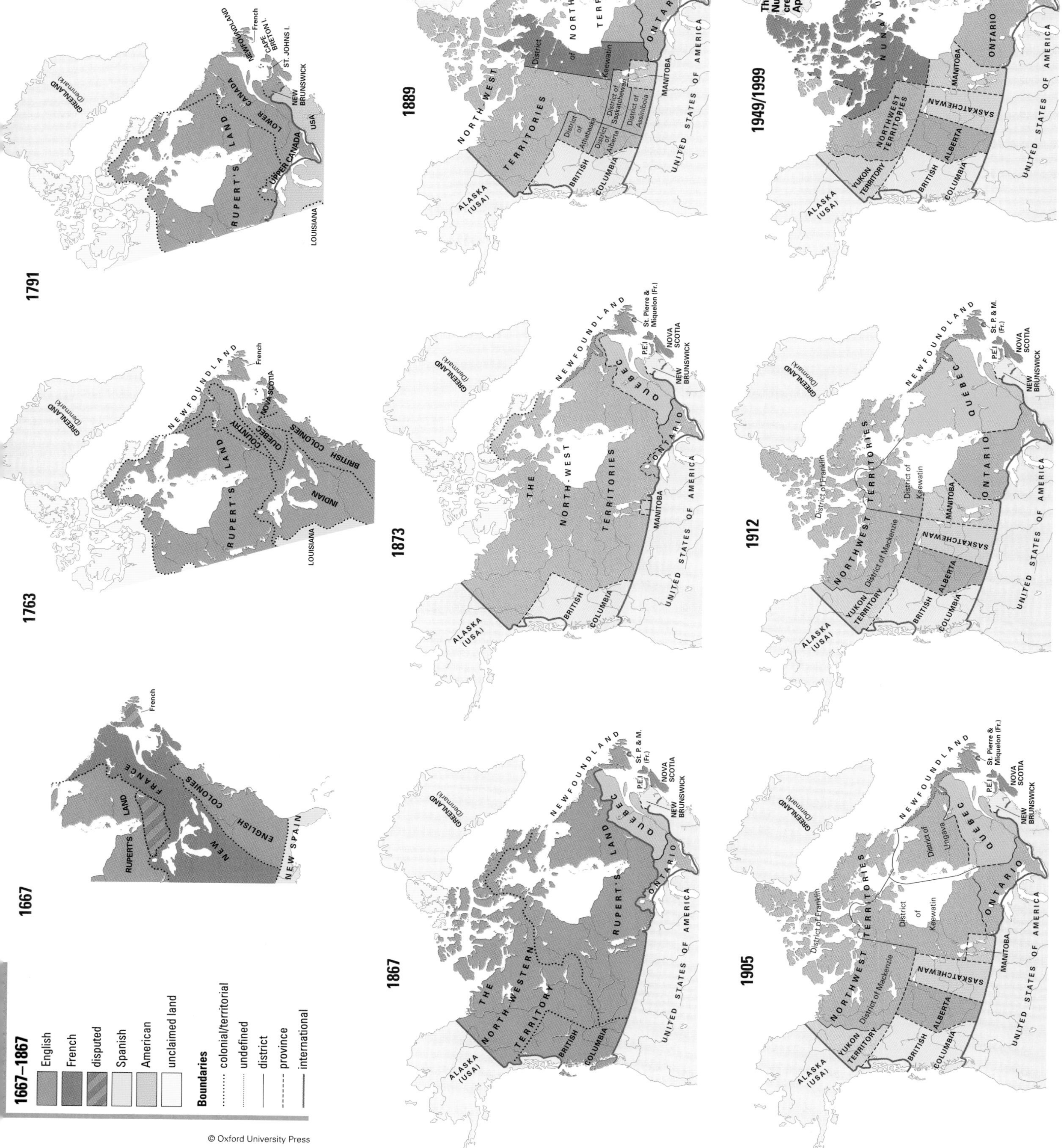

1667–1867

	English
	French
	disputed
	Spanish
	American
	unclaimed land

Boundaries

.... colonial/territorial

··············· undefined

– – – district

– – – – province

─── international

1791

1763

1667

1889

1873

1867

1949/1999

Newfoundland joined Canada in 1949.

The territory of Nunavut was created on April 1, 1999.

1912

1905

© Oxford University Press

physical features
- ~~~ marsh
- ice cap

sea ice
- unnavigable
- pack ice
  - –fall minimum
  - –spring maximum

land height and sea depth

metres
3000
2000
1500
1000
500
300
200
100
0   sea level
200
3000
6000

▲ spot height in metres

boundaries
- ——— international
- ——— province/territory
- ——— national park/ provincial park

communications
- ═══ expressway/other multilane highway
- ——— other highway
- ——— railway
- +++++ canal
- - - - ferry
- ⊕ major airport
- ✈ other airport

settlements
- ⬡ built-up area
- ■ over 1 million inhabitants
- ● more than 100 000 inhabitants
- • smaller urban places

Scale 1 : 2 000 000

0   20   40   60   80   100 km

Conical Orthomorphic Projection   © Oxford University Press

British Columbia

Land area: 925 186km²
Total area: 944 735km²
(9.5% of Canada)

Census Population	
1871	36 247
1891	98 173
1911	392 480
1931	694 263
1951	1 165 210
1971	2 184 620
1991	3 282 061
2001	3 907 738
Rural	15.3%
Urban	84.7%

Census Metropolitan Areas, 2001

Abbotsford	147 370
Vancouver	1 986 965
Victoria (capital)	311 902

Other important urban centres, 2001

Chilliwack	69 776
Kamloops	86 491
Kelowna	147 739
Nanaimo	85 664
Prince George	85 035
Vernon	51 530

Gross Domestic Product
(2001 $113 849 million)

goods producing	%
Agriculture	1.0
Forestry	3.2
Fishing, Hunting, & Trapping	0.2
Mining incl. oil & gas	3.0
Utilities	2.1
Construction	5.1
Manufacturing	10.5

service producing	%
Wholesale & Retail trade	10.5
Transportation & Warehousing	5.8
Information & Cultural industries	4.7
Finance, Insurance, & Real estate	22.7
Other services	25.4
Public administration	5.2

Scale 1: 5 000 000

0   50   100   150   200   250 km

Scale 1 : 300 000

0   3   6   9   12   15 km

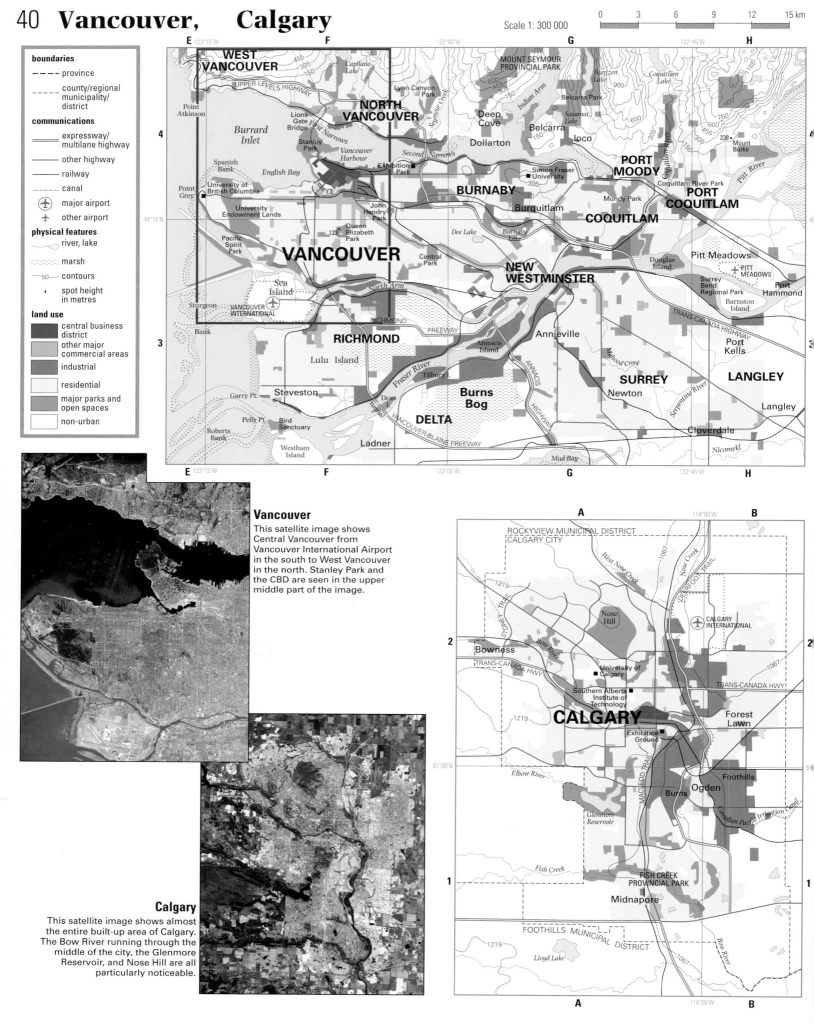

boundaries
— — — province
— — — county/regional municipality/ district

communications
expressway/ multilane highway
other highway
railway
canal
⊕ major airport
✈ other airport

physical features
river, lake
marsh
—50— contours
▴ spot height in metres

land use
central business district
other major commercial areas
industrial
residential
major parks and open spaces
non-urban

WEST VANCOUVER
UPPER LEVELS HIGHWAY
Point Atkinson
Burrard Inlet
Capilano Lake
Lyon Canyon Park
NORTH VANCOUVER
Lions Gate Bridge
First Narrows
Stanley Park
Vancouver Harbour
Second Narrows
Seymour Creek
MOUNT SEYMOUR PROVINCIAL PARK
Deep Cove
Indian Arm
Belcarra Park
Buntzen Lake
Coquitlam Lake
Dollarton
Belcarra
Sasamat Lake
Ioco
Mount Burke
Spanish Bank
English Bay
Exhibition Park
Burnaby Lake
Simon Fraser University
PORT MOODY
Coquitlam River
Pitt River
Point Grey
University of British Columbia
False Ck.
John Hendry Park
Queen Elizabeth Park
BURNABY
Burquitlam
Mundy Park
Coquitlam River Park
PORT COQUITLAM
University Endowment Lands
123
COQUITLAM
Pitt Meadows
PITT MEADOWS
Pacific Spirit Park
Dee Lake
Central Park
NEW WESTMINSTER
Douglas Island
Surrey Bend Regional Park
Port Hammond
VANCOUVER
Barnston Island
Sea Island
North Arm
VANCOUVER INTERNATIONAL
Annieville
TRANS-CANADA HIGHWAY
Sturgeon Bank
RICHMOND
Annacis Island
Mahood Creek
Port Kells
FREEWAY
Lulu Island
Fraser River
Tilbury I.
SURREY
LANGLEY
Garry Pt.
Steveston
Deas I.
Newton
Serpentine River
Langley
Pelly Pt.
Bird Sanctuary
Burns Bog
ANNACIS HIGHWAY
tunnel
VANCOUVER-BLAINE FREEWAY
DELTA
Cloverdale
Roberts Bank
Westham Island
Ladner
Mud Bay
Nicomekl

Vancouver
This satellite image shows Central Vancouver from Vancouver International Airport in the south to West Vancouver in the north. Stanley Park and the CBD are seen in the upper middle part of the image.

ROCKYVIEW MUNICIPAL DISTRICT
CALGARY CITY
West Nose Creek
Nose Creek
DEERFOOT TRAIL
STONEY TRAIL
Nose Hill
CALGARY INTERNATIONAL
Bowness
Bow River
University of Calgary
TRANS-CANADA HWY
Southern Alberta Institute of Technology
TRANS-CANADA HWY
CALGARY
Forest Lawn
Exhibition Ground
Elbow River
Ogden
Foothills
MACLEOD TRAIL
Burns
Glenmore Reservoir
Canadian Pacific Irrigation Canal
Fish Creek
FISH CREEK PROVINCIAL PARK
Midnapore
FOOTHILLS MUNICIPAL DISTRICT
Lloyd Lake
Bow River

Calgary
This satellite image shows almost the entire built-up area of Calgary. The Bow River running through the middle of the city, the Glenmore Reservoir, and Nose Hill are all particularly noticeable.

© Oxford University Press

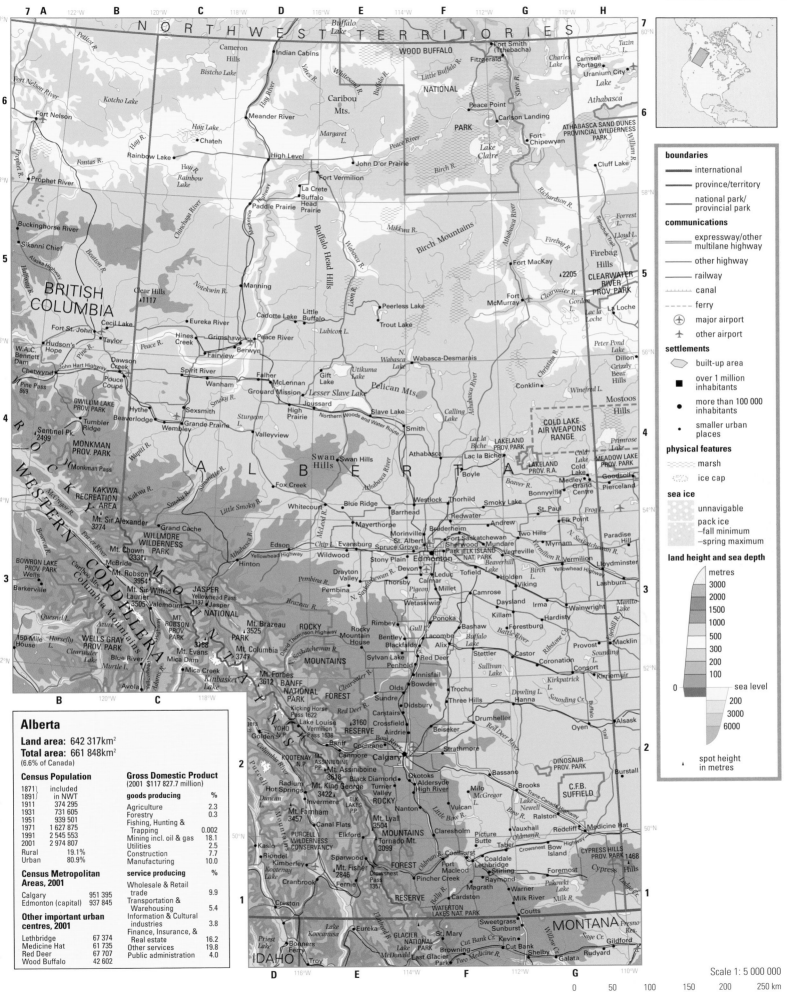

Alberta

Land area: 642 317km²
Total area: 661 848km²
(6.6% of Canada)

Census Population

1871	included
1891	in NWT
1911	374 295
1931	731 605
1951	939 501
1971	1 627 875
1991	2 545 553
2001	2 974 807
Rural	19.1%
Urban	80.9%

Census Metropolitan Areas, 2001

Calgary	951 395
Edmonton (capital)	937 845

Other important urban centres, 2001

Lethbridge	67 374
Medicine Hat	61 735
Red Deer	67 707
Wood Buffalo	42 602

Gross Domestic Product
(2001 $117 827.7 million)

goods producing	%
Agriculture	2.3
Forestry	0.3
Fishing, Hunting & Trapping	0.002
Mining incl. oil & gas	18.1
Utilities	2.5
Construction	7.7
Manufacturing	10.0

service producing	%
Wholesale & Retail trade	9.9
Transportation & Warehousing	5.4
Information & Cultural industries	3.8
Finance, Insurance, & Real estate	16.2
Other services	19.8
Public administration	4.0

boundaries

- international
- province/territory
- national park/ provincial park

communications

- expressway/other multilane highway
- other highway
- railway
- canal
- ferry
- ⊕ major airport
- ✈ other airport

settlements

- built-up area
- ■ over 1 million inhabitants
- ● more than 100 000 inhabitants
- • smaller urban places

physical features

- marsh
- ice cap

sea ice

- unnavigable
- pack ice
  - –fall minimum
  - –spring maximum

land height and sea depth

metres	
3000	
2000	
1500	
1000	
500	
300	
200	
100	
0	sea level
200	
3000	
6000	

▲ spot height in metres

Scale 1: 5 000 000

0 50 100 150 200 250 km

Conical Orthomorphic Projection

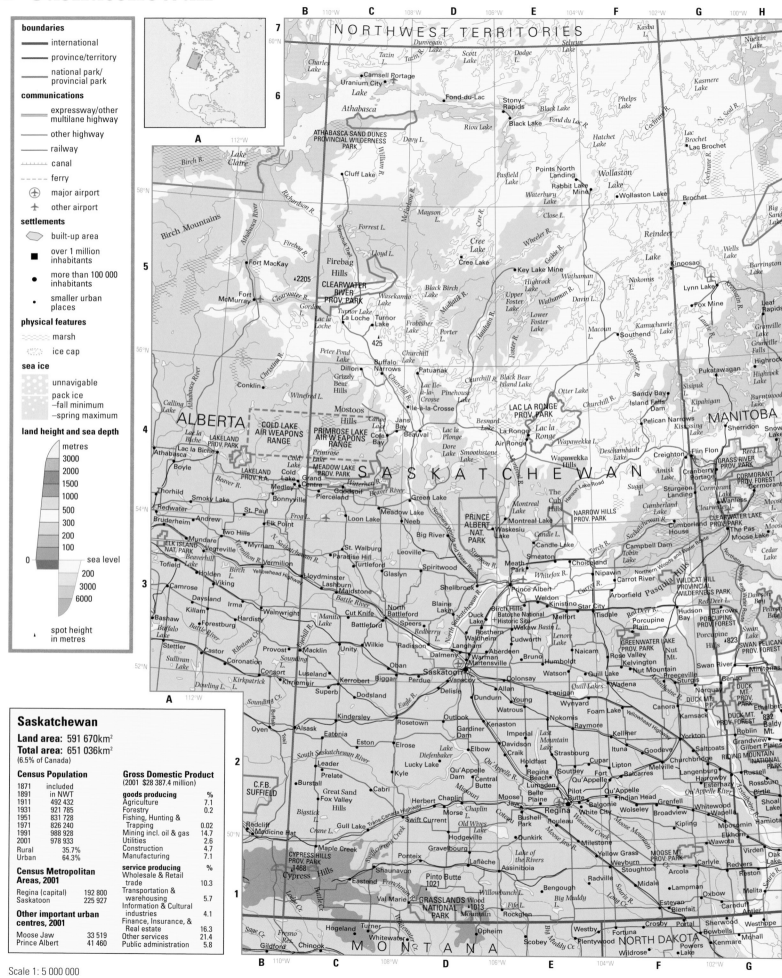

boundaries
— international
— province/territory
— national park/provincial park

communications
═ expressway/other multilane highway
— other highway
— railway
+++++ canal
----- ferry
⊕ major airport
✈ other airport

settlements
⬡ built-up area
■ over 1 million inhabitants
● more than 100 000 inhabitants
• smaller urban places

physical features
▒ marsh
▒ ice cap

sea ice
unnavigable
pack ice
—fall minimum
—spring maximum

land height and sea depth

metres
3000
2000
1500
1000
500
300
200
100
0 sea level
200
3000
6000

▲ spot height in metres

Saskatchewan

Land area: 591 670km²
Total area: 651 036km²
(6.5% of Canada)

Census Population
1871	included
1891	in NWT
1911	492 432
1931	921 785
1951	831 728
1971	826 240
1991	988 928
2001	978 933
Rural	35.7%
Urban	64.3%

Census Metropolitan Areas, 2001
Regina (capital)	192 800
Saskatoon	225 927

Other important urban centres, 2001
Moose Jaw	33 519
Prince Albert	41 460

Gross Domestic Product
(2001 $28 387.4 million)

goods producing	%
Agriculture	7.1
Forestry	0.2
Fishing, Hunting & Trapping	0.02
Mining incl. oil & gas	14.7
Utilities	2.6
Construction	4.7
Manufacturing	7.1

service producing	%
Wholesale & Retail trade	10.3
Transportation & warehousing	5.7
Information & Cultural industries	4.1
Finance, Insurance, & Real estate	16.3
Other services	21.4
Public administration	5.8

Scale 1: 5 000 000

0 50 100 150 200 250 km

Conical Orthomorphic Projection
© Oxford University Press

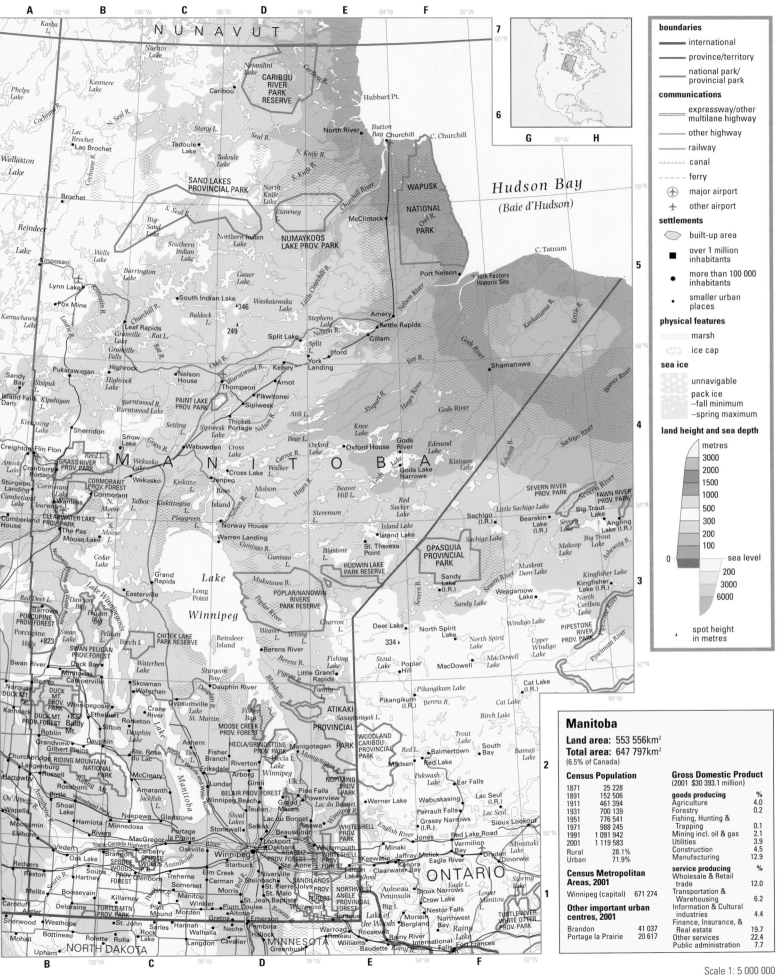

boundaries
— international
— province/territory
— national park/ provincial park

communications
— expressway/other multilane highway
— other highway
— railway
·········· canal
- - - - - ferry
⊕ major airport
✈ other airport

settlements
⬡ built-up area
■ over 1 million inhabitants
● more than 100 000 inhabitants
• smaller urban places

physical features
marsh
ice cap

sea ice
unnavigable
pack ice
–fall minimum
–spring maximum

land height and sea depth
metres
3000
2000
1500
1000
500
300
200
100
0   sea level
200
3000
6000

▲ spot height in metres

Manitoba

Land area: 553 556km²
Total area: 647 797km²
(6.5% of Canada)

Census Population

1871	25 228
1891	152 506
1911	461 394
1931	700 139
1951	776 541
1971	988 245
1991	1 091 942
2001	1 119 583
Rural	28.1%
Urban	71.9%

Census Metropolitan Areas, 2001

Winnipeg (capital) 671 274

Other important urban centres, 2001

Brandon 41 037
Portage la Prairie 20 617

Gross Domestic Product
(2001 $30 393.1 million)

goods producing	%
Agriculture	4.0
Forestry	0.2
Fishing, Hunting & Trapping	0.1
Mining incl. oil & gas	2.1
Utilities	3.9
Construction	4.5
Manufacturing	12.9

service producing	%
Wholesale & Retail trade	12.0
Transportation & Warehousing	6.2
Information & Cultural industries	4.4
Finance, Insurance, & Real estate	19.7
Other services	22.4
Public administration	7.7

Scale 1: 5 000 000

0   50   100   150   200   250 km

Conical Orthomorphic Projection

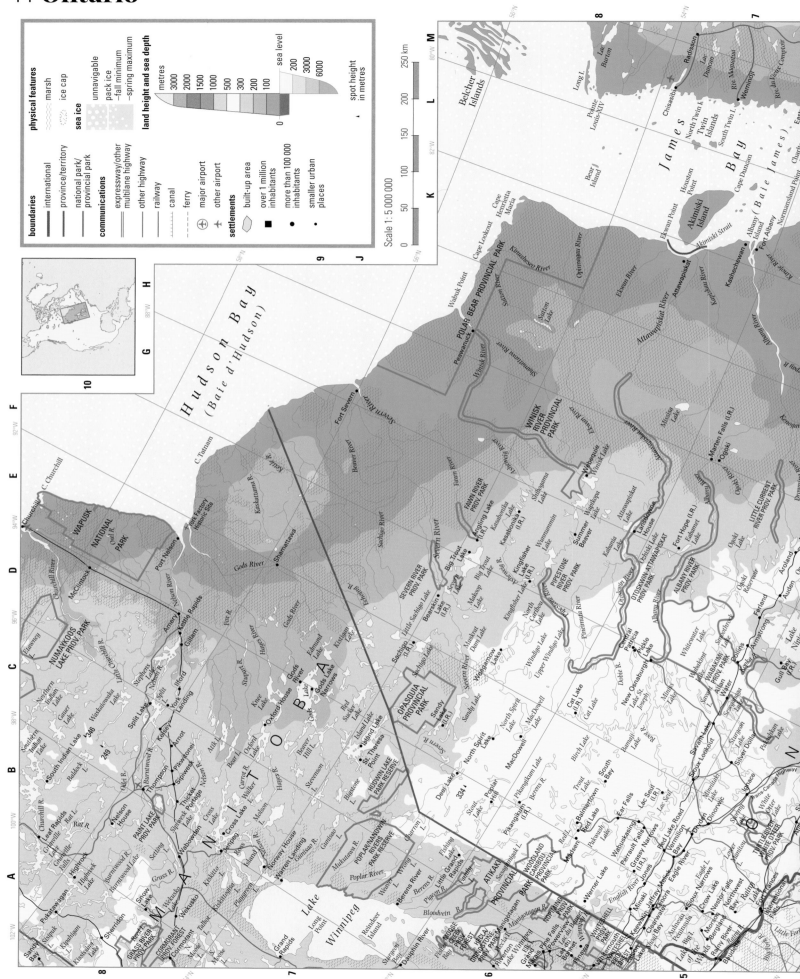

boundaries
international
province/territory
national park/
provincial park

communications
expressway/other
multilane highway
other highway
railway
canal
ferry

physical features
marsh
ice cap

sea ice
unnavigable
pack ice
—fall minimum
—spring maximum

land height and sea depth
metres
3000
2000
1500
1000
500
300
200
100
sea level
200
3000
6000

▲ spot height in metres

settlements
major airport
other airport
built-up area
over 1 million inhabitants
more than 100 000 inhabitants
smaller urban places

Scale 1:5 000 000

0   50   100   150   200   250 km

Conical Orthomorphic Projection   © Oxford University Press

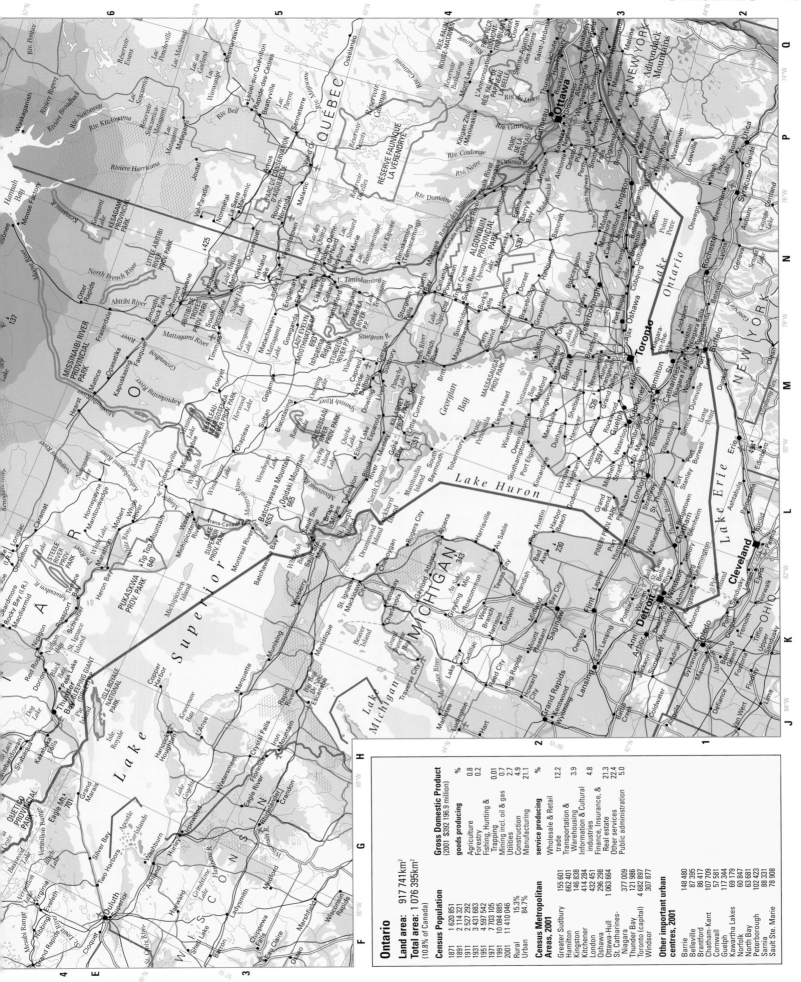

Ontario

Land area: 917 741km²
Total area: 1 076 395km²
(10.8% of Canada)

Census Population

1871	1 620 851
1891	2 114 321
1911	2 527 292
1931	3 431 683
1951	4 597 542
1971	7 703 105
1991	10 084 885
2001	11 410 046
Rural	15.3%
Urban	84.7%

Census Metropolitan Areas, 2001

Greater Sudbury	155 601
Hamilton	662 401
Kingston	146 838
Kitchener	414 284
London	432 451
Oshawa	296 298
Ottawa-Hull	1 063 664
St. Catharines-Niagara	377 009
Thunder Bay	121 986
Toronto (capital)	4 682 897
Windsor	307 877

Other important urban centres, 2001

Barrie	148 480
Belleville	87 395
Brantford	86 417
Chatham-Kent	107 709
Cornwall	57 581
Guelph	117 344
Kawartha Lakes	69 179
Norfolk	60 847
North Bay	63 681
Peterborough	102 423
Sarnia	88 331
Sault Ste. Marie	78 908

Gross Domestic Product
(2001 $392 196.9 million)

goods producing	%
Agriculture	0.8
Forestry	0.2
Fishing, Hunting & Trapping	0.01
Mining incl. oil & gas	0.7
Utilities	2.7
Construction	4.9
Manufacturing	21.1

service producing	%
Wholesale & Retail trade	12.2
Transportation & Warehousing	3.9
Information & Cultural industries	4.8
Finance, Insurance, & Real estate	21.3
Other services	22.4
Public administration	5.0

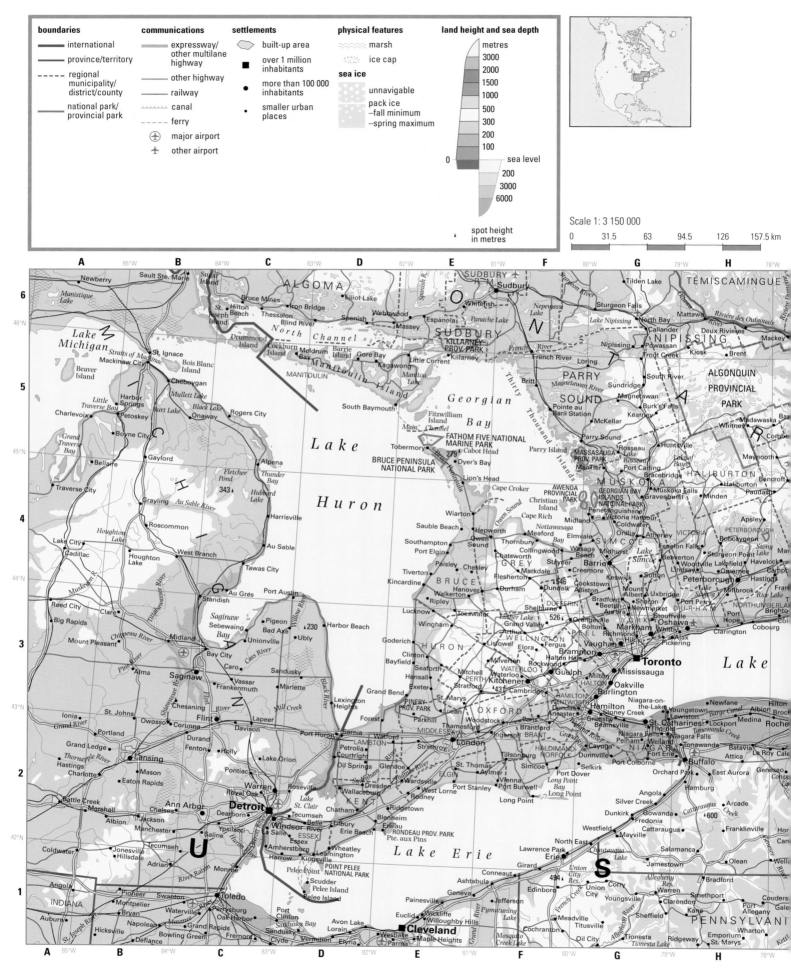

The St. Lawrence Seaway

The St. Lawrence Seaway Authority was established in 1951 for the purpose of constructing, operating, and maintaining a deep waterway between the Port of Montréal and Lake Erie, replacing an earlier network of shallow-draught canals. Two of the seven seaway locks along the St. Lawrence River, in the United States, are operated by the US St. Lawrence Seaway Development Corporation.

The St. Lawrence Seaway was officially opened in 1959. It allows navigation by ships not exceeding 222.5m in length, 23.2m in width, and loaded to a maximum draught of 7.9m in a minimum water depth of 8.2m.

Beginning at Montréal, the Seaway naturally divides into four sections:

1. The Lachine Section required the construction of the 33km South Shore Canal, to by-pass the Lachine Rapids.

The St. Lambert and Côte Ste. Catherine locks provide a lift 13.7m to Lake St. Louis.

2. The Soulanges Section contains the two Beauharnois locks, by-passing the Beauharnois hydro-electric plant to reach Lac Saint-François.

3. The Lac Saint-François Section extends to a point just east of Cornwall, Ontario.

4. The International Rapids Section was developed simultaneously for hydro-electric power generation and navigation. Ontario and the State of New York jointly built the Moses-Saunders Power Dam, the Long Sault and Iroquois control dams, and undertook the flooding of the river above the power dam to form Lake St. Lawrence, the 'head pond' of the generating station.

The Wiley-Dondero Canal and the Snell and Eisenhower locks allow ships to by-pass the Moses-Saunders power station. The Iroquois lock and adjacent control dam are used to adjust the level of Lake St. Lawrence to that of Lake Ontario.

The Welland Canal joins lakes Ontario and Erie and allows ships to by-pass Niagara Falls by means of eight locks. The present Welland Canal, completed in 1932, was later deepened to ensure 7.9m draught navigation throughout the Seaway.

The final section consists of four parallel locks, the 'Soo' locks, on the St. Mary's River and connects Lake Superior to Lake Huron. This section is not part of the St. Lawrence Seaway Authority.

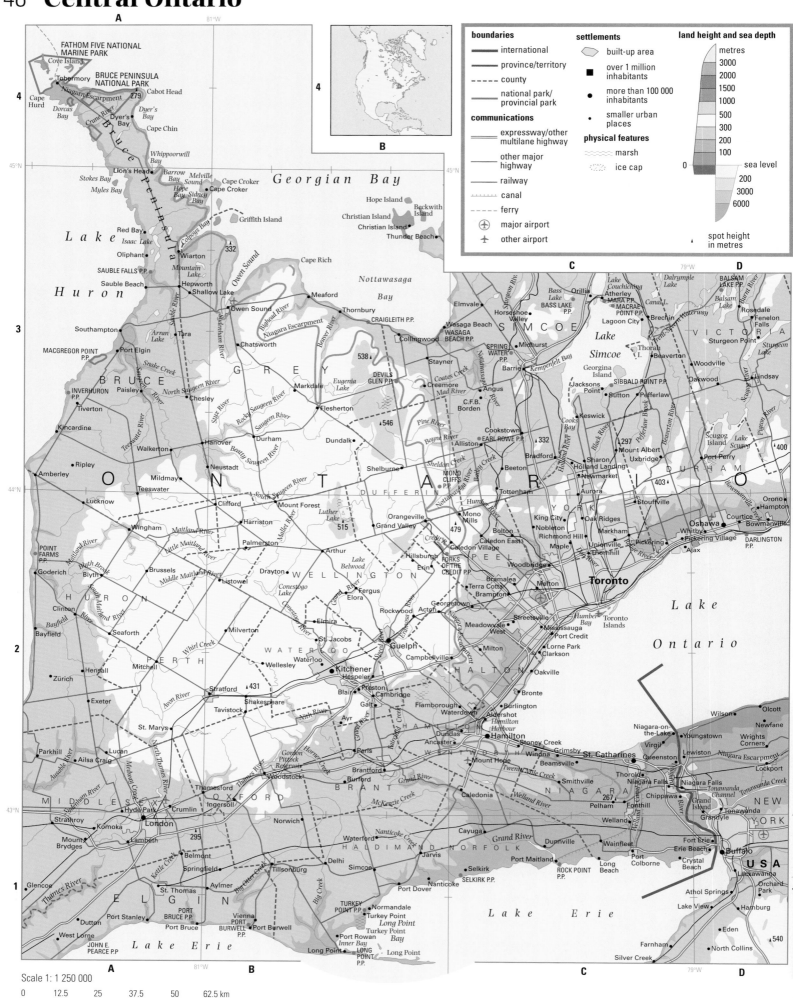

boundaries

― international
― province/territory
--- county
― national park/provincial park

communications

― expressway/other multilane highway
― other major highway
― railway
⊥ canal
--- ferry
✈ major airport
✈ other airport

settlements

⬡ built-up area
■ over 1 million inhabitants
● more than 100 000 inhabitants
• smaller urban places

physical features

marsh
ice cap

land height and sea depth

metres
3000
2000
1500
1000
500
300
200
100
0 sea level
200
3000
6000

▲ spot height in metres

Scale 1: 1 250 000

0   12.5   25   37.5   50   62.5 km

Conical Orthomorphic Projection

© Oxford University Press

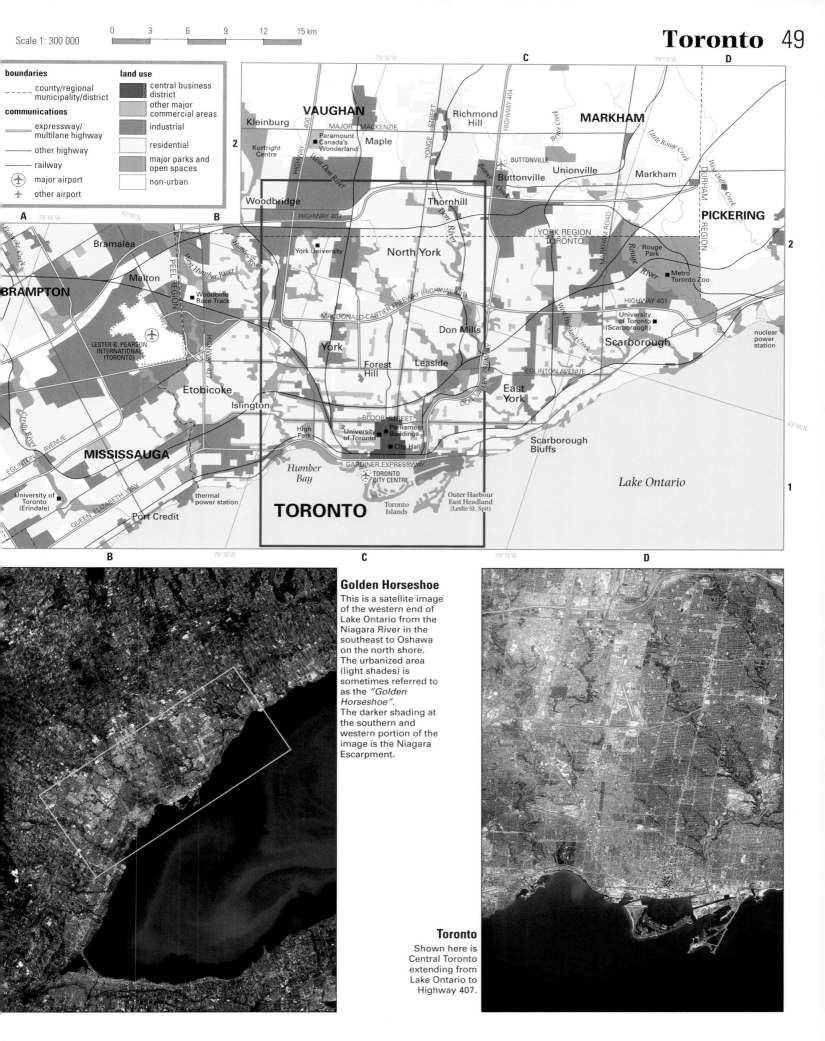

Scale 1 : 300 000

0 3 6 9 12 15 km

boundaries

county/regional
municipality/district

communications

expressway/
multilane highway

other highway

railway

✈ major airport

✈ other airport

land use

central business
district

other major
commercial areas

industrial

residential

major parks and
open spaces

non-urban

A 79°45'W 43°45'N B 79°30'W C 79°15'W D

VAUGHAN

Kleinburg

Kortright
Centre

Woodbridge

HIGHWAY 407

Paramount
Canada's
Wonderland

Maple

MAJOR MACKENZIE

West Don River

Richmond
Hill

YONGE STREET

HIGHWAY 404

BUTTONVILLE

MARKHAM

Bruce Creek

Little Rouge Creek

Thornhill

Don River

Buttonville

Bathurst Creek

Unionville

Markham

DURHAM REGION

West Duffin Creek

PICKERING

York University

North York

YORK REGION
TORONTO

Rouge
Park

Rouge River

Metro
Toronto Zoo

2

BRAMPTON

Bramalea

Malton

PEEL REGION

West Humber River

Humber River

MACDONALD-CARTIER FREEWAY (HIGHWAY 401)

Don Mills

West Highland Creek

HIGHWAY 401

University of Toronto (Scarborough)

Scarborough

nuclear
power
station

Woodbine
Race Track

York

Forest
Hill

Leaside

DON VALLEY PARKWAY

East
York

EGLINTON AVENUE

43°45'N

1

LESTER B. PEARSON
INTERNATIONAL
(TORONTO)

HIGHWAY 427

Etobicoke

Islington

BLOOR STREET

High
Park

University
of Toronto

Parliament
Buildings

City Hall

Scarborough
Bluffs

Scarborough
Bluffs

EGLINTON AVENUE

QUEEN ELIZABETH WAY

Credit River

EGLINTON AVENUE

MISSISSAUGA

University of
Toronto
(Erindale)

Port Credit

thermal
power station

Humber
Bay

GARDINER EXPRESSWAY

TORONTO

TORONTO
CITY CENTRE

Toronto
Islands

Outer Harbour
East Headland
(Leslie St. Spit)

Lake Ontario

B 79°30'W C 79°15'W D

Golden Horseshoe

This is a satellite image of the western end of Lake Ontario from the Niagara River in the southeast to Oshawa on the north shore. The urbanized area (light shades) is sometimes referred to as the *"Golden Horseshoe"*. The darker shading at the southern and western portion of the image is the Niagara Escarpment.

Toronto

Shown here is Central Toronto extending from Lake Ontario to Highway 407.

50 Québec

Conical Orthomorphic Projection

Québec

Land area: 1 356 128km²
Total area: 1 542 056km²
(15.5% of Canada)

Census Population

1871	1 191 516
1891	1 488 535
1911	2 005 776
1931	2 874 662
1951	4 055 681
1971	6 027 765
1991	6 895 963
2001	7 237 479
Rural	19.6%
Urban	80.4%

Gross Domestic Product
(2001 $199 554.5 million)

	%
goods producing	
Agriculture	1.2
Forestry	0.5
Fishing, Hunting &	
Trapping	0.04
Mining incl. oil & gas	0.7
Utilities	4.0
Construction	5.1
Manufacturing	22.2
service producing	
Wholesale & Retail	
trade	11.7
Transportation &	
Warehousing	4.4
Information & Cultural	
industries	5.0
Finance, Insurance, &	
Real estate	16.8
Other services	22.2
Public administration	6.2

Census Metropolitan Areas, 2001

Chicoutimi- Jonquière	154 938
Montréal	3 426 350
Québec (capital)	682 757
Sherbrooke	153 811
Trois-Rivières	137 507

Other important urban centres, 2001

Drummondville	68 451
Granby	60 264
Saint-Hyacinthe	49 536
Saint-Jean-sur- Richelieu	79 600
Shawinigan	57 304

Since the date of this census, Chicoutimi, Jonquière and La Baie have been amalgamated and renamed Saguenay.

52 Atlantic Provinces

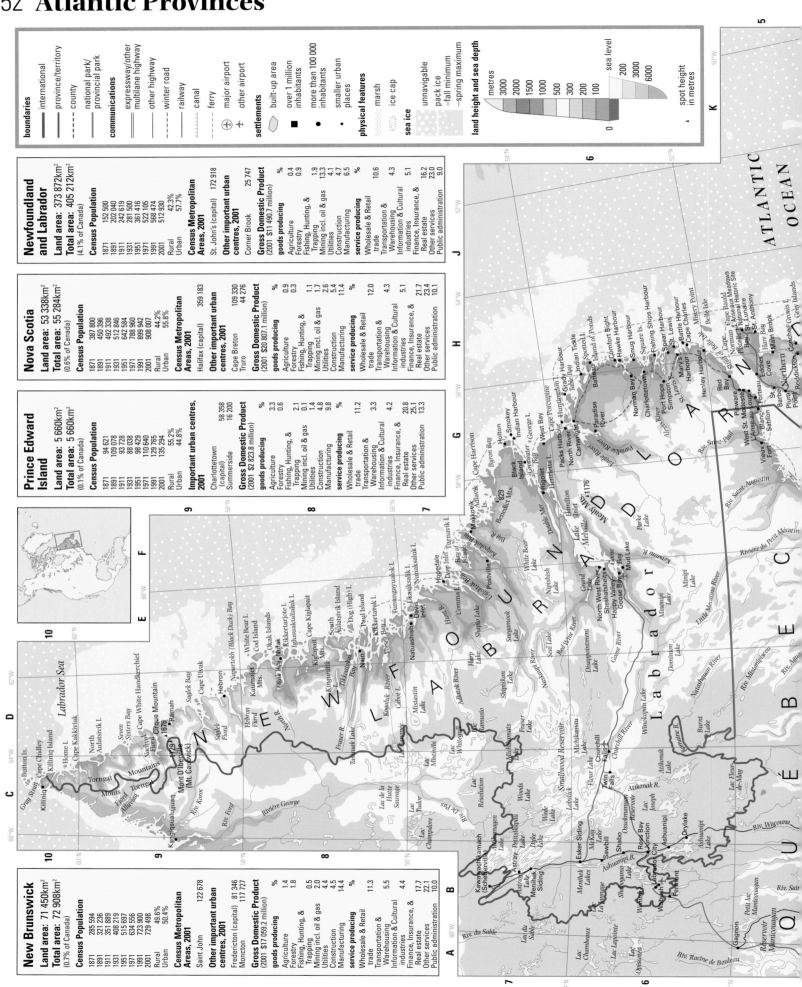

New Brunswick

Land area: 71 450km²
Total area: 72 908km² (0.7% of Canada)

Census Population

Year	Population
1871	285 594
1891	321 236
1911	351 889
1931	408 219
1951	515 697
1971	634 556
1991	723 900
2001	729 498
Rural	49.6%
Urban	50.4%

Census Metropolitan Areas, 2001

Saint John 122 678

Other important urban centres, 2001

Fredericton (capital)	81 346
Moncton	117 727

Gross Domestic Product (2001 $17 059.2 million)

goods producing	%
Agriculture	1.4
Forestry	1.8
Fishing, Hunting, & Trapping	0.5
Mining incl. oil & gas	2.0
Utilities	4.4
Construction	4.5
Manufacturing	14.4
service producing	**%**
Wholesale & Retail trade	11.3
Transportation & Warehousing	5.5
Information & Cultural industries	4.4
Finance, Insurance, & Real estate	17.7
Other services	22.1
Public administration	10.0

Prince Edward Island

Land area: 5 660km²
Total area: 5 660km² (0.1% of Canada)

Census Population

Year	Population
1871	94 021
1891	109 078
1911	93 728
1931	88 038
1951	98 429
1971	110 640
1991	129 765
2001	135 294
Rural	55.2%
Urban	44.8%

Important urban centres, 2001

Charlottetown (capital)	58 358
Summerside	16 200

Gross Domestic Product (2001 $2 823.8 million)

goods producing	%
Agriculture	3.3
Forestry	0.6
Fishing, Hunting, & Trapping	2.1
Mining incl. oil & gas	0.1
Utilities	1.4
Construction	4.8
Manufacturing	9.8
service producing	**%**
Wholesale & Retail trade	11.2
Transportation & Warehousing	3.3
Information & Cultural industries	4.2
Finance, Insurance, & Real estate	20.8
Other services	25.1
Public administration	13.3

Nova Scotia

Land area: 53 338km²
Total area: 55 284km² (0.6% of Canada)

Census Population

Year	Population
1871	387 800
1891	450 396
1911	492 338
1931	512 846
1951	642 584
1971	788 960
1991	899 942
2001	908 007
Rural	44.2%
Urban	55.8%

Census Metropolitan Areas, 2001

Halifax (capital) 359 183

Other important urban centres, 2001

Cape Breton	109 330
Truro	44 276

Gross Domestic Product (2001 $20 807.1 million)

goods producing	%
Agriculture	0.9
Forestry	0.3
Fishing, Hunting, & Trapping	1.1
Mining incl. oil & gas	1.7
Utilities	2.6
Construction	5.4
Manufacturing	11.4
service producing	**%**
Wholesale & Retail trade	12.0
Transportation & Warehousing	4.3
Information & Cultural industries	5.1
Finance, Insurance, & Real estate	21.7
Other services	23.4
Public administration	10.1

Newfoundland and Labrador

Land area: 373 872km²
Total area: 405 212km² (4.1% of Canada)

Census Population

Year	Population
1871	152 500
1891	202 040
1911	242 619
1931	281 500
1951	361 416
1971	522 105
1991	568 474
2001	512 930
Rural	42.3%
Urban	57.7%

Census Metropolitan Areas, 2001

St. John's (capital) 172 918

Other important urban centres, 2001

Corner Brook 25 747

Gross Domestic Product (2001 $11 490.7 million)

goods producing	%
Agriculture	0.4
Forestry	0.9
Fishing, Hunting, & Trapping	1.9
Mining incl. oil & gas	13.3
Utilities	4.1
Construction	4.7
Manufacturing	6.5
service producing	**%**
Wholesale & Retail trade	10.6
Transportation & Warehousing	4.3
Information & Cultural industries	5.1
Finance, Insurance, & Real estate	16.2
Other services	23.0
Public administration	9.0

Nova Scotia and Prince Edward Island

Scale 1: 3 150 000

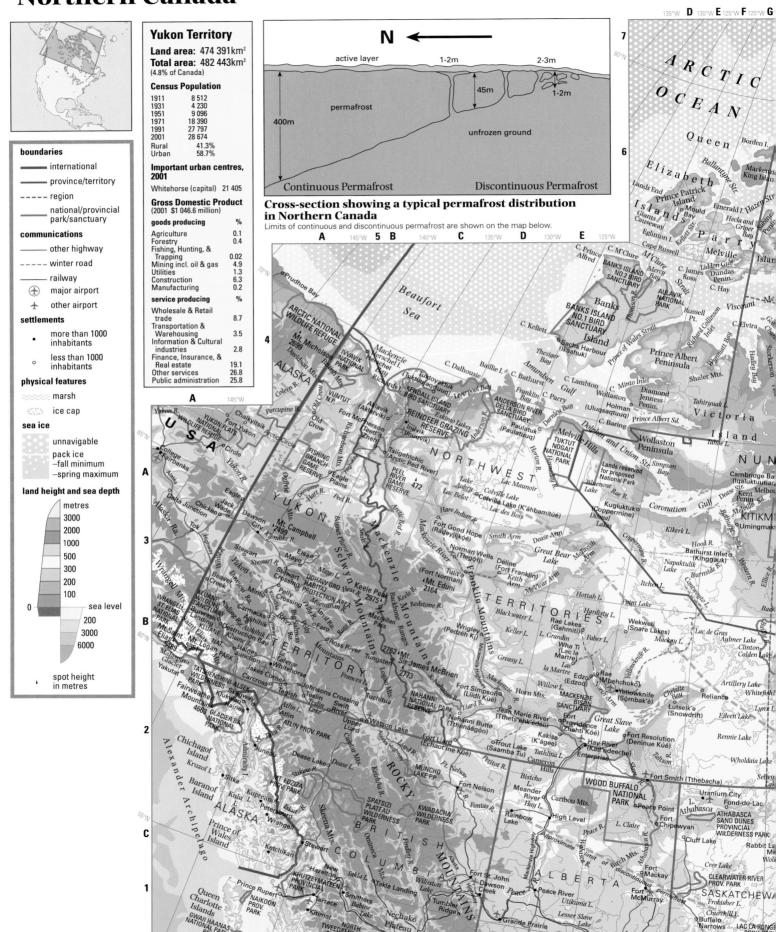

Yukon Territory

Land area: 474 391km²
Total area: 482 443km²
(4.8% of Canada)

Census Population

1911	8 512
1931	4 230
1951	9 096
1971	18 390
1991	27 797
2001	28 674
Rural	41.3%
Urban	58.7%

Important urban centres, 2001

Whitehorse (capital) 21 405

Gross Domestic Product

(2001 $1 046.6 million)

goods producing	%
Agriculture	0.1
Forestry	0.4
Fishing, Hunting, & Trapping	0.02
Mining incl. oil & gas	4.9
Utilities	1.3
Construction	6.3
Manufacturing	0.2

service producing	%
Wholesale & Retail trade	8.7
Transportation & Warehousing	3.5
Information & Cultural industries	2.8
Finance, Insurance, & Real estate	19.1
Other services	26.8
Public administration	25.8

boundaries

— international
— province/territory
--- region
— national/provincial park/sanctuary

communications

— other highway
— winter road
--- railway
⊕ major airport
✈ other airport

settlements

• more than 1000 inhabitants
○ less than 1000 inhabitants

physical features

marsh
ice cap

sea ice

unnavigable
pack ice
–fall minimum
–spring maximum

land height and sea depth

metres
3000
2000
1000
500
300
200
100
0 sea level
200
3000
6000

▲ spot height in metres

Cross-section showing a typical permafrost distribution in Northern Canada

Limits of continuous and discontinuous permafrost are shown on the map below.

Scale 1: 12 000 000

0   120   240   360   480   600 km

Conical Orthomorphic Projection   © Oxford University Press

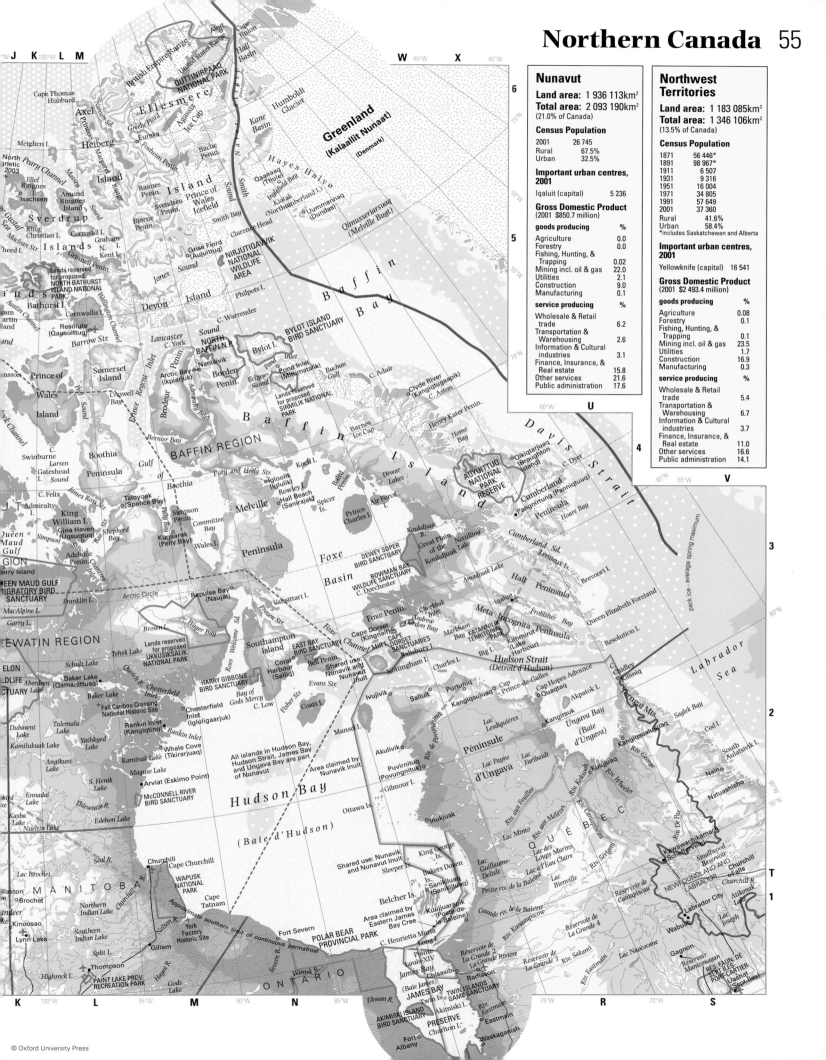

Nunavut

Land area: 1 936 113km²
Total area: 2 093 190km²
(21.0% of Canada)

Census Population

2001	26 745
Rural	67.5%
Urban	32.5%

Important urban centres, 2001

Iqaluit (capital) 5 236

Gross Domestic Product
(2001 $850.7 million)

goods producing	%
Agriculture	0.0
Forestry	0.0
Fishing, Hunting, & Trapping	0.02
Mining incl. oil & gas	22.0
Utilities	2.1
Construction	9.0
Manufacturing	0.1

service producing	%
Wholesale & Retail trade	6.2
Transportation & Warehousing	2.6
Information & Cultural industries	3.1
Finance, Insurance, & Real estate	15.8
Other services	21.6
Public administration	17.6

Northwest Territories

Land area: 1 183 085km²
Total area: 1 346 106km²
(13.5% of Canada)

Census Population

1871	56 446*
1891	98 967*
1911	6 507
1931	9 316
1951	16 004
1971	34 805
1991	57 649
2001	37 360
Rural	41.6%
Urban	58.4%

*includes Saskatchewan and Alberta

Important urban centres, 2001

Yellowknife (capital) 16 541

Gross Domestic Product
(2001 $2 493.4 million)

goods producing	%
Agriculture	0.08
Forestry	0.1
Fishing, Hunting, & Trapping	0.1
Mining incl. oil & gas	23.5
Utilities	1.7
Construction	16.9
Manufacturing	0.3

service producing	%
Wholesale & Retail trade	5.4
Transportation & Warehousing	6.7
Information & Cultural industries	3.7
Finance, Insurance, & Real estate	11.0
Other services	16.6
Public administration	14.1

Scale 1: 300 000

0 3 6 9 12 15 km

boundaries

– – – province

- - - - county/regional
municipality/
district

communications

═══ expressway/
multilane highway

── other highway

── railway

┄┄┄ canal

✈ major airport

✈ other airport

physical features

～～ river, lake

marsh

—50— contours

▴ spot height
in metres

land use

central business
district

other major
commercial areas

industrial

residential

major parks and
open spaces

non-urban

M 73°45'W N 73°30'W P

AÉROPORT INT. DE MONTRÉAL (MIRABEL)

AUTOROUTE DES LAURENTIDES

Blainville

Lorraine

Saint-François

Île Sainte-Thérèse

Varennes

Sainte-Thérèse

Rosemère

CO. TERREBONNE

CO. DEUX MONTAGNES

Boisbriand

Sainte-Rose

VILLE DE LAVAL

Saint-Vincent-de-Paul

Rivière des Mille Îles

Rivière des Prairies

AUTOROUTE FÉLIX-LECLERC

Parc de récréation des Îles-de-Boucherville

Île-de-Boucherville

CO. CHAMBLY

Rivière du Chêne

Île Jésus

Duvernay

AUTOROUTE LAVAL

Pont-Viau

Laval-des-Rapides

RUE SHERBROOKE

Montréal

AUTOROUTE JEAN-LESAGE

Tunnel

Sainte-Eustache

Laval-Ouest

AUTOROUTE CHOMEDEY

Chomedey

Stade Olympique

SAINT-HUBERT

5

Deux-Montagnes

Sainte-Dorothée

MONTRÉAL

Île Ste-Hélène

LONGUEUIL

Sainte-Marthe-sur-le-Lac

45°30'N

Parc québécois d'Oka

Île Bizard

30

Université de Montréal

Université McGill

Mont

Montréal

de

Île des Sœurs

CO. LA PRAIRIE

AUTOROUTE DES CANTONS DE L'EST

Lac des Deux Montagnes

Parc Cap-Saint-Jacques

AÉROPORT INT. DE MONTRÉAL (DORVAL)

AUTOROUTE MÉTROPOLITAINE

Île

Parc Angrignon

Île aux Herons

Fleuve Saint-Laurent

Aboretum Morgan

TRANS CANADA HIGHWAY

Baie de Valois

Île Dorval

Rapides de Lachine

St. Lawrence Seaway

La Prairie

4

Lac Saint Louis

Île Lynch

Kahnawake

Sainte-Catherine

Candiac

L'Île-Perrot

RÉSERVE INDIENNE KAHNAWAKE

30

M 73°45'W N 73°30'W P

Montréal

This view of the entire Montréal
region was taken by the Landsat
7 ETM satellite at an altitude of
705 km on June 8, 2001.

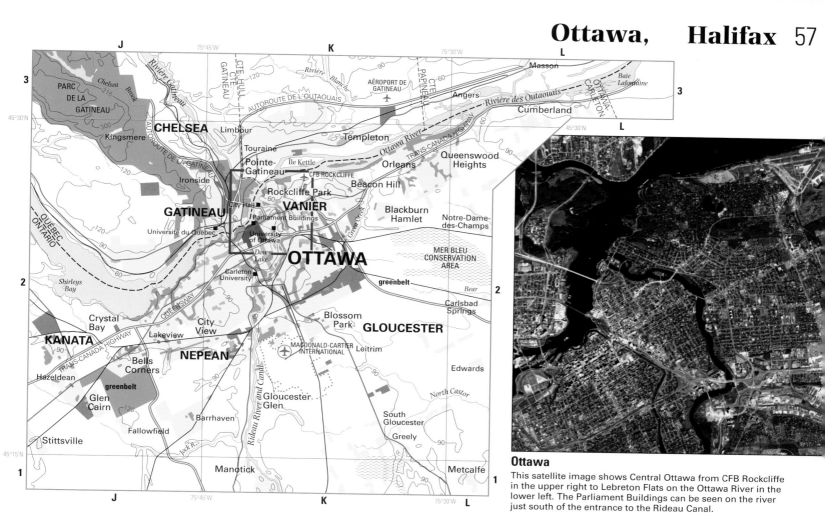

Ottawa

This satellite image shows Central Ottawa from CFB Rockcliffe in the upper right to Lebreton Flats on the Ottawa River in the lower left. The Parliament Buildings can be seen on the river just south of the entrance to the Rideau Canal.

Halifax

This true colour image of the Halifax region taken by the Landsat 7 satellite at an altitude of 705 km, reveals much additional land use information.

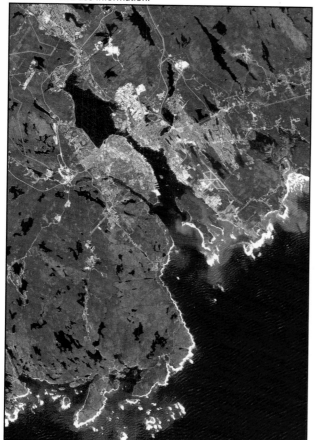

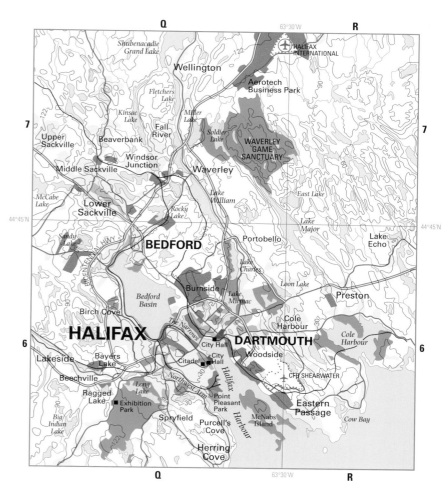

© Oxford University Press

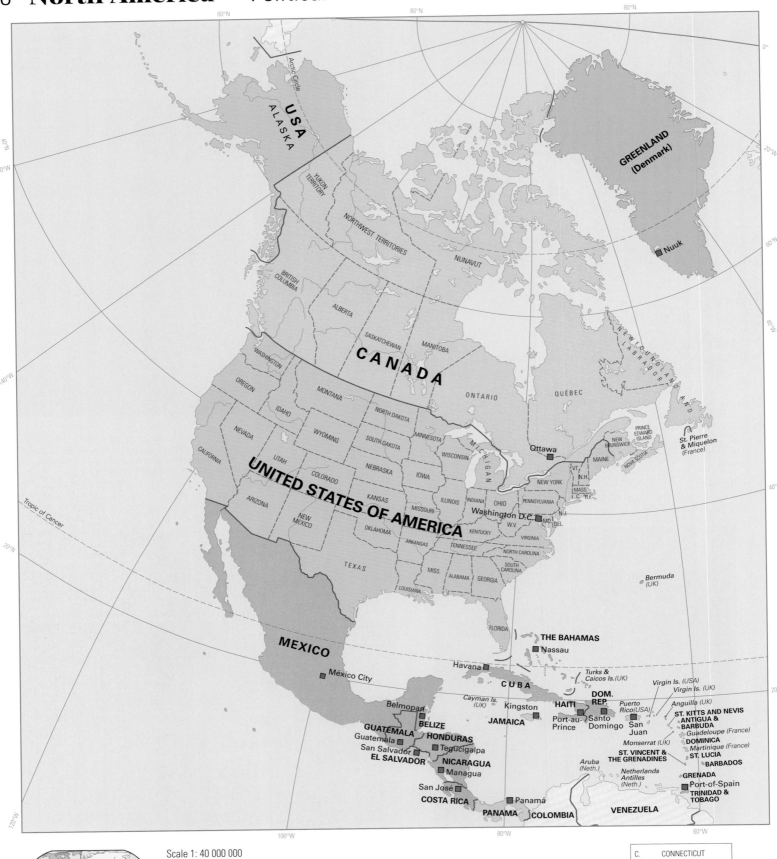

60°N 80°N 80°N 0°

Arctic Circle

USA
ALASKA

GREENLAND
(Denmark)

160°W

20°W

YUKON
TERRITORY

NORTHWEST TERRITORIES

NUNAVUT

Nuuk

BRITISH
COLUMBIA

80°N

ALBERTA

SASKATCHEWAN

MANITOBA

C A N A D A

ONTARIO

QUÉBEC

140°W

WASHINGTON

OREGON

IDAHO

MONTANA

NORTH DAKOTA

MINNESOTA

WISCONSIN

NEW
BRUNSWICK

PRINCE
EDWARD
ISLAND

St. Pierre
& Miquelon
(France)

NEVADA

UTAH

WYOMING

SOUTH DAKOTA

IOWA

Ottawa

MAINE

NOVA SCOTIA

40°N

CALIFORNIA

UNITED STATES OF AMERICA

COLORADO

NEBRASKA

KANSAS

ILLINOIS

MISSOURI

INDIANA

OHIO

PENNSYLVANIA

VT.
N.H.
MASS.
C. R.I.

NEW YORK

Tropic of Cancer

ARIZONA

NEW
MEXICO

OKLAHOMA

ARKANSAS

KENTUCKY

TENNESSEE

VIRGINIA

NORTH CAROLINA

Washington D.C.

N.J.
MD.
DEL.

W.V.

20°N

TEXAS

MISS.

ALABAMA

GEORGIA

SOUTH
CAROLINA

LOUISIANA

Bermuda
(UK)

MEXICO

FLORIDA

THE BAHAMAS

Nassau

México City

Havana

C U B A

Turks &
Caicos Is.(UK)

Virgin Is. (USA)
Virgin Is. (UK)

20°N

Belmopan

Cayman Is.
(UK)

Kingston

HAITI

**DOM.
REP.**

Puerto
Rico(USA)

Anguilla (UK)

ST. KITTS AND NEVIS
ANTIGUA &
BARBUDA

GUATEMALA

BELIZE

JAMAICA

Port-au-
Prince

Santo
Domingo

San
Juan

Guadeloupe (France)

DOMINICA

Guatemala

HONDURAS

Monserrat (UK)

Martinique (France)
ST. LUCIA

San Salvador

Tegucigalpa

ST. VINCENT &
THE GRENADINES

EL SALVADOR

NICARAGUA

Aruba
(Neth.)

BARBADOS

Managua

Netherlands
Antilles
(Neth.)

GRENADA

Port-of-Spain

San José

Panama

TRINIDAD &
TOBAGO

COSTA RICA

PANAMA

COLOMBIA

VENEZUELA

120°W

100°W

80°W

60°W

Scale 1: 40 000 000

0   400   800   1200   1600   2000 km

C.	CONNECTICUT
DEL.	DELAWARE
MASS.	MASSACHUSETTS
MD.	MARYLAND
MISS.	MISSISSIPPI
N.H.	NEW HAMPSHIRE
N.J.	NEW JERSEY
R.I.	RHODE ISLAND
VT.	VERMONT
W.V.	WEST VIRGINIA

——— international boundary

– – – national boundary

- - - disputed boundary

■ capital city

Oblique Mercator Projection   © Oxford University Press

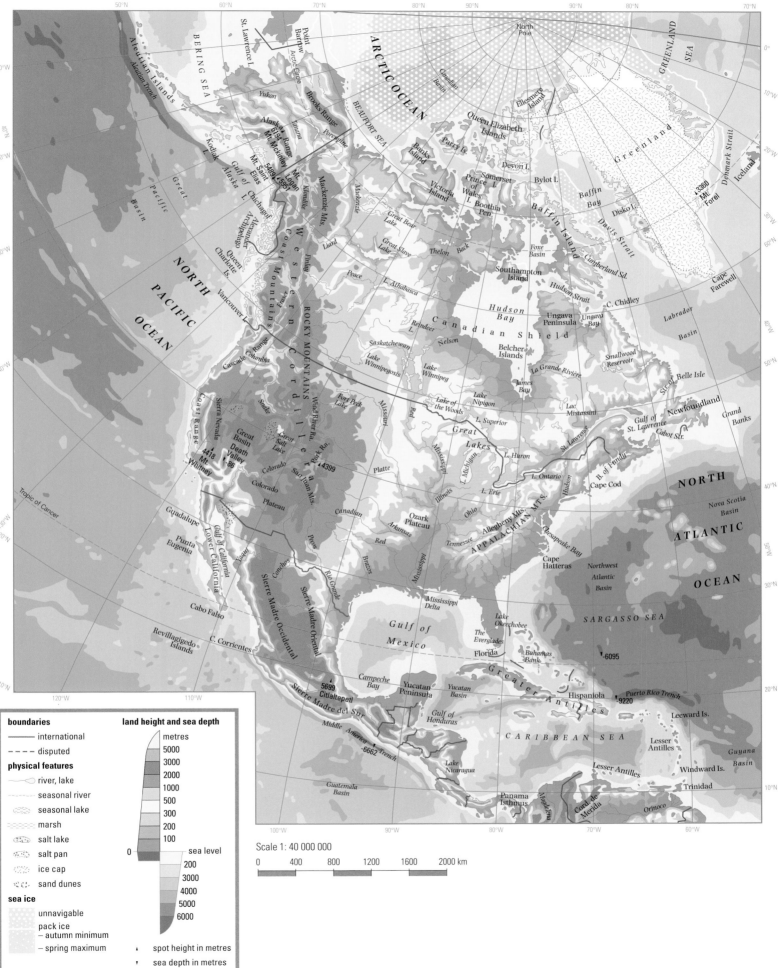

boundaries

——	international
---	disputed

physical features

	river, lake
	seasonal river
	seasonal lake
	marsh
	salt lake
	salt pan
	ice cap
	sand dunes

sea ice

	unnavigable
	pack ice
	– autumn minimum
	– spring maximum

land height and sea depth

metres
5000
3000
2000
1000
500
300
200
100
0   sea level
200
3000
4000
5000
6000

▲ spot height in metres
▼ sea depth in metres

Scale 1: 40 000 000

0   400   800   1200   1600   2000 km

Oblique Mercator Projection   © Oxford University Press

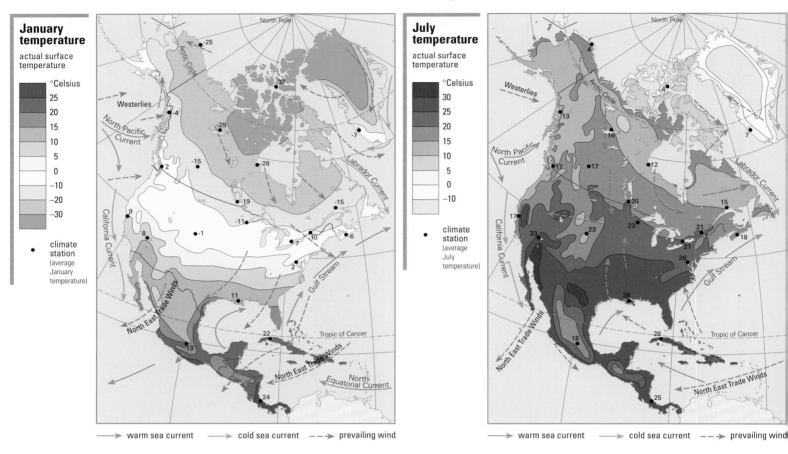

January temperature

actual surface temperature

°Celsius

25
20
15
10
5
0
−10
−20
−30

• climate station
(average January temperature)

July temperature

actual surface temperature

°Celsius

30
25
20
15
10
5
0
−10

• climate station
(average July temperature)

→ warm sea current   → cold sea current   - -→ prevailing wind

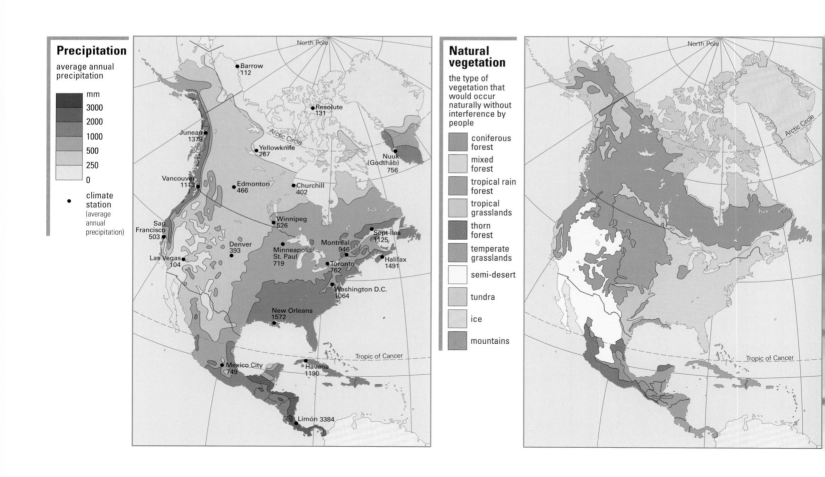

Precipitation

average annual precipitation

mm

3000
2000
1000
500
250
0

• climate station
(average annual precipitation)

Barrow 112
Resolute 131
Juneau 1379
Yellowknife 267
Nuuk (Godthåb) 756
Vancouver 1143
Edmonton 466
Churchill 402
Winnipeg 526
San Francisco 503
Sept-Îles 1125
Denver 393
Montréal 946
Minneapolis/St. Paul 719
Halifax 1491
Las Vegas 104
Toronto 762
Washington D.C. 1064
New Orleans 1572
Mexico City 749
Havana 1190
Limón 3384

Natural vegetation

the type of vegetation that would occur naturally without interference by people

- coniferous forest
- mixed forest
- tropical rain forest
- tropical grasslands
- thorn forest
- temperate grasslands
- semi-desert
- tundra
- ice
- mountains

Oblique Mercator Projection   © Oxford University Pr

Scale 1 : 55 000 000

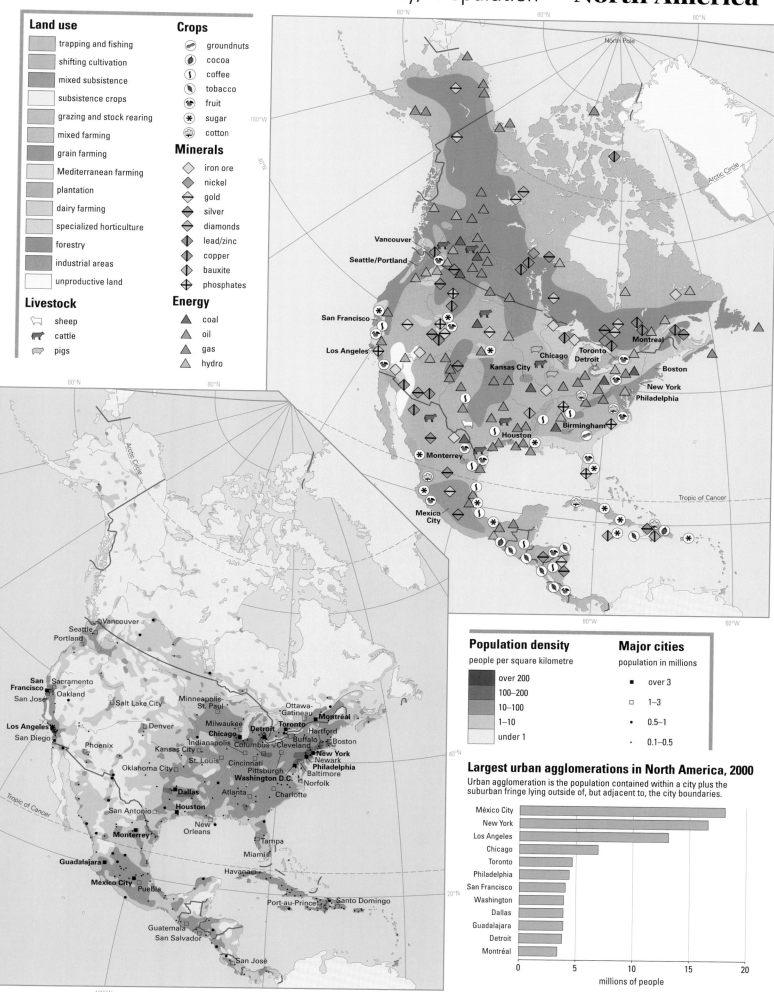

Land use

- trapping and fishing
- shifting cultivation
- mixed subsistence
- subsistence crops
- grazing and stock rearing
- mixed farming
- grain farming
- Mediterranean farming
- plantation
- dairy farming
- specialized horticulture
- forestry
- industrial areas
- unproductive land

Livestock

- sheep
- cattle
- pigs

Crops

- groundnuts
- cocoa
- coffee
- tobacco
- fruit
- sugar
- cotton

Minerals

- iron ore
- nickel
- gold
- silver
- diamonds
- lead/zinc
- copper
- bauxite
- phosphates

Energy

- coal
- oil
- gas
- hydro

Population density

people per square kilometre

- over 200
- 100–200
- 10–100
- 1–10
- under 1

Major cities

population in millions

- over 3
- 1–3
- 0.5–1
- 0.1–0.5

Largest urban agglomerations in North America, 2000

Urban agglomeration is the population contained within a city plus the suburban fringe lying outside of, but adjacent to, the city boundaries.

México City
New York
Los Angeles
Chicago
Toronto
Philadelphia
San Francisco
Washington
Dallas
Guadalajara
Detroit
Montréal

0   5   10   15   20

millions of people

Oblique Mercator Projection   © Oxford University Press

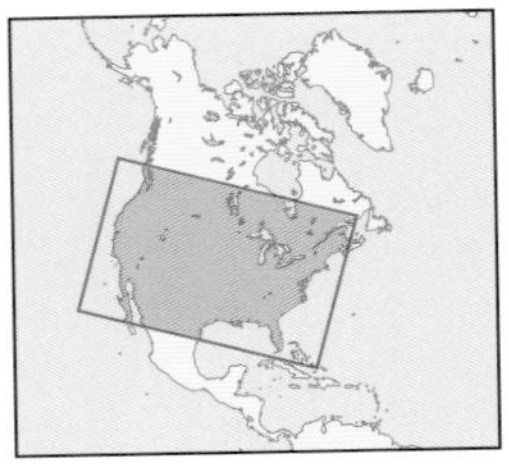

boundaries

— international
--- disputed
— internal

communications

═══ expressway
— major road
— railway
+++ canal
✈ major airport

settlements

■ over 1 million inhabitants
● more than 100 000 inhabitants
• smaller cities

physical features

~ river, lake
--- seasonal river
seasonal lake
marsh
salt lake
salt pan
ice cap
sand dunes

sea ice

unnavigable
pack ice
— fall minimum
— spring maximum

land height and sea depth

metres
5000
3000
2000
1000
500
300
200
100
0 — sea level
200
3000
6000

▲ spot height in metres

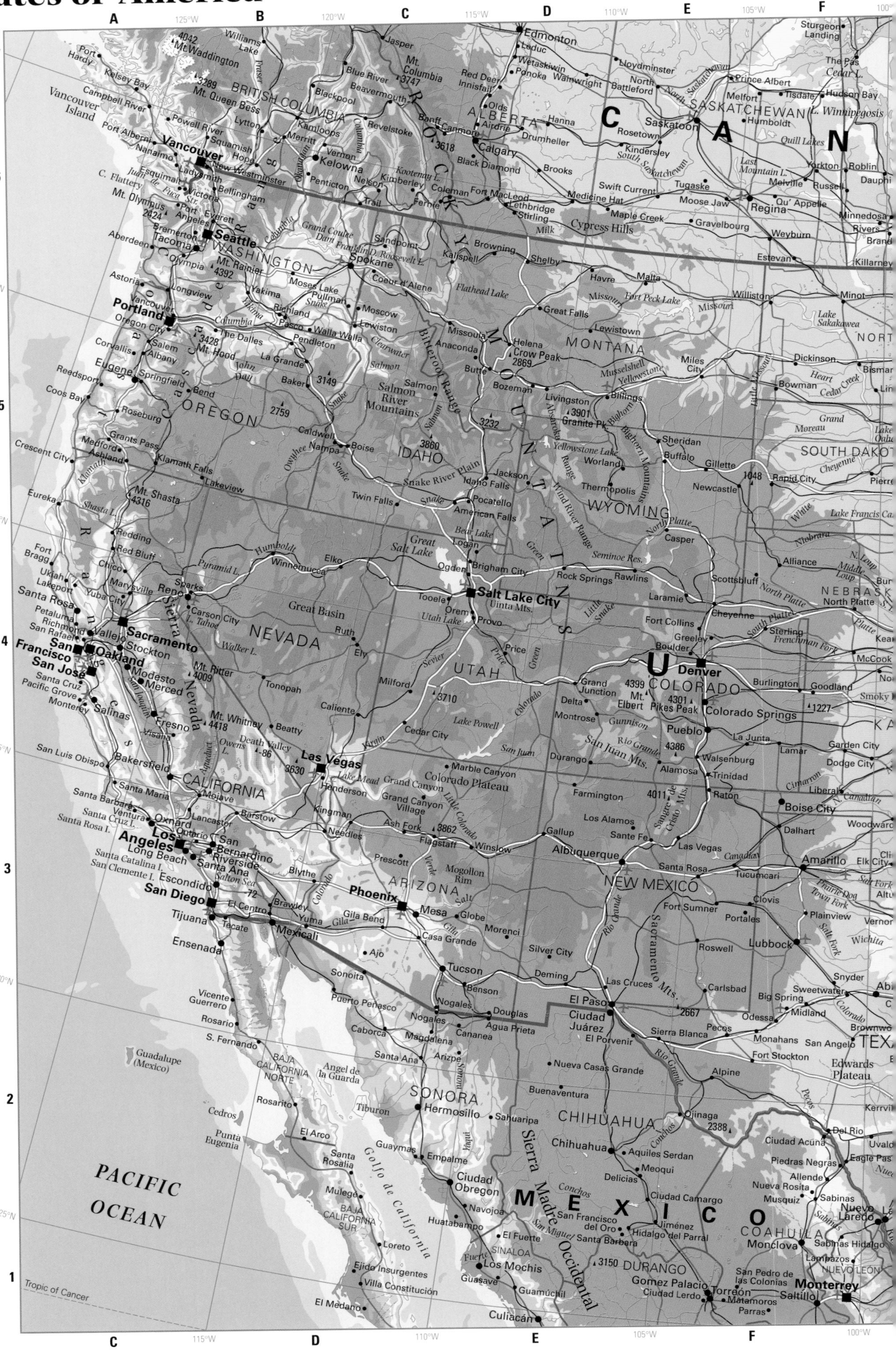

Scale 1: 12 500 000

0   125   250   375   500   625 km

Conical Orthomorphic Projection

© Oxford University Press

PACIFIC OCEAN

BRITISH COLUMBIA
ALBERTA
SASKATCHEWAN
CANADA
WASHINGTON
OREGON
IDAHO
MONTANA
WYOMING
NEVADA
UTAH
CALIFORNIA
ARIZONA
NEW MEXICO
COLORADO
NEBRASKA
SOUTH DAKOTA
TEXAS
MEXICO
SONORA
CHIHUAHUA
COAHUILA
DURANGO
SINALOA
BAJA CALIFORNIA NORTE
BAJA CALIFORNIA SUR
NUEVO LEÓN

Vancouver
Seattle
Tacoma
Portland
Sacramento
San Francisco
Oakland
San Jose
Los Angeles
San Diego
Salt Lake City
Las Vegas
Phoenix
Denver
Edmonton
Calgary
Saskatoon
Regina
Albuquerque
El Paso
Amarillo
Monterrey
Tijuana
Mexicali
Ciudad Juárez
Hermosillo
Chihuahua

Tropic of Cancer

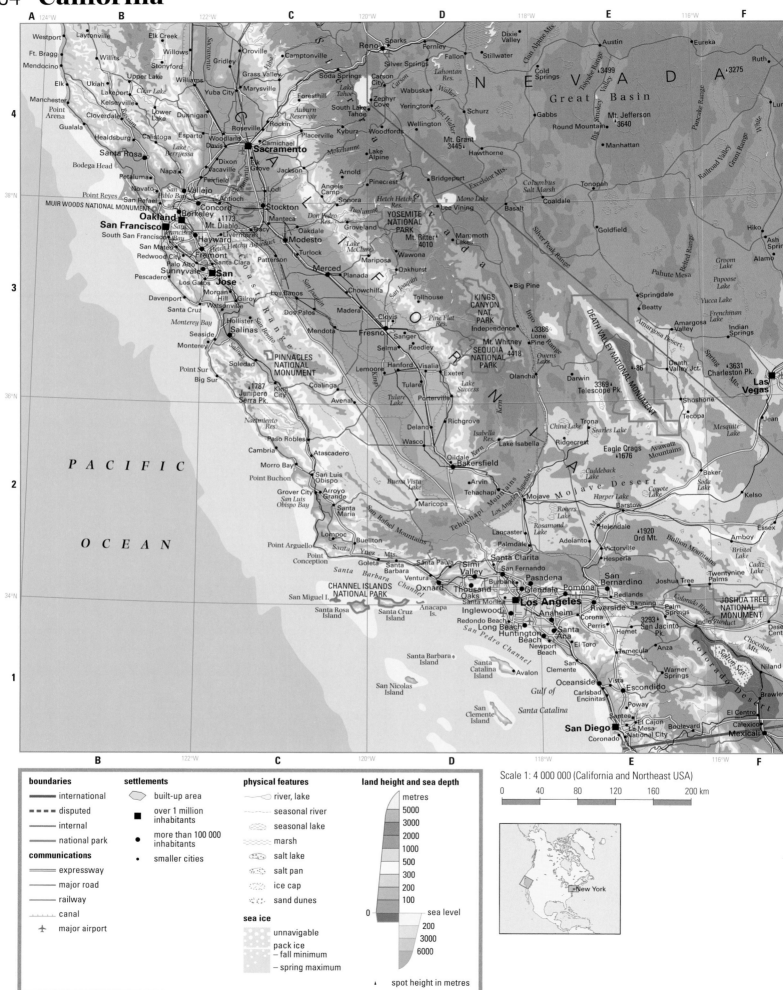

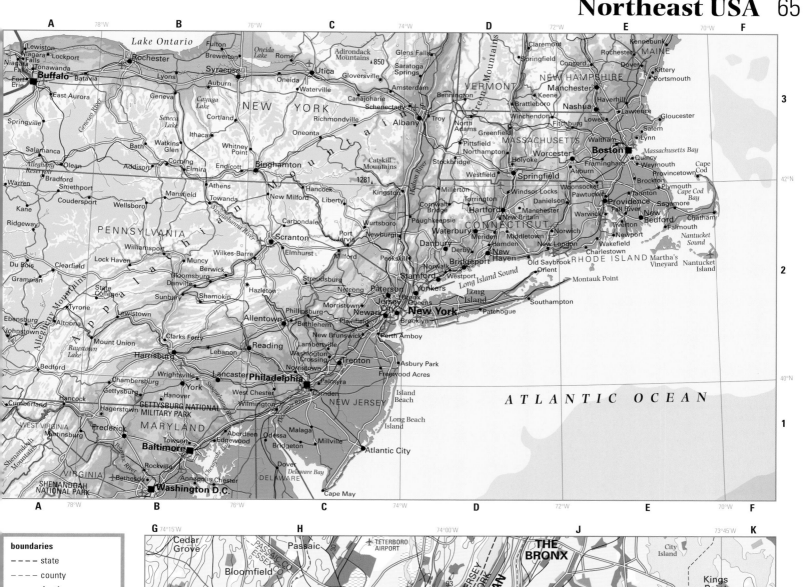

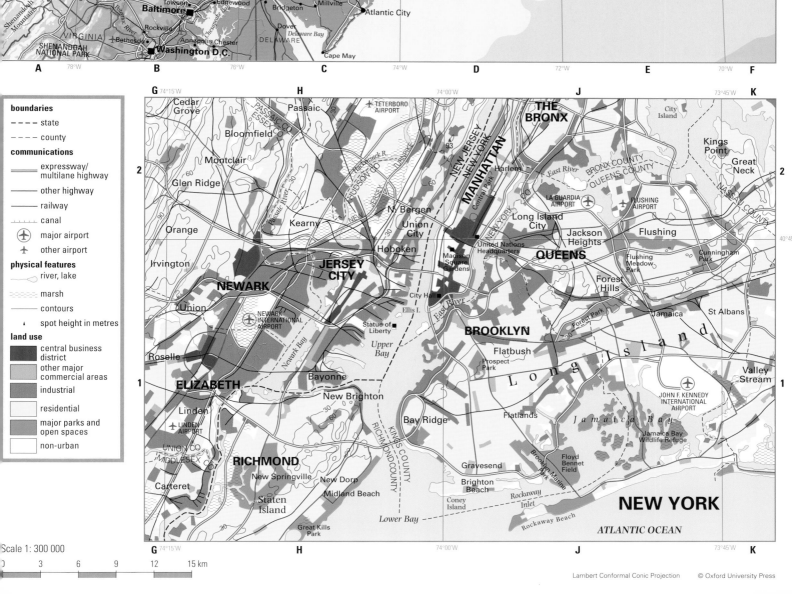

boundaries
- – – – – state
- – – – – county

communications
- ═══ expressway/ multilane highway
- ── other highway
- ── railway
- ┄┄┄ canal
- ✈ major airport
- ✈ other airport

physical features
- river, lake
- marsh
- contours
- ▴ spot height in metres

land use
- central business district
- other major commercial areas
- industrial
- residential
- major parks and open spaces
- non-urban

Scale 1: 300 000

0 3 6 9 12 15 km

Map labels and legend

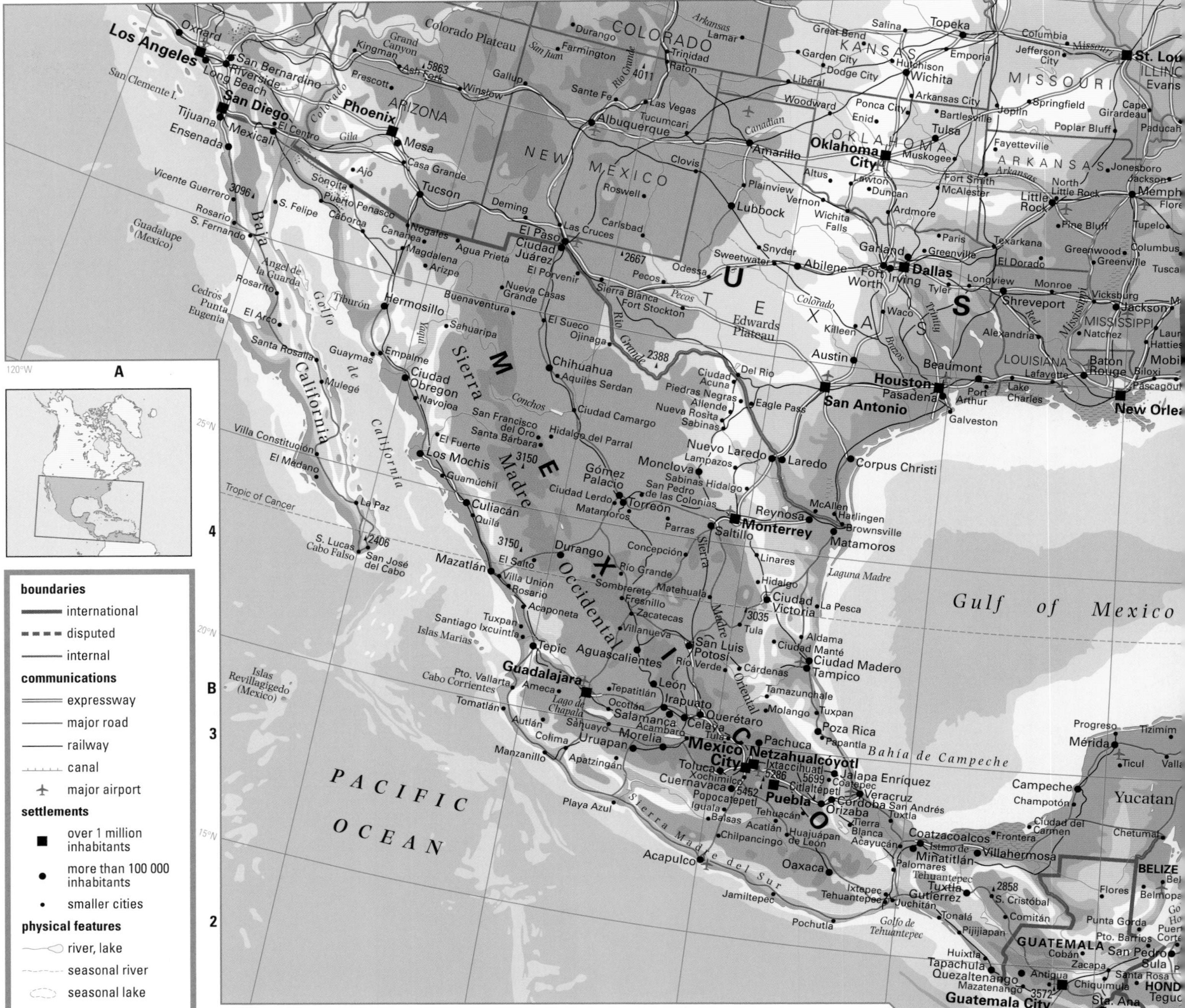

boundaries
— international
-- disputed
— internal

communications
expressway
major road
railway
canal
✈ major airport

settlements
■ over 1 million inhabitants
● more than 100 000 inhabitants
• smaller cities

physical features
river, lake
seasonal river
seasonal lake
marsh
salt lake
salt pan
ice cap
sand dunes

land height and sea depth
metres
5000
3000
2000
1000
500
300
200
100
sea level
0
200
3000
6000

▲ spot height in metres

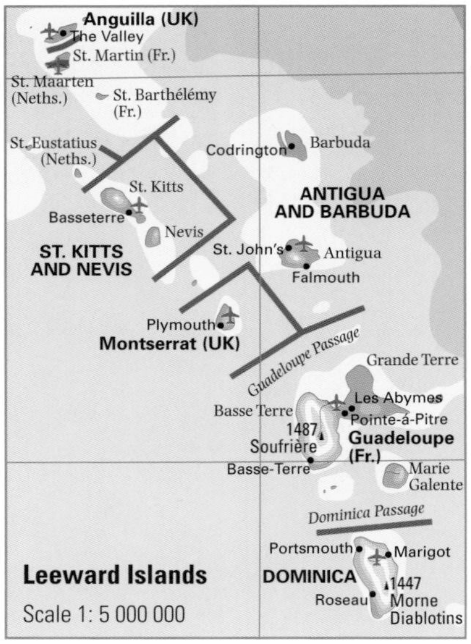

A

Tropic of Cancer

PACIFIC OCEAN

Gulf of Mexico

Bahía de Campeche

Golfo de Tehuantepec

Laguna Madre

Sierra Madre Occidental

Sierra Madre del Sur

Baja California

Golfo de California

Colorado Plateau

Grand Canyon

NEW MEXICO

ARIZONA

COLORADO

KANSAS

OKLAHOMA

TEXAS

MISSOURI

ARKANSAS

LOUISIANA

MISSISSIPPI

ILLINOIS

Yucatan

BELIZE

GUATEMALA

EL SALVADOR

HONDURAS

Major cities and places (selection)
Los Angeles, Oxford, San Bernardino, Riverside, Long Beach, San Diego, Tijuana, Ensenada, Mexicali, El Centro, Phoenix, Mesa, Tucson, Casa Grande, Ajo, Prescott, Kingman, Ash Fork, Winslow, Gallup, Albuquerque, Santa Fe, Las Vegas, Clovis, Roswell, Carlsbad, El Paso, Ciudad Juárez, Las Cruces, Deming, Nogales, Hermosillo, Guaymas, Ciudad Obregón, Navojoa, Los Mochis, Culiacán, Mazatlán, La Paz, Cabo San Lucas, San José del Cabo, Durango, Chihuahua, Torreón, Gómez Palacio, Monterrey, Saltillo, Matamoros, Reynosa, Nuevo Laredo, Laredo, Corpus Christi, Brownsville, McAllen, Harlingen, San Antonio, Houston, Austin, Dallas, Fort Worth, Galveston, Beaumont, Lubbock, Amarillo, Odessa, Del Rio, Eagle Pass, Wichita, Topeka, Oklahoma City, Tulsa, Little Rock, Shreveport, Baton Rouge, New Orleans, Guadalajara, León, Irapuato, Celaya, Querétaro, Morelia, Aguascalientes, San Luis Potosí, Zacatecas, Mexico City, Netzahualcóyotl, Puebla, Cuernavaca, Toluca, Veracruz, Tampico, Ciudad Madero, Acapulco, Oaxaca, Tuxtla Gutiérrez, Villahermosa, Coatzacoalcos, Minatitlán, Campeche, Mérida, Chetumal, Guatemala City, San Salvador, Tegucigalpa

Inset maps

Leeward Islands
Scale 1:5 000 000
Anguilla (UK), The Valley, St. Martin (Fr.), St. Maarten (Neths.), St. Barthélemy (Fr.), St. Eustatius (Neths.), St. Kitts, Nevis, Basseterre, ST. KITTS AND NEVIS, Codrington, Barbuda, ANTIGUA AND BARBUDA, St. John's, Antigua, Falmouth, Montserrat (UK), Plymouth, Guadeloupe (Fr.), Grande Terre, Basse Terre, Soufrière, 1487, Les Abymes, Pointe-à-Pitre, Marie Galente, Guadeloupe Passage, Dominica Passage, DOMINICA, Portsmouth, Marigot, Roseau, Morne Diablotins, 1447

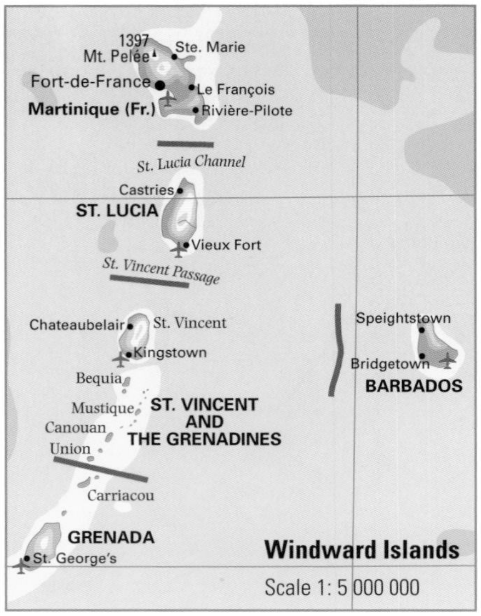

Windward Islands
Scale 1:5 000 000
Mt. Pelée, 1397, Ste. Marie, Fort-de-France, Le François, Rivière-Pilote, Martinique (Fr.), St. Lucia Channel, Castries, ST. LUCIA, Vieux Fort, St. Vincent Passage, Chateaubelair, St. Vincent, Kingstown, Bequia, Mustique, Canouan, Union, ST. VINCENT AND THE GRENADINES, Carriacou, GRENADA, St. George's, Speightstown, Bridgetown, BARBADOS

Panama Canal
Scale 1: 1 500 000

CARIBBEAN SEA

Punta Manzanillo

Portobelo

▲979

Colón Puerto Pilón

Gatún Locks Gatún

Madden Lake

1006 ▲

Palmas Bellas

PANAMA

Escobal

Gatún Lake

Gamboa

Gaillard Cut

Pedro Miguel Locks Miraflores Locks

Panama City

La Chorrera Balboa

PACIFIC OCEAN

CARIBBEAN SEA

PACIFIC OCEAN

Gaillard Cut
maximum elevation 95 m

minimum depth 12 m

sea level

sea level

0   15   30   45   60   75 km

Gatún Locks
(3 pairs)
length 305 m
width 33.5 m
total lift 25.9 m

Pedro Miguel Locks
(1 pair)
length 305 m
width 33.5 m
total lift 9.1 m

Miraflores Locks
(2 pairs)
length 305 m
width 33.5 m
total lift 16.8 m

The canal, opened in 1914, is 82 km long, including approaches (actual canal 64 km). Minimum depth 12 m, minimum width 152 m (Gaillard Cut). Time of passage 8 hours. In 1996, 13 700 vessels used the canal carrying 228 000 000 tonnes of cargo. In 1979 Panama assumed control of the former Canal Zone, with the USA retaining majority representation on the Panama Commission until 1989. Control of the canal reverted to Panama at noon on 31 December 1999.

Indianapolis Dayton
Cincinnati OHIO Parkersburg Baltimore
Louisville WEST Washington Annapolis DELAWARE
Terre Haute INDIANA VIRGINIA D.C. MARYLAND
Lexington Charleston Charlottesville
KENTUCKY Huntington Lynchburg Richmond
Clarksville Johnson Roanoke Hampton
Nashville City Danville Newport News Norfolk
TENNESSEE Knoxville Winston-Salem Portsmouth Chesapeake
Chattanooga Asheville Greensboro Raleigh
Hickory NORTH CAROLINA Cape Hatteras
Gadsden Charlotte Fayetteville
ALABAMA Anniston Rock Hill
Atlanta SOUTH CAROLINA Wilmington
Birmingham Augusta
Columbus Columbia
Montgomery GEORGIA Charleston
Dothan Albany Savannah

ATLANTIC OCEAN

Pensacola Valdosta
Fort Walton Tallahassee Jacksonville
Beach Gainesville St. Augustine
Ocala Daytona Beach
FLORIDA Orlando Cape Canaveral
Tampa Melbourne
St. Petersburg
Sarasota L. Okeechobee West Palm Beach
Fort Myers Miami Grand Bahama
Great Abaco

Key West

Straits of Florida

Nassau Cat I.

THE BAHAMAS San Salvador

Tropic of Cancer

Andros Great Exuma Long Island

Havana Matanzas Crooked I.
(La Habana) Mayaguana
Pinar del Río Güines Sagua la Grande Santa Clara
Le Fé Cienfuegos CUBA Acklins I. Caicos Passage
Sancti Spíritus Caicos Is.
Trinidad Ciego de Morón Nuevitas Great Inagua Turks and
Isla de la Ávila Camagüey Inagua Caicos Is. (UK)
Juventud Victoria de las Tunas Holguín West Indies
Manzanillo Bayamo Guantánamo Port-de-Paix
2005 Santiago Cap Haïtien Santiago San Francisco DOMINICAN
de Cuba 3175 La Vega REPUBLIC
Jérémie Port-au- San Pedro Santo
Grand Cayman Prince Domingo La Romana
(UK) Les Cayes 2680 Mayagüez Puerto
Montego Bay Jacmel Barahona Rico
JAMAICA Hispaniola (USA)
Spanish Town Kingston

CARIBBEAN SEA

Punta Gallinas

Lesser Antilles

Aruba (Neths.) Curaçao (Neths.) Bonaire (Neths.)
Willemstad Isla Margarita
Riohacha Pto. Fijo Punto Fijo Pto. Cumarebo La Asunción Güiria
Santa Marta Coro Churuguara Porlamar Trinidad
Barranquilla Maiquetía Caracas Cumaná Carúpano
Ciénaga Cabimas San Felipe Maracay Petare La Cruz Barcelona
Sabanalarga Maracaibo Barquisimeto Los Teques Maturín
Cartagena Valledupar Lago Yaritagua Valencia La Tucupita
Arjona Cristóbal Machiques de Acarigua Victoria San Juan de Zaraza
Calamar Maracaibo Araure los Morros Valle de El Tigre
San Carlos Mérida San Carlos la Pascua Ciudad Guayana
Sincelejo del Zulia Trujillo Calabozo Ciudad GUYANA
Magangué Valera Guanare Bolívar Embalse
Lorica Monteria de Guri
NICARAGUA Golfo del Cunene

Grand Bahama

Great Abaco

West Indies

Greater Antilles

Windward Passage

Cap Haïtien HAITI

Leeward Is. Virgin Is. (UK/USA) ANTIGUA AND
San St. Thomas Anguilla (UK) BARBUDA
Juan 1389 Barbuda Codrington
Aguadilla Caguas St. John's
La Romana Ponce St. Croix Antigua ST. KITTS
Mayagüez (USA) Montserrat AND NEVIS
(UK) Guadeloupe (Fr.)
Pointe-à-Pitre
Grande Terre
Marie Galente
DOMINICA
Roseau
1397 Martinique (Fr.)
Fort-de-France
Castries ST. LUCIA
St. Vincent 336 BARBADOS
Kingstown Bridgetown
ST. VINCENT AND
THE GRENADINES
840 GRENADA
St. George's

Windward Islands

Port-of-Spain Tobago
TRINIDAD AND
TOBAGO
Trinidad
San Fernando

VENEZUELA

Orinoco Barrancas
Caripito Port Kaituma
Upata Cunuri
El Callao

Scale 1: 16 000 000

0   160   320   480   640   800 km

NICARAGUA
managua
Masaya Laguna de Perlas
Lago de Bluefields
Nicaragua Punta del Mono
COSTA Limón
Puntarenas Alajuela 3432
San José Cartago
Cabo RICA Balboa Panama City
Blanco Palmar Sur Colón Penonomé
David PANAMA Santiago
Pto. Armuelles Penín. de Azuero
Isla de Coiba COLOMBIA

Panama Canal Golfo del Darién
Yarumal
Cisneros

Jamaica
Scale 1: 5 000 000

Montego Bay Falmouth St. Ann's Bay
South Port Maria
Negril Annotto Bay
Point Savanna- Port Antonio
la-Mar Mandeville Blue Mts. Morant
Black River Kingston 2256 Point
May Pen Spanish Morant
Town Port
Portland Point Morant

Trinidad and Tobago
Scale 1: 5 000 000

Tobago
Charlotteville
Scarborough

Dragon's Mouths Galera
Toco Point
Port-of-Spain Arima Sangre
Trinidad Grande
San Fernando Pierreville
Icacos La Brea Galeota Point
Point Serpent's Mouth

South America Political

GUATEMALA
HONDURAS
EL SALVADOR
NICARAGUA
COSTA RICA
PANAMA
Caracas
VENEZUELA
Georgetown
GUYANA
Paramaribo
SURINAME
Cayenne
French Guiana (France)
Bogotá
COLOMBIA
Equator
Quito
ECUADOR
Galapagos Islands (Ecuador)
Rocas Island (Brazil)
Fernando de Noronha (Brazil)
PERU
B R A Z I L
Lima
La Paz
BOLIVIA
Brásília
PARAGUAY
Asunción
Tropic of Capricorn
C H I L E
URUGUAY
Santiago
Buenos Aires
Montevideo
Juan Fernandez Is. (Chile)
ARGENTINA
Stanley
Falkland Islands (UK)
South Georgia (UK)
100°W
80°W
60°W
40°W
0°
20°S
40°S
120°W
60°S
20°W

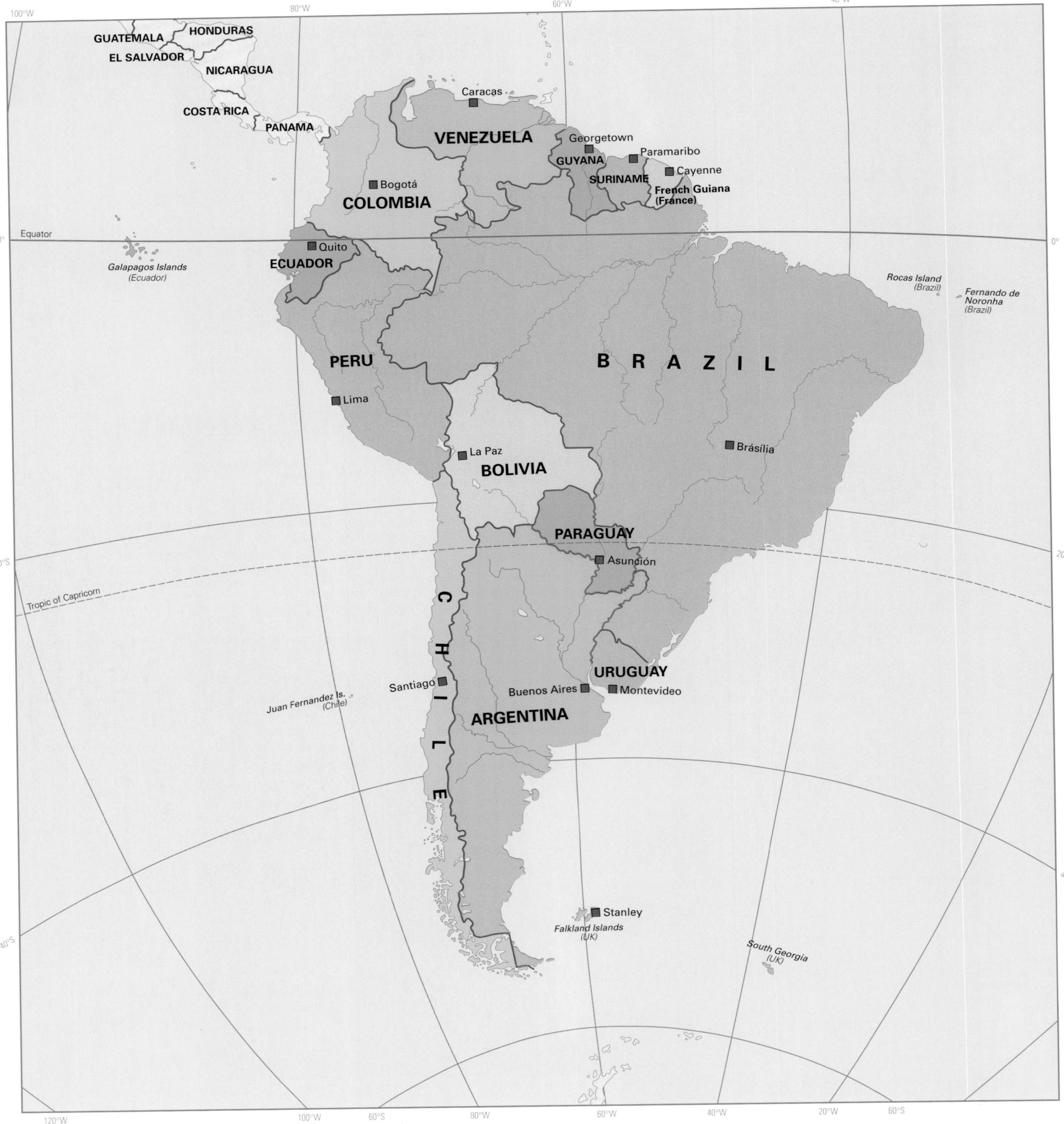

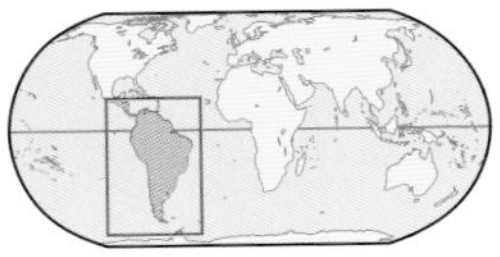

Scale 1: 40 000 000

0 400 800 1200 1600 2000 km

- international boundary
- disputed boundary
- capital city

Oblique Mercator Projection

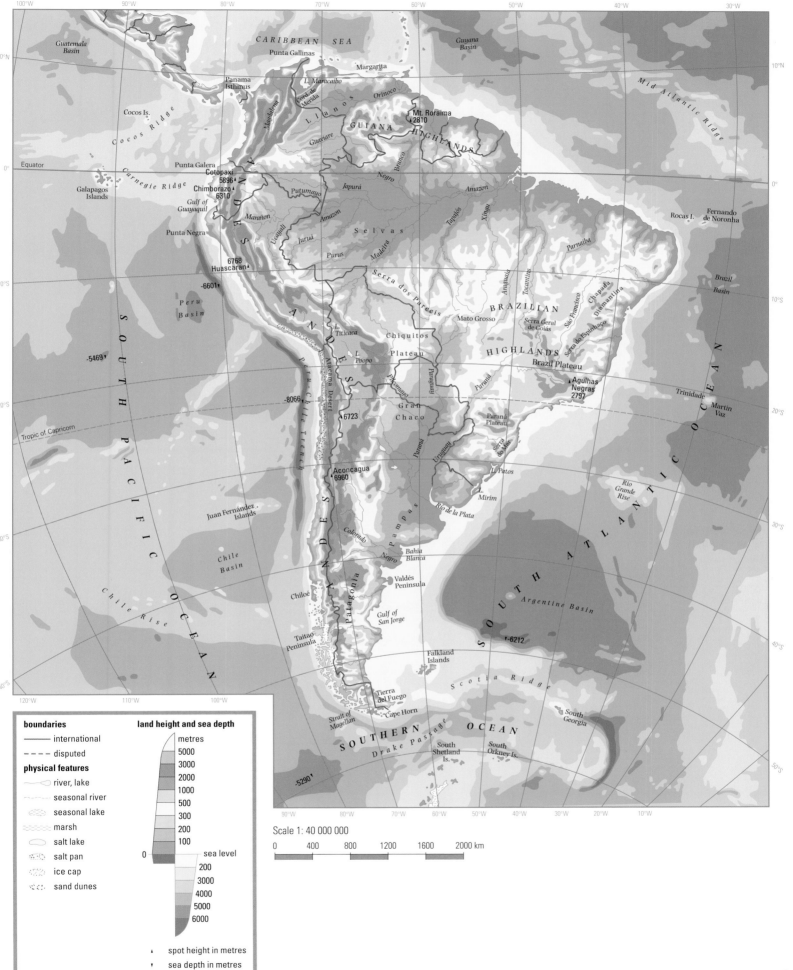

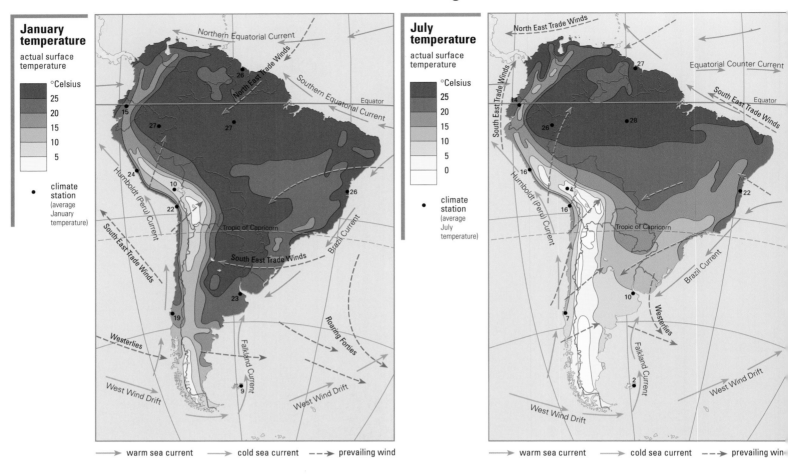

January temperature

actual surface temperature

°Celsius
- 25
- 20
- 15
- 10
- 5

● climate station (average January temperature)

Northern Equatorial Current
North East Trade Winds
Southern Equatorial Current
Equator
Humboldt (Peru) Current
South East Trade Winds
Tropic of Capricorn
South East Trade Winds
Brazil Current
Westerlies
Falkland Current
Roaring Forties
West Wind Drift
West Wind Drift

⟶ warm sea current   ⟶ cold sea current   ⇢ prevailing wind

July temperature

actual surface temperature

°Celsius
- 25
- 20
- 15
- 10
- 5
- 0

● climate station (average July temperature)

North East Trade Winds
Equatorial Counter Current
South East Trade Winds
Equator
South East Trade Winds
Humboldt (Peru) Current
Tropic of Capricorn
Brazil Current
Westerlies
Falkland Current
West Wind Drift
West Wind Drift

⟶ warm sea current   ⟶ cold sea current   ⇢ prevailing win

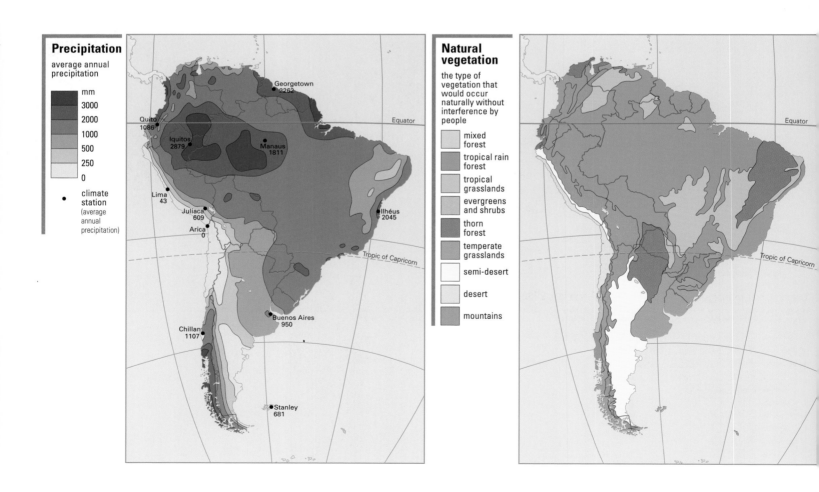

Precipitation

average annual precipitation

mm
- 3000
- 2000
- 1000
- 500
- 250
- 0

● climate station (average annual precipitation)

Georgetown 2262
Quito 1086
Iquitos 2879
Manaus 1811
Lima 43
Juliaca 609
Arica 0
Ilhéus 2045
Buenos Aires 950
Chillan 1107
Stanley 681
Equator
Tropic of Capricorn

Natural vegetation

the type of vegetation that would occur naturally without interference by people

- mixed forest
- tropical rain forest
- tropical grasslands
- evergreens and shrubs
- thorn forest
- temperate grasslands
- semi-desert
- desert
- mountains

Equator
Tropic of Capricorn

Oblique Mercator Projection   © Oxford University P

Scale 1 : 45 000 000

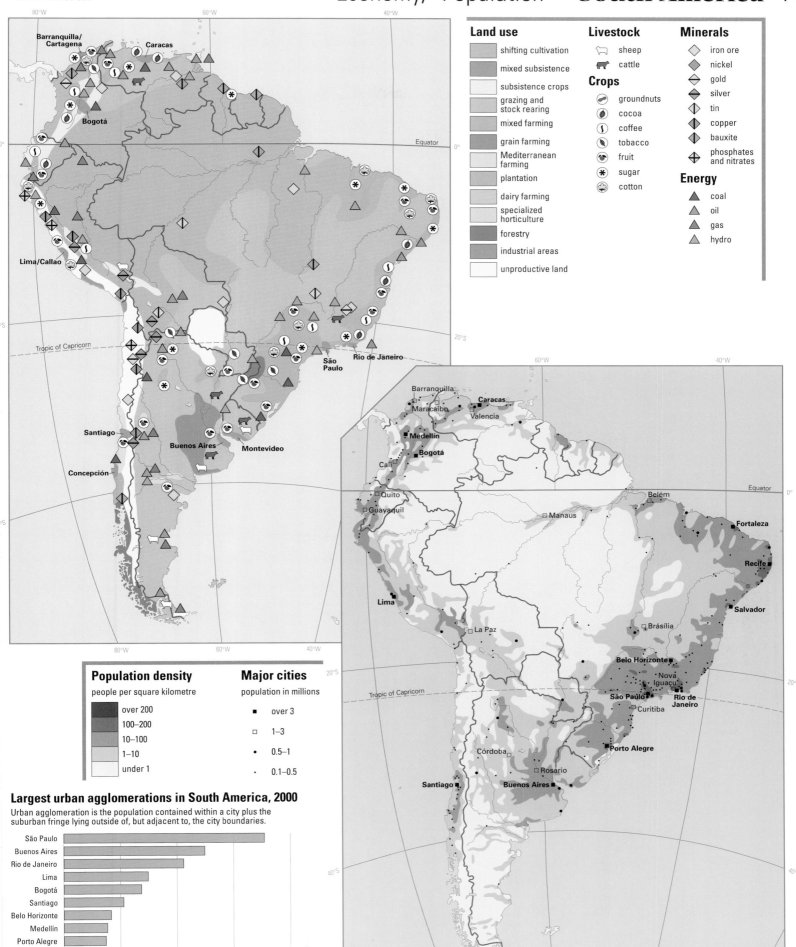

Land use

- shifting cultivation
- mixed subsistence
- subsistence crops
- grazing and stock rearing
- mixed farming
- grain farming
- Mediterranean farming
- plantation
- dairy farming
- specialized horticulture
- forestry
- industrial areas
- unproductive land

Livestock

- sheep
- cattle

Crops

- groundnuts
- cocoa
- coffee
- tobacco
- fruit
- sugar
- cotton

Minerals

- iron ore
- nickel
- gold
- silver
- tin
- copper
- bauxite
- phosphates and nitrates

Energy

- coal
- oil
- gas
- hydro

Population density

people per square kilometre

- over 200
- 100–200
- 10–100
- 1–10
- under 1

Major cities

population in millions

- ■ over 3
- ▫ 1–3
- • 0.5–1
- · 0.1–0.5

Largest urban agglomerations in South America, 2000

Urban agglomeration is the population contained within a city plus the suburban fringe lying outside of, but adjacent to, the city boundaries.

São Paulo
Buenos Aires
Rio de Janeiro
Lima
Bogotá
Santiago
Belo Horizonte
Medellín
Porto Alegre
Recife

0   5   10   15   20
millions of people

© Oxford University Press   Oblique Mercator Projection

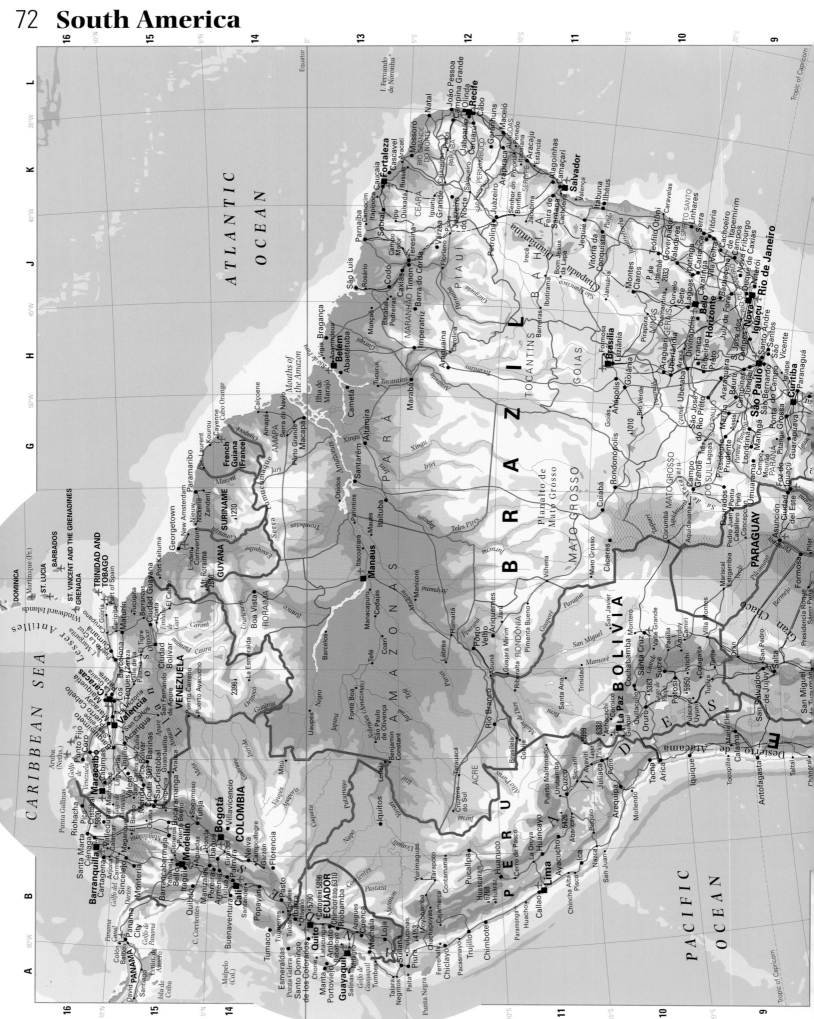

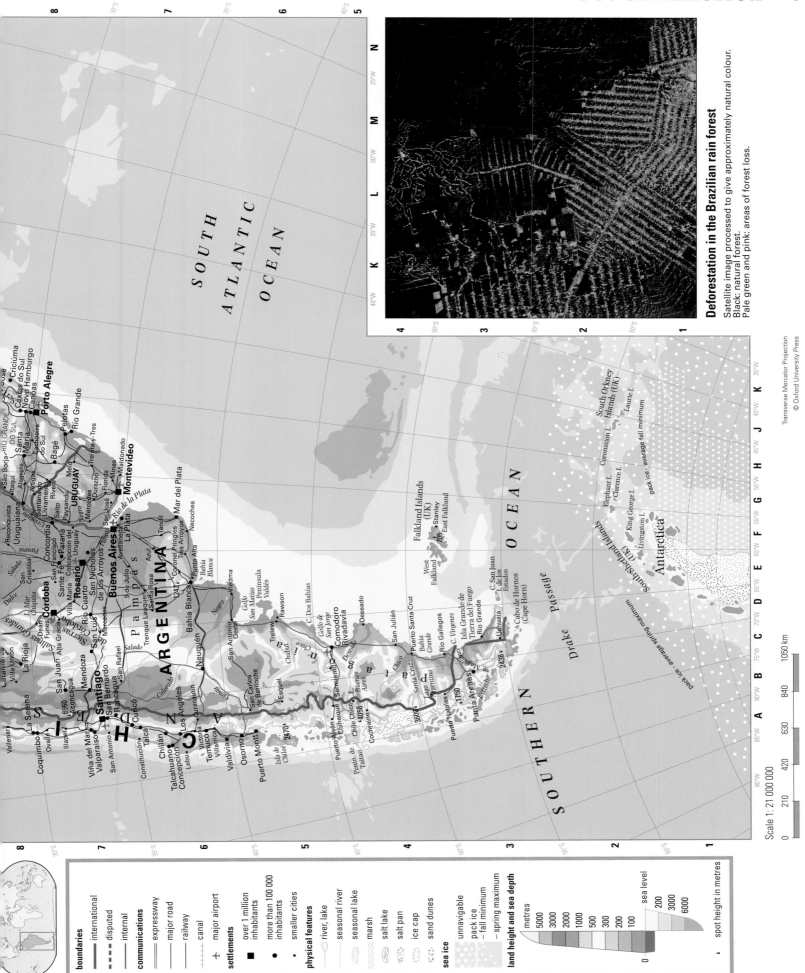

Deforestation in the Brazilian rain forest
Satellite image processed to give approximately natural colour.
Black: natural forest.
Pale green and pink: areas of forest loss.

Scale 1:21 000 000

Transverse Mercator Projection

© Oxford University Press

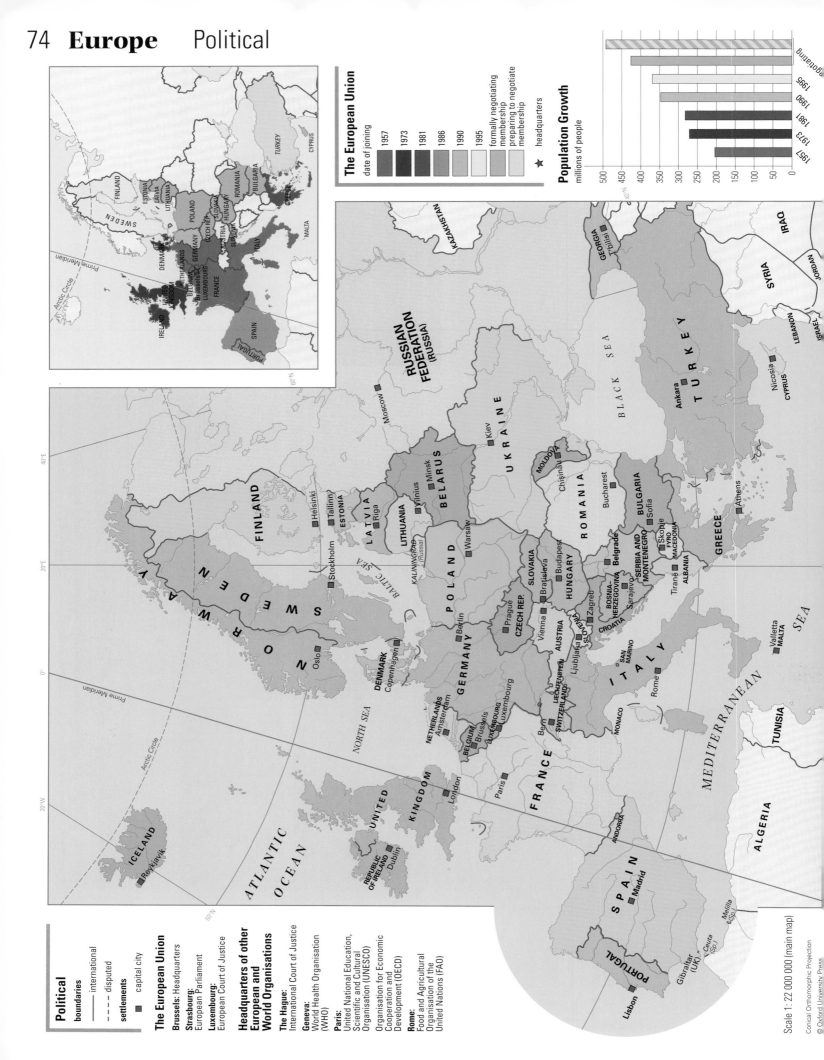

Conical Orthomorphic Projection

© Oxford University Press

Political

boundaries
— international
- - - disputed

settlements
■ capital city

The European Union

Brussels: Headquarters

Strasbourg: European Parliament

Luxembourg: European Court of Justice

Headquarters of other European and World Organisations

The Hague: International Court of Justice

Geneva: World Health Organisation (WHO)

Paris: United National Education, Scientific and Cultural Organisation (UNESCO)

Rome: Food and Agricultural Organisation of the United Nations (FAO)

The European Union

date of joining

| 1957 | 1973 | 1981 | 1986 | 1990 | 1995 | formally negotiating membership | preparing to negotiate membership |

★ headquarters

Population Growth

millions of people

Scale 1: 22 000 000 (main map)

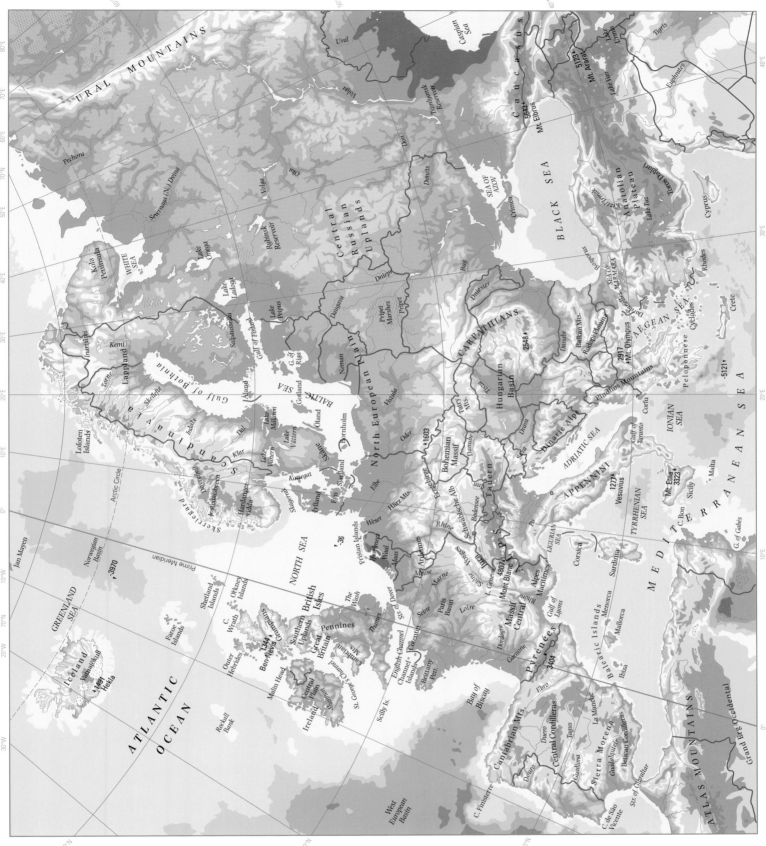

© Oxford University Press

Conical Orthomorphic Projection

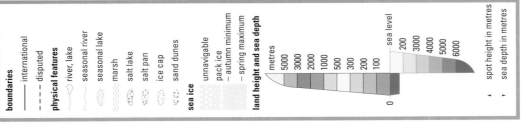

boundaries
— international
-- disputed
physical features
river, lake
seasonal river
seasonal lake
marsh
salt lake
salt pan
ice cap
sand dunes
sea ice
unnavigable
pack ice
— autumn minimum
— spring maximum
land height and sea depth

metres
5000
3000
2000
1000
500
300
200
100
0

sea level
200
3000
4000
5000
6000
metres

· spot height in metres
▸ sea depth in metres

Scale 1: 22 000 000

0   220   440   660   880   1100 km

MAP LABELS:

URAL MOUNTAINS
Pechora
Kola Peninsula
WHITE SEA
Lappland
Kemi
Torne
Inari
Jan Mayen
GREENLAND SEA
Norwegian Basin
3970
Iceland
Hekla
1491
Reykjavik
Faroe Islands
Shetland Islands
Orkney Islands
C. Wrath
Outer Hebrides
Malin Head
Ben Nevis 1344
Southern Uplands
British Isles
Great Britain
Pennines
Central Plain
Ireland
Shannon
Cambrian Mts.
St. George's Channel
Scilly Is.
ATLANTIC OCEAN
Rockall Bank
West European Basin
C. Finisterre
C. de São Vicente
Str. of Gibraltar
ATLAS MOUNTAINS
Grand Erg Occidental
Sierra Morena
Betic Cordilleras
Central Cordilleras
Cantabrian Mts.
Duero
Tagus
Guadiana
Guadalquivir
Ebro
Balearic Islands
Mallorca
Menorca
Ibiza
La Manche
Pyrénées 3404
Gulf of Lyons
Bay of Biscay
Garonne
Dordogne
Massif Central
Rhône
Gironde
Loire
Paris Basin
Seine
Marne
Meuse
Brittany Pen.
Cotentin Pen.
Channel Islands
English Channel
Str. of Dover
The Wash
Thames
NORTH SEA
Frisian Islands
Waal
Maas
Rhine
Ardennes
Vosges
Jura
Mont Blanc 4807
ALPS
Alpes Maritimes
Corsica
LIGURIAN SEA
Sardinia
C. Bon
TYRRHENIAN SEA
Sicily
Mt. Etna 3323
Malta
G. of Gabès
MEDITERRANEAN SEA
Vesuvius 1277
APENNINES
Po
ADRIATIC SEA
Gulf of Taranto
IONIAN SEA
Corfu
Peloponnese
Pindhos Mountains
AEGEAN SEA
Cyclades
Crete
Rhodes
Mt. Olympus 2917
Cyprus
Lake Tuz
Anatolian Plateau
Kizil Irmak
SEA OF MARMARA
Bosporus
Dardanelles
Rodopi Planina
Balkan Mts.
BLACK SEA
Crimea
SEA OF AZOV
Mt. Ararat 5123
Lake Van
Lake Urmia
Tigris
Euphrates
Mt. Elbrus 5642
Caucasus
Caspian Sea
Tsimlyansk Reservoir
Don
Donets
Volga
Ural
Rybinsk Reservoir
Central Russian Uplands
Dniepr
Bug
Dniester
Carpathians 2548
Tisza
Hungarian Basin
Tatry Mts.
Drava
Sava
Dinaric Alps
Tauern 3801
Bodensee
Schwäbische Alb
Bohemian Massif 1603
Erzgebirge
Oder
Elbe
Harz Mts.
Weser
Sjælland
Fyn
Jylland
Kattegat
Skagerrak
Skåne
Bornholm
BALTIC SEA
Öland
Gotland
Lake Vättern
Lake Mälaren
Lake Vänern
Dal
Klar
Gulf of Bothnia
Skellefte
Skellefteå
Indals
SCANDINAVIA
Lofoten Islands
Jostedalsbreen
Hardanger Vidda
Sognefjord
Dovrefjell
Kjølen
Lake Ladoga
Lake Onega
Lake Peipus
Lake Saimaa
Gulf of Finland
Åland
Neman
G. of Riga
Vistula
North European Plain
Daugava
Pripet Marshes
Pripet
Severnaya (N.) Dvina
Ota
36

Scale 1: 50 000 000

© Oxford University Press

Conical Orthomorphic Projection

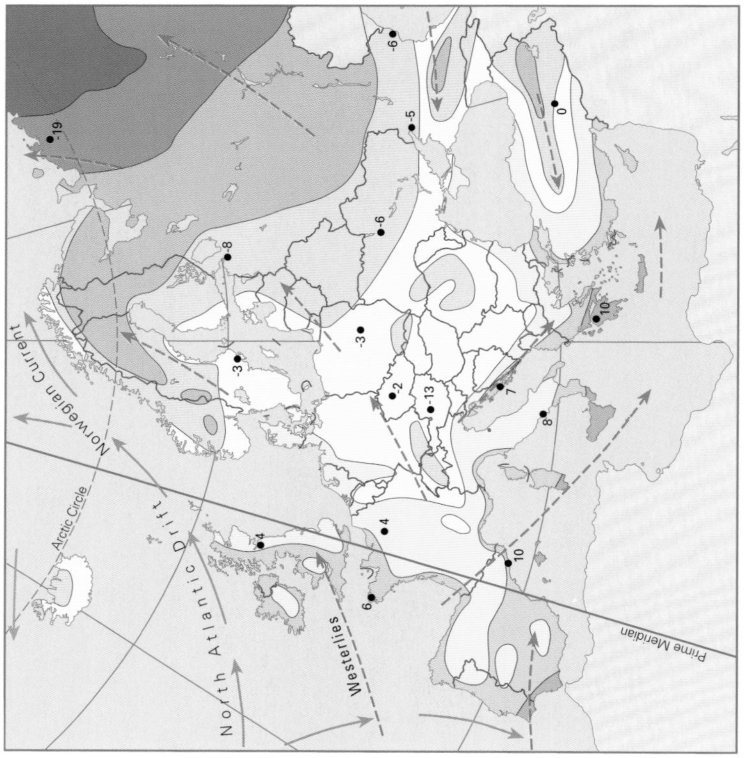

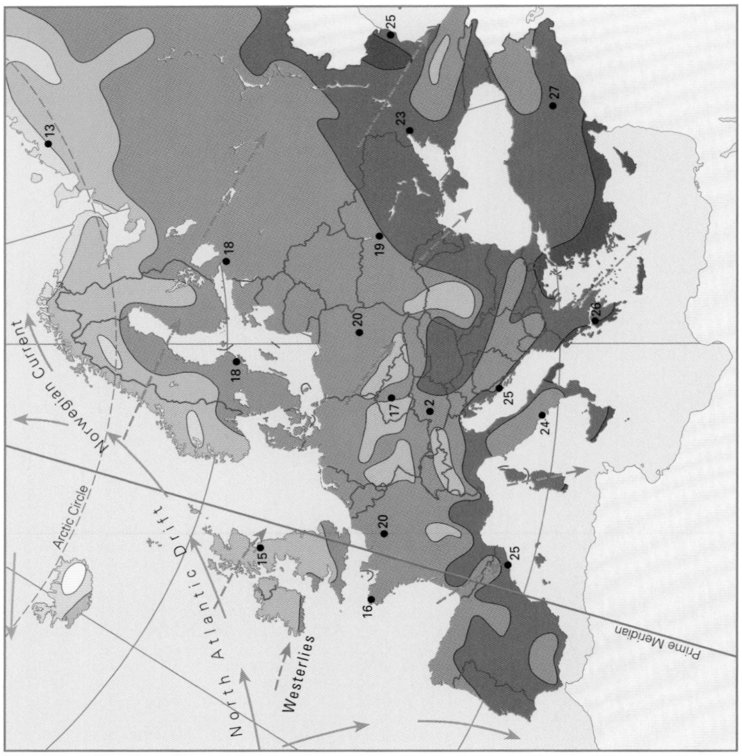

July temperature

actual surface temperature

°Celsius
25
20
15
10
5

• climate station (average July temperature)

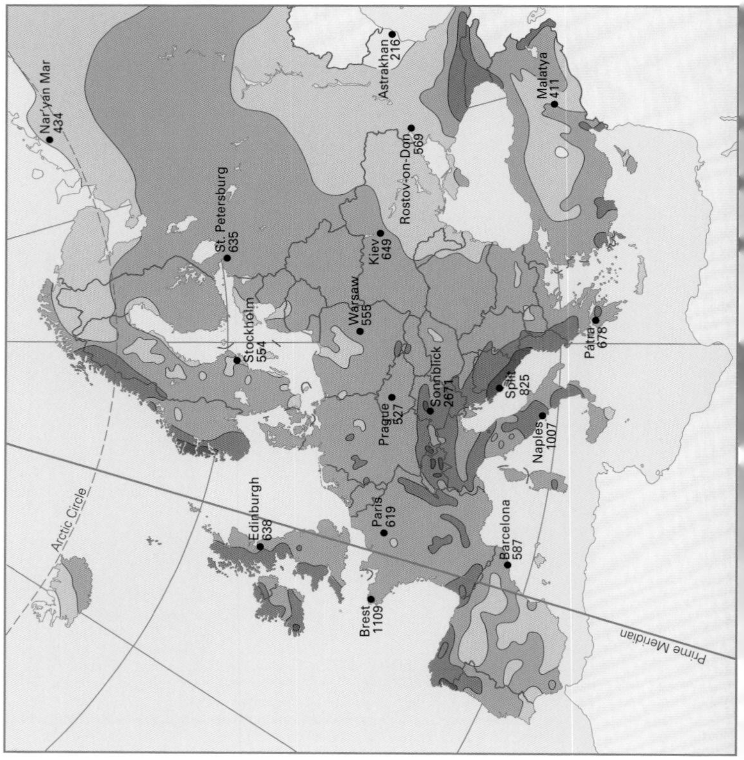

January temperature

actual surface temperature

°Celsius
10
5
0
-5
-10
-15
-20
-25

• climate station (average January temperature)

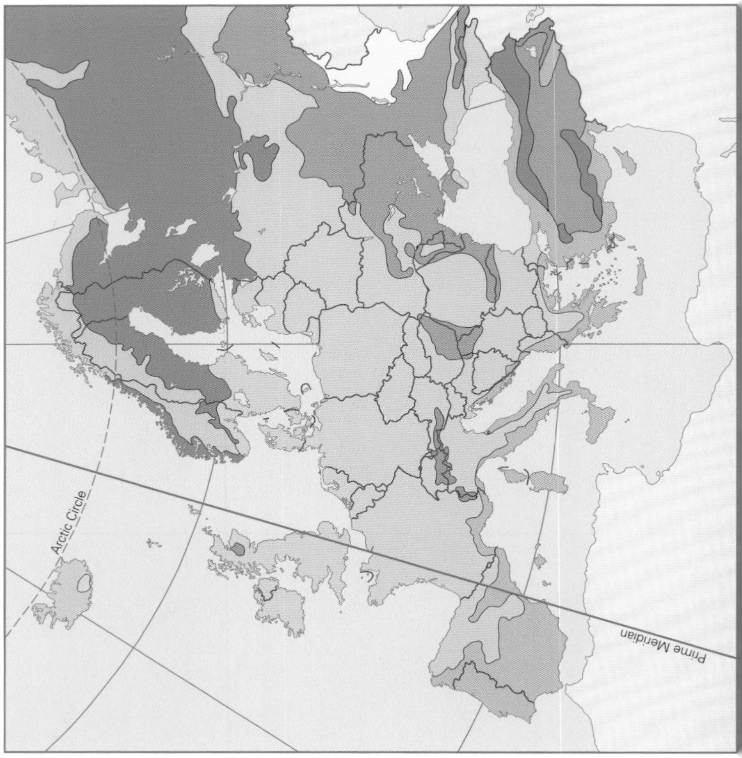

Natural vegetation

the type of vegetation that would occur naturally without interference by people

coniferous forest
mixed forest
evergreens and shrubs
temperate grasslands
semi-desert
tundra
ice
mountains

Precipitation

average annual precipitation

mm
2000
1000
500
250
0

• climate station (average annual precipitation)

Nar'yan Mar 434
St. Petersburg 635
Stockholm 554
Warsaw 555
Kiev 649
Rostov-von-Don 569
Astrakhan 216
Malatya 411
Prague 527
Sornblick 2671
Split 825
Naples 1007
Pátra 678
Edinburgh 638
Paris 619
Barcelona 587
Brest 1109

Prevailing wind
Cold sea current
Warm sea current

Norwegian Current
North Atlantic Drift
Westerlies
Arctic Circle
Prime Meridian

Scale 1: 35 000 000

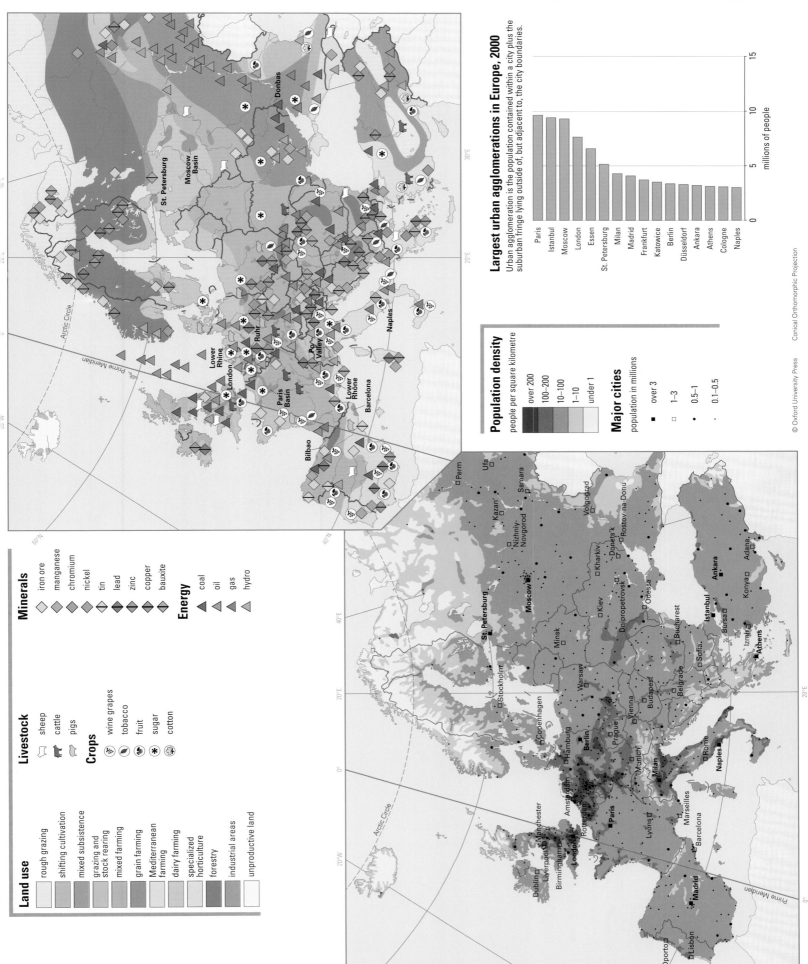

Largest urban agglomerations in Europe, 2000

Urban agglomeration is the population contained within a city plus the suburban fringe lying outside of, but adjacent to, the city boundaries.

millions of people

Paris · Istanbul · Moscow · London · Essen · St. Petersburg · Milan · Madrid · Frankfurt · Katowice · Berlin · Düsseldorf · Ankara · Athens · Cologne · Naples

Population density
people per square kilometre

- over 200
- 100–200
- 10–100
- 1–10
- under 1

Major cities
population in millions

- over 3
- 1–3
- 0.5–1
- 0.1–0.5

© Oxford University Press

Conical Orthomorphic Projection

Land use

- rough grazing
- shifting cultivation
- mixed subsistence
- grazing and stock rearing
- mixed farming
- grain farming
- Mediterranean farming
- dairy farming
- specialized horticulture
- forestry
- industrial areas
- unproductive land

Livestock

- sheep
- cattle
- pigs

Crops

- wine grapes
- tobacco
- fruit
- sugar
- cotton

Minerals

- iron ore
- manganese
- chromium
- nickel
- tin
- lead
- zinc
- copper
- bauxite

Energy

- coal
- oil
- gas
- hydro

Moscow Basin

St. Petersburg

Donbas

Naples

Lower Rhine

Ruhr

Po Valley

London

Lower Rhône

Paris Basin

Barcelona

Bilbao

Arctic Circle

Prime Meridian

Perm · Ufa · Kazan' · Samara · Nizhniy-Novgorod · Volgograd · Rostov-na-Donu

St. Petersburg · Moscow · Minsk · Kiev · Kharkiv · Donets'k · Dnipropetrovsk · Odessa · Volgograd

Ankara · Adana · Konya · Istanbul · Bursa · Izmir · Athens

Stockholm · Copenhagen · Warsaw · Sofia · Belgrade · Bucharest · Budapest · Vienna · Prague · Hamburg · Berlin · Munich · Milan · Rome · Naples

Dublin · Manchester · Liverpool · Birmingham · London · Amsterdam · Rotterdam · Paris · Lyons · Marseilles · Barcelona · Madrid · Oporto · Lisbon

Arctic Circle

Prime Meridian

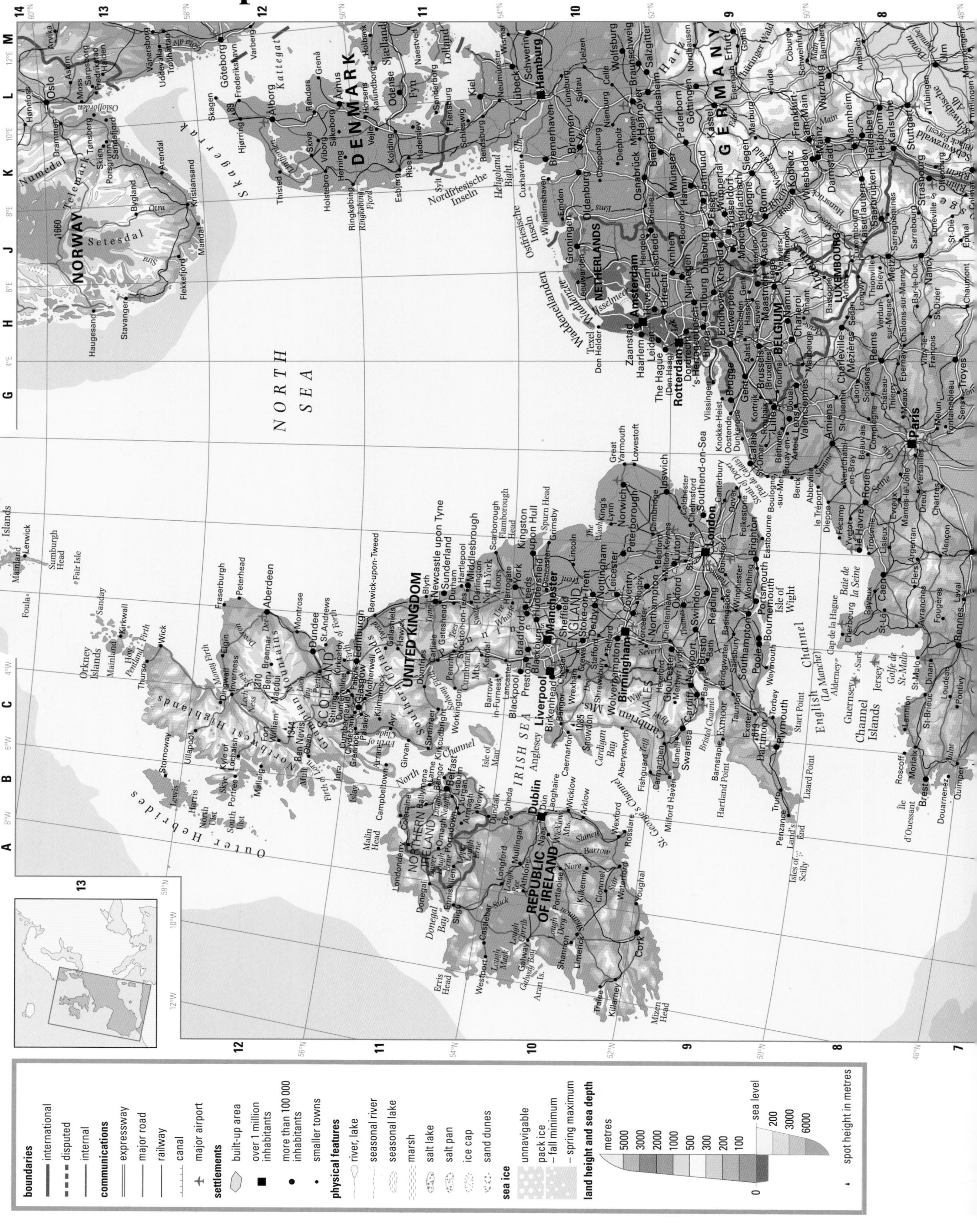

NORTH SEA

NORWAY

DENMARK

GERMANY

NETHERLANDS

BELGIUM

LUXEMBOURG

UNITED KINGDOM

SCOTLAND

ENGLAND

WALES

NORTHERN IRELAND

REPUBLIC OF IRELAND

IRISH SEA

Skagerrak

Kattegat

English Channel (La Manche)

Channel Islands

Outer Hebrides

Shetland Islands

Paris

London

Hamburg

Rotterdam

Amsterdam

Dublin

Belfast

Birmingham

Liverpool

Manchester

© Oxford University Press

boundaries
international
disputed
internal

communications
expressway
major road
railway
canal
major airport

settlements
built-up area
over 1 million inhabitants
more than 100 000 inhabitants
smaller towns

physical features
river, lake
seasonal river
seasonal lake
marsh
salt lake
salt pan
ice cap
sand dunes

sea ice
unnavigable
pack ice — fall minimum
— spring maximum

land height and sea depth
metres
5000
3000
2000
1000
500
300
200
100
sea level
0
200
3000
6000

spot height in metres

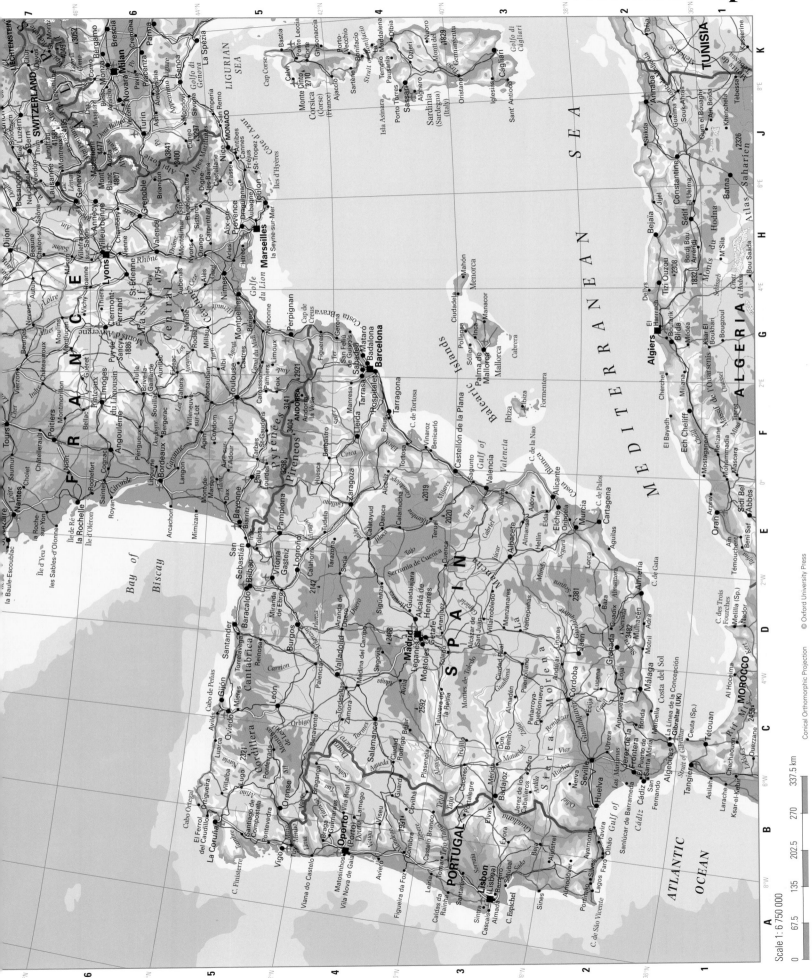

Conical Orthomorphic Projection

Scale 1: 6 750 000

0   67.5   135   202.5   270   337.5 km

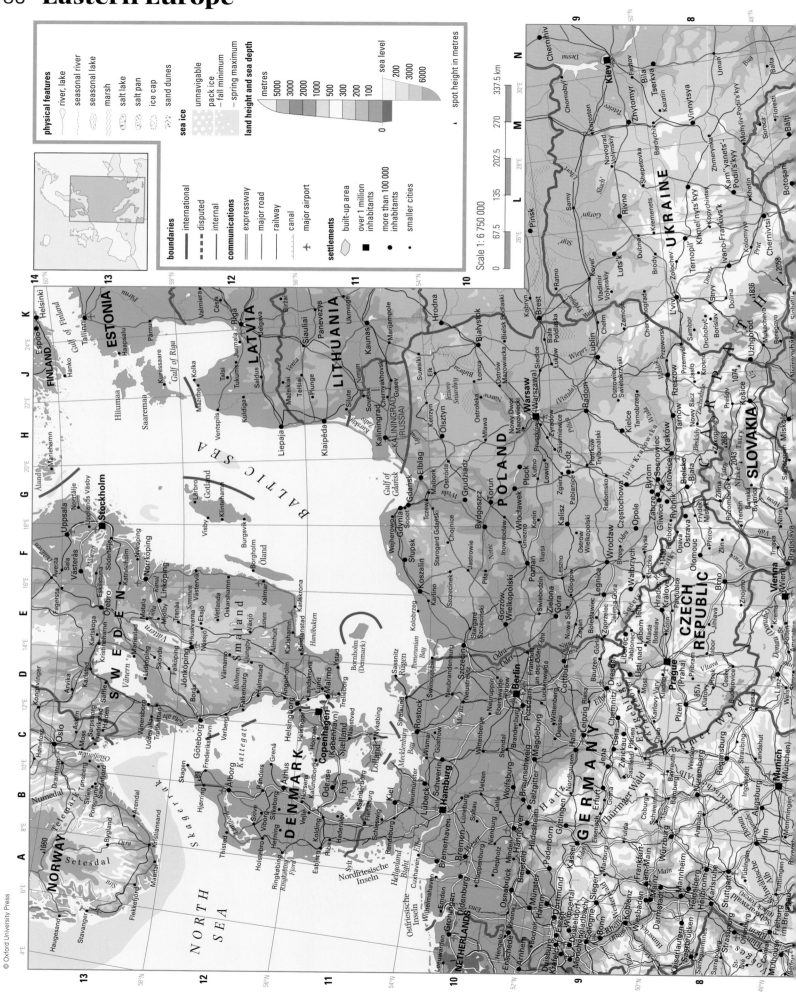

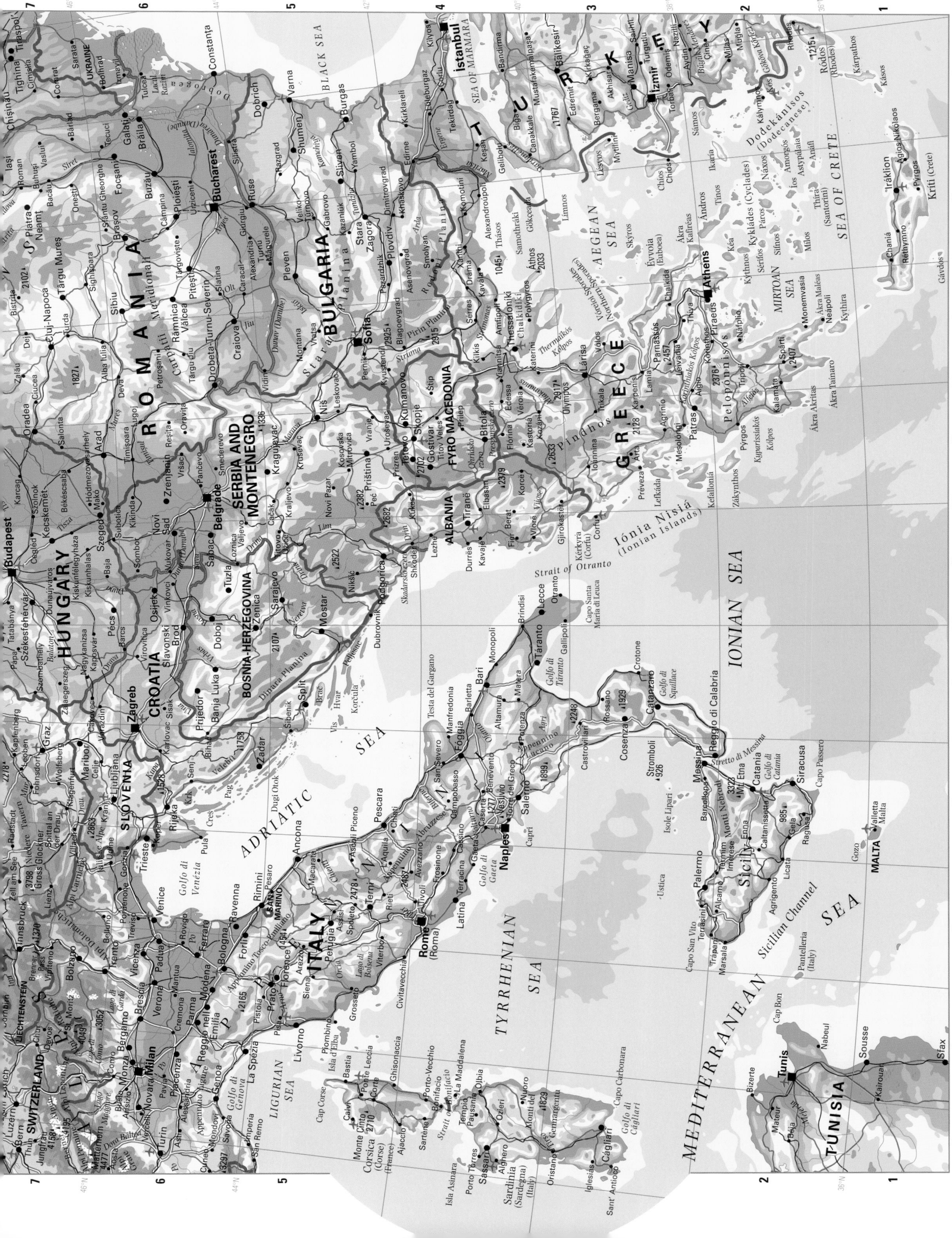

BLACK SEA

TURKEY

İstanbul

İzmir

SEA OF MARMARA

UKRAINE

ROMANIA

Bucharest

BULGARIA

Sofia

SERBIA AND MONTENEGRO

Belgrade

FYRO MACEDONIA

Skopje

ALBANIA

Tiranë

GREECE

Athens

AEGEAN SEA

SEA OF CRETE

Kríti (Crete)

Iráklion

Ródos (Rhodes)

Dodekánisos (Dodecanese)

Kykládes (Cyclades)

MIRTOAN SEA

Peloponnísos

Pindhos

Olympos 2917

Thessaloníki

HUNGARY

Budapest

CROATIA

Zagreb

SLOVENIA

Ljubljana

BOSNIA-HERZEGOVINA

Sarajevo

Mostar

Split

SWITZERLAND

LIECHTENSTEIN

ITALY

Rome (Roma)

Naples

ADRIATIC SEA

TYRRHENIAN SEA

IONIAN SEA

Sicily

Palermo

Catania

Messina

Reggio di Calabria

Taranto

Bari

Brindisi

Lecce

Mt Etna 3323

Strait of Otranto

LIGURIAN SEA

Milan

Turin

Genoa

Venice

Bologna

Florence

SAN MARINO

Corsica (Corse) (France)

Sardinia (Sardegna) (Italy)

Cágliari

MALTA

Valletta

MEDITERRANEAN SEA

Sicilian Channel

TUNISIA

Tunis

Sfax

Ióna Nisiá (Ionian Islands)

Kérkyra (Corfu)

© Oxford University Press

Conical Orthomorphic Projection

Scale 1 : 60 000 000

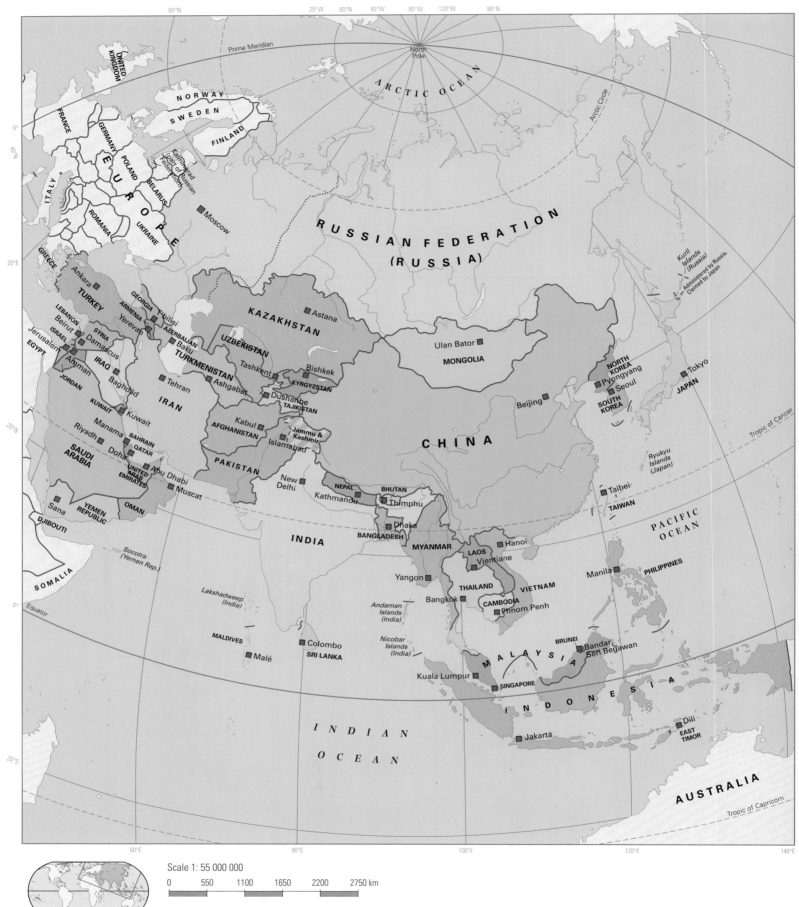

60°N · 20°W · 80°N · 40°W · 80°W · 120°W · 80°N

North Pole

ARCTIC OCEAN

Prime Meridian

Arctic Circle

UNITED KINGDOM

NORWAY

SWEDEN

FINLAND

FRANCE

GERMANY

POLAND

BELARUS

ITALY

E U R O P E

Kaliningrad (part of Russian Federation)

ROMANIA

UKRAINE

●Moscow

RUSSIAN FEDERATION (RUSSIA)

Kuril Islands (Russia)
Administered by Russia, Claimed by Japan

GREECE

Ankara

TURKEY

GEORGIA

ARMENIA

Tbilisi

AZERBAIJAN

Yerevan

Baku

KAZAKHSTAN

●Astana

Ulan Bator ■

MONGOLIA

LEBANON

Beirut

ISRAEL

Damascus

SYRIA

Jerusalem

EGYPT

Amman

IRAQ

JORDAN

Baghdad

UZBEKISTAN

Tashkent

Bishkek

KYRGYZSTAN

Dushanbe

TAJIKISTAN

TURKMENISTAN

Ashgabat

Tehran

IRAN

Beijing ■

NORTH KOREA

Pyongyang

Seoul

SOUTH KOREA

Tokyo ■

JAPAN

KUWAIT

Kuwait

Manama

BAHRAIN

Riyadh

QATAR

Doha

SAUDI ARABIA

Abu Dhabi

UNITED ARAB EMIRATES

Muscat

Kabul

AFGHANISTAN

Jammu & Kashmir

Islamabad

PAKISTAN

C H I N A

Tropic of Cancer

Ryukyu Islands (Japan)

Taibei ■

TAIWAN

Sana

YEMEN REPUBLIC

OMAN

DJIBOUTI

New Delhi

NEPAL

Kathmandu

BHUTAN

Thimphu

PACIFIC OCEAN

SOMALIA

Socotra (Yemen Rep.)

I N D I A

Dhaka

BANGLADESH

MYANMAR

Hanoi

LAOS

Vientiane

Equator

Lakshadweep (India)

Andaman Islands (India)

Yangon

THAILAND

Bangkok

VIETNAM

CAMBODIA

Phnom Penh

Manila

PHILIPPINES

MALDIVES

Malé

Colombo

SRI LANKA

Nicobar Islands (India)

BRUNEI

Bandar Seri Begawan

M A L A Y S I A

Kuala Lumpur

SINGAPORE

I N D O N E S I A

Dili

EAST TIMOR

INDIAN OCEAN

Jakarta

20°S

AUSTRALIA

Tropic of Capricorn

60°E · 80°E · 100°E · 120°E · 140°E

Scale 1 : 55 000 000

0 · 550 · 1100 · 1650 · 2200 · 2750 km

— international boundary

--- disputed boundary

··· continental boundary

■ capital city

Zenithal Equal Area Projection

© Oxford University Press

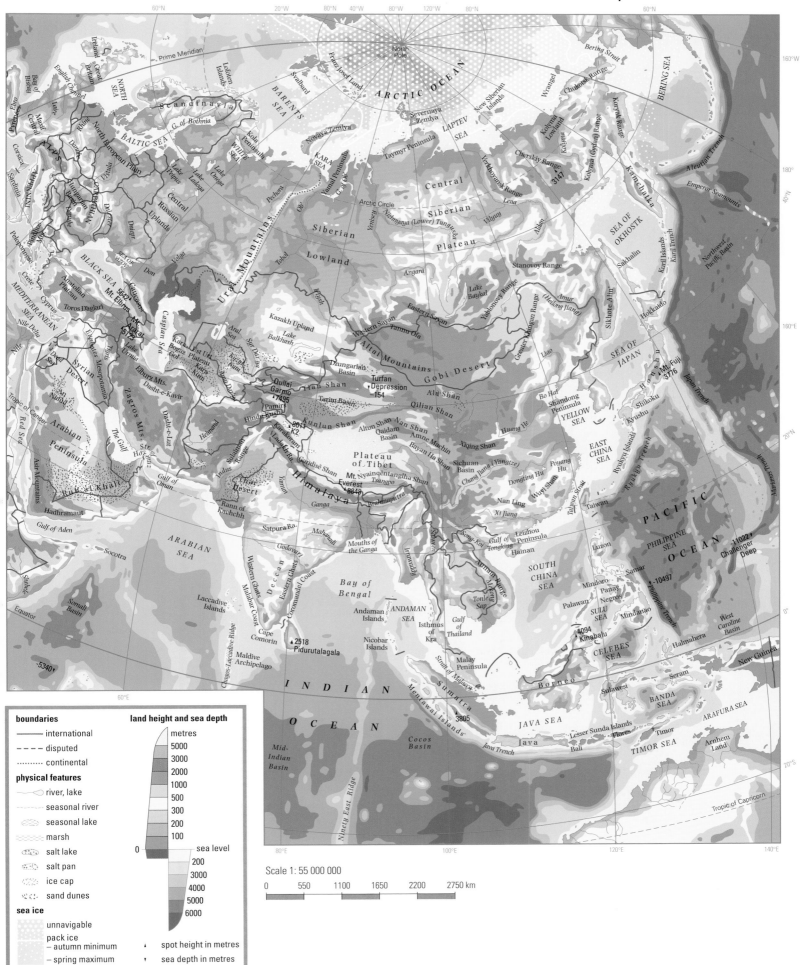

boundaries

———	international
– – –	disputed
··········	continental

physical features

	river, lake
	seasonal river
	seasonal lake
	marsh
	salt lake
	salt pan
	ice cap
	sand dunes

sea ice

	unnavigable
	pack ice
	– autumn minimum
	– spring maximum

land height and sea depth

metres
5000
3000
2000
1000
500
300
200
100
0 — sea level
200
3000
4000
5000
6000

▲ spot height in metres
▼ sea depth in metres

Scale 1: 55 000 000

0   550   1100   1650   2200   2750 km

Zenithal equal Area Projection

© Oxford University Press

Scale 1: 120 000 000

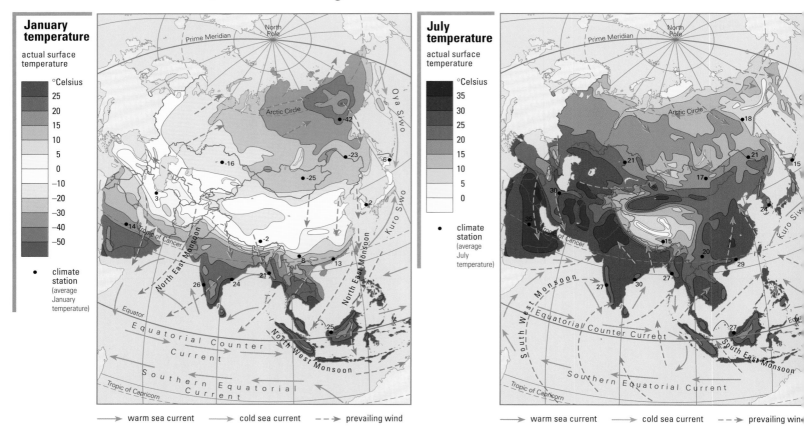

January temperature

actual surface temperature

°Celsius
25
20
15
10
5
0
−10
−20
−30
−40
−50

• climate station (average January temperature)

July temperature

actual surface temperature

°Celsius
35
30
25
20
15
10
5
0

• climate station (average July temperature)

→ warm sea current → cold sea current - - → prevailing wind

→ warm sea current → cold sea current - - → prevailing win

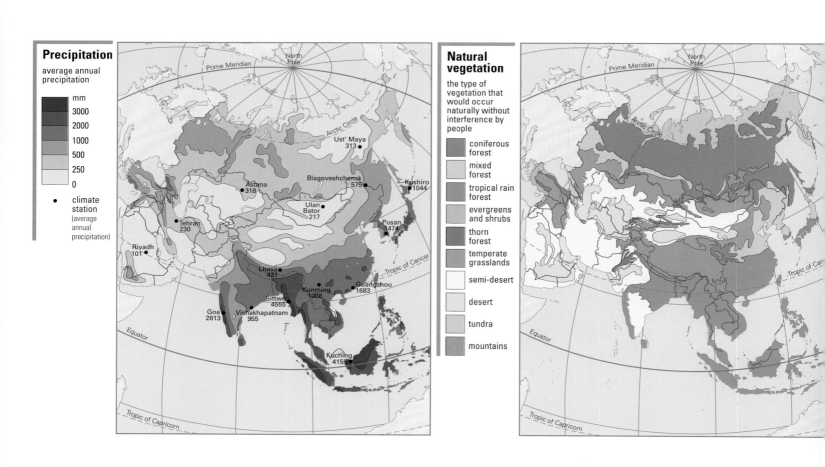

Precipitation

average annual precipitation

mm
3000
2000
1000
500
250
0

• climate station (average annual precipitation)

Ust' Maya 313

Astana 318

Blagoveshchensk 575

Kushiro 1044

Ulan Bator 217

Tehran 230

Pusan 1474

Riyadh 101

Lhasa 421

Kunming 1008

Guangzhou 1683

Sittwe 4555

Goa 2813

Vishakhapatnam 955

Kuching 4155

Natural vegetation

the type of vegetation that would occur naturally without interference by people

coniferous forest
mixed forest
tropical rain forest
evergreens and shrubs
thorn forest
temperate grasslands
semi-desert
desert
tundra
mountains

Zenithal Equal Area Projection   © Oxford University Pr

Scale 1: 75 000 000

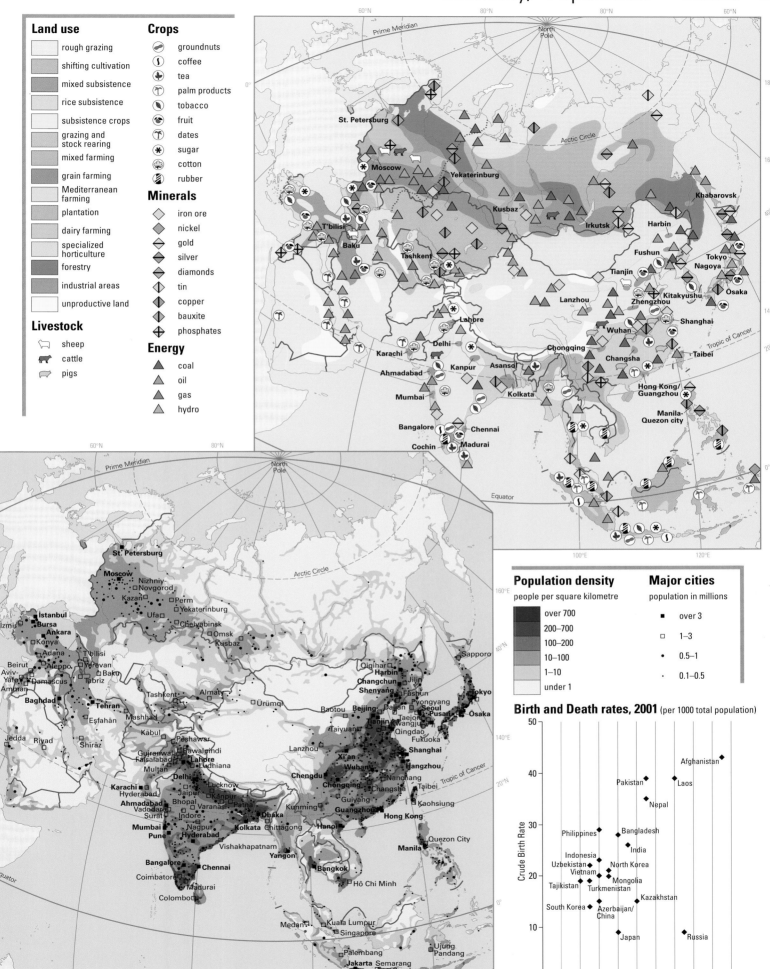

Land use
- rough grazing
- shifting cultivation
- mixed subsistence
- rice subsistence
- subsistence crops
- grazing and stock rearing
- mixed farming
- grain farming
- Mediterranean farming
- plantation
- dairy farming
- specialized horticulture
- forestry
- industrial areas
- unproductive land

Livestock
- sheep
- cattle
- pigs

Crops
- groundnuts
- coffee
- tea
- palm products
- tobacco
- fruit
- dates
- sugar
- cotton
- rubber

Minerals
- iron ore
- nickel
- gold
- silver
- diamonds
- tin
- copper
- bauxite
- phosphates

Energy
- coal
- oil
- gas
- hydro

Population density
people per square kilometre
- over 700
- 200–700
- 100–200
- 10–100
- 1–10
- under 1

Major cities
population in millions
- over 3
- 1–3
- 0.5–1
- 0.1–0.5

Birth and Death rates, 2001 (per 1000 total population)

Afghanistan, Pakistan, Laos, Nepal, Bangladesh, Philippines, India, Indonesia, North Korea, Uzbekistan, Vietnam, Mongolia, Tajikistan, Turkmenistan, Kazakhstan, South Korea, Azerbaijan/China, Japan, Russia

Crude Birth Rate

Crude Death Rate

Zenithal Equal Area Projection

© Oxford University Press

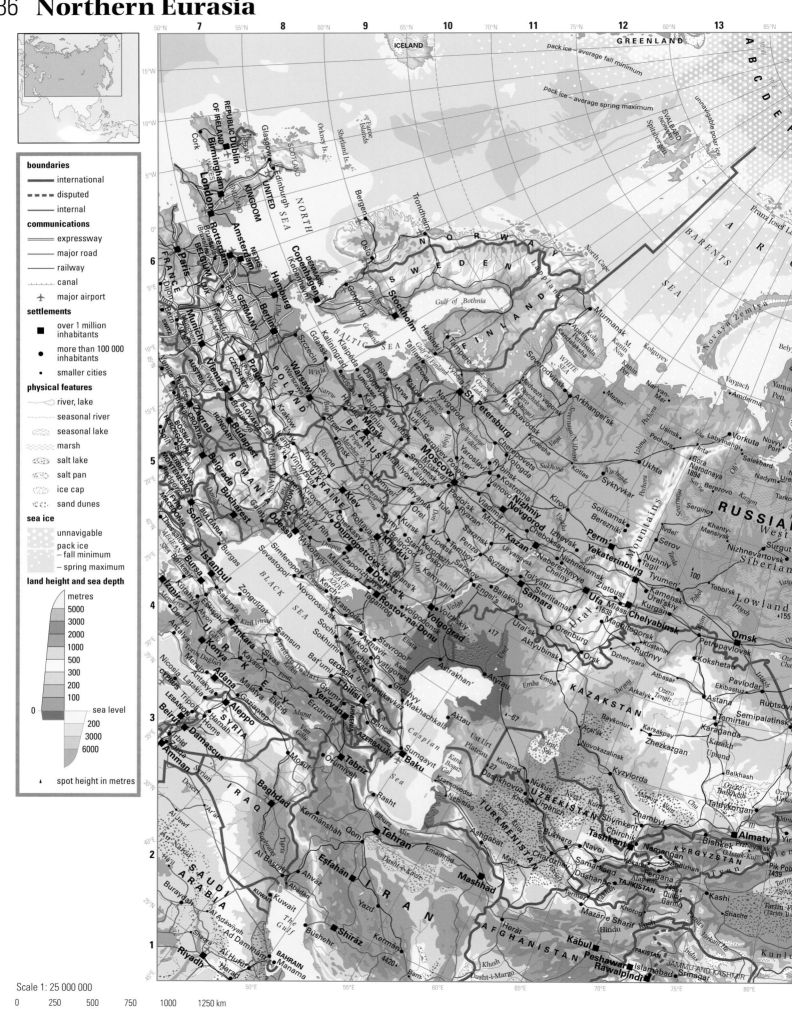

© Oxford University Press

boundaries
— international
--- disputed
— internal

communications
expressway
major road
railway
canal
✈ major airport

settlements
■ over 1 million inhabitants
● more than 100 000 inhabitants
· smaller cities

physical features
river, lake
seasonal river
seasonal lake
marsh
salt lake
salt pan
ice cap
sand dunes

sea ice
unnavigable
pack ice
– fall minimum
– spring maximum

land height and sea depth

metres
5000
3000
2000
1000
500
300
200
100
0 sea level
200
3000
6000

▲ spot height in metres

Scale 1: 25 000 000

0   250   500   750   1000   1250 km

Conical Orthomorphic Projection

13 **12** **11** **10** **9** **8** **7**

85°N 80°N 75°N 70°N 65°N 60°N 55°N

165°W

U S A
A L A S K A

CHUKCHI
SEA
C. Lisburne
Bering Strait
Nome
Norton Sd.
Arctic Circle
Uelen
Chukotskiy
Gulf of
Anadyr'
Providenya
St. Lawrence
(USA)

170°W

EAST
SIBERIAN
SEA
Wrangel
Island
Ayon
Pevek
Chukotsk Range
M. Navarin

175°W

BERING

180°

Aleutian Islands

Ambarchik
Nizhnekolymsk
Bilibino
Markovo
Anadyr'
Koryak Range
SEA

170°E

OCEAN
Severnaya Zemlya
Vise
unnavigable polar ice
New Siberian
Islands
Kolyma
Lowland
Srednekolymsk
Omolon
M. Olyutorskiy
Gizhiga

175°E

LAPTEV
M. Chelyuskin
Indigirka
Kazach'ye
Deputatskiy
Zyryanka
Sredniy
Palana
 Key
Kronotskaya Sopka
4750 Kamchatka

Taymyr
Byrranga Mts.
Nordvik
Tiksi
Bulun
Omoloy
Gora
Pobeda
3147
Seymchan
Shelikhov Bay
Karaginskiy
Petropavlovsk-
Kamchatskiy

6

Peninsula
Ozero
Taymyr
Khatanga
Lena
Zhigansk
Verkhoyansk
Ust'-Nera
Cherskogo Range
Magadan
M. Tolstoy
SEA OF
Oktyabr'skiy

Dikson
Pyasina
Kheta
Khatanga
Olenek
Olenek
Kyutyy
Anabar
Cherskogo Range

G. of Yenisey
insula
Gory
Kamen'
2037
Mts.
Anbar
Zhigansk
Lena
Sangar
Ust'-Maya
Dzhugdzhur Range
OKHOTSK
Kuril Islands

Dudinka
Noril'sk
Central
Olenek
Yakutsk
Amga
Ust'-Maya
Okhotsk
pack ice – average spring maximum
45°N

nburg
Igarka
Kureyka
Putoran Mts.
Vilyuy
Amga
Aldan
Ayan
Sakhalin
Bay
Okha
Aleksandrovsk-
Sakhalinskiy

Taz
rengoy
Turukhansk
Viv
Tura
Siberian
Markha
Vilyuy
Olekminsk
Udo
Nikolayevsk-
na-Amure
Okna
Administered by Russia
Claimed by Japan

FEDERATION
(RUSSIA)
Plateau
Lensk
Aldan
2481
na-Amure
Sakhalin
Poronaysk
Terpeniye Bay
40°N

Podkamennaya (Stony) Tunguska
Chunya
846
Vitim
Lena
Neryungri
Stanovoy Range
Nagornyy
Komsomol'sk-
na-Amure
Amgun'
Sovetskaya
Gavan
Yuzhno-Sakhalinsk
Korsakov

Nizhnyaya (Lower) Tunguska
Tura
823
Mirnyy
Suntar
Berkakit
Tynda
Zeya
Svobodnyy
Belogorsk
Amur
Sikhote-Alin
Kholmsk
Wakkanai

Kel
Belyy Yar
Chulym
Yeniseysk
Angara
Chuna
Ust'-Ilimsk
Kirensk
Mogocha
Skovorodino
Zeya
Blagoveshchensk
Khabarovsk

155°E

pashevo
Anzhero-
Sudzhensk
Achinsk
Kansk
Taishet
Bratsk
Ust'-Kut
Nizhneangarsk
2724
Bukachacha
(Heilong Jiang)
Amur
Ozero Khanka
Asahikawa
4

msk
Kemerovo
Krasnoyarsk
Tayshet
Tulun
Bratsk
Vdkhr.
Chita
Shilka
Sretensk
Nerchinsk
Amur (Heilong Jiang)
Jiamusi
Spassk-Dal'niy
Nakhodka
Vostochnyy
Sapporo
Hakodate
Aomori
Morioka

eninsk
Novosibirsk
Prokop'yevsk
Novokuznetsk
Abakan
Sayanogorsk
Sayan
Cheremkhovo
Angarsk
Irkutsk
Borzya
Hailar
Do Hinggan Ling
(Greater Khingan Range)
Nenjiang
Qiqihar
Harbin
Mudanjiang
Ussuriysk
Vladivostok
Chongjin
SEA OF
JAPAN
Akita
Yamagata
Sendai
Fukushima
Hitachi

Ob'
Biysk
Abakan
Eastern Sayan
Western Sayan
Yenisey
Kyzyl
Manzhouli
Nen Jiang
Jilin
Yanji
JAPAN
Kanazawa
Joetsu

Leninogorsk
Altay
4173
Tannu Ola
Kyzyl
Ulan-Ude
Kyakhta
Yablonovyy
Choybalsan
Qiqihar
Harbin
Changchun
Fushun
Vladivostok
Toyama
Yokohama
Tokyo

Ozero
Zaysan
3816
Altai
Hövsgöl
Nuur
Sühbaatar
Kerulen
Jilin
Shenyang
Anshan
Sinuiju
Pyongyang
Kyoto
Nagoya
Kawasaki

3

-Kamenogorsk
Ulaangom
Uvs Nuur
Selenge
Ulan Bator
Chengde
Yingkou
Hamhung
NORTH KOREA
Kita-Kyushu
Kobe
Osaka

Zaysan
Hovd
Uliastay
MONGOLIA
Saynshand
Erenhot
Chifeng
Tangshan
Pyongyang
Seoul
SOUTH
KOREA
Taegu
Pusan
Hiroshima
Fukuoka
Okayama

Junggar Pendi
(Dzungarian Basin)
Gobi Desert
NEI MONGOL ZIZHIQU
Zhangjiakou
Tangshan
Dalian
Inchon
SOUTH
KOREA
Kwangju
Nagasaki

XINJIANG
Ürümqi
Han Shan
Turpan
-154
Turpan
Depression
Hami
Ala Shan
(INNER MONGOLIAN AUTONOMOUS REGION)
Hohhot
Beijing
Tianjin
Shijiazhuang
Zibo
Qingdao
YELLOW
SEA
Kagoshima

UYGUR
ZIZHIQU
(HUI AUTONOMOUS REGION)
Anxi
Baotou
Yinchuan
NINGXIA
HUIZU
ZIZHIQU
Taiyuan
Jinan
Lianyungang
EAST CHINA
Ryukyu Islands

CHINA
Qilian
Altun Shan
Shan
Anyang
Huang He
Xuzhou
SEA

Qaidam Pendi
(Qaidam Basin)
Xining
Lanzhou
Luoyang
Zhengzhou
Nanyang
Huainan
Hefei
Nanjing
Suzhou
Shanghai

Shan
Golmud
Wei He
Xi'an
Baoji
Xiqing Shan
Nanyang
Wuhu
Hangzhou
Ningbo

6 **5** **4** **3** **2** **1**

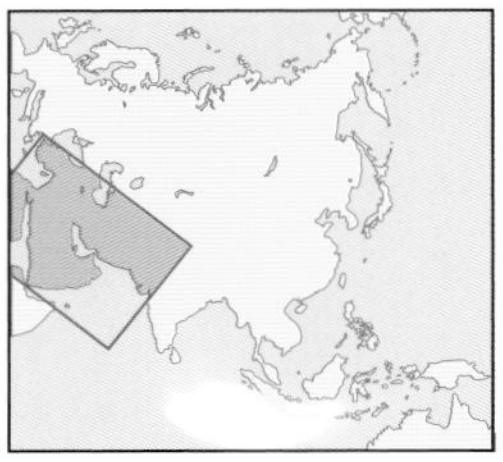

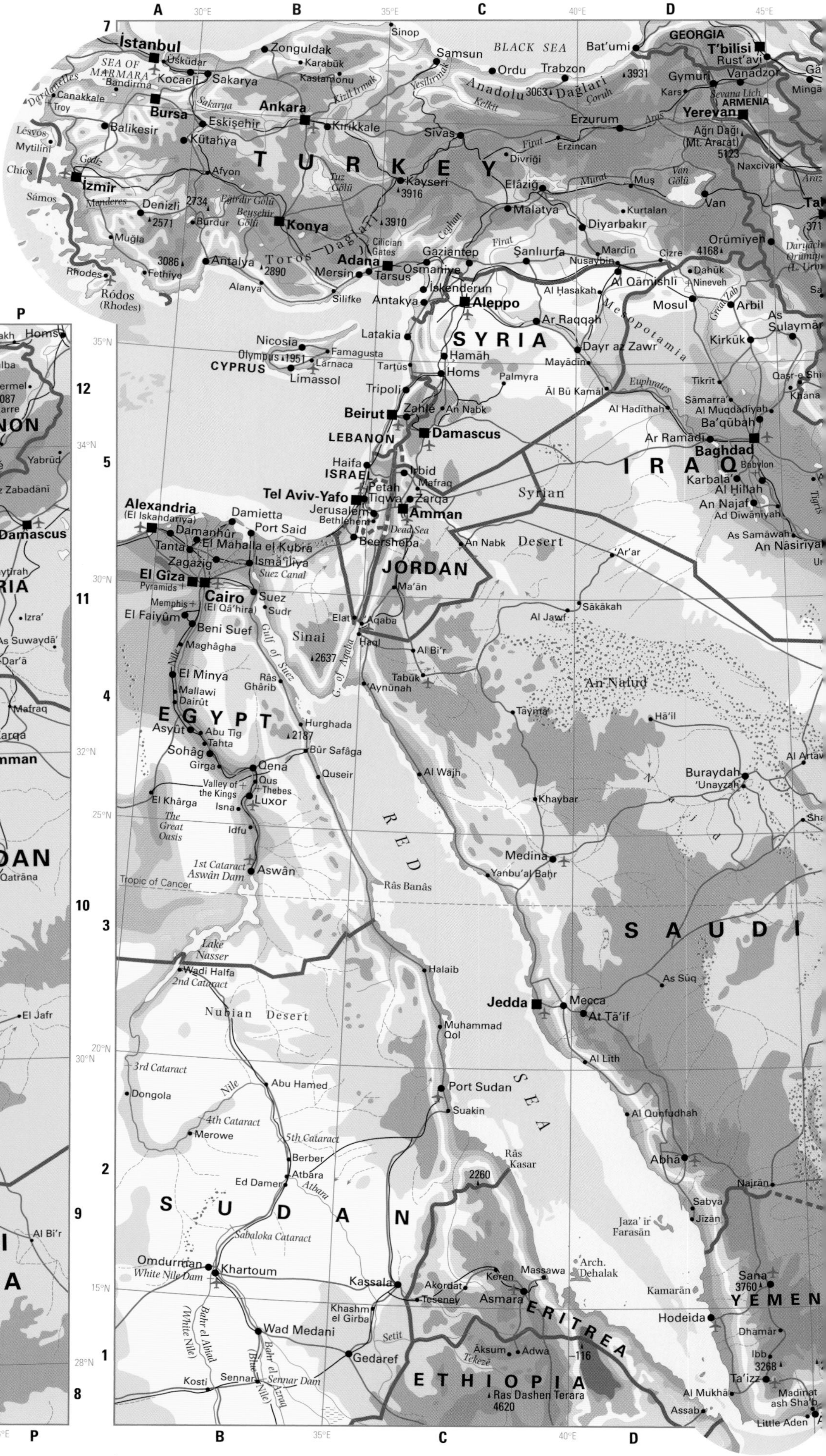

Israel and Lebanon

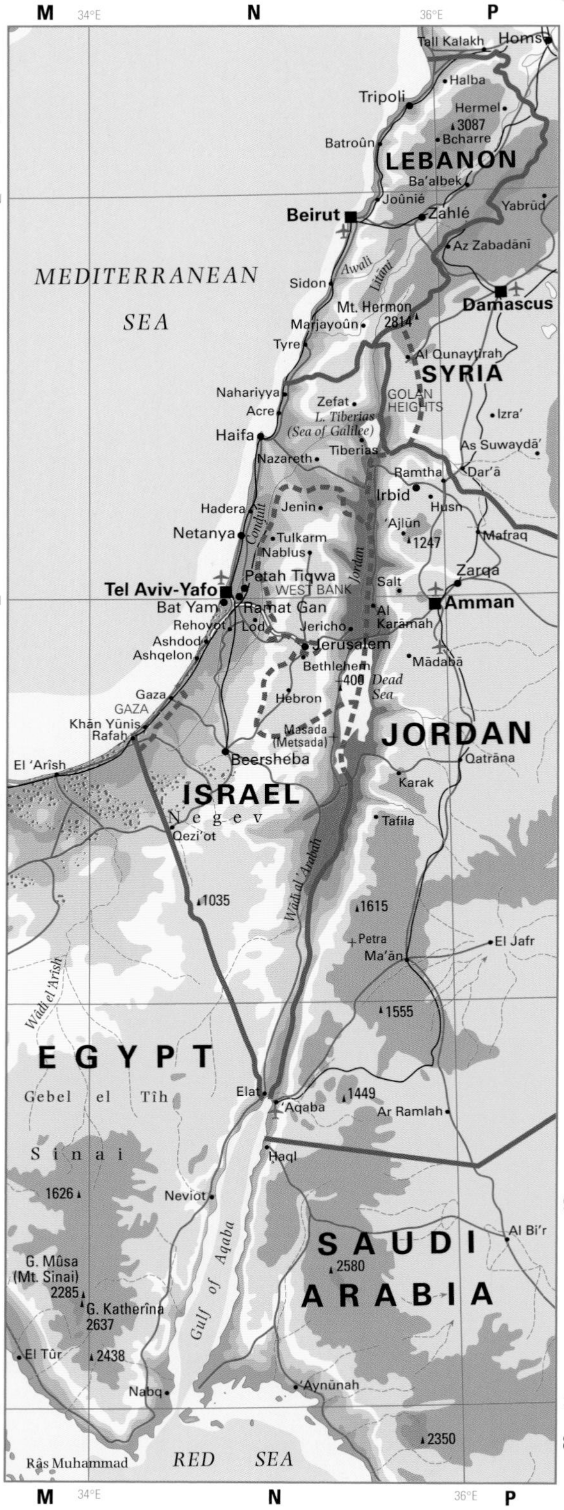

Scale 1: 4 000 000

0 40 80 120 160 200 km

Scale 1: 12 500 000

0 125 250 375 500 625 km

Israel and Lebanon map labels

Tall Kalakh · Homs · Tripoli · Halba · Hermel · 3087 · Batroûn · Bcharre · LEBANON · Ba'albek · Beirut · Jouniè · Zahlé · Yabrûd · Az Zabadāni · MEDITERRANEAN SEA · Sidon · Awali · Damascus · Litani · Mt. Hermon · 2814 · Marjayoûn · Tyre · Al Qunaytirah · GOLAN HEIGHTS · SYRIA · Nahariyya · Zefat · Acre · L. Tiberias (Sea of Galilee) · Izra' · Haifa · Tiberias · As Suwaydā' · Nazareth · Ramtha · Dar'ā · Hadera · Jenin · Irbid · Husn · Netanya · 'Ajlûn · 1247 · Tulkarm · Mafraq · Nablus · Salt · Zarqa · Tel Aviv-Yafo · Petah Tiqwa · WEST BANK · Jordan · Amman · Bat Yam · Ramat Gan · Al Karamah · Rehovot · Lod · Jericho · Mādabā · Ashdod · Jerusalem · Ashqelon · Bethlehem · -400 · Dead Sea · Gaza · GAZA · Hebron · JORDAN · Khān Yûnis · Rafah · Masada (Metsada) · Beersheba · ISRAEL · Karak · El 'Arîsh · Negev · Tafila · Qezi'ot · 1035 · 1615 · Petra · El Jafr · Ma'ān · 1555 · EGYPT · Gebel el Tih · Elat · 1449 · Ar Ramlah · 'Aqaba · Sinai · Haql · 1626 · Neviot · Al Bi'r · G. Mûsa (Mt. Sinai) · SAUDI · 2580 · 2285 · G. Katherina · 2637 · ARABIA · El Tûr · 2438 · Nabq · 'Aynûnah · Râs Muhammad · RED SEA · 2350

Main map labels

BLACK SEA · İstanbul · Üsküdar · Zonguldak · Sinop · Samsun · Bat'umi · GEORGIA · T'bilisi · SEA OF MARMARA · Kocaeli · Sakarya · Karabük · Kastamonu · Ordu · Trabzon · 3931 · Rust'avi · Bandirma · Dardanelles · Bursa · Ankara · Kirikkale · Gymŭri · Vanadzor · ARMENIA · Çanakkale · Troy · Balikesir · Eskişehir · Yeşilirmak · Kizil Irmak · Anadolu Dağlari · 3063 · Kars · Yerevan · Lésvos · Mytilíni · Gediz · Kütahya · TURKEY · Sivas · Erzurum · Erzincan · Firat · Ağri Daği (Mt. Ararat) 5123 · Naxçivan · Chios · İzmir · Afyon · Divriği · Murat · Van Gölü · Sámos · Manderes · Denizli · 2734 · Eğridir Gölü · 3910 · Kayseri · 3916 · Malatya · Muş · Van · Muğla · 2571 · Burdur Gölü · Beyşehir Gölü · Konya · Elâziğ · Kurtalan · Orŭmiyen · 4168 · 3086 · Toros Dağlari · 3910 · Gaziantep · Şanliurfa · Mardin · Nusaybin · Nineveh · Mosul · Arbil · Rhodes · Fethiye · Antalya · 2890 · Adana · Osmaniye · Al Hasakah · Cizre · Dahûk · Ródos (Rhodes) · Alanya · Silifke · Mersin · Tarsus · İskenderun · Aleppo · Al Qāmishli · Great Zab · Kirkŭk · As Sulaymān · Nicosia · 1951 · Famagusta · Latakia · SYRIA · Ar Raqqah · Dayr az Zawr · Mesopotamia · Tikrit · Qasr-e Shirin · Khāna · Olýmpus · Lárnaca · Tartûs · Hamāh · Mayādin · Euphrates · Sāmarrā' · CYPRUS · Limassol · Hama · Homs · Palmyra · Āl Bû Kamāl · Al Muqdādiyah · Ba'qubah · Tripoli · Zahle · An Nabk · Al Hadithah · Ba'qûbah · Beirut · Damascus · Ar Ramadi · Baghdad · Alexandria (El Iskandariya) · Haifa · Irbid · Mafraq · LEBANON · ISRAEL · Karbala · Al Hillah · IRAQ · Damietta · Port Said · Tel Aviv-Yafo · Petah Tiqwa · Zarqa · An Najaf · Damanhûr · Jerusalem · Amman · Ad Diwaniyah · Tanta · Bethlehem · Dead Sea · Beersheba · An Nabk · As Samāwah · An Nāsiriya · El Mahalla el Kubra · Zagazig · Ismā'iliya · JORDAN · 'Ar'ar · El Gîza · Suez Canal · Pyramids · Cairo (El Qâ'hira) · Suez · Ma'ān · Sākākah · Memphis · El Faiyûm · Beni Suef · Gulf of Aqaba · Elat · Al Jawf · Maghâgha · Sinai · Aqaba · Al Bi'r · An Nafud · El Minya · Râs Ghârib · 2637 · Haql · Tabûk · Aynûnah · Tāymā' · Hā'il · EGYPT · Mallawi · Dairût · Hurghada · 2187 · Abu Tig · Tahta · Asyût · Bûr Safâga · Buraydah · Al Artaw · Sohâg · Girga · Qena · 'Unayzah · El Khârga · Qus · Thebes · Luxor · Al Wajh · Khaybar · The Great Oasis · Valley of the Kings · Isna · Quseir · Idfu · RED SEA · Medina · Yanbu' al Bahr · Aswân · 1st Cataract · Aswân Dam · Tropic of Cancer · Râs Bânâs · SAUDI · Lake Nasser · Wadi Halfa · 2nd Cataract · Halaib · Jedda · Mecca · At Tā'if · Al Lith · Nubian Desert · Al Qunfudhah · Dongola · 3rd Cataract · Nile · Abu Hamed · Port Sudan · Suakin · Abhâ · 1449 · 4th Cataract · Merowe · Muhammad Qol · Najrān · SUDAN · Berber · Atbara · 2260 · Sabya · Jīzān · Ed Damer · 5th Cataract · Jaza' ir Farasan · Sabaloka Cataract · Kamarān · Sana · 3760 · Omdurman · Khartoum · Kassala · Keren · Massawa · Arch. Dehalak · Hodeida · White Nile Dam · Akordat · Asmara · ERITREA · YEMEN · Wad Medani · Khashm el Girba · Teseney · ETHIOPIA · Gedaref · Setit · 3268 · Ta'izz · Kosti · Sennar · Sennar Dam · White Nile · Āksum · Ādwa · Ibb · Madinat ash Sha'b · Bahr el Abiad · Blue Nile · -116 · Ras Dashen Terara 4620 · Al Mukhā · Assab · Little Aden

© Oxford University Press

E 50°E F 55°E G 60°E H 65°E J 70°E K 75°E L

TAJIKISTAN

CHINA

TURKMENISTAN

UZBEKISTAN

Navoi
Bukhara
Kattakurgan Samarkand
Kagan Karshi
Dushanbe
Chardzhev
Kerki
Termez
Khorog
Pamirs

Sumqayıt
Baku
Krasnovodsk
Nebitdag
Gyzylarbat
Ashgabat
Abadan
Mary
Tedzhen
Andkhvoy
Sheberghan
Mazar-e Sharif
Konduz
Khanabad
Feyzabad
Chitral
Gilgit
Indus
K2 8611
JAMMU
AND
KASHMIR
7690
8126
Srinagar

ERBAIJAN
Caspian Sea
Länkäran
Astara
Ardabīl
Mīāneh
Rasht
Zanjän
Qazvin
Bandar-e Torkeman
Gorgän
Sabzevar
Sarakhs
Mashhad
Neyshäbür
3147
Herāt
Bālā Morghāb
Meymaneh
Sar-e Pol
Baghlān
5143
Chaghcharān
Charikar
Kābul
Kābul
Jalālābād
Khyber Pass
Mardan
Peshawar
Islāmābād
Rawalpindi
Wah
Kohat
Jhelum
Sialkot
Jammu

Bijär
Karaj
Damāvand 5671
Tehran
Semnän
Emāmrüd
Qom
Damāvand
anandaj
Hamadān
Ghaznī
Banni
Mianwali
Sargodha
Gujranwala
Gujrat
Batala
Amritsar

ermänshäh
Borüjerd
Arāk
Käshän
Tabas
Birjand
Shindand
Miram Shah
Dera Ismail Khan
Jhang Maghiana
Lahore
Kasur

Khorramābād
Esfahān
Yazd
Bäfq
Khäsh
Farāh
Koh-i-Mazar 3738
Zhob
Faisalabad
Sahiwal
Okara
PUNJAB

4548
Qomisheh
Dasht-e Lut
Khush
Registan
Qila Saifullah
Jhang
Dera Ghazi Khan
Multan
Bahawalpur

Al 'Amārah
Ahvāz
Zarand
Kermän
Rafsanjän
Zäbol
Dasht-i-Margo
Helmand
Chaman
Zärgun 3578
Quetta
2641
Ganganagar

Basrah
Khorramshahr
Behbahän
Abädän
Bandar Khomeyni
4420
Bam
Zähedän
Khäsh
Dalbandin
Nushki
Kalat
Sibi
Rahimyar Khan
Bikaner
RAJASTHAN

Jahrah
Kuwait
Al Fuḥayḥil
KUWAIT
Shīräz
Käzerün
Büshehr
Neyriz
Jahrom
Saravan
Iränshahr
2293
Bäluchistan
Kharan
Jacobabad
Shikarpur
Sukkur
Khairpur
Larkana
Jaisalmer
Jodhpur

Khärg
Lär
Kangan
Bandar-e 'Abbās
Khäsh
Bela
Sind
Mirpur Khas
INDIA

The Gulf
Str. of Hormuz
Bandar-e Lengeh
OMAN
Jäsk
Makran
Kotri
Hyderabad
Patan

Al Jubayl
Ad Dammäm
Dhahran
BAHRAIN
Manama
QATAR
Sharjah
Dubai
Chäh Bahär
Karachi
Mouths of the Indus
Rann of Kachchh
GUJARAT

Dir'iyah
Al Mubarraz
Al Hufüf
Doha
Abu Dhabi
Al 'Ayn
Al Buraymi
Maṭrah
Muscat
Tropic of Cancer
Bhuj
Kandla
G. of Kachchh
Jamnagar
Morbi
Rajkot
Bhavnagar

Riyadh
Harad
UNITED ARAB EMIRATES
Ibri
Jabal Akhdar 3018
Nazwä
Sür
Ra's al Hadd
Porbandar
Kathiawar
Veraval
Diu

Ad Dilam
Al Hariq
Layla
Umm as Samim
O M A N
Masirah
ARABIAN SEA

A R A B I A
Rub' Al Khälï
Ra's Madrakah

boundary undefined
Kuria Muria Is.
Ra's Fartak
Say'ün
W. al Masilah
Ṣalälah
Hadhramaut
2112
Habbän
Mukalla
ra
Gulf of Aden
Hadiboh
Socotra (Yemen)
'Abd al Küri
REPUBLIC

Legend

boundaries
━━━ international
- - - disputed
─── internal

communications
═══ expressway
─── major road
─── railway
┼┼┼ canal
✈ major airport

settlements
■ over 1 million inhabitants
● more than 100 000 inhabitants
• smaller cities

physical features
river, lake
seasonal river
seasonal lake
marsh
salt lake
salt pan
ice cap
sand dunes

sea ice
unnavigable
pack ice
— fall minimum
— spring maximum

land height and sea depth
metres
5000
3000
2000
1000
500
300
200
100
0
sea level
200
3000
6000
▲ spot height in metres

© Oxford University Press   Conical Orthomorphic projection

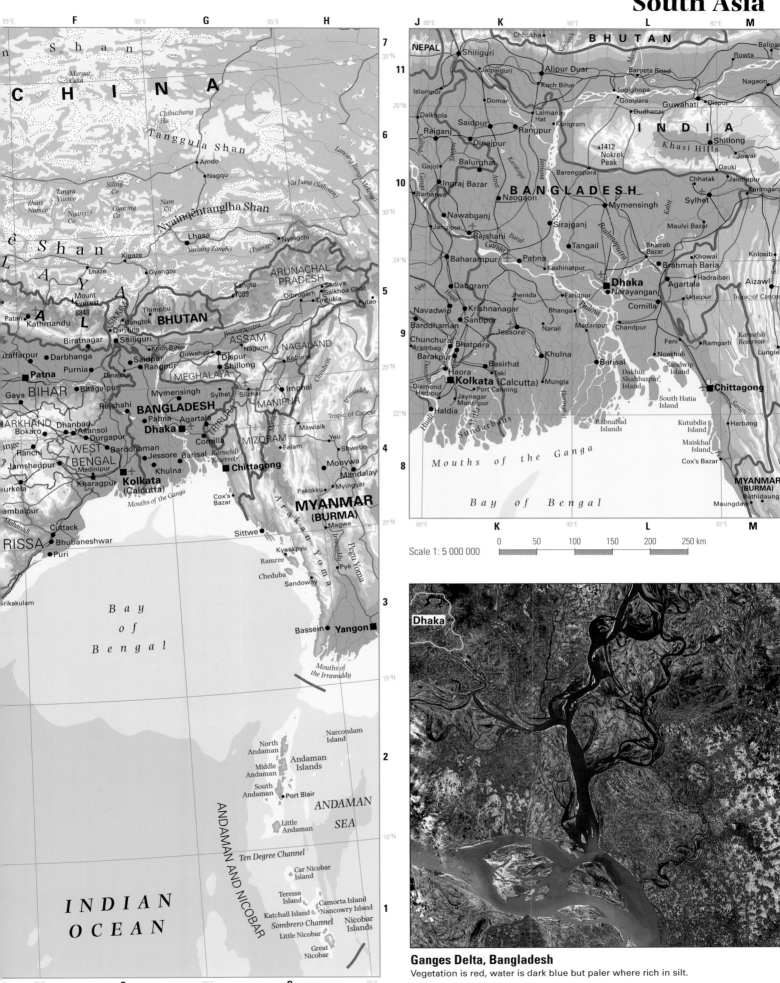

Map labels (left map)

CHINA
Tanggula Shan
Margat Caka
Chibuzhang Hu
Amdo
Nagqu
Nu Jiang (Salween)
Lancang Jiang (Mekong)
Nyainqentanglha Shan
Zhari Namco
Tangra Yumco
Siling Co
Nam Co
Ngangzê Co
Gyaring Co
e Shan
Lhasa
Yarlung Zangbo (Tsangpo)
Nyingchi
Lhaze
Xigaze
Gyangze
ARUNACHAL PRADESH
Sadiya
Kangto ▲7089
Saikhoa Ghat
Mount Everest 8848
Dibrugarh
Tinsukia
Putao
Patan
Kathmandu
Thimphu
SIKKIM
Gangtok
Darjiling
BHUTAN
Brahmaputra
ASSAM
Koch Bihar
Guwahati
Dispur
NAGALAND
Biratnagar
Shiliguri
Saidpur
Rangpur
Nagaon
Kohima
Chindwin
Muzaffarpur
Darbhanga
Purnia
Dinajpur
MEGHALAYA
Shillong
Silchar
Imphal
MANIPUR
BIHAR
Patna
Bhagalpur
Rajshahi
Mymensingh
Sylhet
Irrawaddy
Gaya
BANGLADESH
Pabna
Agartala
TRIPURA
Comilla
Mawlaik
Yeu
JHARKHAND
Dhanbad
Asansol
Dhaka
MIZORAM
Falam
Shwebo
Bokaro
Durgapur
Barddhaman
Monywa
Ranchi
WEST BENGAL
Jessore
Barisal
Karnafuli Reservoir
Mandalay
MYANMAR (BURMA)
Jamshedpur
Medinipur
Khulna
Chittagong
Pakokku
Myingyan
urkela
Kharagpur
Kolkata (Calcutta)
Cox's Bazar
Myitkyina
ambalpur
Mouths of the Ganga
Magwe
RISSA
Cuttack
Sittwe
Pye
Bhubaneswar
Kyaukpyu
Arakan Yoma
Pegu Yoma
Puri
Ramree
Srikakulam
Cheduba
Sandoway
Bay of Bengal
Bassein
Yangon
Mouths of the Irrawaddy
Mahanadi
North Andaman
Narcondam Island
Middle Andaman
Andaman Islands
South Andaman
Port Blair
ANDAMAN SEA
Little Andaman
ANDAMAN AND NICOBAR
Ten Degree Channel
INDIAN OCEAN
Car Nicobar Island
Teressa Island
Katchall Island
Camorta Island
Nancowry Island
Sombrero Channel
Nicobar Islands
Little Nicobar
Great Nicobar

Map labels (right map)

BHUTAN
NEPAL
Chhukha
Shiliguri
Jalpaiguri
Alipur Duar
Barpeta Road
Rowta
Balipar
Islampur
Koch Bihar
Jogighopa
Nagaon
Dalkhola
Saidpur
Rangpur
Kurigram
Goalpara
Guwahati
Dispur
Raiganj
Dinajpur
Lalmani Hat
Dudhnai
INDIA
Gajol
Balurghat
Kurigram
Barengapara
▲1412 Nokrek Peak
Khasi Hills
Shillong
Ingraj Bazar
Atrai
BANGLADESH
Jowai
Barharwa
Naogaon
Mymensingh
Dauki
Jaintiapur
Nawabganj
Sirajganj
Chhatak
Sylhet
Karimganj
Jangipur
Rajshahi
Baral
Tangail
Bhairab Bazar
Brahman Baria
Khowai
Hadraibari
Kolosib
Baharampur
Pabna
Padma
Dhaka
Agartala
Aizawl
Kashinatpur
Narayanganj
Udaipur
Tropic of Cancer
Navadwip
Krishnanagar
Jhenida
Faridpur
Bhanga
Comilla
Barddhaman
Santipur
Jessore
Narail
Madaripur
Chandpur
Feni
Ramgarh
Karnafuli Reservoir
Chunchura
Arambag
Bhatpara
Basirhat
Khulna
Barisal
Feni
Lunglei
Barakpur
Taki
Noakhali
Haora
Kolkata (Calcutta)
Mungla
Dakhin Shahbazpur Island
Sandwip Island
Diamond Harbour
Port Canning
South Hatia Island
Chittagong
Jaynagar
Manjipur
Haldia
Sundarbans
Rabnabad Islands
Kutubdia Island
Harbang
Maiskhal Island
Mouths of the Ganga
Cox's Bazar
MYANMAR (BURMA)
Buthidaung
Bay of Bengal
Maungdaw

Scale 1: 5 000 000

0   50   100   150   200   250 km

Ganges Delta, Bangladesh

Dhaka

Vegetation is red, water is dark blue but paler where rich in silt.

Conical Orthomorphic Projection

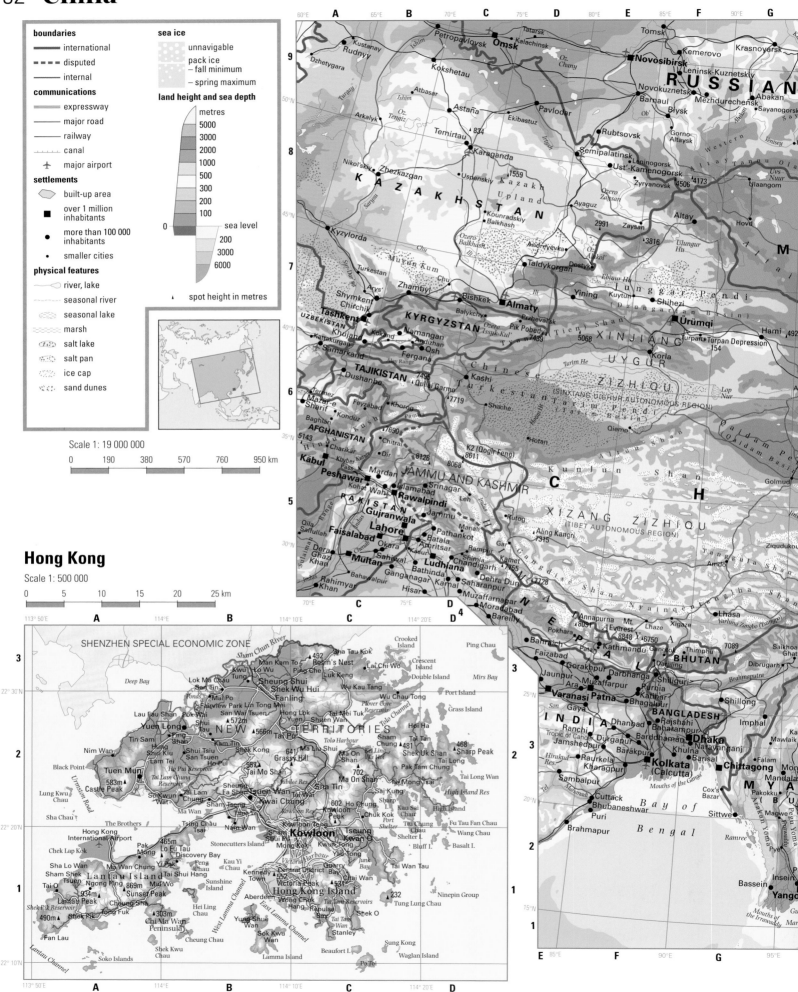

boundaries
— international
--- disputed
— internal

communications
═══ expressway
— major road
— railway
+++ canal
✈ major airport

settlements
⬡ built-up area
■ over 1 million inhabitants
● more than 100 000 inhabitants
• smaller cities

physical features
～ river, lake
⋯ seasonal river
seasonal lake
marsh
salt lake
salt pan
ice cap
sand dunes

sea ice
unnavigable
pack ice
– fall minimum
– spring maximum

land height and sea depth
metres
5000
3000
2000
1000
500
300
200
100
0 sea level
200
3000
6000

▲ spot height in metres

Scale 1: 19 000 000

0 190 380 570 760 950 km

Scale 1: 500 000

0 5 10 15 20 25 km

Gauss Conformal Projection

© Oxford University Press

RUSSIAN FEDERATION (RUSSIA)

MONGOLIA

Gobi Desert

NEI MONGOL ZIZHIQU (INNER MONGOLIAN AUTONOMOUS REGION)

CHINA

NORTH KOREA

SOUTH KOREA

JAPAN

TAIWAN

VIETNAM

LAOS

THAILAND

MYANMAR

SEA OF OKHOTSK

SEA OF JAPAN

YELLOW SEA

EAST CHINA SEA

NORTH PACIFIC OCEAN

SOUTH CHINA SEA

Gulf of Tonking

Luzon Strait

Taiwan Strait

Tropic of Cancer

Selected place names:

Bratsk, Ust-Kut, Nizhneangarsk, Tulun, Cheremkhovo, Usol'ye-Sibirskoye, Angarsk, Irkutsk, Ulan-Ude, Suhbaatar, Ulan Bator, Hövsgöl Nuur, Jiliastay, Saynshand, Erenhot, Choybalsan, Manzhouli, Hailar, Chita, Borzya, Sretensk, Nerchinsk, Mogocha, Skovorodino, Tynda, Mohe, Mangui, Blagoveshchensk, Belogorsk, Svobodnyy, Khabarovsk, Birobidzhan, Komsomol'sk-na-Amure, Sovetskaya Gavan', Aleksandrovsk-Sakhalinskiy, Poronaysk, Sakhalin, Yuzhno-Sakhalinsk, Korsakov, Kholmsk

Qiqihar, Harbin, Daqing, Baicheng, Mudanjiang, Hegang, Jiamusi, Shuangyashan, Jixi, Changchun, Jilin, Huade, Liaoyuan, Fuxin, Chaoyang, Shenyang, Fushun, Benxi, Liaoyang, Anshan, Yingkou, Jinzhou, Jinxi, Chengde, Zhangjiakou, Jining, Xuanhua, Hohhot, Baotou, Wuhai, Datong, Beijing, Tangshan, Tianjin, Qinhuangdao, Dalian, Lushun, Yantai, Weifang, Qingdao, Zibo, Jinan, Tai'an, Shijiazhuang, Baoding, Cangzhou, Dezhou, Taiyuan, Yangquan, Yuci, Xingtai, Handan, Anyang, Hebi, Yinchuan, Shizuishan, Yumen, Lanzhou, Xining, Tianshui, Baoji, Xianyang, Xi'an, Zhengzhou, Luoyang, Kaifeng, Shangqiu, Xuzhou, Xuchang, Nanyang, Pingdingshan, Zhoukou, Huaibei, Bengbu, Huainan, Hefei, Nanjing, Yangzhou, Wuxi, Suzhou, Shanghai, Changzhou, Nantong, Yancheng, Lianyungang, Zaozhuang, Jining, Chengdu, Neijiang, Chongqing, Hechuan, Nanchong, Wanxian, Yichang, Shashi, Wuhan, Huangshi, Nanchang, Jiujiang, Jingdezhen, Changde, Yiyang, Changsha, Xiangtan, Zhuzhou, Hengyang, Ji'an, Fuzhou, Nanping, Sanming, Guiyang, Zunyi, Kunming, Dali, Guilin, Liuzhou, Wuzhou, Nanning, Guangzhou (Canton), Foshan, Shunde, Jiangmen, Zhanjiang, Macao, Hong Kong, Shenzhen, Huizhou, Maoming, Beihai, Haikou, Hainan Dao, Sanya, Qionghai

North Korea: Sinuiju, Dandong, Pyongyang, Nampo, Haeju, Kaesong, Chongjin, Hamhung, Wonsan, Kimchaek, Hungnam

South Korea: Seoul, Inchon, Taejon, Taegu, Pusan, Kwangju, Mokpo, Sunchon, Yosu, Masan, Ulsan, Pohang, Chonju, Cheju do

Japan: Sapporo, Hakodate, Asahikawa, Otaru, Muroran, Aomori, Hachinohe, Akita, Morioka, Sendai, Yamagata, Niigata, Fukushima, Iwaki, Hitachi, Mito, Tokyo, Yokohama, Kawasaki, Nagoya, Kyoto, Osaka, Kobe, Okayama, Hiroshima, Fukuoka, Kita-Kyushu, Nagasaki, Kumamoto, Kagoshima, Miyazaki

Taiwan: Taibei, Chilung, Hsinchu, Taichung, Chiai, Tainan, Kaohsiung, Pingtun

Vietnam: Hanoi, Hai Phong, Nam Dinh, Thanh Hoa, Vinh, Hue, Da Nang, Quang Ngai

Laos / Thailand: Vientiane, Savannakhet, Nong Khai, Udon Thani, Khon Kaen, Nakhon Ratchasima, Ubon Ratchathani, Chiang Mai

Inset map:

3 Gorges Project, 1997–2009

boundaries
— area affected by project
— province

water control
reservoir
dam
* gorge

cities and towns
○ inundated
● others

SHAANXI PROVINCE, HUBEI PROVINCE, SICHUAN PROVINCE, HUNAN PROVINCE

sand dumping site for the proposed Three Gorges Dam

Kai Xian, Wuxi, Wushan, Badong, Xingshan, Zigui, Gezhouba Dam, Wanxian, Fengjie, Yungyang, Qutang Gorge, Wu Gorge, Xiling Gorge, Xiling Gorge, Yichang, Zhong Xian, Fuling, Shizhu, Fengdu, Changshou, Liangbei, Mudong, Chongqing, Baxian, Wulong, Chang Jiang (Yangtze), Daning He

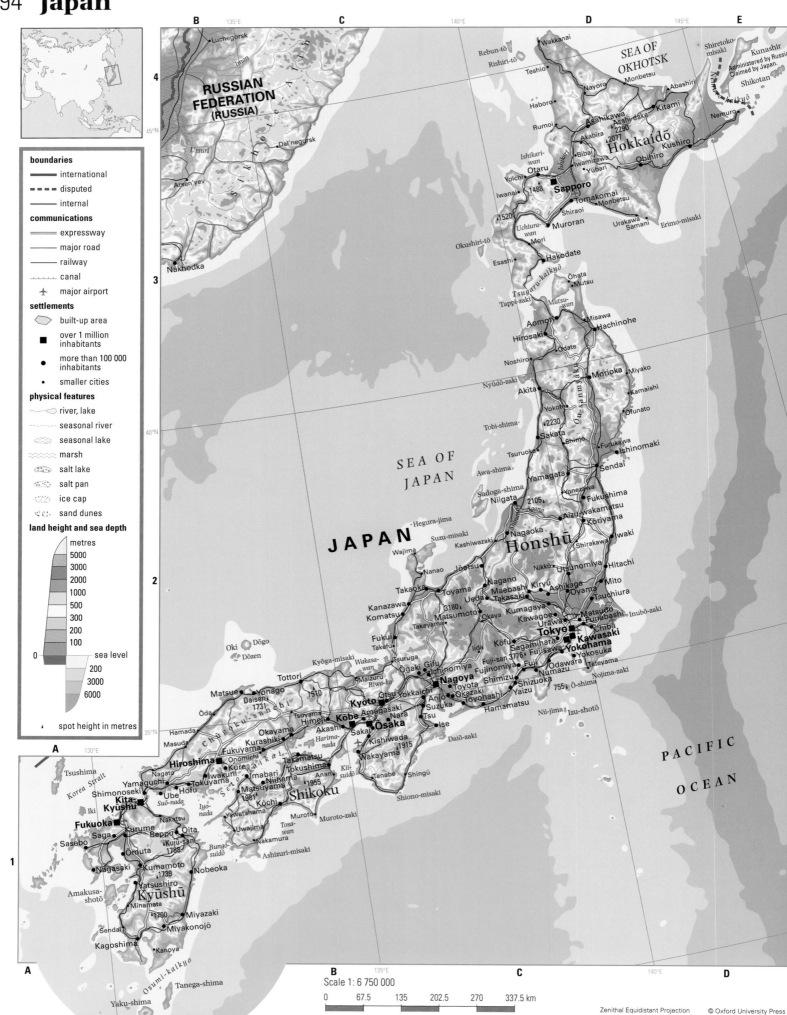

RUSSIAN FEDERATION (RUSSIA)

SEA OF OKHOTSK

Administered by Russia. Claimed by Japan.

Hokkaidō

Sapporo

SEA OF JAPAN

JAPAN

Honshū

Tokyo
Kawasaki
Yokohama

Nagoya

Kyōto
Kōbe
Ōsaka

Hiroshima

Kita-Kyūshū

Fukuoka

Shikoku

Kyūshū

PACIFIC OCEAN

boundaries
— international
--- disputed
— internal

communications
≡ expressway
— major road
— railway
⊥⊥⊥ canal
✈ major airport

settlements
built-up area
■ over 1 million inhabitants
● more than 100 000 inhabitants
• smaller cities

physical features
river, lake
seasonal river
seasonal lake
marsh
salt lake
salt pan
ice cap
sand dunes

land height and sea depth
metres
5000
3000
2000
1000
500
300
200
100
0 sea level
200
3000
6000

▲ spot height in metres

Scale 1: 6 750 000

0   67.5   135   202.5   270   337.5 km

Zenithal Equidistant Projection

© Oxford University Press

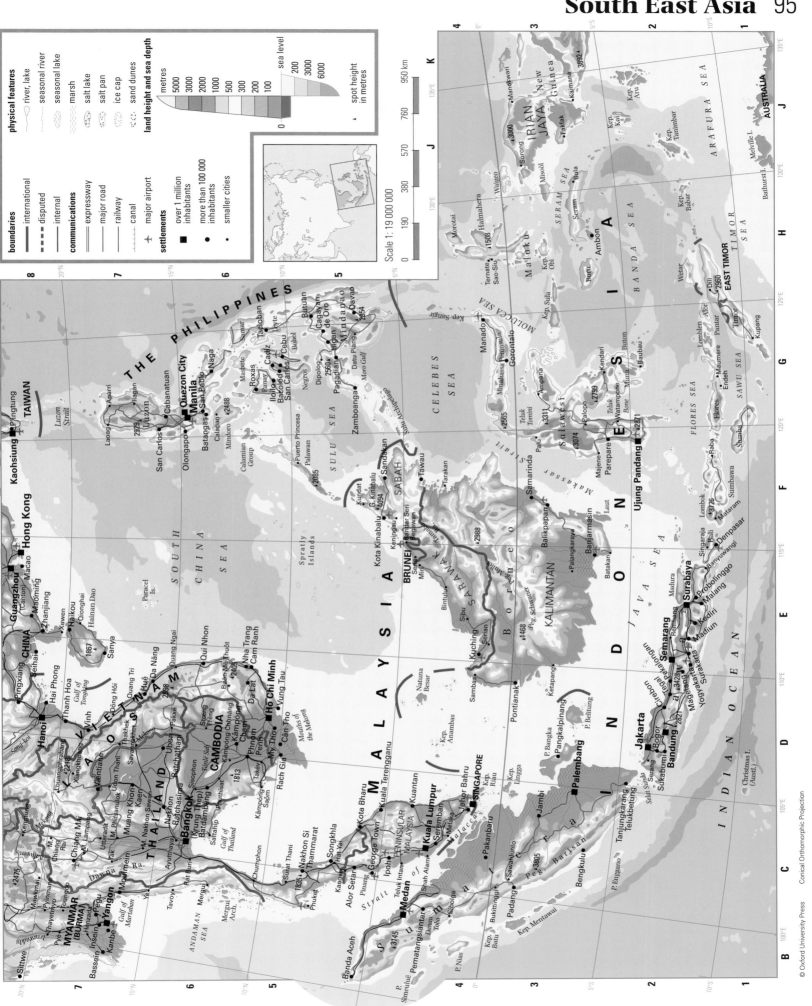

physical features

- river, lake
- seasonal river
- seasonal lake
- marsh
- salt lake
- salt pan
- ice cap
- sand dunes

land height and sea depth

metres
5000
3000
2000
1000
500
300
200
100
sea level
200
3000
6000

spot height in metres

boundaries

- international
- disputed
- internal

communications

- expressway
- major road
- railway
- canal
- major airport

settlements

- over 1 million inhabitants
- more than 100 000 inhabitants
- smaller cities

Scale 1: 19 000 000

0   190   380   570   760   950 km

© Oxford University Press

Conical Orthomorphic Projection

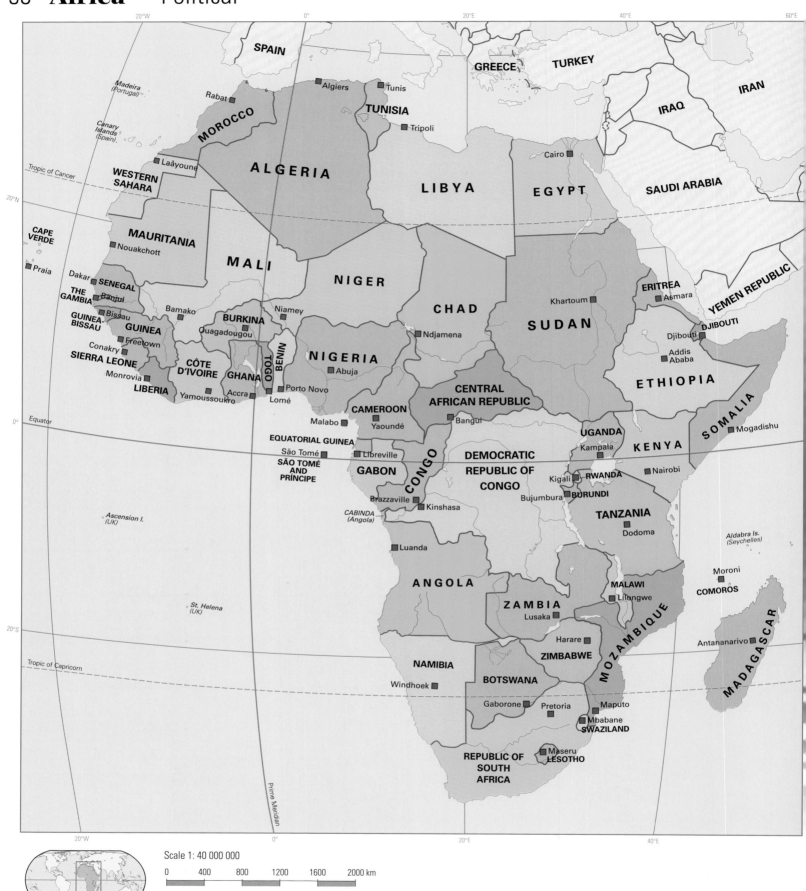

SPAIN

GREECE TURKEY

IRAN

Madeira
(Portugal)

Rabat ■ Algiers ■ Tunis
TUNISIA
■ Tripoli

IRAQ

Canary
Islands
(Spain)

MOROCCO

Tropic of Cancer

Laâyoune ■

ALGERIA

LIBYA

EGYPT

■ Cairo

SAUDI ARABIA

WESTERN
SAHARA

20°N

CAPE
VERDE

MAURITANIA

Nouakchott ■

MALI

NIGER

CHAD

Khartoum ■

S U D A N

ERITREA
Asmara ■

YEMEN REPUBLIC

■ Praia

Dakar ■ SENEGAL
THE Banjul ■
GAMBIA
Bissau ■
GUINEA-
BISSAU GUINEA
Conakry ■ Freetown ■
SIERRA LEONE
Monrovia ■
LIBERIA

Bamako ■
BURKINA
Ouagadougou ■
CÔTE
D'IVOIRE
Yamoussoukro ■

Niamey ■
TOGO
BENIN
NIGERIA
■ Abuja
GHANA
Accra ■ Porto Novo ■
Lomé ■

Ndjamena ■

Djibouti ■ DJIBOUTI
Addis
Ababa ■

ETHIOPIA

SOMALIA

■ Mogadishu

Equator

CENTRAL
AFRICAN REPUBLIC
CAMEROON
Malabo ■ Yaoundé ■ Bangui ■
EQUATORIAL GUINEA
São Tomé ■ Libreville ■
SÃO TOMÉ
AND
PRÍNCIPE GABON CONGO
Brazzaville ■
Kinshasa ■

UGANDA
Kampala ■ KENYA
DEMOCRATIC
REPUBLIC OF
CONGO
RWANDA
Kigali ■
Bujumbura ■ BURUNDI

■ Nairobi

Ascension I.
(UK)

CABINDA
(Angola)

TANZANIA
Dodoma ■

Aldabra Is.
(Seychelles)

Luanda ■

ANGOLA

ZAMBIA
Lusaka ■

MALAWI
Lilongwe ■

Moroni ■
COMOROS

St. Helena
(UK)

20°S

Tropic of Capricorn

NAMIBIA

Windhoek ■

BOTSWANA

Gaborone ■

ZIMBABWE
Harare ■

MOZAMBIQUE

Antananarivo ■

MADAGASCAR

Pretoria ■ Maputo ■
Mbabane ■
SWAZILAND

Prime Meridian

REPUBLIC OF
SOUTH
AFRICA

Maseru ■
LESOTHO

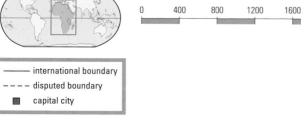

Scale 1: 40 000 000

0   400   800   1200   1600   2000 km

international boundary

disputed boundary

■ capital city

Zenithal Equal Area Projection

© Oxford University Press

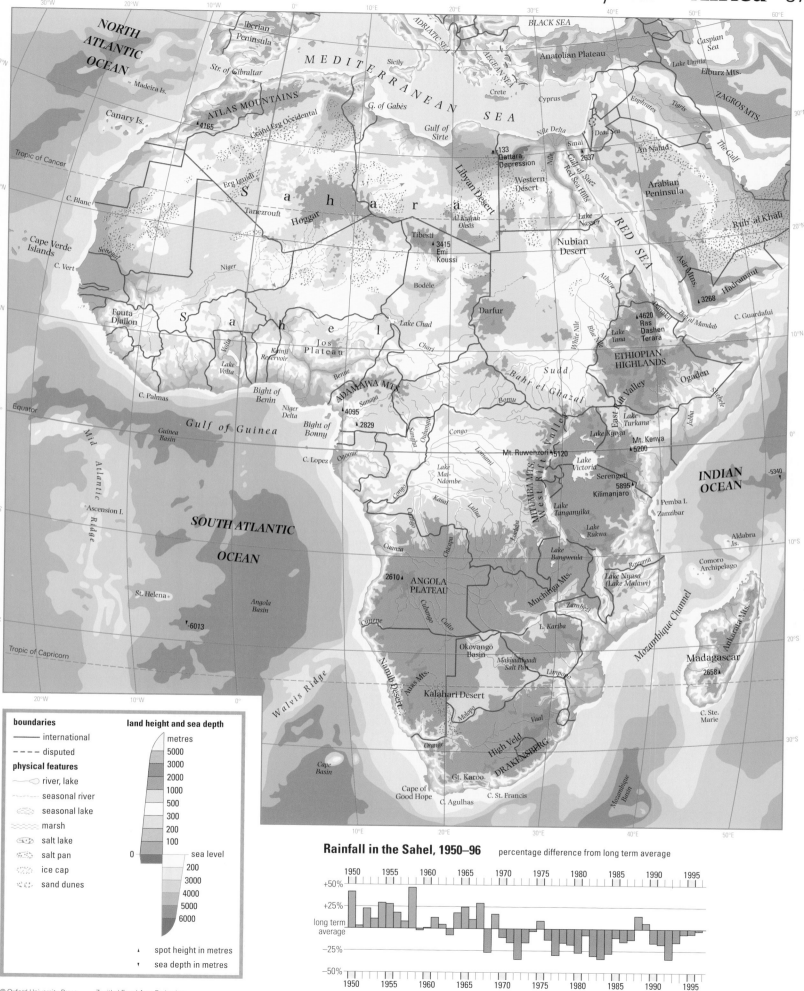

Rainfall in the Sahel, 1950–96 percentage difference from long term average

boundaries
— international
- - - disputed

physical features
river, lake
seasonal river
seasonal lake
marsh
salt lake
salt pan
ice cap
sand dunes

land height and sea depth
metres
5000
3000
2000
1000
500
300
200
100
0 — sea level
200
3000
4000
5000
6000

▲ spot height in metres
▼ sea depth in metres

© Oxford University Press   Zenithal Equal Area Projection

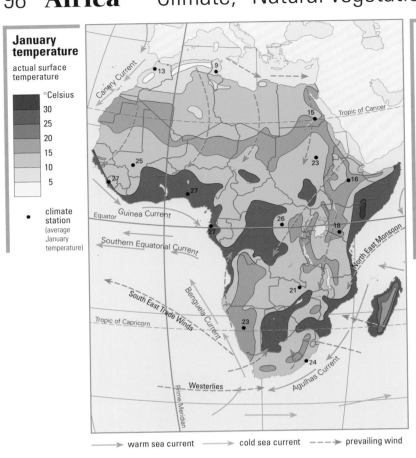

January temperature

actual surface temperature

°Celsius
30
25
20
15
10
5

● climate station (average January temperature)

Canary Current
Guinea Current
Equator
Southern Equatorial Current
South East Trade Winds
Benguela Current
Tropic of Capricorn
Westerlies
Prime Meridian
Agulhas Current
North East Monsoon
Tropic of Cancer

→ warm sea current   → cold sea current   - - - → prevailing wind

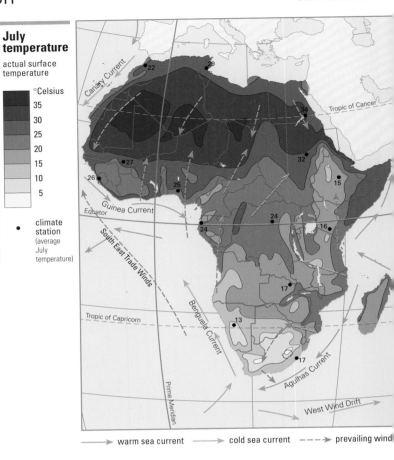

July temperature

actual surface temperature

°Celsius
35
30
25
20
15
10
5

● climate station (average July temperature)

Canary Current
Guinea Current
Equator
South East Trade Winds
Benguela Current
Prime Meridian
Agulhas Current
West Wind Drift
Tropic of Cancer
Tropic of Capricorn

→ warm sea current   → cold sea current   - - - → prevailing wind

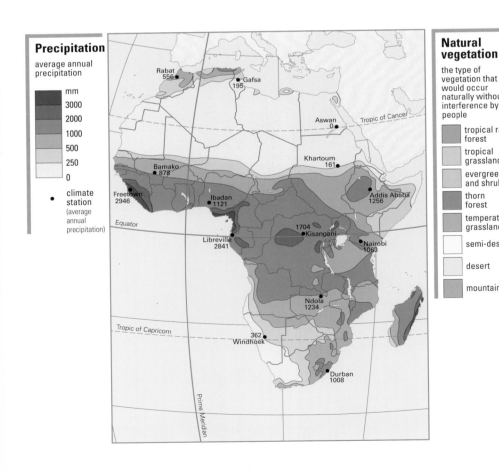

Precipitation

average annual precipitation

mm
3000
2000
1000
500
250
0

● climate station (average annual precipitation)

Rabat 556
Gafsa 195
Aswan 0
Khartoum 161
Bamako 878
Freetown 2946
Ibadan 1121
Addis Ababa 1256
Librevile 2841
Kisangani 1704
Nairobi 1063
Ndola 1234
Windhoek 362
Durban 1008
Equator
Tropic of Cancer
Tropic of Capricorn
Prime Meridian

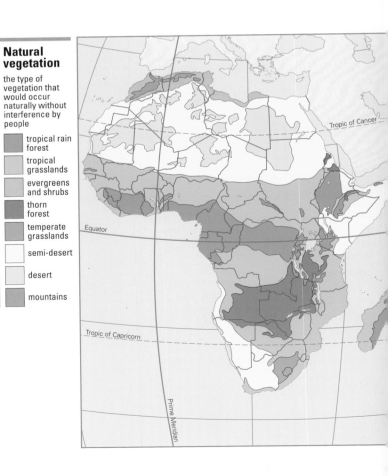

Natural vegetation

the type of vegetation that would occur naturally without interference by people

tropical rain forest

tropical grasslands

evergreens and shrubs

thorn forest

temperate grasslands

semi-desert

desert

mountains

Equator
Tropic of Cancer
Tropic of Capricorn
Prime Meridian

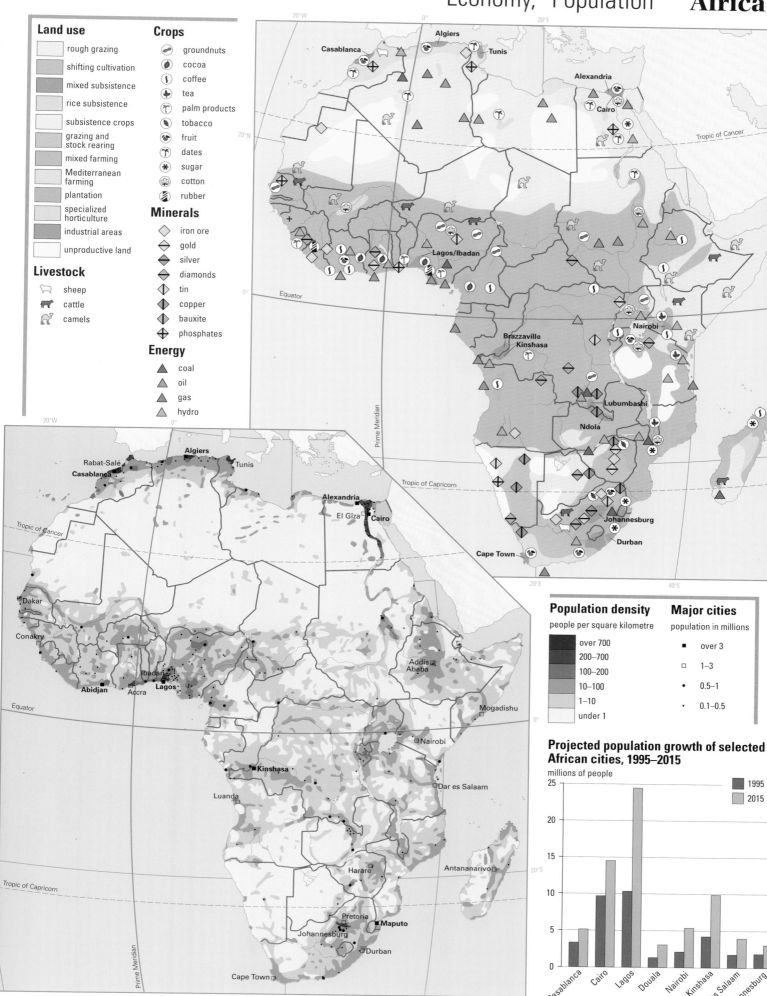

Scale 1 : 55 000 000

Land use

- rough grazing
- shifting cultivation
- mixed subsistence
- rice subsistence
- subsistence crops
- grazing and stock rearing
- mixed farming
- Mediterranean farming
- plantation
- specialized horticulture
- industrial areas
- unproductive land

Livestock

- sheep
- cattle
- camels

Crops

- groundnuts
- cocoa
- coffee
- tea
- palm products
- tobacco
- fruit
- dates
- sugar
- cotton
- rubber

Minerals

- iron ore
- gold
- silver
- diamonds
- tin
- copper
- bauxite
- phosphates

Energy

- coal
- oil
- gas
- hydro

Population density

people per square kilometre

- over 700
- 200–700
- 100–200
- 10–100
- 1–10
- under 1

Major cities

population in millions

- over 3
- 1–3
- 0.5–1
- 0.1–0.5

Projected population growth of selected African cities, 1995–2015

millions of people

- 1995
- 2015

Casablanca, Cairo, Lagos, Douala, Nairobi, Kinshasa, Dar es Salaam, Johannesburg

© Oxford University Press

Zenithal Equal Area Projection

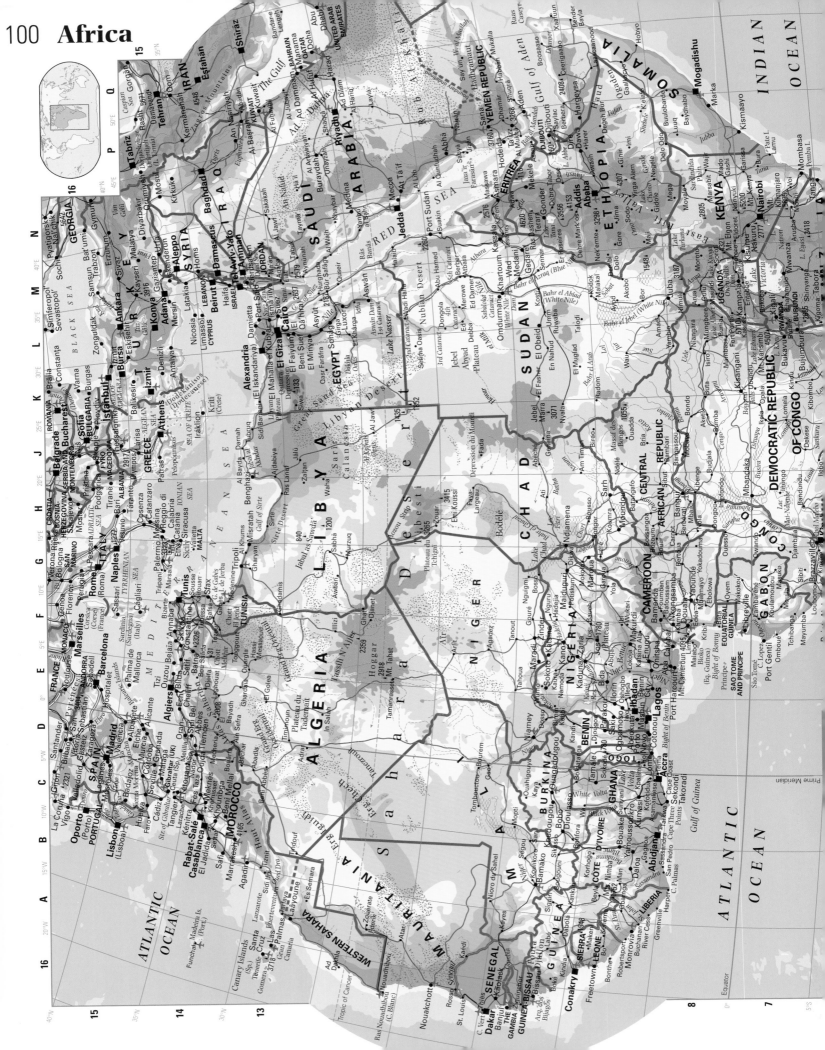

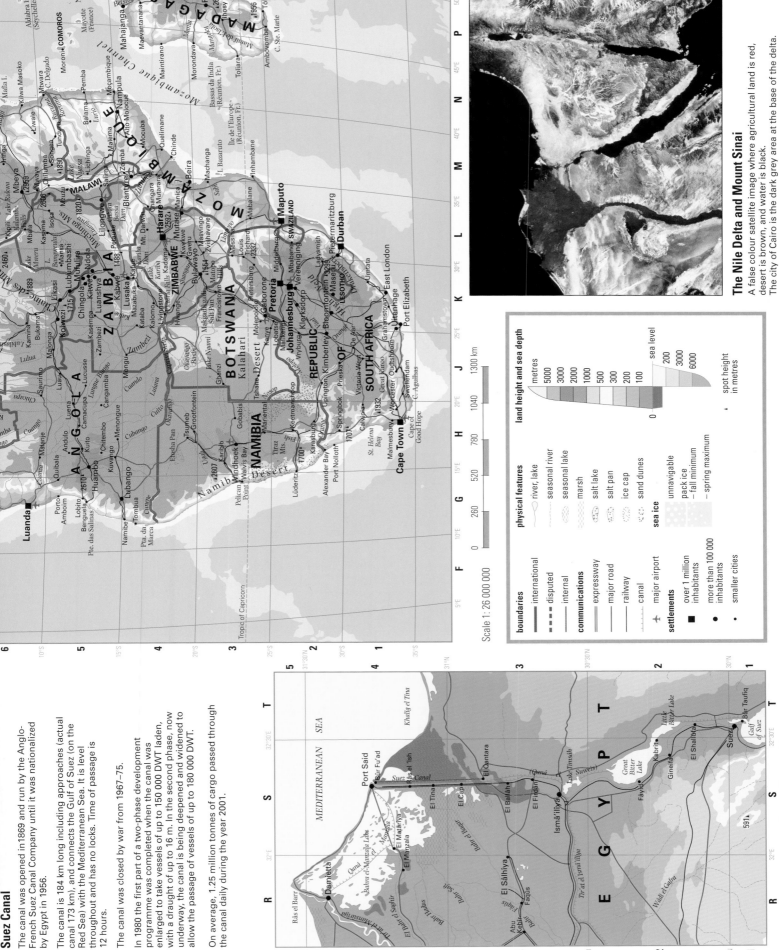

Suez Canal

The canal was opened in 1869 and run by the Anglo-French Suez Canal Company until it was nationalized by Egypt in 1956.

The canal is 184 km long including approaches (actual canal 173 km), and connects the Gulf of Suez (on the Red Sea) with the Mediterranean Sea. It is level throughout and has no locks. Time of passage is 12 hours.

The canal was closed by war from 1967–75.

In 1980 the first part of a two-phase development programme was completed when the canal was enlarged to take vessels of up to 150 000 DWT laden, with a draught of up to 16 m. In the second phase, now underway, the canal is being deepened and widened to allow the passage of vessels of up to 180 000 DWT.

On average, 1.25 million tonnes of cargo passed through the canal daily during the year 2001.

The Nile Delta and Mount Sinai

A false colour satellite image where agricultural land is red, desert is brown, and water is black.
The city of Cairo is the dark grey area at the base of the delta.

Scale 1: 26 000 000

Zenithal Equal Area Projection

© Oxford University Press

land height and sea depth
metres
5000
3000
2000
1000
500
300
200
100
0
sea level
200
3000
6000
spot height in metres

boundaries
international
disputed
internal

communications
expressway
major road
railway
canal
+ major airport

settlements
■ over 1 million inhabitants
● more than 100 000 inhabitants
• smaller cities

physical features
river, lake
seasonal river
seasonal lake
marsh
salt lake
salt pan
ice cap
sand dunes

sea ice
unnavigable
pack ice
— fall minimum
— spring maximum

Scale 1: 1 500 000
0 15 30 45 km

Scale 1: 26 000 000
0 260 520 780 1040 1300 km

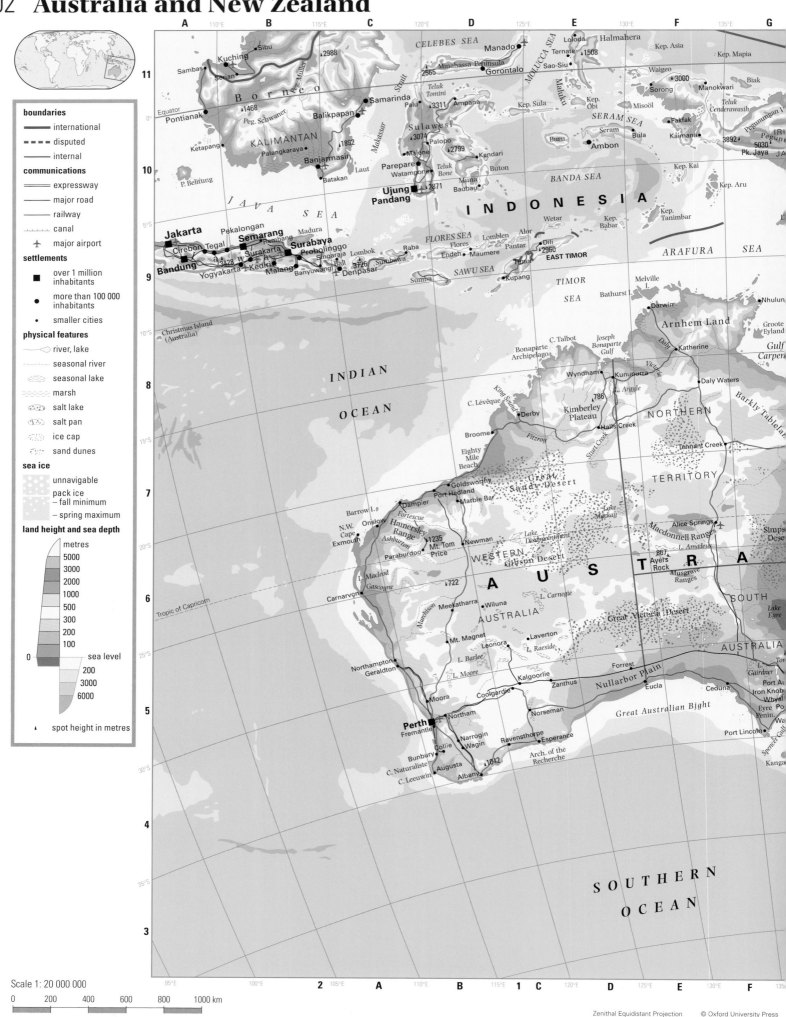

boundaries
▬▬▬	international
▬ ▬ ▬	disputed
▬▬	internal

communications
	expressway
	major road
	railway
	canal
✈	major airport

settlements
■	over 1 million inhabitants
●	more than 100 000 inhabitants
•	smaller cities

physical features
	river, lake
	seasonal river
	seasonal lake
	marsh
	salt lake
	salt pan
	ice cap
	sand dunes

sea ice
	unnavigable
	pack ice – fall minimum
	– spring maximum

land height and sea depth

metres
5000
3000
2000
1000
500
300
200
100
0 — sea level
200
3000
6000

▲ spot height in metres

Scale 1: 20 000 000

0   200   400   600   800   1000 km

Zenithal Equidistant Projection   © Oxford University Press

Australia and New Zealand

Jayapura
Ninigo Group
Kaniet Is.
Hermit Is.
Admiralty Is.
Saint Matthias Group
Lyra Reef
New
3993
Wuvulu
Wewak
Sepik
BISMARCK SEA
Bismarck Archipelago
New Ireland
Nuguria Is.
Rabaul
New Britain
Green Is.
Tauu Is.
Nukumanu Is.
Butaritari
Abaiang
Tarawa
Abemama
Aranuka
Nonouti
Beru
Nikunau
Onotoa
Tabiteuea
Tamana
Arorae
Equator

NAURU
Banaba (Kiribati)

Mount Hagen
Madang
Goroka
Mendi
Kikori
Lae
Wau
Kerema
Popondetta
Daru
Gulf of Papua
Port Moresby
Owen Stanley Range
D'Entrecasteaux Islands
Woodlark I.
Louisiade Archipelago
2743
Kieta
Bougainville Island
Choiseul
New Georgia Is.
Santa Isabel
Ontong Java Atoll
Stewart Is.
Honiara
2391
Guadalcanal
Malaita
San Cristobal
Rennell

PAPUA NEW GUINEA
SOLOMON SEA
SOLOMON
ISLANDS

KIRIBATI

Nanumea
Niutao
Nanumanga
Nui
Nukufetau
Funafuti
TUVALU
Nulakita

C. York
Weipa
Cape York Peninsula
C. Melville
Cooktown
Mitchell
Gilbert
Cairns
Innisfail
Ingham
Townsville
Bowen
Charters Towers
Richmond
Hughenden
Mackay
Cloncurry
Winton
Longreach
Barcaldine
Blackall
Emerald
Mount Morgan
Gladstone
Yeppoon
Rockhampton
Monto
Bundaberg
Taroom
Maryborough
Gympie

Duff Is.
Indispensable Reefs
Cherry
Mitre
Rotuma I.

CORAL SEA

Banks Islands
Espiritu Santo
Maéwo
Aoba
Pentecost I.
Malekula
Ambrym
Épi
Vila
Erromango
Tanna
Anatom

VANUATU
Îles Chesterfield
Île Loyauté
Lifou
Maré
Matthew
Hunter
Walpole

Vanua Levu
Labassa
Lautoka
Viti Levu
Suva
Kadavu
1324

FIJI
Ceva-i-Ra

QUEENSLAND
Thomson
Diamantina
Barcoo
Charleville
Quilpie
Mitchell
Roma
Chinchilla
Dalby
Cunnamulla
Toowoomba
Darling Downs
Warwick
Goondiwindi
Brisbane
Gold Coast
Lismore
Grafton
Moree
Bourke
Armidale
Tamworth
Nyngan
Dubbo
Port Macquarie
Taree

Capricorn Channel
Tropic of Capricorn
Minerva Reefs

NEW SOUTH WALES
Cobar
Broken Hill
terborough
Wompah
Parroo
Warrego
Grey Range
Range
Great Dividing Range
Darling
Cooper
Orange
Bathurst
Lithgow
Maitland
Newcastle
Sydney
Wollongong

Norfolk I. (Aust.)
Lord Howe I. (Aust.)

delaide
Murray Bridge
Mildura
Wangaratta
Albury
Wagga Wagga
Murrumbidgee
Lachlan
Murray
Goulburn
Canberra
ACT
Queanbeyan
2230
Mt. Kosciusko

Kermadec Is. (NZ)
Raoul
Macauley I.
Curtis I.

VICTORIA
Bendigo
Ballarat
Melbourne
Geelong
Mount ambier
Portland
Warrnambool
Moe
Hotsham
Snowy Mts.
Great Dividing
Gippsland
Cape Howe

TASMAN SEA

Three Kings Is.
North Cape
Kaitaia
North Island
Dargaville
Whangarei
Auckland
Takapuna
Hamilton
Tauranga
East Cape
New Plymouth
Rotorua
2518
1754
2997
Napier
Gisborne
Hastings
Wanganui

King I.
Bass Strait
Furneaux Group
Burnie
Devenport
Launceston
1617
Queenstown
Mt. Ossa
TASMANIA
Hobart
S.E. Cape

Palmerston North
Nelson
Picton
Porirua
Lower Hutt
Wellington
Greymouth
2885
Cook Strait

South Island
Mt. Cook
3764
Southern Alps
Christchurch
Queenstown
Timaru
Dunedin

NEW ZEALAND

C. Providence
Fiordland
Stewart I.
Invercargill
Chatham Is. (NZ)
Pitt I.

PACIFIC OCEAN

© Oxford University Press

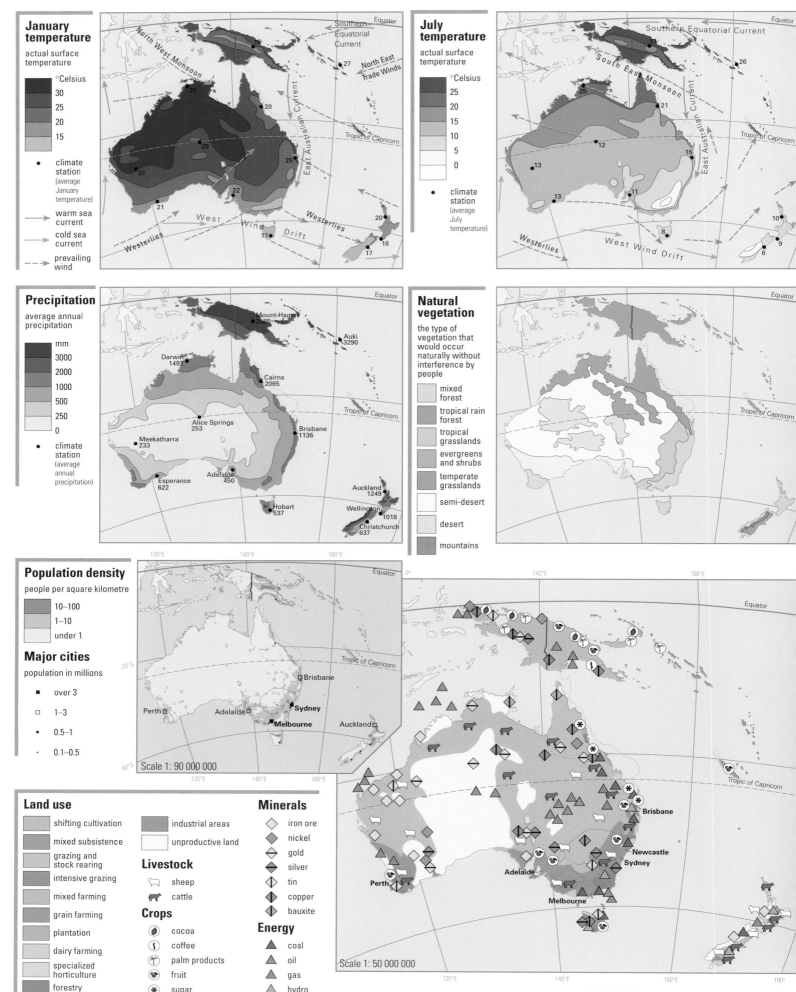

January temperature

actual surface temperature

°Celsius
30
25
20
15

● climate station (average January temperature)

→ warm sea current
→ cold sea current
⇢ prevailing wind

July temperature

actual surface temperature

°Celsius
25
20
15
10
5
0

● climate station (average July temperature)

Precipitation

average annual precipitation

mm
3000
2000
1000
500
250
0

● climate station (average annual precipitation)

Mount Hagen 2586
Auki 3290
Darwin 1492
Cairns 2065
Alice Springs 253
Brisbane 1136
Meekatharra 233
Esperance 622
Adelaide 450
Auckland 1249
Hobart 537
Wellington 1018
Christchurch 637

Natural vegetation

the type of vegetation that would occur naturally without interference by people

mixed forest
tropical rain forest
tropical grasslands
evergreens and shrubs
temperate grasslands
semi-desert
desert
mountains

Population density

people per square kilometre

10–100
1–10
under 1

Major cities

population in millions

■ over 3
□ 1–3
● 0.5–1
· 0.1–0.5

Brisbane
Perth
Adelaide
Sydney
Melbourne
Auckland

Scale 1: 90 000 000

Land use

shifting cultivation
mixed subsistence
grazing and stock rearing
intensive grazing
mixed farming
grain farming
plantation
dairy farming
specialized horticulture
forestry
industrial areas
unproductive land

Livestock

sheep
cattle

Crops

cocoa
coffee
palm products
fruit
sugar

Minerals

iron ore
nickel
gold
silver
tin
copper
bauxite

Energy

coal
oil
gas
hydro

Scale 1: 50 000 000

Perth
Adelaide
Melbourne
Newcastle
Sydney
Brisbane

Modified Zenithal Equidistant Projection   © Oxford University Press

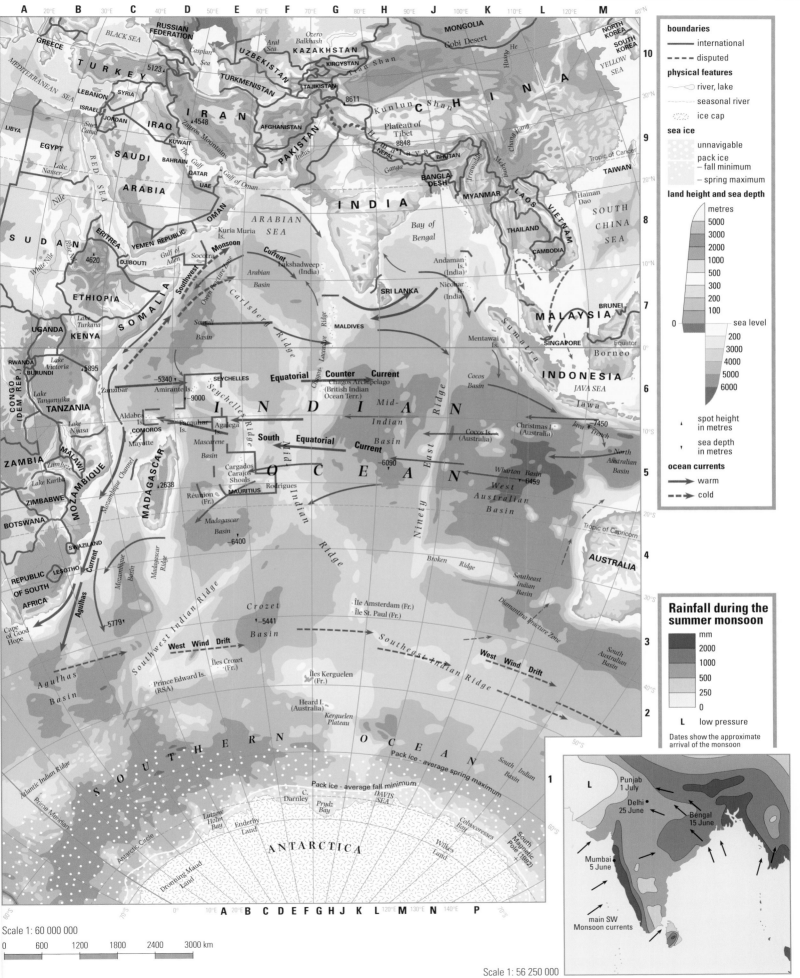

boundaries
— international
- - - disputed

physical features
river, lake
seasonal river
ice cap

sea ice
unnavigable
pack ice
– fall minimum
– spring maximum

land height and sea depth
metres
5000
3000
2000
1000
500
300
200
100
0 — sea level
200
3000
4000
5000
6000

▲ spot height in metres
▼ sea depth in metres

ocean currents
→ warm
- → cold

Rainfall during the summer monsoon
mm
2000
1000
500
250
0
L low pressure

Dates show the approximate arrival of the monsoon

Scale 1: 56 250 000

Punjab 1 July
Delhi 25 June
Bengal 15 June
Mumbai 5 June
main SW Monsoon currents

Scale 1: 60 000 000
0 600 1200 1800 2400 3000 km

© Oxford University Press   Modified Zenithal Equidistant Projection

boundaries
—— international
- - - disputed

communications
—— major road
✈ major airport

settlements
● more than 100 000 inhabitants
• smaller cities

physical features
river, lake
seasonal river
ice cap

sea ice
unnavigable
pack ice
– fall minimum
– spring maximum

land height and sea depth
metres
5000
3000
2000
1000
500
300
200
100
0 — sea level
200
3000
4000
5000
6000

▴ spot height in metres
▾ sea depth in metres

ocean currents
→ warm
- -▸ cold

Fiji

Scale 1: 7 500 000

Scale 1: 60 000 000

0 600 1200 1800 2400 3000 km

© Oxford University Press

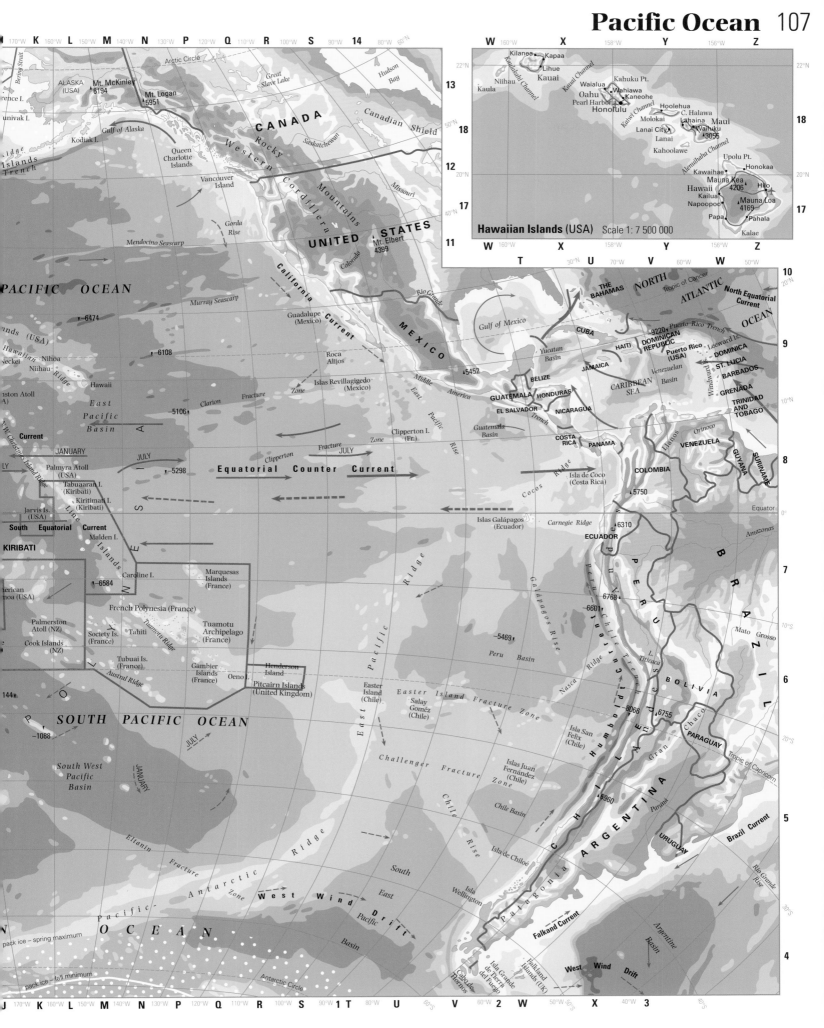

Hawaiian Islands (USA) Scale 1 : 7 500 000

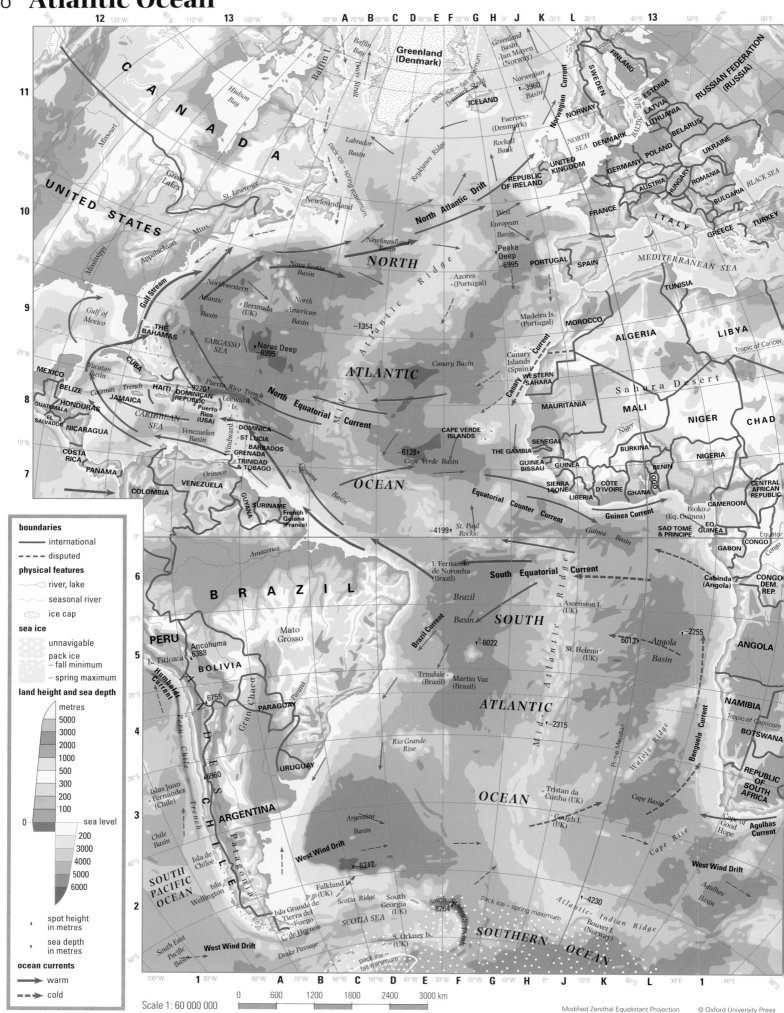

boundaries
—— international
- - - disputed

physical features
～ river, lake
- - - seasonal river
ice cap

sea ice
unnavigable
pack ice
– fall minimum
– spring maximum

land height and sea depth
metres
5000
3000
2000
1000
500
300
200
100
0 sea level
200
3000
4000
5000
6000

▲ spot height in metres
▼ sea depth in metres

ocean currents
→ warm
- -→ cold

Scale 1: 60 000 000

0   600   1200   1800   2400   3000 km

Modified Zenithal Equidistant Projection

© Oxford University Press

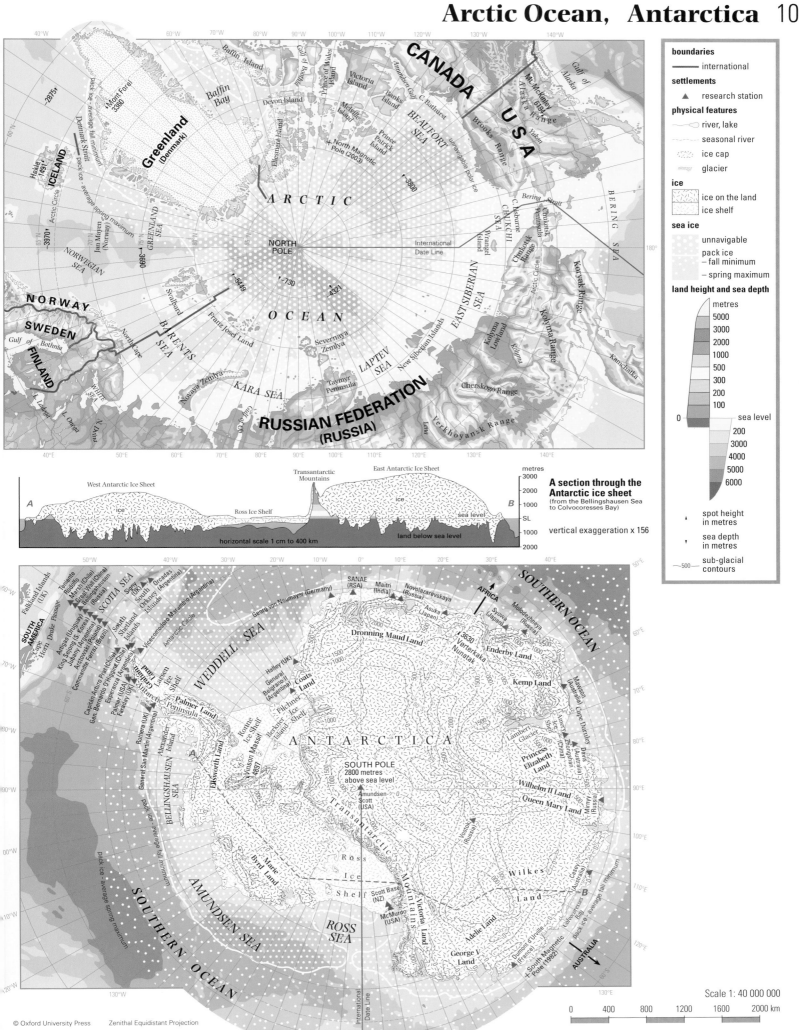

boundaries
— international

settlements
▲ research station

physical features
～ river, lake
⋯ seasonal river
ice cap
glacier

ice
ice on the land
ice shelf

sea ice
unnavigable
pack ice
− fall minimum
− spring maximum

land height and sea depth

metres
5000
3000
2000
1000
500
300
200
100
0 — sea level
200
3000
4000
5000
6000

▲ spot height in metres
▼ sea depth in metres
—500— sub-glacial contours

Arctic Ocean map labels

ICELAND · Hekla 1491 · Mont Forel 3380 · 2875 · Denmark Strait · Greenland (Denmark) · Baffin Bay · Baffin Island · Devon Island · Ellesmere Island · Prince of Wales Island · Victoria Island · North Magnetic Pole (2003) · Melville Island · Banks Island · Prince Patrick Island · Amundsen Gulf · C. Bathurst · BEAUFORT SEA · CANADA · Mt. McKinley 6194 · Alaska Range · Brooks Range · Yukon · Gulf of Alaska · USA · Gulf of Boothia · −3600 · A R C T I C · NORTH POLE · International Date Line · O C E A N · Bering Strait · C. Lisburne · Chukchi Peninsula · CHUKCHI SEA · Wrangel Island · BERING SEA · Koryak Range · Kamchatka · Kolyma Range · Kolyma · Kolyma Lowland · Cherskogo Range · EAST SIBERIAN SEA · New Siberian Islands · LAPTEV SEA · Lena · Verkhoyansk Range · RUSSIAN FEDERATION (RUSSIA) · Taymyr Peninsula · KARA SEA · Severnaya Zemlya · Novaya Zemlya · Franz Josef Land · Svalbard · BARENTS SEA · North Cape · NORWEGIAN SEA · Jan Mayen (Norway) · −3970 · −3690 · GREENLAND SEA · Arctic Circle · 65°N · 75°N · −730 · −4921 · −5449 · WHITE SEA · L. Ladoga · L. Onega · N. Dvina · Gulf of Bothnia · FINLAND · SWEDEN · NORWAY · unnavigable polar ice · pack ice − average fall minimum · pack ice − average spring maximum

A section through the Antarctic ice sheet
(from the Bellingshausen Sea to Colvocoresses Bay)

West Antarctic Ice Sheet · Transantarctic Mountains · East Antarctic Ice Sheet · A · B · ice · Ross Ice Shelf · ice · sea level · SL · land below sea level · metres 3000 2000 1000 SL 1000 2000

horizontal scale 1 cm to 400 km · vertical exaggeration x 156

Antarctica map labels

SOUTHERN OCEAN · Falkland Islands (UK) · SOUTH AMERICA · C. Horn · Drake Passage · Tenienta Rodolfo Marsh (Chile) · Great Wall (China) · Bellingshausen (Russia) · SCOTIA SEA · Signy (UK) · South Orkney Islands (Argentina) · Arctowski (Poland) · Arturo Prat (Chile) · King Seiong (S. Korea) · Jubany (Argentina) · Artigas (Uruguay) · Commandte Ferraz (Brazil) · South Shetland Islands · Vicecomodoro Marambio (Argentina) · Antarctic Circle · Esperanza (Argentina) · Gen. Bernardo O'Higgins (Chile) · Palmer USA · Faraday (UK) · Rothera (UK) · General San Martin (Argentina) · Capitán Arturo Prat (Chile) · Larsen Ice Shelf · WEDDELL SEA · SANAE (RSA) · Maitri (India) · Novolazarevskaya (Russia) · Georg von Neumayer (Germany) · AFRICA · SOUTHERN OCEAN · Dronning Maud Land · Asuka (Japan) · Syowa (Japan) · Molodezhnaya (Russia) · −3630 · Vorterkaka Nunatak · Enderby Land · Halley (UK) · General Belgrano II (Argentina) · Coats Land · Kemp Land · Mawson (Australia) · Cape Darnley · Pilchner Ice Shelf · Berkner Island · Ronne Ice Shelf · Palmer Land · Antarctic Peninsula · Alexander Island · Ellsworth Land · Vinson Massif 4897 · A N T A R C T I C A · SOUTH POLE 2800 metres above sea level · Amundsen-Scott (USA) · Lambert Glacier · Davis (Australia) · Zhongshan (China) · Princess Elizabeth Land · Wilhelm II Land · Queen Mary Land · Mirny (Russia) · BELLINGSHAUSEN SEA · Transantarctic Mountains · Vostok (Russia) · Casey (Australia) · Wilkes Land · Marie Byrd Land · Ross Ice Shelf · Scott Base (NZ) · McMurdo (USA) · Victoria Land · Adélie Land · George V Land · Dumont d'Urville (France) · South Magnetic Pole (1982) · AUSTRALIA · AMUNDSEN SEA · ROSS SEA · SOUTHERN OCEAN · pack ice − average fall minimum · pack ice − average spring maximum

Scale 1: 40 000 000

0 400 800 1200 1600 2000 km

Zenithal Equidistant Projection

Equatorial scale 1: 95 000 000 (main map)

——— international boundary

• capital city

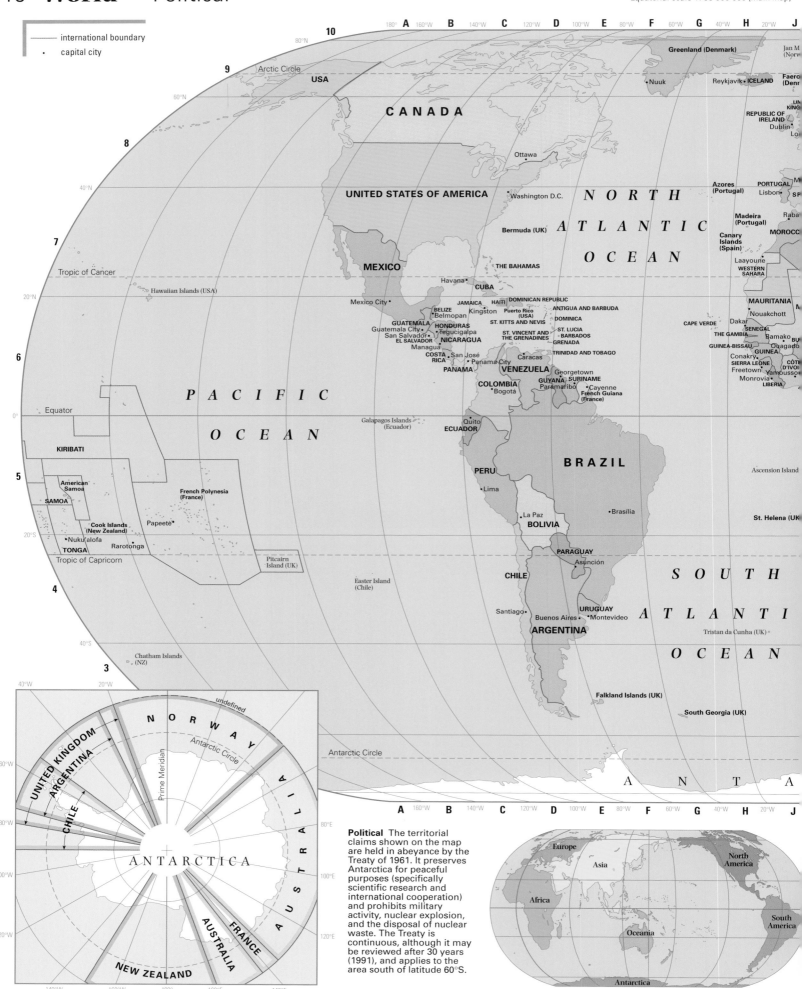

Political The territorial claims shown on the map are held in abeyance by the Treaty of 1961. It preserves Antarctica for peaceful purposes (specifically scientific research and international cooperation) and prohibits military activity, nuclear explosion, and the disposal of nuclear waste. The Treaty is continuous, although it may be reviewed after 30 years (1991), and applies to the area south of latitude 60°S.

© Oxford University Press

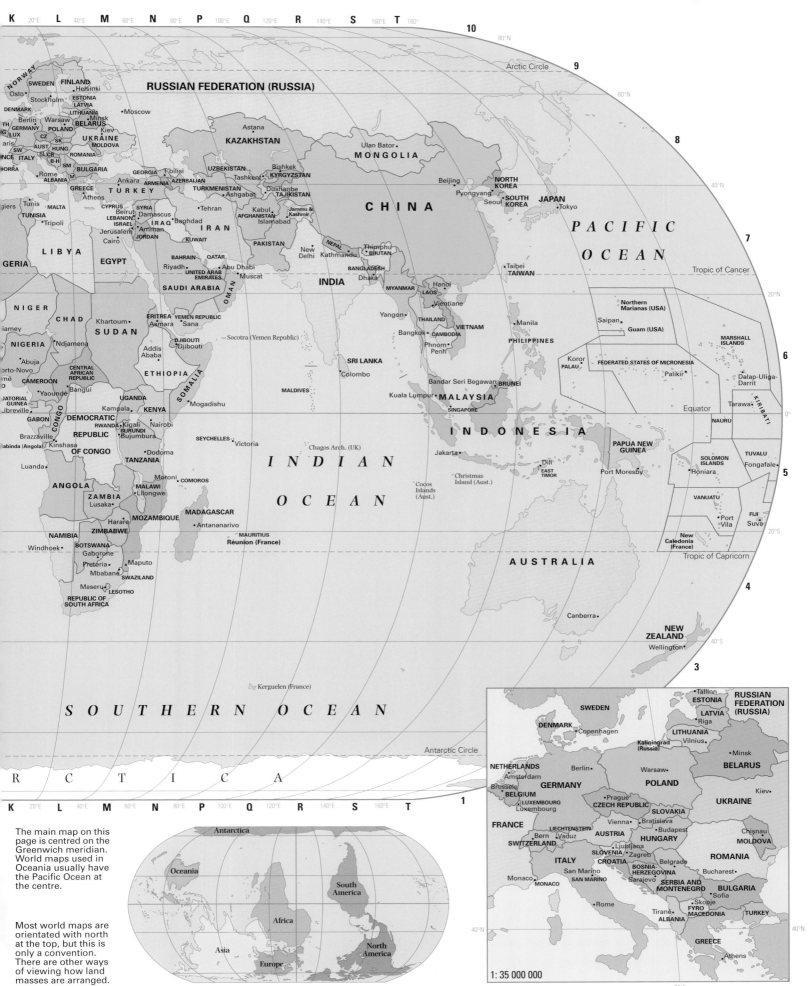

The main map on this page is centred on the Greenwich meridian. World maps used in Oceania usually have the Pacific Ocean at the centre.

Most world maps are orientated with north at the top, but this is only a convention. There are other ways of viewing how land masses are arranged.

1: 35 000 000

© Oxford University Press   Eckert IV Projection

Equatorial scale 1: 95 000 000

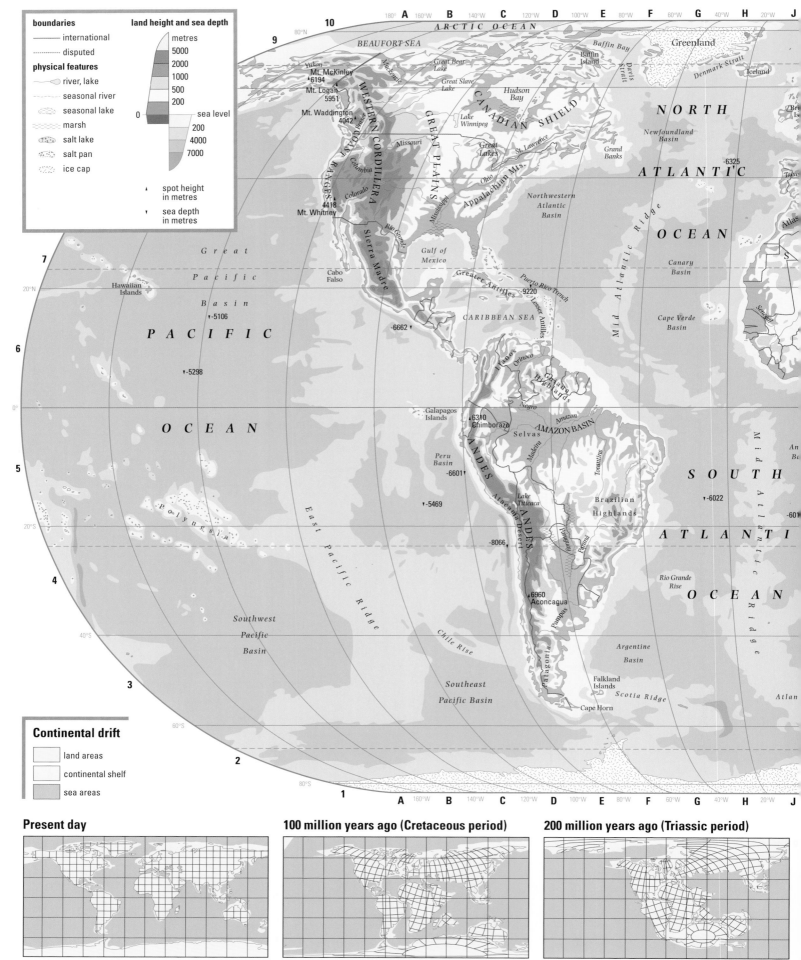

boundaries
—————— international
.... disputed
physical features
river, lake
seasonal river
seasonal lake
marsh
salt lake
salt pan
ice cap

▲ spot height
in metres
▼ sea depth
in metres

land height and sea depth

metres
5000
2000
1000
500
200
0 ——— sea level
200
4000
7000

ARCTIC OCEAN
BEAUFORT SEA
Yukon
Mt. McKinley
▲6194
Mt. Logan
5951
Mt. Waddington
▲4042
Fraser
Columbia
Colorado
▲4418
Mt. Whitney
Rio Grande
Sierra Madre
Cabo Falso
WESTERN CORDILLERA
COAST RANGES
Mackenzie
Great Bear Lake
Great Slave Lake
Lake Winnipeg
Missouri
Mississippi
Ohio
GREAT PLAINS
CANADIAN SHIELD
Hudson Bay
Great Lakes
St. Lawrence
Appalachian Mts.
Gulf of Mexico
Greater Antilles
Puerto Rico Trench
-9220
Lesser Antilles
CARIBBEAN SEA
Orinoco
Llanos
Guiana Highlands
Negro
Amazon
AMAZON BASIN
Selvas
Madeira
Tocantins
Brazilian Highlands
Paraguay
Paraná
Pampas
Patagonia
ANDES
Atacama Desert
Lake Titicaca
▲6310
Chimborazo
▲6960
Aconcagua
Galapagos Islands
Cape Horn
Falkland Islands
Scotia Ridge

NORTH
ATLANTIC
OCEAN
Baffin Bay
Baffin Island
Davis Strait
Greenland
Denmark Strait
Iceland
Newfoundland Basin
Grand Banks
Northwestern Atlantic Basin
-6325
Canary Basin
Cape Verde Basin
Mid Atlantic Ridge
SOUTH
ATLANTIC
OCEAN
-6022
-601
Rio Grande Rise
Argentine Basin
Mid Atlantic Ridge
Atlas
Senegal
An
Ba

Great Pacific Basin
Hawaiian Islands
▼-5106
▼-5298
PACIFIC
OCEAN
Polynesia
East Pacific Ridge
Southwest Pacific Basin
Southeast Pacific Basin
Chile Rise
-6662
Peru Basin
▼-6601
▼-5469
-8066
Mid

80°N
80°N
20°N
0°
20°S
40°S
60°S
80°S

180° 160°W 140°W 120°W 100°W 80°W 60°W 40°W 20°W

Continental drift
land areas
continental shelf
sea areas

Present day

100 million years ago (Cretaceous period)

200 million years ago (Triassic period)

© Oxford University Press

The equatorial circumference of the globe is 40 075 km

ARCTIC OCEAN

BARENTS SEA

Scandinavia

Lake Onega
Lake Ladoga

NORTH SEA
BALTIC SEA

North European Plain

Mont Blanc
4807
ALPS
Carpathians
Appennini
Balkan MTS.

MEDITERRANEAN SEA

Danube

BLACK SEA
CAUCASUS
Anatolian Plateau

Sahara
Hoggar

Qattara Depression
-133

Dead Sea
-400

ZAGROS MTS.
The Gulf

Arabian Peninsula

Tibesti

RED SEA
Nile
Asir Mts.
Rub' al Khali

Jos Plateau
Lake Chad
Darfur
Benue
Adamawa Mts.

Blue Nile
White Nile

Ethiopian Highlands

CONGO BASIN
Congo
Kasai

Somali Basin

ARABIAN SEA

Lake Victoria
5895
Kilimanjaro
Lake Tanganyika
Lake Nyasa
Zambezi

▼-5340

Seychelles Ridge

Chagos-Laccadive Ridge

Western Ghats
Eastern Ghats

Deccan

Sri Lanka

Bay of Bengal

Mid-Indian Basin

INDIAN OCEAN

▼-6090

Ninety East Ridge

Cocos Basin

West Australian Basin

Madagascar
Mozambique Channel

Namib Desert
Walvis Ridge

Kalahari Desert
Orange
Limpopo
Drakensberg

Cape of Good Hope

Southwest Indian Ridge

Crozet Basin

Southeast Indian Ridge

Kerguelen

Indian Ridge

SOUTHERN OCEAN

URAL MOUNTAINS

Siberian Lowland

Central Siberian Plateau

Yenisey
Ob'
Volga
Ural
Irtysh

Aral Sea
TURANIAN PLAIN
Caspian Sea

KAZAKH UPLAND
Lake Balkhash

ALTAI
Lake Baykal

TIEN SHAN

Hindu Kush
8611
K2

Nan Shan

Gobi Desert

Plateau of Tibet

Mt. Everest
8848
HIMALAYA
INDO-GANGETIC PLAIN
Indus
Ganga

Huang He

Irrawaddy
Mekong

Chang Jiang

SOUTH CHINA SEA

Borneo
4094
Kinabalu

Sumatra

JAVA SEA

SULAWESI
BANDA SEA

ARAFURA SEA

Great Sandy Desert
Macdonnell Ranges

Great Victoria Desert

Darling
Murray

Great Dividing Range

South Australian Basin

TASMAN SEA

S. ALPS
South Island
North Island

Lena
Cherskiy Range

SEA OF OKHOTSK
Kamchatka
BERING SEA

Sakhalin
Amur
Hokkaido
Kuril Trench
SEA OF JAPAN
Honshu

YELLOW SEA
EAST CHINA SEA

Taiwan

PHILIPPINE SEA
-8724
-11022

Philippine Trench

Northwest Pacific Basin

PACIFIC OCEAN

Micronesia

West Caroline Basin

New Guinea

Melanesia

CORAL SEA

North Fiji Basin
-7570

Lord Howe Rise

South Fiji Basin

Record breakers
Climate
Physical geography

Highest surface wind ever recorded Mt. Washington, USA 231 mph

ighest snowfall in a single season Mt. Baker, USA 2896cm, 1998–99

Largest desert Sahara, North Africa 1 350 000 km²

Highest waterfall Angel Falls, Venezuela 979m drop

Driest place Arica, Chile 14 years without rainfall

Highest temperature ever recorded El Aisisa, Libya 58°C

Deepest land depression Dead Sea shore 400m below sea level

Highest mountain Mt. Everest 8848m

Wettest place Mawsynram, India Annual average rainfall 1187cm

Deepest ocean trench Marianas Trench 8724m deep

Longest river Nile 6695 km

Lowest temperature ever recorded Vostock, Antarctica -88°C

January temperature

actual surface temperature

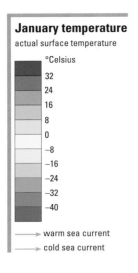

°Celsius

32
24
16
8
0
-8
-16
-24
-32
-40

→ warm sea current
→ cold sea current

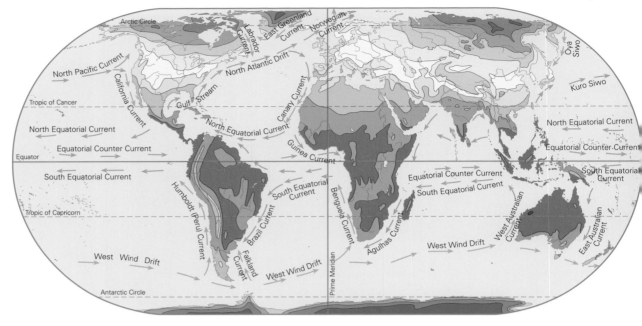

July temperature

actual surface temperature

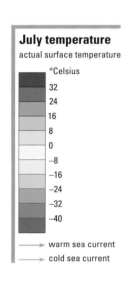

°Celsius

32
24
16
8
0
-8
-16
-24
-32
-40

→ warm sea current
→ cold sea current

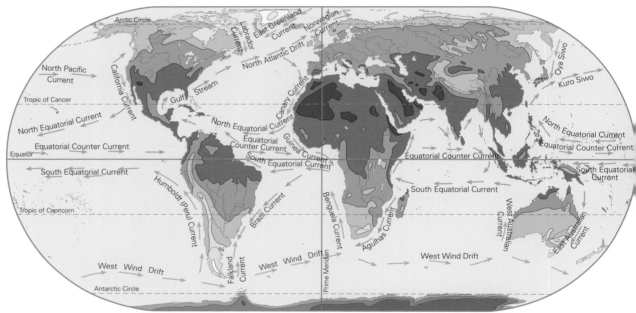

Antarctic ozone 'hole'

Three dimensional image of ozone depletion over Antarctica in September, 1998. The lowest ozone concentration is shown in blue.

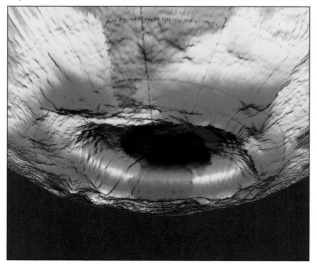

Global warming

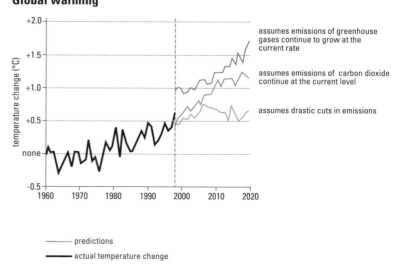

assumes emissions of greenhouse gases continue to grow at the current rate

assumes emissions of carbon dioxide continue at the current level

assumes drastic cuts in emissions

— predictions
— actual temperature change

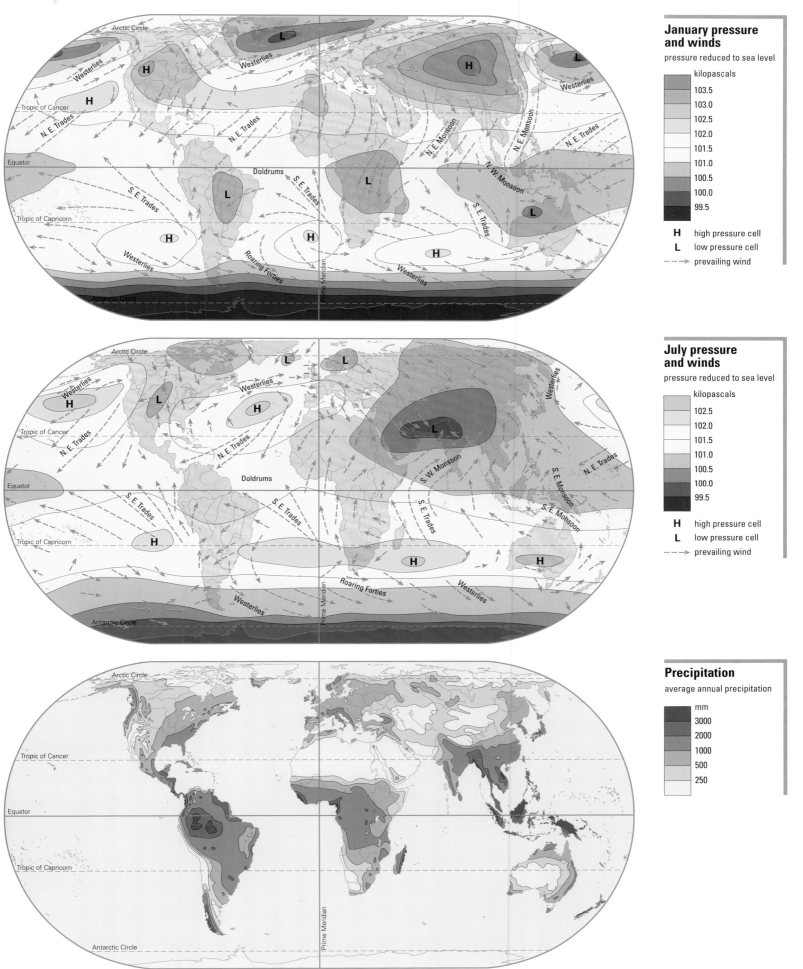

January pressure and winds

pressure reduced to sea level

kilopascals

103.5
103.0
102.5
102.0
101.5
101.0
100.5
100.0
99.5

H high pressure cell
L low pressure cell
--> prevailing wind

July pressure and winds

pressure reduced to sea level

kilopascals

102.5
102.0
101.5
101.0
100.5
100.0
99.5

H high pressure cell
L low pressure cell
--> prevailing wind

Precipitation

average annual precipitation

mm

3000
2000
1000
500
250

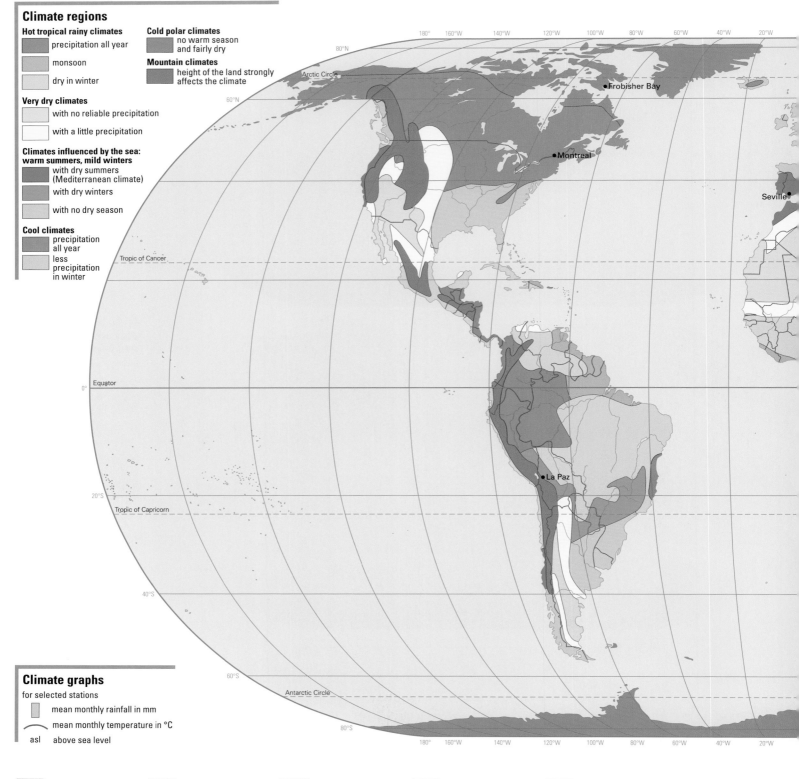

Climate regions

Hot tropical rainy climates
- precipitation all year
- monsoon
- dry in winter

Very dry climates
- with no reliable precipitation
- with a little precipitation

Climates influenced by the sea: warm summers, mild winters
- with dry summers (Mediterranean climate)
- with dry winters
- with no dry season

Cool climates
- precipitation all year
- less precipitation in winter

Cold polar climates
- no warm season and fairly dry

Mountain climates
- height of the land strongly affects the climate

Climate graphs

for selected stations

- mean monthly rainfall in mm
- mean monthly temperature in °C

asl above sea level

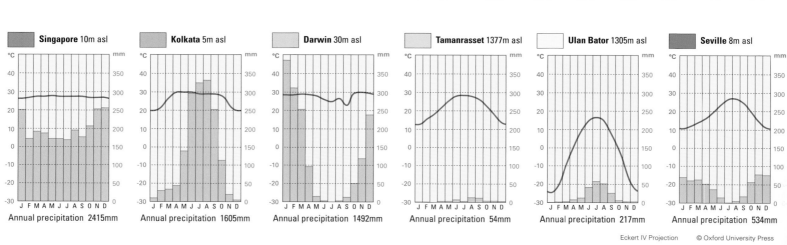

Singapore 10m asl	**Kolkata** 5m asl	**Darwin** 30m asl	**Tamanrasset** 1377m asl	**Ulan Bator** 1305m asl	**Seville** 8m asl
Annual precipitation 2415mm	Annual precipitation 1605mm	Annual precipitation 1492mm	Annual precipitation 54mm	Annual precipitation 217mm	Annual precipitation 534mm

Eckert IV Projection   © Oxford University Press

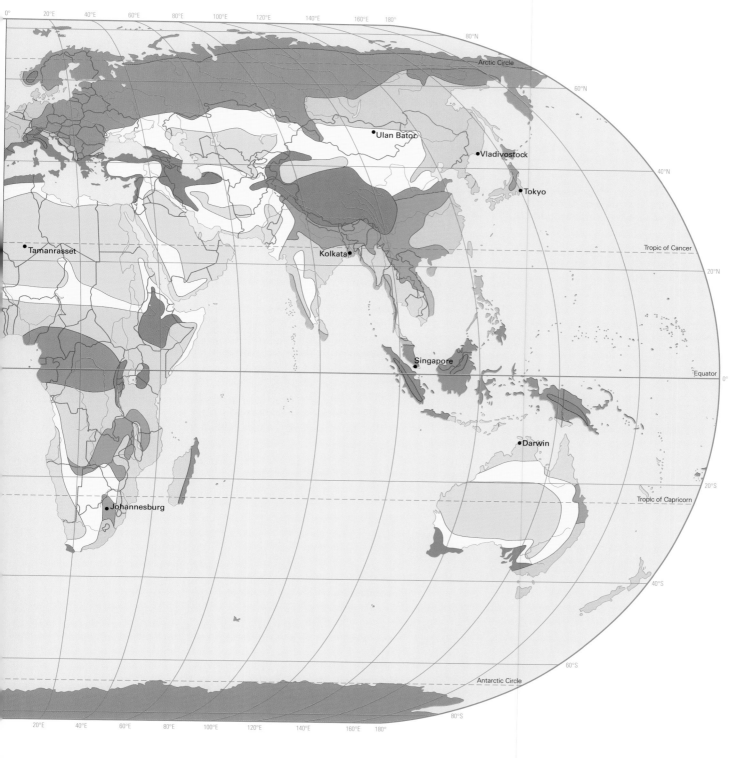

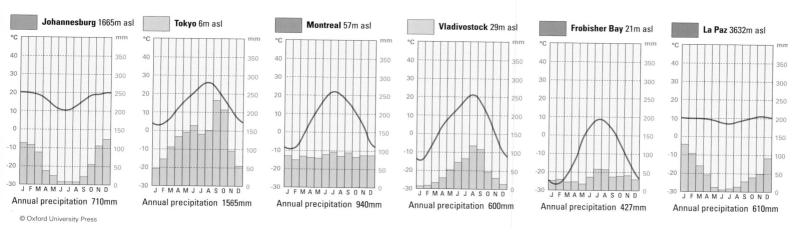

| Johannesburg 1665m asl | Tokyo 6m asl | Montreal 57m asl | Vladivostock 29m asl | Frobisher Bay 21m asl | La Paz 3632m asl |

Annual precipitation 710mm

Annual precipitation 1565mm

Annual precipitation 940mm

Annual precipitation 600mm

Annual precipitation 427mm

Annual precipitation 610mm

Climate data

Averages are for 1961–1990

Denver 1626m — climate station and its height above sea level
Temperature (°C)
 high — average daily maximum temperature
 mean — average monthly temperature
 low — average daily minimum temperature
Rainfall (mm) — average monthly precipitation

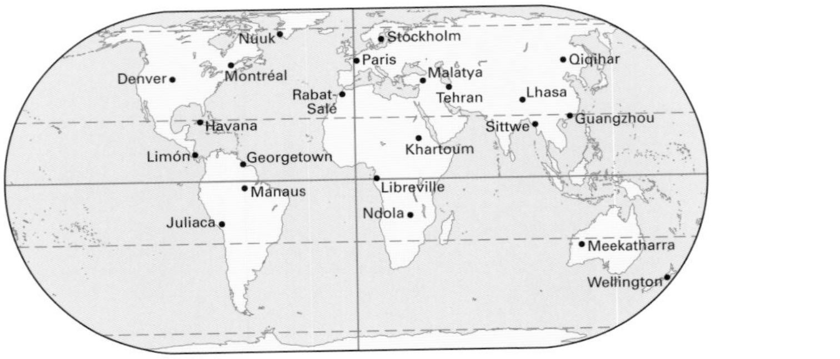

Denver 1626m

	Jan	Feb	Mar	Apr	May	Jun	Jul	Aug	Sep	Oct	Nov	Dec	YEAR
high	6.2	8.1	11.2	16.6	21.6	27.4	31.2	29.9	24.9	19.1	11.4	6.9	17.9
mean	-1.3	0.8	3.9	9.0	14.0	19.4	23.1	21.9	16.8	10.8	3.9	-0.6	10.1
low	-8.8	-6.6	-3.4	1.4	6.4	11.3	14.8	13.8	8.7	2.4	-3.7	-8.1	2.4
Rainfall	13	15	33	43	61	46	49	38	32	25	22	16	393

Georgetown 2m

	Jan	Feb	Mar	Apr	May	Jun	Jul	Aug	Sep	Oct	Nov	Dec	YEAR
high	28.6	28.9	29.2	29.5	29.4	29.2	29.6	30.2	30.8	30.8	30.2	29.1	29.6
mean	26.1	26.4	26.7	27.0	26.8	26.5	26.6	27.0	27.5	27.6	27.2	26.4	26.8
low	23.6	23.9	24.2	24.4	24.3	23.8	23.5	23.8	24.2	24.4	24.2	23.8	24.0
Rainfall	185	89	111	141	286	328	268	201	98	107	186	262	2262

Guangzhou 42m

	Jan	Feb	Mar	Apr	May	Jun	Jul	Aug	Sep	Oct	Nov	Dec	YEAR
high	18.3	18.4	21.6	25.5	29.4	31.3	32.7	32.6	31.4	28.6	24.4	20.5	26.2
mean	13.3	14.3	17.7	21.9	25.6	27.3	28.5	28.3	27.1	24.0	19.4	15.0	21.9
low	5.0	6.6	10.7	16.1	20.7	23.5	25.7	25.2	22.6	17.6	11.9	6.5	16.0
Rainfall	43	65	85	182	284	258	228	221	172	79	42	24	1683

Havana 50m

	Jan	Feb	Mar	Apr	May	Jun	Jul	Aug	Sep	Oct	Nov	Dec	YEAR
high	25.8	26.1	27.6	28.6	29.8	30.5	31.3	31.6	31.0	29.2	27.7	26.5	28.8
mean	22.2	22.4	23.7	24.8	26.1	26.9	27.6	27.8	27.4	26.2	24.5	23.0	25.2
low	18.6	18.6	19.7	20.9	22.4	23.4	23.8	24.1	23.8	23.0	21.3	19.5	21.6
Rainfall	64	69	46	54	98	182	106	100	144	181	88	58	1190

Juliaca 3827m

	Jan	Feb	Mar	Apr	May	Jun	Jul	Aug	Sep	Oct	Nov	Dec	YEAR
high	16.7	16.7	16.5	16.8	16.6	16.0	16.0	17.0	17.6	18.6	18.8	17.7	17.1
mean	10.2	10.1	9.9	8.7	6.4	4.5	4.3	5.8	8.1	9.5	10.2	10.4	8.2
low	3.6	3.5	3.2	0.6	-3.8	-7.0	-7.5	-5.4	-1.4	0.3	1.5	3.0	-0.8
Rainfall	133	109	99	43	10	3	2	6	22	41	55	86	609

Khartoum 380m

	Jan	Feb	Mar	Apr	May	Jun	Jul	Aug	Sep	Oct	Nov	Dec	YEAR
high	30.8	33.0	36.8	40.1	41.9	41.3	38.4	37.3	39.1	39.3	35.2	31.8	37.1
mean	23.2	25.0	28.7	31.9	34.5	34.3	32.1	31.5	32.5	32.4	28.1	24.5	29.9
low	15.6	17.0	20.5	23.6	27.1	27.3	25.9	25.3	26.0	25.5	21.0	17.1	22.7
Rainfall	0	0	0	0.5	4	5	46	75	25	5	1	0	161

Lhasa 3650m

	Jan	Feb	Mar	Apr	May	Jun	Jul	Aug	Sep	Oct	Nov	Dec	YEAR
high	6.9	9.0	12.1	15.6	19.3	22.7	22.1	21.1	19.7	16.3	11.2	7.7	15.3
mean	-2.1	1.1	4.6	8.1	11.9	15.5	15.3	14.5	12.8	8.1	2.2	-1.7	7.5
low	-10.1	-6.8	-3.0	0.9	5.0	9.3	10.1	9.4	7.5	1.3	-4.9	-9.0	0.8
Rainfall	1	1	2	5	27	72	119	123	58	10	2	1	421

Libreville 15m

	Jan	Feb	Mar	Apr	May	Jun	Jul	Aug	Sep	Oct	Nov	Dec	YEAR
high	29.5	30.0	30.2	30.1	29.4	27.6	26.4	26.8	27.5	28.0	28.4	29.0	28.6
mean	26.8	27.0	27.1	26.6	26.7	25.4	24.3	24.3	25.4	25.7	25.9	26.2	26.0
low	24.1	24.0	23.9	23.1	24.0	23.2	22.1	21.8	23.4	23.4	23.4	23.4	23.3
Rainfall	250	243	363	339	247	54	7	14	104	427	490	303	2841

Limón 3m

	Jan	Feb	Mar	Apr	May	Jun	Jul	Aug	Sep	Oct	Nov	Dec	YEAR
high	27.9	28.6	29.6	29.6	28.5	27.5	27.7	27.7	27.2	27.0	27.1	27.7	28.0
mean	24.0	24.3	25.0	25.8	26.1	25.9	25.2	25.6	25.7	25.4	25.1	24.3	25.2
low	20.3	20.3	20.9	21.6	22.2	22.3	22.1	22.1	22.2	21.9	21.6	20.9	21.5
Rainfall	319	201	193	287	281	276	408	289	163	198	367	402	3384

Malatya 849m

	Jan	Feb	Mar	Apr	May	Jun	Jul	Aug	Sep	Oct	Nov	Dec	YEAR
high	2.9	5.3	11.1	18.2	23.5	29.2	33.8	33.4	28.9	20.9	11.8	5.7	18.7
mean	-0.4	1.5	6.9	13.0	17.8	22.9	27.0	26.5	22.0	14.8	7.6	2.4	13.5
low	-3.2	-1.7	2.4	7.7	11.8	16.1	19.8	19.4	15.2	9.5	3.7	-0.3	8.4
Rainfall	42	36	60	61	50	22	3	2	6	40	47	42	411

Manaus 84m

	Jan	Feb	Mar	Apr	May	Jun	Jul	Aug	Sep	Oct	Nov	Dec	YEAR
high	30.5	30.4	30.6	30.7	30.8	31.0	31.3	32.6	32.9	32.8	32.1	31.3	31.4
mean	26.1	26.0	26.1	26.3	26.3	26.4	26.5	27.0	27.5	27.6	27.3	26.7	26.7
low	23.1	23.1	23.2	23.3	23.3	23.0	22.7	23.0	23.5	23.7	23.7	23.5	23.3
Rainfall	260	288	314	300	256	114	88	58	83	126	183	217	2287

Meekatharra 518m

	Jan	Feb	Mar	Apr	May	Jun	Jul	Aug	Sep	Oct	Nov	Dec	YEAR
high	38.1	36.5	34.5	29.2	23.6	19.7	18.9	21.0	25.4	29.4	33.1	36.5	28.8
mean	31.2	30.1	28.0	23.2	17.8	14.3	13.2	14.8	18.4	22.2	25.9	29.3	22.4
low	24.3	23.7	21.5	17.1	11.9	8.9	7.5	8.5	11.4	15.0	18.6	22.1	15.9
Rainfall	26	30	22	17	27	36	25	12	6	7	14	11	233

Montréal 57m

	Jan	Feb	Mar	Apr	May	Jun	Jul	Aug	Sep	Oct	Nov	Dec	YEAR
high	-5.7	-4.4	1.6	10.6	18.5	23.6	26.1	24.8	19.9	13.3	5.4	-3.0	10.9
mean	-10.3	-8.8	-2.4	5.7	12.9	18.0	20.8	19.4	14.5	8.3	1.6	-6.9	6.1
low	-14.6	-13.5	-6.7	0.8	7.4	12.9	15.6	14.3	9.6	4.1	-1.5	-10.8	1.5
Rainfall	63.3	56.4	67.6	74.8	68.3	82.5	85.6	100.3	86.5	75.4	93.4	85.6	939.7

Ndola 1270m

	Jan	Feb	Mar	Apr	May	Jun	Jul	Aug	Sep	Oct	Nov	Dec	YEAR
high	26.6	26.9	27.4	27.5	26.6	25.1	25.2	27.5	30.5	31.5	29.4	27.0	27.6
mean	20.8	20.8	21.0	20.5	18.6	16.5	16.7	19.2	22.5	23.7	22.5	21.0	20.3
low	17.1	17.1	16.5	14.4	10.8	7.9	7.8	10.2	13.6	16.2	17.1	17.2	13.8
Rainfall	29.3	249	170	46	4	1	0	0	3	32	130	306	1234

Nuuk 70m

	Jan	Feb	Mar	Apr	May	Jun	Jul	Aug	Sep	Oct	Nov	Dec	YEAR
high	-4.4	-4.5	-4.8	-0.8	3.5	7.7	10.6	9.9	6.3	1.7	-1.0	-3.3	1.7
mean	-7.4	-7.8	-8.0	-3.9	0.6	3.9	6.5	6.1	3.5	-0.6	-3.6	-6.2	-1.4
low	-10.1	-10.6	-10.6	-6.1	-1.5	1.3	3.8	3.8	1.6	-2.5	-5.8	-8.7	-3.8
Rainfall	39	47	50	46	55	62	82	89	88	70	74	54	756

Paris 65m

	Jan	Feb	Mar	Apr	May	Jun	Jul	Aug	Sep	Oct	Nov	Dec	YEAR
high	6.0	7.6	10.8	14.4	18.2	21.5	24.0	23.8	20.8	16.0	10.1	6.8	15.0
mean	3.4	4.2	6.6	9.5	13.2	16.4	18.4	18.0	15.3	11.4	6.7	4.2	10.6
low	0.9	1.3	2.9	5.0	8.3	11.2	12.9	12.7	10.6	7.7	3.8	1.7	6.6
Rainfall	54	46	54	47	63	58	84	52	54	56	56	56	650

Qiqihar 148m

	Jan	Feb	Mar	Apr	May	Jun	Jul	Aug	Sep	Oct	Nov	Dec	YEAR
high	-12.7	-7.8	2.3	12.9	21.0	26.2	27.8	26.1	20.1	11.1	-1.3	-10.4	9.6
mean	-19.2	-14.8	-4.5	6.1	14.4	20.3	22.8	20.9	14.0	4.8	-7.1	-16.2	3.5
low	-24.5	-20.9	-11.0	-0.9	7.3	14.2	17.9	16.2	8.5	-0.7	-12.0	-21.2	-2.3
Rainfall	1	2	5	15	31	64	138	94	45	19	4	3	421

Rabat Sale 75m

	Jan	Feb	Mar	Apr	May	Jun	Jul	Aug	Sep	Oct	Nov	Dec	YEAR
high	17.2	17.7	19.2	20.0	22.1	24.1	26.8	27.1	26.4	24.0	20.6	17.7	21.9
mean	12.6	13.1	14.2	15.2	17.4	19.8	22.2	22.4	21.5	19.0	15.9	13.2	17.2
low	8.0	8.6	9.2	10.4	12.7	15.4	17.6	17.7	16.7	14.1	11.1	8.7	12.5
Rainfall	77	74	61	62	25	7	1	1	6	44	97	101	556

Sittwe 5m

	Jan	Feb	Mar	Apr	May	Jun	Jul	Aug	Sep	Oct	Nov	Dec	YEAR
high	28.0	29.4	31.4	34.1	31.5	29.5	28.9	28.9	30.1	31.1	30.3	28.5	30.1
mean	21.4	22.7	24.8	28.9	28.3	27.1	26.8	26.7	27.4	27.6	25.7	22.6	25.8
low	14.7	15.9	18.2	23.6	25.1	24.6	24.7	24.5	24.6	24.0	21.0	16.6	21.5
Rainfall	11	8	5	44	268	1091	1155	1025	537	289	105	17	4555

Stockholm 52m

	Jan	Feb	Mar	Apr	May	Jun	Jul	Aug	Sep	Oct	Nov	Dec	YEAR
high	-0.7	-0.6	3.0	8.6	15.7	20.7	21.9	20.4	15.1	9.9	4.5	1.1	10.0
mean	-2.8	-3.0	0.1	4.6	10.7	15.6	17.2	16.2	11.9	7.5	2.6	-1.0	6.6
low	-5.0	-5.3	-2.7	1.1	6.3	11.3	13.4	12.7	9.0	5.3	0.7	-3.2	3.6
Rainfall	39	27	26	30	30	45	72	66	55	50	53	46	539

Tehran 1191m

	Jan	Feb	Mar	Apr	May	Jun	Jul	Aug	Sep	Oct	Nov	Dec	YEAR
high	7.2	9.9	15.4	21.9	28.0	34.1	36.8	35.4	31.5	24.0	16.5	9.8	22.5
mean	3.0	5.3	10.3	16.4	22.1	27.5	30.4	29.2	25.3	18.5	11.6	5.6	17.1
low	-1.1	0.7	5.2	10.9	16.1	20.9	24.0	23.0	19.2	12.9	6.7	1.3	11.7
Rainfall	37	34	37	28	15	3	3	1	1	14	21	36	230

Wellington 8m

	Jan	Feb	Mar	Apr	May	Jun	Jul	Aug	Sep	Oct	Nov	Dec	YEAR
high	21.3	21.1	19.8	17.3	14.8	12.8	12.0	12.7	14.2	15.9	17.8	19.6	16.6
mean	17.8	17.7	16.6	14.3	11.9	10.1	9.2	9.8	11.2	12.8	14.5	16.4	13.5
low	14.4	14.3	13.5	11.3	9.1	7.3	6.4	6.9	8.3	9.7	11.3	13.2	10.5
Rainfall	67	48	76	87	99	113	111	106	82	81	74	74	1018

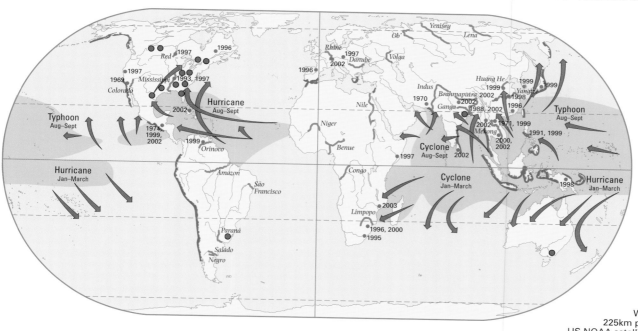

Storms and floods

→ paths of revolving tropical storms

areas affected by tropical storms

coasts vulnerable to tsunamis (seismic sea waves)

major river flood plains susceptible to flooding

• major floods

● areas affected by tornadoes

Hurricane Floyd, Florida

Winds in this hurricane reached 225km per hour and caused 40 deaths. US NOAA satellite image, 15 September, 1999.

Water

Surplus

Enough water to support vegetation and crops without irrigation.

large surplus
surplus

Deficiency

Not enough water to support vegetation and crops without irrigation. After long periods of deficiency these areas may lose their natural vegetation.

deficiency
chronic deficiency

Distribution of the Earth's Water

	Volume (km³)	Average residence time
Oceans and seas	1 370 000 000	4 000+ years
Glaciers and ice caps	30 000 000	1000's of years
Groundwater	4 000 000–60 000 000	from days to tens of thousands of years
Atmospheric water	113 000	8 to 10 days
Freshwater lakes	125 000	days to years
Saline lakes and inland seas	104 000	–
River channels	1 700	2 weeks
Swamps and marshes	3 600	years
Biological water (in plants and animals)	65 000	a few days
Moisture in soil	65 000	2 weeks to 1 year

Mozambique floods

These images from the Landsat 7 satellite show the Limpopo river before and after flooding. Torrential rain between 4 and 7 February, 2000 added to already high levels of seasonal rainfall. Tropical cyclone Eline hit the southern coast of Mozambique on 21 February bringing even more rain. Over a million people were made homeless and 100 000 hectares of agricultural land flooded. 992 kms of roads were swept away.

Before flooding, August, 1999

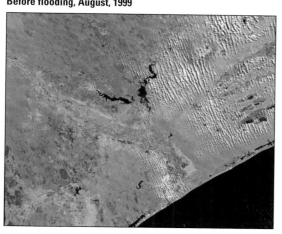

After flooding, March 2000

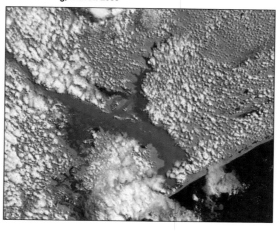

Limpopo River

Eckert IV Projection   © Oxford University Press

Equatorial scale 1: 105 000 000

Ecosystems

vegetation types are those which would occur naturally without interference by people

coniferous forest
cone bearing trees

deciduous and mixed forest
leaf shedding and coniferous trees

tropical rain forest
many species of lush, tall trees

tropical grasslands (savannah)
tall grass parkland with scattered trees

evergreen trees and shrubs
plants and small trees with leathery leaves

thorn forest
low trees and shrubs with spines or thorns

temperate grasslands
prairies, steppes, pampas, and veld

semi-desert
short grasses and drought-resistant scrub

desert
sand and stones, very little vegetation

tundra
moss and lichen, with few trees

ice
no vegetation

mountains
thin soils, steep slopes, and high altitude affects type of vegetation

ice
Aerial view of Jameson Land, towards Liverpool Land, Greenland

deciduous and mixed forest
Mixed forest, Trois-Rivières, Québec, Canada

temperate grasslands
Prairie, South Dakota, USA

tropical rain forest
Monteverde Cloud Forest Reserve, Costa Rica

thorn forest
Acacia thorns, Hwange, Zimbabwe

© Oxford University Press

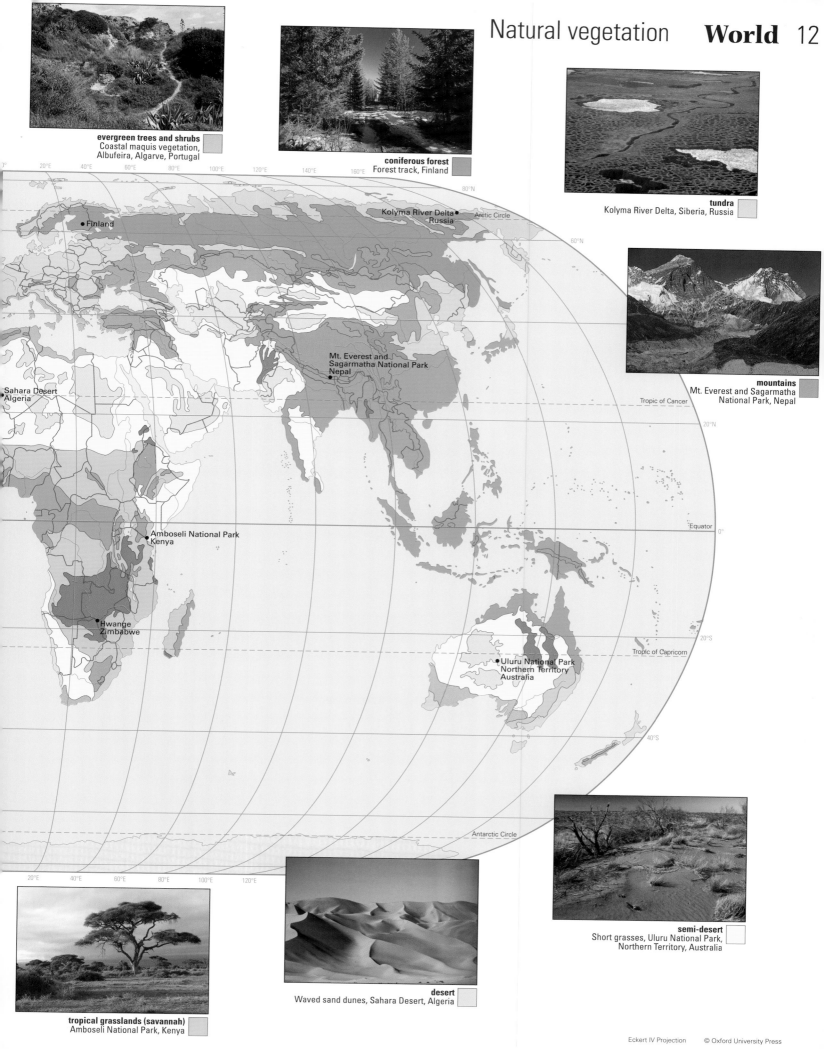

evergreen trees and shrubs
Coastal maquis vegetation,
Albufeira, Algarve, Portugal

coniferous forest
Forest track, Finland

tundra
Kolyma River Delta, Siberia, Russia

mountains
Mt. Everest and Sagarmatha
National Park, Nepal

semi-desert
Short grasses, Uluru National Park,
Northern Territory, Australia

desert
Waved sand dunes, Sahara Desert, Algeria

tropical grasslands (savannah)
Amboseli National Park, Kenya

Finland

Kolyma River Delta
Russia

Arctic Circle

Mt. Everest and
Sagarmatha National Park
Nepal

Sahara Desert
Algeria

Tropic of Cancer

Amboseli National Park
Kenya

Equator

Hwange
Zimbabwe

Uluru National Park
Northern Territory
Australia

Tropic of Capricorn

Antarctic Circle

Eckert IV Projection   © Oxford University Press

Plate tectonics

plate boundaries

≡ ridge zones (moving apart)

◄▲ trench zones (colliding)

--- passive

— transform faults

→ direction of plate movement

▲ volcanoes active between 1900 and 2000

⁂ areas of deep focus earthquakes

EURASIAN PLATE

HELLENIC PLATE

IRANIAN PLATE

ARABIAN PLATE

CARIBBEAN PLATE

COCOS PLATE

AFRICAN PLATE

East African Rift System

NASCA PLATE

Mid-Atlantic Ridge

Peru-Chile Trench

SOUTH AMERICAN PLATE

INDIAN

Indian Ocean Ridge

Mid-Atlantic Ridge

ANTARCTIC PLATE

SCOTIA PLATE

ANTARCTIC PLATE

Structure of the Earth

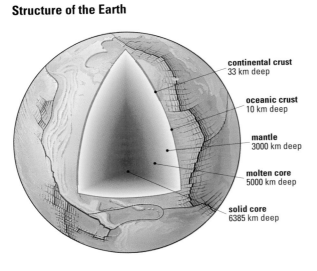

continental crust
33 km deep

oceanic crust
10 km deep

mantle
3000 km deep

molten core
5000 km deep

solid core
6385 km deep

Cross section of a strato volcano

(e.g. Mt. Vesuvius, Italy)

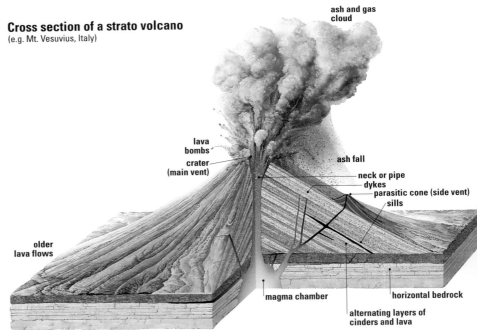

ash and gas cloud

lava bombs

crater (main vent)

ash fall

neck or pipe

dykes

parasitic cone (side vent)

sills

older lava flows

magma chamber

alternating layers of cinders and lava

horizontal bedrock

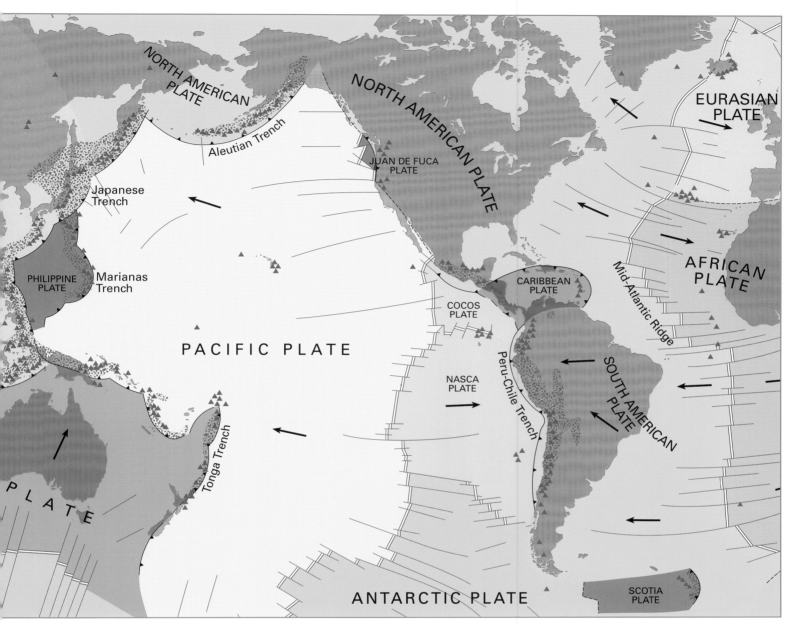

PACIFIC PLATE

NORTH AMERICAN PLATE

NORTH AMERICAN PLATE

EURASIAN PLATE

AFRICAN PLATE

SOUTH AMERICAN PLATE

ANTARCTIC PLATE

PHILIPPINE PLATE

Japanese Trench

Marianas Trench

Aleutian Trench

JUAN DE FUCA PLATE

CARIBBEAN PLATE

COCOS PLATE

NASCA PLATE

Peru-Chile Trench

Tonga Trench

Mid-Atlantic Ridge

SCOTIA PLATE

PLATE

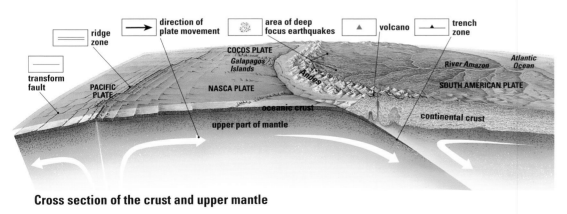

ridge zone	direction of plate movement	area of deep focus earthquakes

volcano · trench zone · transform fault

Cross section of the crust and upper mantle

COCOS PLATE
Galapagos Islands
PACIFIC PLATE
NASCA PLATE
Andes
River Amazon
Atlantic Ocean
SOUTH AMERICAN PLATE
oceanic crust
continental crust
upper part of mantle

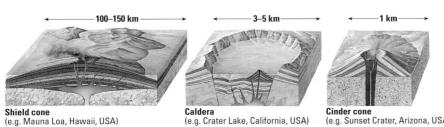

Shield cone
(e.g. Mauna Loa, Hawaii, USA)
100–150 km

Caldera
(e.g. Crater Lake, California, USA)
3–5 km

Cinder cone
(e.g. Sunset Crater, Arizona, USA)
1 km

Deadliest earthquakes, 1990–2002
force measured on the Richter scale

Year	Place	Force	Deaths
1990	Northwestern Iran	7.7	37 000
1990	Luzon, Philippines	7.7	1660
1991	Afghanistan/Pakistan	6.8	1000
1991	Uttar Pradesh, India	6.1	1500
1992	Erzincan, Turkey	6.7	2000
1992	Flores Island, Indonesia	7.5	2500
1993	Maharashtra, India	6.3	9800
1994	Cauca, Colombia	6.8	1000
1995	Kobe, Japan	7.2	5500
1995	Sakhalin Island, Russia	7.6	2000
1997	Ardabil, Iran	unknown	>1000
1997	Khorash, Iran	7.1	>1600
1998	Takhar, Afghanistan	6.1	>3800
1998	Northeastern Afghanistan	7.1	>3000
1999	Western Colombia	6.0	1124
1999	Izmit, Turkey	7.4	>17 000
1999	Central Taiwan	7.6	2295
1999	Ducze, Turkey	7.2	>700
2001	Gujarat, India	6.9	>20 000
2002	Baghlan, Afghanistan	6.0	>2000

Desertification and tropical deforestation

- existing areas of desert
- areas with a high risk of desertification
- areas with a moderate risk of desertification
- existing areas of tropical rain forest
- former areas of tropical rain forest

Countries losing greatest areas of forest ('000 hectares) 1990 – 2000

Brazil	2309
Indonesia	1312
Sudan	959
Zambia	851
Mexico	631
Congo Dem. Rep.	532
Myanmar	517

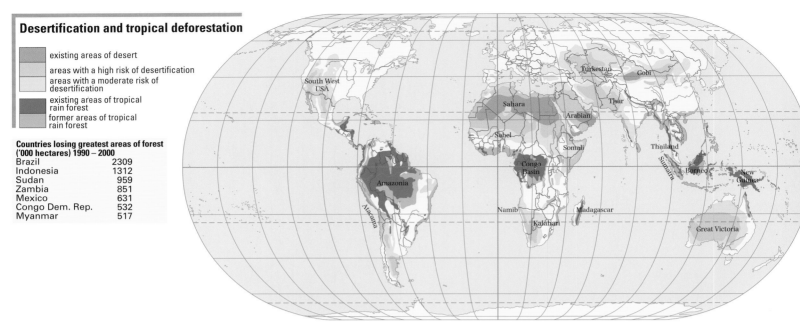

Lake Chad, West Africa, 1973–1997

Lake Chad was once the sixth-largest lake in the world, but persistent drought since the 1960's has shrunk it to about one tenth of its former size. Wetland marsh (shown on the satellite images as red) has now largely replaced open water (shown in blue). The lake is shallow and very responsive to the high variability of rainfall in the region. People living around Lake Chad do not have secure food supplies. Farming and irrigation projects have been affected by fluctuations in the level of the lake.

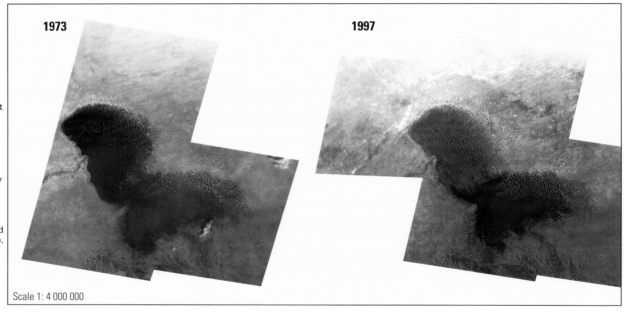

1973   1997

Scale 1: 4 000 000

Acid rain

Sulphur and nitrogen emissions
Oxides of sulphur and nitrogen produced by burning fossil fuel react with rain to form dilute sulphuric and nitric acids

- areas with high levels of fossil fuel burning
- cities where sulphur dioxide emissions are recorded and exceed World Health Organization recommended levels

Areas of acid rain deposition
Annual mean values of pH in precipitation

- pH less than 4.2 (most acidic)
- pH 4.2–4.6
- pH 4.6–5.0
- other areas where acid rain is becoming a problem

Lower pH values are more acidic. 'Clean' rain water is slightly acidic with a pH of 5.6. The pH scale is logarithmic, so that a value of 4.6 is ten times as acidic as normal rain.

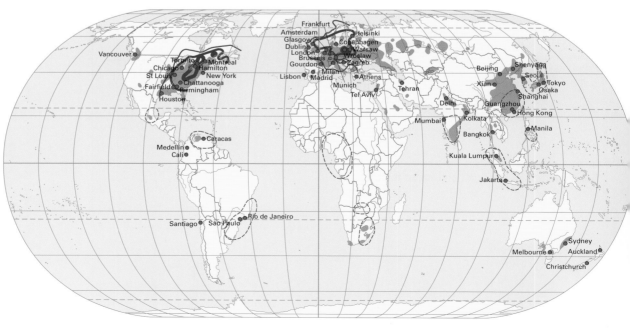

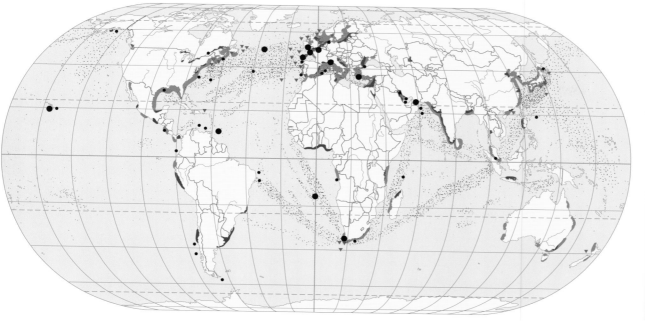

Sea pollution

Major oil spills

- ● over 100 000 tonnes
- ・ under 100 000 tonnes
- ⬦ frequent oil slicks from shipping

Other sea pollution

- severe pollution
- moderate pollution
- ▼ deep sea dump sites

Major oil spills ('000 tonnes)

1977	*Ekofisk* well blow-out, North Sea	270
1979	*Ixtoc 1* well blow-out, Gulf of Mexico	600
1979	Collision of *Atlantic Empress* and *Aegean Captain*, off Tobago, Caribbean	370
1983	*Nowruz* well blow-out, The Gulf	600
1989	*Exxon Valdez* spills oil off the coast of Alaska	250
1991	Release of oil by Iraqi troops, *Sea Island* terminal, The Gulf	799
2002	*Prestige* oil tanker sinks off the coast of Spain	77

Summary of atmospheric greenhouse gases

Gas	Anthropogenic sources	Concentrations preindustrial 1860	Concentrations 2000	Annual rate of increase	Lifetime in atmosphere	Contribution to global warming
carbon dioxide (CO_2)	fossil fuels, deforestation, soil destruction	286-288 ppm	369 ppm	1.4 ppm (0.4%)	50-200 years	54%
methane (CH_4)	domesticated livestock, biomass, rice cultivation, oil and gas production, mining	848 ppb	1784 ppb	17 ppm (1.0%)	23 years	12%
halocarbons eg. chlorofluorocarbons (CFC 11 & 12) and hydro-fluorocarbons (HFC)	refrigeration, air conditioning, solvents, aerosols	0 0	263 CFC 11 544 CFC 12 ppt	11 ppt (5.0%) CFC 11 19 ppt (5.0%) CFC 12	10s to 1000s years	21%
nitrous oxide (N_2O)	fossil fuels, deforestation, fertilizer use	285 ppb	315 ppb	0.6 ppb (0.2%)	114 years	6%
ozone and other trace gases (O_3)	photochemicals, processes, cars, power plants, solvents	25 ppb	29 ppb	unknown	hours to days in upper troposphere	7%

ppm = parts per million; ppb = parts per billion; ppt = parts per trillion
Halocarbons are carbon compounds containing halogens such as chlorine, fluorine, and bromine. They are a product of human activities.
Each greenhouse gas differs in its ability to absorb heat in the atmosphere. CFCs and HFCs are the most heat absorbent. CH_4 traps 27 times and N_2O 270 times more heat than CO_2.

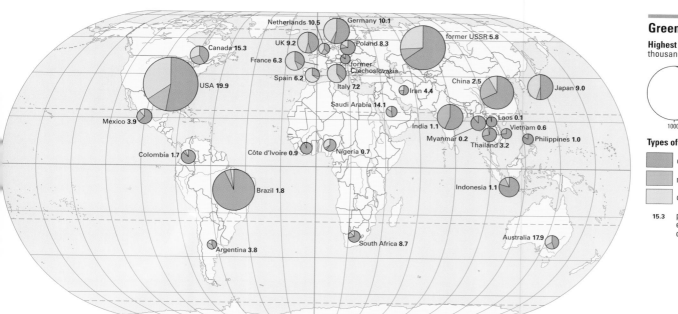

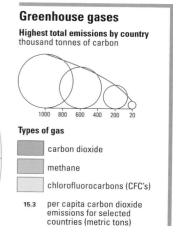

Greenhouse gases

Highest total emissions by country
thousand tonnes of carbon

1000   800   600   400   200   20

Types of gas

- carbon dioxide
- methane
- chlorofluorocarbons (CFC's)

15.3   per capita carbon dioxide emissions for selected countries (metric tons)

   Eckert IV Projection

Population density
people per square kilometre

- over 200
- 100–200
- 50–100
- 5–50
- 1–5
- under 1

Major cities
population in millions

- ■ over 10
- ⊡ 5–10
- □ 1–5

Further information on this topic is located in the World Statistics section which begins on page 176.

Population structure, 2000

World

males | Age | females

6 5 4 3 2 1 0 0 1 2 3 4 5
percent of total population

Total population: 6 079 727 906
Land area: 148 940 000km²

Kenya

males | Age | females

8 7 6 5 4 3 2 1 0 0 1 2 3 4 5 6 7 8
percent of total population

Total population: 30 340 000
Land area: 580 367km²

Brazil

males | Age | females

6 5 4 3 2 1 0 0 1 2 3 4 5 6
percent of total population

Total population: 172 860 000
Land area: 8 547 403km²

Japan

males | Age | females

5 4 3 2 1 0 0 1 2 3 4 5 6
percent of total population

Total population: 126 550 000
Land area: 377 801km²

Italy

males | Age | females

5 4 3 2 1 0 0 1 2 3 4 5
percent of total population

Total population: 57 634 000
Land area: 301 268km²

China

males | Age | females

6 5 4 3 2 1 0 0 1 2 3 4 5
percent of total population

Total population: 1 261 832 000
Land area: 9 596 961km²

USA

males | Age | females

5 4 3 2 1 0 0 1 2 3 4 5
percent of total population

Total population: 275 563 000
Land area: 9 158 960km²

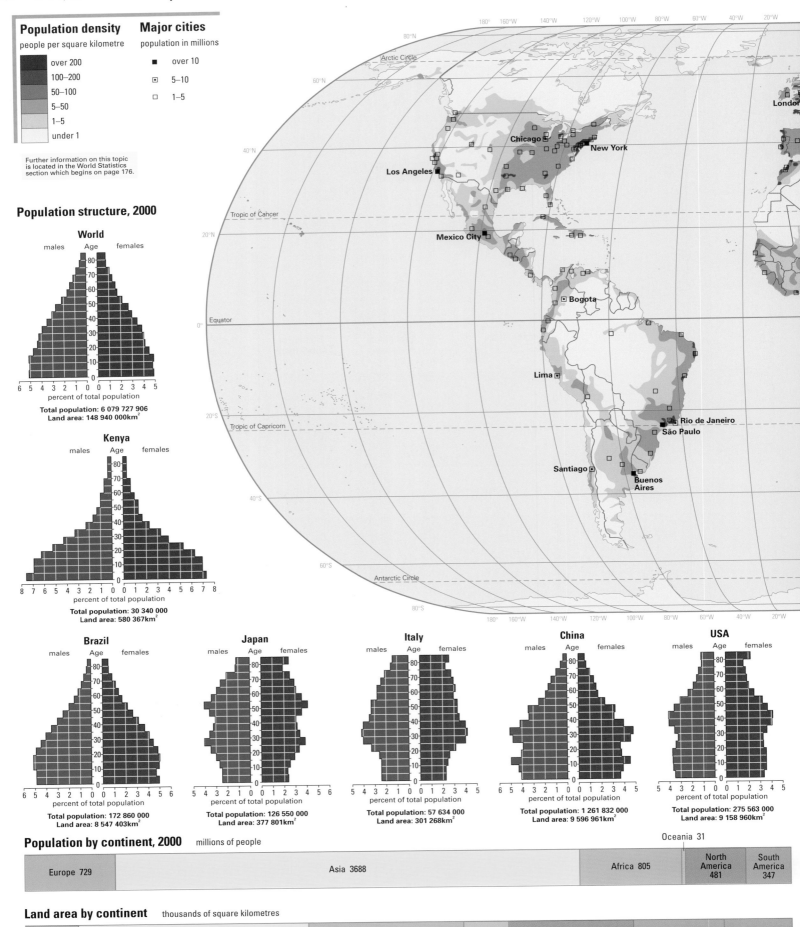

Population by continent, 2000 millions of people

Europe 729	Asia 3688	Africa 805	North America 481	South America 347

Oceania 31

Land area by continent thousands of square kilometres

Europe 10 498	Asia 44 387	Africa 30 335	Oceania 8503	North America 24 241	South America 17 832	Antarctica 13 340

Eckert IV Projection   © Oxford University Press

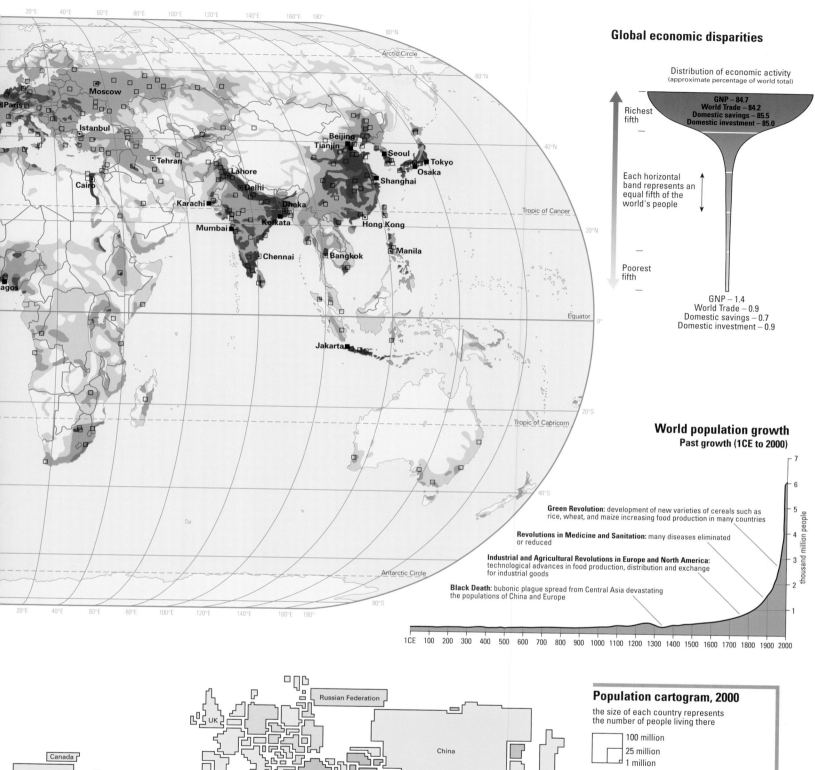

Global economic disparities

Distribution of economic activity
(approximate percentage of world total)

Richest fifth

GNP – 84.7
World Trade – 84.2
Domestic savings – 85.5
Domestic investment – 85.0

Each horizontal band represents an equal fifth of the world's people

Poorest fifth

GNP – 1.4
World Trade – 0.9
Domestic savings – 0.7
Domestic investment – 0.9

Paris
Moscow
Istanbul
Tehran
Cairo
Karachi
Mumbai
Lahore
Delhi
Dhaka
Kolkata
Chennai
Bangkok
Beijing
Tianjin
Seoul
Tokyo
Osaka
Shanghai
Hong Kong
Manila
Jakarta
agos

Arctic Circle
80°N
60°N
40°N
Tropic of Cancer
20°N
Equator
0°
Tropic of Capricorn
20°S
40°S
Antarctic Circle
80°S

20°E 40°E 60°E 80°E 100°E 120°E 140°E 160°E 180°

World population growth
Past growth (1CE to 2000)

Green Revolution: development of new varieties of cereals such as rice, wheat, and maize increasing food production in many countries

Revolutions in Medicine and Sanitation: many diseases eliminated or reduced

Industrial and Agricultural Revolutions in Europe and North America: technological advances in food production, distribution and exchange for industrial goods

Black Death: bubonic plague spread from Central Asia devastating the populations of China and Europe

thousand million people

1CE 100 200 300 400 500 600 700 800 900 1000 1100 1200 1300 1400 1500 1600 1700 1800 1900 2000

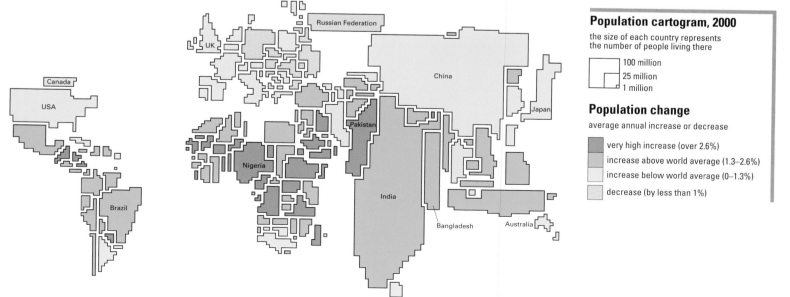

Russian Federation
UK
Canada
USA
China
Japan
Pakistan
Nigeria
India
Brazil
Bangladesh
Australia

Population cartogram, 2000

the size of each country represents the number of people living there

100 million
25 million
1 million

Population change

average annual increase or decrease

very high increase (over 2.6%)

increase above world average (1.3–2.6%)

increase below world average (0–1.3%)

decrease (by less than 1%)

Population change, 1990–2000

percentage population gain or loss

- over 40% gain
- 30–40% gain
- 20–30% gain
- 10–20% gain
- under 10% gain
- 0–10% loss

Population change refers to the growth or decline of a national population over the period 1990 to 2000 resulting from natural increase (births - deaths) and net migration (immigration - emigration).

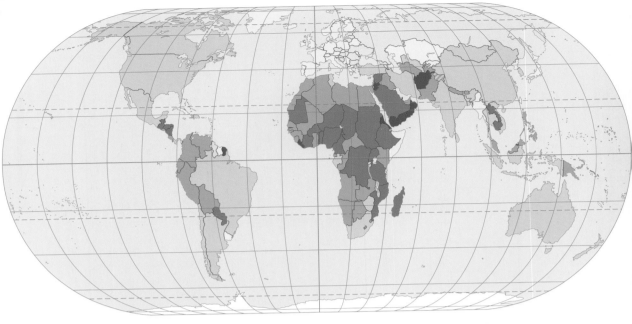

Urban population, 2000

percentage of the population living in urban areas

- over 80%
- 60–80%
- 40–60%
- 20–40%
- under 20%

Selected highly urban
Belgium 98%
Kuwait 97%
Israel 91%
Uruguay 91%
Argentina 90%
United Kingdom 89%

Canada 80%

Selected least urban
Thailand 21%
Vietnam 20%
Cambodia 16%
Uganda 14%
Nepal 12%
Rwanda 5%

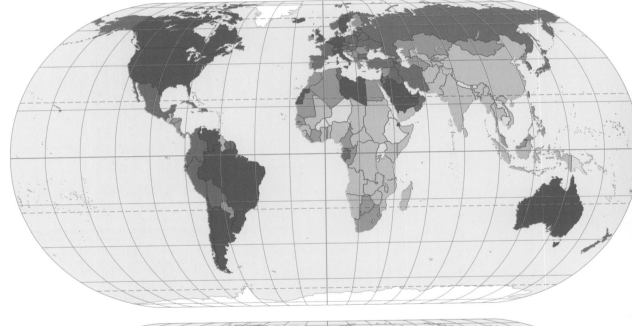

Fertility rate, 2000

average number of children born to childbearing women, over their lifetime, assuming the rates remained constant

- over 6 children
- 5–5.9 children
- 4–4.9 children
- 3–3.9 children
- 2–2.9 children
- 1–1.9 children

 countries with over 40% of the total population under the age of 15 in 2000

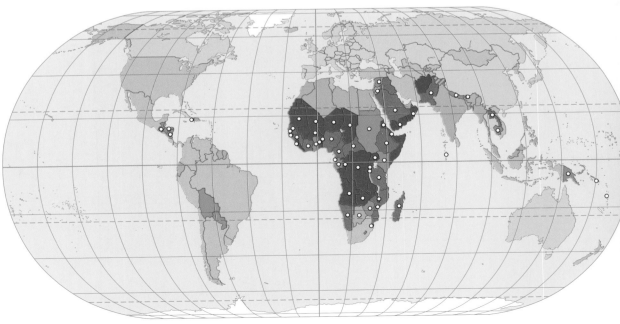

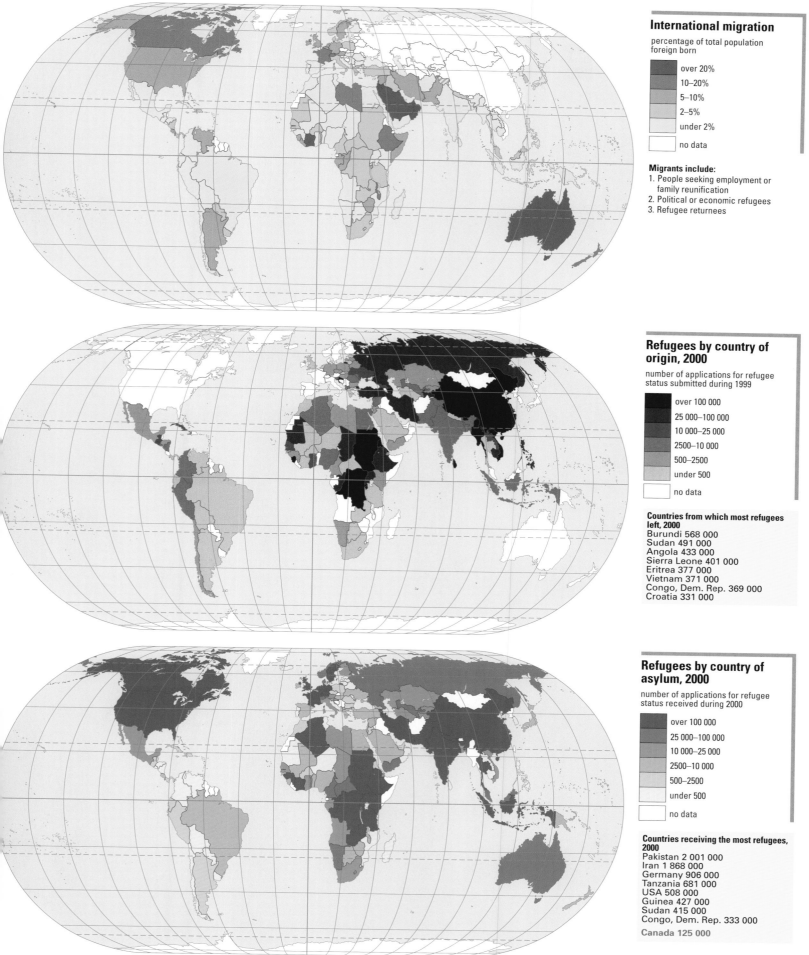

International migration

percentage of total population
foreign born

- over 20%
- 10–20%
- 5–10%
- 2–5%
- under 2%
- no data

Migrants include:
1. People seeking employment or
   family reunification
2. Political or economic refugees
3. Refugee returnees

Refugees by country of origin, 2000

number of applications for refugee
status submitted during 1999

- over 100 000
- 25 000–100 000
- 10 000–25 000
- 2500–10 000
- 500–2500
- under 500
- no data

Countries from which most refugees left, 2000

Burundi 568 000
Sudan 491 000
Angola 433 000
Sierra Leone 401 000
Eritrea 377 000
Vietnam 371 000
Congo, Dem. Rep. 369 000
Croatia 331 000

Refugees by country of asylum, 2000

number of applications for refugee
status received during 2000

- over 100 000
- 25 000–100 000
- 10 000–25 000
- 2500–10 000
- 500–2500
- under 500
- no data

Countries receiving the most refugees, 2000

Pakistan 2 001 000
Iran 1 868 000
Germany 906 000
Tanzania 681 000
USA 508 000
Guinea 427 000
Sudan 415 000
Congo, Dem. Rep. 333 000

Canada 125 000

Purchasing power, 2000

Purchasing Power Parity (PPP) in US$
Based on Gross Domestic Product (GDP)
per person, adjusted for the local cost
of living

- over 25 000
- 10 000–25 000
- 5000–10 000
- 2500–5000
- 1000–2500
- under 1000
- no data

Highest purchasing power
Luxembourg $50 061
United States $34 142
Norway $29 918
Ireland $29 866
Iceland $29 581

Canada $27 840

Lowest purchasing power
Ethiopia $668
Malawi $615
Burundi $591
Tanzania $523
Sierra Leone $490

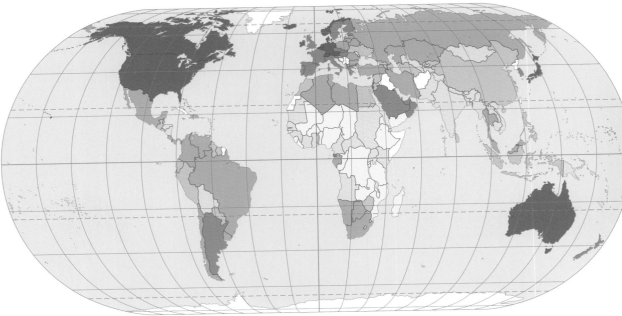

Literacy, 2000

percentage of people aged 15 and above
who can, with understanding, both read
and write a short, simple statement on
their person daily life

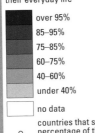

- over 95%
- 85–95%
- 75–85%
- 60–75%
- 40–60%
- under 40%
- no data
- ○ countries that spend a greater percentage of their GDP on the military than on education

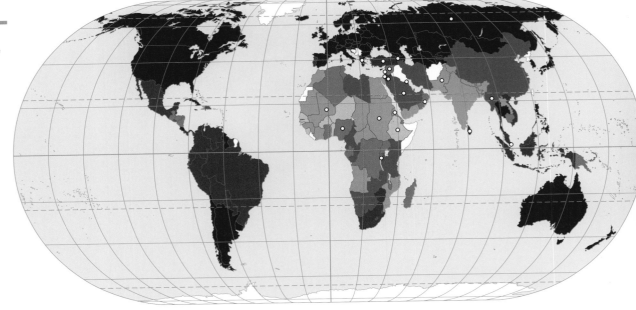

Life expectancy, 2000

average expected lifespan of babies
born in 2000

- over 75 years
- 70–75 years
- 65–70 years
- 60–65 years
- 55–60 years
- 50–55 years
- under 50 years
- no data
- ○ countries with infant mortality rates exceeding 56 per 1000 live births (This is the world average rate.)

Canada 6 per 1000 live births

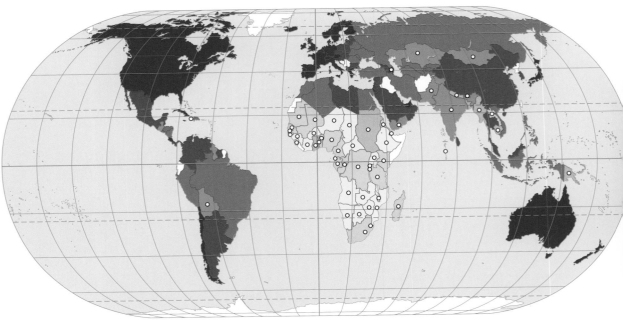

Eckert IV Projection   © Oxford University Press

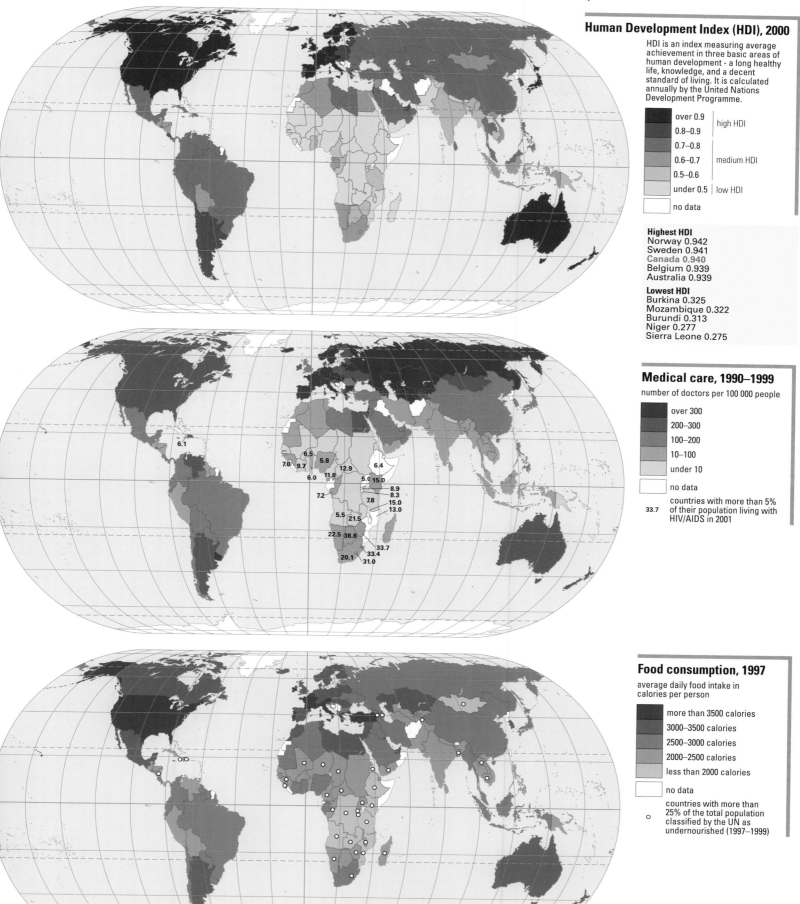

Human Development Index (HDI), 2000

HDI is an index measuring average achievement in three basic areas of human development - a long healthy life, knowledge, and a decent standard of living. It is calculated annually by the United Nations Development Programme.

over 0.9	high HDI
0.8–0.9	
0.7–0.8	
0.6–0.7	medium HDI
0.5–0.6	
under 0.5	low HDI
no data	

Highest HDI
Norway 0.942
Sweden 0.941
Canada 0.940
Belgium 0.939
Australia 0.939

Lowest HDI
Burkina 0.325
Mozambique 0.322
Burundi 0.313
Niger 0.277
Sierra Leone 0.275

Medical care, 1990–1999

number of doctors per 100 000 people

over 300
200–300
100–200
10–100
under 10
no data

33.7 countries with more than 5% of their population living with HIV/AIDS in 2001

Food consumption, 1997

average daily food intake in calories per person

more than 3500 calories
3000–3500 calories
2500–3000 calories
2000–2500 calories
less than 2000 calories
no data

○ countries with more than 25% of the total population classified by the UN as undernourished (1997–1999)

© Oxford University Press

Agriculture

Commercial farming

- cereals dominant
- mixed farming and dairy
- mixed farming, fruit and vegetables
- mixed farming, cash crops
- ranching and stock raising

Mainly subsistence farming

- staples: cassava, yam, potatoes
- staples: millet, sorghum, barley, rye
- nomadic herding

Small holding

- rice dominant
- other cereals dominant
- mixed farming and livestock
- mixed farming, fruit and vegetables
- mixed farming, cash crops
- stock raising

Forests

- commercially exploited

Non-agricultural land

- ice, tundra, swamp, desert, montane and coniferous forest

Scale 1: 190 000 000

Agriculture's contribution to Gross Domestic Product (GDP)

percentage of GDP, for selected countries, 2000 (GDP is the annual total value of all goods and services in a country, excluding transactions with other countries)

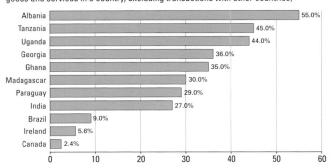

Country	%
Albania	55.0%
Tanzania	45.0%
Uganda	44.0%
Georgia	36.0%
Ghana	35.0%
Madagascar	30.0%
Paraguay	29.0%
India	27.0%
Brazil	9.0%
Ireland	5.6%
Canada	2.4%

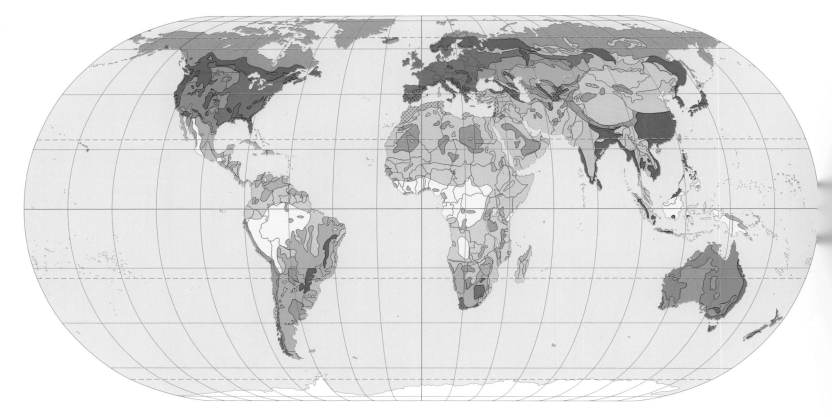

Employment in agriculture

percentage of the labour force

- over 80%
- 60–80%
- 30–60%
- 10–30%
- under 10%
- no data

Highest employment in agriculture
Bhutan 94%
Nepal 94%
Burkina 92%
Burundi 92%
Rwanda 92%

Canada 3%

Lowest employment in agriculture
Bahrain 2%
Brunei 2%
United Kingdom 2%
Kuwait 1%
Singapore 0%

Scale 1: 240 000 000

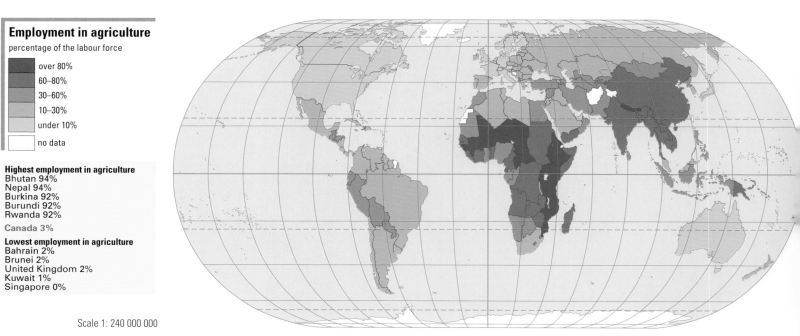

Eckert IV Projection   © Oxford University Press

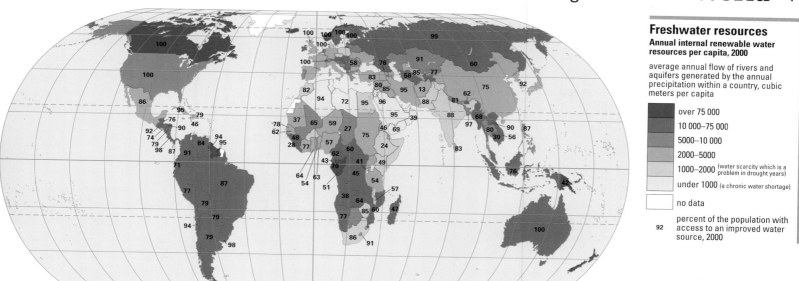

Freshwater resources
Annual internal renewable water resources per capita, 2000

average annual flow of rivers and aquifers generated by the annual precipitation within a country, cubic meters per capita

- over 75 000
- 10 000–75 000
- 5000–10 000
- 2000–5000
- 1000–2000 (water scarcity which is a problem in drought years)
- under 1000 (a chronic water shortage)
- no data

92   percent of the population with access to an improved water source, 2000

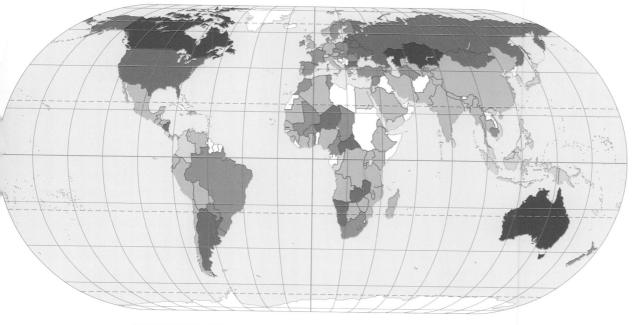
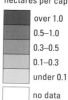

Arable land

hectares per capita, 1995–1997

- over 1.0
- 0.5–1.0
- 0.3–0.5
- 0.1–0.3
- under 0.1
- no data

Arable land includes land under crops, meadows for mowing or for pasture, land under market or kitchen gardens, and land temporarily fallow.

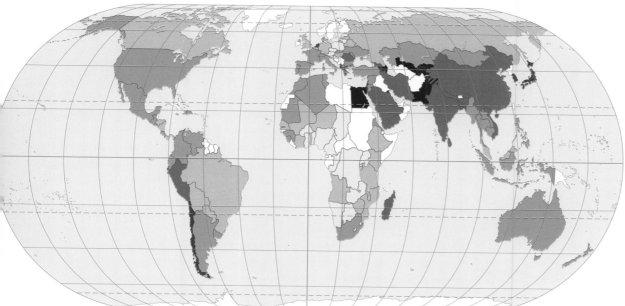
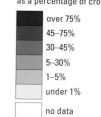

Irrigated land

areas permanently provided with water as a percentage of cropland, 1995–1997

- over 75%
- 45–75%
- 30–45%
- 5–30%
- 1–5%
- under 1%
- no data

Industrialization, 2000

Industrialized high income economies
Most people live in cities and have high standards of living based on manufacturing and services. High levels of energy consumption

Industrializing upper-middle income economies
Manufacturing and industrial development are growing alongside traditional economies. Most people have rising incomes.

Industrializing lower-middle income economies
Manufacturing and industrial development are growing alongside traditional economies. Most people have relatively low incomes.

Agricultural low income economies
Most people live in rural areas and depend on agriculture. Little industrial development. Low incomes.

○ Major oil exporting countries

International aid, 2000

Official development assistance (ODA) given or received per person in $US

Countries giving aid

over $100 per person

$50–$100 per person

under $50 per person

Countries receiving aid

under $10 per person

$10–$100 per person

over $100 per person

no data

Countries giving most aid (total $US)
Japan $13 508 000 000
USA $9 955 000 000
Germany $5 030 000 000
United Kingdom $4 501 000 000
France $4 105 000 000
Canada $1 744 000 000

Countries receiving most aid (total $US)
China $1 735 000 000
Indonesia $1 731 000 000
Vietnam $1 699 500 000
Russian Federation $1 564 600 000
Poland $1 396 200 000

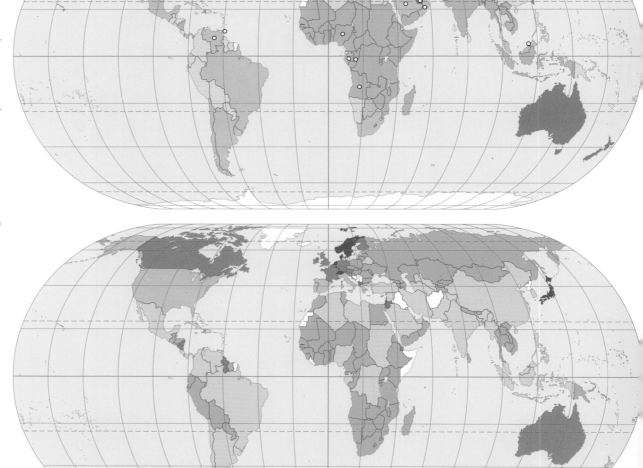

Employment

percentage of the labour force

over 80%

60–80%

30–60%

10–30%

under 10%

no data

Scale 1: 480 000 000

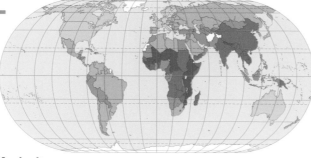

Agriculture

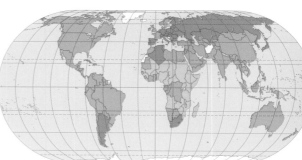

Indust

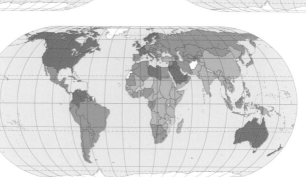

Services

World trade cartogram, 1999
the size of each country represents its share of total world trade

- 1% of world trade
- 0.1% of world trade

Change in share of world trade, 1990–1999

over 50%	growth
5–50%	
0–5% growth or decline	little or no change
5–50	decline
over 50%	

Only those countries with more than 0.01% share in world trade are shown

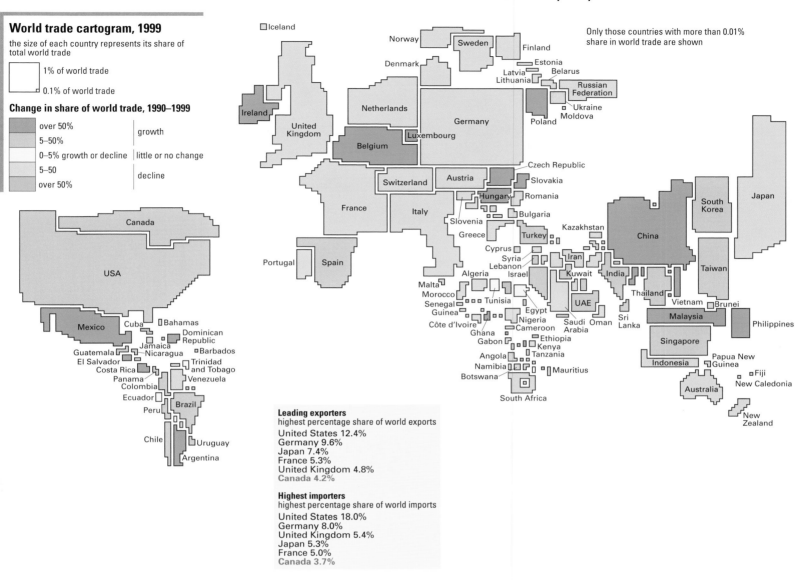

Leading exporters
highest percentage share of world exports
United States 12.4%
Germany 9.6%
Japan 7.4%
France 5.3%
United Kingdom 4.8%
Canada 4.2%

Highest importers
highest percentage share of world imports
United States 18.0%
Germany 8.0%
United Kingdom 5.4%
Japan 5.3%
France 5.0%
Canada 3.7%

Sector	includes
Primary	Farming, fishing, forestry, mining and quarrying
Secondary	Manufacturing industry, building and construction
Tertiary	Transport and distribution, wholesale and retail, administration and finance, services

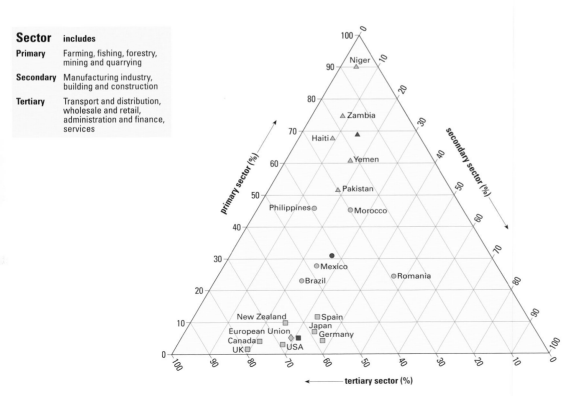

Employment by economic sector

Average for country categories

- ▲ Low income economies
- ● Middle income economies
- ■ High income economies

Selected countries and the European Union

- △ Low income countries
- ○ Middle income countries
- ▢ High income countries
- ◇ European Union

Scale 1: 240 000 000

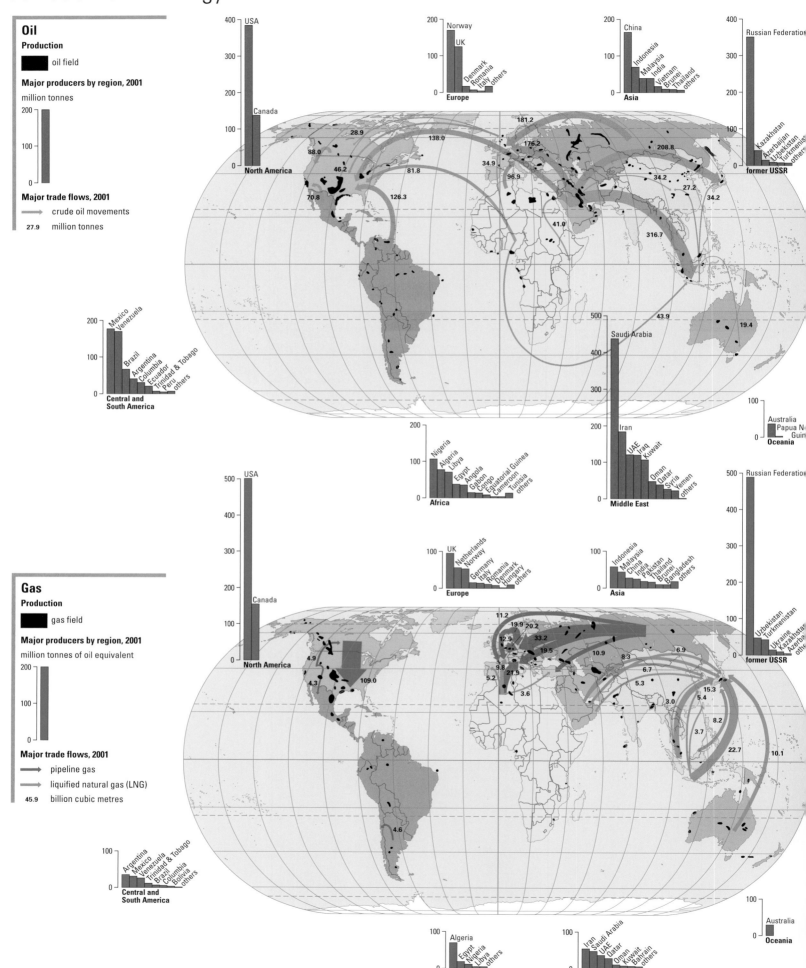

Oil

Production

■ oil field

Major producers by region, 2001

million tonnes

Major trade flows, 2001

→ crude oil movements

27.9 million tonnes

Gas

Production

■ gas field

Major producers by region, 2001

million tonnes of oil equivalent

Major trade flows, 2001

→ pipeline gas

→ liquified natural gas (LNG)

45.9 billion cubic metres

Eckert IV Projection

© Oxford University Press

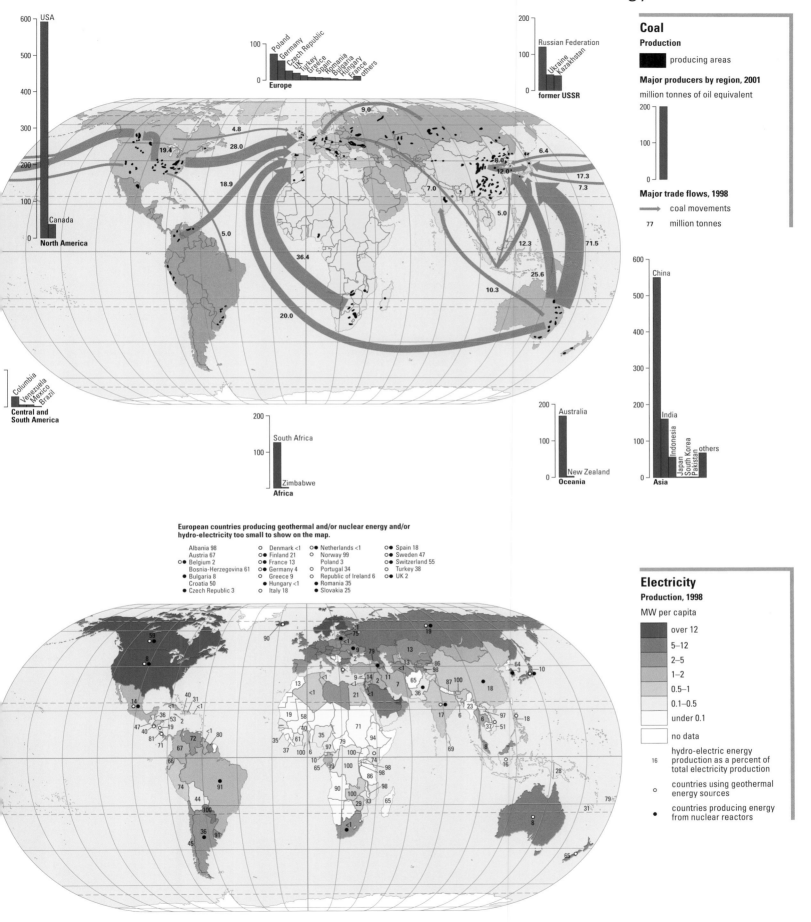

Coal

Production

■ producing areas

Major producers by region, 2001

million tonnes of oil equivalent

Major trade flows, 1998

→ coal movements

77 million tonnes

USA

Canada

North America

Columbia
Venezuela
Mexico
Brazil
Central and South America

Poland
Germany
Czech Republic
UK
Turkey
Greece
Spain
Bulgaria
Romania
Hungary
France
others
Europe

Russian Federation
Ukraine
Kazakhstan
former USSR

South Africa
Zimbabwe
Africa

Australia
New Zealand
Oceania

China
India
Indonesia
Japan
South Korea
Pakistan
others
Asia

European countries producing geothermal and/or nuclear energy and/or hydro-electricity too small to show on the map.

Albania 98
Austria 67
○●Belgium 2
Bosnia-Herzegovina 61
●Bulgaria 8
Croatia 50
●Czech Republic 3

○ Denmark <1
○● Finland 21
○● France 13
○● Germany 4
○ Greece 9
● Hungary <1
○ Italy 18

○● Netherlands <1
○ Norway 99
○ Poland 3
○ Portugal 34
● Republic of Ireland 6
● Romania 35
● Slovakia 25

○● Spain 18
○● Sweden 47
○● Switzerland 55
○ Turkey 38
○● UK 2

Electricity

Production, 1998

MW per capita

over 12
5–12
2–5
1–2
0.5–1
0.1–0.5
under 0.1
no data

16 hydro-electric energy production as a percent of total electricity production

○ countries using geothermal energy sources

● countries producing energy from nuclear reactors

Energy production, 2000

kg oil equivalent per person

- over 25 000
- 2500–25 000
- 1000–2500
- 100–1000
- under 100
- no data

Highest energy producers
kg oil equivalent per person

Qatar 94 758
United Arab Emirates 71 971
Kuwait 65 096
Brunei 63 244
Norway 56 907
Saudi Arabia 23 974
Oman 23 293
Trinidad & Tobago 17 778
Bahrain 16 167
Libya 16 129
Canada 14 547
Gabon 14 513
Australia 12 575
Turkmenistan 11 344
Venezuela 9483

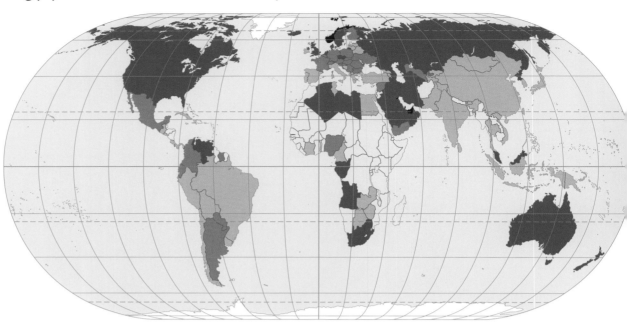

Oil reserves
Proven recoverable reserves
World total: 142 100 000 000 tonnes

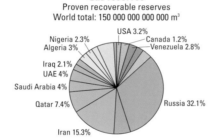

China 2.3%
USA 2.6%
Nigeria 2.2%
Canada 0.6%
Libya 2.7%
Venezuela 7.8%
Mexico 2.8%
Iran 8.7%
Russia 4.7%
UAE 8.8%
Kuwait 9.4%
Saudi Arabia 25.2%
Iraq 10.6%

Gas reserves
Proven recoverable reserves
World total: 150 000 000 000 000 m³

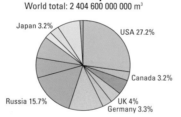

Nigeria 2.3%
USA 3.2%
Algeria 3%
Canada 1.2%
Venezuela 2.8%
Iraq 2.1%
UAE 4%
Saudi Arabia 4%
Russia 32.1%
Qatar 7.4%
Iran 15.3%

Coal reserves
Proven recoverable reserves
World total: 984 211 000 000 tonnes

Australia 9.2%
USA 25.1%
India 7.6%
China 11.6%
Canada 0.9%
Brazil 1.2%
Germany 6.8%
South Africa 5.6%
Poland 1.5%
Kazakhstan 3.5%
Ukraine 3.5%
Russia 3.5%

Oil consumption
World total: 3 503 600 000 tonnes

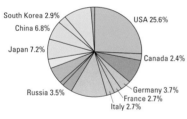

South Korea 2.9%
USA 25.6%
China 6.8%
Japan 7.2%
Canada 2.4%
Russia 3.5%
Germany 3.7%
France 2.7%
Italy 2.7%

Gas consumption
World total: 2 404 600 000 000 m³

Japan 3.2%
USA 27.2%
Canada 3.2%
Russia 15.7%
UK 4%
Germany 3.3%

Coal consumption
World total: 2 186 000 000 tonnes oil equivalent

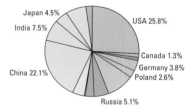

Japan 4.5%
USA 25.8%
India 7.5%
Canada 1.3%
China 22.1%
Germany 3.8%
Poland 2.6%
Russia 5.1%

Energy consumption, 2000

kg oil equivalent per person

- over 10 000
- 2500–10 000
- 1000–2500
- 250–1000
- under 250
- no data

Highest energy consumers
kg oil equivalent per person

Qatar 22 177
United Arab Emirates 18 362
Bahrain 14 590
Kuwait 12 538
Iceland 11 576
Canada 10 447
Singapore 10 116

Lowest energy consumers
kg oil equivalent per person

Afghanistan 25
Burkina 24
Ethiopia 22
Cambodia 16
Chad 8

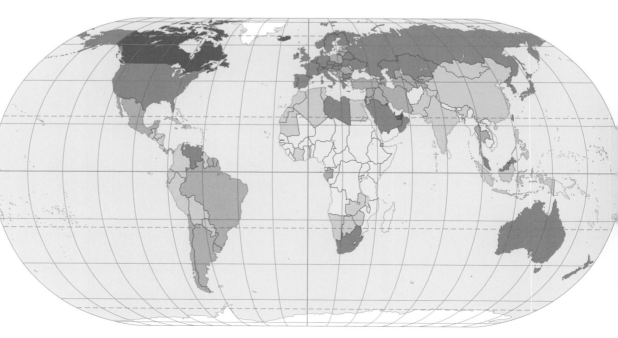

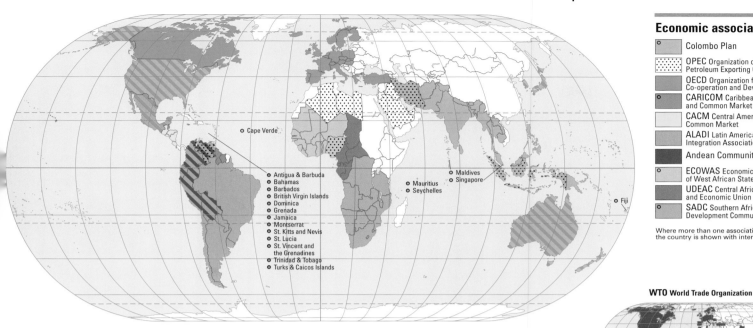

Economic associations

- Colombo Plan
- OPEC Organization of Petroleum Exporting Countries
- OECD Organization for Economic Co-operation and Development
- CARICOM Caribbean Community and Common Market
- CACM Central American Common Market
- ALADI Latin American Integration Association
- Andean Community
- ECOWAS Economic Community of West African States
- UDEAC Central African Customs and Economic Union
- SADC Southern African Development Community

Where more than one association is involved, the country is shown with interlocking shading.

Antigua & Barbuda
- Antigua & Barbuda
- Bahamas
- Barbados
- British Virgin Islands
- Dominica
- Grenada
- Jamaica
- Montserrat
- St. Kitts and Nevis
- St. Lucia
- St. Vincent and the Grenadines
- Trinidad & Tobago
- Turks & Caicos Islands

Cape Verde
Mauritius
Seychelles
Maldives
Singapore
Fiji

UNCTAD

United Nations Conference on Trade and Development

Almost all nations (191) are now members, Western Sahara is the only non-member.

EU

European Union

For members see page 74.

United Nations

The following countries are **non-members**

Northern Marianas
Switzerland†
Taiwan
Vatican City†
Western Sahara

† observer status

Headquarters of selected World Organizations

Brussels:
The European Union
North Atlantic Treaty Organization (NATO)

The Hague:
International Court of Justice

New York:
United Nations

Paris:
United National Education, Scientific and Cultural Organization (UNESCO)

Organization for Economic Co-operation and Development (OECD)

Rome:
Food and Agricultural Organization of the United Nations (FAO)

Geneva:
World Health Organization (WHO)
World Trade Organization (WTO)

Washington:
Organization of American States (OAS)

Addis Ababa:
Organization of African Unity (OAU)

Cairo:
Arab League

Singapore:
Asia Pacific Economic Co-operation (APEC)

Strasbourg:
Council of Europe
European Parliament

WTO World Trade Organization

WTO World Trade Organization

- Antigua & Barbuda
- Azerbaijan†
- Bahamas
- Bahrain
- Barbados
- Brunei
- Burundi
- Cyprus
- Dominica
- Fiji
- Grenada
- Israel
- Jamaica
- Kiribati
- Kuwait
- Laos†
- Liechtenstein
- Luxembourg
- Maldives
- Malta
- Mauritius
- Qatar
- St. Kitts and Nevis
- St. Lucia
- St. Vincent and the Grenadines
- Samoa
- Seychelles
- Singapore
- Solomon Islands
- Somalia†
- Sudan†
- Tajikistan†
- Trinidad & Tobago
- Turkmenistan†
- Vanuatu

†observer status

Commonwealth of Nations

Commonwealth of Nations

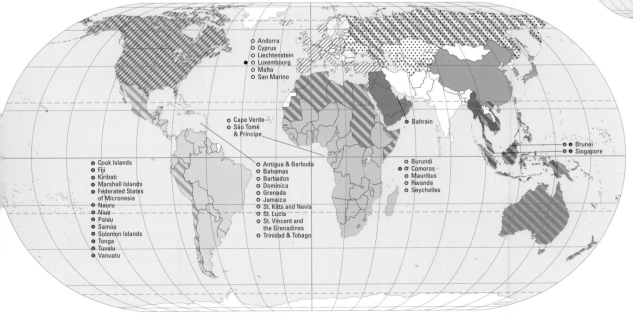

Andorra
Cyprus
Liechtenstein
Luxembourg
Malta
San Marino

Cape Verde
São Tomé & Príncipe
Bahrain
Brunei
Singapore

Cook Islands
Fiji
Kiribati
Marshall Islands
Federated States of Micronesia
Nauru
Niue
Palau
Samoa
Solomon Islands
Tonga
Tuvalu
Vanuatu

Antigua & Barbuda
Bahamas
Barbados
Dominica
Grenada
Jamaica
St. Kitts and Nevis
St. Lucia
St. Vincent and the Grenadines
Trinidad & Tobago

Burundi
Comoros
Mauritius
Rwanda
Seychelles

International organizations

- South Pacific Forum
- ASEAN Association of South East Asian Nations
- OAS Organization of American States
- Arab League
- OAU Organization of African Unity
- NATO North Atlantic Treaty Organization
- Council of Europe
- APEC Asia Pacific Economic Co-operation
- CIS Commonwealth of Independent States

Where more than one organization is involved, the country is shown with interlocking shading.

Internet users, 2000

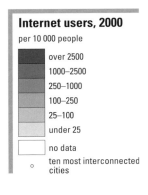

per 10 000 people

- over 2500
- 1000–2500
- 250–1000
- 100–250
- 25–100
- under 25
- no data
- ○ ten most interconnected cities

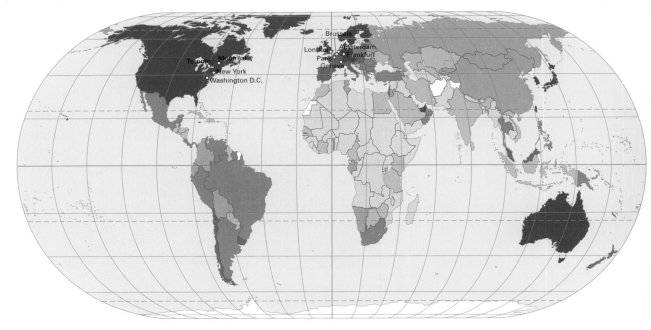

Internet traffic, 2000

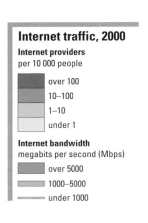

Internet providers
per 10 000 people

- over 100
- 10–100
- 1–10
- under 1

Internet bandwidth
megabits per second (Mbps)

- over 5000
- 1000–5000
- under 1000

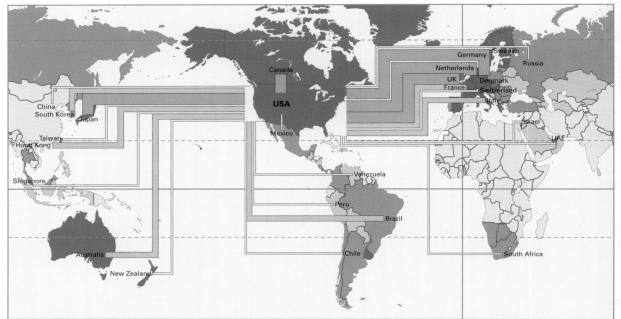

Internet traffic flow

The 'arc map' shows Internet traffic between 50 countries. Arcs are coloured to show Internet traffic between countries. The height of each arc is proportional to the volume of Internet traffic flowing over a link, so the highest arcs represent the greatest volume of traffic.

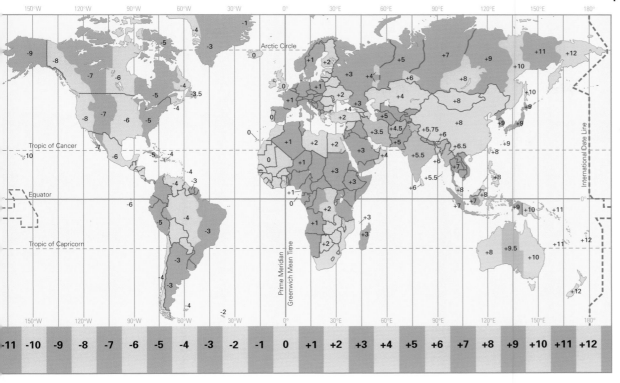

Time zones, 2001

Minus numbers show hours behind Greeenwich Mean Time (GMT). Plus numbers show hours ahead of GMT.

- even numbers of hours difference from GMT
- odd numbers of hours difference from GMT
- half an hour difference from adjacent zone
- less than half an hour difference from adjacent zone

Longitude is measured from the **prime meridian** which passes through Greenwich. There are 24 standard time zones, each of 15° of longitude. The edges of these time zones often follow political boundaries.

The **international date line** marks the point where one calendar day ends and another begins. A traveller crossing from east to west moves forward one day. Crossing from west to east the calendar goes back one day.

| -11 | -10 | -9 | -8 | -7 | -6 | -5 | -4 | -3 | -2 | -1 | 0 | +1 | +2 | +3 | +4 | +5 | +6 | +7 | +8 | +9 | +10 | +11 | +12 |

Flying time

Typical flight times by air between cities in hours and minutes
ooo means there is no direct flight available, early 2002

7.55	15.45	20.30	27.40	7.10	5.25	4.55	17.30	1.25	7.25	21.05	22.45	16.55	**Toronto**
3.35	ooo	4.55	ooo	12.40	10.40	15.50	12.35	15.55	12.50	7.05	10.00	**Tokyo**
2.55	16.35	8.50	14.30	22.45	14.35	ooo	14.40	21.45	22.25	8.55	**Sydney**
6.15	ooo	4.05	10.30	14.40	18.45	ooo	6.30	22.05	14.15	**Singapore**
0.20	13.50	12.45	10.55	1.10	12.30	12.20	12.10	7.40	**Paris**
5.20	13.25	19.25	16.25	7.20	6.00	6.00	20.05	**New York**
ooo	ooo	7.45	20.15	10.30	ooo	ooo	**Mumbai**
ooo	13.10	ooo	ooo	11.05	4.15	**Mexico City**
3.30	16.40	14.50	ooo	13.00	**Los Angeles**
0.25	14.50	13.30	10.50	**London**
ooo	ooo	13.00	**Johannesburg**
3.00	ooo	**Hong Kong**
ooo	**Buenos Aires**
Beijing

Transport

Air transport
- —— major air route
- • major airport

Sea transport
- —— major shipping lane
- • major port

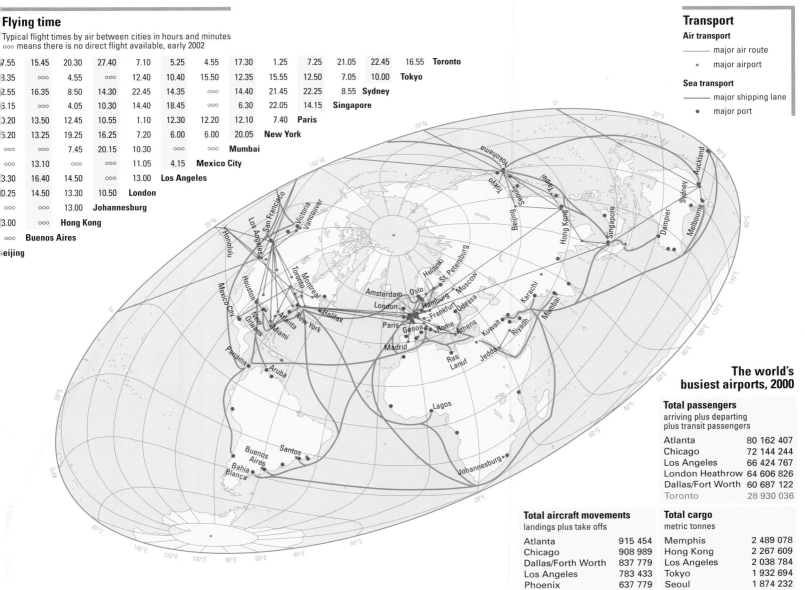

The world's busiest airports, 2000

Total passengers
arriving plus departing plus transit passengers

Atlanta	80 162 407
Chicago	72 144 244
Los Angeles	66 424 767
London Heathrow	64 606 826
Dallas/Fort Worth	60 687 122
Toronto	28 930 036

Total aircraft movements
landings plus take offs

Atlanta	915 454
Chicago	908 989
Dallas/Forth Worth	837 779
Los Angeles	783 433
Phoenix	637 779
Toronto	426 506

Total cargo
metric tonnes

Memphis	2 489 078
Hong Kong	2 267 609
Los Angeles	2 038 784
Tokyo	1 932 694
Seoul	1 874 232
New York	1 817 727

Scale 1: 125 000 000 (main map)

Selected tourist destinations

The locations shown represent a limited selection of important tourism sites.

- 🏛 cultural/historical sites
- ✳ natural heritage sites
- ⬤ resorts
- ⬤ tourist cities
- —— main cruise routes

land height

metres
2000
500
0

Top tourist destinations, 2001

	arrivals (000's)	% change 2000–2001
France	76 500	1.2
Spain	49 500	3.4
USA	45 500	-10.6
Italy	39 000	-5.3
China	33 200	6.2
United Kingdom	23 400	-7.4
Russian Federation	21 200	0.0
Mexico	19 800	-4.0
Canada	19 700	-0.1
Austria	18 200	1.1

Market share, 2001

percent of all international tourist arrivals

France	11.0%
Spain	7.1%
USA	6.6%
Italy	5.6%
China	4.8%
UK	3.4%
Russia	3.0%
Mexico	2.9%
Canada	2.8%
Austria	2.6%

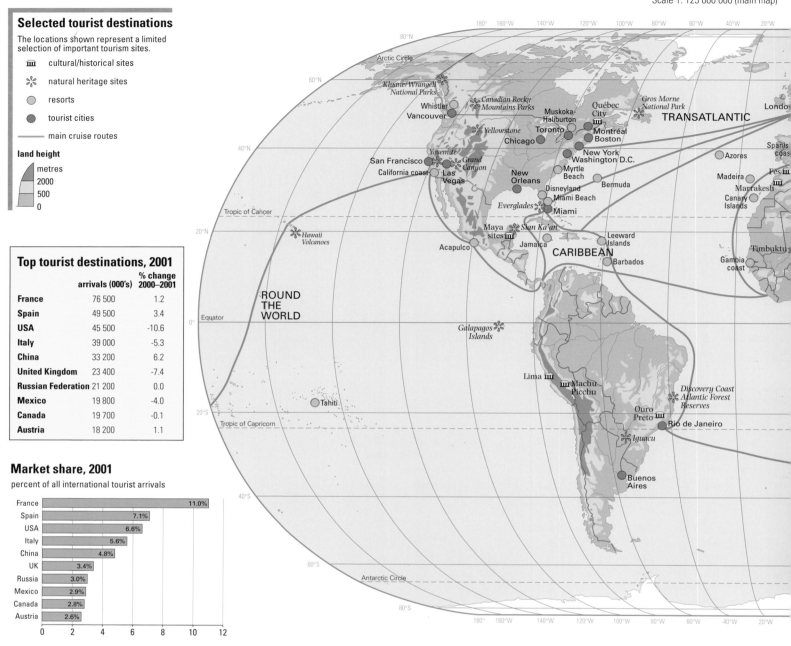

Earnings from tourism, 1999

tourist receipts in million $US

- over 5000
- 1000–5000
- 250–1000
- 100–250
- under 100
- no data

Highest tourist earnings (millions)
USA $74 881
Spain $32 400
France $31 507
Italy $28 359
Canada $10 171

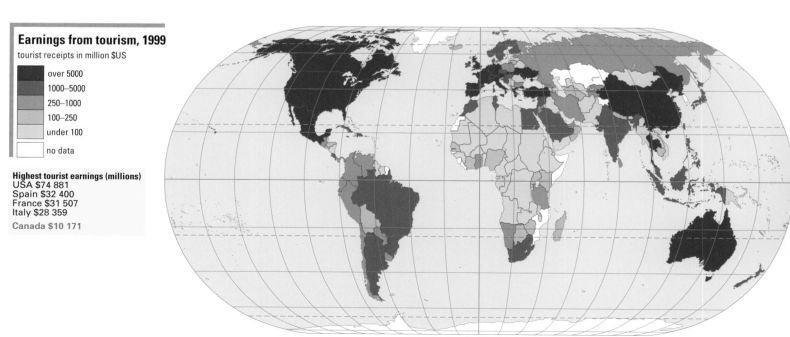

Eckert IV Projection   © Oxford University Press

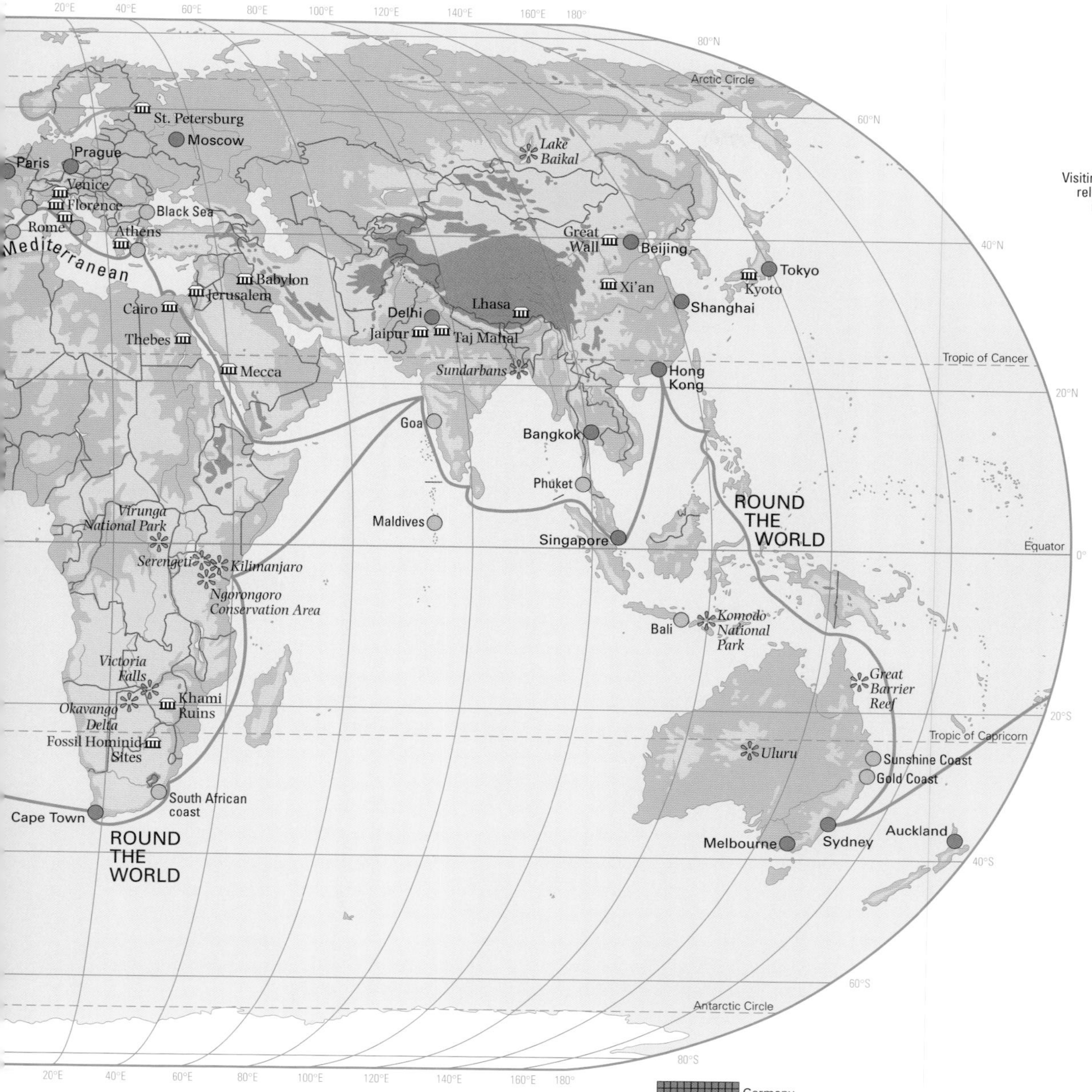

International tourism by purpose of visit, 1998

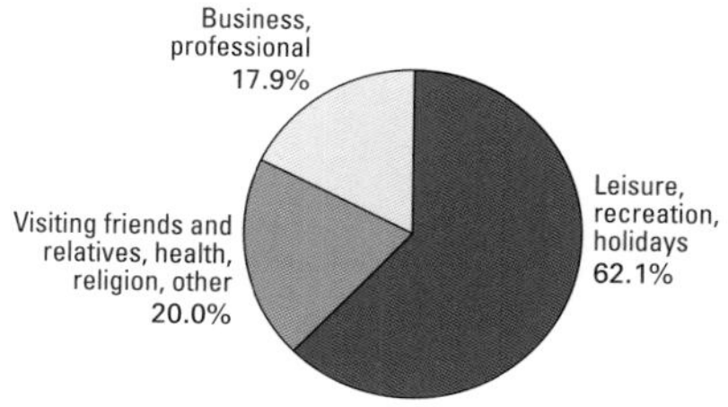

Business, professional 17.9%

Visiting friends and relatives, health, religion, other 20.0%

Leisure, recreation, holidays 62.1%

International tourism by mode of transport, 1998

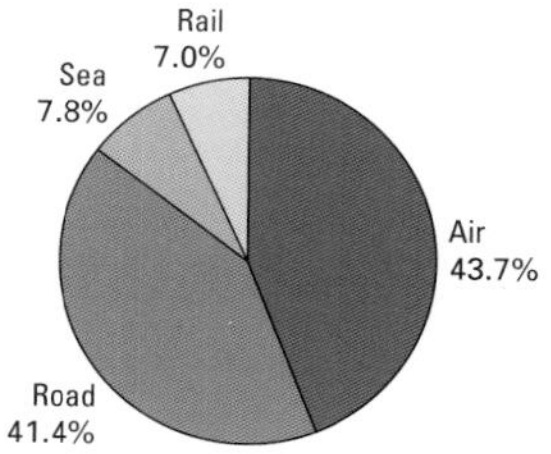

Rail 7.0%

Sea 7.8%

Air 43.7%

Road 41.4%

Map labels (top globe)

St. Petersburg
Moscow
Paris
Prague
Venice
Florence
Rome
Athens
Black Sea
Mediterranean
Cairo
Thebes
Jerusalem
Babylon
Mecca
Lake Baikal
Great Wall
Beijing
Xi'an
Shanghai
Tokyo
Kyoto
Lhasa
Delhi
Jaipur
Taj Mahal
Sundarbans
Hong Kong
Goa
Bangkok
Phuket
Maldives
Singapore
ROUND THE WORLD
Tropic of Cancer
Equator
Virunga National Park
Serengeti
Kilimanjaro
Ngorongoro Conservation Area
Victoria Falls
Okavango Delta
Khami Ruins
Fossil Hominid Sites
Cape Town
South African coast
ROUND THE WORLD
Bali
Komodo National Park
Great Barrier Reef
Uluru
Sunshine Coast
Gold Coast
Melbourne
Sydney
Auckland
Tropic of Capricorn
Arctic Circle
Antarctic Circle

Tourists, 1998

□ one square represents 500 000 tourists

Origin

- Europe
- North and South America
- Asia and Oceania
- Africa
- no data

only countries with at least 500 000 tourists are shown

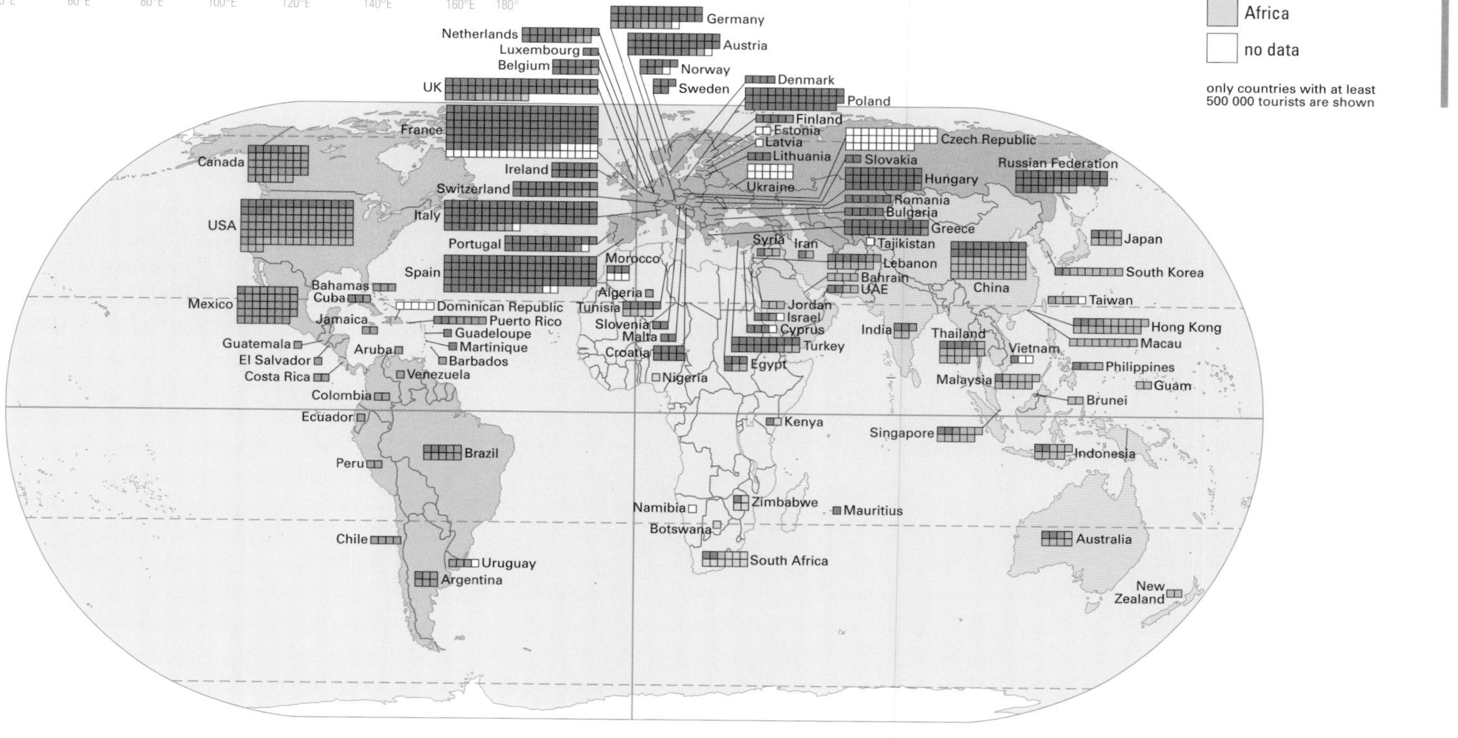

Map labels (bottom globe)

Netherlands
Luxembourg
Belgium
UK
France
Ireland
Switzerland
Italy
Portugal
Spain
Canada
USA
Mexico
Bahamas
Cuba
Jamaica
Guatemala
El Salvador
Costa Rica
Colombia
Ecuador
Peru
Chile
Uruguay
Argentina
Brazil
Germany
Austria
Norway
Sweden
Denmark
Poland
Finland
Estonia
Latvia
Lithuania
Ukraine
Morocco
Algeria
Tunisia
Dominican Republic
Puerto Rico
Guadeloupe
Martinique
Barbados
Aruba
Venezuela
Slovenia
Malta
Croatia
Nigeria
Namibia
Botswana
Zimbabwe
Mauritius
South Africa
Kenya
Egypt
Syria
Iran
Israel
Cyprus
Jordan
Lebanon
Bahrain
UAE
Tajikistan
Turkey
India
Czech Republic
Slovakia
Hungary
Romania
Bulgaria
Greece
Russian Federation
China
Japan
South Korea
Taiwan
Hong Kong
Macau
Thailand
Vietnam
Philippines
Guam
Malaysia
Brunei
Singapore
Indonesia
Australia
New Zealand

© Oxford University Press

Selected tourist sites

The locations shown represent a limited selection of important tourism sites.

- 🏛 cultural/historical centres
- ✳ sites of natural beauty
- 🔴 National Parks[†]
- 🔴 coastal tourism areas and resorts
- 🟠 ski and mountain areas and resorts
- △ leisure parks
- ⭐

land height

metres
- 2000
- 500
- 0

[†] All Canadian parks and reserves are shown on page 25.

Florida Scale 1 : 8 000 000

Marineland, Daytona Beach, Jacksonville, John F. Kennedy Space Centre, Cape Canaveral, Orlando, Walt Disney World Resort Complex, Palm Beach, Fort Lauderdale, Miami Beach, Universal Studios, Lake Okeechobee, Biscayne National Park, Tampa, Busch Gardens, St. Petersburg, Tampa Bay, Sarasota, Charlotte Harbour, Fort Myers, Big Cypress National Preserve, The Everglades, Miami, Everglades National Park, FLORIDA, Florida Keys, Key West, Straits of Florida, Gulf of Mexico

The Caribbean Scale 1 : 18 000 000

Leeward Islands, Virgin Is., Cane Garden Bay (UK/USA), Trunk Bay, Shoal Bay, Anguilla (UK), St. Jean, St. Croix (USA), ST. KITTS AND NEVIS, Montserrat (UK), Barbuda, ANTIGUA AND BARBUDA, Antigua, Grande Terre, Guadeloupe (Fr.), Marie Galante, DOMINICA, Le Diamant, Martinique (Fr.), ST. LUCIA, BARBADOS, ST. VINCENT AND THE GRENADINES, St. Vincent, GRENADA, Grand Anse Beach, Tobago, TRINIDAD AND TOBAGO, Trinidad, Port-of-Spain, Windward Islands, Lesser Antilles, CARIBBEAN SEA, Puerto Rico (USA), San Juan, Liquilla Beach, La Romana, Santo Domingo, DOMINICAN REPUBLIC, HAITI, Port-au-Prince, West Indies, Netherland Antilles, Aruba (Neth.), Curaçao (Neths.), Bonaire (Neths.), Mayaguana, Crooked I., Acklins I., Long Island, Great Exuma, Great Inagua, Turks and Caicos Is., Windward Passage, THE BAHAMAS, Santa Lucia, Cayo Santa Maria, Varadero, Cayo Largo, CUBA, Havana, Isla de la Juventud, Cayman Islands (UK), Grand Cayman, Seven Mile Beach, Greater Antilles, JAMAICA, Montego Bay, Negril Beach, Kingston

Montego Bay, Jamaica

Scale 1 : 40 000 000 (main map)

Main map labels:

ATLANTIC OCEAN, PACIFIC OCEAN, CANADA, UNITED STATES, MEXICO, ROCKY MOUNTAINS, Baja California, Gulf of Mexico, Great Lakes, Arctic Circle, Tropic of Cancer

L'Anse aux Meadows, Gros Morne, Cape Breton Highlands National Park, Louisbourg, Halifax, Bay of Fundy, Quebec, Montreal, White Mts., Mont Tremblant, Chromedome Mountain, Killington, Boston, New York, Six Flags Hurricane Harbour, Washington D.C., Niagara Falls, Mont Rolland, Haliburton, Muskoka, Paramount Canada's Wonderland, Cedar Point, Chicago, Kings Island, Kings Dominion, Fort Sumter, Great Smoky Mountains, Blue Ridge, National Museum, Six Flags Over Georgia, Walt Disney World, Universal Studios, Everglades National Park, Memphis, New Orleans, Astro World, Houston, Six Flags Fiesta Texas, Alamo, Monterrey, Guadalajara, San Miguel de Allende, Querétaro, Teotihuacán, Mexico City, Morelia, Lago de Pátzcuaro, Oaxaca, Puerto Escondido, Acapulco, Lago de Chapala, Mazatlán, San Blas, Guaymas, Puerto Vallarta, Chihuahua, Cancún, Isla de Cozumel, Chichén Itzá, Yucatán Peninsula, Tulum, Uxmal, Palenque, San Cristóbal de las Casas, Tula

Six Flags Great America, Grand Ole Opry, Camp Snoopy, Fort Garry, Wapusk National Park, Tuktut Nogait National Park, Nahanni National Park Reserve, Wood Buffalo National Park, Columbia Icefield, Canadian Rocky Mountain Parks, Jasper National Park, Banff, Lake Louise, Selkirk, Glacier National Park, Little Bighorn Battlefield, Yellowstone National Park, Mount Rushmore, Copper Mountain, Rocky Mountain National Park, Winter Park, Vail, Aspen, Steamboat, Snowmass, Navajo and Apache lands, Grand Canyon National Park, Las Vegas, Death Valley, Knott's Berry Farm, Mammoth Mountain, Salt Lake City, Sun Valley, Whistler, Kluane National Park, Klondike, Vancouver, Seattle, Squaw Valley, San Francisco, Sea World, Santa Cruz, Santa Monica Beach, Universal Studios, Los Angeles, Tijuana

Kingston

Montego Bay, Jamaica

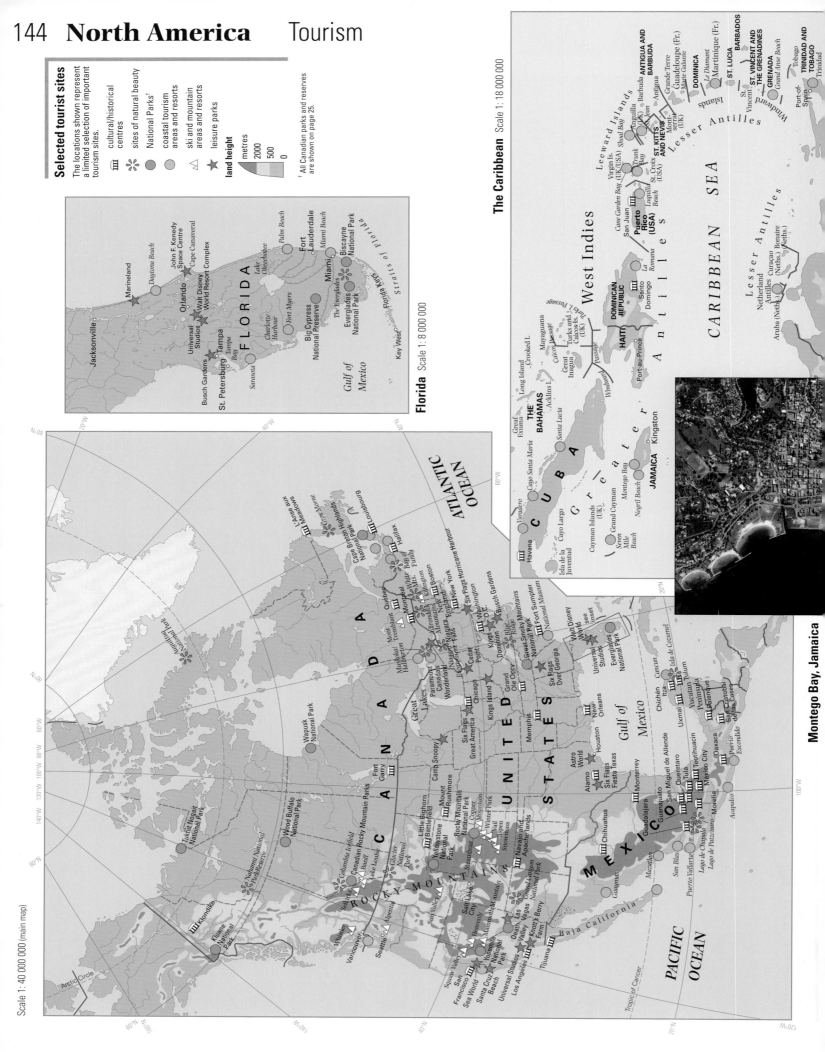

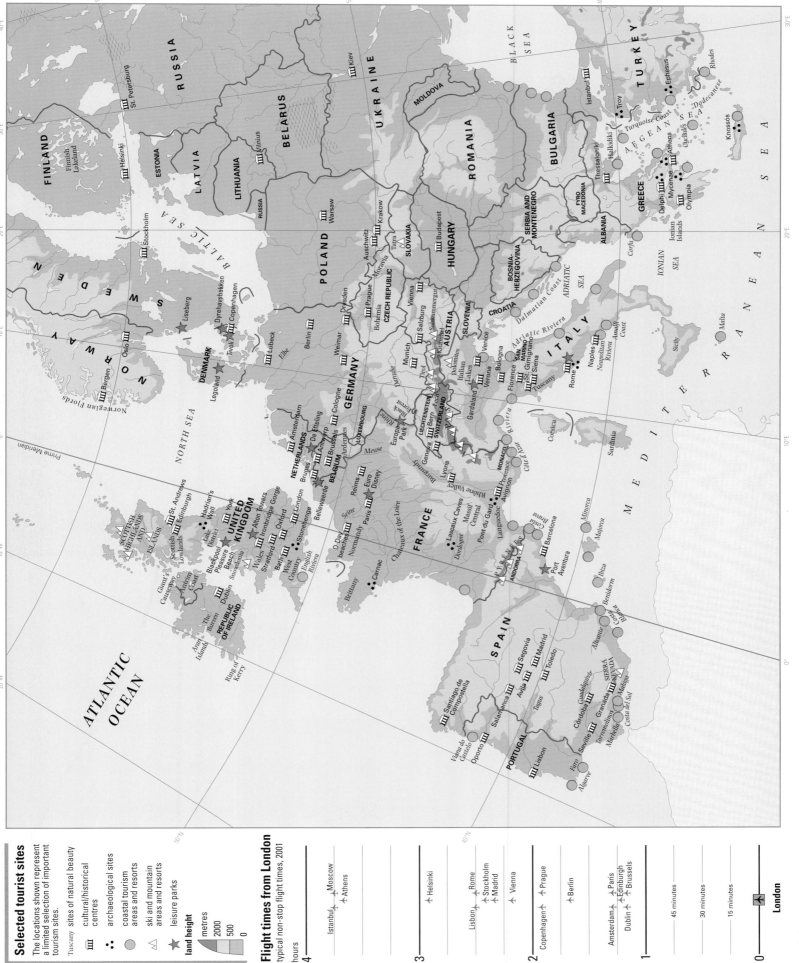

Scale 1 : 17 000 000

Selected tourist sites

The locations shown represent a limited selection of important tourism sites.

Tuscany sites of natural beauty

▦ cultural/historical centres

∴ archaeological sites

⬤ coastal tourism areas and resorts

△ ski and mountain areas and resorts

★ leisure parks

land height

metres
2000
500
0

Flight times from London

typical non-stop flight times, 2001

hours

4 ──────────

✈ Moscow
✈ Athens
Istanbul

3 ──────────

✈ Helsinki
✈ Rome
✈ Stockholm
✈ Madrid
Lisbon
✈ Vienna

2 ──────────

Copenhagen✈   ✈ Prague
✈ Berlin

Amsterdam✈ ✈ Paris
Dublin✈   ✈ Edinburgh   ✈ Brussels

1 ──────────

45 minutes ──────────

30 minutes ──────────

15 minutes ──────────

0 ────────── ✈ London

Scale 1: 55 000 000 (main map)

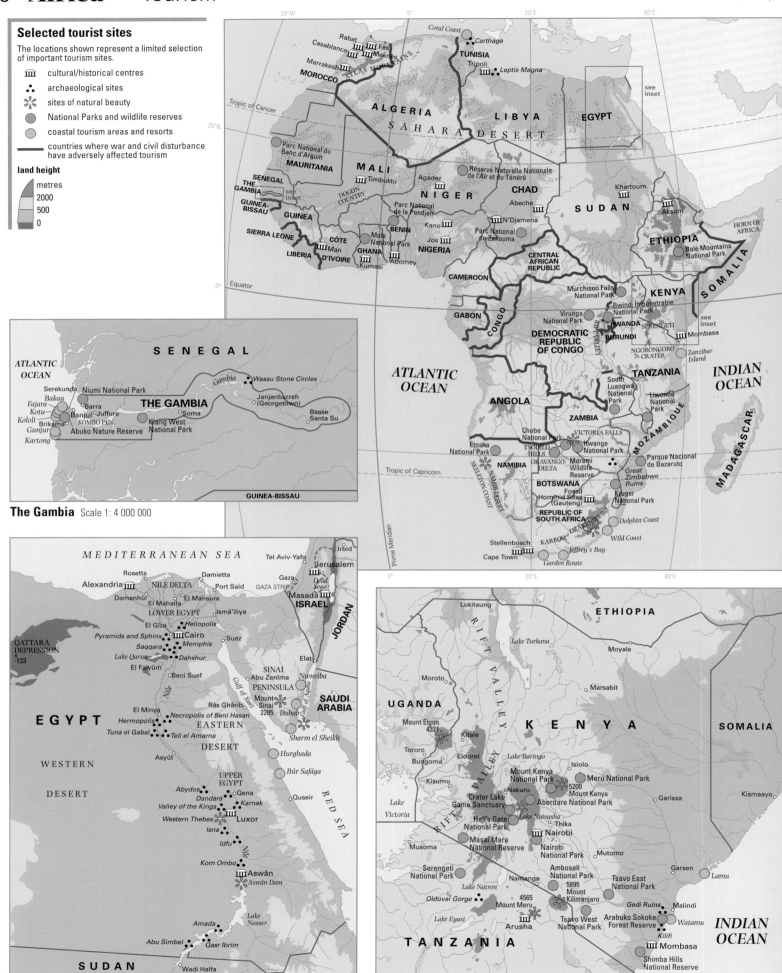

Selected tourist sites

The locations shown represent a limited selection of important tourism sites.

- 🏛 cultural/historical centres
- ⋮ archaeological sites
- ✳ sites of natural beauty
- ⬤ National Parks and wildlife reserves
- ◯ coastal tourism areas and resorts
- ▬▬ countries where war and civil disturbance have adversely affected tourism

land height

metres
2000
500
0

The Gambia Scale 1: 4 000 000

Nile Valley and Eastern Egypt Scale 1: 10 000 000

Kenya Scale 1: 10 000 000

Zenithal Equal Area Projection   © Oxford University Press

Land

1. Land and Freshwater Area

Province or Territory	Total Area (km²)	Land (km²)	Fresh Water (km²)	% of Total Area
Newfoundland & Labrador	405 212	373 872	31 340	4.1
Prince Edward Island	5 660	5 660	—	0.1
Nova Scotia	55 284	53 338	1 946	0.6
New Brunswick	72 908	71 450	1 458	0.7
Quebec	1 542 056	1 365 128	176 928	15.4
Ontario	1 076 395	917 741	158 654	10.8
Manitoba	647 797	553 556	94 241	6.5
Saskatchewan	651 036	591 670	59 366	6.5
Alberta	661 848	642 317	19 531	6.6
British Columbia	944 735	925 186	19 549	9.5
Yukon	482 443	474 391	8 052	4.8
Northwest Territories	1 346 106	1 183 085	163 021	13.5
Nunavut	2 093 190	1 936 113	157 077	21.0
Canada	**9 984 670**	**9 093 507**	**891 163**	**100.0**

— = nil

SOURCE: Adapted from the Statistics Canada website <http://www.statcan.ca/english/Pgdb/phys01.htm>, "Land and Freshwater Area".

Population

3. Total Population Growth, 1851 to 2001

Year	Population (000)	Average Annual Rate of Population Growth (%)
1851	2 436.3	—
1861	3 229.6	2.9
1871	3 689.3	1.3
1881	4 324.8	1.6
1891	4 833.2	1.1
1901	5 371.3	1.1
1911	7 206.6	3.0
1921	8 787.9	2.0
1931	10 376.8	1.7
1941	11 506.7	1.0
1951[1]	14 009.4	1.7
1961	18 238.2	2.5
1971	21 568.3	1.5
1981	24 343.2	1.1
1991	27 296.9	1.5
2001[2]	30 007.1	1.0

— = nil

[1]Newfoundland included for the first time. [2]Data from Statistics Canada 2001 Census.
SOURCE: Adapted from the Statistics Canada publication "Canada Year Book", Catalogue 11-402, 1992.

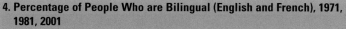

4. Percentage of People Who are Bilingual (English and French), 1971, 1981, 2001

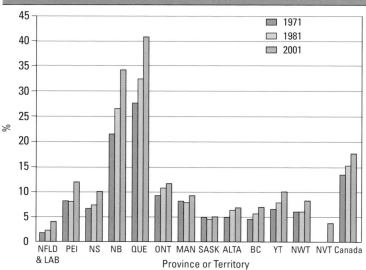

SOURCE: Adapted from the Statistics Canada website <http://www.statcan.ca/Daily/English/971202/d971202.htm>, "English-French Bilingualism Rate".

2. Primary Land Cover in Canada

Land Cover Class	Predominant Cover in the Class	Area[1] (000 km²)	% of Canada Total
Forest and taiga	Closed canopy forest and/or open stands of trees with secondary occurrences of wetland, barren land, or others	4 218	42.2
Tundra/sparse vegetation	Well-vegetated to sparsely vegetated or barren land, mostly in arctic or alpine environments	2 303	23.0
Wetland	Treed and non-treed fens, bogs, swamps, marshes, shallow open water, and coastal and shore marshes	1 396	14.0
Fresh water	Lakes, rivers, streams, and reservoirs	891	8.9
Cropland	Cropland, pasture land and orchards	681	6.6
Rangeland	Generally nonfenced pasture land, grazing land; includes natural grassland that is not necessarily used for agriculture	203	2.0
Ice/snow	Permanent ice and snow fields (glaciers, ice caps)	199	2.0
Built-up	Urban and industrial land	94	1.0
Total		**9 985**	**100.0**

NOTE: Data for this table are derived from satellite imagery and may deviate slightly from other sources of data. [1]Includes the area of all land and fresh water.
SOURCE: Adapted from a variety of sources (1991 to 2002) including the Environment Canada publication *The State of Canada's Environment* and the Statistics Canada website <http://www.statcan.ca/english/Pgdb/phys01.htm>, "Land and Freshwater Area".

5. Population by Mother Tongue,[1] 1991, 1996, 2001

Official Language	1991	1996	2001
English	16 169 875	16 890 615	17 352 315
French	6 502 860	6 636 660	6 703 325
Non-Official Language			
Chinese	498 845	715 640	853 745
Indo-Iranian[2]	301 335	430 485	627 860
Italian	510 990	484 500	469 485
German	466 245	450 140	438 080
Spanish	177 425	212 890	245 500
Portuguese	212 090	211 290	213 815
Polish	189 815	213 410	208 375
Arabic	107 750	148 555	199 940
Aboriginal	172 610	186 935	187 675
Tagalog (Filipino)	99 715	133 215	174 060
Ukrainian	187 010	162 695	148 090
Dutch	149 870	143 705	128 670
Vietnamese	78 570	106 515	122 055
Greek	126 205	121 180	120 365
Russian	35 300	57 495	94 555
Tamil	30 535	66 835	92 010
Korean	36 185	54 540	85 070
Hungarian	79 770	77 235	75 555
Croatian	39 660	50 105	54 880
Finnish	27 705	24 735	22 405
Total single response	26 686 850	28 125 560	29 257 885
Total multiple response	307 190	402 560	381 145
Canada	**26 994 045**	**28 528 125**	**29 639 035**

NOTE: Data is listed in order of 2001 population values.
[1]The mother tongue is the language learned at home in childhood and still understood by the individual at the time of the census. Also note that "mother tongue" is the official term used in the census. [2]Includes the following principal languages: Punjabi (271 220), Persian (Farsi) (94 095), and Urdu (80 895).
SOURCE: Adapted from the Statistics Canada 1991, 1996, and 2001 Census.

6. Population Growth, 1961, 1971, 1981, 1991, 2001, and Population Density, 2001, by Province and Territory

Province or Territory	1961	1971	1981	1991	2001	Population Density (km²) 2001
Newfoundland & Labrador	457 853	522 104	567 181	568 474	512 930	1.3
Prince Edward Island	104 629	111 641	122 506	129 765	135 294	24.0
Nova Scotia	737 007	788 960	847 882	899 942	908 007	16.4
New Brunswick	597 936	634 557	696 403	723 900	729 498	10.0
Quebec	5 259 211	6 027 764	6 438 403	6 895 963	7 237 479	5.8
Ontario	6 236 092	7 703 106	8 625 107	10 084 885	11 410 046	10.6
Manitoba	921 686	988 247	1 026 241	1 091 942	1 119 583	1.7
Saskatchewan	925 181	926 242	968 313	988 928	978 933	1.5
Alberta	1 331 944	1 627 874	2 237 724	2 545 553	2 974 807	4.5
British Columbia	1 629 082	2 184 021	2 744 467	3 282 061	3 907 738	4.1
Yukon	14 628	18 388	23 153	27 797	28 674	0.06
Northwest Territories	22 998	34 807	45 741	57 649	37 360	0.03
Nunavut	n.a.	n.a.	n.a.	n.a.	26 745	0.01
Canada	**18 238 247**	**21 568 310**	**24 343 181**	**27 296 859**	**30 007 094**	**3.0**

n.a. = not available
SOURCE: Adapted from the Statistics Canada publications "Canada Year Book", Catalogue 11-402, various years and "A National Overview – Population and Dwelling Counts (Data Products: 1996 Census of Population)", Catalogue 93-357, 27 March 1997.

7. Interprovincial Migration, 1977 to 2000

Year(s)	NFLD & LAB	PEI	NS	NB	QUE	ONT	MAN	SASK	ALTA	BC	YT	NWT	NVT[1]
1977–81	-21 086	-1 451	-8 185	-13 680	-156 817	-60 890	-42 115	-11 729	190 719	131 176	-2 363	-3 579	n.a.
1982–86	-14 117	811	7 442	835	-67 235	165 460	-2 395	-7 057	-82 737	3 226	-2 393	-1 840	n.a.
1987–91	-11 355	-65	-607	-2 063	-45 406	28 876	-39 533	-69 397	-13 198	154 126	871	-2 249	n.a.
1992–95	-18 730	1 826	-5 454	-3 015	-37 711	-32 592	-18 977	-19 418	242	135 036	-129	-1 078	n.a.
1996[2]	-8 380	315	-246	-1 263	-14 711	-5 942	-2 638	-1 160	13 902	20 665	168	-710	n.a.
1997[3]	-9 279	-466	-3 555	-1 688	-17 789	5 149	-7 008	-3 288	33 834	5 554	-433	-1 231	n.a.
1998[3]	-7 972	-76	-1 491	-2 847	-15 674	11 118	-2 801	-327	43 381	-20 984	-1 455	-852	n.a.
1999[3]	-2 865	669	1 440	80	-13 553	16 624	-1 435	-6 230	13 985	-8 129	-577	14	-23
2000[4]	-3 534	255	-208	15	-14 724	21 940	-2 410	-8 426	21 951	-14 123	-727	-113	104

n.a. = not available
[1] Nunavut became a territory in 1999. [2] Updated postcensal estimates. [3] Updated data. [4] Preliminary data.
SOURCE: Susan Girvan, *The Canadian Global Almanac 2002*, "Where Canadians Move Within Canada", Toronto: Macmillan Canada, p.69.

8. Births, Deaths, Migration, Infant Mortality, and Life Expectancy, 2001

Demographic Category	NFLD & LAB	PEI	NS	NB	QUE	ONT	MAN	SASK	ALTA	BC	YT	NWT	NVT	Canada
Birth rate/1000	8.7	9.1	9.8	10.1	9.7	11.1	12.3	12.3	11.8	9.9	11.9	16.6	25.7	10.7
Death rate/1000	8.5	9.1	9.0	8.8	7.2	7.4	9.0	9.1	5.8	6.8	4.8	3.8	5.5	7.3
Number of immigrants (000)	0.44	0.19	1.8	0.88	36.7	150.0	4.8	1.8	16.1	39.4	0.05	0.07	0.01	252.1
Number of emigrants (000)	0.38	0.05	0.7	0.31	12.2	32.2	1.8	1.1	7.8	8.8	0.1	0.09	0.06	65.5
Interprovincial in-migration (000)	10.6	2.9	18.3	13.7	24.8	85.8	17.6	18.5	79.4	50.0	1.5	2.6	1.5	327.1
Interprovincial out-migration (000)	14.2	2.8	19.2	13.8	36.6	67.9	20.7	29.0	53.6	62.7	2.3	3.2	1.3	327.1
Infant mortality rate/1000	5.9	7.9	4.5	6.4	5.5	5.0	6.8	7.1	4.8	4.2	5.1	18.7	18.7	5.3
Life expectancy at birth (in years) [1998] M	74.8	75.0	75.1	74.9	75.3	76.6	75.2	75.6	76.4	77.0	73.4	70.3	n.a.[1]	76.1
F	80.1	79.9	80.4	81.1	81.3	81.6	80.8	81.6	81.9	82.1	78.7	75.9	n.a.[1]	81.5

n.a. = not available
[1] Life expectancy data for Nunavut is included in the Northwest Territories data.
SOURCE: Adapted from the Statistics Canada website <http://www.statcan.ca/Daily/English/010523/d010525e.htm>, 23 May 2001 and from the Statistics Canada publication "Annual Demographic Statistics", 2001, Catalogue 91-213.

9. Composition of Canadian Families, 1971, 1981, 1991, 1996, 2001

Family Type	1971 Number of Families (000)	1971 %	1981 Number of Families (000)	1981 %	1991 Number of Families (000)	1991 %	1996 Number of Families (000)	1996 %	2001 Number of Families (000)	2001 %
Without children at home	1 545	30.5	2 013	31.8	2 580	35.1	2 730	34.8	3 059	36.5
With children at home[1]	3 526	69.5	4 312	68.2	4 776	64.9	5 108	65.2	5 312	63.5
One child	1 045	20.6	1 580	25.0	1 945	26.4	2 106	26.9	2 285	27.3
Two children	1 077	21.2	1 648	26.1	1 927	26.2	2 047	26.1	2 087	24.9
Three children	677	13.4	730	11.5	691	9.4	729	9.3	939[2]	11.2[2]
Four children	367	7.2	243	3.8	165	2.2	175	2.2	n.a.	n.a.
Five children or more	186	3.7	70	1.1	33	0.4	51	0.7	n.a.	n.a.
Total families[3]	**5 071**	**100.0**	**6 325**	**100.0**	**7 356**	**100.0**	**7 838**	**100.0**	**8 371**	**100.0**

NOTE: Entries may not add to totals in all cases due to statistical discrepancies.
n.a. = not available
[1] In 1971, 9.3% of all families with children were lone parent families; by 2001, this had risen to 15.7%. [2] Refers to 3 or more children; further breakdown not available. [3] Based on the census family definition: a husband and wife (without children or with children who never married) or a parent with one or more children who never married, living together in the same home.
SOURCE: Adapted from JR Colombo, *The Canadian Global Almanac 1997*, Toronto: Macmillan Canada, November 1996 and the Statistics Canada publication "Number of Children at Home (8) and Family Structure (7) for Census Families in Private Households, for Canada, Provinces, Territories, Census Metropolitan Areas and Census Agglomerations, 2001 Census – 20% Sample Data", Catalogue 95F0312, 22 October 2002.

10. Components of Population Growth, 1960 to 2001

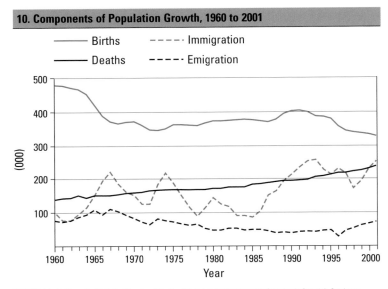

SOURCE: Adapted from the Statistics Canada publication "Report on the Demographic Situation in Canada", Catalogue 91-209, various years.

11. Aging of the Canadian Population, 1921 to 2001 (%)

Year	Age 0–64	65 and Over	Ratio of 65 and Over to 0–64	Average Annual Change
1921	95.2	4.8	5.0	—
1931	94.4	5.6	5.9	0.86
1941	93.3	6.7	7.1	1.27
1951	92.2	7.8	8.4	1.26
1956	92.3	7.7	8.4	-0.04
1961	92.4	7.6	8.3	-0.25
1966	92.3	7.7	8.3	0.15
1971	91.9	8.1	8.8	0.93
1976	91.3	8.7	9.5	1.48
1981	90.3	9.7	10.7	2.40
1986	89.3	10.7	11.9	2.38
1991	88.4	11.6	13.1	2.42
1996	87.8	12.2	13.8	2.60
2001	87.0	13.0	14.9	2.04

— = nil
SOURCE: Adapted from the Statistics Canada publications "Age, Sex and Marital Status", 1991, Catalogue 93-310, 6 July 1992 and "Report on the Demographic Situation in Canada", Catalogue 91-209, 1991 and 2001.

12. Average Total Income by Selected Family Types, 1991 and 2000

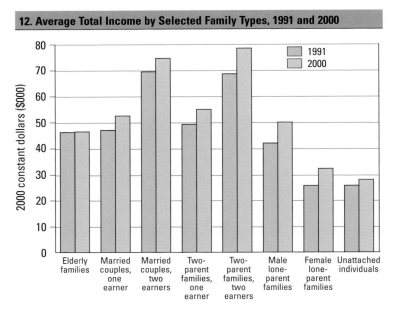

SOURCE: Adapted from the Statistics Canada publication "Income in Canada", Catalogue 75-202, 2000, pp.11 and 36.

13. Total Population by Aboriginal Identity,[1] 2001

Province or Territory	Aboriginal Population[2]	North American Indian	Métis	Inuit
Newfoundland & Labrador	18 775	7 040	5 480	4 560
Prince Edward Island	1 345	1 035	220	20
Nova Scotia	17 010	12 920	3 135	350
New Brunswick	16 990	11 495	4 290	155
Quebec	79 400	51 125	15 855	9 530
Ontario	188 315	131 560	48 340	1 375
Manitoba	150 045	90 340	56 800	340
Saskatchewan	130 185	83 745	43 695	235
Alberta	156 225	84 995	66 060	1 090
British Columbia	170 025	118 295	44 265	800
Yukon	6 540	5 600	535	140
Northwest Territories	18 730	10 615	3 580	3 910
Nunavut	22 720	95	55	22 560
Canada	**976 305**	**608 850**	**292 305**	**45 070**

[1]The Aboriginal identity population comprises those persons who reported identifying with at least one Aboriginal group, that is, North American Indian, Métis, or Inuit, and/or who reported being a Treaty Indian or a Registered Indian, as defined by the *Indian Act* of Canada, and/or who reported being a member of an Indian Band or First Nation. [2]Includes the Aboriginal groups (North American Indian, Métis, and Inuit), multiple Aboriginal responses, and Aboriginal responses not included elsewhere.
SOURCE: Adapted from the Statistics Canada publication "Aboriginal Identity (8), Age Groups (11B) and Sex (3) for Population, for Canada, Provinces, Territories, Census Metropolitan Areas and Census Agglomerations, 2001 Census – 20% Sample Data", Catalogue 97F0011, 21 January 2003.

14. Status Indian Population,[1] 2000

Province or Territory	Number of Bands	On Reserve	On Crown Land	Off Reserve	Total Indian Population
Atlantic Provinces	31	17 053	22	9 322	26 397
Quebec	39	43 046	1 228	19 041	63 315
Ontario	126	76 872	1 474	75 600	153 946
Manitoba	62	68 357	1 737	37 052	107 146
Saskatchewan	70	52 291	1 802	52 018	106 111
Alberta	44	53 641	2 904	28 828	85 373
British Columbia	198	56 359	442	53 728	110 529
Yukon	16	699	3 173	3 761	7 633
Northwest Territories[2]	26	238	10 655	4 156	15 049
Canada	**612**	**368 556**	**23 437**	**283 506**	**675 499**

[1]Status Indians are those individuals registered with Indian and Northern Affairs Canada under the *Indian Act*. [2]Any Status Indians living in Nunavut are included in the totals for the Northwest Territories.
SOURCE: Susan Girvan, *The Canadian Global Almanac 2002*, "Status Indian Population, 2000", Toronto: Macmillan Canada, p.48.

15. Largest Aboriginal Bands in Canada, 2000

Band, Province	Population[1]
Six Nations of the Grand River,[2] ONT	20 876
Mohawks of Akwesasne, ONT	9 500
Blood, ALTA	9 051
Kahnawake, QUE	8 888
Saddle Lake, ALTA	7 648
Lac La Ronge, SASK	7 126
Peguis, MAN	7 077
Mohawks of the Bay of Quinte, ONT	7 046
Peter Ballantyne Cree Nation, SASK	6 901
Wikwemikong, ONT	6 479

[1]Registered Indian population as of 31 December 2000. [2]This Six Nations Band consists of the following 13 registry groups: Bay of Quinte Mohawk, Bearfoot Onondaga, Deleware, Konadaha Seneca, Lower Cayuga, Lower Mohawk, Nibarondasa Seneca, Oneida, Onondaga Clear Sky, Tuscarora, Upper Cayuga, Upper Mohawk, Walker Mohawk.
SOURCE: Susan Girvan, *The Canadian Global Almanac 2002*, "Largest Native Bands in Canada, 2000", Toronto: Macmillan Canada, p.48.

16. Population by Ethnic Origin, 2001[1] (000)

Ethnic Origin	NFLD & LAB	PEI	NS	NB	QUE	ONT	MAN	SASK	ALTA	BC	YT	NWT	NVT	Canada
British Isles	266.0	84.3	491.6	302.1	547.8	4 454.0	404.6	387.5	1 267.5	1 737.2	13.7	11.5	3.8	9 971.6
European	14.7	12.8	161.6	63.0	743.5	3 882.5	529.8	517.7	1 364.1	1 423.2	10.4	7.4	1.2	8 732.0
Western European	7.7	9.3	115.8	40.6	153.8	1 447.2	259.8	311.6	733.6	700.8	5.5	3.9	0.5	3 790.0
German	6.3	5.4	89.5	27.5	88.7	965.5	200.4	275.1	576.4	500.7	4.1	3.0	0.4	2 742.8
Dutch (Netherlands)	1.4	4.1	35.0	13.4	18.0	436.0	51.4	32.3	149.2	180.6	1.0	0.8	0.1	923.3
Eastern European	2.1	1.4	20.7	6.3	130.4	980.9	236.4	207.1	507.1	422.6	3.2	2.4	0.3	2 520.8
Ukrainian	0.6	0.3	6.3	2.0	24.0	290.9	157.7	121.7	285.7	178.9	1.5	1.3	0.1	1 071.1
Polish	0.7	0.6	8.8	2.4	47.0	386.1	73.9	51.5	137.6	107.3	0.6	0.7	0.1	817.1
Southern European	3.3	1.3	21.1	9.8	409.1	1 445.9	44.4	17.2	132.1	245.1	1.1	0.9	0.2	2 331.3
Italian	1.2	0.6	11.2	5.6	249.2	781.4	18.6	7.6	67.7	126.4	0.5	0.4	0.1	1 270.4
Portuguese	0.7	0.1	2.4	1.2	48.8	248.3	11.1	1.0	13.9	30.1	0.08	0.09	0.05	357.7
Other European	3.0	1.5	14.9	10.3	101.8	412.2	83.7	104.1	277.2	321.8	2.6	1.5	0.4	1 334.9
Scandinavian	2.4	1.2	9.8	8.3	13.4	147.1	64.8	98.4	247.2	260.8	2.3	1.3	0.3	857.2
Jewish	0.4	0.2	3.9	1.4	82.5	196.3	15.1	2.1	15.4	31.3	0.1	0.06	0.01	348.6
French[2]	27.8	29.9	155.2	210.3	2 123.2	1 240.1	139.4	109.9	333.7	332.6	3.9	3.9	0.8	4 710.6
East and Southeast Asian	1.7	0.4	6.5	3.0	132.3	840.7	53.3	16.5	184.3	547.3	0.7	1.1	0.1	1 787.7
Chinese	1.1	0.2	3.7	2.1	63.0	518.6	14.3	9.3	108.1	373.8	0.3	0.3	0.05	1 094.7
Filipino	0.3	0.04	0.8	0.4	19.7	165.0	31.7	3.3	36.2	69.4	0.3	0.5	0.04	327.6
Aboriginal	28.1	2.7	33.4	28.5	159.9	308.1	160.3	135.0	199.0	216.1	7.0	19.0	22.9	1 319.9
South Asian	1.1	0.1	3.5	1.7	62.6	592.5	14.1	4.2	72.4	210.4	0.2	0.2	0.03	963.2
East Indian	0.9	0.1	2.9	1.3	34.1	413.4	12.1	3.3	61.2	183.7	0.2	0.2	0.03	713.3
Pakistani	0.03	0	0.3	0.07	8.0	52.8	0.6	0.5	5.5	6.3	0	0	0	74.0
Caribbean	0.3	0.3	2.7	1.1	108.5	347.9	8.3	1.8	17.3	15.6	0.1	0.1	0.04	503.8
Arab	0.9	0.7	9.4	3.1	135.8	149.5	3.2	2.4	28.0	14.9	0.05	0.1	0.02	348.0
African	0.5	0.2	10.4	2.2	48.7	173.7	7.5	3.5	22.6	25.0	0.07	0.2	0.1	294.7
Latin, Central, and South American	0.08	0.1	1.0	0.6	65.2	114.7	7.0	2.4	21.6	31.6	0.08	0.06	0.01	244.4
West Asian	0.1	0.04	1.1	0.4	41.0	118.8	1.7	0.9	9.0	31.8	0.05	0.06	0.02	205.0
Oceania	0.05	0.08	0.7	0.2	1.2	12.1	1.0	0.7	8.1	24.3	0.1	0.07	0	48.6
Total[3]	**508.1**	**133.4**	**897.6**	**719.7**	**7 125.6**	**11 285.6**	**1 103.7**	**963.2**	**2 941.2**	**3 868.9**	**28.5**	**37.1**	**26.7**	**29 639.0**

NOTE: Due to rounding, individual values may not add up to totals.
[1]Includes both single and multiple responses. This means that the values shown indicate the number of respondents who reported each ethnic origin, either as their only response or in addition to one or more other ethnic origins. Total responses represent the sum of single responses and multiple responses received in the census. [2]Includes both French and Acadian origins. [3]Represents total population. The sum of specific groups is not equal to the total population due to multiple counts.
SOURCE: Adapted from the Statistics Canada publication "Ethnic Origin (232), Sex (3), and Single and Multiple Responses (3) for Population, for Canada, Provinces, Territories, Census Metropolitan Areas and Census Agglomerations, 2001 Census – 20% Sample Data", Catalogue 97F0010, 21 January 2003.

17. Population by Sex and Age Group, 2001 (000)

Sex and Age Group	NFLD & LAB	PEI	NS	NB	QUE	ONT	MAN	SASK	ALTA	BC	YT	NWT	NVT	Canada
Male	**251.0**	**65.8**	**439.1**	**356.7**	**3 532.8**	**5 577.1**	**549.6**	**481.8**	**1 486.6**	**1 919.1**	**14.5**	**19.1**	**13.8**	**14 706.9**
0–4	12.7	3.9	24.3	19.4	192.3	343.3	36.4	31.0	95.3	105.4	0.85	1.5	1.7	868.1
5–9	15.0	4.7	28.4	22.6	232.7	396.4	41.1	35.4	106.9	123.9	1.0	1.8	1.7	1 011.5
10–14	17.9	5.0	31.5	24.8	234.2	405.0	42.3	39.4	114.1	132.7	1.2	1.8	1.7	1 051.5
15–24	36.8	9.5	58.9	49.3	482.0	754.6	77.7	73.5	223.8	261.1	2.0	2.9	2.4	2 034.4
25–34	31.8	8.0	55.3	46.4	460.0	760.7	71.4	56.8	216.4	253.0	1.8	3.0	2.3	1 966.8
35–44	41.2	10.3	74.1	60.1	617.5	963.8	88.2	73.7	259.5	320.4	2.7	3.5	1.8	2 516.7
45–54	41.1	9.9	67.8	56.0	548.1	801.5	77.3	66.0	213.3	297.0	2.6	2.6	1.2	2 184.5
55–64	26.5	6.6	45.6	36.4	371.0	520.6	49.4	41.8	120.8	188.9	1.4	1.2	0.65	1 410.8
65–74	17.1	4.6	31.2	24.1	248.7	383.6	36.8	34.7	83.9	139.5	0.63	0.57	0.26	1 005.6
75–84	8.9	2.5	17.5	14.1	120.9	202.3	22.7	22.4	42.3	77.3	0.21	0.23	0.09	531.5
85+	2.0	0.73	4.6	3.6	25.6	45.3	6.5	7.0	10.4	19.8	0.06	0.05	0.02	125.6
Female	**262.0**	**69.5**	**468.9**	**372.8**	**3 704.6**	**5 833.0**	**570.0**	**497.2**	**1 488.2**	**1 988.6**	**14.2**	**18.2**	**12.9**	**15 300.3**
0–4	12.1	3.7	23.1	18.3	183.5	327.9	34.3	29.9	91.2	100.3	0.85	1.5	1.6	828.2
5–9	14.1	4.4	27.5	21.5	224.6	376.3	39.3	33.9	101.6	117.2	1.0	1.8	1.6	964.7
10–14	17.1	5.0	30.3	23.5	224.5	383.9	40.4	37.6	108.6	126.6	1.1	1.7	1.6	1 001.7
15–24	36.5	9.5	59.0	48.1	467.5	733.3	75.6	70.7	214.3	253.2	1.9	2.8	2.3	1 974.7
25–34	34.8	8.5	60.0	48.4	461.8	797.8	71.8	58.3	213.8	265.6	2.1	3.1	2.3	2 028.2
35–44	44.0	11.0	78.3	62.1	626.5	995.7	89.0	75.6	259.0	335.8	3.0	3.4	1.7	2 584.9
45–54	41.9	10.2	70.5	57.1	561.9	833.7	78.5	64.9	207.6	302.7	2.5	2.3	1.1	2 234.8
55–64	26.5	6.6	47.0	36.5	390.0	543.4	50.7	42.8	120.3	190.6	1.1	1.0	0.57	1 457.3
65–74	18.4	5.1	35.5	28.0	298.5	434.5	41.8	37.9	89.3	147.2	0.52	0.49	0.17	1 137.2
75–84	12.4	3.9	26.9	21.0	197.2	301.7	34.2	31.5	60.1	109.0	0.24	0.22	0.06	798.4
85+	4.3	1.8	10.9	8.3	68.9	104.8	14.5	14.1	22.5	40.2	0.08	0.09	0.01	290.3

SOURCE: Adapted from the Statistics Canada publication "Age Groups (12) and Sex (3) for Population, for Canada, Provinces and Territories, 1921 to 2001 Censuses – 100% Data", Catalogue 97F0003, 16 July 2002.

18. Population of Census Metropolitan Areas, 1961, 1971, 1981, 1991, 2001

Census Metropolitan Area	Area (km²) 1996	1961	1971	1981	1991	2001
Toronto	5 868	1 919 409	2 628 043	3 130 392	3 893 046	4 682 897
Montreal	4 024	2 215 627	2 743 208	2 862 286	3 127 242	3 426 350
Vancouver	2 821	826 798	1 082 352	1 268 183	1 602 502	1 986 965
Ottawa–Hull[1]	5 686	457 038	602 510	743 821	920 857	1 063 664
Calgary	5 083	279 062	403 319	625 966	754 033	951 395
Edmonton	9 536	359 821	495 702	740 882	839 924	937 845
Quebec	3 150	379 067	480 502	583 820	645 550	682 757
Winnipeg	4 078	476 543	540 262	592 061	652 354	671 274
Hamilton	1 358	401 071	498 523	542 095	599 760	662 401
London	2 105	226 669	286 011	326 817	381 522	432 451
Kitchener	824	154 864	226 846	287 801	356 421	414 284
St. Catharines–Niagara	1 400	257 796	303 429	342 645	364 552	377 009
Halifax	2 508	193 353	222 637	277 727	320 501	359 183
Victoria	633	155 763	195 800	241 450	287 897	311 902
Windsor	862	217 215	258 643	250 885	262 075	307 877
Oshawa	894	n.a.	120 318	186 446	240 104	296 298
Saskatoon	5 322	95 564	126 449	175 058	210 023	225 927
Regina	3 422	113 749	140 734	173 226	191 692	192 800
St. John's	790	106 666	131 814	154 835	171 859	172 918
Sudbury	2 612	127 446	155 424	156 121	157 613	155 601
Chicoutimi–Jonquière[1]	1 723	127 616	133 703	158 229	160 928	154 938
Sherbrooke	979	n.a.	n.a.	125 183	139 194	153 811
Kingston	1 629	n.a.	n.a.	n.a.	136 401	146 838
Trois-Rivières	872	n.a.	n.a.	125 343	136 303	137 507
Saint John	3 509	98 083	106 744	121 012	124 981	122 678
Thunder Bay	2 295	102 085	112 093	121 948	124 427	121 986

NOTE: Data is listed in order of 2001 population values.
n.a. = not available
[1]Since this information was published by Statistics Canada, Chicoutimi–Jonquière has been renamed Saguenay and Ottawa–Hull has been renamed Ottawa–Gatineau.
SOURCE: Adapted from the Statistics Canada publication "Canada Year Book", Catalogue 11-402, various years.

19. Employment, Unemployment, and Participation Rates,[1] 2001

Province[2]	Population Over 15 Years (000)	Labour Force (000)	Employed (000)	Unemployed (000)	Participation Rate (%)	Unemployment Rate (%)
Newfoundland & Labrador	439.4	251.9	211.3	40.6	57.3	16.1
Prince Edward Island	110.5	74.7	65.9	8.9	67.6	11.9
Nova Scotia	751.6	468.9	423.3	45.6	62.4	9.7
New Brunswick	605.7	376.7	334.4	42.2	62.2	11.2
Quebec	5 984.6	3 806.9	3 474.5	332.3	63.6	8.7
Ontario	9 455.4	6 364.4	5 962.7	401.6	67.3	6.3
Manitoba	862.4	587.1	557.9	29.3	68.1	5.0
Saskatchewan	761.7	501.5	472.4	29.2	65.8	5.8
Alberta	2 366.7	1 710.7	1 632.1	78.7	72.3	4.6
British Columbia	3 279.9	2 103.5	1 942.4	161.1	64.1	7.7
Canada	**24 617.8**	**16 246.3**	**15 076.8**	**1 169.6**	**66.0**	**7.2**

[1]The participation rate is the percentage of the population (over 15 years of age) in the labour force and includes both employed and unemployed. [2]Data for the three territories is not available.
SOURCE: Adapted from the Statistics Canada website <http://www.statcan.ca/english/Pgdb/labor07a.htm>, "Labour Force, Employed and Unemployed, Numbers and Rates".

20. Distribution of Employed People by Industry and by Province, 2001

Province[1]	Employees (000)										
	All Industries	Agriculture	Forestry, Fishing, Mining, Oil and Gas	Utilities	Construction	Manufacturing	Trade	Transportation and Warehousing	Finance, Insurance, Real Estate and Leasing	Public Administration	Other
Newfoundland & Labrador	211.3	1.0	14.9	2.8	10.9	16.4	39.6	12.4	7.9	15.8	89.6
Prince Edward Island	65.9	4.0	2.8	0.2	4.7	6.3	10.0	2.4	2.1	5.8	27.5
Nova Scotia	423.3	7.3	13.6	2.6	25.7	43.5	77.0	21.2	20.1	25.9	186.3
New Brunswick	334.4	6.0	12.0	4.6	19.2	39.0	55.0	19.0	12.8	21.8	145.1
Quebec	3 474.5	59.8	39.0	28.3	139.6	642.5	557.7	173.4	183.8	209.1	1 441.3
Ontario	5 962.7	83.7	37.8	49.7	343.3	1 087.6	923.7	276.2	394.5	274.8	2 491.3
Manitoba	557.9	30.0	6.8	6.1	27.4	70.8	86.5	36.4	28.8	34.2	230.8
Saskatchewan	472.4	51.3	17.7	3.6	24.9	29.8	73.4	26.0	26.8	28.0	191.0
Alberta	1 632.1	59.5	105.2	13.4	132.7	142.3	251.2	99.4	81.5	62.3	684.5
British Columbia	1 942.4	25.9	43.3	11.7	114.9	196.2	309.5	106.9	116.2	88.8	929.0
Canada	**15 076.8**	**328.6**	**293.1**	**123.0**	**843.3**	**2 274.5**	**2 383.6**	**773.2**	**874.5**	**766.4**	**6 416.5**

[1]Data for the three territories is not available.
SOURCE: Adapted from the Statistics Canada website <http://www.statcan.ca/english/Pgdb/labor21a.htm>, "Distribution of Employed People, by Industry, by Province".

21. Employment by Industry and by Sex, 2001

Industry	Number Employed (000)		
	Both Sexes	Men	Women
Agriculture	328.6	234.0	94.6
Forestry, fishing, mining, oil and gas	293.1	246.4	46.7
Utilities	123.0	91.6	31.4
Construction	843.3	753.9	89.4
Manufacturing	2 274.5	1 635.3	639.2
Trade	2 383.6	1 234.9	1 148.6
Transportation and warehousing	773.2	586.6	186.6
Finance, insurance, real estate and leasing	874.5	355.6	518.9
Public administration	766.4	406.9	359.5
Other	6 416.5	2 564.4	3 852.1
Total all industries	**15 076.8**	**8 109.7**	**6 967.1**

SOURCE: Adapted from the Statistics Canada website <http://www.statcan.ca/english/Pgdb/labor10a.htm>, "Employment by Industry and Sex".

22. Persons in Low Income Before Tax, 1981, 1991, 1996, 2000 (000)

Persons and Age Group	1981	1991	1996	2000
All persons	**3 737**	**4 360**	**5 385**	**4 422**
Under 18 years of age	1 049	1 244	1 484	1 139
18 to 64 years of age	1 952	2 476	3 237	2 688
65 years of age and over	737	641	664	594
Persons in economic families	**2 670**	**2 983**	**3 788**	**2 915**
Under 18 years of age	1 049	1 244	1 484	1 139
18 to 64 years of age	1 359	1 586	2 112	1 648
65 years of age and over	262	153	192	128
Unattached individuals	**1 067**	**1 377**	**1 597**	**1 506**
Under 65 years of age	592	890	1 125	1 040
65 years of age and over	474	488	473	466

SOURCE: Adapted from JR Colombo, *The Canadian Global Almanac 1997*, Toronto: Macmillan Canada, November 1996 and the Statistics Canada website <www.statcan.ca/english/Pgdb/famil41b.htm>, "Persons in low income before tax".

23. Immigration by Level (Principal Applicants and Dependants), 1999 to 2001

Immigrants	1999 Number	1999 %	2000 Number	2000 %	2001 Number	2001 %
Spouse	32 823	17.28	35 246	15.51	37 709	15.06
Parents and grandparents	14 485	7.63	17 753	7.81	21 261	8.49
Others	7 958	4.19	7 542	3.32	7 674	3.07
Total family	**55 266**	**29.10**	**60 541**	**26.64**	**66 644**	**26.62**
Skilled workers	92 437	48.67	118 509	52.13	137 085	54.76
Business immigrants	13 015	6.85	13 660	6.01	14 580	5.82
Provincial/territorial nominees	477	0.25	1 253	0.55	1 274	0.51
Total economic	**105 929**	**55.77**	**133 422**	**58.69**	**152 939**	**61.09**
Live-in caregivers	3 260	1.72	2 783	1.22	2 623	1.05
Post-determination refugee claimants	189	0.10	163	0.07	82	0.03
Deferred removal orders	833	0.44	297	0.13	123	0.05
Retirees	9	0.00	0	0.00	0	0.00
Total other	**4 291**	**2.26**	**3 243**	**1.42**	**2 828**	**1.13**
Total immigrants	**165 486**	**87.13**	**197 206**	**86.75**	**222 411**	**88.84**
Government assisted refugees[1]	7 444	3.92	10 666	4.69	8 693	3.47
Privately sponsored refugees	2 330	1.23	2 912	1.28	3 570	1.43
Refugees landed in Canada	11 792	6.21	12 990	5.71	11 891	4.75
Dependants abroad[2]	2 808	1.48	3 490	1.54	3 740	1.49
Total refugees	**24 374**	**12.84**	**30 058**	**13.22**	**27 894**	**11.14**
Total immigrants/refugees	**189 860**	**99.97**	**227 264**	**99.98**	**250 305**	**99.98**
Total	**189 922**	**100.00**	**227 313**	**100.00**	**250 346**	**100.00**

[1]Includes Kosovo refugees who arrived in 1999 as part of a special movement and who obtained permanent resident status in 2000. [2]Dependants (of a refugee landed in Canada) who live abroad.
SOURCE: Adapted with the permission of the Minister of Public Works and Government Services Canada, 2003, from Citizenship and Immigration Canada web site <http://www.cic.gc.ca/English/pub/facts2001/1imm-03.html>.

24. Total Population by Visible Minority, 2001

Province or Territory	Total Population[1]	Total Visible Minorities[2]	Chinese	South Asian	Black	Filipino
Newfoundland & Labrador	508 075	3 850	920	1 005	845	260
Prince Edward Island	133 385	1 180	205	110	370	35
Nova Scotia	897 565	34 525	3 290	2 895	19 670	655
New Brunswick	719 710	9 425	1 530	1 415	3 845	355
Quebec	7 125 580	497 975	56 830	59 505	152 195	18 550
Ontario	11 285 550	2 153 045	481 505	554 870	411 090	156 515
Manitoba	1 103 700	87 115	11 930	12 880	12 820	30 490
Saskatchewan	963 150	27 580	8 085	4 090	4 165	3 025
Alberta	2 941 150	329 925	99 100	69 585	31 390	33 940
British Columbia	3 868 875	836 445	365 490	210 290	25 460	64 005
Yukon	28 520	1 020	225	205	120	235
Northwest Territories	37 100	1 545	255	190	175	235
Nunavut	26 665	210	40	25	65	35
Canada	**29 639 030**	**3 983 845**	**1 029 395**	**917 070**	**662 215**	**308 575**

[1]Counts for the non-visible minority population are not shown as a separate data column in this table but are included in the total population data for each geographic area. [2]Includes population counts for all visible minority groups, including the four groups whose counts are shown separately in this table.
SOURCE: Adapted from the Statistics Canada publication "Visible Minority Groups (15) and Sex (3) for Population, for Canada, Provinces, Territories, Census Metropolitan Areas and Census Agglomerations, 2001 Census - 20% Sample Data", Catalogue 97F0010, 21 January 2003.

25. Numbers of Immigrants and Immigration Rates, Canada, 1944 to 2000

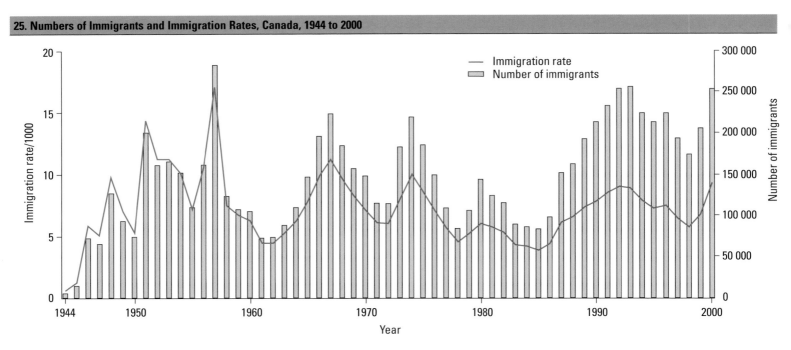

SOURCE: Adapted from the Statistics Canada publication "Report on the demographic situation in Canada", Catalogue 91-209, various years.

26. Immigration by Top Ten Source Countries and Source Area (Principal Applicants and Dependants), 1999 to 2001

Source Country	1999		2000		2001	
	Number	%	Number	%	Number	%
China, People's Republic of	29 112	15.33	36 715	16.15	40 296	16.10
India	17 429	9.18	26 086	11.48	27 812	11.11
Pakistan	9 295	4.89	14 182	6.24	15 339	6.13
Philippines	9 170	4.83	10 086	4.44	12 903	5.15
Korea, Republic of	7 216	3.80	7 626	3.35	9 604	3.84
United States	5 528	2.91	5 814	2.56	5 894	2.35
Iran	5 907	3.11	5 608	2.47	5 736	2.29
Romania	3 461	1.82	4 425	1.95	5 585	2.23
Sri Lanka	4 723	2.49	5 841	2.57	5 514	2.20
United Kingdom	4 478	2.36	4 647	2.04	5 345	2.14
Taiwan	5 464	2.88	3 511	1.54	3 111	1.24
Yugoslavia	1 490	0.78	4 723	2.08	2 786	1.11
Total for top ten only	**98 322**	**51.78**	**121 328**	**53.38**	**134 028**	**53.54**
Total other countries	**91 600**	**48.22**	**105 985**	**46.62**	**116 318**	**46.46**
Total	**189 922**	**100.00**	**227 313**	**100.00**	**250 346**	**100.00**
Source Area						
Asia and Pacific	96 437	50.78	120 539	53.03	132 711	53.01
Africa and the Middle East	33 490	17.63	40 815	17.96	48 078	19.20
Europe	38 930	20.50	42 885	18.87	43 204	17.26
South and Central America	15 221	8.01	16 944	7.45	20 129	8.04
United States	5 528	2.91	5 814	2.56	5 894	2.35
Not stated	316	0.17	316	0.14	330	0.13
Total	**189 922**	**100.00**	**227 313**	**100.00**	**250 346**	**100.00**

NOTE: Data is listed in order of 2001 values.
SOURCE: Adapted with the permission of the Minister of Public Works and Government Services Canada, 2003, from Citizenship and Immigration Canada web site <http://www.cic.gc.ca/English/pub/facts2001/1imm-05.html>.

27. Approximate Geographic Distribution of the Population

Selected Parallels of Latitude	%
South of 49°	70.0
Between 49° and 54°	27.6
Between 54° and 60°	2.1
North of 60°	0.3
Selected Distances North of Canada–US Border	
0–150 km	72.0
151–300 km	13.4
301–600 km	10.4
Over 600 km	4.2

SOURCE: Statistics Canada, various sources.

Agriculture

28. Farm Cash Receipts from Farming Operations, 2001[1] ($000)

	NFLD & LAB	PEI	NS	NB	QUE	ONT	MAN	SASK	ALTA	BC	Canada[2]
Wheat excluding durum	—	2 355	1 572	1 089	11 462	88 540	425 874	916 906	586 248	9 292	2 043 338
CWB[3] payments	—	—	—	—	—	13 968	127 049	276 628	190 979	3 581	612 205
Canola	—	—	—	—	2 381	8 276	352 436	768 525	573 792	12 854	1 718 264
Floriculture and nursery	9 729	2 171	34 606	46 414	174 996	856 877	35 766	24 321	112 610	400 937	1 698 427
Vegetables	2 789	10 961	19 001	6 498	273 383	682 966	28 292	2 298	63 623	259 286	1 349 097
Potatoes	1 197	125 982	8 194	103 934	97 105	71 935	127 987	34 748	107 364	51 655	730 101
Corn	—	—	2 075	—	223 218	376 959	19 080	—	492	—	621 824
Barley	—	5 292	563	3 388	27 392	8 979	89 310	305 596	177 868	3 386	621 774
CWB payments	—	—	—	—	—	—	2 887	69 436	34 066	945	107 334
Soybeans	—	1 090	—	—	82 992	447 430	—	—	—	—	531 512
Durum wheat	—	—	—	—	—	—	9 401	385 984	82 669	—	478 054
CWB payments	—	—	—	—	—	—	4 647	254 045	53 736	—	312 428
Dry peas	—	—	—	—	—	—	21 776	229 059	74 590	1 284	326 709
Oats	—	451	195	523	12 623	4 389	101 300	136 016	36 337	2 396	294 230
Tobacco	—	—	—	—	16 831	244 454	—	—	—	—	261 285
Other berries and grapes	89	2 468	14 497	6 781	56 768	59 661	350	722	1 326	77 224	219 886
Hay and clover	43	578	363	388	12 770	28 900	19 955	27 433	99 400	22 606	212 436
Lentils	—	—	—	—	—	—	2 494	184 971	2 010	—	189 475
Forest products	55	937	12 838	6 482	68 341	19 347	1 172	4 562	26 007	36 940	176 681
Apples	x	x	10 262	2 253	29 557	88 133	16	x	x	44 977	175 318
Flaxseed	—	—	—	—	—	—	48 167	109 395	3 875	—	161 437
Maple products	—	—	1 184	3 384	123 181	10 666	—	—	—	—	138 415
Total crops	**15 748**	**154 647**	**122 566**	**192 357**	**1 309 295**	**3 159 825**	**1 487 182**	**3 849 844**	**2 290 583**	**1 010 936**	**13 592 978**
Cattle	2 078	25 435	32 484	32 237	241 627	1 126 077	505 909	812 268	3 920 815	264 875	6 963 805
Dairy	27 173	52 484	95 861	68 251	1 543 895	1 369 058	157 999	114 736	348 378	364 478	4 142 313
Hogs	1 237	33 528	38 991	38 229	1 130 021	954 995	785 471	251 932	570 062	46 722	3 851 188
Hens and chickens	x	x	55 162	44 440	421 392	491 060	63 347	45 350	132 120	228 180	1 508 066
Calves	232	420	2 390	2 290	200 992	96 744	94 814	343 548	30 899	79 971	852 300
Eggs	10 580	3 380	23 709	15 746	96 964	220 580	61 794	21 577	40 515	70 559	565 404
Miscellaneous livestock	x	x	2 001	1 705	40 774	89 242	33 469	49 368	51 373	33 296	302 289
Turkeys	x	x	6 497	4 169	57 955	114 944	17 270	9 361	23 718	27 778	261 761
Total livestock	**65 478**	**123 179**	**280 793**	**212 724**	**3 771 364**	**4 551 286**	**1 819 396**	**1 694 920**	**5 188 716**	**1 143 148**	**18 851 004**
Insurance, stabilization, and other payments	712	58 542	17 531	6 412	607 992	777 175	382 147	1 022 437	819 427	59 863	3 752 238
Total receipts	**81 938**	**336 368**	**420 890**	**411 493**	**5 688 651**	**8 488 286**	**3 688 725**	**6 567 201**	**8 298 726**	**2 213 947**	**36 196 220**

x = confidential to meet secrecy requirements of the Statistics Act; — = nil
[1]Those listed have total production exceeding $60 million. [2]Information about the territories is excluded because of the small number of farms. [3]Canadian Wheat Board.
SOURCE: Adapted from the Statistics Canada publication "Agriculture Economic Statistics", May 2002, Catalogue 21-603, 28 June 2002, p.54.

29. Cash Receipts and Net Income from Farming by Province, 1983, 1989, 1995, 2000 ($000 000)

Province[1]	Cash Receipts				Net Income[2]			
	1983	1989	1995	2000	1983	1989	1995	2000
Newfoundland & Labrador	35	58	67	73	5	11	12	10
Prince Edward Island	172	256	311	326	25	78	87	42
Nova Scotia	236	315	329	414	26	72	53	87
New Brunswick	200	272	287	366	31	66	45	60
Quebec	2 710	3 649	4 379	5 423	485	918	1 074	1 215
Ontario	4 990	5 663	6 158	7 579	811	941	1 002	1 580
Manitoba	1 798	2 102	2 461	3 137	215	295	361	643
Saskatchewan	4 026	4 475	5 250	5 781	703	760	1 386	1 175
Alberta	3 751	4 509	5 846	7 337	412	783	1 378	1 516
British Columbia	915	1 164	1 527	2 077	38	176	206	476
Canada	**18 832**	**22 462**	**26 614**	**32 513**	**2 751**	**4 099**	**5 602**	**6 803**

[1]Information about the territories is excluded because of the small number of farms. [2]Income excludes the value of inventory change.
SOURCE: Adapted from the Statistics Canada publication "Agriculture Economic Statistics", May 2002, Catalogue 21-603, 28 June 2002.

30. Farm Cash Receipts, 2001 ($000 000)

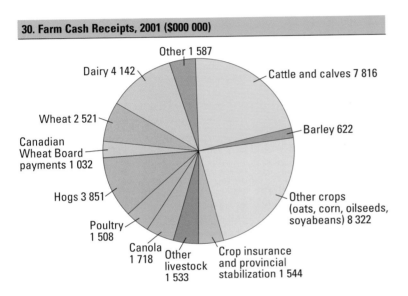

Other 1 587
Dairy 4 142
Cattle and calves 7 816
Wheat 2 521
Canadian Wheat Board payments 1 032
Barley 622
Hogs 3 851
Other crops (oats, corn, oilseeds, soyabeans) 8 322
Poultry 1 508
Canola 1 718
Other livestock 1 533
Crop insurance and provincial stabilization 1 544

Total cash receipts 2001 = 36 196

SOURCE: Adapted from the Statistics Canada website <http://www.statcan.ca/english/Pgdb/prim06.htm>, "Farm Cash Receipts".

31. Number of Farms and Average Size, 1901 to 2001

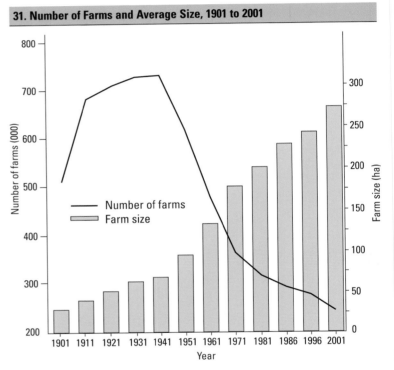

SOURCE: Adapted from the Statistics Canada 1996 and 2001 Census of Agriculture.

32. Agricultural Land Use, 2001

Province[1]	Farmland Area (000 ha)	% Change 1996 to 2001	% Classed as Class 1, 2, or 3 (1996)	Number of Farms	Average Farm Size (ha)	% Change 1986 to 2001	Cropland Area (000 ha)	Summer Fallow Area (000 ha)	Tame or Seeded Pasture (000 ha)
Newfoundland & Labrador	40.6	-7.3	0.005	643	63	+12.5	8.4	0.1	2.5
Prince Edward Island	261.5	-1.4	71.2	1 845	142	+48.0	175.5	0.2	11.8
Nova Scotia	407.0	-4.7	20.7	3 923	104	+7.2	119.2	0.6	22.9
New Brunswick	388.0	+0.5	17.9	3 034	128	+11.3	148.9	0.6	18.2
Quebec	3 417.0	-1.1	1.4	32 139	106	+20.5	1 850.0	4.9	182.9
Ontario	5 466.2	-2.7	6.8	59 728	92	+21.1	3 656.7	14.2	313.1
Manitoba	7 601.8	-1.9	8.0	21 071	361	+27.6	4 714.8	255.7	383.5
Saskatchewan	26 265.6	-1.1	25.0	50 598	519	+24.1	15 376.0	3 131.6	1 405.7
Alberta	21 067.5	+0.2	16.2	53 652	393	+9.8	9 728.2	1 235.6	2 230.9
British Columbia	2 587.1	+2.3	1.0	20 290	128	+1.6	617.5	36.8	233.0
Canada	**67 502.5**	**-0.8**	**4.6**	**246 923**	**273**	**+18.2**	**36 395.0**	**4 680.4**	**4 804.5**

[1]Information about the territories is excluded because of the small number of farms.
SOURCE: Adapted from the Statistics Canada 1996 and 2001 Census.

33. Wheat Statistics,[1] 1984 to 2000 (000 t)

	1984	1985	1986	1987	1988	1989	1990	1991	1992	1993	1994	1995	1996	1997	1998	1999	2000[2]
Carryover from previous crop year	9 190	7 598	8 569	12 731	7 305	5 032	6 442	10 285	9 803	12 193	11 117	5 940	6 633	9 047	6 009	7 435	7 739
Production	21 199	24 252	31 378	25 992	15 996	24 334	32 709	31 946	28 879	27 232	23 122	24 102	29 801	24 280	24 082	26 900	26 804
Total supply	30 389	31 850	39 947	38 723	23 301	29 366	39 151	42 253	39 967	39 452	34 242	30 042	36 646	33 378	30 171	34 349	34 604
Exports	17 542	17 683	20 783	23 519	12 413	17 418	21 913	25 376	20 328	19 304	20 761	16 198	19 366	19 996	14 722	18 313	16 756
Domestic use	5 250	5 598	6 433	7 899	5 856	5 581	6 766	7 074	7 448	9 054	7 542	7 866	8 234	7 375	8 014	8 662	8 337
Carryover at the end of the crop year	7 598	8 569	12 731	7 305	5 032	6 442	10 285	9 803	12 193	11 117	5 940	6 633	9 047	6 009	7 435	7 375	9 518

[1]The crop year begins 1 August and ends 31 July. [2]Preliminary data from the Statistics Canada publication "Grain Trade of Canada", Catalogue 22-201, 2000–2001.
SOURCE: Adapted from the Statistics Canada publication "Canada Year Book", Catalogue 11-402, various years; the Canada Grain Council publication *Statistical Handbook*, various years; and the Canadian Wheat Board publication *CWB Annual Report*, various years.

34. Canadian Bulk Wheat Exports,[1] 1990 to 2000 (000 t)

Country or Region	Average 1990 to 1999	1999/2000
Iran	1 419	3 492
Japan	1 338	1 242
United States	1 026	1 158
Mexico	551	814
Indonesia	759	693
China	3 322	661
Venezuela	279	482
Philippines	230	436
United Kingdom	266	410
Total all countries	**15 973**	**14 569**

[1]The crop year begins 1 August and ends 31 July.
SOURCE: Canada Grains Council, *Statistical Handbook 2000*. Reprinted by permission of Canada Grains Council.

35. World Wheat Production, 1990, 1995, 2000 (000 000 t)

Country or Region	1990	1995	2000
China	98.2	103.0	102.0
India	49.7	65.4	74.3
Russian Federation	108.0	30.1	67.2
United States	74.5	59.4	60.9
France	33.6	30.9	37.5
Canada	32.7	25.0	25.5
Australia	15.1	17.0	21.0
Pakistan	14.4	17.0	21.0
Turkey	20.0	15.5	17.5
Argentina	10.9	8.6	15.5
Ukraine	30.4	16.3	11.0
World total	**592.4**	**541.7**	**580.0**

NOTE: Data is listed in order of 2000 production values.
SOURCE: Adapted from the Canada Grains Council publication *Statistical Handbook*, various years and the Canadian Wheat Board publication *CWB Annual Report*, various years.

36. World Wheat Imports and Exports, 1981, 1990, 1998

Country or Region	Imports (000 000 t)			
	1981	1990	1998	10-Year Average 1989 to 1998
China	13.2	9.6	2.7[2]	10.4
Former USSR[1]	19.6	14.5	1.7	10.1
Egypt	6.0	6.0	7.1	6.5
Japan	5.6	5.5	5.6	5.7
Brazil	4.6	2.8	5.5	4.5
Iran	1.4	4.1	3.7	3.9
South Korea	1.9	4.1	3.6	3.7
Algeria	2.3	3.5	4.3	3.5
Indonesia	1.5	2.0	3.7	2.7
Pakistan	n.a.	1.1	3.6	2.3
Morocco	n.a.	1.9	2.6	1.8
Iraq	1.6	0.2	2.5	1.5
World total	**100.7**	**90.6**	**100.6**	**95.8**

Country or Region	Exports (000 000 t)			
	1981	1990	1998	10-Year Average 1989 to 1998
United States	48.8	28.3	28.0	32.5
Canada	28.5	21.9	21.1	19.2
European Union	13.9	18.5	13.0	17.5
Australia	11.4	11.9	15.1	11.7
Argentina	4.3	5.1	8.9	6.1
World total	**100.7**	**90.6**	**100.6**	**95.8**

NOTE: Data is listed in order of 10-year average values.
n.a. = not available
[1]Historical data are not available from the individual republics. [2]1997 data.
SOURCE: Adapted from the Canada Grains Council publication *Statistical Handbook*, various years and the Canadian Wheat Board publication *CWB Annual Report*, various years.

37. Natural Resources Summary, 2000

	Forestry	Minerals[1]	Energy	Total Natural Resources	Canada
Gross Domestic Product (GDP in current $ billions)	$20.8 (2.3%)	$30.4 (3.4%)	$55.2 (6.2%)	$106.4 (12.0%)	$886.9 (100%)
Direct employment (thousands of people)	373 (2.5%)	395 (2.6%)	201 (1.3%)	969 (6.5%)	14 910 (100%)
New investments (capital only) ($ billions)	$4.3 (2.4%)	$7.2 (4.0%)	$32.5 (18.2%)	$44.0 (24.7%)	$178.3 (100%)
Trade ($ billions)					
Domestic exports (excluding re-exports)	$47.4 (12.3%)	$47.3 (12.3%)	$54.4 (14.2%)	$149.1 (38.8%)	$384.1 (100%)
Imports	$10.0 (2.8%)	$49.5 (13.6%)	$18.9 (5.2%)	$78.4 (21.6%)	$363.2 (100%)
Balance of trade[2] (including re-exports)	+$37.5	-$0.9	+$35.6	+$72.2	+$54.5

[1]The minerals industry now includes mineral extraction and concentrating, smelting and refining, non-metals and metals-based semi-fabricating industries, and metals fabricating industries. Minerals include uranium mining; energy includes coal mining. [2]Balance of trade shown in this table is the merchandise balance, which represents the difference between the total exports and imports of goods. Services and capital flows are excluded.
SOURCE: Adapted from the Natural Resources Canada website <www.nrcan.gc.ca/statistics/factsheet.htm>, "Facts for 2000 as of July 2001".

Forestry and Fishing

38. Forest Land, Harvests, and Forest Fires, 1999

Province or Territory	Total Area (000 000 ha)	Area of Forest (000 000 ha)	Area of Productive Forest (000 000 ha)	Total Area Harvested (000 ha) (% Clear-cut)	Total Volume of Roundwood Harvested (000 m³)	Forest Fire Losses as a % of Productive Forest (Annual Average 1990 to 1999)
Newfoundland & Labrador	40.6	22.5	11.3	17.0 (100)	2.7	0.3
Prince Edward Island	0.6	0.3	0.3	6.0 (100)	0.7	0.2
Nova Scotia	5.5	3.9	3.8	50.0 (96)	6.2	0.2
New Brunswick	7.3	6.1	6.0	111.0 (72)	11.3	0.3
Quebec	154.1	83.9	54.0	384.0 (85)	45.6	0.6
Ontario	106.9	58.0	42.2	202.0 (94)	24.8	0.6
Manitoba	65.0	26.3	15.2	16.0 (100)	2.2	1.5
Saskatchewan	65.2	28.8	12.6	21.0 (100)	3.3	1.7
Alberta	66.1	38.2	25.7	42.0 (100)	19.4	0.5
British Columbia	94.8	60.6	51.7	176.0 (96)	77.0	0.05
Yukon	48.3	27.5	7.5	0.5 (100)	0.1	2.1
Northwest Territories[1]	342.6	61.4	14.3	0.6 (100)	0.07	1.6
Canada	**997.1**	**417.6**	**244.6**	**1 025.0 (89)**	**193.0**	**1.1**

[1]Nunavut has no forests.
SOURCE: Natural Resources Canada, *Compendium of Canadian Forestry Statistics* and *State of Canada's Forests 2002*, Catalogue FO-6/2001-2002E.

39. Wood Pulp Market in Canada, 1992 to 2001

SOURCE: Natural Resources Canada, *State of Canada's Forests 2002*, "Wood Pulp", Catalogue FO-6/2001-2002E, p.22.

40. Lumber Market in Canada, 1992 to 2001

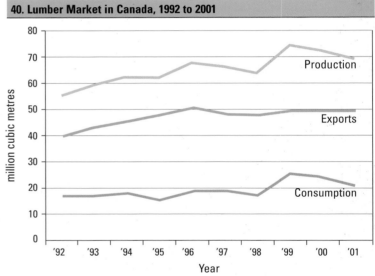

SOURCE: Natural Resources Canada, *State of Canada's Forests 2002*, "Lumber", Catalogue FO-6/2001-2002E, p.22.

41. Newsprint Market in Canada, 1992 to 2001

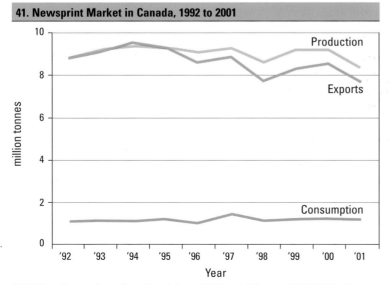

SOURCE: Natural Resources Canada, *State of Canada's Forests 2002*, "Newsprint", Catalogue FO-6/2001-2002E, p.24.

42. Exports of Forest Products, 1992 to 2001

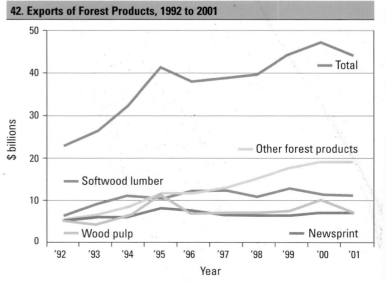

SOURCE: Natural Resources Canada, *State of Canada's Forests 2002*, "Exports of Forest Products", Catalogue FO-6/2001-2002E, p.23.

43. Fish Catches, 1994 and 2001

Species	Atlantic Coast				Pacific Coast			
	Quantity (000 t)		Value ($000 000)		Quantity (000 t)		Value ($000 000)	
	1994	2001	1994	2001	1994	2001	1994	2001
Cod	22.70	40.30	29.60	58.50	3.10	0.80	1.80	0.60
Flatfishes	15.20	25.10	18.00	21.80	6.30	5.50	4.40	6.50
Haddock	7.00	15.60	14.00	27.90	—	—	—	—
Hake	14.70	23.00	9.00	17.60	103.80	61.00	14.80	12.30
Halibut	1.30	1.70	8.00	12.10	5.30	4.50	33.60	20.60
Pollock	15.60	7.20	10.90	5.60	3.60	1.70	1.20	0.80
Redfish	50.70	19.70	15.70	12.60	14.90	21.60	12.60	29.80
Turbot	11.00	13.80	14.40	14.90	2.10	8.30	0.40	2.40
Other	6.20	11.30	4.00	7.90	8.30	11.10	32.30	31.90
Total groundfish	**144.30**	**157.60**	**123.50**	**178.70**	**147.40**	**114.20**	**101.00**	**104.90**
Herring	206.80	199.30	27.70	42.00	39.30	24.20	63.70	16.80
Mackerel	20.60	24.50	7.00	10.50	—	0.02	—	—
Salmon	0.10	—	0.70	—	65.40	22.90	195.20	30.90
Swordfish	—	1.10	—	8.50	—	—	—	—
Tuna	0.60	0.90	9.70	13.40	0.60	3.10	1.40	12.00
Other	21.90	24.50	28.70	6.70	1.00	0.20	0.80	0.80
Total pelagic	**250.10**	**250.30**	**73.70**	**81.10**	**106.70**	**50.40**	**261.30**	**59.80**
Clams	26.10	26.90	27.00	28.50	4.00	2.50	37.40	37.70
Crab	64.90	107.50	272.80	407.80	5.60	5.70	24.20	36.80
Lobster	41.40	51.40	354.20	638.70	—	—	—	—
Mussels	6.10	11.80	6.50	15.40	—	—	—	—
Oysters	2.60	3.00	4.60	7.80	5.30	—	4.20	—
Scallops	91.40	90.50	138.70	122.00	0.10	0.04	0.50	0.30
Shrimps	48.70	125.60	99.20	261.30	4.20	4.20	15.60	33.80
Other	9.50	6.30	8.50	8.60	7.20	5.10	11.60	9.20
Total shellfish	**290.70**	**423.00**	**911.60**	**1 749.80**	**26.40**	**17.60**	**93.60**	**117.80**
Total all fisheries	**717.50**	**847.80**	**1 123.30**	**1 761.40**	**280.80**	**182.70**	**473.10**	**295.20**

— = nil

SOURCE: Adapted from the Statistics Canada publication "Canada Year Book", Catalogue 11-402, 1997 and the Department of Fisheries and Oceans.

Mining

44. Production of Leading Minerals, 2001 ($000 000)

Mineral	NFLD & LAB	PEI	NS	NB	QUE	ONT	MAN	SASK	ALTA	BC	YT	NWT	NVT	Canada
Gold	20.5	—	—	3.5	452.0	1 052.0	89.8	20.3	0.3	321.9	39.5	54.0	58.8	2 112.4
Nickel	—	—	—	—	232.4	1 117.9	413.1	—	—	—	—	—	—	1 763.3
Copper	—	—	—	22.2	244.4	450.5	122.7	1.9	—	678.9	—	—	—	1 520.6
Zinc	—	—	—	429.1	362.0	104.4	131.2	1.7	—	154.6	—	—	233.4	1 416.4
Iron ore	768.3	—	—	—	x	—	—	—	—	x	—	—	—	1 155.2
Uranium	—	—	—	—	—	—	—	675.6	—	—	—	—	—	675.6
Platinum group	—	—	—	—	x	x	x	—	—	—	—	—	—	568.8
Silver	0.1	—	—	45.9	50.6	28.3	7.2	0.2	—	132.0	0.2	0.2	3.3	267.9
Lead	—	—	—	58.0	—	—	—	—	—	26.6	—	—	23.7	108.3
Cobalt	—	—	—	—	9.6	53.5	15.1	—	—	—	—	—	—	78.2
Molybdenum	—	—	—	—	—	—	—	—	—	77.1	—	—	—	77.1
Total metals	**788.8**	**—**	**—**	**562.3**	**2 157.6**	**3 388.1**	**823.9**	**699.5**	**0.3**	**1 411.8**	**39.7**	**54.2**	**319.2**	**10 245.4**
Potash (K$_2$O)	—	—	—	x	—	—	—	—	x	—	—	—	—	1 581.5
Cement	—	—	x	—	248.9	546.4	—	—	x	232.6	—	—	—	1 312.5
Sand and gravel[1]	12.1	1.3	11.7	10.4	77.3	390.3	26.9	44.9	206.4	166.7	3.4	1.8	—	953.2
Stone[1]	27.7	—	52.0	17.2	240.4	471.8	17.1	x	x	47.9	—	2.5	—	884.1
Diamonds	—	—	—	—	—	—	—	—	—	—	—	846.9	—	846.9
Salt	—	—	x	x	x	289.0	—	38.4	19.8	—	—	—	—	449.5
Peat	0.2	3.3	x	47.4	48.2	—	x	x	33.5	x	—	—	—	167.9
Asbestos	—	—	—	—	132.2	—	—	—	—	—	—	—	—	132.2
Sulphur	x	—	x	4.3	9.4	19.8	—	0.3	0.7	2.1	—	—	—	36.7
Total non-metals	**42.9**	**4.6**	**238.7**	**207.1**	**1 332.6**	**2 116.2**	**78.1**	**1 601.7**	**559.8**	**515.8**	**3.4**	**851.3**	**—**	**7 552.3**
Natural gas and by-products	—	—	972.1	—	—	69.4	—	1 242.7	30 652.2	5 447.2	54.5	58.4	—	38 496.6
Crude oil	1 971.4	—	150.7	—	—	61.1	145.7	4 287.0	18 234.8	711.0	—	379.8	—	25 941.3
Coal	—	—	53.7	19.8	—	—	—	145.0	385.4	943.0	—	—	—	1 546.8
Total fuels	**1 971.4**	**—**	**1 176.5**	**19.8**	**—**	**130.5**	**145.7**	**5 674.6**	**49 272.4**	**7 101.2**	**54.5**	**438.2**	**—**	**65 984.7**
Total all minerals	**2 803.1**	**4.6**	**1 415.2**	**789.2**	**3 490.2**	**5 634.8**	**1 047.7**	**7 975.9**	**49 832.5**	**9 028.8**	**97.7**	**1 343.7**	**319.2**	**83 782.4**

— = nil; n.a. = not available; x = confidential to meet secrecy requirements of the Statistics Act
[1]Does not include shipments to Canadian cement, lime, and clay plants.
SOURCE: Adapted from the Statistics Canada publication "Canada's Mineral Production, Preliminary Estimate", 2001, Catalogue 26-202, 18 April 2002, Table 1.

45. Mineral Reserves, 1994 to 1998

Mineral	Reserves					Production
	1994	1995	1996	1997	1998	1998
Crude petroleum (000 000 m³)[1]	1 259.0	1 383.0	1 372.0	1 387.0	1 448.0	128.5[4]
Natural gas (000 000 000 m³)[1]	2 232.2	1 897.8	1 929.0	1 841.0	1 809.0	187.2
Crude bitumen (000 000 m³)[1]	158.8	169.6	197.5	211.1	229.8	n.a.[5]
Coal (megatonnes)[1]	8 623.0	8 623.0	8 623.0	8 623.0	8 623.0	75.4
Copper (000 t)[2]	9 533.0	9 250.0	9 667.0	9 032.0	8 402.0	690.7
Nickel (000 t)[2]	5 334.0	5 832.0	5 632.0	5 122.0	5 683.0	198.0
Lead (000 t)[2]	3 861.0	3 660.0	3 450.0	2 344.0	1 845.0	150.0
Zinc (000 t)[2]	14 514.0	14 712.0	13 660.0	10 588.0	10 159.0	991.6
Molybdenum (000 t)[2]	148.0	129.0	144.0	149.0	121.0	8.1
Silver (t)[2]	19 146.0	19 073.0	18 911.0	16 697.0	15 738.0	1 140.0
Gold (t)[2]	1 513.0	1 540.0	1 510.0	1 724.0	1 415.0	164.8
Uranium (000 t)[3]	397.0	381.0	369.0	331.0	312.0	10.0

n.a. = not available

[1]Proved reserves recoverable with present technology and prices. [2]Proven and probable reserves. [3]Reserves recoverable from mineable ore. [4]Includes crude bitumen. [5]Included in the production data for crude petroleum.
SOURCE: Adapted from the Statistics Canada website <http://www.statcan.ca/english/Pgdb/phys09.htm>, "Mineral Reserves".

46. Canada's World Role as a Producer of Certain Important Minerals, 1999

Mineral	Values (% of World Total)	World Total	Rank of Five Leading Countries				
			1	2	3	4	5
Potash (K₂O equivalent) (mine production)	000 t (%)	25 849	**Canada** **8 304** **(32.1)**	CIS[1] 7 665 (29.7)	Germany 3 545 (13.7)	Israel 1 700 (6.6)	United States 1 300 (5.0)
Uranium (U concentrates) (mine production)	t (%)	31 651	**Canada** **8 214**[2] **(26.0)**	Australia 5 987 (18.9)	Niger 2 916 (9.2)	Namibia 2 687 (8.5)	Uzbekistan 2 100 (6.6)
Nickel (mine production)	000 t (%)	1 088	Russia 235 (21.6)	**Canada** **186** **(17.1)**	Australia 126 (11.6)	New Caledonia 110 (10.1)	Indonesia 89 (8.2)
Gypsum (mine production)	000 t (%)	109 686	United States 19 400 (17.7)	**Canada** **9 886** **(9.0)**	China 9 200 (8.4)	Iran 9 000 (8.2)	Thailand 9 000 (8.2)
Asbestos (mine production)	000 t (%)	1 998	CIS 683 (34.2)	China 400 (20.0)	**Canada** **340** **(17.0)**	Brazil 200 (10.0)	Zimbabwe 137 (6.9)
Titanium concentrate	000 t (%)	6 220	Australia 2 212 (35.6)	South Africa 1 230 (19.8)	**Canada** **950** **(15.3)**	Norway 590 (9.5)	India 394 (6.3)
Zinc (mine production)	000 t (%)	8 076	China 1 476 (18.3)	Australia 1 163 (14.4)	**Canada** **1 021** **(12.6)**	Peru 900 (11.1)	United States 843 (10.4)
Cadmium (refined production)	t (%)	19 152	Japan 2 567 (13.4)	China 2 000 (10.4)	**Canada** **1 911** **(10.0)**	Mexico 1 275 (6.7)	Belgium 1 235 (6.4)
Platinum group metals (mine production)	kg (%)	377 712	South Africa 224 900 (59.5)	Russia 115 700 (30.6)	**Canada** **13 872** **(3.7)**	United States 12 720 (3.4)	Japan 6 250 (1.7)
Aluminum (primary metal)	000 t (%)	23 654	United States 3 779 (16.0)	Russia 3 146 (13.3)	China 2 599 (11.0)	**Canada** **2 390** **(10.1)**	Australia 1 719 (7.3)
Salt (mine production)	000 t (%)	199 278	United States 41 400 (20.8)	China 31 000 (15.6)	Germany 15 200 (7.6)	**Canada** **12 678** **(6.4)**	India 9 500 (4.8)
Gold (mine production)	t (%)	2 501	South Africa 449 (18.0)	United States 341 (13.6)	Australia 300 (12.0)	China 170 (6.8)	**Canada** **158** **(6.3)**
Lead (mine production)	000 t (%)	3 018	Australia 681 (22.6)	China 549 (18.2)	United States 520 (17.2)	Peru 271 (9.0)	**Canada** **162** **(5.4)**
Copper (mine production)	000 t (%)	12 684	Chile 4 383 (34.6)	United States 1 603 (12.6)	Indonesia 790 (6.2)	Australia 718.9 (5.7)	**Canada** **620** **(4.9)**
Molybdenum (Mo content) (mine production)	t (%)	126 532	United States 43 700 (34.5)	China 30 000 (23.7)	Chile 27 300 (21.6)	Mexico 7 100 (5.6)	**Canada** **5 932** **(4.7)**

[1]CIS = Commonwealth of Independent States. [2]Includes tonnes of uranium recovered by Elliot Lake producers from refinery/conversion facility wastes.
SOURCE: Natural Resources Canada, *Canadian Minerals Yearbook 2000*, p.64.8, Table 7.

Energy

47. Coal,[1] Supply and Demand, 1960, 1970, 1980, 1991, 2001 (10^6 t)

	1960	1970	1980	1991	2001
Production	10.0	15.1	36.7	71.1	70.5
Imports	11.5	18.0	15.6	12.4	25.4
Total supply	**21.5**	**33.1**	**52.3**	**83.5**	**95.9**
Domestic	20.4	25.7	37.3	49.4	57.3
Exports	0.9	4.3	15.3	34.1	30.2
Total demand	**21.3**	**30.0**	**52.6**	**83.5**	**87.5**

[1]Includes bituminous, sub-bituminous, and lignite.
SOURCE: Adapted from the Statistics Canada publications "Canada Year Book", Catalogue 11-402, 1997 and "Coal and Coke Statistics", Catalogue 45-002, various years.

48. Electricity, Supply and Demand, 1960, 1970, 1980, 1991, 2000 (10^9 kWh)

	1960	1970	1980	1991	2000
Production	114.0	204.7	367.3	489.2	585.8
Imports	1.0	3.2	2.9	6.2	15.3
Total supply	**115.0**	**207.9**	**370.2**	**495.4**	**601.1**
Domestic	109.0	202.3	239.9	470.8	550.2
Exports	6.0	5.6	30.3	24.6	50.6
Total demand	**115.0**	**207.9**	**370.2**	**495.4**	**600.8**

SOURCE: Adapted from the Statistics Canada publications "Canada Year Book", Catalogue 11-402, 1997 and "Electric Power Statistics", Catalogue 57-001, various years.

49. Marketable Natural Gas, Supply and Demand, 1960, 1970, 1980, 1991, 2001 (10^9 m^3)

	1960	1970	1980	1991	2001
Production	12.5	52.9	69.8	105.2	171.4
Imports	0.2	0.3	5.6	0.3	3.9
Total supply	**12.7**	**53.2**	**75.4**	**105.5**	**175.3**
Domestic	9.4	29.5	43.3	54.8	85.5
Exports	3.1	22.1	22.6	47.6	108.2
Total demand	**12.5**	**51.6**	**75.4**	**102.4**	**194.6**

SOURCE: Adapted from the Statistics Canada publications "Canada Year Book", Catalogue 11-402, 1997 and "Supply and Disposition of Crude Oil and Natural Gas", Catalogue 26-006, various years.

50. Petroleum, Supply and Demand, 1960, 1970, 1980, 1991, 2001 (10^6 m^3)

	1960	1970	1980	1991	2001
Production	36.5	80.2	89.5	96.7	129.0
Imports	21.2	33.1	32.2	31.5	53.5
Total supply	**57.7**	**113.3**	**121.7**	**128.2**	**182.5**
Domestic	46.8	74.3	109.8	84.4	103.1
Exports	10.7	38.9	11.9	44.2	79.6
Total demand	**57.5**	**113.2**	**121.7**	**128.6**	**182.5**

SOURCE: Adapted from the Statistics Canada publications "Canada Year Book", Catalogue 11-402, 1997 and "Supply and Disposition of Crude Oil and Natural Gas", Catalogue 26-006, various years.

51. Electricity Production and Consumption, 1960, 1970, 1980, 2000 (GWh)

Province or Territory	1960		1970		1980		2000	
	Production	Consumption	Production	Consumption	Production	Consumption	Production	Consumption
Newfoundland & Labrador	1 512	1 427	4 854	4 770	46 374	8 545	43 598	11 817
Prince Edward Island	79	79	250	250	127	518	48	1 037
Nova Scotia	1 814	1 733	3 511	3 706	6 868	6 814	11 625	11 505
New Brunswick	1 738	1 684	5 142	4 221	9 323	8 838	19 295	16 134
Quebec	50 433	44 002	75 877	69 730	97 917	118 254	179 757	191 819
Ontario	35 815	37 157	63 857	69 488	110 283	106 509	153 221	153 696
Manitoba	3 742	4 021	8 449	8 601	19 468	13 927	32 500	21 051
Saskatchewan	2 204	2 124	6 011	5 402	9 204	9 827	17 488	18 629
Alberta	3 443	3 472	10 035	9 880	23 451	23 172	54 535	59 363
British Columbia	13 409	13 413	26 209	25 761	43 416	42 789	68 683	64 052
Yukon	89	89	224	220	381	381	298	298
Northwest Territories	100	100	304	308	494	494	765[1]	765[1]
Canada	**114 378**	**109 304**	**204 723**	**202 337**	**367 306**	**340 068**	**581 813**	**550 166**

[1]Includes Nunavut.
SOURCE: Adapted from the Statistics Canada publication "Electric Power Statistics", Catalogue 57-001, various years.

52. Primary Energy Supply, 1988 to 1999 (annual petajoules[1])

Year	Petroleum	Natural Gas[2]	Coal	Hydro-electricity	Nuclear Energy[3]	Steam & Biomass	Total
1988	3 878	3 465	1 614	1 096	281	516	11 222
1989	3 769	3 654	1 718	1 039	271	507	11 337
1990	3 765	3 732	1 673	1 058	248	477	11 343
1991	3 765	3 980	1 748	1 099	288	482	11 763
1992	3 932	4 415	1 554	1 128	274	483	12 218
1993	4 117	4 901	1 651	1 154	319	471	13 098
1994	4 300	5 353	1 735	1 176	366	548	13 979
1995	4 458	5 648	1 801	1 198	332	554	14 573
1996	4 591	5 852	1 832	1 268	315	552	14 999
1997	4 843	5 953	1 897	1 250	280	554	15 381
1998	5 022	6 125	1 651	1 183	243	571	15 402
1999	4 779	6 189	1 589	1 232	250	609	15 288

[1]A petajoule is one quadrillion joules (10^{15}). [2]Includes butane, propane, and pentane plus. [3]3.6 MJ/kWh.
SOURCE: Susan Girvan, *The Canadian Global Almanac 2002*, "Primary Energy Supply", Toronto: Macmillan Canada, p.222.

53. Energy Summary, 1994 and 2000 (petajoules[1])

	1994	2000
Primary production	13 941	15 768
Net supply[2]	8 418	9 426
Producer's own consumption	976	1 257
Non-energy use	745	789
Energy use (final demand)	6 697	7 379
Industrial	2 086	2 287
Transportation	2 027	2 280
Agriculture	195	232
Residential	1 277	1 288
Public administration	145	131
Commercial and institutional	967	1 162

[1]A 30-litre gasoline fill-up contains about one gigajoule of energy. A petajoule is one million gigajoules. [2]Net supply of primary and secondary sources.
SOURCE: Adapted from the Statistics Canada publication "Canada Year Book", Catalogue 11-402, 1997 and from the Statistics Canada website <http://www.statcan.ca/english/Pgdb/manuf19.htm>, "Energy Summary".

54. Marketable Natural Gas, Remaining Established Reserves in Canada, 2000

Area	Remaining Reserves at 1999-12-31	Gross Additions 2000	Net Production 2000	Remaining Reserves at 2000-12-31	Net Changes in Reserves during 2000
	(000 000 m³ at 101.325 kPa and 15°C)				
British Columbia	238 973	30 495	19 989	249 479	10 506
Alberta	1 311 707	91 973	140 731	1 262 949	-48 758
Saskatchewan	68 595	13 697	6 659	75 633	7 038
Ontario	11 993	178	580	11 591	-402
Quebec	105	n.a.	n.a.	105	0
New Brunswick	0	n.a.	n.a.	0	0
Mainland Territories	17 025	100	1 046	16 079	-946
Eastcoast Offshore	70 500	n.a.	3 417	67 083	-3 417
Total	**1 718 898**	**136 443**	**172 422**	**1 682 919**	**-35 979**

n.a. = not available
SOURCE: Abridged from Canadian Association of Petroleum Producers, *CAPP Statistical Handbook*, "Marketable Natural Gas Remaining Established Reserves in Canada", Pub. No. 2001-9999, November 2001.

55. Conventional Crude Oil and Equivalent, Remaining Established Reserves in Canada, 2000 (000 m³)

	Remaining Reserves at 1999-12-31	Gross Additions 2000	Net Production 2000	Remaining Reserves at 2000-12-31	Net Changes in Reserves during 2000
British Columbia	27 687	2 569	2 618	27 638	-49
Alberta	341 343	31 242	42 185	330 400	-10 943
Saskatchewan	169 113	36 957	23 955	182 115	13 002
Manitoba	4 273	863	620	4 516	243
Ontario	1 859	353	231	1 981	122
Quebec	0	n.a.	n.a.	0	0
New Brunswick	0	n.a.	n.a.	0	0
Mainland Territories	11 614	1 546	1 365	11 795	181
Eastcoast Offshore	138 008	30 020	8 394	159 634	21 626
Total conventional areas	**693 897**	**103 550**	**79 368**	**718 079**	**24 182**
Mackenzie/Beaufort	53 950	n.a.	n.a.	53 950	0
Arctic Islands	0	n.a.	n.a.	0	0
Total frontier areas	**53 950**	**0**	**0**	**53 950**	**0**
Total crude oil	**747 847**	**103 550**	**79 368**	**772 029**	**24 182**
British Columbia	5 198	933	654	5 477	279
Alberta	81 148	12 789	9 658	84 279	3 131
Saskatchewan	287	34	41	280	-7
Manitoba	0	0	n.a.	0	0
Mainland Territories	3 360	-315	71	2 974	-386
Eastcoast Offshore	10 784	n.a.	92	10 692	-92
Total pentanes plus	**100 777**	**13 441**	**10 516**	**103 702**	**2 925**
Total crude oil & equivalent	**848 624**	**116 991**	**89 884**	**875 731**	**27 107**

n.a. = not available
SOURCE: Canadian Association of Petroleum Producers, *CAPP Statistical Handbook*, "Conventional Crude Oil and Equivalent Remaining Established Reserves in Canada", Pub. No. 2001-9999, November 2001.

56. Developed Non-Conventional Oil, Remaining Established Reserves in Canada, 2000 (000 m³)

	Remaining Reserves at 1999-12-31	Gross Additions 2000	Net Production 2000	Remaining Reserves at 2000-12-31	Net Changes in Reserves during 2000
Mining—integrated synthetic crude oil[1] (Alberta)	799 910	14 742	18 393	796 259	-3 651
In-situ—bitumen[2] (Alberta)	248 058	55 129	16 361	286 826	38 768
Total developed non-conventional oil	**1 047 968**	**69 871**	**34 754**	**1 083 085**	**35 117**
Total conventional & non-conventional oil	**1 896 592**	**186 862**	**124 638**	**1 958 816**	**62 224**

[1]Developed synthetic crude oil reserves are those recoverable from developed commercial projects. [2]Developed bitumen reserves are those recoverable from developed experimental/demonstration and commercial projects.
SOURCE: Canadian Association of Petroleum Producers, *CAPP Statistical Handbook*, "Developed Non-Conventional Oil Remaining Established Reserves in Canada", Pub. No. 2001-9999, November 2001.

57. Installed Electrical Generating Capacity by Fuel Type and Region, 1960, 1970, 1990, 2000

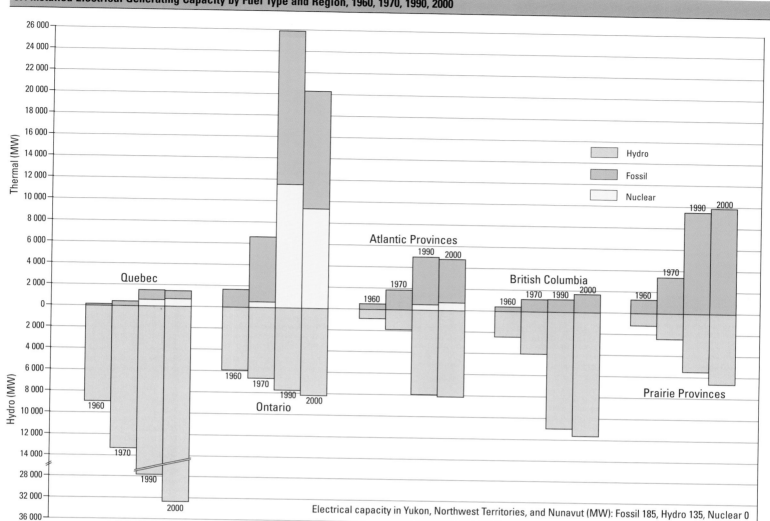

NOTE: Not to scale.
SOURCE: Adapted from the Natural Resources Canada publication *Electrical Power in Canada*, 1975, 1990, and 1999 and the Statistics Canada publication *Electric Power Generation, Transmission, and Distribution*, Catalogue 57-2002, 2000.

Manufacturing

58. Summary Statistics, Annual Census of Manufacturers, 1965, 1970, 1975, 1980, 1984, 1990, 1994, 1999

Year	Number of Establishments[1]	Production and Related Workers		Cost of Fuel & Electricity ($000 000)	Cost of Materials & Supplies Used ($000 000)	Value of Shipments of Goods of Own Manufacture ($000 000)	Value Added ($000 000)
		Number	Wages ($000 000)				
1965	33 310	1 115 892	5 012.4	675.6	18 622.2	33 889.4	14 927.8
1970	31 928	1 167 063	7 232.3	903.3	25 700.0	46 380.9	20 047.8
1975	30 100	1 271 786	12 699.2	1 805.4	51 177.9	88 427.0	36 105.5
1980	35 495	1 346 187	22 162.3	4 448.9	99 897.6	168 058.7	65 851.8
1984	36 464	1 240 816	28 294.6	7 306.4	136 133.6	230 070.1	88 667.7
1990	39 864	1 393 324	40 406.5	7 936.1	168 664.3	298 918.5	122 972.5
1994	31 974	1 243 026	41 405.0	9 151.6	202 655.0	352 834.7	142 858.8
1999	29 822	1 487 098	53 163.5	11 018.4	277 802.9	488 729.4	202 930.2

[1]The increase in the number of establishments between 1975 and 1980 was largely a result of the addition of 4 962 small establishments by improved coverage.
SOURCE: Adapted from the Statistics Canada publications "Manufacturing Industries of Canada, National and Provincial Areas", Catalogue 31-203, various years and "Canada Year Book", Catalogue 11-402, 1976-77 and 1992.

59. Principal Statistics on Manufacturing Industries by Province and Territory, 1999

Province or Territory	Number of Establishments	Number of Employees	Salaries & Wages ($000 000)	Cost of Fuel & Electricity ($000 000)	Cost of Materials, Supplies, & Goods For Resale ($000 000)	Value of Shipments & Other Revenue ($000 000)	Value Added ($000 000)
Newfoundland & Labrador	260	11 948	341.9	89.2	952.6	1 969.4	947.1
Prince Edward Island	143	4 189	95.3	24.4	686.1	1 029.1	329.8
Nova Scotia	634	30 377	939.2	299.8	4 161.2	7 430.8	3 008.3
New Brunswick	598	28 942	889.6	371.2	5 460.3	8 905.2	3 093.8
Quebec	8 738	391 934	12 373.9	3 370.9	59 239.4	114 800.8	53 982.5
Ontario	11 647	735 371	28 382.5	4 336.8	156 972.1	267 738.7	106 851.1
Manitoba	970	52 051	1 557.0	233.8	5 669.6	10 140.3	4 217.5
Saskatchewan	698	19 307	626.7	190.5	3 828.0	6 172.2	2 085.8
Alberta	2 481	89 685	3 105.8	884.0	21 239.5	34 822.8	13 415.4
British Columbia	3 615	122 999	4 843.1	1 217.1	19 578.4	35 686.3	14 981.7
Yukon, Northwest Territories, and Nunavut	38	295	8.5	0.7	15.7	33.8	17.3
Canada	**29 822**	**1 487 098**	**53 163.5**	**11 018.4**	**277 802.9**	**488 729.4**	**202 930.2**

SOURCE: Adapted from the Statistics Canada publication "Manufacturing Industries of Canada, National and Provincial Areas", 1999, Catalogue 31-203, 18 June 2002.

Trade

60. Exports from Canada, Principal Nations, 1987, 1991, 1995, 2001 ($000 000)

Country or Region	1987	1991	1995	2001
United States	91 756	103 449	196 161	325 034
Japan	7 036	7 111	11 857	8 067
United Kingdom	2 850	2 920	3 748	4 700
China	1 432	1 849	3 212	3 920
Germany[1]	1 515	2 125	3 150	2 691
Mexico	n.a.	n.a.	1 107	2 353
France	1 037	1 350	1 888	2 035
South Korea	1 167	1 861	2 695	1 950
Belgium	1 123	1 073	1 823	1 837
Italy	843	1 017	1 768	1 550
Netherlands	1 021	1 655	1 584	1 541
Hong Kong	480	817	1 377	1 063
Taiwan	n.a.	n.a.	1 683	965
Australia	689	628	1 139	954
Brazil	n.a.	n.a.	1 265	874
Total all countries	**121 462**	**138 079**	**247 703**	**373 554**

NOTE: Data is listed in order of 2001 export values.
n.a. = not available
[1]Figure for 1987 does not include the former East Germany.
SOURCE: Adapted from the Statistics Canada publication "Exports by Country", Catalogue 65-003, various years.

61. Imports to Canada, Principal Nations, 1987, 1991, 1995, 2001 ($000 000)

Country or Region	1987	1991	1995	2001
United States	76 716	86 235	150 705	218 408
Japan	8 351	10 249	12 103	14 647
China	812	1 852	4 639	12 712
Mexico	1 165	2 574	5 341	12 110
United Kingdom	4 276	4 182	5 470	11 631
Germany[1]	3 649	3 734	4 801	7 955
France	1 590	2 670	3 125	5 510
South Korea	1 912	2 110	3 204	4 601
Taiwan	2 166	2 212	2 792	4 410
Italy	1 793	1 792	3 270	4 034
Norway	n.a.	n.a.	2 314	3 500
Malaysia	n.a.	n.a.	1 549	1 894
Sweden	n.a.	n.a.	1 305	1 708
Thailand	n.a.	n.a.	1 014	1 689
Australia	n.a.	n.a.	1 283	1 608
Total all countries	**116 238**	**135 284**	**225 493**	**343 056**

NOTE: Data is listed in order of 2001 import values.
n.a. = not available
[1]Figure for 1987 does not include the former East Germany.
SOURCE: Adapted from the Statistics Canada publication "Imports by Country", Catalogue 65-006, various years.

62. Principal Commodities, Imported and Exported, 2001 ($000 000)

Commodity	Imports	Exports
Aircraft, spacecraft and parts	7 820	12 699
Aluminum and articles thereof	3 492	8 072
Electrical machinery and parts	40 250	19 592
Furniture, bedding, etc.	5 586	8 083
Iron and steel products	11 602	8 485
Mineral fuels	19 301	57 372
Nuclear reactors, boilers, mechanical appliances, engines	61 857	30 790
Optical and photo equipment	12 165	4 284
Organic chemicals	5 678	3 510
Paper and paperboard	6 314	17 826
Pharmaceutical products	6 139	2 056
Plastic products	11 695	11 458
Pulp wood and cellulose	542	7 291
Vehicles, rolling stock, parts and accessories	59 194	80 433
Wood and articles thereof	3 012	18 972
Total all commodities	**343 056**	**373 554**

SOURCE: Adapted from the Statistics Canada publications "Imports by Country", 2001, Catalogue 65-006, March 2002 and "Exports by Country", 2001, Catalogue 65-003, March 2002.

The Economy

63. Gross Domestic Product by Industry,[1] 1980, 1990, 2001 (%)

Industry	1980	1990	2001
Agricultural, fishing, trapping, and forestry	2.3	3.0	2.3
Mining	4.1	4.0	3.9
Manufacturing	17.7	18.1	17.3
Construction	5.7	6.4	5.3
Trade (wholesale and retail)	11.4	11.5	11.5
Finance, insurance, and real estate	13.4	15.7	19.6
Transportation	4.6	4.7	4.6
Professional, community, and personal services	22.2	23.1	22.3
Public administration	7.2	6.7	5.6
Other (utilities, and information and cultural industries)	11.4	6.8	7.6

[1]Based on per cent of Canada's GDP.
SOURCE: Adapted from the Statistics Canada publication "Canadian Economic Observer", Catalogue 11-010, various years.

64. Gross Domestic Product by Province and Territory,[1] 1970, 1980, 1990, 2001 (%)

Province or Territory	1970	1980	1990	2001
Newfoundland & Labrador	1.4	1.3	1.3	1.3
Prince Edward Island	0.3	0.3	0.3	0.3
Nova Scotia	2.5	2.0	2.5	2.3
New Brunswick	1.9	1.6	2.0	1.7
Quebec	25.5	23.3	23.1	21.0
Ontario	42.0	37.1	40.8	40.6
Manitoba	4.2	3.6	3.5	3.2
Saskatchewan	3.4	4.0	3.1	3.1
Alberta	8.0	13.9	10.7	13.9
British Columbia	10.6	12.4	12.2	12.0
Yukon, Northwest Territories, and Nunavut	0.3	0.4	0.5	0.6

[1]Based on per cent of Canada's GDP.
SOURCE: Adapted from the Statistics Canada publication "Canadian Economic Observer", Catalogue 11-010, various years.

65. Inflation Rates, 1915 to 2001

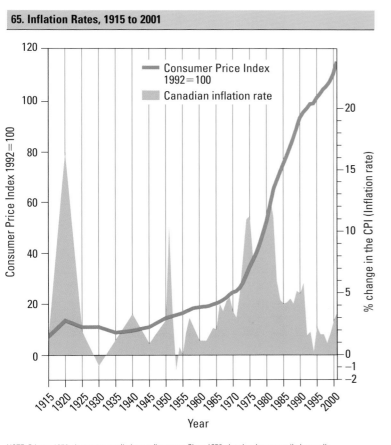

NOTE: Prior to 1950, data was compiled every five years. Since 1950, data has been compiled annually.
SOURCE: Adapted from Susan Girvan, *The Canadian Global Almanac 2002*, "Canadian Inflation Rate by Year" and "Canadian Consumer Price Index by Year", Toronto: Macmillan Canada, pp.202-203.

66. Foreign Investment in Canada, 1970, 1990, 2000 ($000 000)

Country or Region	1970	1990	2000
United States	22 054	84 311	185 238
Other European Union	1 617	14 339	58 653
United Kingdom	2 641	18 217	19 268
Other OECD[1]	580	5 871	9 229
Japan	103	5 203	8 442
Total	**27 374**	**130 932**	**291 520**

NOTE: Data is listed in order of 2000 investment values.
[1]OECD = Organization for Economic Cooperation and Development. Member countries are shown on the map on page 139.
SOURCE: Susan Girvan, *The Canadian Global Almanac 2002*, Toronto: Macmillan Canada, p.218.

67. Canadian Investment Abroad, 1970, 1990, 2000 ($000 000)

Country or Region	1970	1990	2000
United States	3 518	60 049	154 033
Other European Union	304	7 098	31 222
United Kingdom	636	13 527	25 301
Other OECD[1]	142	3 996	15 316
Japan	48	917	5 502
Total	**6 520**	**98 402**	**301 357**

NOTE: Data is listed in order of 2000 investment values.
[1]OECD = Organization for Economic Cooperation and Development. Member countries are shown on the map on page 139.
SOURCE: Susan Girvan, *The Canadian Global Almanac 2002*, Toronto: Macmillan Canada, p.219.

Transportation and Tourism

68. St. Lawrence Seaway Traffic by Commodity and by Nationality, 2001[1]

Commodities	Upbound (000 t)	Sources and Destinations of Upbound Commodities (%)	Downbound (000 t)	Sources and Destinations of Downbound Commodities (%)
Corn	—		1 499.5	Can to Can 2 US to Can 55 Can to For 2 US to For 41
Flaxseed	—		531.7	Can to For 89 US to For 11
Soybeans	—		1 800.0	Can to Can 4 US to Can 67 Can to For 9 US to For 20
Wheat	—		6 710.0	Can to Can 57 US to Can 8 US to For 23 Can to For 12
Total agricultural	**43.9**	For to Can 58 For to US 42	**11 756.4**	Can to Can to 34 Can to For 20 US to Can 22 US to For 24
Aluminum ore and concentrates	152.5	Can to Can 4 For to Can 60 For to US 36	—	
Bituminous coal	—		4 803.6	US to Can 93 Can to Can 7
Coke	63.5	Can to Can 63 For to US 37	885.2	US to Can 78 Can to For 12 Can to Can 10
Gypsum	445.0	Can to Can 100	—	
Iron ore	8 386.0	Can to Can 67 Can to US 33	270.9	US to Can 100
Salt	124.1	Can to Can 86 For to Can 9 For to US 5	2 144.1	Can to Can 54 Can to US 11 US to Can 35
Stone and gravel	527.4	Can to Can 6 Can to US 91 For to Can 1 For to US 1	629.4	Can to Can 68 US to Can 32
Total mine	**10 168.5**	Can to Can 62 Can to US 34 For to Can 2 For to US 2	**19 305.5**	Can to Can 24 Can to US 3 Can to For 1 US to Can 71 US to For 1
Cement and cement clinker	2 701.1	Can to Can 1 Can to US 96 For to Can 2 For to US 1	—	
Chemicals	227.8	Can to Can 4 US to Can 16 For to Can 47 For to US 33	360.0	Can to For 42 Can to Can 18 Can to US 18 US to Can 21 US to For 1
Fuel oil	375.6	Can to Can 68 Can to US 32	592.2	Can to Can 89 Can to US 9 US to Can 2
Gasoline	687.1	Can to Can 59 For to Can 18 Can to US 14 US to Can 9	8.8	Can to Can 100
Iron and steel products	3 059.4	Can to US 3 For to Can 30 For to US 67	58.0	US to US 2 Can to For 66 US to For 32
Sugar	577.2	Can to Can 22 For to Can 77 For to US 1	—	
Total manufactures[2]	**9 001.6**	Can to Can 13 Can to US 38 US to Can 2 For to Can 20 For to US 27	**1 551.4**	Can to Can 54 Can to US 8 Can to For 20 US to Can 16 US to For 2
Grand total	**19 234.1**	Can to Can 39 Can to US 35 US to Can 1 For to Can 11 For to US 14	**22 471.2**	Can to Can 31 Can to US 2 Can to For 12 US to Can 42 US to For 13

— = nil
[1]Includes traffic through both the Montreal–Lake Ontario section and the Welland Canal section. [2]Includes unclassified cargoes.
SOURCE: The St. Lawrence Seaway Management Corporation. Reprinted by permission.

69. Cargo Loaded and Unloaded at Leading Canadian Ports, Major Commodities, 1999 (000 t)

Port	Domestic Cargo		International Cargo		Total
	Loaded	Unloaded	Loaded	Unloaded	
Vancouver	724	504	62 583 (coal, wheat, sulphur)	5 995 (machinery/equipment)	69 806
Halifax	1 876	912	5 520 (gypsum)	14 250 (crude petroleum)	22 558
Sept-Îles–Pointe-Noire	4 103 (iron ore)	624	15 429 (iron ore)	899	21 055
Montreal–Contrecoeur	1 230	3 987 (iron ore, wheat, salt)	6 067 (wheat, food products)	9 086 (iron, steel, machinery/ equipment, gasoline, miscellaneous chemicals)	20 370
Port Cartier	3 078 (iron ore)	1 502 (wheat)	13 941 (iron ore)	1 407 (fodder and feed)	19 928
Saint John	1 336 (fuel oil)	739	7 530 (fuel oil, gasoline)	10 084 (crude petroleum)	19 689
Quebec–Lévis	1 768 (fuel oil)	1 220 (wheat)	3 519 (wheat, iron ore)	9 780 (crude petroleum)	16 287
Port Hawkesbury	85	16	8 036 (crude petroleum, gypsum, cement)	5 481 (crude petroleum)	13 618
Nanticoke	318	983	310	10 654 (coal)	12 265
Hamilton	634	5 970 (iron ore)	363	4 472 (coal)	11 439

SOURCE: Adapted from the Statistics Canada publication "Shipping in Canada", 1999, Catalogue 54-205, October 2001.

70. Manufacturing Activity, Value of Shipments of Goods of Own Manufacture, 1999

Major Industry Group	Value ($000 000)
Food	52 939
Beverage and tobacco products	11 537
Rubber and plastic products	19 011
Leather and allied products	880
Primary textile	4 065
Textile products	2 431
Clothing	6 816
Wood	29 841
Furniture and fixture	9 708
Paper and allied products	31 941
Printing and publishing	9 626
Primary metal	31 111
Fabricated metal products	24 101
Machinery, except electrical	22 339
Transportation equipment	127 021
Aerospace products	11 356
Motor vehicle	77 508
Heavy-duty trucks	7 970
Motor vehicle parts and accessories	28 581
Railroad rolling stocks	3 930
Shipbuilding and repair	574
Electrical, computer, and electronic products	37 847
Non-metallic products	8 926
Petroleum and coal	20 519
Chemical products	32 393
Other manufacturing	5 677
Total all major industries	**488 729**

SOURCE: Adapted from the Statistics Canada publication "Manufacturing Industries of Canada, National and Provincial Areas", 1999, Catalogue 31-203, 18 June 2002.

71. Principal Seaway Ports,[1] 1995 and 2001 (000 t)[2]

Port	Inbound Cargo		Outbound Cargo	
	1995	2001	1995	2001
Canadian ports	**30 289**	**26 022**	**26 622**	**24 471**
Baie-Comeau	2 643	1 248	v.s.	v.s.
Goderich	v.s.	v.s.	758	1 046
Hamilton	11 044	9 947	702	666
Montreal[3]	2 198	1 775	96	442
Nanticoke	n.a.	477	n.a.	304
Picton	239	182	567	491
Pointe-Noire	380	263	3 845	3 753
Port Cartier	4 664	2 733	2 113	2 068
Quebec City	2 247	955	1 008	883
Sept-Îles	821	217	3 950	2 222
Sorel	404	307	116	133
Thorold	299	235	7	v.s.
Thunder Bay	9	v.s.	6 702	6 145
Toronto[4]	798	3 751	19	1 623
Trois-Rivières	803	424	78	v.s.
Windsor	179	v.s.	1 373	773
US ports	**11 986**	**9 941**	**16 375**	**12 449**
Ashtabula	710	563	660	1 186
Chicago	1 168	871	1 357	429
Cleveland	2 044	1 692	400	339
Conneault	v.s.	v.s.	725	1 174
Detroit	1 935	2 311	472	130
Duluth	230	270	4 510	3 613
Essexville	n.a.	400	n.a.	v.s.
Indiana–Burns Harbor	3 047	1 735	566	225
Milwaukee	228	141	769	363
Oswego	n.a.	366	n.a.	v.s.
Sandusky	v.s.	v.s.	1 660	992
Toledo	264	229	3 579	2 673

v.s. = very small/unreported; n.a. = not available
[1]Area includes all ports or installations within a 20 km radius of the main harbour. [2]Tonnage figures are limited to cargo volumes moved through seaway lock structures. [3]Includes Cote Ste. Catherine. [4]Includes Port Credit, Lakeview, Bowmanville, Clarkson, and Oakville.
SOURCE: The St. Lawrence Seaway Management Corporation. Reprinted by permission.

72. Top Ten Countries (Other than the US) Visited by Canadians for One or More Nights, 1986, 1991, 2000

Rank	1986	1991	2000
1	United Kingdom	United Kingdom	United Kingdom
2	France	Mexico	Mexico
3	Mexico	France	France
4	West Germany	Germany	Germany
5	Netherlands	Netherlands	Cuba
6	Switzerland	Cuba	Italy
7	Italy	Dominican Republic	Dominican Republic
8	Austria	Italy	Netherlands
9	Jamaica	Switzerland	Spain
10	Dominican Republic	Hong Kong	Hong Kong

SOURCE: Adapted from the Statistics Canada publication "International Travel", 2000, Catalogue 66-201, November 2001.

73. Visits and Expenditures of Canadian Residents in Selected Countries (Other than the US), 2000

Country or Region	Visits (000)	%	Spending ($000 000)
Austria	95	1.4	66.8
Belgium	117	1.7	53.7
Denmark	43	0.6	19.0
France	493	7.2	565.8
Germany	323	4.7	235.7
Greece	76	1.1	57.5
Ireland (Rep.)	104	1.5	115.3
Italy	254	3.7	337.7
Netherlands	176	2.5	115.6
Portugal	83	1.2	82.0
Spain	161	2.3	174.6
Switzerland	143	2.1	101.0
United Kingdom	884	12.2	975.9
Yugoslavia	5	0.1	1.8
Other	440	6.4	309.6
Total Europe	**3 357**	**48.7**	**3 212.1**
Total Africa	**158**	**2.3**	**216.8**
Hong Kong	101	1.5	97.0
Japan	128	1.9	191.5
Other	443	6.4	599.0
Total Asia	**672**	**9.7**	**887.5**
Total Central America	**123**	**1.8**	**95.5**
Bahamas	125	1.8	60.6
Barbados	78	1.1	49.1
Bermuda	66	1.0	93.3
Cuba	274	4.0	210.4
Dominican Republic	200	2.9	152.6
Jamaica	87	1.3	59.3
Other	552	8.0	219.2
Total Bermuda and Caribbean	**1 302**	**20.0**	**884.0**
Total South America	**198**	**2.9**	**248.5**
Mexico	840	12.2	725.9
Other	11	0.2	4.4
Total North America	**851**	**12.3**	**730.4**
Total Oceania and other ocean islands	**149**	**2.2**	**285.0**
Total	**6 895**	**100.0**	**6 515.9**

SOURCE: Adapted from the Statistics Canada publication "International Travel", 2000, Catalogue 66-201, November 2001.

74. Visits and Expenditures of Canadian Residents Returning from the US by Selected States, 2000

State	Visits (000)	%	Spending ($000 000)
Arizona	361	1.1	299.4
California	1 176	3.7	925.4
Colorado	178	0.6	107.6
Connecticut	212	0.7	48.1
District of Columbia	229	0.7	105.4
Florida	2 168	6.8	2 113.0
Georgia	796	2.5	143.4
Hawaii	371	1.2	487.9
Idaho	517	1.6	42.3
Illinois	724	2.3	246.3
Kentucky	445	1.4	33.7
Louisiana	139	0.4	99.0
Maine	884	2.8	162.5
Maryland	503	1.6	58.9
Massachusetts	702	2.2	214.3
Michigan	2 195	6.9	251.6
Minnesota	810	2.5	145.9
Montana	566	1.8	102.4
Nevada	865	2.7	577.4
New Hampshire	797	2.5	61.4
New Jersey	377	1.2	107.5
New York	4 446	13.9	686.7
North Carolina	764	2.4	102.7
North Dakota	505	1.6	55.5
Ohio	873	2.7	122.0
Oregon	404	1.3	79.1
Pennsylvania	1 372	4.3	166.9
South Carolina	656	2.1	209.0
Tennessee	475	1.5	73.8
Texas	431	1.4	330.9
Utah	182	0.6	39.7
Vermont	1 361	4.3	110.0
Virginia	797	2.5	105.0
Washington	2 007	6.3	269.5
Wisconsin	305	1.0	50.1
Other states	2 268	7.1	366.9
Total	**31 875**	**100.0**	**9 091.2**

SOURCE: Adapted from the Statistics Canada publication "International Travel", 2000, Catalogue 66-201, November 2001.

75. Trip Characteristics of US Residents Entering Canada, Staying One or More Nights in Province Visited, 2000

	Atlantic Provinces	Quebec	Ontario	Manitoba	Saskatchewan	Alberta	British Columbia	Canada
Number of province-visits (000)	1 154	2 256	7 593	330	218	1 073	4 002	16 627
Spending in province ($000 000)	480	1 147	2 904	172	113	724	1 908	7 448
Average spending per province-visit ($)	416.00	508.50	382.50	521.30	517.30	674.80	476.60	448.00
Number of visit-nights (000)	4 368	7 866	25 167	1 227	853	4 739	14 430	58 649
Average number of nights	3.8	3.5	3.3	3.7	3.9	4.4	3.6	3.5
Average spending per visit-night ($)	109.90	145.90	115.40	140.20	132.10	152.80	132.20	127.00
Region of Residence (000)								
New England	513	922	378	9	6	30	78	1 936
Middle Atlantic	160	564	2 038	11	9	83	169	3 034
South Atlantic	159	226	660	17	18	103	279	1 462
East North Central	119	217	3 153	48	40	123	239	3 940
West North Central	43	69	489	185	57	72	172	1 085
East South Central	28	32	128	8	7	20	45	269
West South Central	41	72	214	10	13	84	184	618
Mountain	41	39	165	17	33	265	376	936
Pacific	49	112	358	23	30	274	2 313	3 158
Other states	2	2	9	2	6	20	149	189
Total	**1 154**	**2 256**	**7 593**	**330**	**218**	**1 073**	**4 002**	**16 627**
Purpose of Trip (000)								
Business, convention, and employment	69	430	1 314	35	29	186	393	2 456
Visiting friends or relatives	311	427	1 287	62	48	183	679	2 997
Other pleasure, recreation, or holiday	719	1 239	4 235	163	105	581	2 516	9 558
Other	55	161	758	69	36	123	414	1 615
Total	**1 154**	**2 256**	**7 593**	**330**	**218**	**1 073**	**4 002**	**16 627**
Quarter of Entry (000)								
I	43	382	959	42	12	117	600	2 155
II	254	565	2 081	95	56	267	1 059	4 377
III	749	853	3 214	137	111	552	1 737	7 352
IV	109	456	1 339	56	38	138	606	2 743
Total	**1 154**	**2 256**	**7 593**	**330**	**218**	**1 073**	**4 002**	**16 627**
Type of Transportation (000)								
Automobile	626	1 301	5 165	226	133	509	2 375	10 335
Plane	203	663	1 686	92	68	485	965	4 162
Bus	85	213	419	11	4	34	136	901
Other methods	240	80	324	1	11	46	526	1 229
Total	**1 154**	**2 256**	**7 593**	**330**	**218**	**1 073**	**4 002**	**16 627**

SOURCE: Adapted from the Statistics Canada publication "International Travel", 2000, Catalogue 66-201, November 2001, p.25.

76. Trip Characteristics of Residents of Countries Other than the US Entering Canada, Staying One or More Nights in Province Visited, 2000

	Atlantic Provinces	Quebec	Ontario	Manitoba	Saskatchewan	Alberta	British Columbia	Canada
Number of province-visits (000)	435	1 082	1 986	96	65	834	1 461	5 959
Spending in province ($000 000)	337	917	1 643	71	35	730	1 457	5 188
Average spending per province-visit ($)	774.60	847.80	827.50	730.80	530.10	875.00	996.90	870.70
Number of visit-nights (000)	3 566	8 758	18 162	787	511	6 129	11 253	49 167
Average number of nights	8.2	8.1	9.1	8.2	7.8	7.4	7.7	8.3
Average spending per visit-night ($)	94.40	104.70	90.50	89.60	67.60	119.00	129.40	105.50
Area of Residence (000)								
Europe	329	704	1 044	62	35	446	595	3 215
France	19	340	141	6	4	19	18	546
Germany	79	72	153	11	5	84	124	527
Italy	17	37	54	4	—	9	32	153
Netherlands	25	13	48	3	4	49	51	193
Scandinavia	19	9	30	3	2	13	23	99
United Kingdom	121	111	421	23	15	210	242	1 143
Other Europe	49	122	196	12	7	63	106	554
Africa	13	27	31	1	2	9	12	95
Asia	49	205	601	20	17	280	622	1 794
Japan	19	60	201	7	8	146	261	702
Other Asia	30	145	400	14	9	134	361	1 092
Central America	1	6	10	v.s.	—	2	3	20
Bermuda and Caribbean	11	26	81	3	5	5	12	142
South America	4	39	69	2	1	20	33	169
North America	14	49	74	2	v.s.	4	52	196
Oceania and other ocean islands	15	27	76	6	5	67	132	328
Australia	14	22	63	5	4	55	108	272
Other	v.s.	5	13	1	1	12	24	56
Total	**435**	**1 082**	**1 986**	**96**	**65**	**834**	**1 461**	**5 959**
Purpose of Trip (000)								
Business, convention, and employment	64	221	390	18	13	88	173	968
Visiting friends or relatives	116	288	661	38	26	145	284	1 558
Other pleasure, recreation, or holiday	241	536	835	33	21	568	939	3 174
Other	13	37	99	7	5	33	65	260
Total	**435**	**1 082**	**1 986**	**96**	**65**	**834**	**1 461**	**5 959**
Quarter of Entry (000)								
I	33	127	200	12	6	85	218	680
II	143	265	583	22	22	230	398	1 664
III	205	495	873	45	25	419	594	2 656
IV	53	195	330	18	12	100	251	958
Total	**435**	**1 082**	**1 986**	**96**	**65**	**834**	**1 461**	**5 959**

v.s. = very small/too small to be expressed; — = nil
SOURCE: Adapted from the Statistics Canada publication "International Travel", 2000, Catalogue 66-201, November 2001, p.31.

77. Trips of One or More Nights between Canada and the US, 1987 to 2000

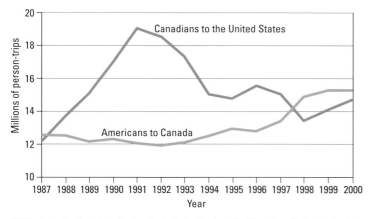

SOURCE: Adapted from the Statistics Canada publication "International Travel", 2000, Catalogue 66-201, November 2001.

78. Trips of One or More Nights between Canada and the US by Purpose of Trip, 2000

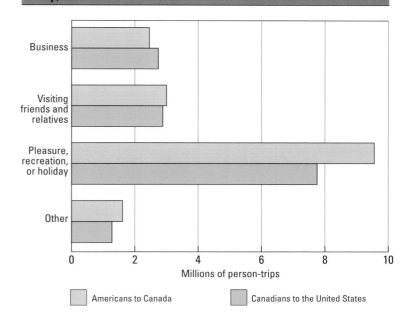

SOURCE: Adapted from the Statistics Canada publication "International Travel", 2000, Catalogue 66-201, November 2001.

Conservation and Pollution

79. Biophysical Characteristics of Terrestrial Ecozones

Terrestrial Ecozone	Land Area (km²)	Landforms	Vegetation/Productivity	Surface Materials/Soils	Climate Characteristics
Boreal Shield	1 876 142	Plains; some hills	Evergreen forest; mixed evergreen-deciduous forest	Canadian Shield rock; moraine; lacustrine; podzols;[1] brunisols[2]	Cold; moist
Taiga Shield	1 367 722	Plains; some hills	Open evergreen-deciduous trees; some lichen-shrub tundra	Canadian Shield rock; moraine; cryosols;[3] brunisols[2]	Cold; moist to semi-arid; discontinuous permafrost
Atlantic Maritime	202 619	Hills and coastal plains	Mixed deciduous-evergreen forest stands	Moraine; colluvium; marine; brunisols;[2] podzols;[1] luvisols[4]	Cool; wet
Arctic Cordillera	244 584	Mountains	Mainly unvegetated; some shrub-herb tundra	Ice; snow; colluvium; rock; cryosols[3]	Extremely cold; dry; continuous permafrost
Northern Arctic	1 529 827	Plains; hills	Herb-lichen tundra	Moraine; rock; marine; cryosols[3]	Very cold; dry; continuous permafrost
Southern Arctic	851 673	Plains; hills	Shrub-herb tundra	Moraine; rock; marine; cryosols[3]	Cold; dry; continuous permafrost
Mixedwood Plains	113 971	Plains; some hills	Mixed deciduous-evergreen forest	Moraine; marine; rock; luvisols;[4] brunisols[2]	Cool to mild; moist
Hudson Plains	374 270	Plains	Wetlands; some herb-moss-lichen tundra; evergreen forest	Organic; marine; cryosols[3]	Cold to mild; semi-arid; discontinuous permafrost
Boreal Plains	704 719	Plains; some foothills	Mixed evergreen-deciduous forest	Moraine, lacustrine; organic; luvisols;[4] brunisols[2]	Cold; moist
Prairies	464 070	Plains; some hills	Grass; scattered deciduous forest (aspen parkland)	Moraine; chernozems[5]	Cold; semi-arid
Taiga Plains	610 541	Plains; some foothills	Open to closed mixed evergreen-deciduous forest	Organic; moraine; lacustrine; cryosols;[3] brunisols[2]	Cold; semi-arid to moist; discontinuous permafrost
Montane Cordillera	490 234	Mountains; interior plains	Evergreen forest; alpine tundra; interior grassland	Moraine; colluvium; rock; luvisols;[4] brunisols[2]	Moderately cold; moist to arid
Pacific Maritime	213 000	Mountains; minor coastal plains	Coastal evergreen forest	Colluvium; moraine; rock; podzols;[1] brunisols[2]	Mild; temperate; very wet to cold alpine
Boreal Cordillera	470 476	Mountains; some hills	Largely evergreen forest; some tundra; open woodland	Colluvium; moraine; rock; podzols;[1] cryosols[3]	Moderately cold; moist
Taiga Cordillera	267 283	Mountains	Shrub-herb-moss-lichen tundra	Colluvium; moraine; rock; cryosols;[3] gleysols[6]	Very cold winters; cool summers; minimal precipitation

[1]Podzols are acid and well-weathered soils. [2]Brunisols are soils with minimal weathering. [3]Cryosols are frozen soils. [4]Luvisols are temperate-region soils with clay-rich sublayers. [5]Chernozems are organically rich, relatively fertile grassland soils. [6]Gleysols are soils developed under wet conditions and characterized by reduced iron and other elements.
SOURCE: Adapted from the Statistics Canada publication "Human Activity and the Environment", 2000, Catalogue 11-509, June 2000, p. 23.

80. Greenhouse Gas Emissions by Principal Greenhouse Gases and Major Sector, 1990, 1995, 1997, 2000, and Projections

Greenhouse Gas and Major Sector	1990	1995	1997	2000	Projection 2005	2010	2015	2020
				(megatonnes of CO_2-equivalent emissions)				
Carbon dioxide (CO_2) emissions	**461**	**495**	**520**	**537**	**567**	**595**	**636**	**662**
Transportation	140	150	162	168	178	189	204	219
Total industrial	104	109	107	116	122	130	137	144
Power generation	95	99	111	110	115	119	124	122
Fossil fuel industries	46	60	59	67	78	84	95	98
Residential and agricultural	43	45	47	43	41	40	41	43
Commercial and public administration	26	30	30	32	33	34	34	35
Methane (CH_4) emissions	**75**	**87**	**90**	**90**	**91**	**92**	**96**	**97**
Fossil fuel industries	28	35	39	39	39	39	40	39
Agroecosystems	20	22	23	23	24	24	26	27
Waste	19	21	21	21	21	22	23	24
Residential and agricultural	5	5	6	5	6	6	6	7
Nitrous oxide (N_2O) emissions	**57**	**63**	**64**	**57**	**59**	**62**	**64**	**65**
Agroecosystems	34	38	39	43	45	48	49	50
Transportation	7	9	9	9	8	8	8	9
Total industrial	12	12	12	1	1	1	1	1
Residential and agricultural	1	1	1	1	2	2	2	2

NOTE: Data is listed in order of 2000 emission values.
SOURCE: *Canada's Emissions Outlook: 1997-2020*, Natural Resources Canada. Reprinted by permission.

81. Greenhouse Gas Emissions Summary by Province and Territory, 2000

	NFLD & LAB	PEI	NS	NB	QUE	ONT	MAN	SASK	ALTA	BC	YT	NWT & NVT	Canada
						(kilotonnes of CO_2-equivalent emissions[1])							
Fossil fuel combustion	8 040	1 620	19 400	18 800	61 800	167 000	12 800	37 200	156 000	48 200	418	1 620	533 000
Fossil fuel industries	1 380	0	989	1 520	3 610	6 550	1	4 400	44 400	3 540	82	156	66 800
Electricity and heat generation	920	58	8 830	8 560	579	40 300	984	14 500	51 000	2 280	17	321	128 000
Mining	915	5	54	133	922	469	29	2 140	4 160	355	0	80	9 270
Manufacturing	241	134	660	1 320	11 000	22 600	1 130	893	12 400	7 560	0	2	57 900
Construction	11	6	28	40	190	439	62	49	171	76	2	0	1 080
Transportation	3 650	871	5 900	5 640	33 500	63 900	7 430	11 200	31 000	26 300	248	754	190 000
Residential	553	318	1 800	853	6 000	19 100	1 390	1 980	8 280	4 600	31	125	45 000
Commercial and institutional	324	198	922	614	5 720	12 500	1 680	1 710	4 790	3 200	37	179	31 900
Other	48	32	237	66	262	902	63	281	361	315	1	0	2 570
Fugitive emissions (fossil fuels)[2]	120	0	390	30	440	1 700	530	11 000	34 000	6 100	53	120	54 000
Industrial processes	85	2	270	230	13 000	18 000	470	2 000	11 000	3 200	0	4	51 000
Agriculture	80	430	610	530	7 700	11 000	6 900	11 000	19 000	2 500	0	0	60 000
Waste	430	91	700	600	6 700	8 300	600	610	1 200	5 000	8	19	24 000
Other[3]	48	5	64	61	510	580	117	215	345	861	50	61	2 500
Total	**8 810**	**2 150**	**21 500**	**20 200**	**90 400**	**207 000**	**21 400**	**61 800**	**223 000**	**65 900**	**529**	**1 830**	**726 000**

NOTE: Due to rounding, individual values may not add up to totals (zero values may represent estimated quantities too small to display).
[1] CO_2-equivalent emissions are the weighted sum of all greenhouse gas emissions. The following global warming potentials are used as the weights: CO_2 = 1; CH_4 = 21; N_2O = 310; HFC = 140–11 700; PFC = 6 500–9 200; SF_6 = 23 900. [2] Includes intentional and unintentional emissions from production, processing, transmission, storage, and use of fuels, including those from flaring of natural gas at oil and gas production facilities. [3] Includes emissions from use of solvents, from land use change, and from forestry.
SOURCE: Adapted from Olsen, K., et al, *Canada's Greenhouse Gas Inventory 1990–2000*, Appendix E, Greenhouse Gas Division, Environment Canada, Ottawa, ON, June 2002, Catalogue No. EN-49-5-5/5-9-2-2000E. Adapted with the permission of the Minister of Public Works and Government Services, 2003.

82. Characteristics of Canada's National Parks System, 1997

National Park/National Park Reserve/ Marine Conservation Area, Province	Number of Visitors (person-visits[1])	Area (km[2])	Visitors per Park Area (person-visits/km[2])	Number of Trails	Length of Trails (km)	Stress Reported From Visitor/Tourism Facilities[2]
Gros Morne, NFLD	120 943	1 805.0	61	19	74	yes
Terra Nova, NFLD	232 616	399.9	500	26	79	yes
Prince Edward Island, PEI	749 212[3]	21.5	30 233	15	42	yes
Cape Breton Highlands, NS	379 894[(e)]	948.0	559	35	217	yes
Kejimkujik, NS	56 592	403.7	421	42	144	yes
Fundy, NB	220 725	205.9	1 068	26	111	yes
Kouchibouguac, NB	229 562	239.2	711	15	93	yes
Forillon, QUE	173 914	240.4	749	15	83	yes
Mauricie, QUE	215 888	536.1	504	81	67	yes
Mingan Archipelago, QUE (R)	19 860	150.7	186	8	4	yes
Saguenay–St. Lawrence, QUE (M)	377 382	1 138.0	n.r.	2	1	n.a.
Bruce Peninsula, ONT	207 444	154.0	714	8	12	yes
Fathom Five, ONT (M)	399 054	113.0	n.r.	n.r.	n.r.	n.a.
Georgian Bay Islands, ONT	69 252	25.6	1 992	15	51	yes
Point Pelee, ONT	384 682	15.0	28 661	17	29	yes
Pukaskwa, ONT	7 940	1 877.8	9	5	66	yes
St. Lawrence Islands, ONT	63 278	8.7	5 057	7	9	yes
Riding Mountain, MAN	353 134	2 973.1	118	48	673	yes
Wapusk, MAN	n.a.	11 475.0	n.a.	n.a.	n.a.	no
Grasslands, SASK	3 451	906.4	2	3	13	no
Prince Albert, SASK	172 194	3 874.3	49	35	381	yes
Banff, ALTA	4 453 021	6 641.0	599	154	1 215	yes
Elk Island, ALTA	152 852	194.0	1 495	13	86	yes
Jasper, ALTA	2 100 089	10 878.0	120	109	1 772	yes
Waterton Lakes, ALTA	330 939	505.0	693	33	211	yes
Glacier, BC	101 924	1 349.3	119	51[4]	201[4]	yes
Gwaii Haanas, BC (R, M)	2 077	1 495.0[5]	1	n.a.	n.a.	no
Kootenay, BC	1 113 795	1 406.4	853	39	261	yes
Mount Revelstoke, BC	163 687	259.7	616	51[4]	201[4]	yes
Pacific Rim, BC (R)	836 120	285.8[5]	1 241	21	339	no
Yoho, BC	678 189	1 313.1	495	71	266	yes
Ivvavik, YT	152	9 750.0	v.s.	n.a.	n.a.	no
Kluane, YT	69 924	22 013.3	3	18	235	no
Vuntut, YT	n.a.	4 345.0	n.a.	n.a.	n.a.	no
Aulavik, NWT	20	12 200.0	v.s.	n.a.	n.a.	no
Auyittuq, NWT (R)	470	19 707.4[6]	v.s.	1	100	no
Ellesmere Island, NWT	462	37 775.0	v.s.	n.a.	n.a.	no
Nahanni, NWT (R)	4 605	4 765.2	v.s.	4	12	no
Tuktut Nogait, NWT	n.a.	16 340.0	n.a.	n.a.	n.a.	n.a.
Wood Buffalo, NWT and ALTA	6 040	44 802.0	v.s.	10	67	yes
Total	**14 451 383**	**222 283.0[7]**	**n.a.**	**n.r.**	**n.r.**	**n.r.**

v.s. = very small/too small to be expressed; n.a. = not available; n.r. = not relevant/not appropriate; e = estimated data; R = national park reserve: an area set aside as a national park pending settlement of any outstanding Aboriginal land claim; M = marine conservation area

[1]Considered to be each time a person enters a park reporting unit for the purpose of recreation. Same-day re-entries by visitors staying overnight in the reporting unit do not constitute new person-visits. [2]Stress from visitor/tourism facilities was reported if: (1) it had a definite ecological impact; (2) the scale of the impact was greater than 1 km[2]; and (3) the trend in the intensity of the stress was either increasing or stable. [3]Excludes visits to Green Gables House. [4]Combined total of Glacier and Mount Revelstoke national parks. [5]Excludes marine portion. [6]Park area measurement pending review by Surveyor General. [7]Excludes Fathom Five and Saguenay–St. Lawrence Marine Conservation areas, as well as marine portions of Gwaii Haanas (3 570 km[2]) and Pacific Rim Park (214 km[2]) reserves.

SOURCE: Adapted from the Statistics Canada publication "Human Activity and the Environment", 2000, Catalogue 11-509, June 2000, p. 306.

83. Species at Risk in Canada, 2001[1]

Status	Birds	Terrestrial Mammals	Marine Mammals	Fish	Amphibians & Reptiles	Molluscs	Lepidoptera (Butterflies & Moths)	Plants	Lichens & Mosses	Total
Extinct	3	1	1	6	0	1	0	0	0	12
Extirpated	2	2	2	2	3	1	3	2	0	17
Endangered	20	9	7	10	10	7	3	49	3	118
Threatened	8	8	6	21	13	1	2	34	1	94
Special concern	21	17	8	37	13	1	2	44	3	146
Total	**54**	**37**	**24**	**76**	**39**	**11**	**10**	**129**	**7**	**387**[2]

[1]See map on page 25 for additional information. [2]This number includes the 12 species that are already extinct.
SOURCE: Environment Canada, *Hinterland Who's Who: Endangered Species in Canada 2002*, "Species at Risk in Canada (November 2001)", Catalogue CW69-4/76-2002E, p.3.

Climate

84. Annual Average "Number of Days with" and Hours of Bright Sunshine

Station	Average[1] Number of Days with:[2]								Bright Sunshine[3] (hours)
	Winds (>63 km/h)	Hail[4]	Thunder[5]	Fog[6]	Freezing Temperatures[7]	Freezing Precipitation[8]	Rain[9]	Snow[10]	
Goose Bay	1	*	9	14	215	13	102	97	1 564.9
St. John's	23	*	3	124	176	38	156	88	1 497.4
Charlottetown	6	*	9	47	169	17	124	68	1 818.4
Halifax	3	*	9	122	163	19	125	64	1 885.0
Saint John	6	*	11	106	173	12	124	59	1 865.3
Kuujjuarapik	3	*	6	45	243	10	83	100	1 497.8
Quebec	*	*	24	35	180	15	115	73	1 851.7
Sept-Îles	9	*	7	51	206	8	93	72	1 990.6
Montreal	1	*	25	20	155	13	114	62	2 054.0
Ottawa	*	*	24	35	165	16	107	62	2 008.5
Thunder Bay	*	*	26	38	204	8	88	61	2 202.8
Toronto	*	*	27	35	155	10	99	47	2 045.4
Windsor	2	*	33	37	136	9	105	45	n.a.
The Pas	*	*	23	15	209	12	65	73	2 167.5
Winnipeg	1	3	27	20	195	12	72	57	2 321.4
Churchill	11	*	7	48	258	19	58	100	1 827.9
Regina	9	1	23	29	204	14	59	58	2 331.1
Saskatoon	*	*	19	25	202	9	57	59	2 449.7
Calgary	6	3	25	22	201	5	58	62	2 314.4
Edmonton	*	3	22	17	185	8	70	59	2 263.7
Penticton	*	*	12	1	129	1	78	29	2 032.2
Vancouver	*	*	6	45	55	1	156	15	1 919.6
Prince Rupert	4	8	2	37	107	0	218	35	1 224.1
Alert	10	0	0	46	338	5	10	93	1 767.4
Inuvik	*	*	1	24	267	6	36	99	1 898.8
Yellowknife	*	*	5	21	226	13	46	82	2 276.6
Whitehorse	*	*	6	16	224	1	52	120	1 843.8
Resolute	25	0	*	62	324	13	20	82	1 505.1

* = a value less than 0.5 (but not zero); n.a. = not available
[1]Average, mean, or normal refer to the value of the particular element averaged over the period from 1951-1980. [2]A "day with" is counted once per day regardless of the number of individual occurrences of that phenomenon that day. [3]Bright sunshine is reported in hours and tenths. [4]Hail is a piece of ice with a diameter of 5 mm or more. [5]Thunder is reported when thunder is heard or lightning or hail is seen. [6]Fog is a suspension of small water droplets in air that reduces the horizontal visibility at eye level to less than 1 km. [7]Freezing temperature is a temperature below 0°C. [8]Freezing precipitation is rain or drizzle of any quantity that freezes on impact. [9]Rain is a measurable amount of liquid water (rain, showers, or drizzle) equal to or greater than 0.2 mm. [10]Snow is a measurable amount of solid precipitation (snow, snow grains, ice crystals, or ice and snow pellets) equal to or greater than 0.2 cm.
SOURCE: Adapted from David Phillips, *The Climates of Canada*, Catalogue EN56-1/1990E, Ottawa: Canadian Government Publishing, 1990 and the Environment Canada publications *Canadian Climate Normals 1961-1990* and *Principal Station Data.*

85. Average Monthly Precipitation[1] (mm)

Station	Jan	Feb	Mar	Apr	May	June	July	Aug	Sept	Oct	Nov	Dec	Annual
Goose Bay	64.9	57.0	68.6	57.1	66.4	100.9	119.4	98.3	90.6	78.8	79.9	77.6	959.5
St. John's West	179.4	154.9	146.3	124.5	107.0	93.5	77.8	113.8	117.0	149.0	152.8	163.5	1 579.5
Charlottetown	97.1	82.3	83.1	88.3	94.2	87.5	78.5	90.1	91.9	112.4	115.0	116.7	1 137.1
Halifax	146.9	119.1	122.6	124.4	110.5	98.4	96.8	109.6	94.9	128.9	154.4	167.0	1 473.5
Saint John	128.3	102.6	109.9	109.7	123.1	104.8	103.7	103.0	111.3	122.5	146.2	167.6	1 432.8
Kuujjuarapik	28.1	21.1	21.1	25.1	36.4	57.3	72.7	89.0	93.6	73.3	62.1	35.1	614.9
Quebec	90.0	74.4	85.0	75.5	99.9	110.2	118.5	119.6	123.7	96.0	106.1	108.9	1 207.7
Sept-Îles	86.8	68.9	80.9	93.4	96.3	92.4	90.8	99.6	111.5	100.8	99.6	107.0	1 127.9
Montreal	63.3	56.4	67.6	74.8	68.3	82.5	85.6	100.3	86.5	75.4	93.4	85.6	939.7
Ottawa	50.8	49.7	56.6	64.8	76.8	84.3	86.5	87.8	83.6	74.7	81.0	72.9	869.5
Thunder Bay	32.4	25.6	40.9	47.1	69.3	84.0	79.9	88.5	86.4	60.9	49.4	39.3	703.5
Toronto	55.2	52.6	65.2	65.4	68.0	67.0	71.0	82.5	76.2	63.3	76.1	76.5	818.9
Windsor	50.3	53.7	72.0	80.3	75.7	97.0	85.3	85.7	86.7	57.9	75.4	81.6	901.6
The Pas	16.6	15.1	21.0	26.2	33.6	63.1	69.1	65.0	58.3	37.5	26.6	19.8	451.9
Winnipeg	19.3	14.8	23.1	35.9	59.8	83.8	72.0	75.3	51.3	29.5	21.2	18.6	504.4
Churchill	17.3	12.8	18.3	22.6	30.5	44.5	50.7	60.5	52.6	46.5	35.5	19.7	411.6
Regina	14.7	13.0	16.5	20.4	50.8	67.3	58.9	40.0	34.4	20.3	11.7	15.9	364.0
Saskatoon	15.9	12.9	16.0	19.7	44.2	63.4	58.0	36.8	32.1	16.9	14.1	17.2	347.2
Calgary	12.2	9.9	14.7	25.1	52.9	76.9	69.9	48.7	48.1	15.5	11.6	13.2	398.8
Edmonton	22.9	15.5	15.9	21.8	42.8	76.1	101.0	69.5	47.5	17.7	16.0	19.2	465.8
Penticton	27.3	20.6	20.4	25.8	33.0	34.4	23.3	28.4	23.0	15.7	24.3	32.1	308.5
Vancouver	149.8	123.6	108.8	75.4	61.7	45.7	36.1	38.1	64.4	115.3	169.9	178.5	1 167.4
Prince Rupert	250.8	216.5	188.2	181.0	142.0	119.5	112.9	162.8	244.7	378.9	284.4	269.8	2 551.6
Alert	7.8	5.2	6.8	9.4	9.9	12.7	25.0	23.8	24.3	13.2	8.8	7.4	154.2
Inuvik	15.6	11.1	10.8	12.6	19.1	22.2	34.1	43.9	24.2	29.6	17.5	16.8	257.4
Yellowknife	14.9	12.6	10.6	10.3	16.6	23.3	35.2	41.7	28.8	34.8	23.9	14.7	267.3
Whitehorse	16.9	11.9	12.1	8.3	14.4	31.2	38.5	39.3	35.2	23.0	18.9	18.9	268.8
Resolute	3.5	3.2	4.7	6.2	8.3	12.7	23.4	31.5	22.8	13.1	5.7	4.6	139.6

[1]These are statistics for the 1961–1990 period.
SOURCE: Environment Canada web site <http://www.msc-smc.ec.gc.ca/climate/climate_normals/index_e.cfm>. Reproduced with the permission of the Minister of Public Works and Government Services Canada, 2003.

86. Average Daily Temperature[1] (°C)

Station	Jan	Feb	Mar	Apr	May	June	July	Aug	Sept	Oct	Nov	Dec	Annual
Goose Bay	-17.3	-15.5	-9.2	-1.8	5.1	10.9	15.5	14.2	9.0	2.5	-4.0	-13.4	-0.3
St. John's West	-4.0	-4.6	-2.0	1.8	6.4	11.3	15.8	15.6	11.8	7.3	3.3	-1.4	5.1
Charlottetown	-7.2	-7.5	-3.0	2.7	9.2	14.8	18.8	18.4	14.0	8.6	3.1	-3.6	5.7
Halifax	-5.8	-6.0	-1.7	3.6	9.4	14.7	18.3	18.1	13.8	8.5	3.2	-3.0	6.1
Saint John	-8.2	-7.7	-2.6	3.2	9.1	13.8	16.9	16.7	12.7	7.5	2.1	-5.0	4.9
Kuujjuarapik	-22.8	-23.1	-17.5	-7.1	1.2	6.3	10.2	10.6	7.2	2.1	-5.0	-16.6	-4.5
Quebec	-12.4	-11.0	-4.6	3.3	10.8	16.3	19.1	17.6	12.5	6.5	-0.5	-9.1	4.0
Sept-Îles	-14.6	-13.0	-6.8	0.0	5.9	11.6	15.2	14.2	9.2	3.4	-2.7	-11.0	0.9
Montreal	-10.3	-8.8	-2.4	5.7	12.9	18.0	20.8	19.4	14.5	8.3	1.6	-6.9	6.1
Ottawa	-10.7	-9.2	-2.6	5.9	13.0	18.1	20.8	19.4	14.7	8.3	1.5	-7.2	6.0
Thunder Bay	-15.0	-12.8	-5.6	2.7	9.0	13.9	17.7	16.4	11.2	5.4	-2.6	-11.3	2.4
Toronto	-4.5	-3.8	1.0	7.5	13.8	18.9	22.1	21.1	16.9	10.7	4.9	-1.5	8.9
Windsor	-5.0	-3.9	1.7	8.1	14.4	19.7	22.4	21.3	17.4	10.9	4.7	-1.9	9.1
The Pas	-21.4	-17.5	-10.0	0.5	8.7	14.8	17.7	16.4	9.9	3.5	-7.7	-18.0	-0.3
Winnipeg	-18.3	-15.1	-7.0	3.8	11.6	16.9	19.8	18.3	12.4	5.7	-4.7	-14.6	2.4
Churchill	-26.9	-25.4	-20.2	-10.0	-1.1	6.1	11.8	11.3	5.5	-1.4	-12.5	-22.7	-7.1
Regina	-16.5	-12.9	-6.0	4.1	11.4	16.4	19.1	18.1	11.6	5.1	-5.1	-13.6	2.6
Saskatoon	-17.5	-13.9	-7.0	3.9	11.5	16.2	18.6	17.4	11.2	4.8	-6.0	-14.7	2.0
Calgary	-9.6	-6.3	-2.5	4.1	9.7	14.0	16.4	15.7	10.6	5.7	-3.0	-8.3	3.9
Edmonton	-14.2	-10.8	-5.4	3.7	10.3	14.2	16.0	15.0	9.9	4.6	-5.7	-12.2	2.1
Penticton	-2.0	0.7	4.5	8.7	13.3	17.6	20.3	19.9	14.7	8.7	3.2	-1.1	9.0
Vancouver	3.0	4.7	6.3	8.8	12.1	15.2	17.2	17.4	14.3	10.0	6.0	3.5	9.9
Prince Rupert	0.8	2.5	3.7	5.5	8.4	10.9	12.9	13.3	11.3	8.0	3.8	1.7	6.9
Alert	-31.9	-33.6	-33.1	-25.1	-11.6	-1.0	3.4	1.0	-9.7	-19.5	-27.0	-29.5	-18.1
Inuvik	-28.8	-28.5	-24.1	-14.1	-0.7	10.6	13.8	10.5	3.3	-8.2	-21.5	-26.1	-9.5
Yellowknife	-27.9	-24.5	-18.5	-6.2	5.0	13.1	16.5	14.1	6.7	-1.4	-14.8	-24.1	-5.2
Whitehorse	-18.7	-13.1	-7.2	0.3	6.6	11.6	14.0	12.3	7.3	0.7	-10.0	-15.9	-1.0
Resolute	-32.0	-33.0	-31.2	-23.5	-11.0	-0.6	4.0	1.9	-5.0	-15.2	-24.3	-29.0	-16.6

[1]These are statistics for the 1961–1990 period.
SOURCE: Environment Canada web site <http://www.msc-smc.ec.gc.ca/climate/climate_normals/index_e.cfm>. Reproduced with the permission of the Minister of Public Works and Government Services Canada, 2003.

The datasets below are explained on pages 182/183

	ooo	no data
	per capita	for each person

	Land		Population									Employment		
	Area	Arable and permanent crops	Total	Density	Change	Births	Deaths	Fertility	Infant mortality	Life expectancy	Urban	Agriculture	Industry	Services
	2002	2002	2002	2002	1990–2000	2002	2002	2000	2000	2000	2000	1990	1990	1990
	thousand km²	% of total	millions	persons per km²	%	births per 1000	deaths per 1000	children per mother	per 1000 live births	years	%	%	%	%
Afghanistan	652	12.4	27.8	42.6	75.5	41	17	6.0	145	45	22	ooo	ooo	ooo
Albania	29	24.3	3.5	120.7	7.1	19	6	2.8	27	72	46	55	23	22
Algeria	2382	3.5	32.3	13.6	23.1	22	5	3.1	50	69	49	26	31	43
Andorra	0.5	2.2	0.07	136.0	26.5	10	6	1.2	4	ooo	93	ooo	ooo	ooo
Angola	1247	2.8	10.6	8.5	25.9	46	26	6.9	172	38	32	75	8	17
Antigua and Barbuda	0.4	18.2	0.07	167.5	6.0	19	6	2.4	13	70	37	ooo	ooo	ooo
Argentina	2780	9.8	38.3	13.8	13.2	18	8	2.6	18	73	90	12	32	56
Armenia	30	18.8	3.3	110.0	-0.6	12	10	1.1	25	73	67	18	43	39
Australia	7741	6.2	19.5	2.5	12.6	13	7	1.7	6	79	85	6	26	68
Austria	84	17.6	8.2	97.6	5.4	10	10	1.3	5	78	65	8	38	54
Azerbaijan	87	22.9	7.8	89.7	7.6	19	10	2.0	74	72	51	31	29	40
Bahamas, The	14	0.7	0.3	21.4	14.7	19	9	2.4	15	72	84	5	16	79
Bahrain	0.7	8.7	0.7	937.1	26.7	20	4	2.8	13	72	88	2	30	68
Bangladesh	144	58.6	135.7	942.4	17.6	30	9	3.3	54	59	21	65	16	19
Barbados	0.4	39.5	0.3	690.0	4.4	13	9	1.6	12	73	38	14	30	56
Belarus	208	30.4	10.3	49.5	1.5	10	14	1.3	17	68	70	20	40	40
Belgium	33	25.2	10.3	312.1	2.7	11	10	1.6	6	78	97	3	28	69
Belize	23	3.9	0.3	11.3	30.5	31	6	3.2	34	72	49	33	19	48
Benin	113	16.4	6.8	60.2	37.4	44	14	6.3	98	50	39	63	8	29
Bhutan	47	3.4	2.1	44.7	25.5	35	14	5.6	77	66	15	94	2	4
Bolivia	1099	2.0	8.4	7.6	24.0	26	8	4.2	62	62	63	47	18	35
Bosnia-Herzegovina	51	12.7	4.0	77.7	-13.3	13	8	1.6	24	68	40	ooo	ooo	ooo
Botswana	582	0.6	1.6	2.7	20.9	26	29	3.9	74	41	49	46	20	34
Brazil	8547	7.6	179.9	21.0	14.4	18	6	2.4	32	68	81	23	23	54
Brunei	6	1.2	0.4	58.3	30.3	20	3	2.7	6	74	67	2	24	74
Bulgaria	111	40.7	7.6	68.5	-12.3	8	14	1.2	14	72	68	13	48	39
Burkina	274	12.6	12.9	47.1	32.2	45	19	6.8	105	47	15	92	2	6
Burundi	28	39.5	6.0	213.0	14.6	40	18	6.5	114	47	8	92	3	5
Cambodia	181	21.0	12.9	71.2	36.2	27	9	4.0	95	56	16	74	8	18
Cameroon	475	15.1	15.4	32.4	31.1	36	15	5.2	95	55	48	70	9	21
Canada	9971	4.6	31.9	3.2	12.6	11	8	1.4	6	79	78	3	25	72
Cape Verde	4	10.2	0.4	100.0	14.9	28	7	4.0	30	68	53	30	30	40
Central African Republic	623	3.2	3.6	5.8	25.3	36	19	5.1	115	45	39	80	3	17
Chad	1284	2.8	9.0	7.0	40.0	48	16	6.6	118	50	21	83	4	13
Chile	757	3.0	15.5	20.5	15.4	16	6	2.3	10	75	86	19	25	56
China	9598	14.1	1286.5	134.0	10.8	13	7	1.8	32	71	36	72	15	13
Colombia	1139	3.8	41.0	36.0	20.8	22	6	2.6	25	71	71	27	23	50
Comoros	2	52.9	0.6	307.0	34.8	39	9	6.8	61	56	29	78	9	13
Congo	342	0.6	2.9	8.5	27.7	30	14	6.3	81	50	41	49	15	36
Congo, Dem. Rep.	2345	3.4	55.0	23.5	36.8	46	15	7.0	128	48	29	68	13	19
Costa Rica	51	9.9	3.8	74.5	22.6	20	4	2.6	10	77	45	26	27	47
Côte d'Ivoire	322	22.8	16.6	51.6	34.1	40	18	5.2	102	46	46	60	10	30
Croatia	57	28.1	4.4	77.2	-5.0	13	11	1.4	8	74	54	16	34	50
Cuba	111	40.3	11.2	100.9	5.7	12	7	1.6	7	75	75	19	30	51
Cyprus	9	15.5	0.8	85.2	11.3	13	8	1.8	6	77	66	14	30	56
Czech Republic	79	42.2	10.3	130.4	-0.4	9	11	1.1	5	75	77	11	45	44
Denmark	43	53.4	5.4	125.6	3.8	12	11	1.7	4	76	72	6	28	66
Djibouti	23	ooo	0.5	19.4	22.1	41	19	6.1	102	46	83	ooo	ooo	ooo
Dominica	0.8	20.0	0.07	87.5	-1.6	17	7	1.8	14	73	71	ooo	ooo	ooo
Dominican Republic	49	32.2	8.6	175.5	18.9	24	7	3.1	42	69	61	25	29	46
Ecuador	284	10.6	13.4	47.2	25.2	25	5	3.3	25	71	62	33	19	48
Egypt	1001	3.3	73.3	73.2	21.8	25	5	3.5	37	66	43	40	22	38
El Salvador	21	38.5	6.4	304.8	20.1	28	6	3.5	34	70	58	36	21	43
Equatorial Guinea	28	8.2	0.5	17.9	28.8	37	13	5.9	103	50	37	66	11	23
Eritrea	118	4.3	4.3	36.4	40.5	40	13	6.0	73	55	16	80	5	15

Wealth · Energy and trade · Quality of life

GNP (2000, billion US$)	Purchasing power (2000, US$)	Growth of PP (1990–2000, %)	Energy consumption (1999, kg oil equivalent per capita)	Imports (1999, US$ per capita)	Exports (1999, US$ per capita)	Aid received (given) (2000, million US$)	Human Development Index (2000)	Health care (1990–1999, doctors per 100 000)	Food consumption (1997, daily calories per capita)	Safe water (2000, % access)	Illiteracy male (1998, %)	Illiteracy female (1998, %)	Higher education (1996, students per 100 000)	Cars (2000, people per car)	Country
2.9	3506	2.7	311	170	344	142	—	—	—	13	—	—	165	644	Afghanistan
48.3	5308	-0.1	944	420	312	319	0.733	129	2961	76	9	24	1087	36	Albania
—	—	—	595	398	515	162	0.697	85	2853	94	24	46	1238	34	Algeria
3.1	2187	-1.8	—	—	—	—	—	—	—	100	—	—	—	2	Andorra
—	—	—	—	—	—	307	0.403	8	1903	38	—	—	—	111	Angola
—	10 541	2.8	—	—	—	10	0.800	—	2365	91	—	—	—	—	Antigua and Barbuda
275.5	12 377	3.0	1727	740	869	76	0.844	268	3093	79	3	3	3317	7	Argentina
2.0	2559	-2.5	485	101	242	216	0.754	316	2371	84	1	3	1886	1900	Armenia
394.1	25 693	2.9	5690	3801	4364	(987)	0.939	240	3224	100	—	—	5682	2	Australia
204.2	26 765	1.7	3513	11 719	11 840	(423)	0.926	302	3536	100	—	—	2988	2	Austria
4.9	2936	-7.3	1575	158	237	139	0.741	360	2236	—	—	—	2289	30	Azerbaijan
—	17 012	0.1	—	—	—	6	0.826	152	2443	96	—	—	—	4	Bahamas, The
—	15 084	1.7	9000	—	—	49	0.831	100	—	—	—	—	1402	5	Bahrain
49.9	1602	3.0	139	43	61	1172	0.478	20	2085	97	49	71	397	2808	Bangladesh
—	15 494	1.7	—	—	—	0	0.871	125	3176	100	—	—	2535	7	Barbados
30.0	7544	-1.4	2381	655	685	40	0.788	443	3225	100	0	—	3168	9	Belarus
252.5	27 178	1.8	5735	18 856	17 811	(820)	0.939	395	3619	—	—	—	3551	2	Belgium
0.7	5606	1.6	—	—	—	15	0.784	55	2907	76	—	—	—	29	Belize
2.4	990	1.8	323	83	122	239	0.420	6	2487	63	46	77	256	260	Benin
0.4	1412	3.4	—	—	—	53	0.494	16	—	62	—	—	—	—	Bhutan
8.3	2424	1.6	562	154	234	477	0.653	130	2174	79	9	22	—	65	Bolivia
—	—	—	518	—	—	1063	—	—	—	—	—	—	—	34	Bosnia-Herzegovina
5.3	7184	2.3	—	1903	1570	31	0.572	24	2183	70	27	22	587	59	Botswana
606.8	7625	1.5	1068	323	369	322	0.757	127	2974	83	16	16	1424	11	Brazil
—	16 779	-0.7	4341	—	—	1	0.856	85	2857	—	—	—	516	2	Brunei
12.4	5710	-1.5	2218	733	830	311	0.779	345	2686	100	1	2	3110	5	Bulgaria
2.6	976	2.4	—	27	62	336	0.325	3	2121	—	68	87	83	744	Burkina
0.7	591	-4.7	—	9	20	93	0.313	—	1685	52	45	63	—	650	Burundi
3.1	1446	2.0	—	84	105	399	0.543	30	2048	30	43	80	85	788	Cambodia
8.6	1703	-0.8	419	148	151	380	0.512	7	2111	62	20	33	—	152	Cameroon
647.1	27 840	1.9	7929	8957	8354	(1744)	0.940	229	3119	100	—	—	5953	2	Canada
0.6	4863	3.3	—	—	—	94	0.715	17	3015	74	—	—	—	133	Cape Verde
1.1	1172	-0.5	—	41	64	76	0.375	4	2016	60	43	68	—	422	Central African Republic
1.5	871	-0.8	—	38	61	131	0.365	3	2032	27	21	69	51	853	Chad
69.9	9417	5.2	1688	1260	1173	49	0.831	110	2796	94	4	5	2546	15	Chile
1240.9	3976	9.2	868	169	147	1735	0.726	162	2897	75	9	25	473	369	China
88.0	6248	1.1	676	324	312	187	0.772	116	2597	91	9	9	1640	43	Colombia
0.2	1588	-2.4	—	—	—	19	0.511	7	1858	96	—	—	—	1	Comoros
1.8	825	-3.4	245	578	618	33	0.512	25	2143	51	14	29	—	119	Congo
5.0	765	-8.2	293	28	26	184	0.431	7	1755	45	29	53	212	525	Congo, Dem. Rep.
14.4	8650	3.0	818	1998	1752	12	0.820	141	2649	98	5	5	2830	22	Costa Rica
10.5	1630	0.4	388	326	252	352	0.428	9	2610	77	47	64	568	88	Côte d'Ivoire
20.1	8091	1.8	1864	1727	2083	66	0.809	229	2445	95	1	3	1911	5	Croatia
—	—	3.7	1117	—	—	44	0.795	—	2480	95	—	—	1013	574	Cuba
9.1	20 824	3.1	3057	—	—	55	0.883	255	3429	100	—	—	1193	4	Cyprus
50.6	13 991	1.0	3754	3222	3300	438	0.849	303	3244	—	—	—	2009	3	Czech Republic
171.0	27 627	2.1	3773	12 394	10 959	(1664)	0.926	290	3407	100	—	—	3349	3	Denmark
0.5	2377	-3.9	—	—	—	71	0.445	14	2084	100	—	—	26	55	Djibouti
0.2	5880	—	—	—	—	16	0.779	—	3059	97	—	—	—	23	Dominica
18.0	6033	4.2	904	940	1093	62	0.727	216	2288	79	17	17	2223	53	Dominican Republic
15.3	3203	-0.3	705	408	317	147	0.732	170	2679	71	8	11	—	123	Ecuador
95.2	3635	2.5	709	196	306	1328	0.642	202	3287	95	35	58	1895	52	Egypt
12.5	4497	2.6	651	490	727	180	0.706	107	2562	74	19	25	1935	67	El Salvador
0.5	15 073	18.9	—	—	—	21	0.679	25	—	43	—	—	—	143	Equatorial Guinea
0.7	837	1.1	—	17	157	176	0.421	3	1622	46	34	62	90	760	Eritrea

The datasets below are explained on pages 182/183.

ooo	no data	
per capita	for each person	

	Land		Population									Employment		
	Area	Arable and permanent crops	Total	Density	Change	Births	Deaths	Fertility	Infant mortality	Life expectancy	Urban	Agriculture	Industry	Services
	2002		2002	2002	1990–2000	2002	2002	2000	2000	2000	2000	1990	1990	1990
	thousand km²	% of total	millions	persons per km²	%	births per 1000	deaths per 1000	children per mother	per 1000 live births	years	%	%	%	%
Estonia	45	25.2	1.4	31.1	-9.0	9	13	1.3	17	71	69	14	41	45
Ethiopia	1104	9.7	65.3	59.1	32.7	40	20	5.9	117	52	15	86	2	12
Fiji	18	15.6	0.9	47.6	12.8	23	6	3.3	18	67	46	46	15	39
Finland	338	6.4	5.2	15.4	3.6	11	10	1.7	4	77	60	8	31	61
France	552	35.4	59.9	108.5	4.6	13	9	1.9	4	79	74	5	29	66
French Guiana	91	0.1	0.2	2.0	48.9	22	5	3.4	ooo	76	79	ooo	ooo	ooo
Gabon	268	1.8	1.3	4.9	13.0	37	11	4.3	60	52	73	51	16	33
Gambia, The	11	17.7	1.5	136.4	42.2	41	13	5.9	92	52	37	82	8	10
Georgia	70	15.3	5.0	70.9	-8.0	11	15	1.2	24	73	56	26	31	43
Germany	357	33.7	82.4	230.8	4.3	9	10	1.3	4	78	86	4	38	58
Ghana	239	22.2	20.2	84.5	27.2	27	10	4.3	58	58	37	59	13	28
Greece	132	29.3	10.6	80.3	4.4	10	10	1.3	5	78	59	23	27	50
Greenland	342	ooo	0.06	0.2	1.1	16	8	ooo	ooo	ooo	ooo	ooo	ooo	ooo
Grenada	0.3	32.4	0.09	296.7	-3.3	23	8	2.4	21	65	34	ooo	ooo	ooo
Guatemala	109	17.5	13.5	123.9	31.2	36	7	4.8	44	66	39	52	17	31
Guinea	246	6	8.8	35.8	25.8	43	16	5.5	112	45	26	87	2	11
Guinea-Bissau	36	9.7	1.3	36.1	29.1	39	17	5.8	132	45	22	85	2	13
Guyana	215	2.3	0.7	3.3	-6.0	18	9	2.5	55	65	36	22	25	53
Haiti	28	32.8	7.4	264.3	13.9	34	14	4.7	81	49	35	68	9	23
Honduras	112	16.3	6.5	58.0	31.0	32	6	4.4	32	66	46	41	20	39
Hungary	93	54.2	10.1	108.6	-2.3	9	13	1.3	8	71	64	15	38	47
Iceland	103	0.07	0.3	2.7	8.5	14	7	2.0	4	79	93	ooo	ooo	ooo
India	3288	51.6	1034.2	314.5	19.2	24	9	3.2	69	61	28	64	16	20
Indonesia	1905	16.3	231.3	121.4	19.2	22	6	2.7	35	67	39	55	14	31
Iran	1633	11.8	67.5	41.3	17.8	17	6	2.6	36	70	64	39	23	38
Iraq	438	12.2	24.0	54.8	25.0	34	6	5.3	104	59	68	16	18	66
Ireland	70	15.4	3.9	55.7	8.2	15	8	1.9	6	77	58	14	29	57
Israel	21	20.9	6.0	285.7	29.5	19	6	3.0	6	78	91	4	29	67
Italy	301	37.9	57.9	192.4	1.6	9	10	1.3	6	79	90	9	31	60
Jamaica	11	24.9	2.7	245.5	7.7	18	5	2.4	17	71	50	25	23	52
Japan	378	12.9	127.1	336.2	2.4	10	8	1.3	4	81	78	7	34	59
Jordan	89	4.3	5.3	59.6	53.2	25	3	3.6	28	70	79	15	23	62
Kazakhstan	2717	11.1	16.7	6.1	0.2	18	11	1.8	60	66	56	22	32	46
Kenya	580	7.8	31.2	53.8	27.7	30	16	4.4	77	48	20	80	7	13
Kiribati	0.7	50.7	0.1	137.1	28.9	32	9	4.5	53	62	37	ooo	ooo	ooo
Kuwait	18	0.4	2.1	116.7	-7.9	22	2	4.2	9	73	100	1	25	74
Kyrgyzstan	199	7.2	4.8	24.1	6.7	26	9	2.4	53	69	35	32	27	41
Laos	237	4.0	5.8	24.5	30.6	37	13	5.4	90	52	17	78	6	16
Latvia	65	29.1	2.4	36.9	-10.0	8	15	1.2	17	71	69	16	40	44
Lebanon	10	29.6	3.7	370.0	13.7	20	6	2.5	28	71	88	7	31	62
Lesotho	30	10.7	1.9	63.3	23.7	28	24	4.3	92	53	16	40	28	32
Liberia	111	2.9	3.3	29.7	44.5	46	18	6.6	157	50	45	ooo	ooo	ooo
Libya	1760	1.2	5.4	3.1	23.6	28	4	3.9	17	75	86	11	23	66
Liechtenstein	0.2	25.0	0.03	150.0	11.8	11	7	1.4	10	ooo	23	ooo	ooo	ooo
Lithuania	65	46.0	3.6	55.4	-2.2	10	13	1.3	17	73	68	18	41	41
Luxembourg	3	ooo	0.4	133.3	14.5	12	9	1.7	5	78	88	ooo	ooo	ooo
Macedonia, FYRO	26	24.7	2.1	80.8	7.8	13	8	1.9	22	73	60	21	40	39
Madagascar	587	5.3	16.5	28.1	34.6	42	12	5.8	86	54	22	78	7	15
Malawi	118	16.9	11.4	96.6	12.7	45	22	6.4	117	39	20	87	5	8
Malaysia	330	23.1	22.7	68.8	24.5	24	5	3.2	8	73	57	27	23	50
Maldives	0.3	10.0	0.3	1066.7	39.3	37	8	5.8	59	61	25	32	31	37
Mali	1240	3.8	11.3	9.1	29.9	48	19	7.0	142	46	26	86	2	12
Malta	0.3	28.1	0.4	1333.3	9.1	13	8	1.7	5	77	91	ooo	ooo	ooo
Marshall Islands	0.2	16.7	0.06	300.0	47.3	34	5	6.6	63	65	65	ooo	ooo	ooo
Mauritania	1026	0.5	2.8	2.7	34.4	43	13	6.0	120	51	54	55	10	35

Wealth   Energy and trade   Quality of life

GNP	Purchasing power	Growth of PP	Energy consumption	Imports	Exports	Aid received (given)	Human Development Index	Health care	Food consumption	Safe water	Illiteracy male	Illiteracy female	Higher education	Cars	
2000	2000	1990–2000	1999	1999	1999	2000	2000	1990–1999	1997	2000	1998	1998	1996	2000	
billion US$	US$	%	kg oil equivalent per capita	US$ per capita	US$ per capita	million US$		doctors per 100 000 people	daily calories per capita	% access	%	%	students per 100 000 people	people per car	
4.9	10 066	1.0	3286	2816	3034	64	0.826	297	2849	°°°	°°°	°°°	2965	3	Estonia
6.7	668	2.4	290	14	29	693	0.327	°°°	1858	24	58	70	74	1433	Ethiopia
1.8	4668	0.7	°°°	°°°	°°°	29	0.758	48	2865	47	°°°	°°°	757	17	Fiji
129.0	24 996	2.4	6461	9328	7279	(371)	0.930	299	3100	100	°°°	°°°	4418	3	Finland
1429.4	24 223	1.3	4351	6420	5773	(4105)	0.928	303	3518	100	°°°	°°°	3541	2	France
°°°	°°°	°°°	°°°	°°°	°°°	°°°	°°°	°°°	°°°	°°°	°°°	°°°	°°°	7	French Guiana
4.0	6237	0.1	1342	2135	1489	12	0.637	°°°	2556	70	°°°	°°°	649	7	Gabon
0.4	1649	-0.3	°°°	189	240	49	0.405	4	2350	62	°°°	°°°	148	186	Gambia, The
3.2	2664	-12.4	512	142	242	170	0.748	436	2614	76	°°°	°°°	3149	12	Georgia
2057.6	25 103	1.2	4108	7635	7382	(5030)	0.925	350	3382	°°°	°°°	°°°	2603	2	Germany
6.8	1964	1.8	377	131	195	609	0.548	6	2611	64	22	40	°°°	214	Ghana
126.2	16 501	1.8	2552	1402	2415	(226)	0.885	392	3649	°°°	2	5	3138	4	Greece
°°°	°°°	°°°	°°°	°°°	°°°	°°°	°°°	°°°	°°°	°°°	°°°	°°°	°°°	°°°	Greenland
0.3	7580	2.9	°°°	°°°	°°°	17	0.747	°°°	2768	94	°°°	°°°	°°°	°°°	Grenada
19.2	3821	1.4	548	297	429	264	0.631	93	2339	92	25	40	804	84	Guatemala
3.3	1982	1.7	°°°	95	112	153	0.414	13	2231	48	°°°	°°°	112	488	Guinea
0.2	755	-1.1	°°°	47	67	80	0.349	17	2430	49	°°°	°°°	°°°	267	Guinea-Bissau
0.7	3963	5.0	°°°	°°°	°°°	108	0.708	18	2530	94	°°°	°°°	956	32	Guyana
4.0	1467	-2.7	265	70	152	208	0.471	8	1869	46	50	54	°°°	252	Haiti
5.5	2453	0.3	522	346	463	449	0.638	83	2403	90	27	27	985	165	Honduras
47.5	12 416	1.9	2474	2777	2859	252	0.835	357	3313	99	1	1	1903	4	Hungary
8.1	29 581	1.8	11 434	°°°	°°°	0	0.936	326	3117	°°°	°°°	°°°	2918	2	Iceland
471.2	2358	4.1	482	53	66	1487	0.577	48	2496	88	33	57	638	218	India
119.9	3043	2.5	658	260	196	1731	0.684	16	2886	76	9	20	1157	86	Indonesia
104.6	5884	1.9	1651	283	218	130	0.721	85	2836	95	18	33	1763	44	Iran
°°°	°°°	°°°	1263	°°°	°°°	76	°°°	°°°	2619	85	°°°	°°°	°°°	35	Iraq
87.1	29 866	6.5	3726	21 493	18 128	(235)	0.925	219	3565	°°°	°°°	°°°	3702	3	Ireland
99.6	20 131	2.2	3029	5789	6538	800	0.896	385	3278	99	2	6	3571	5	Israel
1154.3	23 626	1.4	2932	5083	4680	(1376)	0.913	554	3507	°°°	1	2	3299	2	Italy
6.4	3639	0.4	1597	1291	1511	10	0.742	140	2553	71	18	10	768	23	Jamaica
4337.3	26 755	1.1	4070	3650	3107	(13 508)	0.933	193	2932	96	°°°	°°°	3131	3	Japan
8.2	3966	1.0	1028	690	976	552	0.717	166	3014	96	6	17	°°°	28	Jordan
17.6	5871	-3.1	2374	430	419	189	0.750	353	3085	91	°°°	°°°	2859	°°°	Kazakhstan
10.7	1022	-0.5	499	85	101	512	0.513	13	1976	49	12	27	°°°	174	Kenya
0.08	°°°	°°°	°°°	°°°	°°°	21	°°°	°°°	°°°	47	°°°	°°°	°°°	°°°	Kiribati
°°°	15 799	-1.4	8984	6982	6040	3	0.813	189	3096	100	17	22	1750	3	Kuwait
1.3	2711	-5.1	504	106	141	215	0.712	301	2447	77	°°°	°°°	1088	36	Kyrgyzstan
1.5	1575	3.9	°°°	87	107	281	0.485	24	2108	90	38	70	260	540	Laos
6.9	7045	-2.3	1586	1214	1502	91	0.800	282	2864	°°°	0	0	2248	5	Latvia
16.2	4308	4.2	1280	505	2421	197	0.755	210	3277	100	9	21	2712	5	Lebanon
1.2	2031	2.1	°°°	103	395	42	0.535	5	2243	91	29	7	234	350	Lesotho
°°°	°°°	°°°	°°°	°°°	°°°	94	°°°	°°°	°°°	°°°	°°°	°°°	°°°	310	Liberia
°°°	7570	°°°	2370	1358	980	15	0.773	128	3289	72	°°°	°°°	°°°	11	Libya
°°°	°°°	°°°	°°°	°°°	°°°	°°°	°°°	°°°	°°°	°°°	°°°	°°°	°°°	2	Liechtenstein
10.7	7106	-2.9	2240	1145	1442	99	0.808	395	3261	°°°	0	1	2251	4	Lithuania
19.3	50 061	4.1	8083	°°°	°°°	(127)	0.925	272	°°°	°°°	°°°	°°°	640	2	Luxembourg
3.5	5086	-1.5	°°°	721	963	252	0.772	204	2664	99	°°°	°°°	1557	7	Macedonia, FYRO*
4.0	840	-0.9	°°°	57	76	322	0.469	11	2021	47	28	42	188	288	Madagascar
1.9	615	1.8	°°°	51	86	445	0.400	°°°	2043	57	27	56	58	644	Malawi
78.5	9068	4.4	1878	4247	3369	45	0.782	66	2977	95	9	18	1048	6	Malaysia
0.3	4485	5.4	°°°	°°°	°°°	19	0.743	40	2485	100	°°°	°°°	°°°	°°°	Maldives
2.6	797	1.3	°°°	55	80	360	0.386	5	2029	65	54	69	134	557	Mali
3.5	17 273	4.0	2544	°°°	°°°	21	0.875	261	3398	100	°°°	°°°	2183	2	Malta
0.1	°°°	°°°	°°°	°°°	°°°	63	°°°	°°°	°°°	°°°	°°°	°°°	°°°	°°°	Marshall Islands
1.0	1677	1.2	°°°	130	148	212	0.438	14	2622	37	48	69	365	280	Mauritania

The datasets below are explained on pages 182/183.

	Land		**Population**										**Employment**		
	Area	Arable and permanent crops	Total	Density	Change	Births	Deaths	Fertility	Infant mortality	Life expectancy	Urban	Agriculture	Industry	Services
	2002	2002	2002	2002	1990–2000	2002	2002	2000	2000	2000	2000	1990	1990	1990
	thousand km²	% of total	millions	persons per km²	%	births per 1000	deaths per 1000	children per mother	per 1000 live births	years	%	%	%	%
Mauritius	2	52.0	1.2	600.0	9.9	16	7	2.0	17	71	43	17	43	40
Mexico	1958	13.9	103.4	52.8	18.8	22	5	2.8	25	75	74	28	24	48
Micronesia, Fed. States	0.7	51.4	0.1	142.9	22.6	31	6	4.6	20	66	27	ooo	ooo	ooo
Moldova	34	64.4	4.4	129.4	0.8	14	13	1.4	27	68	46	33	30	37
Monaco	0.002	ooo	0.03	15 000	5.7	10	13	ooo	5	ooo	100	ooo	ooo	ooo
Mongolia	1567	0.8	2.7	1.7	18.0	21	7	2.2	62	63	57	32	22	46
Morocco	447	21.2	31.2	69.8	22.0	24	6	3.4	41	69	55	45	25	30
Mozambique	802	4.2	17.3	21.6	33.8	39	29	5.6	126	72	28	83	8	9
Myanmar	677	15.0	42.3	62.5	8.4	20	12	3.3	78	56	27	73	10	17
Namibia	824	1.0	1.9	2.3	25.7	35	18	5.0	56	46	27	49	15	36
Nauru	0.02	ooo	0.01	500.0	24.8	27	7	3.7	25	61	100	ooo	ooo	ooo
Nepal	147	20.2	25.9	176.2	27.8	33	10	4.8	72	57	11	94	0	6
Netherlands	41	22.9	16.1	392.7	6.3	12	9	1.7	5	78	62	5	26	69
New Zealand	271	12.1	3.9	14.4	13.7	14	8	2.0	6	77	77	10	25	65
Nicaragua	130	21.1	5.0	38.5	32.1	27	5	4.3	37	68	57	28	26	46
Niger	1267	4.0	10.8	8.5	32.1	50	22	7.5	159	41	17	90	4	6
Nigeria	924	33.3	130.5	141.2	33.4	39	14	5.8	110	52	36	43	7	50
Northern Marianas	0.5	17.4	0.08	154.0	6.3	20	2	ooo	ooo	ooo	ooo	ooo	ooo	ooo
North Korea	121	16.6	22.2	183.5	8.3	19	7	2.3	23	70	59	38	32	30
Norway	324	2.7	4.5	13.9	5.6	12	10	1.8	4	78	74	6	25	69
Oman	213	0.4	2.7	12.7	42.9	38	4	6.1	12	71	72	44	24	32
Pakistan	796	27.5	147.7	185.6	24.2	30	9	5.6	85	60	33	52	19	29
Palau	0.5	21.7	0.02	40.0	23.4	19	7	2.5	28	67	71	ooo	ooo	ooo
Panama	76	8.7	2.9	38.2	17.6	21	6	2.6	20	74	56	26	16	58
Papua New Guinea	463	1.5	5.2	11.2	28.8	32	8	4.8	79	56	15	79	7	14
Paraguay	407	5.6	5.9	14.5	31.9	31	5	4.3	26	73	52	39	22	39
Peru	1285	3.3	27.9	21.7	22.9	23	6	2.9	40	69	72	36	18	46
Philippines	300	33.5	83.0	276.7	24.8	27	6	3.5	30	67	47	46	15	39
Poland	323	44.6	38.6	119.5	1.4	10	10	1.4	9	73	62	27	36	37
Portugal	92	29.4	10.1	109.8	1.3	12	10	1.5	6	76	48	18	34	48
Qatar	11	1.9	0.8	72.1	54.6	16	4	3.9	12	72	91	3	32	65
Romania	238	41.3	22.3	93.7	-2.0	11	12	1.3	19	71	55	24	47	29
Russian Federation	17 075	7.4	145.0	8.5	-1.4	10	14	1.2	18	66	73	14	42	44
Rwanda	26	42.4	7.7	296.2	3.8	40	22	5.8	100	39	5	92	3	5
St. Kitts and Nevis	0.4	22.2	0.04	100.0	-6.3	19	9	2.5	21	69	43	ooo	ooo	ooo
St. Lucia	0.6	27.4	0.2	333.3	12.0	21	5	2.1	17	71	30	ooo	ooo	ooo
St. Vincent & the Grenadines	0.4	28.2	0.1	250.0	8.4	18	6	2.2	21	72	44	ooo	ooo	ooo
Samoa	3.0	43.0	0.2	66.7	5.3	16	6	4.5	21	68	33	ooo	ooo	ooo
San Marino	0.06	16.7	0.03	500.0	14.8	11	8	1.3	6	80	89	ooo	ooo	ooo
Sao Tome and Principe	1.0	42.7	0.2	170.0	33.9	42	7	6.2	58	65	44	ooo	ooo	ooo
Saudi Arabia	2150	1.8	23.5	10.9	39.0	37	6	5.7	24	67	83	19	20	61
Senegal	197	11.5	10.3	52.3	25.7	37	11	5.7	80	52	43	77	8	15
Serbia and Montenegro	102	36.5	10.7	104.9	9.2	13	11	1.6	20	72	52	ooo	ooo	ooo
Seychelles	0.5	15.6	0.08	160.0	8.0	17	7	2.0	13	70	63	ooo	ooo	ooo
Sierra Leone	72	7.5	5.6	77.8	23.8	44	21	6.3	180	45	37	68	15	17
Singapore	1	1.6	4.5	4500.0	37.6	13	4	1.6	4	78	100	0	36	64
Slovakia	49	32.5	5.4	110.2	2.8	10	9	1.3	8	73	57	12	32	56
Slovenia	20	10.0	1.9	95.0	1.7	9	10	1.2	4	76	50	6	46	48
Solomon Islands	29	2.1	0.5	17.2	39.4	33	4	5.7	21	67	13	77	7	16
Somalia	638	1.7	7.8	12.2	8.7	47	18	7.3	125	46	28	ooo	ooo	ooo
South Africa	1221	12.9	42.7	35.0	13.7	19	17	2.9	55	53	54	14	32	54
South Korea	99	19.1	48.0	484.8	10.7	13	6	1.5	5	74	79	18	35	47
Spain	506	36.6	40.2	79.4	1.6	10	9	1.2	5	78	64	12	33	55
Sri Lanka	66	29.0	19.6	297.0	11.9	16	6	2.1	17	72	22	48	21	31
Sudan	2506	6.7	37.1	14.8	31.7	37	10	4.9	66	56	27	70	8	22

Legend:
- ooo — no data
- per capita — for each person

Wealth | Energy and trade | Quality of life

GNP	Purchasing power	Growth of PP	Energy consumption	Imports	Exports	Aid received (given)	Human Development Index	Health care	Food consumption	Safe water	Illiteracy male	Illiteracy female	Higher education	Cars	
2000	2000	1990–2000	1999	1999	1999	2000	2000	1990–1999	1997	2000	1998	1998	1996	2000	
billion US$	US$	%	kg oil equivalent per capita	US$ per capita	US$ per capita	million US$		doctors per 100 000 people	daily calories per capita	% access	%	%	students per 100 000 people	people per car	
4.2	10 017	4.0	ooo	2217	2331	20	0.772	85	2917	100	ooo	ooo	632	26	Mauritius
498.0	9023	1.4	1543	1475	1557	-54	0.796	186	3097	86	7	11	1739	11	Mexico
0.2	ooo	ooo	ooo	ooo	ooo	108	ooo	ooo	ooo	ooo	ooo	ooo	ooo	ooo	Micronesia, Fed. States
1.4	2109	-9.5	656	135	175	123	0.701	350	2567	100	1	2	2143	25	Moldova
ooo	ooo	ooo	ooo	ooo	ooo	ooo	ooo	ooo	ooo	100	ooo	ooo	ooo	2	Monaco
0.9	1783	-0.3	ooo	204	252	218	0.655	243	1917	60	28	49	1767	104	Mongolia
33.8	3546	0.6	352	350	393	419	0.602	46	3078	82	40	66	1167	29	Morocco
3.7	854	3.9	404	350	88	876	0.322	ooo	1832	60	42	73	40	233	Mozambique
ooo	1027	4.8	273	24	37	107	0.552	30	2862	68	11	21	590	1274	Myanmar
3.6	6431	1.8	645	889	1072	152	0.610	30	2183	77	18	20	735	31	Namibia
ooo	ooo	ooo	ooo	ooo	ooo	7	ooo	ooo	ooo	ooo	ooo	ooo	ooo	ooo	Nauru
5.3	1327	2.4	358	49	63	390	0.490	4	2366	81	43	78	485	ooo	Nepal
400.3	25 657	2.2	4686	15 644	14 256	(3135)	0.935	251	3284	100	ooo	ooo	3018	3	Netherlands
50.1	20 070	1.8	4770	4454	4631	(113)	0.917	218	3395	ooo	ooo	ooo	3318	2	New Zealand
2.1	2366	0.6	539	161	387	562	0.635	86	2186	79	34	31	1209	98	Nicaragua
2.0	746	-1.0	ooo	26	38	211	0.277	4	2097	59	78	93	ooo	590	Niger
32.8	896	-0.4	705	119	103	185	0.462	19	2735	57	30	48	ooo	151	Nigeria
ooo	ooo	ooo	ooo	ooo	ooo	0	ooo	ooo	ooo	ooo	ooo	ooo	ooo	ooo	Northern Marianas
ooo	ooo	ooo	ooo	ooo	ooo	201	ooo	ooo	ooo	100	ooo	ooo	ooo	ooo	North Korea
151.2	29 918	3.1	5965	12 171	12 098	(1264)	0.942	413	3357	100	ooo	ooo	4239	3	Norway
ooo	13 356	0.3	3607	2783	2062	46	0.751	133	ooo	39	ooo	ooo	695	13	Oman
64.6	1928	1.2	444	61	81	703	0.499	57	2476	88	42	71	ooo	161	Pakistan
ooo	ooo	ooo	ooo	ooo	ooo	29	ooo	ooo	ooo	79	ooo	ooo	ooo	ooo	Palau
9.3	6000	2.3	835	2375	2655	17	0.787	167	2430	87	8	9	3025	15	Panama
3.7	2280	1.4	ooo	444	367	275	0.535	7	2224	42	29	45	ooo	136	Papua New Guinea
8.0	4426	-0.4	773	582	633	82	0.740	110	2566	79	6	9	948	66	Paraguay
53.9	4799	2.9	519	293	339	401	0.747	93	2302	77	6	16	3268	48	Peru
78.7	3971	1.1	549	506	477	578	0.754	123	2366	87	5	5	2958	110	Philippines
162.2	9051	4.5	2416	998	1353	1396	0.833	236	3366	ooo	0	0	1865	5	Poland
110.7	17 290	2.5	2365	3405	4661	(271)	0.880	312	3667	82	6	11	3242	3	Portugal
ooo	18 789	ooo	28 262	ooo	ooo	1	0.803	126	ooo	ooo	ooo	ooo	1518	4	Qatar
37.4	6423	-0.4	1622	441	508	432	0.775	184	3253	58	1	3	1819	10	Romania
241.1	8377	-4.6	4121	587	363	1565	0.781	421	2904	99	0	1	3006	9	Russian Federation
2.0	943	-2.1	ooo	12	37	322	0.403	ooo	2056	41	29	43	ooo	889	Rwanda
0.3	12 510	4.7	ooo	ooo	ooo	4	0.814	ooo	2771	98	ooo	ooo	ooo	8	St. Kitts and Nevis
0.6	5703	0.9	ooo	ooo	ooo	11	0.772	ooo	2734	98	ooo	ooo	ooo	21	St. Lucia
0.3	5555	2.6	ooo	ooo	ooo	6	0.733	ooo	2472	93	ooo	ooo	ooo	16	St. Vincent & the Grenadines
0.2	5041	1.9	ooo	ooo	ooo	27	0.715	34	ooo	99	ooo	ooo	ooo	56	Samoa
ooo	ooo	ooo	ooo	ooo	ooo	ooo	ooo	ooo	ooo	ooo	ooo	ooo	ooo	1	San Marino
0.04	1792	-0.8	ooo	ooo	ooo	35	0.632	ooo	2138	ooo	ooo	ooo	ooo	3	Sao Tome and Principe
139.4	11 367	-1.2	4204	2673	2123	31	0.759	166	2783	95	17	36	1455	11	Saudi Arabia
4.7	1510	0.9	318	136	168	424	0.431	8	2418	78	55	74	297	104	Senegal
ooo	ooo	ooo	1258	ooo	ooo	638	ooo	ooo	ooo	ooo	16	31	1625	5	Serbia and Montenegro
0.5	12 508	1.1	ooo	ooo	ooo	18	0.811	ooo	2487	ooo	ooo	ooo	ooo	12	Seychelles
0.6	490	-6.5	ooo	16	33	182	0.275	7	2035	28	ooo	ooo	ooo	131	Sierra Leone
99.4	23 356	4.7	5742	33 984	30 053	1	0.885	163	ooo	100	4	12	2730	10	Singapore
20.0	11 243	1.9	3335	2241	2436	113	0.835	353	2984	100	ooo	ooo	1897	4	Slovakia
20.0	17 367	2.8	3277	5261	5702	61	0.879	228	3101	100	0	0	2657	3	Slovenia
0.3	1648	-1.0	ooo	ooo	ooo	68	0.622	ooo	2122	71	ooo	ooo	ooo	ooo	Solomon Islands
ooo	ooo	ooo	ooo	ooo	ooo	ooo	ooo	ooo	ooo	ooo	ooo	ooo	ooo	876	Somalia
129.2	9401	-0.2	2597	761	685	488	0.695	56	2990	86	15	16	1841	11	South Africa
421.1	17 380	4.7	3871	3645	3057	-198	0.882	136	3155	92	1	14	6106	6	South Korea
590.1	19 472	2.3	3005	4119	4277	(1195)	0.913	424	3310	ooo	2	4	4254	2	Spain
16.6	3530	3.9	406	291	352	276	0.741	37	2302	83	6	12	474	87	Sri Lanka
9.4	1797	5.6	503	26	49	225	0.499	9	2395	75	ooo	ooo	ooo	398	Sudan

	◦◦◦	no data
	per capita	for each person

	Land		Population									Employment		
	Area	**Arable and permanent crops**	**Total**	**Density**	**Change**	**Births**	**Deaths**	**Fertility**	**Infant mortality**	**Life expectancy**	**Urban**	**Agriculture**	**Industry**	**Services**
			2002	2002	1990–2000	2002	2002	2000	2000	2000	2000	1990	1990	1990
	thousand km²	% of total	millions	persons per km²	%	births per 1000	deaths per 1000	children per mother	per 1000 live births	years	%	%	%	%
Suriname	163	0.4	0.4	2.5	9.2	20	7	3.0	27	71	69	21	18	61
Swaziland	17	10.4	1.2	70.6	27.1	30	19	5.9	62	40	25	40	22	38
Sweden	450	6.1	8.9	19.8	3.7	10	11	1.5	3	80	84	◦◦◦	◦◦◦	◦◦◦
Switzerland	41	10.6	7.3	178.0	6.2	10	9	1.5	3	80	68	6	35	59
Syria	185	29.7	17.2	93.0	31.1	30	5	4.1	25	70	50	33	24	43
Taiwan	36	◦◦◦	22.5	625.0	9.4	13	6	1.7	◦◦◦	75	77	◦◦◦	◦◦◦	◦◦◦
Tajikistan	143	6.0	6.7	46.9	20.8	33	9	2.4	54	68	27	41	23	36
Tanzania	945	4.9	35.3	37.4	34.6	40	17	5.6	90	53	22	84	5	11
Thailand	513	35.1	63.6	124.0	11.2	17	7	1.8	26	72	30	64	14	22
Togo	57	40.5	5.3	93.0	36.0	36	11	5.8	80	55	31	66	10	24
Tonga	0.8	64.0	0.1	125.0	11.1	24	6	4.2	18	71	32	◦◦◦	◦◦◦	◦◦◦
Trinidad and Tobago	5	23.8	1.1	220.0	-1.9	13	8	1.7	17	71	72	11	31	58
Tunisia	164	31.2	9.8	59.8	16.9	17	5	2.3	24	72	62	28	33	39
Turkey	775	34.4	67.3	86.8	17.1	18	6	2.5	40	69	66	53	18	29
Turkmenistan	488	3.5	4.7	9.6	23.2	28	9	2.2	52	67	44	37	23	40
Tuvalu	0.02	◦◦◦	0.01	500.0	18.2	21	7	3.1	40	67	18	◦◦◦	◦◦◦	◦◦◦
Uganda	241	28.3	24.9	103.3	35.7	47	17	6.9	83	42	15	85	5	10
Ukraine	604	55.7	48.4	80.1	-4.9	10	16	1.1	17	68	68	20	40	40
United Arab Emirates	84	1.6	2.4	28.6	21.5	18	4	3.5	8	74	84	8	27	65
United Kingdom	245	24.6	59.9	244.5	3.3	11	10	1.7	6	77	90	2	29	69
United States of America	9364	18.6	287.7	30.7	10.3	14	9	2.1	7	77	75	3	28	69
Uruguay	177	7.4	3.4	19.2	7.4	17	9	2.3	15	74	92	14	27	59
Uzbekistan	447	10.8	25.6	57.3	20.0	26	8	2.7	45	70	38	34	25	41
Vanuatu	12	9.8	0.2	16.7	23.3	25	8	4.6	37	65	21	◦◦◦	◦◦◦	◦◦◦
Venezuela	912	3.8	24.3	26.6	21.8	20	5	2.9	20	73	87	12	27	61
Vietnam	332	22.2	80.6	242.8	18.8	20	6	2.3	31	66	24	71	14	15
Western Sahara	252	0.008	0.3	1.2	28.1	46	17	6.8	◦◦◦	◦◦◦	95	◦◦◦	◦◦◦	◦◦◦
Yemen	528	3.2	18.7	35.4	45.4	43	9	7.2	86	59	26	61	17	22
Zambia	753	7.0	10.2	13.4	22.1	40	24	6.1	112	37	38	75	8	17
Zimbabwe	391	8.6	12.5	32.0	12.3	31	21	4.0	60	40	32	68	8	24

Explanation of datasets

Land

Area does not include areas of lakes and seas

Arable and permanent crops percentage of total land area used for arable and permanent crops

Population

Total estimate for mid 2002

Density the total population of a country divided by its land area

Change percentage change in population between 1990 and 2000. Negative numbers indicate a decrease

Births number of births per one thousand people in one year

Deaths number of deaths per one thousand people in one year

Fertility average number of children born to child bearing women

Infant mortality number of deaths of children under one year per 1000 live births

Life expectancy number of years a baby born now can expect to live

Urban percentage of the population living in towns and cities

Employment

Agriculture percentage of the labour force employed in agriculture

Industry percentage of the labour force employed in industry

Services percentage of the labour force employed in services

Macedonia, FYRO*   Former Yugoslav Republic of Macedonia

Wealth | Energy and trade | Quality of life

GNP	Purchasing power	Growth of PP	Energy consumption	Imports	Exports	Aid received (given)	Human Development Index	Health care	Food consumption	Safe water	Illiteracy male	Illiteracy female	Higher education	Cars	
2000	2000	1990–2000	1999	1999	1999	2000	2000	1990–1999	1997	2000	1998	1998	1996	2000	
billion US$	US$	%	kg oil equivalent per capita	US$ per capita	US$ per capita	million US$		doctors per 100 000 people	daily calories per capita	% access	%	%	students per 100 000 people	people per car	
ooo	3799	3.0	ooo	ooo	ooo	34	0.756	25	2665	95	ooo	ooo	ooo	8	Suriname
1.4	4492	0.2	ooo	ooo	ooo	13	0.577	15	2483	ooo	ooo	ooo	630	38	Swaziland
237.5	24 277	1.6	5769	12 213	10 735	(1799)	0.941	311	3194	100	ooo	ooo	3116	2	Sweden
273.7	28 769	0.2	3738	16 526	14 843	(890)	0.928	323	3223	100	ooo	ooo	2072	2	Switzerland
16.0	3556	2.8	1143	329	313	158	0.691	144	3351	80	13	42	1559	107	Syria
ooo	ooo	ooo	ooo	6034	5795	0	ooo	ooo	ooo	ooo	ooo	ooo	ooo	5	Taiwan
1.1	1152	-11.8	543	122	113	0142	0.667	201	2001	69	1	1	1895	ooo	Tajikistan
9.3	523	0.1	457	33	62	1045	0.440	4	1995	54	17	36	57	735	Tanzania
121.8	6402	3.3	1169	1123	886	641	0.762	24	2360	80	3	7	2252	37	Thailand
1.4	1442	-0.4	313	101	146	70	0.493	8	2469	54	28	62	315	174	Togo
0.2	ooo	ooo	ooo	ooo	ooo	21	ooo	ooo	ooo	100	ooo	ooo	ooo	19	Tonga
5.7	8964	2.3	6205	2611	2312	-2	0.805	79	2661	86	ooo	ooo	787	6	Trinidad and Tobago
20.1	6363	3.0	811	916	963	223	0.722	70	3283	99	21	42	1341	24	Tunisia
201.5	6974	2.1	1093	676	721	325	0.742	121	3525	83	7	25	2301	17	Turkey
4.0	3956	-8.0	2677	287	426	32	0.741	300	2306	58	ooo	ooo	2072	ooo	Turkmenistan
ooo	ooo	ooo	ooo	ooo	ooo	7	ooo	ooo	ooo	100	ooo	ooo	ooo	ooo	Tuvalu
6.8	1208	3.8	ooo	30	76	819	0.444	ooo	2085	50	24	46	179	923	Uganda
34.7	3816	-8.8	2973	347	310	541	0.748	229	2795	55	0	1	2996	10	Ukraine
ooo	17 935	-1.6	9977	ooo	ooo	4	0.812	181	3390	ooo	ooo	ooo	801	7	United Arab Emirates
1463.5	23 509	2.2	3871	6282	6687	(4501)	0.928	164	3276	100	ooo	ooo	3237	2	United Kingdom
9645.6	34 142	2.2	8159	3345	4272	(9955)	0.939	279	3699	100	ooo	ooo	5341	2	United States of America
20.3	9035	2.6	976	1055	1197	17	0.831	370	2816	98	3	2	2458	11	Uruguay
15.2	2441	-2.4	2024	125	121	186	0.727	309	2433	85	7	17	ooo	ooo	Uzbekistan
0.2	2802	-0.9	ooo	ooo	ooo	46	0.542	ooo	2700	88	ooo	ooo	ooo	50	Vanuatu
104.1	5794	-0.6	2253	899	690	77	0.770	236	2321	84	7	9	ooo	13	Venezuela
30.7	1996	6.0	454	180	181	1700	0.688	48	2484	56	5	9	678	562	Vietnam
ooo	ooo	ooo	ooo	ooo	ooo	ooo	ooo	ooo	ooo	ooo	ooo	ooo	ooo	ooo	Western Sahara
6.7	893	2.3	184	137	158	265	0.479	23	2051	69	34	77	419	101	Yemen
3.0	780	-2.1	626	85	97	795	0.433	7	1970	64	8	17	238	107	Zambia
5.8	2635	0.4	821	196	180	178	0.551	14	2145	85	ooo	ooo	661	61	Zimbabwe

Explanation of datasets

Wealth

GNP Gross National Product (GNP) is the total value of goods and services produced in a country plus income from abroad.

Purchasing power Gross Domestic Product (GDP) is the total value of goods and services produced in a country. Purchasing power parity (PPP) is GDP per person, adjusted for the local cost of living

Growth of PP average annual growth (or decline, shown as a negative value in the table) in purchasing power. This figure shows whether people are becoming better or worse off

Energy and trade

Energy consumption consumption of energy per person shown as the equivalent in kilograms of oil

Imports total value of imports per person shown in US dollars

Exports total value of exports per person shown in US dollars

Aid received (given) amount of economic aid a country has received. Negative values indicate that the repayment of loans exceeds the amount of aid received. Figures in brackets show aid given

Quality of life

HDI Human Development Index (HDI) measures the relative social and economic progress of a country. It combines life expectancy, adult literacy, average number of years of schooling, and purchasing power. Economically more developed countries have an HDI approaching 1.0. Economically less developed countries have an HDI approaching 0.

Health care number of doctors in each country per 100 000 people

Food consumption average number of calories consumed by each person each day

Safe water percentage of the population with access to safe drinking water

Illiteracy percentage of men and women who are unable to read and write

Higher education number of students in higher education per 100 000 people

Cars the number of people for every car

How to use the gazetteer

To find a place on an atlas map use either the grid code or latitude and longitude.

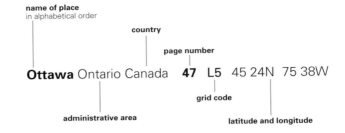

name of place
in alphabetical order

country

page number

Ottawa Ontario Canada **47** L5 45 24N 75 38W

administrative area

grid code

latitude and longitude

Grid code

Ottawa Ontario Canada **47** L5 45 24N 75 38W

Ottawa is in grid square L5

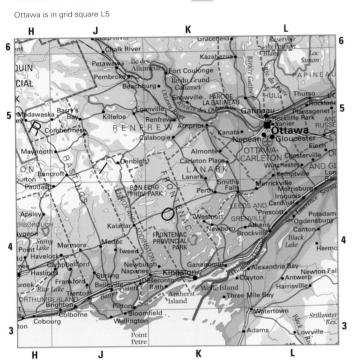

Latitude and longitude

Ottawa Ontario Canada **47** L5 45 24N 75 38W

Ottawa is at latitude 45 degrees, 24 minutes north and 75 degrees, 38 minutes west

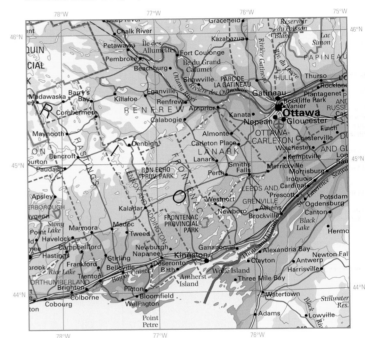

Abbreviations used in the gazetteer

admin.	administrative area	*mt.*	mountain, peak, or spot height	
Aust.	Australia			
b.	bay or harbour	*mts.*	mountains	
Bahamas	The Bahamas	Neths.	Netherlands	
bor.	borough	NZ	New Zealand	
c.	cape, point, or headland	*p.*	peninsula	
can.	canal	Philippines	The Philippines	
CAR	Central African Republic	*plat.*	plateau	
CDR	Congo Democratic Republic	PNG	Papua New Guinea	
		Port.	Portugal	
Col.	Colombia	*r.*	river	
Czech Rep.	Czech Republic	*res.*	reservoir	
d.	desert	RoI	Republic of Ireland	
dep.	depression	RSA	Republic of South Africa	
Dom. Rep.	Dominican Republic	Russia	Russian Federation	
Eq. Guinea	Equatorial Guinea	*salt l.*	salt lake	
est.	estuary	*sd.*	sound, strait, or channel	
Fr.	France	SM	Serbia and Montenegro	
g.	gulf	Sp.	Spain	
geog. reg.	geographical region	*St.*	Saint	
hist. site	historical site	*Ste.*	Sainte	
i.	island	Switz.	Switzerland	
in.	inlet	*tn.*	town	
I.R.	Indian Reservation	UAE	United Arab Emirates	
is.	islands	UK	United Kingdom	
ist.	isthmus	USA	United States of America	
l.	lake, lakes, lagoon	*vol.*	volcano	
m.s.	manned meteorological station	W. Indies	West Indies	
		Yemen	Yemen Republic	

Abbreviations used on the maps

A.C.T.	Australian Capital Territory	P.	Pulau
Arch.	Archipelago	Peg.	Pegunungan
Arq.	Arquípelago	Pen.; Penin.	Peninsula
Aust.	Australia	Pk.	Peak
C.	Cape; Cabo; Cap	Port.	Portugal
Col.	Colombia	P.P.	Provincial Park
Cr.	Creek	PROV. PARK	Provincial Park
Czech Rep.	Czech Republic	Pt.	Point
D.C.	District of Columbia	Pte.	Pointe
E.	East	Pto.	Porto; Puerto
Eq. Guinea	Equatorial Guinea	R.	River; Rio
Fr.	France	Ra.	Range
FYROM	Former Yugoslav Republic of Macedonia	R.A.	Recreational Area
		Res	Reservoir
G.	Gunung; Gebel; Gulf	RÉS. FAUN.	Réserve Faunique
Hwy.	Highway	Riv.	Rivière
I.	Island; Île; Isla; Ilha	RSA	Republic of South Africa
Is.	Islands; Îles; Islas; Ilhas	Russia	Russian Federation
Kep.	Kepulauan	S.	South
L.	Lake; Lac; Lago	Sd.	Sound
Mt.	Mount; Mountain; Mont	Sp.	Spain
Mts.	Mountains; Monts	St.	Saint
N.	North	Sta.	Santa
NAT. PARK	National Park	Ste.	Sainte
Neths	Netherlands	UK	United Kingom
N.P.	National Park	USA	United States of America
NZ	New Zealand	Yemen	Yemen Republic

A

Abbotsford British Columbia 38 H4 49 02N 122 18W
Abitibi *admin.* Québec 47 K8/L8 48 20N 76 00W
Abitibi-De Troyes Provincial Park Ontario 45 L5 48 50N 80 40W
Abitibi River Ontario 45 L5 49 40N 81 20W
Acton Ontario 48 B2 43 38N 80 04W
Acton Vale Québec 47 P5 45 40N 72 35W
Adams Lake British Columbia 39 L2 51 10N 119 30W
Adams River British Columbia 39 L2 51 40N 119 00W
Adlatok River Newfoundland and Labrador 52 D7 55 28N 62 50W
Adlavik Islands Newfoundland and Labrador 52 F7 54 55N 58 40W
Admiralty Inlet Nunavut 55 N5 72 30N 86 00W
Advocate Harbour *tn.* Nova Scotia 53 M12 45 20N 64 45W
Agassiz Ice Cap Nunavut 55 Q7 80 15N 76 00W
Agassiz Provincial Forest Manitoba 43 D1 49 50N 96 20W
Aguasabon River Ontario 45 H5 48 50N 87 00W
Ailsa Craig *tn.* Ontario 48 A2 43 08N 81 34W
Ainslie, Lake Nova Scotia 53 M12 46 10N 61 10W
Airdrie Alberta 41 E2 51 20N 114 00W
Ajax Ontario 48 C2 43 48N 79 00W
Akimiski Island Nunavut 55 P1 52 30N 81 00W
Akimiski Island Bird Sanctuary Nunavut 55 P1 53 00N 81 00W
Akimiski Strait Northwest Territories/Ontario 44 L7 52 40N 82 00W
Aklavik (Akłarvik) Northwest Territories 54 D4 68 15N 135 02W
Akpotak Island Northwest Territories 50 F9 60 30N 68 00W
Akulivik Québec 50 A9 60 53N 78 15W
Albany Island Ontario 44 L7 52 15N 81 34W
Albany River Ontario 44 K6 51 40N 83 20W
Albany River Provincial Park Ontario 44 G6 51 30N 88 30W
Alberni Inlet *admin.* British Columbia 38 H4 49 05N 124 52W
Albert *admin.* New Brunswick 53 L12 45 40N 65 10W
Alberta *province* 41
Alberton Prince Edward Island 53 M12 46 50N 64 08W
Aldershot Ontario 48 C2 43 17N 79 51W
Aldersyde Alberta 41 F2 50 44N 113 53W
Alert Bay *tn.* British Columbia 39 G2 50 34N 126 58W
Alexandria Ontario 47 M5 45 19N 74 38W
Alexis Creek *tn.* British Columbia 39 J3 52 05N 123 12W
Alexis River Newfoundland and Labrador 52 G6 52 50N 57 40W
Alfred Ontario 47 M5 45 34N 74 53W
Alfred, Mount British Columbia 38 H5 50 13N 124 07W
Algoma *admin.* Ontario 46 C6/D6 48 00N 84 00W
Algonquin Provincial Park Ontario 46 H5 45 50N 78 30W
Alix Alberta 41 F3 52 25N 113 11W
Allan Saskatchewan 42 D2 51 54N 106 02W
Allan Water *tn.* Ontario 44 F6 50 14N 90 12W
Alliston Ontario 48 C3 44 09N 79 51W
Alma New Brunswick 53 M12 45 36N 64 58W
Alma Québec 51 E3 48 32N 71 41W
Almonte Ontario 47 K5 45 14N 76 12W
Alouette Lake British Columbia 38 H4 49 22N 121 22W
Alsask Saskatchewan 42 C2 51 22N 110 00W
Alsek Ranges *mts.* British Columbia 38 A6/B6 59 30N 137 30W
Altona Manitoba 43 D1 49 06N 97 35W
Alvin British Columbia 38 H4 49 25N 122 34W
Amadjuak Lake Nunavut 55 R3 65 00N 71 08W
Amaranth Manitoba 43 C2 50 36N 98 43W
Amberley Ontario 48 A3 44 02N 81 44W
Amery Manitoba 43 E5 56 45N 94 00W
Amherst Nova Scotia 53 M12 45 50N 64 14W
Amherstburg Ontario 46 C2 42 06N 83 07W
Amherst Island Ontario 47 K4 44 08N 76 43W
Amisk Lake Saskatchewan 42 F4 54 30N 102 15W
Amos Québec 51 A3 48 04N 78 08W
Amqui Québec 51 G3 48 30N 67 30W
Amund Ringnes Islands Nunavut 55 L6 78 00N 96 00W
Amundsen Gulf Northwest Territories 54 E5 70 30N 125 00W
Anahim Lake *tn.* British Columbia 39 H3 52 25N 125 18W
Ancaster Ontario 48 C2 43 13N 79 58W
Anderson River Northwest Territories 54 E4 69 42N 129 01W
Anderson River Delta Bird Sanctuary Northwest Territories 54 E4 69 50N 128 00W
Andrew Alberta 41 F3 53 52N 112 14W
Andrew Gordon Bay Nunavut 55 R3 60 27N 75 30W
Angers Québec 57 L3 45 32N 75 29W
Angikuni Lake Nunavut 55 L3 62 00N 99 45W
Angling Lake *I.R.* Ontario 44 G7 53 50N 89 30W
Anguille, Cape Newfoundland and Labrador 53 F3 47 55N 59 24W
Angus Ontario 48 C3 44 19N 79 53W
Annacis Island British Columbia 40 G3 49 09N 122 59W
Annapolis *admin.* Nova Scotia 53 L11 44 40N 65 20W
Annapolis Royal Nova Scotia 53 L11 44 44N 65 32W
Annieville British Columbia 40 G3 49 10N 122 54W
Antigonish Nova Scotia 53 M12 45 39N 62 00W
Antigonish *admin.* Nova Scotia 53 M12 45 30N 62 10W
Anvil Range Yukon Territory 54 D3 62 25N 133 15W
Apsley Ontario 46 H4 44 45N 78 06W
Arborfield Saskatchewan 42 F3 53 06N 103 39W
Arborg Manitoba 43 D2 50 55N 97 12W
Arcola Saskatchewan 42 F1 49 38N 102 26W
Arctic Bay *(Ikpiarjuk) tn.* Nunavut 55 N5 73 05N 85 20W
Arctic Red River Northwest Territories 54 D4 66 00N 132 00W
Argenteuil *admin.* Québec 47 M5 45 50N 74 40W
Argentia Newfoundland and Labrador 53 J3 47 17N 53 59W
Arichat Nova Scotia 53 M12 45 31N 61 00W
Aristazabal Island British Columbia 38 F3 52 40N 129 40W
Armstrong British Columbia 39 L2 50 27N 119 14W
Armstrong Ontario 44 G6 50 20N 89 02W
Arnold's Cove *tn.* Newfoundland and Labrador 53 H3 47 45N 54 00W
Arnot Manitoba 43 D4 55 46N 96 42W
Arnprior Ontario 47 K5 45 26N 76 21W
Aroland Ontario 44 H6 50 14N 86 59W
Aroostook New Brunswick 53 B3 46 45N 67 40W
Arran Lake Ontario 48 A3 44 29N 81 16W
Arrowsmith, Mount British Columbia 38 H4 49 00N 124 00W
Arthabaska *admin.* Québec 47 P5 45 58N 72 11W
Arthur Ontario 48 B2 43 50N 80 32W
Artillery Lake Northwest Territories 54 J3 63 09N 107 52W
Arviat *(Eskimo Point)* Nunavut 55 M3 61 10N 94 05W
Asbestos Québec 47 Q5 45 46N 71 56W
Ashcroft British Columbia 39 K2 50 41N 121 17W
Ashern Manitoba 43 C2 51 10N 98 20W
Asheweig River Ontario 44 H7 53 50N 87 50W
Ashihik Lake Yukon Territory 54 C3 61 00N 135 05W
Ashuanipi Newfoundland and Labrador 52 B6 52 46N 66 05W
Ashuanipi Lake Newfoundland and Labrador 52 B6 52 45N 66 15W
Ashuanipi River Newfoundland and Labrador 52 B6 53 50N 66 30W
Aspy Bay Nova Scotia 53 M12 46 50N 60 20W
Assiniboia Saskatchewan 42 E1 49 39N 105 59W
Assiniboine River Manitoba/Saskatchewan 43 C1 49 40N 98 50W
Aston, Cape Nunavut 55 S5 70 00N 67 15W
Astray Newfoundland and Labrador 52 B7 54 36N 66 42W
Astray Lake Newfoundland and Labrador 52 B7 54 36N 66 42W
Athabasca Alberta 41 F4 54 44N 113 15W
Athabasca, Lake Alberta/Saskatchewan 42 C6 59 00N 109 00W
Athabasca River Alberta 41 G5 57 30N 111 40W
Athabasca Sand Dunes Provincial Wilderness Park Saskatchewan 42 C6 59 10N 108 30W
Athens Ontario 47 L4 44 38N 75 57W
Atherley Ontario 48 C3 44 36N 79 21W
Athol Nova Scotia 53 M12 45 40N 64 10W
Atikaki Provincial Park Manitoba 43 E2 51 30N 95 30W
Atik Lake Manitoba 43 D4 55 20N 96 10W
Atikokan Ontario 44 F5 48 45N 91 38W
Atikonak Lake Newfoundland and Labrador 52 C6 52 40N 64 32W
Atikonak River Newfoundland and Labrador 52 C6 53 20N 64 50W
Atkinson, Point British Columbia 40 E4 49 20N 123 16W
Atlin British Columbia 38 D6 59 31N 133 41W
Atlin Lake British Columbia 38 D6 59 31N 133 41W
Atlin Provincial Park British Columbia 38 D6 59 10N 133 50W
Atna Peak British Columbia 39 F3 53 53N 128 07W
Attawapiskat Ontario 44 K7 53 00N 82 30W
Attawapiskat Lake Ontario 44 H7 52 18N 87 54W
Attawapiskat River Ontario 44 K7 53 00N 84 00W
Aubry, Lake Northwest Territories 54 E4 67 23N 126 30W
Auden Ontario 44 H6 50 14N 87 54W
Aulac New Brunswick 53 M12 45 50N 64 20W
Aulavik National Park Northwest Territories 54 G5 73 30N 118 00W
Aulneau Peninsula Ontario 44 D5 49 23N 94 29W
Aupaluk Québec 50 F8 59 12N 69 35W
Aurora Ontario 48 C3 43 00N 79 28W
Ausable River Ontario 48 A2 43 06N 81 36W
Austin Channel Nunavut 55 K6 75 35N 103 25W
Auyuittuq National Park Reserve Nunavut 55 S4 67 00N 67 00W
Avalon Peninsula Newfoundland and Labrador 53 J3 47 30N 53 30W
Avalon Wilderness Reserve Newfoundland and Labrador 53 J3 47 10N 52 40W
Avola British Columbia 39 L2 51 47N 119 19W
Avon River Ontario 48 A2 43 20N 81 10W
Awenda Provincial Park Ontario 48 B3 44 50N 80 00W
Axel Heiberg Island Nunavut 55 M6 80 00N 90 00W
Aylmer Ontario 48 B1 42 47N 80 58W
Aylmer Lake Northwest Territories 54 J3 64 05N 108 30W
Ayr Ontario 48 B2 43 17N 80 26W
Azure Lake British Columbia 39 K3 52 22N 120 07W

B

Babine Lake British Columbia 39 H4 54 45N 125 05W
Babine Mountains Recreation Area British Columbia 39 G4 54 50N 126 55W
Babine River British Columbia 39 G4 55 44N 127 29W
Bache Peninsula Nunavut 55 Q6 79 08N 76 00W
Backbone Ranges *mts.* Northwest Territories 54 E3 64 30N 130 00W
Back River Nunavut 54 J4 65 00N 105 00W
Baddeck Nova Scotia 53 M12 46 06N 60 45W
Badger Newfoundland and Labrador 53 G4 49 00N 56 04W
Baffin Bay Nunavut 55 S5 72 00N 64 00W
Baffin Island Nunavut 55 Q5 70 00N 75 00W
Baffin Region Nunavut 55 N5 71 30N 88 00W
Baie-Comeau *tn.* Québec 51 F3 49 12N 68 10W
Baie des Chaleurs *b.* Québec/New Brunswick 51 H2 47 59N 65 50W
Baie de Valois *b.* Québec 56 M4 45 27N 73 17W
Baie d'Ungava Québec/Northwest Territories 50 G8 59 00N 67 30W
Baie James *b.* Québec/Northwest Territories 51 A5 52 00N 79 00W
Baie Lafontaine *b.* Ontario 57 L3 45 32N 75 18W
Baie-St.-Paul *tn.* Québec 47 R7 47 27N 70 30W
Baie-Trinité *tn.* Québec 51 G3 49 25N 67 20W
Baie Vert *b.* Nova Scotia 53 M12 46 00N 64 00W
Baie Vert *tn.* Newfoundland and Labrador 53 G4 49 55N 56 12W
Baie Verte Peninsula Newfoundland and Labrador 53 G4 49 45N 56 15W
Bailey Creek Ontario 48 C3 44 01N 79 56W
Baillie Island Northwest Territories 54 E5 70 35N 128 10W
Baillie River Northwest Territories/Nunavut 54 J3 64 40N 105 50W
Baird Peninsula Nunavut 55 Q4 68 55N 76 04W
Baker Lake Nunavut 55 L3 64 00N 95 00W
Baker Lake *(Qamanittuaq) tn.* Nunavut 55 L3 64 20N 96 10W
Balcarres Saskatchewan 42 F2 50 49N 103 32W
Baldock Lake Manitoba 43 C5 56 30N 98 25W
Baldy Mountain Manitoba 43 B2 51 27N 100 45W
Balgonie Saskatchewan 42 E2 50 31N 104 15W
Ballantyne Strait Northwest Territories 54 G6 77 25N 114 20W
Balmertown Ontario 44 E6 51 04N 93 41W
Balsam Lake Ontario 48 D3 44 37N 78 51W
Balsam Lake Provincial Park Ontario 48 D3 44 30N 78 50W
Bamaji Lake Ontario 44 F6 51 09N 91 25W
Bancroft Ontario 46 J5 45 03N 77 51W
Banff Alberta 41 E2 51 10N 115 34W
Banff National Park Alberta 41 D2/E2 51 00N 116 00W
Banks Island British Columbia 38 E3 53 30N 130 00W
Banks Island Northwest Territories 54 F4 73 15N 121 30W
Banks Island No 1 Bird Sanctuary Northwest Territories 54 F4 72 30N 124 50W
Banks Island No 2 Bird Sanctuary Northwest Territories 54 F4 73 30N 124 00W
Barachois Pond Provincial Park Newfoundland and Labrador 53 F4 48 28N 58 20W
Baring, Cape Northwest Territories 54 G5 70 02N 117 20W
Barkerville British Columbia 39 K3 53 06N 121 35W
Barkley Sound British Columbia 38 G4 48 58N 125 11W
Barnes Ice Cap Nunavut 55 R5 70 00N 74 00W
Barnfield British Columbia 38 G4 48 50N 125 07W
Barnston Island British Columbia 40 H3 49 11N 122 42W
Barrage Daniel-Johnson Québec 51 F4 50 39N 68 45W
Barr'd Islands *tn.* Newfoundland and Labrador 53 H4 49 44N 54 11W
Barrhaven Ontario 57 J2 45 16N 75 47W
Barrhead Alberta 41 E4 54 10N 114 22W
Barrie Ontario 48 C3 44 22N 79 42W
Barrie Island Ontario 46 D5 45 56N 82 39W
Barrière British Columbia 39 K2 51 10N 120 07W
Barrington Nova Scotia 53 L11 43 34N 65 35W
Barrington Lake Manitoba 43 B5 57 00N 100 15W
Barrow Bay Ontario 48 A3 44 58N 81 11W
Barrows Manitoba 43 B2 52 50N 101 26W
Barrow Strait Nunavut 55 M5 74 24N 94 10W
Barrys Bay *tn.* Ontario 46 J5 45 27N 77 41W
Bashaw Alberta 41 F3 52 35N 112 58W
Basin Lake Saskatchewan 42 E3 52 40N 105 10W
Bassano Alberta 41 F2 50 47N 112 28W
Bass Lake Ontario 48 C3 44 36N 79 31W
Bass Lake Provincial Park Ontario 48 C3 44 30N 79 40W
Batchawana Bay *tn.* Ontario 45 J4 46 53N 84 36W
Batchawana Mountain Ontario 45 J4 47 04N 84 24W
Bath New Brunswick 53 B3 46 30N 67 36W
Bath Ontario 47 K4 44 11N 76 47W
Bathurst, Cape Northwest Territories 54 E5 70 31N 127 53W
Bathurst New Brunswick 53 C3 47 37N 65 40W
Bathurst Inlet Nunavut 54 J4 66 49N 108 00W
Bathurst Inlet *(Kinggauk) tn.* Nunavut 54 J4 66 50N 108 01W
Bathurst Island Nunavut 55 K6 76 00N 100 00W
Batoche National Historic Site Saskatchewan 42 E3 52 45N 106 00W
Batteau Newfoundland and Labrador 52 H6 53 24N 55 47W
Battle Creek Saskatchewan 42 C1 49 20N 109 30W
Battleford Saskatchewan 42 C3 52 45N 108 20W
Battle Harbour *tn.* Newfoundland and Labrador 52 H6 52 16N 55 35W
Battle River Alberta/Saskatchewan 42 C3 52 50N 109 10W
Bauld, Cape Newfoundland and Labrador 52 H5 51 40N 55 25W
Bay Bulls *tn.* Newfoundland and Labrador 53 J3 47 19N 52 50W
Bay de Verde *tn.* Newfoundland and Labrador 53 J4 48 03N 52 54W
Bay du Nord Wilderness Reserve Newfoundland and Labrador 53 H4 48 10N 54 55W
Bayers Lake Nova Scotia 57 Q6 44 38N 63 39W
Bayfield Ontario 48 A2 43 33N 81 41W
Bayfield River Ontario 48 A2 43 34N 81 38W
Bay Roberts *tn.* Newfoundland and Labrador 53 J3 47 36N 53 16W
Beachburg Ontario 47 K5 45 44N 76 51W
Beacon Hill *tn.* Ontario 57 K2 45 28N 75 35W
Beale, Cape British Columbia 38 G4 48 46N 125 10W
Beamsville Ontario 48 C2 43 10N 79 31W
Bear *r.* Ontario 57 L2 45 22N 75 29W
Beardmore Ontario 45 H5 49 36N 87 59W
Bear Island Northwest Territories 44 L8 64 01N 83 13W
Bear Lake Manitoba 43 D4 55 10N 96 30W
Bear River *tn.* Nova Scotia 53 L11 44 34N 65 40W
Bearskin Lake *I.R.* Ontario 44 F7 53 50N 90 55W
Beatton River British Columbia 39 K5 57 18N 121 15W
Beatty Saugeen River Ontario 48 B3 44 08N 80 54W
Beattyville Québec 51 B3 48 53N 77 10W
Beauce *admin.* Québec 47 R6 46 15N 71 00W
Beauceville Québec 47 R6 46 12N 70 45W
Beaufort Sea 54 C5 72 00N 139 30W
Beauharnois Québec 47 N5 45 18N 73 52W
Beaupré Québec 47 R7 47 03N 70 56W
Beauséjour Manitoba 43 D2 50 04N 96 30W
Beauval Saskatchewan 42 D4 55 09N 107 35W
Beaverbank Nova Scotia 57 Q7 44 48N 63 39W
Beaver Creek Ontario 49 C2 43 51N 79 23W
Beaver Creek *tn.* Yukon Territory 54 B3 60 20N 140 45W
Beaverdell British Columbia 39 L1 49 25N 119 09W
Beaverhill Lake Alberta 41 F3 53 27N 112 32W
Beaver Hill Lake Manitoba 43 E4 54 20N 95 20W
Beaverlodge Alberta 41 C4 55 13N 119 26W
Beaver River Alberta/Saskatchewan 42 C4 54 20N 108 40W
Beaver River Ontario 48 B3 44 21N 80 33W
Beaverton Ontario 48 C3 44 25N 79 10W
Beaverton River Ontario 48 C3 44 08N 79 06W
Bécancour Québec 47 P6 46 20N 72 30W
Beckwith Island Ontario 48 B3 44 53N 80 06W
Bedford Nova Scotia 53 M11 44 44N 61 41W
Bedford Basin Nova Scotia 57 Q6 44 41N 63 37W
Beechey Head *c.* British Columbia 38 H4 48 19N 123 39W
Beechville Nova Scotia 57 Q6 44 37N 63 42W
Beeton Ontario 48 C3 44 04N 79 46W
Beiseker Alberta 41 F2 51 23N 113 32W
Belair Provincial Forest Manitoba 43 D2 50 38N 96 40W
Belcher Islands Nunavut 55 Q2 56 00N 79 30W
Bella Bella British Columbia 39 F3 52 06N 128 06W
Bella Coola British Columbia 39 G3 52 30N 126 50W
Bella Coola River British Columbia 39 G3 52 22N 126 35W
Bellcarra British Columbia 40 G4 49 19N 122 56W
Belle Bay Newfoundland and Labrador 53 H3 47 37N 55 18W
Bellechasse *admin.* Québec 47 R6 46 40N 70 50W
Belledune New Brunswick 53 C3 47 50N 65 45W
Belle Isle *i.* Newfoundland and Labrador 52 H5 51 57N 55 21W
Belle Isle, Strait of Newfoundland and Labrador 52 G5 51 30N 56 30W
Belle Plaine Saskatchewan 42 E2 50 25N 105 09W
Belle River *tn.* Ontario 46 D2 42 18N 82 43W
Belleville Ontario 47 J4 44 10N 77 23W
Bell-Irving River British Columbia 38 F5 56 42N 129 40W
Bell Island Newfoundland and Labrador 52 H5 50 50N 55 50W
Bell Peninsula Nunavut 55 P3 63 00N 82 00W
Bells Corners Ontario 57 J2 45 19N 75 49W
Belly River Alberta 41 F1 49 10N 113 40W
Belmont Ontario 48 A1 42 52N 81 06W
Beloeil Québec 47 N5 45 34N 73 15W
Belwood, Lake Ontario 48 B2 43 46N 80 20W
Benedict Mountains Newfoundland and Labrador 52 F7 54 45N 58 45W
Bengough Saskatchewan 42 E1 49 25N 105 10W
Benito Manitoba 43 B2 51 55N 101 30W
Bentley Alberta 41 E3 52 28N 114 04W
Berens River Manitoba/Ontario 43 D3 52 10N 96 40W
Berens River *tn.* Manitoba 43 D3 52 22N 97 00W
Beresford New Brunswick 53 C3 47 40N 65 40W
Bergland Ontario 44 D5 48 57N 94 23W
Bernier Bay Nunavut 55 N5 71 05N 88 15W
Berthier *admin.* Québec 47 M7 47 40N 75 20W
Bertrand New Brunswick 53 C3 47 45N 65 05W
Berwick Nova Scotia 53 M12 45 03N 64 44W

Berwyn Alberta	**41**	D5	56 09N	117 44W
Besnard Lake Saskatchewan	**42**	D4	55 30N	106 10W
Betsiamites Québec	**51**	F3	48 56N	68 40W
Bible Hill *tn.* Nova Scotia	**53**	M12	45 20N	63 10W
Bienfait Saskatchewan	**42**	F1	49 09N	102 48W
Big Bay *tn.* British Columbia	**38**	G5	50 24N	125 08W
Big Creek Ontario	**48**	B1	42 43N	80 33W
Big Creek Provincial Park British Columbia	**39**	J2	51 10N	123 10W
Biggar Saskatchewan	**42**	D3	52 03N	107 59W
Bighead River Ontario	**48**	B3	44 30N	80 47W
Big Indian Lake Nova Scotia	**57**	Q6	44 35N	63 42W
Big Island Nunavut	**55**	R3	62 43N	70 43W
Big Island Ontario	**44**	D5	49 10N	94 30W
Big Muddy Lake Saskatchewan	**42**	E1	49 10N	104 50W
Big Otter Creek Ontario	**48**	B1	42 46N	80 51W
Big River Newfoundland and Labrador	**52**	F7	54 50N	59 40W
Big River *tn.* Saskatchewan	**42**	D3	53 50N	107 01W
Big Salmon Range *mts.* Yukon Territory	**54**	D3	62 40N	134 59W
Big Sand Lake Manitoba	**43**	C5	57 50N	99 30W
Big Silver Creek British Columbia	**38**	H4	49 50N	121 50W
Bigstick Lake Saskatchewan	**42**	C2	50 20N	109 50W
Bigstone Lake Manitoba	**43**	E3	53 30N	95 50W
Big Trout Lake Ontario	**44**	F7	53 50N	90 00W
Big Trout Lake *tn.* Ontario	**44**	G7	53 40N	89 50W
Birch Cove Nova Scotia	**57**	Q6	44 40N	63 39W
Birch Hills *tn.* Saskatchewan	**42**	E3	53 00N	105 00W
Birch Island Manitoba	**43**	C3	52 20N	99 50W
Birch Lake Alberta	**41**	G3	53 19N	111 35W
Birch Lake Ontario	**44**	E6	51 20N	92 20W
Birch Mountains Alberta	**41**	F5	57 20N	113 55W
Birch River Alberta	**41**	F6	58 20N	113 20W
Birken British Columbia	**38**	H5	50 29N	112 36W
Birtle Manitoba	**43**	B2	50 26N	101 04W
Biscotasing Ontario	**45**	K4	47 17N	82 06W
Bishop's Falls *tn.* Newfoundland and Labrador	**53**	H4	49 01N	55 30W
Bistcho Lake Alberta	**41**	C6	59 45N	118 50W
Bjorne Peninsula Nunavut	**55**	N6	77 37N	87 00W
Black Bear Island Lake Saskatchewan	**42**	E4	55 45N	105 50W
Black Birch Lake Saskatchewan	**42**	D5	56 55N	107 25W
Blackburn Hamlet Ontario	**57**	K2	45 26N	75 33W
Black Diamond Alberta	**41**	E2	50 45N	114 12W
Blackfalds Alberta	**41**	F3	52 23N	113 47W
Black Island *tn.* Newfoundland and Labrador	**52**	G7	54 30N	58 50W
Black Lake Saskatchewan	**42**	E6	59 10N	104 30W
Black Lake *tn.* Québec	**47**	Q6	46 03N	71 21W
Black Lake *tn.* Saskatchewan	**42**	E6	59 05N	105 35W
Black River Ontario	**48**	C3	44 48N	79 08W
Blacks Harbour New Brunswick	**53**	B2	45 03N	66 49W
Blackville New Brunswick	**53**	C3	46 44N	65 51W
Blackwater Lake Northwest Territories	**54**	F3	64 00N	123 05W
Blaine Lake *tn.* Saskatchewan	**42**	D3	52 50N	106 54W
Blainville Québec	**47**	N5	45 39N	73 52W
Blair Ontario	**48**	B2	43 23N	80 23W
Blanc-Sablon Québec	**50**	L4	51 26N	57 08W
Blenheim Ontario	**46**	E2	42 20N	82 00W
Blind River *tn.* Ontario	**46**	D6	46 10N	82 58W
Bloodvein River Manitoba	**43**	D2	51 50N	96 40W
Bloomfield Ontario	**47**	J3	43 59N	77 14W
Blossom Park *tn.* Ontario	**57**	K2	45 21N	75 37W
Blubber Bay *tn.* British Columbia	**38**	H4	49 48N	124 37W
Bluenose Lake Nunavut	**54**	G4	68 30N	119 35W
Blue Ridge *tn.* Alberta	**41**	E4	54 08N	115 22W
Blue River *tn.* British Columbia	**39**	L3	52 05N	119 09W
Blyth Ontario	**48**	A2	43 43N	81 26W
Blyth Brook Ontario	**48**	A2	43 45N	81 31W
Bobcaygeon Ontario	**46**	H4	44 32N	78 33W
Boisbriand Québec	**56**	M5	45 35N	73 51W
Boissevain Manitoba	**43**	B1	49 14N	100 02W
Bolton Ontario	**48**	C2	43 53N	79 44W
Bonavista Newfoundland and Labrador	**53**	J4	48 39N	53 07W
Bonavista Bay Newfoundland and Labrador	**53**	J4	48 45N	53 30W
Bonavista Peninsula Newfoundland and Labrador	**53**	J4	48 30N	53 30W
Bon Echo Provincial Park Ontario	**47**	J4	44 55N	77 15W
Bonnet Plume River Yukon Territory	**54**	D4	65 25N	135 00W
Bonnyville Alberta	**41**	G4	54 16N	110 44W
Boothia, Gulf of Nunavut	**55**	N4	69 00N	88 00W
Boothia Peninsula Nunavut	**55**	M5	70 30N	94 30W
Borden-Carleton Prince Edward Island	**53**	M12	46 20N	63 40W
Borden Island Northwest Territories/Nunavut	**54**	H6	78 30N	111 30W
Borden Peninsula Nunavut	**55**	P5	73 00N	82 30W
Boston Bar British Columbia	**39**	K1	49 52N	121 25W
Botwood Newfoundland and Labrador	**53**	H4	49 09N	55 21W
Bouctouche New Brunswick	**53**	M12	46 30N	64 40W
Boundary Range *mts.* British Columbia	**38**	D6	58 00N	133 00W
Bowden Alberta	**41**	E2	51 55N	114 02W
Bowen Island British Columbia	**38**	H4	49 23N	123 26W
Bow Island *tn.* Alberta	**41**	G1	49 52N	111 22W
Bowman Bay Wildlife Sanctuary Nunavut	**55**	R4	66 00N	74 00W
Bowmanville Ontario	**48**	D2	43 55N	78 43W
Bowmanville Creek Ontario	**48**	D3	44 02N	78 47W
Bowness Alberta	**40**	A2	51 05N	114 14W
Bow River Alberta	**41**	F2	50 47N	111 55W
Bowron Lake Provinvial Park British Columbia	**39**	K3	53 00N	121 00W
Bowron River British Columbia	**39**	K3	53 38N	121 40W
Bowser British Columbia	**38**	H4	49 26N	124 41W
Boyle Alberta	**41**	F4	54 35N	112 49W
Boyne River Ontario	**48**	B3	44 07N	80 07W
Bracebridge Ontario	**46**	G5	45 02N	79 19W
Bradford Ontario	**48**	C3	44 07N	79 34W
Bralorne British Columbia	**39**	J2	50 46N	122 51W
Bramalea Ontario	**48**	C2	43 44N	79 44W
Brampton Ontario	**48**	C2	43 42N	79 46W
Brandon Manitoba	**43**	C1	49 50N	99 57W
Brant *admin.* Ontario	**48**	B2	43 03N	80 29W
Brantford Ontario	**48**	B2	43 09N	80 17W
Bras d'Or Lake Nova Scotia	**53**	M12	45 50N	60 50W
Brazeau, Mount Alberta	**41**	D3	52 33N	117 21W
Brazeau River Alberta	**41**	D3	52 50N	116 20W
Brechin Ontario	**48**	C3	44 32N	79 11W
Brent Ontario	**46**	H6	46 02N	78 29W
Breton Cove *tn.* Nova Scotia	**53**	M12	46 30N	60 30W
Brevoort Island Nunavut	**55**	T3	63 19N	64 08W
Bridge River British Columbia	**39**	J2	50 55N	123 25W
Bridgetown Nova Scotia	**53**	L11	44 50N	65 20W
Bridgewater Nova Scotia	**53**	M11	44 23N	64 32W
Brier Island Nova Scotia	**53**	L11	44 20N	66 20W
Brighton Ontario	**46**	J4	44 07N	77 45W
Brisay Québec	**50**	E6	54 25N	70 42W
Bristol New Brunswick	**53**	B3	46 28N	67 38W
Britannia Beach *tn.* British Columbia	**38**	H4	49 38N	123 10W
British Columbia *province*	**38/39**			
British Empire Range *mts.* Nunavut	**55**	P7	82 30N	84 50W
British Mountains	**54**	B4	69 00N	141 00W
Britt Ontario	**46**	F5	45 46N	80 33W
Broadview Saskatchewan	**42**	F2	50 22N	102 31W
Brochet Manitoba	**43**	B5	57 55N	101 40W
Brockville Ontario	**47**	L4	44 35N	75 41W
Brodeur Peninsula Nunavut	**55**	N5	72 00N	87 30W
Brome *admin.* Québec	**47**	P5	45 10N	72 10W
Bromont Québec	**47**	P5	45 18N	72 38W
Bronte Ontario	**48**	C2	43 23N	79 43W
Brookfield Nova Scotia	**53**	M12	45 15N	63 18W
Brooklyn Nova Scotia	**53**	M11	44 04N	64 42W
Brooks Alberta	**41**	G2	50 35N	111 54W
Brooks Peninsula British Columbia	**39**	G2	50 05N	127 45W
Brooks Peninsula Provincial Park British Columbia	**39**	G2	50 15N	127 50W
Brown Lake Nunavut	**55**	M4	65 54N	91 15W
Bruce *admin.* Ontario	**48**	A3	44 15N	81 24W
Bruce Creek Ontario	**49**	C2	43 55N	79 20W
Bruce Mines *tn.* Ontario	**46**	C6	46 18N	83 48W
Bruce Peninsula Ontario	**48**	A3/A4	45 00N	81 20W
Bruce Peninsula National Park Ontario	**48**	A4	45 00N	81 20W
Bruderheim Alberta	**41**	F3	53 47N	112 56W
Brunette Island Newfoundland and Labrador	**53**	H3	47 16N	55 55W
Bruno Saskatchewan	**42**	E3	52 17N	105 31W
Brussels Ontario	**48**	A2	43 44N	81 15W
Buchan Gulf Nunavut	**55**	R5	71 47N	74 16W
Buchans Newfoundland and Labrador	**53**	G4	48 49N	56 53W
Buckinghorse River *tn.* British Columbia	**39**	J5	57 25N	122 50W
Buffalo Head Hills Alberta	**41**	E5	57 25N	115 55W
Buffalo Head Prairie Alberta	**41**	D6	58 04N	116 30W
Buffalo Lake Alberta	**41**	F3	52 27N	112 54W
Buffalo Narrows *tn.* Saskatchewan	**42**	C4	55 52N	108 28W
Buffalo River Alberta	**41**	E6	59 25N	114 35W
Buffalo Trail Alberta	**41**	G2	51 45N	110 35W
Bulkley River British Columbia	**39**	G4	55 00N	127 10W
Buntzen Lake British Columbia	**40**	G4	49 20N	124 51W
Burden, Mount British Columbia	**39**	J5	56 10N	123 09W
Burford Ontario	**48**	B2	43 46N	80 25W
Burgeo Newfoundland and Labrador	**53**	G3	47 37N	57 37W
Burin Newfoundland and Labrador	**53**	H3	47 02N	55 10W
Burin Peninsula Newfoundland and Labrador	**53**	H3	47 00N	55 40W
Burk's Falls *tn.* Ontario	**46**	G5	45 37N	79 25W
Burlington Ontario	**48**	C2	43 19N	79 48W
Burnaby British Columbia	**38**	H4	49 16N	122 58W
Burnaby Lake British Columbia	**40**	G3	49 14N	122 57W
Burns Alberta	**40**	A1	50 59N	114 02W
Burnside Nova Scotia	**57**	Q6	44 41N	63 35W
Burnside River Northwest Territories	**54**	J4	66 20N	109 30W
Burns Lake *tn.* British Columbia	**39**	H4	54 14N	125 45
Burnt Islands *tn.* Newfoundland and Labrador	**53**	F3	47 50N	58 00W
Burnt Lake Québec	**51**	J5	52 15N	63 50W
Burnt River Ontario	**48**	D3	44 41N	78 43W
Burntwood Lake Manitoba	**43**	B4	55 20N	100 10W
Burntwood River Manitoba	**43**	D4	55 50N	97 40W
Burquitlam British Columbia	**40**	G4	49 15N	122 56W
Burrard Inlet British Columbia	**40**	F4	49 19N	123 14W
Burstall Saskatchewan	**42**	C2	50 40N	109 56W
Bushell Park *tn.* Saskatchewan	**42**	E2	50 25N	105 30W
Butedale British Columbia	**39**	F3	53 12N	128 45W
Bute Inlet British Columbia	**38**	H5	50 31N	124 59W
Buttle Lake British Columbia	**38**	G4	49 47N	125 30W
Button Bay Manitoba	**43**	E6	58 50N	94 30W
Button Islands Northwest Territories	**50**	H9	60 35N	64 40W
Buttonville Ontario	**49**	C2	43 51N	79 22W
Byam Channel Nunavut	**55**	K6	75 10N	105 00W
Byam Martin Island Nunavut	**55**	K6	75 15N	104 15W
Bylot Island Nunavut	**55**	Q5	73 30N	79 00W
Bylot Island Bird Sanctuary Nunavut	**55**	Q5	73 20N	79 00W
Byron Bay Newfoundland and Labrador	**52**	G7	54 40N	57 40W

C

Cabano Québec	**51**	F2	47 40N	68 56W
Cabot Head Ontario	**48**	A4	45 15N	81 17W
Cabot Lake Newfoundland and Labrador	**52**	D8	56 09N	62 37W
Cabot Strait Nova Scotia/Newfoundland and Labrador	**53**	F3	47 10N	59 30W
Cabri Saskatchewan	**42**	C2	50 38N	108 28W
Cache Creek *tn.* British Columbia	**39**	K2	50 46N	121 17W
Cadotte Lake *tn.* Alberta	**41**	D5	56 25N	116 28W
Calabogie Ontario	**47**	K5	45 18N	76 43W
Calais New Brunswick	**53**	B2	45 10N	67 15W
Caledon East Ontario	**48**	C2	43 52N	79 53W
Caledonia Nova Scotia	**53**	L11	44 24N	65 02W
Caledonia Ontario	**48**	C2	43 05N	79 57W
Caledon Village Ontario	**48**	C2	43 51N	79 59W
Calgary Alberta	**41**	E2	51 05N	114 05W
Callander Ontario	**46**	G6	46 13N	79 22W
Calling Lake Alberta	**41**	F4	55 15N	113 20W
Calmar Alberta	**41**	F3	53 16N	113 49W
Calvert Island British Columbia	**39**	F2	51 30N	128 00W
Cambridge Ontario	**48**	B2	43 22N	80 20W
Cambridge Bay *(Iqaluktuutiaq) tn.* Northwest Territories	**54**	K4	69 09N	105 00W
Cambridge-Narrows New Brunswick	**53**	C2	45 50N	65 55W
Cameron Hills Alberta	**41**	C6	59 48N	118 00W
Campbell Dam Saskatchewan	**42**	F3	53 40N	103 20W
Campbellford Ontario	**46**	J4	44 18N	77 48W
Campbell Lake British Columbia	**38**	G4	49 59N	125 30W
Campbell, Mount Yukon Territory	**54**	C3	64 23N	138 43W
Campbell River *tn.* British Columbia	**38**	G5	50 00N	125 18W
Campbells Cove *tn.* Prince Edward Island	**53**	M12	46 30N	62 15W
Campbellton New Brunswick	**53**	B3	48 00N	66 41W
Campbellton Newfoundland and Labrador	**53**	H4	49 17N	54 56W
Campbellville Ontario	**48**	C2	43 29N	79 59W
Camperville Manitoba	**43**	B2	51 00N	100 08W
Campobello Island New Brunswick	**53**	B2	44 50N	66 50W
Camrose Alberta	**41**	F3	53 01N	112 50W
Camsell Portage Saskatchewan	**42**	C6	59 39N	109 12W
CANADA	**10/11**			
Canal Flats *tn.* British Columbia	**39**	N2	50 09N	115 50W
Canal Lake Ontario	**48**	C3	44 34N	79 02W
Candiac Québec	**56**	N4	45 24N	73 31W
Candle Lake Saskatchewan	**42**	E3	53 55N	105 10W
Candle Lake *tn.* Saskatchewan	**42**	E3	53 50N	105 10W
Canmore Alberta	**41**	E2	51 07N	115 18W
Canning Nova Scotia	**53**	M12	45 10N	64 26W
Canoe Lake Saskatchewan	**42**	C4	55 10N	108 30W
Canora Saskatchewan	**42**	F2	51 38N	102 28W
Canso Nova Scotia	**53**	M12	45 20N	61 00W
Canso, Cape Nova Scotia	**53**	M12	45 19N	60 59W
Cap-aux-Meules *tn.* Québec	**53**	E3	47 25N	62 00W
Cap-Chat *tn.* Québec	**51**	G3	49 06N	66 42W
Cap de Nouvelle-France *c.* Québec	**50**	D10	61 30N	73 45W
Cap Dufferin *c.* Québec	**50**	A8	58 35N	78 32W
Cape Breton *admin.* Nova Scotia	**53**	M12	45 50N	60 00W
Cape Breton Highlands National Park Nova Scotia	**53**	M12	46 45N	60 40W
Cape Breton Island Nova Scotia	**53**	M12	46 45N	60 00W
Cape Charles *tn.* Newfoundland and Labrador	**52**	H6	52 13N	55 38W
Cape Croker *tn.* Ontario	**48**	A3	44 56N	81 01W
Cape Dorset *(Kingnait) tn.* Nunavut	**55**	Q3	64 10N	76 40W
Cape Dorset Sanctuaries Nunavut	**55**	Q3	63 50N	77 00W
Cape Le Havre Island Nova Scotia	**53**	M11	44 10N	64 20W
Cape North *tn.* Nova Scotia	**53**	M12	46 55N	60 30W
Cape Parry *m.s.* Northwest Territories	**54**	F5	70 08N	124 34W
Cape Sable Island Nova Scotia	**53**	L11	43 30N	65 40W
Cape St. George *tn.* Newfoundland and Labrador	**53**	F4	48 28N	59 15W
Cape Scott Provincial Park British Columbia	**39**	F2	50 42N	128 20W
Cape Smith *tn.* Nunavut	**50**	A9	60 44N	78 29W
Cape Tormentine *tn.* New Brunswick	**53**	M12	46 08N	63 47W
Cap Gaspé *c.* Québec	**51**	H3	48 46N	64 10W
Cap Hopes Advance *c.* Québec	**50**	F9	61 00N	69 40W
Capilano Lake British Columbia	**40**	F4	49 22N	123 06W
Cap Pelé *tn.* New Brunswick	**53**	M12	46 10N	64 10W
Cap Prince-de-Galles *c.* Québec	**50**	E9	61 42N	71 30W
Cap-Saint-Ignace *c.* Québec	**47**	R7	47 00N	70 29W
Capstick Nova Scotia	**53**	M12	47 00N	60 31W
Caramat Ontario	**45**	H5	49 37N	86 09W
Caraquet New Brunswick	**53**	C3	47 48N	64 59W
Carberry Manitoba	**43**	C1	49 52N	99 20W
Carbonear Newfoundland and Labrador	**53**	J3	47 44N	53 13W
Carcross Yukon Territory	**54**	D3	60 11N	134 41W
Cardigan Prince Edward Island	**53**	M12	46 14N	62 37W
Cardinal Ontario	**47**	L4	44 47N	75 23W
Cardston Alberta	**41**	F1	49 12N	113 18W
Cariboo Mountains British Columbia	**39**	K3	53 20N	120 50W
Caribou Manitoba	**43**	D6	59 20N	97 50W
Caribou Mountains Alberta	**41**	E6	59 00N	115 30W
Caribou River Manitoba	**43**	E6	59 30N	95 30W
Caribou River Park Reserve Manitoba	**43**	D6	59 30N	96 40W
Carleton Québec	**51**	G3	48 08N	66 10W
Carleton *admin.* New Brunswick	**53**	B3	46 10N	66 52W
Carleton, Mount New Brunswick	**53**	B3	47 24N	66 52W
Carleton Place Ontario	**47**	K5	45 15N	75 45W
Carlsbad Springs Ontario	**57**	L2	45 22N	75 29W
Carlson Landing Alberta	**41**	G6	58 59N	111 45W
Carlyle Saskatchewan	**42**	F1	49 39N	102 18W
Carmacks Yukon Territory	**54**	C3	62 04N	136 21W
Carman Manitoba	**43**	D1	49 32N	97 59W
Carmanah Walbran Provincial Park British Columbia	**38**	H4	48 37N	124 35W
Carmanville Newfoundland and Labrador	**53**	H4	49 24N	54 18W
Carnduff Saskatchewan	**42**	G1	49 11N	101 50W
Carp Lake British Columbia	**39**	J4	54 48N	123 20W
Carp Lake Provincial Park British Columbia	**39**	J4	54 08N	123 30W
Carrot River Manitoba	**43**	D4	54 50N	96 40W
Carrot River Saskatchewan	**42**	E3	53 05N	104 15W
Carrot River *tn.* Saskatchewan	**42**	F3	53 18N	103 32W
Carstairs Alberta	**41**	E2	51 34N	114 06W
Cartmel, Mount British Columbia	**39**	F5	57 45N	129 12W
Cartwright Newfoundland and Labrador	**52**	G6	53 42N	57 01W
Cascade Range *mts.* British Columbia	**38**	H4	50 48N	121 15W
Cascade Recreation Area British Columbia	**38**	H4	49 16N	120 56W
Cascumpec Bay Prince Edward Island	**53**	M12	46 45N	64 00W
Casselman Ontario	**47**	L5	45 19N	78 07W
Cassiar British Columbia	**38**	F6	59 15N	129 49W
Cassiar Highway British Columbia	**38**	F5	57 30N	130 10W
Cassier Mountains British Columbia	**38/39**	E6/F6	59 50N	131 50W
Castlegar British Columbia	**39**	M1	49 18N	117 41W
Castor Alberta	**41**	G3	52 13N	111 53W
Catalina Newfoundland and Labrador	**53**	J4	48 31N	53 05W
Cat Arm Reservoir Newfoundland and Labrador	**53**	G5	50 10N	56 40W
Cathedral Provincial Park British Columbia	**39**	K1	49 05N	120 11W
Cat Lake Ontario	**44**	F6	51 30N	91 50W
Cat Lake *I.R.* Ontario	**44**	F6	51 40N	91 50W
Caubvick, Mt. Newfoundland and Labrador	**52**	D9	58 50N	64 40W
Causapscal Québec	**51**	G3	48 22N	67 14W
Cavendish Prince Edward Island	**53**	M12	46 30N	63 20W
Cayuga Ontario	**48**	C1	42 57N	79 50W
Cecil Lake *tn.* British Columbia	**39**	K5	56 19N	120 40W
Cedar Lake Manitoba	**43**	B3	53 40N	100 30W
Central Bedeque Prince Edward Island	**53**	M12	46 20N	63 40W
Central Butte Saskatchewan	**42**	D2	50 50N	106 30W
Central Patricia Ontario	**44**	F6	51 30N	90 09W

Central Saanich British Columbia **38** H4 48 32N 123 25W
Centreville Newfoundland and Labrador **53** J4 49 01N 53 53W
Centreville Nova Scotia **53** M12 45 10N 64 30W
C.F.B. Borden Ontario **48** C3 44 18N 79 53W
C.F.B. Suffield Alberta **41** G2 50 35N 110 47W
Chalk River *tn.* Ontario **47** J6 46 01N 77 27W
Chambly Québec **47** N5 45 27N 73 19W
Champlain *admin.* Québec **47** N7 48 20N 74 20W
Chandler Québec **51** H3 48 21N 64 41W
Channel-Port aux Basques Newfoundland and Labrador **53** F3 47 34N 59 09W
Chantrey Inlet Nunavut **55** L4 67 48N 96 20W
Chapais Québec **51** C3 49 47N 74 54W
Chapleau Ontario **45** K4 47 50N 83 24W
Chapleau-Nemegosenda River Provincial Park Ontario **45** K5 48 25N 83 00W
Chaplin Saskatchewan **42** D2 50 29N 106 40W
Chaplin Lake Saskatchewan **42** D2 50 25N 106 30W
Charles Island Nunavut **55** R3 62 39N 74 15W
Charles Lake Alberta **41** G6 59 50N 110 33W
Charles, Lake Nova Scotia **57** Q6 44 43N 63 32W
Charlevoix-Est *admin.* Québec **47** R7 47 50N 70 20W
Charlevoix-Ouest *admin.* Québec **47** R7 47 57N 71 05W
Charlo New Brunswick **53** B3 47 55N 66 20W
Charlotte *admin.* New Brunswick **53** B2 45 20N 67 20W
Charlotte Lake British Columbia **39** H3 52 11N 125 19W
Charlottetown Newfoundland and Labrador **52** G6 52 06N 56 07W
Charlottetown Prince Edward Island **53** M12 46 14N 63 09W
Charlton Island Northwest Territories **44** M7 52 00N 79 30W
Charron Lake Manitoba **43** E3 52 40N 95 40W
Chase British Columbia **39** L2 50 49N 119 41W
Châteauguay Québec **47** N5 45 20N 73 42W
Chateh Alberta **41** C6 58 42N 118 55W
Chatham Ontario **46** D2 42 24N 82 11W
Chatham Sound British Columbia **38** E4 54 30N 130 30W
Chatsworth Ontario **48** B3 44 27N 80 54W
Chedabucto Bay Nova Scotia **53** M12 45 20N 61 10W
Cheepay River Ontario **44** K6 50 50N 83 40W
Chelsea Québec **57** J2 45 29N 75 48W
Chelsea Brook Québec **57** J3 45 31N 75 51W
Chemainus British Columbia **38** H4 48 54N 123 42W
Chemainus River British Columbia **38** H4 48 58N 124 09W
Cheslatta Lake British Columbia **39** H3 53 44N 125 20W
Chesley Ontario **48** A3 44 18N 81 07W
Chester Nova Scotia **53** M11 44 33N 64 16W
Chesterfield Inlet Nunavut **55** M3 63 21N 90 42W
Chesterfield Inlet *(Igluligaarjuk) tn.* Nunavut **55** M3 63 21N 90 42W
Chesterville Ontario **47** L5 45 06N 75 14W
Cheticamp Nova Scotia **53** M12 46 37N 60 59W
Cheticamp Island Nova Scotia **53** M12 46 40N 61 05W
Chetwynd British Columbia **39** K4 55 38N 121 40W
Chevery Québec **50** L4 50 29N 59 41W
Chibougamau Québec **51** C3 49 56N 74 24W
Chicoutimi *admin.* Québec **47** R8 48 10N 71 10W
Chidley, Cape Newfoundland and Labrador **52** C10 60 23N 64 26W
Chignecto Bay Nova Scotia **53** M12 45 40N 64 40W
Chignecto, Cape Nova Scotia **53** M12 45 20N 64 55W
Chignecto Game Sanctuary Nova Scotia **53** M12 45 30N 64 35W
Chilanko Forks British Columbia **39** H3 52 04N 124 00W
Chilcotin River British Columbia **39** J2 51 54N 123 20W
Chilko Lake British Columbia **39** H2 51 15N 124 59W
Chilko River British Columbia **39** J2 51 59N 124 05W
Chilliwack British Columbia **38** H4 49 06N 121 56W
Chilliwack Lake British Columbia **38** H4 49 04N 121 22W
Chilliwack River British Columbia **38** H4 49 04N 121 52W
Chin, Cape Ontario **48** A4 45 05N 81 17W
Chinchaga River Alberta **41** C5 57 30N 119 00W
Chip Lake Alberta **41** E3 53 40N 115 23W
Chipman New Brunswick **53** C3 46 11N 65 54W
Chippawa Ontario **48** C2 43 03N 79 04W
Chisasibi Québec **51** A5 53 50N 79 01W
Chitek Lake Park Reserve Manitoba **43** C3 52 30N 99 30W
Choiceland Saskatchewan **42** E3 53 30N 104 33W
Chomedey Québec **56** M5 45 32N 73 46W
Chorkbak Inlet Nunavut **55** R3 64 30N 74 25W
Chown, Mount Alberta **41** C3 53 24N 119 25W
Christian Island Ontario **48** B3 44 50N 80 14W
Christian Island *tn.* Ontario **48** B3 44 49N 80 10W
Christie Bay Northwest Territories **54** H3 62 32N 111 10W
Christina River Alberta **41** G4 55 50N 111 59W
Churchbridge Saskatchewan **42** G2 50 55N 101 38W
Churchill Manitoba **43** E6 58 45N 94 00W
Churchill, Cape Manitoba **43** F6 59 00N 93 00W
Churchill Falls *tn.* Newfoundland and Labrador **52** D6 53 35N 64 00W
Churchill Lake Saskatchewan **42** C5 56 05N 108 15W
Churchill Peak British Columbia **39** H6 58 20N 125 02W
Churchill River Manitoba/Saskatchewan **43** E6 58 00N 95 00W
Churchill River Newfoundland and Labrador **52** D6 53 20N 63 40W
Churn Creek Provincial Park British Columbia **39** J2 51 25N 122 30W
Chute-aux-Outardes Québec **51** F3 49 17N 68 25W
Cirque Mountain Newfoundland and Labrador **52** D9 58 56N 63 33W
City View Ontario **57** K2 45 21N 75 44W
Claire, Lake Alberta **41** F6/G6 58 30N 112 00W
Clarence Head *c.* Nunavut **55** Q6 76 47N 77 47W
Clarenville Newfoundland and Labrador **53** J4 48 10N 53 58W
Claresholm Alberta **41** F2 50 04N 113 29W
Clarke City Québec **51** G4 50 11N 66 39W
Clark's Harbour *tn.* Nova Scotia **53** L11 43 25N 65 38W
Clarkson Ontario **48** C2 43 30N 79 38W
Clayoquot Sound British Columbia **39** G1 49 12N 126 05W
Clear Hills Alberta **41** C5 56 40N 119 30W
Clearwater British Columbia **39** K2 51 37N 120 03W
Clearwater Bay *tn.* Ontario **44** D5 49 39N 94 48W
Clearwater Lake British Columbia **39** K3 52 13N 120 20W
Clearwater Lake Manitoba **43** B4 53 50N 101 40W
Clearwater Lake Provincial Park Manitoba **43** B4 54 00N 101 00W
Clearwater River Alberta **41** E2 51 59N 115 20W
Clearwater River Alberta **41** G5 56 47N 110 59W
Clearwater River Provincial Park Saskatchewan **42** C5 57 10N 108 10W
Clifford Ontario **48** B2 43 58N 80 00W
Clinton British Columbia **39** K2 51 05N 121 38W
Clinton Ontario **48** A2 43 36N 81 33W
Clinton-Colden Lake Northwest Territories **54** J3 64 58N 107 27W
Close Lake Saskatchewan **42** E5 57 50N 104 40W
Cloverdale British Columbia **40** H3 49 05N 122 46W
Cluff Lake *tn.* Saskatchewan **42** C6 58 20N 109 35W
Clyde River *(Kangiqtugaapik) tn.* Nunavut **55** S5 70 30N 68 30W
Coaldale Alberta **41** F1 49 43N 112 37W
Coalhurst Alberta **41** F1 49 45N 112 56W
Coal River British Columbia **39** G6 59 56N 127 11W
Coast Mountains British Columbia **38/39** E5/H2 58 10N 132 40W
Coates Creek Ontario **48** B3 44 22N 80 07W
Coaticook Québec **47** Q5 45 08N 71 40W
Coats Island Nunavut **55** P3 63 30N 83 00W
Cobalt Ontario **45** M4 47 24N 79 41W
Cobble Hill *tn.* British Columbia **38** H4 48 41N 123 39W
Cobequid Bay Nova Scotia **53** M12 45 20N 63 50W
Cobequid Mountains Nova Scotia **53** M12 45 30N 64 50W
Cobourg Ontario **45** M2 43 58N 78 11W
Cochrane Alberta **41** E2 51 11N 114 28W
Cochrane Ontario **45** L5 49 04N 81 02W
Cochrane River Manitoba/Saskatchewan **42** F6 58 50N 102 20W
Cockburn Island Ontario **46** C5 45 55N 83 22W
Cod Island Newfoundland and Labrador **52** E8 57 47N 61 47W
Colborne Ontario **46** J4 44 00N 77 53W
Colchester *admin.* Nova Scotia **53** M12 45 30N 63 30W
Cold Lake Alberta **41** G4 54 00N 110 00W
Cold Lake *tn.* Alberta **41** G4 54 28N 110 15W
Cold Lake Air Weapons Range Alberta **41** G4 55 10N 110 25W
Coldspring Head Nova Scotia **53** M12 45 55N 63 50W
Coldstream British Columbia **39** L2 50 10N 119 12W
Coldwater Ontario **46** G4 44 43N 79 39W
Cole Harbour Nova Scotia **57** R6 44 40N 63 27W
Cole Harbour *tn.* Nova Scotia **57** R6 44 40N 63 30W
Collingwood Ontario **48** B3 44 30N 80 14W
Collins Ontario **44** G6 50 17N 89 27W
Colonsay Saskatchewan **42** E3 52 00N 105 52W
Colpoys Bay Ontario **48** A3 44 48N 81 04W
Columbia, Mount British Columbia/Alberta **41** D3 52 09N 117 25W
Columbia Mountains British Columbia **39**K3/M2 53 12N 120 49W
Columbia River British Columbia **39** M2 51 15N 116 58W
Colville Lake Northwest Territories **54** E4 67 10N 126 00W
Colville Lake *(K'áhbamítúe) tn.* Northwest Territories **54** E4 67 02N 126 07W
Colwood British Columbia **38** H4 48 27N 123 28W
Combermere Ontario **46** J5 45 22N 77 37W
Comfort Bight *tn.* Newfoundland and Labrador **52** H6 53 09N 55 48W
Comma Island Newfoundland and Labrador **52** E7 55 20N 60 20W
Committee Bay Nunavut **55** N4 68 30N 86 30W
Comox British Columbia **38** H4 49 41N 124 56W
Comox Lake British Columbia **38** G4 49 37N 125 10W
Compton *admin.* Québec **47** Q5 45 20N 71 40W
Conception Bay Newfoundland and Labrador **53** J3 47 45N 53 00W
Conception Bay South *tn.* Newfoundland and Labrador **53** J3 47 30N 53 00W
Conche Newfoundland and Labrador **52** H5 50 53N 55 54W
Conestogo Lake Ontario **48** B2 43 47N 80 44W
Conestogo River Ontario **48** B2 43 41N 80 42W
Conklin Alberta **41** G4 55 38N 111 05W
Conne River *tn.* Newfoundland and Labrador **53** H3 47 50N 55 20W
Consort Alberta **41** G3 52 01N 110 46W
Contrecoeur Québec **47** N5 45 51N 73 15W
Contwoyto Lake Nunavut **54** J4 65 42N 110 50W
Cook's Bay Ontario **48** C3 44 53N 79 31W
Cookstown Ontario **48** C3 44 12N 79 42W
Coppermine River Nunavut **54** H4 67 10N 115 00W
Coquihalla Highway British Columbia **38** H4 49 25N 121 20W
Coquitlam British Columbia **40** G4 49 15N 122 52W
Coquitlam Lake British Columbia **40** G4 49 21N 122 46W
Coquitlam River British Columbia **40** G4 49 17N 122 45W
Coral Harbour *(Salliq) tn.* Nunavut **55** P3 64 10N 83 15W
Cormorant Manitoba **43** B4 54 14N 100 35W
Cormorant Lake Manitoba **43** B4 54 10N 101 30W
Cormorant Provincial Forest Manitoba **43** B4 54 10N 100 50W
Corner Brook *tn.* Newfoundland and Labrador **53** G4 48 58N 57 58W
Cornwall Ontario **47** M5 45 02N 74 45W
Cornwall Prince Edward Island **53** M12 46 10N 63 10W
Cornwallis Island Nunavut **55** L6 75 00N 97 30W
Coronation Alberta **41** G3 52 05N 111 27W
Coronation Gulf Nunavut **54** H4 68 15N 112 30W
Cortes Island British Columbia **38** H5 50 07N 125 01W
Couchiching, Lake Ontario **48** C3 44 39N 79 22W
Courtenay British Columbia **38** H4 49 40N 124 58W
Courtice Ontario **48** D2 43 57N 78 48W
Courtright Ontario **46** D2 42 49N 82 28W
Coutts Alberta **41** G1 49 00N 112 00N
Cove Island Ontario **48** A4 45 19N 81 44W
Cowansville Québec **47** P5 45 13N 72 44W
Cow Bay Nova Scotia **57** R6 44 36N 63 26W
Cow Head *tn.* Newfoundland and Labrador **53** G4 49 55N 57 48W
Cowichan Bay *tn.* British Columbia **38** H4 48 44N 123 40W
Cowichan Lake British Columbia **38** H4 48 50N 124 04W
Cowichan River British Columbia **38** H4 48 48N 123 58W
Cox's Cove *tn.* Newfoundland and Labrador **53** F4 49 07N 58 04W
Craigellachie British Columbia **39** L2 50 59N 118 38W
Craigleith Provinicial Park Ontario **48** B3 44 30N 80 15W
Craik Saskatchewan **42** E2 51 03N 105 50W
Cranberry Portage Manitoba **43** B4 54 36N 101 22W
Cranbrook British Columbia **39** N1 49 29N 115 48W
Crane Lake Saskatchewan **42** C2 50 10N 109 20W
Crane River Ontario **48** A4 45 53N 81 31W
Crane River *tn.* Manitoba **43** C2 51 30N 99 18W
Credit River Ontario **48** B2 43 50N 80 02W
Cree Lake Saskatchewan **42** D5 57 30N 106 30W
Creemore Ontario **48** B3 44 20N 80 07W
Cree River Saskatchewan **42** D5 58 00N 106 30W
Creighton Saskatchewan **42** G4 54 46N 101 50W
Cresswell Bay Nunavut **55** M5 72 40N 93 30W
Creston British Columbia **39** M1 49 05N 116 32W
Crofton British Columbia **38** H4 48 52N 123 38W
Croker, Cape Ontario **48** B3 44 58N 80 59W
Crossfield Alberta **41** E2 51 26N 114 02W
Cross Lake Manitoba **43** D4 54 50N 97 20W
Cross Lake *tn.* Manitoba **43** D4 54 38N 97 45W
Crow Lake Ontario **44** E5 49 10N 93 56W
Crowsnest Highway Alberta **41** G1 49 50N 111 55W
Crowsnest Pass Alberta/British Columbia **39** N1 49 40N 114 41W
Crumlin Ontario **48** A2 43 01N 81 08W
Crystal Bay Ontario **57** J2 45 21N 75 51W
Crystal Beach *tn.* Ontario **48** C1 42 52N 79 03W
Cub Hills, The Saskatchewan **42** E4 54 20N 104 40W
Cudworth Saskatchewan **42** E3 52 31N 105 44W
Cumberland British Columbia **38** H4 49 37N 124 59W
Cumberland Ontario **57** L3 45 31N 75 23W
Cumberland *admin.* Nova Scotia **53** M12 45 30N 64 10W
Cumberland House *tn.* Saskatchewan **42** F3 53 57N 102 20W
Cumberland Lake Saskatchewan **42** F4 54 10N 102 30W
Cumberland Peninsula Nunavut **55** T4 67 00N 65 00W
Cumberland Sound Nunavut **55** S4 65 30N 66 00W
Cupar Saskatchewan **42** E2 50 57N 104 12W
Cushing, Mount British Columbia **39** G5 57 36N 126 51W
Cut Knife Saskatchewan **42** C3 52 45N 109 01W
Cypress Hills Alberta/Saskatchewan **41** G1 49 30N 110 00W
Cypress Hills Provincial Park Alberta/Saskatchewan **41** G1 49 38N 110 00W

D

Dalhousie New Brunswick **53** B4 48 03N 66 22W
Dalhousie, Cape Northwest Territories **54** E5 70 14N 129 42W
Dalmeny Saskatchewan **42** D3 52 22N 106 46W
Dalrymple Lake Ontario **48** C3 44 41N 79 07W
Daniel's Harbour *tn.* Newfoundland and Labrador **53** G5 50 14N 57 35W
Danville Québec **47** P5 45 48N 72 01W
Darlington Provincial Park Ontario **48** D2 44 00N 78 50W
Darnley Bay Northwest Territories **54** F4 69 30N 123 30W
Dartmouth Nova Scotia **53** M11 44 40N 63 35W
Dauphin Manitoba **43** B2 51 09N 100 05W
Dauphin, Cape Nova Scotia **53** M12 46 20N 60 25W
Dauphin Lake Manitoba **43** C2 51 10N 99 30W
Dauphin River Manitoba **43** D2 51 50N 98 20W
Dauphin River *tn.* Manitoba **43** D2 51 50N 98 00W
Davidson Saskatchewan **42** E2 51 15N 105 59W
David Thompson Highway Alberta **41** D3 52 15N 116 35W
Davin Lake Saskatchewan **42** F5 56 45N 103 40W
Davis Inlet *tn.* Newfoundland and Labrador **52** E7 55 51N 60 52W
Davis Strait Greenland/Nunavut **55** T4 65 00N 65 00W
Davy Lake Saskatchewan **42** C6 58 50N 108 10W
Dawson Bay Manitoba **43** B3 52 50N 100 50W
Dawson City Yukon Territory **54** C3 64 04N 139 24W
Dawson Creek *tn.* British Columbia **39** K4 55 44N 120 15W
Dawson, Mount British Columbia **39** M2 51 08N 117 26W
Dawson Range *mts.* Yukon Territory **54** C3 63 00N 139 30W
Dawsons Landing British Columbia **39** G2 51 28N 127 33W
Daysland Alberta **41** F3 52 52N 112 15W
Ddhaw Gro Habitat Protection Area Yukon Territory **54** C3 62 25N 135 50W
Dean Channel British Columbia **39** G3 52 18N 127 35W
Dean River British Columbia **39** G3 52 45N 122 30W
Dease Arm *b.* Northwest Territories **54** F4 66 52N 122 00W
Dease Lake British Columbia **38** E6 58 05N 130 04W
Dease Lake *tn.* British Columbia **38** E6 58 28N 130 00W
Dease River British Columbia **38** F6 59 05N 129 40W
Dease Strait Nunavut **54** J4 68 40N 108 00W
Deas Island British Columbia **40** F3 49 07N 123 04W
Déception Québec **50** C10 62 10N 74 45W
Dee Lake British Columbia **40** G3 49 14N 122 59W
Deep Cove British Columbia **40** G4 49 19N 122 58W
Deep Inlet Newfoundland and Labrador **52** E7 55 22N 60 14W
Deep River *tn.* Ontario **47** J6 46 06N 77 30W
Deer Island New Brunswick **53** B2 45 00N 67 00W
Deer Lake Ontario **44** D7 52 38N 94 25W
Deer Lake *tn.* Newfoundland and Labrador **53** G4 49 11N 57 27W
Delhi Ontario **48** B1 42 51N 80 30W
Déline *(Fort Franklin)* Northwest Territories **54** F4 65 11N 123 26W
Delisle Saskatchewan **42** D2 51 56N 107 10W
Deloraine Manitoba **43** B1 49 11N 100 30W
Delta British Columbia **38** H4 49 06N 123 01W
Dempster Highway Yukon Territory **54** C4 65 30N 138 10W
Denbigh Ontario **47** J5 45 08N 77 15W
Denetiah Provincial Park British Columbia **39** G6 58 30N 127 30W
Denman Island British Columbia **38** H4 49 32N 124 49W
Deschambault Lake Saskatchewan **42** F4 54 50N 103 50W
Deseronto Ontario **47** J4 44 12N 77 03W
Desmaraisville Québec **51** B3 49 30N 76 18W
Desolation Sound Marine Park British Columbia **38** H5 50 08N 124 45W
Destruction Bay *tn.* Yukon Territory **54** C3 61 16N 138 50W
Détroit de Jacques-Cartier *sd.* Québec **51** J3 50 10N 64 10W
Détroit d'Honguedo *sd.* Québec **51** H3 49 30N 64 20W
Détroit d'Hudson *sd.* Québec/Northwest Territories **50** F9 62 00N 70 00W
Deux-Montagnes Québec **56** M5 45 32N 73 56W
Deux Rivières Ontario **46** H6 46 15N 78 17W
Devil's Glen Provincial Park Ontario **48** B3 44 20N 80 30W
Devon Alberta **41** F3 53 22N 113 44W
Devon Island Nunavut **55** N6 75 47N 88 00W
Dewar Lakes Nunavut **55** R4 68 30N 71 20W
Dewey Soper Bird Sanctuary Nunavut **55** R4 66 20N 68 50W
Diamond Jennes Peninsula Northwest Territories **54** G5 71 20N 117 00W
Didsbury Alberta **41** E2 51 40N 114 08W
Diefenbaker, Lake Saskatchewan **42** D2 51 10N 107 30W
Dieppe New Brunswick **53** M12 46 10N 64 40W
Digby Nova Scotia **53** L11 44 37N 65 47W
Digby *admin.* Nova Scotia **53** L11 44 30N 65 40W
Digby Neck *p.* Nova Scotia **53** L11 44 30N 66 00W
Dillon Saskatchewan **42** C6 55 56N 108 54W

Dingwall Nova Scotia	53	M12	46 50N	60 30W
Dinorwic Ontario	44	E5	49 41N	92 30W
Dinosaur Provincial Park Alberta	41	G2	50 47N	111 25W
Disappointment Lake Newfoundland and Labrador	52	D6	53 49N	62 31W
Dismal Lakes Nunavut	54	G4	67 26N	117 07W
Disraeli Québec	47	Q5	45 54N	71 22W
Dixon Entrance *sd.* British Columbia/USA	38	D4/E4	54 28N	132 50W
Doaktown New Brunswick	53	B3	46 34N	66 06W
Dobie River Ontario	44	F6	51 30N	90 05W
Dodge Lake Saskatchewan	42	E6	59 50N	105 25W
Dodsland Saskatchewan	42	C2	51 48N	108 51W
Dog Creek *tn.* British Columbia	39	J2	51 35N	122 18W
Dog (High) Island Newfoundland and Labrador	52	E8	56 38N	61 10W
Dog Lake Manitoba	43	C2	51 00N	98 20W
Dog Lake Ontario	45	G5	48 50N	89 30W
Dolbeau Québec	51	D3	48 52N	72 15W
Dollarton British Columbia	40	G4	49 18N	122 58W
Dolphin and Union Strait Nunavut	54	G4	69 05N	114 45W
Dominion Nova Scotia	53	M12	46 14N	60 01W
Dominion Lake Newfoundland and Labrador	52	E6	52 40N	61 43W
Don Mills Ontario	49	C1	43 44N	79 22W
Donnacona Québec	47	Q6	46 41N	71 45W
Don River Ontario	48	C2	43 48N	79 24W
D'Or, Cape Nova Scotia	53	M12	45 20N	64 50W
Dorcas Bay Ontario	48	A4	45 10N	81 38W
Dorchester New Brunswick	53	M12	45 54N	64 32W
Dorchester *admin.* Québec	47	R6	46 20N	70 40W
Dorchester, Cape Nunavut	55	Q4	65 27N	77 27W
Dore Lake Saskatchewan	42	D4	54 50N	107 20W
Dorion Ontario	45	G5	48 49N	88 33W
Double Mer *in.* Newfoundland and Labrador	52	F7	54 04N	59 10W
Douglas Island British Columbia	40	G3	49 13N	122 46W
Dowling Lake Alberta	41	F2	51 44N	112 00W
Downtown, Mount British Columbia	39	H3	52 45N	124 53W
Dows Lake Ontario	57	K2	45 24N	75 42W
Drayton Ontario	48	B2	43 45N	80 40W
Drayton Valley *tn.* Alberta	41	E3	53 13N	114 59W
Dresden Ontario	46	D2	42 34N	82 11W
Driftwood Ontario	45	L5	49 08N	81 20W
Drowning River Ontario	44	J6	50 30N	86 00W
Drumheller Alberta	41	F2	51 28N	112 40W
Drummond *admin.* Québec	47	P5	45 50N	72 40W
Drummondville Québec	47	P5	45 52N	72 30W
Dryden Ontario	44	E5	49 48N	92 48W
Drylake *tn.* Newfoundland and Labrador	52	C7	52 38N	65 59W
Dubawnt Lake Nunavut	55	K3	63 15N	102 00W
Dubreuilville Ontario	45	J5	48 21N	84 32W
Duck Bay *tn.* Manitoba	43	B3	52 10N	100 10W
Duck Lake *tn.* Saskatchewan	42	D3	52 52N	106 12W
Duck Mountain Provincial Forest Manitoba	43	B2	51 20N	100 50W
Duck Mountain Provincial Park Manitoba	43	B2	51 40N	101 00W
Duck Mountain Provincial Park Saskatchewan	42	G2	51 40N	101 40W
Dufferin *admin.* Ontario	48	B3	44 00N	80 20W
Duncan British Columbia	38	H4	48 46N	123 40W
Duncan, Cape Northwest Territories	44	L7	52 40N	80 50W
Duncan Lake British Columbia	39	M2	50 23N	116 57W
Dundalk Ontario	48	B3	44 10N	80 24W
Dundas Ontario	48	C2	43 16N	79 57W
Dundas Island British Columbia	38	E4	54 33N	131 20W
Dundas Peninsula Northwest Territories	54	H5	74 50N	111 30W
Dundurn Saskatchewan	42	D2	51 49N	106 30W
Dunkirk Saskatchewan	42	E2	50 04N	105 41W
Dunnville Ontario	48	C1	42 54N	79 36W
Dunville Newfoundland and Labrador	53	J3	47 16N	53 54W
Duparquet Québec	51	A3	48 32N	79 14W
Durham Ontario	48	B3	44 11N	80 49W
Durham *admin.* Ontario	48	C3/D3	44 04N	79 11W
Durrell Newfoundland and Labrador	53	H4	49 40N	54 44W
Dutton Ontario	48	A1	42 39N	81 30W
Duvernay Québec	56	N5	45 34N	73 41W
Dyer, Cape Nunavut	55	T4	66 37N	61 16W
Dyer's Bay Ontario	48	A4	45 10N	81 18W
Dyer's Bay *tn.* Ontario	48	A4	45 09N	81 20W
Dyke Lake Newfoundland and Labrador	52	B7	54 30N	66 18W

E

Eabamet Lake Ontario	44	H6	51 32N	87 46W
Eagle Lake Ontario	44	E5	49 35N	93 00W
Eagle Plains *tn.* Yukon Territory	54	C4	66 30N	136 50W
Eagle River Newfoundland and Labrador	52	G6	53 10N	58 00W
Eagle River Saskatchewan	42	D2	51 35N	107 40W
Eagle River *tn.* Ontario	44	E5	49 50N	93 12W
Ear Falls *tn.* Ontario	44	E6	50 38N	93 13W
Earl Rowe Provincial Park Ontario	48	C3	44 15N	79 45W
East Angus Québec	47	Q5	45 30N	71 40W
East Bay Bird Sanctuary Nunavut	55	P3	66 20N	74 00W
East Chezzetcook Nova Scotia	53	M11	44 34N	63 14W
Eastend Saskatchewan	42	C1	49 32N	108 50W
Eastern Passage *tn.* Nova Scotia	57	R6	44 36N	63 29W
Easterville Manitoba	43	C3	53 00N	99 40W
East Lake Nova Scotia	57	R7	44 46N	63 29W
Eastmain Québec	51	A5	52 10N	78 30W
East Point Prince Edward Island	53	M12	46 27N	61 59W
Eastport Newfoundland and Labrador	53	J4	48 39N	53 45W
East Thurlow Island British Columbia	38	G5	50 24N	125 26W
East York *bor.* Metropolitan Toronto Ontario	49	C2	43 43N	79 20W
Eatonia Saskatchewan	42	C2	51 13N	109 22W
Echoing River Ontario	44	F8	54 30N	92 00W
Eclipse Sound Nunavut	55	Q5	72 38N	79 00W
Ecum Secum Nova Scotia	53	M11	44 58N	62 08W
Eddies Cove *tn.* Newfoundland and Labrador	52	G5	51 25N	56 27W
Edehon Lake Nunavut	55	L3	60 25N	97 15W
Edgewood British Columbia	39	L1	49 47N	118 08W
Edmonton Alberta	41	F3	53 34N	113 25W
Edmund Lake Manitoba	43	F4	54 50N	93 30W
Edmundston New Brunswick	53	A3	47 22N	68 20W
Edson Alberta	41	D3	53 35N	116 26W
Eduni, Mount Northwest Territories	54	E3	64 13N	128 10W
Edwards Ontario	57	L2	45 19N	75 48W
Edziza, Mount British Columbia	38	E5	57 43N	130 42W
Edzo *(Edzoò)* Northwest Territories	54	G3	63 50N	116 00W
Eganville Ontario	47	J5	45 32N	77 06W
Eglington Island Northwest Territories	54	G6	75 48N	118 30W
Egmont British Columbia	38	H4	49 45N	123 55W
Egmont Bay Prince Edward Island	53	M12	46 30N	64 20W
Egmont, Cape Nova Scotia	53	M12	46 50N	60 20W
Eileen Lake Northwest Territories	54	J3	62 16N	107 37W
Ekwan Point Ontario	44	K7	53 20N	82 10W
Ekwan River Ontario	44	K7	53 30N	83 40W
Elaho River British Columbia	38	H5	50 14N	123 33W
Elbow Saskatchewan	42	D2	51 08N	106 36W
Elbow River Alberta	40	A1	50 59N	114 13W
Elgin *admin.* Ontario	48	A1	42 38N	81 36W
Elkford British Columbia	39	N2	50 02N	114 55W
Elkhorn Manitoba	43	B1	49 58N	101 14W
Elk Island Manitoba	43	D2	50 50N	96 40W
Elk Island National Park Alberta	41	F3	53 36N	112 53W
Elk Lake *tn.* Ontario	45	L4	47 44N	80 20W
Elk Lakes Provincial Park British Columbia	39	N2	50 00N	115 00W
Elk Point *tn.* Alberta	41	G3	53 54N	110 54W
Ellef Ringnes Island Nunavut	55	K6	78 30N	102 00W
Ellesmere Island Nunavut	55	P6	77 30N	82 30W
Ellice River Nunavut	54	J4	66 20N	105 00W
Elliot Lake *tn.* Ontario	46	D6	46 25N	82 40W
Elm Creek *tn.* Manitoba	43	D1	49 41N	97 59W
Elmira Ontario	48	B2	43 36N	80 34W
Elmira Prince Edward Island	53	M12	46 26N	62 05W
Elmvale Ontario	48	C3	44 35N	79 52W
Elora Ontario	48	B2	43 42N	80 26W
Elrose Saskatchewan	42	C2	51 12N	108 01W
Elsa Yukon Territory	54	C3	63 55N	135 29W
Elvira, Cape Nunavut	54	J5	73 16N	107 10W
Embree Newfoundland and Labrador	53	H4	49 18N	55 02W
Emerald Island Northwest Territories	54	H6	76 48N	114 10W
Emerson Manitoba	43	D1	49 00N	97 11W
Endako British Columbia	39	H4	54 10N	125 21W
Enderby British Columbia	39	L2	50 32N	119 10W
Enfield Nova Scotia	53	M11	44 56N	63 34W
Englee Newfoundland and Labrador	52	G5	50 44N	56 06W
Englehart Ontario	45	M4	47 50N	79 52W
English Bay British Columbia	40	F4	49 17N	123 12W
English River Ontario	44	D6	50 20N	94 50W
Ennadai Lake Nunavut	55	K3	60 58N	101 20W
Enterprise Northwest Territories	54	G3	60 34N	116 15W
Eramosa River Ontario	48	B2	43 33N	80 11W
Erieau Ontario	46	E2	42 16N	81 56W
Erie Beach *tn.* Ontario	46	D2	42 16N	82 00W
Erie Beach *tn.* Ontario	48	D1	42 53N	78 56W
Erie, Lake Ontario/USA	46	E2	42 15N	81 00W
Eriksdale Manitoba	43	C2	50 52N	98 07W
Erin Ontario	48	B2	43 48N	80 04W
Escuminac, Point New Brunswick	53	C3	47 04N	64 49W
Esker Siding Newfoundland and Labrador	52	B6	53 53N	66 25W
Eskimo Lakes Northwest Territories	54	D4	68 30N	132 30W
Espanola Ontario	46	E6	46 15N	81 46W
Esquimalt British Columbia	38	H4	48 25N	123 29W
Essex Ontario	46	D2	42 10N	82 49W
Essex *admin.* Ontario	46	D2	42 10N	82 50W
Esterhazy Saskatchewan	42	F2	50 40N	102 02W
Estevan Saskatchewan	42	F1	49 09N	103 00W
Eston Saskatchewan	42	C2	51 09N	108 42W
Etawney Lake Manitoba	43	D5	57 50N	96 40W
Ethelbert Manitoba	43	B2	51 32N	100 25W
Etobicoke *bor.* Metropolitan Toronto Ontario	49	B1	43 38N	79 30W
Etobicoke Creek Ontario	49	A1	43 43N	79 47W
Eugenia Lake Ontario	48	B3	44 20N	80 30W
Eureka *m.s.* Nunavut	55	N6	79 59N	85 57W
Eureka River *tn.* Alberta	41	C5	56 25N	118 48W
Eutsuk Lake British Columbia	39	G3	53 12N	126 32W
Evansburg Alberta	41	E3	53 36N	115 01W
Evans, Mount Alberta	41	C3	52 26N	118 07W
Evans Strait Nunavut	55	P3	63 15N	82 30W
Exeter Ontario	48	A2	43 21N	81 30W
Exploits River Newfoundland and Labrador	53	G4	48 40N	56 30W
Eyehill River Saskatchewan	42	C3	52 25N	109 50W

F

Faber Lake Northwest Territories	54	G3	63 56N	117 15W
Fairchild Creek Ontario	48	B2	43 13N	80 11W
Fairview Alberta	41	C5	56 03N	118 28W
Fairweather Mountain British Columbia/USA	38	B6	58 50N	137 55W
Falcon Lake *tn.* Manitoba	43	E1	49 44N	95 18W
Falher Alberta	41	D4	55 44N	117 12W
Fallowfield Ontario	57	J2	45 17N	75 51W
Fall River *tn.* Nova Scotia	53	M11	44 49N	63 36W
False Creek British Columbia	40	F4	49 16N	123 08W
Family Lake Manitoba	43	E2	51 50N	95 40W
Farnham Québec	47	P5	45 17N	72 59W
Farnham, Mount British Columbia	39	M2	50 27N	116 37W
Faro Yukon Territory	54	D3	62 30N	133 00W
Fathom Five National Marine Park Ontario	48	A4	54 20N	81 35W
Fauquier Ontario	45	L5	49 19N	81 59W
Fawn River Ontario	44	G8	54 20N	88 40W
Fawn River Provincial Park Ontario	44	G8	54 10N	89 25W
Felix, Cape Nunavut	55	L4	69 54N	97 58W
Fenelon Falls *tn.* Ontario	48	D3	44 32N	78 45W
Fergus Ontario	48	B2	43 43N	80 24W
Ferland Ontario	44	G6	50 18N	88 25W
Ferme-Neuve Québec	47	L6	46 42N	75 28W
Fermont Québec	51	G5	52 00N	68 00W
Fernie British Columbia	39	N1	49 30N	115 00W
Ferryland Newfoundland and Labrador	53	J3	47 01N	54 53W
Fife Lake Saskatchewan	42	E1	49 10N	105 455W
Finch Ontario	47	L5	45 08N	75 05W
Finlay Ranges *mts.* British Columbia	39	H5	57 10N	126 00W
Finlay River British Columbia	39	G5	57 20N	125 40W
Fiordland Recreation Area British Columbia	39	F3	52 00N	127 00W
Firebag Hills Saskatchewan	42	C5	57 15N	109 50W
Firebag River Alberta	41	G5	57 30N	110 40W
Fish Creek Alberta	40	A1	50 55N	114 10W
Fish Creek Provincial Park Alberta	40	A1	50 55N	114 04W
Fisher Bay Manitoba	43	D2	51 30N	97 30W
Fisher Branch *tn.* Manitoba	43	D2	51 04N	97 38W
Fisher, Mount British Columbia	39	N1	49 35N	115 20W
Fisher Strait Nunavut	55	P3	63 00N	84 00W
Fishing Branch Game Reserve Yukon Territory	54	C4	66 30N	139 30W
Fishing Lake Manitoba	43	E3	52 10N	95 40W
Fishing Ships Harbour *tn.* Newfoundland and Labrador	52	H6	52 36N	55 47W
Fitzgerald Alberta	41	G6	59 51N	111 36W
Fitzwilliam Island Ontario	46	E5	45 29N	81 45W
Fjord Alluviaq Québec	50	H8	59 30N	65 30W
Flamborough Ontario	48	C2	43 20N	79 57W
Flathead River British Columbia	39	N1	48 30N	114 10W
Flesherton Ontario	48	B3	44 16N	80 32W
Fletchers Lake Nova Scotia	57	Q7	44 51N	63 35W
Fleur de Lys Newfoundland and Labrador	53	G5	50 07N	56 08W
Fleuve Saint-Laurent *r.* Québec	51	F3	48 20N	69 20W
Flin Flon Manitoba	43	B4	54 50N	102 00W
Florenceville New Brunswick	53	B3	46 20N	67 20W
Flores Island British Columbia	39	G1	49 20N	126 10W
Flour Lake Newfoundland and Labrador	52	C6	53 44N	64 50W
Foam Lake *tn.* Saskatchewan	42	F2	51 38N	103 31W
Foch British Columbia	38	H5	50 07N	124 31W
Fogo Newfoundland and Labrador	53	H4	49 43N	54 17W
Fogo Island Newfoundland and Labrador	53	H4	49 40N	54 10W
Foleyet Ontario	45	K5	48 05N	82 26W
Fond du Lac Saskatchewan	42	D6	59 20N	107 09W
Fond du Lac River Saskatchewan	42	E6	59 05N	104 40W
Fontas River British Columbia	39	K6	58 20N	121 25W
Fonthill *tn.* Ontario	48	C2	43 02N	79 17W
Foothills *tn.* Alberta	40	B1	50 59N	113 58W
Forbes, Mount Alberta	41	D2	51 52N	116 55W
Foremost Alberta	41	G1	49 29N	111 25W
Forest Ontario	46	E3	43 06N	82 00W
Forestburg Alberta	41	G3	52 35N	112 04W
Forest Hill Ontario	49	C1	43 42N	79 25W
Forest Lawn Alberta	40	B2	51 02N	113 58W
Forestville Québec	51	F3	48 45N	69 04W
Forks of the Credit Provincial Park Ontario	48	B2	43 49N	80 02W
Forrest Lake Saskatchewan	42	C5	57 35N	109 10W
Fort Albany Ontario	44	L7	52 12N	81 40W
Fort Babine British Columbia	39	G4	55 20N	126 35W
Fort Chipewyan Alberta	41	G6	58 46N	111 09W
Fort Coulange Québec	47	K5	45 51N	76 46W
Forteau Newfoundland and Labrador	52	G5	51 28N	56 58W
Fort Erie Ontario	48	D1	42 55N	78 56W
Fort Frances Ontario	44	E5	48 37N	93 23W
Fort Fraser British Columbia	39	H4	54 03N	124 30W
Fort Good Hope *(Rádeyįlįkóé)* Northwest Territories	54	E4	66 16N	128 37W
Fort Hope *I.R.* Ontario	44	H6	51 37N	87 55W
Fort Langley British Columbia	38	H4	49 11N	122 38W
Fort Liard *(Echaot'ine Kúé)* Northwest Territories	54	F3	60 14N	123 28W
Fort MacKay Alberta	41	G5	57 11N	111 37W
Fort Macleod Alberta	41	F1	49 44N	113 24W
Fort McMurray Alberta	41	G5	56 45N	111 27W
Fort McPherson *(Teetl'it Zheh)* Northwest Territories	54	D4	67 29N	134 50W
Fort Nelson British Columbia	39	J6	58 48N	122 44W
Fort Nelson River British Columbia	39	J6	59 20N	124 05W
Fort Providence *(Zhahti Kóé)* Northwest Territories	54	G3	61 03N	117 40W
Fort Qu'Appelle Saskatchewan	42	F2	50 46N	103 54W
Fort Resolution *(Denínue Kúé)* Northwest Territories	54	H3	61 10N	113 39W
Fort St. James British Columbia	39	H4	54 26N	124 15W
Fort St. John British Columbia	39	K5	56 14N	120 55W
Fort Saskatchewan Alberta	41	F3	53 42N	113 12W
Fort Severn Ontario	44	H9	56 00N	87 40W
Fort Simpson *(Łíídlı Kúé)* Northwest Territories	54	F3	61 46N	121 15W
Fort Smith *(Tthebacha)* Northwest Territories	54	H3	60 01N	111 55W
Fortune Newfoundland and Labrador	53	H3	47 04N	55 50W
Fortune Bay Newfoundland and Labrador	53	H3	47 15N	55 30W
Fort Vermilion Alberta	41	E6	58 22N	115 59W
Fort Ware British Columbia	39	H5	57 30N	125 43W
Fosheim Peninsula Nunavut	55	P6	80 00N	85 00W
Foster, Mount British Columbia	38	C6	59 49N	135 35W
Foster River Saskatchewan	42	E5	56 20N	105 45W
Fourchu Nova Scotia	53	M12	45 43N	60 17W
Fox Creek *tn.* Alberta	41	D4	54 24N	116 48W
Foxe Basin *b.* Nunavut	55	P4	66 20N	79 00W
Foxe Channel Nunavut	55	P3	64 40N	80 00W
Foxe Peninsula Nunavut	55	Q3	65 00N	76 00W
Fox Mine *tn.* Manitoba	43	B5	56 39N	101 38W
Fox River Manitoba	43	F5	56 00N	93 50W
Fox Valley *tn.* Saskatchewan	42	C2	50 29N	109 29W
Frances Lake Yukon Territory	54	E3	61 20N	129 30W
François Lake British Columbia	39	H3	54 00N	125 47W
Frankford Ontario	46	J4	44 12N	77 36W
Franklin Bay Northwest Territories	54	E5	69 45N	126 00W
Franklin Lake Nunavut	55	L4	66 56N	96 03W
Franklin Mountains Northwest Territories	54	F3	61 15N	123 50W
Fraserdale Ontario	45	L5	49 51N	81 37W
Fraser Lake Newfoundland and Labrador	52	D7	54 24N	63 40W
Fraser Lake *tn.* British Columbia	39	H4	54 00N	124 50W
Fraser Plateau British Columbia	39	J3	52 32N	124 10W
Fraser River British Columbia	39	J2	51 36N	122 25W
Fraser River Newfoundland and Labrador	52	D8	56 50N	63 50W
Fredericton New Brunswick	53	B2	45 57N	66 40W
Fredericton Junction New Brunswick	53	B2	45 40N	66 38W
Freels, Cape Newfoundland and Labrador	53	J4	49 15N	53 29W
Freeport Nova Scotia	53	L11	44 17N	66 19W
Frenchman River Saskatchewan	42	D1	49 30N	108 00W
Frenchman's Cove *tn.* Newfoundland and Labrador	53	F4	49 04N	58 10W
French River Ontario	46	F6	46 00N	81 00W
French River *tn.* Ontario	46	F6	46 03N	80 34W
Freshwater Newfoundland and Labrador	53	J3	47 15N	53 59W
Frobisher Bay Nunavut	55	S3	62 15N	65 00W
Frobisher Lake Saskatchewan	42	C5	57 00N	108 00W
Frog Lake Alberta	41	G3	53 55N	110 20W
Frontenac *admin.* Ontario	47	K4	44 40N	76 45W
Frontenac *admin.* Québec	47	R5	45 40N	70 50W
Frontenac Provincial Park Ontario	47	K4	44 32N	76 29W
Frozen Strait Nunavut	55	P4	66 08N	85 00W
Fruitvale British Columbia	39	M1	49 08N	117 28W
Fundy, Bay of New Brunswick/Nova Scotia	53	L11	45 00N	66 00W
Fundy National Park New Brunswick	53	L12	45 40N	65 10W

Fury and Hecla Strait Nunavut 55 P4 69 56N 84 00W

G

Gabarus Bay Nova Scotia 53 M12 45 50N 60 10W
Gabriola Island British Columbia 38 H4 49 10N 123 51W
Gage, Cape Prince Edward Island 53 M12 46 50N 64 20W
Gagetown New Brunswick 53 B2 45 46N 66 29W
Gagnon Québec 51 F4 51 56N 68 16W
Galiano Island British Columbia 38 H4 48 57N 123 25W
Galt Ontario 48 B2 43 21N 80 19W
Gambier Island British Columbia 38 H4 49 30N 123 25W
Gambo Newfoundland and Labrador 53 H4 48 46N 54 14W
Gananoque Ontario 47 K4 44 20N 76 10W
Gander Newfoundland and Labrador 53 H4 48 57N 54 34W
Gander Lake Newfoundland and Labrador 53 H4 48 55N 54 35W
Ganges British Columbia 38 H4 48 51N 123 31W
Gardiner Dam Saskatchewan 42 D2 51 15N 106 40W
Gardner Canal British Columbia 38 F3 53 30N 128 50W
Garibaldi Lake British Columbia 38 H4 49 55N 122 57W
Garibaldi, Mount British Columbia 38 H4 49 53N 123 00W
Garibaldi Provincial Park British Columbia 38 H4 49 58N 122 45W
Garnish Newfoundland and Labrador 53 H3 47 14N 55 22W
Garry Lake Nunavut 55 K4 66 20N 100 00W
Garry Point British Columbia 46 F3 49 07N 123 14W
Gaspé Québec 51 H3 48 50N 64 30W
Gaspereau Lake Nova Scotia 53 M11 44 50N 64 30W
Gataga River British Columbia 39 G6 58 30N 126 40W
Gateshead Island Nunavut 55 K5 70 36N 100 26W
Gatineau Québec 47 L5 45 29N 75 39W
Gatineau *admin.* Québec 47 L6 45 47N 76 05W
Gauer Lake Manitoba 43 D5 57 10N 97 30W
Gaultois Newfoundland and Labrador 53 H3 47 36N 55 54W
Geikie River Saskatchewan 42 E5 57 20N 104 40W
George, Cape Nova Scotia 53 M12 45 50N 61 50W
George Island Newfoundland and Labrador 52 G7 54 16N 57 20W
Georgetown Ontario 48 C2 43 39N 79 56W
Georgetown Prince Edward Island 53 M12 46 12N 62 32W
Georgian Bay Ontario 46 E5 45 00N 81 00W
Georgian Bay Islands National Park Ontario 46 G4 44 53N 79 52W
Georgia, Strait of British Columbia 38 H4 49 39N 124 34W
Georgina Island Ontario 48 C3 44 22N 79 17W
Geraldton Ontario 45 H5 49 44N 86 59W
Germansen Landing British Columbia 39 H4 55 47N 124 42W
Giant's Causeway Northwest Territories 54 F6 75 46N 121 11W
Giants Tomb Island Ontario 48 B3 44 55N 80 00W
Gibsons *tn.* British Columbia 38 H4 49 24N 123 30W
Gifford Island British Columbia 39 G2 50 45N 126 20W
Gift Lake *tn.* Alberta 41 E4 55 50N 115 50W
Gilbert Plains *tn.* Manitoba 43 B2 51 09N 100 28W
Gil Island British Columbia 38 F3 53 10N 129 15W
Gillam Manitoba 43 E5 56 25N 94 45W
Gillies Bay *tn.* British Columbia 38 H4 49 42N 124 28W
Gimli Manitoba 43 D2 50 39N 97 00W
Gitnadoix River Recreation Area British Columbia 39 F4 54 05NN 129 00W
Gjoa Haven *(Uqsuqtuq)* *tn.* Nunavut 55 L4 68 39N 96 09W
Glace Bay *tn.* Nova Scotia 53 M12 46 11N 59 58W
Glacial Mountain British Columbia 38 F6 58 15N 129 25W
Glacier National Park British Columbia 39 M2 51 00N 117 00W
Gladstone Manitoba 43 C2 50 14N 98 56W
Gladstone Provincial Park British Columbia 39 L1 49 15N 118 10W
Gladys Lake British Columbia 38 D6 59 50N 132 52W
Glaslyn Saskatchewan 42 C3 53 23N 108 22W
Glenboro Manitoba 43 C1 49 35N 99 20W
Glen Cairn Ontario 57 J2 45 15N 75 45W
Glencoe Ontario 48 A1 42 45N 81 44W
Glenmore Reservoir Alberta 40 A1 50 58N 114 08W
Glenwood Newfoundland and Labrador 53 H4 48 59N 54 53W
Gloucester Ontario 47 L5 45 21N 75 39W
Gloucester *admin.* New Brunswick 53 C3 47 30N 65 50W
Gloucester Glen Ontario 57 K2 45 17N 75 41W
Glover Island Newfoundland and Labrador 53 G4 48 46N 57 43W
Glovertown Newfoundland and Labrador 53 H4 48 41N 54 02W
Goat Island British Columbia 38 H5 50 03N 124 28W
Goderich Ontario 48 A2 43 43N 81 43W
Gods Lake Manitoba 43 E4 54 40N 94 20W
Gods Lake *tn.* Manitoba 43 E4 54 45N 94 00W
Gods Mercy, Bay of Nunavut 55 N3 63 30N 88 10W
Gods River Manitoba 43 F4 56 20N 92 50W
Gogama Ontario 45 L4 47 40N 81 43W
Goldboro Nova Scotia 53 M12 45 12N 61 35W
Gold Bridge British Columbia 39 J2 50 51N 122 51W
Golden British Columbia 39 M2 51 19N 116 55W
Golden Ears Provincial Park British Columbia 38 H4 49 28N 122 25W
Golden Hinde *mt.* British Columbia 39 H1 49 35N 125 40W
Gold River British Columbia 39 G1 49 41N 125 59W
Goldsmith Channel Nunavut 54 J5 73 00N 106 00W
Golfe du Saint-Laurent Québec 51 J3 48 40N 63 20W
Goodeve Saskatchewan 42 F2 51 03N 103 11W
Good Hope British Columbia 39 G2 50 59N 124 01W
Good Hope Lake British Columbia 39 F6 56 15N 129 20W
Good Hope Mountain British Columbia 39 J2 51 08N 124 10W
Goodsoil Saskatchewan 42 C4 54 24N 109 12W
Goose Bay *tn.* Newfoundland and Labrador 52 E6 53 15N 60 20W
Goose River Newfoundland and Labrador 52 E6 53 30N 61 50W
Gordon Horne Peak British Columbia 39 L2 51 47N 118 50W
Gordon Lake Alberta 41 G5 56 30N 110 25W
Gordon Pittock Reservoir Ontario 48 B2 43 11N 80 43W
Gordon River British Columbia 38 H4 48 38N 124 25W
Gore Bay *tn.* Ontario 46 D5 45 55N 82 28W
Goshen Nova Scotia 53 M12 45 20N 62 55W
Gowganda Ontario 45 L4 47 39N 80 46W
Gracefield Québec 47 K6 46 05N 76 05W
Grady Harbour *tn.* Newfoundland and Labrador 52 G6 53 48N 56 25W
Graham Island British Columbia 38 D3 53 50N 132 40W
Graham Island Nunavut 55 M6 77 25N 90 30W
Graham Laurier Provincial Park British Columbia 39 J5 56 30N 123 30W
Granby Québec 47 P5 45 22N 72 43W
Granby Provincial Park British Columbia 39 L1 49 45N 118 30W
Granby River British Columbia 39 L1 49 27N 118 25W
Grand Bank Newfoundland and Labrador 53 H3 47 06N 55 46W
Grand Bay-Westfield *tn.* New Brunswick 53 L12 45 19N 66 14W
Grand Bend Ontario 46 E3 43 21N 81 45W
Grand Centre Alberta 41 G4 54 25N 110 13W
Grande-Anse New Brunswick 53 C3 47 50N 65 10W
Grande-Anse Québec 47 P7 47 05N 72 55W
Grande Cache Alberta 41 C3 53 50N 119 08W
Grande Prairie Alberta 39 L4 55 10N 118 40W
Grande-Rivière *tn.* Québec 51 H3 48 23N 64 31W
Grande Rivière de la Baleine *r.* Québec 50 C6 55 15N 77 00W
Grand Étang Nova Scotia 53 M12 46 00N 61 00W
Grande-Vallée *tn.* Québec 51 H3 49 15N 65 10W
Grand Falls/Grand Sault *tn.* New Brunswick 53 B3 47 02N 67 46W
Grand Falls-Windsor *tn.* Newfoundland and Labrador 53 H4 48 56N 55 40W
Grand Forks British Columbia 39 L1 49 02N 118 30W
Grandin, Lake Northwest Territories 54 G3 63 50N 119 50W
Grand Jardin Newfoundland and Labrador 53 F4 48 28N 59 13W
Grand Lake New Brunswick 53 B2 46 00N 66 40W
Grand Lake Newfoundland and Labrador 52 E6 53 40N 60 30W
Grand Lake Newfoundland and Labrador 53 G4 49 00N 57 20W
Grand Manan *tn.* New Brunswick 53 L11 44 41N 66 46W
Grand Manan Island New Brunswick 53 L11 44 45N 66 40W
Grand Marais Manitoba 43 D2 50 30N 96 35W
Grand-Mère Québec 47 P6 46 36N 72 41W
Grand Narrows *tn.* Nova Scotia 53 M12 45 55N 60 50W
Grand Prairie *tn.* Alberta 41 C4 55 10N 118 52W
Grand Rapids *tn.* Manitoba 43 C3 53 12N 99 19W
Grand River Ontario 48 C1 42 51N 79 34W
Grand Valley *tn.* Ontario 48 B2 43 54N 80 10W
Grandview Manitoba 43 B2 51 11N 100 51W
Granisle British Columbia 39 G4 54 56N 126 18W
Granite Bay *tn.* British Columbia 38 G5 50 00N 125 00W
Granite Lake Newfoundland and Labrador 53 G4 48 11N 57 01W
Granville Falls Manitoba 43 B5 56 10N 100 20W
Granville Lake Manitoba 43 B5 56 00N 101 00W
Grasslands National Park Saskatchewan 42 D1 49 10N 107 30W
Grass River Manitoba 43 C4 54 50N 99 20W
Grass River Provincial Park Manitoba 43 B4 54 40N 101 40W
Grassy Narrows *I.R.* Ontario 44 E6 50 10N 93 55W
Gravelbourg Saskatchewan 42 D1 49 53N 106 33W
Gravenhurst Ontario 46 G4 44 55N 79 22W
Grayling River British Columbia 39 H6 59 43N 125 55W
Greasy Lake Northwest Territories 54 F3 62 55N 122 15W
Great Bear Lake Northwest Territories 54 F4 66 00N 120 00W
Great Central Lake British Columbia 38 G4 49 22N 125 10W
Great Plain of the Koukdjuak Nunavut 55 R4 66 25N 72 50W
Great Pubnico Lake Nova Scotia 53 L11 43 50N 65 30W
Great Sand Hills Saskatchewan 42 C2 50 35N 109 20W
Great Slave Lake Northwest Territories 54 H3 62 00N 114 00W
Great Village Nova Scotia 53 M12 45 25N 63 36W
Greely Ontario 57 K2 45 16N 75 33W
Greely Fiord Nunavut 55 P7 80 30N 85 00W
Green Creek Ontario 57 K2 45 25N 75 35W
Green Gables Prince Edward Island 53 M12 46 28N 63 20W
Green Lake British Columbia 39 K2 51 26N 121 12W
Green Lake *tn.* Saskatchewan 42 D4 54 18N 107 49W
Greenville British Columbia 38 F4 55 05N 129 35W
Greenwater Lake Provincial Park Saskatchewan 42 F3 52 35N 103 25W
Greenwood British Columbia 39 L1 49 08N 118 41W
Greenwood Nova Scotia 53 M11 45 00N 64 50W
Grenfell Saskatchewan 42 F2 50 24N 102 56W
Grenville Québec 47 M5 45 40N 74 38W
Gretna Manitoba 43 D1 49 01N 97 34W
Grey *admin.* Ontario 48 B3 44 22N 80 33W
Grey Islands Newfoundland and Labrador 52 H5 50 50N 55 35W
Grey, Point British Columbia 40 E4 49 16N 123 17W
Grey River Newfoundland and Labrador 53 G3 47 50N 56 50W
Griffith Island Ontario 48 B3 44 50N 80 54W
Grimsby Ontario 48 C2 43 12N 79 35W
Grimshaw Alberta 41 D5 56 11N 117 36W
Grinnell Peninsula Nunavut 55 L6 76 40N 95 00W
Grise Fiord *(Aujuittuq)* *tn.* Nunavut 55 P6 76 25N 82 57W
Grizzly Bear Hills Saskatchewan 42 C4 55 50N 109 30W
Groais Island Newfoundland and Labrador 52 H5 50 57N 55 36W
Gros Morne *mt.* Newfoundland and Labrador 53 G4 49 36N 57 47W
Gros Morne National Park Newfoundland and Labrador 53 G4 49 40N 58 40W
Groswater Bay Newfoundland and Labrador 52 G7 54 20N 57 40W
Grouard Mission Alberta 41 D4 55 30N 116 10W
Groundhog River Ontario 45 K5 49 00N 82 10W
Guelph Ontario 48 B2 43 34N 80 16W
Gull Bay *I.R.* Ontario 44 G5 49 50N 89 00W
Gull Lake Alberta 41 F3 52 34N 114 00W
Gull Lake *tn.* Saskatchewan 42 C2 50 05N 108 30W
Gunisao Lake Manitoba 43 D3 53 30N 96 40W
Gunisao River Manitoba 43 D3 53 30N 96 50W
Guysborough Nova Scotia 53 M12 45 23N 61 30W
Guysborough *admin.* Nova Scotia 53 M12 45 20N 61 40W
Gwaii Haanas National Park Reserve British Columbia 38 E3 52 30N 130 40W
Gwillim Lake Provincial Park British Columbia 39 K4 55 00N 121 00W
Gypsumville Manitoba 43 C2 51 47N 98 38W
Gyrfalcon Islands Northwest Territories 50 F8 59 05N 69 00W

H

Hadley Bay Nunavut 54 J5 72 22N 108 30W
Hagensborg British Columbia 39 G3 52 30N 126 30W
Haileybury Ontario 45 M4 47 27N 79 38W
Haines Junction Yukon Territory 54 C3 60 45N 137 21W
Hakai Recreation Area British Columbia 39 G2 50 40N 128 00W
Haldimand-Norfolk *admin.* Ontario 48 B1/C1 42 37N 80 39W
Halfway Point *tn.* Newfoundland and Labrador 53 F4 48 59N 58 06W
Halfway River British Columbia 39 J5 56 42N 122 30W
Haliburton Ontario 46 H5 45 03N 78 31W
Haliburton *admin.* Ontario 46 H5 45 05N 78 50W
Halifax Nova Scotia 53 M11 44 40N 63 41W
Halifax *admin.* Nova Scotia 53 M12 45 00N 63 00W
Halifax Harbour Nova Scotia 57 Q6 44 39N 63 33W
Hall Beach *(Sanirajak)* *tn.* Nunavut 55 P4 68 46N 81 12W
Hall Peninsula Nunavut 55 S3 68 40N 66 00W
Halls Harbour Nova Scotia 53 M12 45 12N 64 37W
Halton *admin.* Ontario 48 C2 43 26N 79 57W
Hamilton Ontario 48 C2 43 15N 79 50W
Hamilton Harbour Ontario 48 C2 43 16N 80 50W
Hamilton Inlet Newfoundland and Labrador 52 F6 54 18N 57 30W
Hamilton Sound Newfoundland and Labrador 53 H4 49 30N 54 15W
Hamilton-Wentworth *admin.* Ontario 48 B2/C2 43 14N 80 09W
Hamiota Manitoba 43 B2 50 11N 100 38W
Hampden Newfoundland and Labrador 53 G4 49 33N 56 51W
Hampton New Brunswick 53 L12 45 30N 65 50W
Hampton Ontario 48 D2 43 52N 78 43W
Hanna Alberta 41 G2 51 38N 111 56W
Hannah Bay Ontario 45 L6/M6 51 20N 80 00W
Hanover Ontario 48 A3 44 10N 81 03W
Hanson Lake Road Saskatchewan 42 E4 54 20N 104 35W
Hants *admin.* Nova Scotia 53 M12 45 10N 63 40W
Hantsport Nova Scotia 53 M12 45 04N 64 12W
Happy Valley-Goose Bay Newfoundland and Labrador 52 E6 53 18N 60 16W
Harbour Breton *tn.* Newfoundland and Labrador 53 H3 47 29N 55 50W
Harbour Deep *tn.* Newfoundland and Labrador 53 G5 50 22N 56 31W
Harbour Grace *tn.* Newfoundland and Labrador 53 J3 47 42N 53 13W
Hardisty Alberta 41 G3 52 40N 111 18W
Hardisty Lake Northwest Territories 54 G3 64 30N 117 45W
Hare Bay Newfoundland and Labrador 52 H5 51 15N 55 45W
Hare Bay *tn.* Newfoundland and Labrador 53 J4 48 51N 54 00W
Hare Indian River Northwest Territories 54 E4 66 40N 128 00W
Haro Strait British Columbia 38 H4 48 36N 123 17W
Harp Lake Newfoundland and Labrador 52 E7 55 05N 61 50W
Harrington Harbour *tn.* Québec 50 L4 50 31N 59 30W
Harrison, Cape Newfoundland and Labrador 52 G7 54 57N 57 57W
Harrison Hot Springs *tn.* British Columbia 38 H4 49 17N 121 47W
Harrison Lake British Columbia 38 H4 49 30N 122 10W
Harriston Ontario 48 B2 43 54N 80 52W
Harrow Ontario 46 D2 42 02N 82 55W
Harrowby Manitoba 43 B2 50 45N 101 28W
Harry Gibbons Bird Sanctuary Nunavut 55 N3 63 50N 86 00W
Hartland New Brunswick 53 B3 46 18N 67 31W
Hartney Manitoba 43 B1 49 29N 100 31W
Hart River Yukon Territory 54 C4 65 40N 137 10W
Hastings Ontario 46 J4 44 18N 77 57W
Hastings *admin.* Ontario 46 J4/J5 44 45N 77 40W
Hatchet Lake Saskatchewan 42 F6 58 50N 103 30W
Haultain River Saskatchewan 42 D5 56 20N 106 20W
Havelock Ontario 46 J4 44 26N 77 53W
Havre-Aubert Québec 53 E3 47 15N 61 51W
Havre Saint-Pierre Québec 51 J4 50 20N 63 38W
Hawke Harbour *tn.* Newfoundland and Labrador 52 H6 53 03N 55 49W
Hawkes Bay *tn.* Newfoundland and Labrador 53 G5 50 36N 57 10W
Hawkesbury Ontario 47 M5 45 36N 74 37W
Hay, Cape Northwest Territories 54 H5 74 25N 113 00W
Hayes River Manitoba 43 F4 55 20N 93 50W
Hay Lake Alberta 41 C6 58 52N 119 20W
Hay River Alberta/Northwest Territories 41 C6 58 20N 119 00W
Hay River *(Kátł'odeeche)* *tn.* Northwest Territories 54 G3 60 51N 115 42W
Hazeldean Ontario 57 J2 45 18N 75 55W
Hazelton British Columbia 39 G4 55 17N 127 42W
Hazen Strait Northwest Territories/Nunavut 54 J6 77 00N 110 00W
Head of Bay d'Espoir Newfoundland and Labrador 53 H3 47 56N 55 45W
Hearst Ontario 45 K5 49 42N 83 40W
Heart's Content Newfoundland and Labrador 53 J3 47 53N 53 22W
Hebron Newfoundland and Labrador 52 D9 58 12N 62 38W
Hebron Nova Scotia 53 L11 43 57N 66 03W
Hebron Fiord *in.* Newfoundland and Labrador 52 D9 58 09N 62 45W
Hecate Strait British Columbia 38 E3 53 40N 131 10W
Hecla and Griper Bay Northwest Territories/Nunavut 54 H6 76 25N 113 00W
Hecla/Grindstone Provincial Park Manitoba 43 D2 51 10N 96 30W
Hecla Island Manitoba 43 D2 51 00N 96 30W
Henley Harbour *tn.* Newfoundland and Labrador 52 H6 52 00N 55 51W
Henrietta Island Newfoundland and Labrador 52 F7 54 05N 58 28W
Henrietta Maria, Cape Ontario 44 K8 55 00N 82 30W
Henry Kater Peninsula Nunavut 55 S4 69 20N 67 20W
Hensall Ontario 48 A2 43 26N 81 31W
Hepworth Ontario 48 A3 44 37N 81 09W
Herbert Saskatchewan 42 D2 50 26N 107 12W
Heriot Bay *tn.* British Columbia 38 G5 50 06N 125 12W
Hermitage Sandyville Newfoundland and Labrador 53 H3 47 33N 55 56W
Heron Bay *I.R.* Ontario 45 H5 48 40N 86 17W
Herring Cove Nova Scotia 53 M11 44 35N 63 35W
Herschel Yukon Territory 54 C4 69 34N 139 00W
Herschel Island Yukon Territory 54 C4 69 34N 139 00W
Hespeler Ontario 48 B2 43 26N 80 20W
Hess River Yukon Territory 54 D3 63 25N 133 50W

Hibbard Québec	47	M7	47 53N	74 03W
Hickman, Mount British Columbia	38	E5	57 15N	131 07W
Highlands British Columbia	38	H4	48 30N	123 30W
High Level *tn.* Alberta	41	D6	58 10N	117 20W
High Prairie *tn.* Alberta	41	D4	55 26N	116 29W
High River *tn.* Alberta	41	F2	50 35N	113 52W
Highrock Manitoba	43	B4	55 50N	100 22W
Highrock Lake Manitoba	43	B4	55 45N	100 20W
Highrock Lake Saskatchewan	42	E5	57 00N	105 20W
Hillsborough New Brunswick	53	M12	45 56N	64 40W
Hillsburgh Ontario	48	B2	43 46N	80 10W
Hilton Beach *tn.* Ontario	46	C6	46 16N	83 56W
Hinds Lake Reservoir Newfoundland and Labrador	53	G4	49 10N	56 50W
Hines Creek *tn.* Alberta	41	C5	56 15N	118 36W
Hinton Alberta	41	D3	53 25N	117 34W
Hoare Bay Nunavut	55	T4	65 17N	62 55W
Hodgeville Saskatchewan	42	D2	50 07N	106 58W
Hog Island Prince Edward Island	53	M12	46 53N	63 50W
Holden Alberta	41	F3	53 14N	112 14W
Holdfast Saskatchewan	42	E2	50 58N	105 28W
Holland Landing Ontario	48	C3	44 05N	79 29W
Holland River Ontario	48	C3	44 01N	79 39W
Holman *(Uluqsaqtuuq)* Northwest Territories	54	G5	70 44N	117 44W
Holton Newfoundland and Labrador	52	G7	54 35N	57 16W
Holyrood Newfoundland and Labrador	53	J3	47 23N	53 08W
Homathko River British Columbia	39	H2	51 00N	125 05W
Home Bay Nunavut	55	S4	69 00N	87 00W
Home Island Newfoundland and Labrador	52	C10	60 10N	64 14W
Hope British Columbia	38	H4	49 21N	121 28W
Hope Bay Ontario	48	A3	44 55N	81 14W
Hopedale Newfoundland and Labrador	52	E7	55 28N	60 13W
Hope Island British Columbia	39	G2	50 55N	127 55W
Hope Island Ontario	48	B3	44 54N	80 11W
Hopes Advance Bay Québec	50	F8	59 20N	69 40W
Hopewell Nova Scotia	53	M12	45 29N	62 41W
Hopewell Islands Nunavut	50	A8	58 20N	78 10W
Hornaday River Northwest Territories	54	F4	69 00N	123 00W
Hornby Island British Columbia	38	H4	49 31N	124 40W
Hornepayne Ontario	45	J5	49 13N	84 47W
Horner Creek Ontario	48	B2	43 12N	80 35W
Horn Mountains Northwest Territories	54	G3	62 15N	119 15W
Horsefly Lake British Columbia	39	K3	52 25N	121 00W
Horse Islands Newfoundland and Labrador	53	H5	50 13N	55 48W
Horseshoe Bay *tn.* British Columbia	38	H4	49 22N	123 17W
Horseshoe Valley Ontario	48	C3	44 34N	79 41W
Horton River Northwest Territories	54	F4	68 50N	123 50W
Horwood Lake Ontario	45	K5	48 00N	82 20W
Hottah Lake Northwest Territories	54	G4	65 04N	118 30W
Houston British Columbia	39	G4	54 24N	126 39W
Houston Point Northwest Territories	44	L7	58 20N	81 00W
Howe Sound British Columbia	38	H4	49 30N	123 25W
Howie Centre Nova Scotia	53	M12	46 05N	60 15W
Howley Newfoundland and Labrador	53	G4	49 10N	57 07W
Hubbards Nova Scotia	53	M11	44 38N	64 03W
Hubbart Point Manitoba	43	E6	59 21N	94 41W
Hudson Bay *(Baie d'Hudson)* Canada	55	N3/P2	60 00N	85 00W
Hudson Bay *tn.* Saskatchewan	42	F3	52 45N	102 45W
Hudson's Hope British Columbia	39	K5	56 00N	121 59W
Hudson Strait *(Detroit d'Hudson)* Nunavut	55	R3	62 00N	70 00W
Hudwin Lake Park Reserve Manitoba	43	E3	53 15N	95 00W
Hugh Keenleyside Dam British Columbia	39	M1	49 33N	118 00W
Hull *admin.* Québec	47	L5	45 40N	75 40W
Humber Bay Ontario	48	C2	43 36N	79 27W
Humber River Ontario	48	C2	43 58N	79 37W
Humboldt Saskatchewan	42	E3	52 12N	105 07W
150 Mile House British Columbia	39	K3	52 05N	121 56W
100 Mile House British Columbia	39	K2	51 36N	121 18W
Hunter Island British Columbia	39	F2	51 57N	128 05W
Hunter River *tn.* Prince Edward Island	53	M12	46 20N	63 20W
Huntingdon Québec	47	M5	45 05N	74 11W
Huntingdon *admin.* Québec	47	M5	45 00N	74 20W
Huntingdon Island Newfoundland and Labrador	52	G6	53 47N	56 55W
Hunt River Newfoundland and Labrador	52	E7	55 20N	61 10W
Huntsville Ontario	46	G5	45 20N	79 13W
Hurd, Cape Ontario	48	A4	45 14N	81 44W
Huron *admin.* Ontario	48	A2	43 27N	81 35W
Huron, Lake Ontario/USA	46	D4/D5	45 00N	83 00W
Hyde Park Ontario	48	A2	43 00N	81 20W
Hythe Alberta	41	C4	55 18N	119 33W

I

Igloolik *(Iglulik)* Nunavut	55	P4	69 23N	81 46W
Iglusuaktalialuk Island Newfoundland and Labrador	52	E8	57 20N	61 30W
Ignace Ontario	44	F5	49 26N	91 40W
Île-à-la-Crosse *tn.* Saskatchewan	42	D4	55 28N	107 53W
Île aux Coudres *i.* Québec	47	R7	47 23N	70 20W
Île aux Herons Québec	56	N4	45 26N	73 35W
Île Bizard *i.* Québec	56	M4	45 29N	73 54W
Île d'Anticosti *i.* Québec	51	J3	49 20N	62 30W
Île de Montréal *i.* Québec	56	M4	45 30N	73 43W
Île des Allumettes *i.* Québec	47	J5	45 55N	77 08W
Île des Soeurs *i.* Québec	56	N4	45 28N	73 33W
Île d'Orléans *i.* Québec	47	R6	46 55N	71 00W
Île Dorval *i.* Québec	56	N4	45 26N	73 44W
Île Jésus *i.* Québec	56	N5	45 35N	73 45W
Île Kettle *i.* Québec	57	K2	45 28N	75 39W
Île Lamèque *i.* New Brunswick	53	C3	47 50N	64 40W
Île Lynch *i.* Québec	56	M4	45 25N	73 54W
Île Ste. Hélène *i.* Québec	56	N5	45 31N	73 32W
Île Sainte-Thérèse *i.* Québec	56	P5	45 39N	73 28W
Îles-de-Boucherville *is.* Québec	56	P5	45 36N	73 28W
Îles de la Madeleine *is.* Québec	53	E3	47 40N	61 50W
Îles du Grand Calumet *is.* Québec	47	K5	45 30N	76 35W
Ilford Manitoba	43	E5	56 04N	95 40W
Indian Arm *b.* British Columbia	40	G4	49 19N	122 55W
Indian Arm Provincial Park British Columbia	38	H4	49 22N	122 45W
Indian Cabins Alberta	41	D6	59 52N	117 02W
Indian Harbour *tn.* Newfoundland and Labrador	52	G7	54 27N	57 13W
Indian Head *tn.* Saskatchewan	42	F2	50 35N	103 37W
Indian Tickle Newfoundland and Labrador	52	H6	53 34N	56 00W
Ingenika River British Columbia	39	G5	56 48N	126 11W
Ingersoll Ontario	48	B2	43 03N	80 53W
Ingonish Nova Scotia	53	M12	46 42N	60 22W
Inklin River British Columbia	38	D6	58 54N	132 50W
Inner Bay Ontario	48	B1	42 35N	80 26W
Innisfail Alberta	41	F3	52 01N	113 59W
Inside Passage British Columbia	38/39	F3	53 38N	129 40W
Inukjuak Québec	50	A8	58 40N	78 15W
Inuvik *(Inuuvik)* Northwest Territories	54	D4	68 16N	133 40W
Inverhuron Provincial Park Ontario	48	A3	44 20N	81 30W
Invermere British Columbia	39	M2	50 30N	116 00W
Inverness Nova Scotia	53	M12	46 14N	61 19W
Inverness *admin.* Nova Scotia	53	M12	46 00N	61 30W
Ioco *tn.* British Columbia	40	G4	49 18N	122 51W
Iqaluit Nunavut	55	S3	60 00N	65 00W
Irma Alberta	41	G3	52 55N	111 14W
Iron Bridge *tn.* Ontario	46	C6	46 17N	83 14W
Ironside Québec	57	J2	45 27N	75 46W
Iroquois Ontario	47	L4	44 51N	75 19W
Iroquois Falls *tn.* Ontario	45	L5	48 47N	80 41W
Irvines Landing British Columbia	38	H4	49 37N	124 02W
Isaac Lake Ontario	48	A3	44 46N	81 13W
Isachsen Nunavut	55	K6	78 47N	103 30W
Ishpatina Ridge Ontario	45	L4	47 19N	80 44W
Iskut River British Columbia	38	E5	56 45N	131 10W
Island Falls Dam Saskatchewan	42	F4	55 30N	102 20W
Island Lake Manitoba	43	E3	53 50N	94 00W
Island Lake *tn.* Manitoba	43	E3	53 50N	94 00W
Island of Ponds *tn.* Newfoundland and Labrador	52	H6	53 20N	55 50W
Islands, Bay of Newfoundland and Labrador	52	F7	55 09N	59 49W
Islands, Bay of Newfoundland and Labrador	53	F4	49 10N	58 14W
Isle aux Morts *tn.* Newfoundland and Labrador	53	F3	47 35N	58 59W
Isle Madame *i.* Nova Scotia	53	M12	45 30N	60 50W
Isle Royale *i.* Ontario	45	G4	48 10N	88 30W
Isle Royale National Park Ontario	45	G4	48 10N	88 30W
Islington Ontario	49	B1	43 38N	79 32W
Itcha Ilgachuz Provincial Park British Columbia	39	H3	52 50N	125 00W
Itchen Lake Northwest Territories	54	H4	65 33N	112 50W
Ituna Saskatchewan	42	F2	51 09N	103 24W
Ivujivik Québec	50	B10	62 25N	77 54W
Ivvavik National Park Yukon Territory	54	C4	69 20N	139 30W

J

Jackfish Lake Manitoba	43	C2	50 30N	99 20W
Jackson's Arm *tn.* Newfoundland and Labrador	53	G4	49 53N	56 47W
Jacksons Point *tn.* Ontario	48	C3	44 18N	79 22W
Jaffray Melick Ontario	44	D5	49 49N	94 25W
Jakes Corner *tn.* Yukon Territory	54	D3	60 20N	133 58W
James Bay Ontario/Québec	44	L7/M7	53 45N	81 00W
James Ross, Cape Northwest Territories	54	H4	74 40N	114 25W
James Ross Strait Nunavut	55	L4	69 40N	96 00W
Jans Bay *tn.* Saskatchewan	42	C4	55 09N	108 08W
Jarvis Ontario	48	B1	42 52N	80 08W
Jasper Alberta	41	C3	52 55N	118 05W
Jasper National Park Alberta	41	C3/D3	53 00N	118 00W
Jean Marie River *(Tthets'éhk'édéli)* *tn.* Northwest Territories	54	F3	61 32N	120 38W
Jellicoe Ontario	45	H5	49 41N	87 31W
Jennings River British Columbia	38	E6	59 33N	131 40W
Jenpeg Manitoba	43	C4	54 30N	98 00W
Jervis Inlet British Columbia	38	H4	49 47N	124 04W
Jock River Ontario	57	J2	45 15N	75 46W
Joe Batt's Arm *tn.* Newfoundland and Labrador	53	H4	49 44N	54 10W
Joggins Nova Scotia	53	M12	45 42N	64 27W
John D'or Prairie Alberta	41	E6	58 30N	115 08W
John E. Pearce Provincial Park Ontario	48	A1	42 37N	81 27W
John Hart Highway British Columbia	39	K4	55 40N	121 38W
Johnsons Crossing *tn.* Yukon Territory	54	D3	60 29N	133 17W
Johnstone Strait British Columbia	39	G2/H2	50 23N	126 30W
Joliette Québec	47	N6	46 02N	73 27W
Joliette *admin.* Québec	47	L7	47 40N	75 40W
Jones Ontario	44	D5	49 59N	94 05W
Jones Sound Nunavut	55	N6	76 00N	88 00W
Jordan Lake Nova Scotia	53	L11	44 05N	65 20W
Jordan River *tn.* British Columbia	38	H4	48 26N	123 59W
Joussard Alberta	41	E4	55 25N	115 59W
Joutel Québec	51	A3	49 28N	78 28W
Juan de Fuca Strait British Columbia	38	H4	48 30N	124 31W
Judique Nova Scotia	53	M12	45 55N	61 30W

K

Kabania Lake Ontario	44	G7	52 12N	88 20W
Kabinakagami, Lake Ontario	45	J5	48 54N	84 25W
Kabinakagami River Ontario	45	J5	49 10N	84 10W
Kagawong Ontario	46	D5	45 54N	82 15W
Kahnawake Québec	56	N4	45 25N	73 42W
Kaipokok Bay Newfoundland and Labrador	52	F7	54 00N	59 35W
Kakabeta Falls *tn.* Ontario	45	G5	48 24N	89 40W
Kakisa *(K'ágee)* Northwest Territories	54	G3	60 58N	117 30W
Kakkiviak, Cape Newfoundland and Labrador	52	C10	60 05N	64 15W
Kakwa Recreation Area British Columbia	39	K4	54 05N	120 20W
Kakwa River Alberta	41	C4	54 15N	119 45W
Kaladar Ontario	47	J4	44 39N	77 07W
Kaleden British Columbia	39	L1	49 20N	119 38W
Kamilukuak Lake Nunavut	55	K3	62 22N	101 40W
Kaminak Lake Nunavut	55	M3	62 10N	95 00W
Kamloops British Columbia	39	K2	50 39N	120 24W
Kamloops Lake British Columbia	39	K2	50 45N	120 40W
Kamouraksa Québec	47	S7	47 34N	69 51W
Kamouraksa *admin.* Québec	47	S7	47 10N	69 50W
Kamsack Saskatchewan	42	G2	51 34N	101 51W
Kamuchawie Lake Saskatchewan	42	F5/G5	56 20N	102 20W
Kanaaupscow Québec	50	B5	54 02N	76 40W
Kanata Ontario	47	L5	45 20N	75 53W
Kangiqsualujjuaq Québec	50	G8	58 48N	66 08W
Kangiqsujuaq Québec	50	E9	61 40N	71 59W
Kangirsuk Québec	50	E9	60 00N	70 00W
Kapiskau River Ontario	44	K7	52 30N	82 50W
Kapuskasing Ontario	45	K5	49 25N	82 26W
Kapuskasing River Ontario	45	K5	48 40N	82 50W
Kasabonika *I.R.* Ontario	44	G7	53 32N	88 37W
Kasabonika Lake Ontario	44	G7	53 35N	88 35W
Kasba Lake Northwest Territories/Nunavut	55	K3	60 18N	102 07W
Kashechewan *I.R.* Ontario	44	L7	52 18N	81 37W
Kaskattama River Manitoba	43	G5	56 25N	91 10W
Kaslo British Columbia	39	M1	49 54N	116 57W
Kasmere Lake Manitoba	43	B6	59 30N	101 10W
Katannilik Territorial Park Nunavut	55	S3	63 00N	69 55W
Kates Needle *mt.* British Columbia	38	D5	57 02N	132 05W
Kaumajet Mountains Newfoundland and Labrador	52	D8	57 48N	61 51W
Kawawachikamach Québec	50	G6	54 50N	67 00W
Kazabazua Québec	47	K5	45 56N	76 01W
Kearney Ontario	46	G5	45 35N	79 17W
Kechika River British Columbia	39	G6	58 44N	127 25W
Kedgwick New Brunswick	53	B3	47 38N	67 21W
Keele Peak Yukon Territory	54	D3	63 25N	130 17W
Keele River Northwest Territories	54	E3	64 15N	126 00W
Keewatin Ontario	44	D5	49 47N	94 30W
Keewatin Region Nunavut	55	K4/L4		
Keewatin River Manitoba	43	B5	56 59N	100 59W
Keith Arm *b.* Northwest Territories	54	F4	65 20N	122 15W
Kejimkujik National Park Nova Scotia	53	L11	44 20N	65 20W
Keller Lake Northwest Territories	54	F3	64 00N	121 30W
Kellett, Cape Northwest Territories	54	E5	71 59N	126 00W
Kellett Strait Northwest Territories	54	G6	75 45N	117 30W
Kelliher Saskatchewan	42	F2	51 15N	103 41W
Kelowna British Columbia	39	L1	49 50N	119 29W
Kelsey Manitoba	43	D5	56 04N	96 30W
Kelsey Bay *tn.* British Columbia	39	H2	50 22N	125 29W
Kelvington Saskatchewan	42	F3	52 10N	103 30W
Kemano British Columbia	39	G3	53 39N	127 58W
Kempenfelt Bay Ontario	48	C3	44 22N	79 39W
Kemptville Ontario	47	L5	45 01N	75 38W
Kenamu River Newfoundland and Labrador	52	E6	52 50N	60 20W
Kenaston Saskatchewan	42	D2	51 30N	106 15W
Kendall Island Bird Sanctuary Northwest Territories	54	C4	69 30N	135 00W
Kennebecasis River New Brunswick	53	L12	45 30N	65 55W
Kennedy Lake British Columbia	38	G4	49 12N	125 32W
Kennetcook Nova Scotia	53	M12	45 10N	63 43W
Kenney Dam British Columbia	39	H3	53 38N	124 59W
Kenogami River Ontario	45	J6	50 50N	84 30W
Kenogamissi Lake Ontario	45	L5	48 15N	81 33W
Kenora Ontario	44	D5	49 47N	94 26W
Kensington Prince Edward Island	53	M12	46 26N	63 39W
Kent *admin.* New Brunswick	53	C3	46 30N	65 20W
Kent *admin.* Ontario	46	D2	42 25N	82 10W
Kent Peninsula Nunavut	54	J4	68 30N	106 00W
Kentville Nova Scotia	53	M12	45 04N	64 30W
Keremeos British Columbia	39	L1	49 12N	119 50W
Kerrobert Saskatchewan	42	C2	51 56N	109 09W
Kesagami Lake Ontario	45	L6	50 00N	80 00W
Kesagami Provincial Park Ontario	45	L6	50 30N	80 10W
Kesagami River Ontario	45	L6	50 30N	80 10W
Keswick Ontario	48	C3	44 15N	79 28W
Kettle Creek Ontario	48	A1	42 47N	81 13W
Kettle Rapids *tn.* Manitoba	43	E5	56 25N	94 30W
Kettle River British Columbia	39	L1	49 10N	119 02W
Kettle River Manitoba	43	H5	56 40N	89 50W
Kettlestone Bay Québec	50	B9	61 20N	77 54W
Keyano Québec	50	D5	53 52N	73 30W
Key Lake Mine *tn.* Saskatchewan	42	E5	57 10N	105 30W
Khutzeymateen Provincial Park British Columbia	38	F4	54 45N	129 50W
Kicking Horse Pass Alberta/British Columbia	39	M2	51 28N	116 23W
Kiglapait, Cape Newfoundland and Labrador	52	E9	57 06N	61 22W
Kiglapait Mountains Newfoundland and Labrador	52	E8	57 06N	61 35W
Kikerk Lake Nunavut	54	H4	66 55N	113 20W
Kikkertarjote Island Newfoundland and Labrador	52	E8	57 30N	61 28W
Kikkertavak Island Newfoundland and Labrador	52	E8	56 22N	61 35W
Killaloe Ontario	47	J5	45 33N	77 26W
Killam Alberta	41	G3	52 47N	111 51W
Killarney Manitoba	43	C1	49 12N	99 40W
Killarney Ontario	46	E5	45 59N	81 30W
Killarney Provincial Park Ontario	46	E6	46 00N	81 00W
Killiniq Northwest Territories	50	H9	60 30N	64 50W
Killiniq Island Newfoundland and Labrador	52	C10	60 24N	64 31W
Kimberley British Columbia	39	N1	49 40N	115 58W
Kimmirut *(Lake Harbour)* Nunavut	55	S3	62 50N	69 50W
Kinbasket Lake British Columbia	39	M2	51 57N	118 02W
Kincardine Ontario	48	A3	44 11N	81 38W
Kincolith British Columbia	38	F4	55 00N	129 57W
Kincora Prince Edward Island	53	M12	46 20N	63 40W
Kindersley Saskatchewan	42	C2	51 27N	109 08W
King Christian Island Nunavut	55	K6	77 45N	102 00W
King City Ontario	48	C2	43 54N	79 31W
Kingcome Inlet British Columbia	39	G2	50 58N	125 15W
Kingfisher Lake Ontario	44	G7	53 05N	89 49W
Kingfisher Lake *I.R.* Ontario	44	G7	53 02N	89 50W
King George, Mount British Columbia	39	N2	50 36N	115 26W
King Island British Columbia	39	G3	52 10N	127 35W
Kings *admin.* New Brunswick	53	L12	45 30N	65 40W
Kings *admin.* Nova Scotia	53	M11	44 50N	64 50W
Kings *admin.* Prince Edward Island	53	M12	46 20N	62 40W
Kingsburg Nova Scotia	53	M11	44 20N	64 10W
Kings Landing New Brunswick	53	B2	45 50N	67 00W
Kingsmere Québec	57	J2	45 29N	75 50W
Kingston Ontario	47	K4	44 14N	76 30W
Kingsville Ontario	46	D2	42 02N	82 45W
Kingurutik Lake Newfoundland and Labrador	52	D8	56 49N	62 20W
King William Island Nunavut	55	L4	69 00N	97 30W

Kinistino Saskatchewan 42 E3 52 28N 105 01W
Kinoje River Ontario 44 L6 51 40N 81 50W
Kinoosao Saskatchewan 42 F5 57 07N 102 02W
Kinsac Lake Nova Scotia 57 Q7 44 50N 63 38W
Kinusheseo River Ontario 44 K8 54 30N 83 50W
Kiosk Ontario 46 H6 46 05N 78 53W
Kipahigan Lake Manitoba 43 B4 55 20N 101 50W
Kipling Saskatchewan 42 F2 50 08N 102 40W
Kirkland Lake Ontario 45 L5 48 10N 80 02W
Kirkpatrick Lake Alberta 41 G2 51 52N 111 18W
Kirriemuir Alberta 41 G2 51 56N 110 18W
Kiskittogisa Lake Manitoba 43 C4 54 10N 98 50W
Kiskitto Lake Manitoba 43 C4 54 20N 98 50W
Kispiox British Columbia 39 G4 55 21N 127 41W
Kississing Lake Manitoba 43 B4 55 10N 101 30W
Kistigan Lake Manitoba 43 F4 54 50N 92 40W
Kitchener Ontario 48 B2 43 27N 80 03W
Kitikmeot Region Nunavut 54/55 J4/K4
Kitimat British Columbia 38 F4 54 05N 128 38W
Kitlope Heritage Conservancy Park British Columbia 39 G3 53 00N 127 30W
Klappan River British Columbia 38 F6 57 50N 129 40W
Kleinburg Ontario 49 B2 43 50N 79 36W
Klemtu British Columbia 39 F3 52 32N 128 24W
Klinaklini River British Columbia 39 H2 51 18N 125 45W
Klondike Highway Yukon Territory 54 C3 62 55N 136 10W
Klondike River Yukon Territory 54 C3 64 20N 138 50W
Kluane Lake Yukon Territory 54 C3 62 20N 139 00W
Kluane National Park Yukon Territory 54 C3 60 30N 139 00W
Kluane Wildlife Sanctuary Yukon Territory 54 B3 61 30N 139 50W
Knee Lake Manitoba 43 E4 55 10N 94 40W
Knight Inlet British Columbia 39 H2 50 45N 125 36W
Knox, Cape British Columbia 38 D4 54 09N 133 05W
Koch Island Nunavut 55 Q4 69 38N 78 15W
Kogaluc Bay Québec 50 B8 56 10N 63 30W
Kogaluk River Newfoundland and Labrador 52 D8 56 10N 63 30W
Kokanee Glacier Park British Columbia 39 M1 49 45N 117 10W
Komoka Ontario 48 A1 42 56N 81 26W
Kootenay Lake British Columbia 39 M1 49 35N 116 30W
Kootenay National Park British Columbia 39 M2 51 15N 116 25W
Kopka River Ontario 44 G6 50 00N 90 00W
Kotcho Lake British Columbia 39 K6 59 05N 121 10W
Kouchibouguac National Park New Brunswick 53 C3 46 45N 64 50W
Koukdjuuak River Nunavut 55 R4 66 50N 72 50W
Kovik Bay Québec 50 B9 61 35N 77 54W
Kugaaruk *(Pelly Bay)* Nunavut 55 N4 68 32N 89 48W
Kugluktuk *(Coppermine)* Nunavut 54 H4 65 00N 110 00W
Kunghit Island British Columbia 38 E3 52 02N 131 02W
Kuujjuaq Québec 50 F8 58 25N 68 55W
Kuujjuarapik Québec 50 B6 55 15N 77 41W
Kwadacha Recreation Area British Columbia 39 H5 57 35N 125 30W
Kwadacha Wilderness Park British Columbia 39 H5 57 50N 125 00W
Kwataboahegan River Ontario 45 K6 51 10N 82 30W
Kyle Saskatchewan 42 C2 50 50N 108 02W
Kyuquot Souund British Columbia 39 G1 50 02N 127 22W

L

Labelle Québec 47 M6 46 17N 74 45W
Labelle *admin.* Québec 47 L6 46 30N 75 40W
Laberge, Lake Yukon Territory 54 D3 61 10N 134 59W
Labrador *geog. reg.* Newfoundland and Labrador 52 D6/E6 54 00N 64 00W
Labrador City Newfoundland and Labrador 52 B6 52 57N 66 55W
Labrador Sea 55 T2/U2 59 30N 60 00W
Lac Abitibi *l.* Ontario/Québec 45 M5 48 40N 79 40W
Lac Albanel *l.* Québec 51 D4 51 N 73 20W
Lac à l'Eau Claire *l.* Québec 50 C7 56 20N 74 30W
Lac Anuc *l.* Québec 50 C8 59 15N 75 10W
Lac Assinica *l.* Québec 51 C4 50 20N 75 12W
Lac au Goéland *l.* Québec 51 B3 49 45N 76 55W
Lac Aylmer *l.* Québec 47 Q5 45 50N 71 20W
Lac Bacqueville *l.* Québec 50 D8 58 05N 74 00W
Lac Batiscan *l.* Québec 47 Q7 47 23N 71 53W
Lac Bécard *l.* Québec 50 D9 60 05N 73 45W
Lac Belot *l.* Northwest Territories 54 E4 66 53N 126 16W
Lac Bérard *l.* Québec 50 E8 58 25N 70 05W
Lac Bermen *l.* Québec 50 F5 53 40N 69 00W
Lac Berté *l.* Québec 51 F4 50 52N 68 35W
Lac Bienville *l.* Québec 50 D6 55 30N 73 00W
Lac Bourdel *l.* Québec 50 C7 56 42N 74 15W
Lac Boyd *l.* Québec 51 B5 52 45N 76 45W
Lac Brochet *l.* Manitoba 43 B6 58 40N 101 20W
Lac Brochet *tn.* Manitoba 43 B6 58 45N 101 30W
Lac Brome *l.* Québec 47 P5 45 15N 72 30W
Lac Brome *tn.* Québec 47 P5 45 13N 72 30W
Lac Burton *l.* Québec 50 A6 54 45N 79 25W
Lac Cambrien *l.* Québec 50 F7 56 30N 69 22W
Lac Cananée *l.* Québec 50 H7 56 05N 64 05W
Lac Chaconipau *l.* Québec 50 F7 56 20N 68 45W
Lac Champdoré *l.* Québec 50 H5 55 50N 65 50W
Lac Champlain *l.* Québec/IUSA 47 N4 45 08N 73 08W
Lac Châtelain *l.* Québec 50 C9 60 20N 74 20W
Lac Chavigny *l.* Québec 50 C8 58 10N 75 10W
Lac Chibougamau *l.* Québec 51 C3 49 55N 74 20W
Lac Couture *l.* Québec 50 C9 60 00N 75 20W
Lac de Gras *l.* Northwest Territories 54 J3 64 10N 109 00W
Lac de la Hutte Sauvage *l.* Québec 50 H7 56 18N 65 00W
Lac des Bois *l.* Northwest Territories 54 E4 65 00N 127 00W
Lac des Commissaires *l.* Québec 47 P8 48 09N 72 13W
Lac des Deux Montagnes *l.* Québec 56 M4 45 30N 73 58W
Lac des Loups Marins *l.* Québec 50 D7 56 30N 73 30W
Lac des Mille Lacs *l.* Ontario 44 F5 48 53N 90 22W
Lac des Quinze *l.* Québec 51 A2 47 45N 79 15W
Lac des Trente et Un Milles *l.* Québec 47 L6 46 18N 75 43W
Lac d'Iberville *l.* Québec 50 D6 55 55N 73 25W
Lac du Bonnet *l.* Manitoba 43 E2 50 30N 95 50W
Lac du Bonnet *tn.* Manitoba 43 D2 50 16N 96 03W
Lac Duncan *l.* Québec 51 A5 53 25N 78 00W
Lac du Sable *l.* Québec 50 G6 54 25N 67 59W
Lac Édouard *l.* Québec 47 P7 47 40N 72 16W
Lac-Etchemin *tn.* Québec 47 R6 46 23N 70 32W
Lac Faribault *l.* Québec 50 E8 59 10N 72 00W
Lac Fleur-de-May *l.* Newfoundland and Labrador 52 C6 52 00N 65 02W
Lac Goatanaga *l.* Québec 47 J7 47 42N 77 28W
Lac Guillaume-Delisle *l.* Québec 50 B7 56 15N 77 20W
Lachute Québec 47 M5 51 00N 71 00W
Lac Île-à-la Crosse *l.* Saskatchewan 42 D4 55 40N 107 30W
Lac Jeannin *l.* Québec 50 G7 56 25N 66 30W
Lac Joseph *l.* Newfoundland and Labrador 52 C6 52 45N 65 18W
Lac Kempt *l.* Québec 47 M7 47 28N 74 08W
Lac Kénogami *l.* Québec 51 E3 48 22N 71 25W
Lac Kipawa *l.* Québec 45 M4 46 55N 79 06W
Lac Klotz *l.* Québec 50 D9 60 30N 73 30W
Lac la Biche *l.* Alberta 41 F4 54 55N 112 58W
Lac la Biche *tn.* Alberta 41 G4 54 46N 111 58W
Lac la Croix *l.* Ontario 45 F5 48 21N 92 09W
Lac la Loche *l.* Saskatchewan 42 C5 56 30N 109 40W
Lac la Martre *l.* Northwest Territories 54 G3 63 20N 118 30W
Lac la Plonge *l.* Saskatchewan 42 D4 55 05N 107 00W
Lac la Ronge *l.* Saskatchewan 42 E4 55 10N 105 00W
Lac la Ronge Provincial Park Saskatchewan 42 E4 55 20N 104 45W
Lac le Moyne *l.* Québec 50 F7 57 10N 68 33W
Lac Le Roy *l.* Québec 50 C8 58 35N 75 25W
Lac Lesdiguière *l.* Québec 50 C9 60 00N 74 20W
Lac Magpie *l.* Québec 51 H4 51 00N 64 40W
Lac Maicasagi *l.* Québec 51 B4 50 00N 76 45W
Lac Manitou *l.* Québec 51 H4 50 50N 65 20W
Lac Manouane *l.* Québec 51 E4 50 45N 70 45W
Lac Matagami *l.* Québec 51 B3 49 55N 77 50W
Lac Maunoir *l.* Northwest Territories 54 E4 67 30N 125 55W
Lac-Mégantic *tn.* Québec 47 R5 45 34N 70 53W
Lac Memphrémagog *l.* Québec 47 P5 45 05N 72 13W
Lac Mesgouez *l.* Québec 51 C4 51 25N 75 00W
Lac Minto *l.* Québec 50 C7 57 5N 75 00W
Lac Mistassini *l.* Québec 51 D4 51 00N 73 20W
Lac Mistinibi *l.* Québec 50 H6 55 50N 64 20W
Lac Mitchinamécus *l.* Québec 47 M7 47 20N 75 00W
Lac Musquaro *l.* Québec 51 K4 50 50N 60 50W
Lac Nantais *l.* Québec 50 C9 61 10N 74 20W
Lac Naococane *l.* Québec 51 E5 52 53N 70 40W
Lac Nichicapau *l.* Québec 50 F7 56 42N 68 28W
Lac Nichicun *l.* Québec 51 E5 53 05N 71 05W
Lacombe Alberta 41 F3 52 28N 113 44W
Lac Opiscotéo *l.* Québec 51 F5 53 15N 68 20W
Lac Otelnuk *l.* Québec 50 F7 56 10N 68 20W
Lac Parent *l.* Québec 47 J8 48 30N 77 08W
Lac Payne *l.* Québec 50 C8 59 25N 74 25W
Lac Pélican *l.* Québec 50 D8 59 57N 73 40W
Lac Péribonka *l.* Québec 51 E4 50 10N 71 23W
Lac Plétipi *l.* Québec 51 E4 51 0N 70 10W
Lac Poncheville *l.* Québec 51 B4 50 12N 77 00W
Lac Potherie *l.* Québec 50 D8 58 50N 72 25W
Lac Qilalugalik *l.* Québec 50 B8 58 35N 76 00W
Lac Ramusio *l.* Québec 50 J6 55 10N 63 59W
Lac Résolution *l.* Québec 50 H6 55 15N 64 40W
La Crete Alberta 41 D6 58 11N 116 30W
Lac Roberts *l.* Québec 50 E9 60 25N 70 25W
Lac Saindon *l.* Québec 50 D6 55 35N 73 30W
Lac Sainte-Anne *l.* Québec 51 G4 50 5N 68 00W
Lac Saint-François *l.* Québec 47 Q5 45 56N 71 08W
Lac Saint-Jean *l.* Québec 51 D3/E3 48 35N 72 00W
Lac-St.-Jean-Est *admin.* Québec 47 Q8 48 20N 71 40W
Lac-St.-Jean-Ouest *admin.* Québec 47 N8/P8 48 20N 72 20W
Lac Saint-Louis *l.* Québec 56 M4 45 25N 73 49W
Lac Saint-Patrice *l.* Québec 47 J6 46 20N 77 30W
Lac Saint-Pierre *l.* Québec 47 P6 46 12N 72 49W
Lac Sakami *l.* Québec 51 B5 53 20N 76 50W
Lac Seul *I.R.* Ontario 44 E6 50 15N 92 15W
Lac Seul *l.* Ontario 44 E6 50 20N 92 00W
Lac Simard *l.* Québec 51 A2 47 40N 78 50W
Lac Simon *l.* Québec 47 L5 45 55N 75 05W
Lac Soscumica *l.* Québec 51 B4 50 15N 77 35W
Lac Tasiaalujjuak *l.* Québec 50 E8 59 35N 71 59W
Lac Tasiat *l.* Québec 50 C8 59 05N 75 25W
Lac Tasiataq *l.* Québec 50 E8 58 40N 71 40W
Lac Tassialouc *l.* Québec 50 D8 58 59N 74 00W
Lac Témiscaminque *l.* Québec 51 A2 47 28N 79 30W
Lac Tiblemont *l.* Québec 47 J8 48 17N 77 20W
Lac Tudor *l.* Québec 50 H6 55 58N 65 30W
Lac Wakuach *l.* Québec 50 G6 55 35N 67 40W
Lac Waswanipi *l.* Québec 51 B3 49 35N 76 36W
Lac Wayagamac *l.* Québec 47 P7 47 23N 72 35W
Lac Whitegull *l.* Québec 50 H6 55 25N 64 30W
Ladner British Columbia 38 H4 49 06N 123 05W
Lady Evelyn-Smoothwater Provincial Park Ontario 45 L4 47 20N 80 30W
Ladysmith British Columbia 38 H4 48 57N 123 50W
Laflèche Saskatchewan 42 D1 49 44N 106 32W
Lagoon City Ontario 48 C3 44 31N 79 11W
La Grande 2 *dam* Québec 51 B5 53 45N 77 38W
La Grande 3 *dam* Québec 51 B5 53 40N 76 09W
La Grande 4 *dam* Québec 50 D5 53 59N 72 50W
La Grande Rivière *r.* Québec 51 C5 53 34N 74 36W
La Guadeloupe Québec 47 R5 45 58N 70 57W
Lake Country *tn.* British Columbia 39 L2 50 02N 119 25W
Lake Cowichan *tn.* British Columbia 38 H4 48 50N 124 04W
Lake Echo *tn.* Nova Scotia 57 R6 44 44N 63 24W
Lakefield Ontario 46 H4 44 26N 78 16W
Lakeland Provincial Park Alberta 41 G4 54 45N 112 25W
Lakeland Provincial Recreation Area Alberta 41 G4 54 45N 111 15W
Lake Louise *tn.* Alberta 41 D2 51 25N 116 14W
Lake of Bays *tn.* Ontario 46 G5 45 00N 79 00W
Lake of the Rivers Saskatchewan 42 E1 49 50N 105 30W
Lakeside Nova Scotia 57 Q6 44 38N 63 42W
Lake Superior Provincial Park Ontario 45 J4 47 35N 85 45W
Lakeview Newfoundland and Labrador 53 J3 47 20N 54 10W
Lakeview Ontario 57 J2 45 20N 75 48W
La Loche Saskatchewan 42 C5 56 31N 109 27W
La Malbaie Québec 47 R7 47 39N 70 11W
Lamaline Newfoundland and Labrador 53 H3 46 52N 55 49W
Lambeth Ontario 48 A1 42 54N 81 20W
Lambton *admin.* Ontario 46 D2 42 45N 82 05W
Lambton, Cape Northwest Territories 54 F4 71 05N 123 09W
Lampman Saskatchewan 42 F1 49 23N 102 48W
Lanark Ontario 47 K5 45 01N 74 30W
Lanark *admin.* Ontario 47 K5 45 05N 76 20W
Lancaster Ontario 47 M5 45 08N 74 30W
Lancaster Sound Nunavut 55 N5 74 00N 87 30W
Land's End Northwest Territories 54 F6 76 22N 122 33W
Langenburg Saskatchewan 42 G2 50 50N 101 42W
Langham Saskatchewan 42 D3 52 22N 106 55W
Langley British Columbia 38 H4 49 06N 122 38W
Lanigan Saskatchewan 42 E2 51 50N 105 01W
L'Annonciation Québec 47 M6 46 24N 74 52W
Lansdowne House *tn.* Ontario 44 H7 52 05N 88 00W
L'Anse-au-Loup Newfoundland and Labrador 52 G5 51 31N 56 45W
L'Anse aux Meadows National Historic Site Newfoundland and Labrador 52 H5 51 36N 55 32W
L'Anse Pleureuse Québec 51 H3 49 15N 65 40W
Lantzville British Columbia 38 H4 49 15N 124 05W
La Pocatière Québec 47 R7 47 22N 70 03W
La Poile Newfoundland and Labrador 53 F3 47 41N 58 42W
La Prairie Québec 56 P4 45 25N 73 29W
Larder Lake *tn.* Ontario 45 M5 48 05N 79 38W
L'Ardoise Nova Scotia 53 M12 45 37N 60 46W
Lark Harbour *tn.* Newfoundland and Labrador 53 F4 49 06N 58 23W
La Ronge Saskatchewan 42 E4 55 07N 105 18W
Larrys River *tn.* Nova Scotia 53 M12 45 15N 61 25W
Larsen Sound Nunavut 55 L5 70 35N 98 00W
La Salle Ontario 46 C2 42 15N 83 05W
La Sarre Québec 51 A3 48 50N 79 20W
La Scie Newfoundland and Labrador 53 H4 49 57N 55 36W
Lashburn Saskatchewan 42 C3 53 08N 109 36W
Lasqueti Island British Columbia 38 H4 49 28N 124 20W
Last Mountain Lake Saskatchewan 42 E2 51 40N 106 55W
La Tabatière Québec 50 L4 50 50N 58 57W
Latchford Ontario 45 M4 47 20N 79 49W
La Tuque Québec 47 P7 47 26N 72 47W
Laurie River Manitoba 43 B5 56 30N 101 30W
Lauzon Québec 47 Q6 46 49N 71 10W
Laval Québec 47 N5 45 38N 73 45W
Laval-des-Rapides Québec 56 N5 45 33N 73 42W
Laval-Ouest Québec 56 M5 45 33N 73 50W
Lawn Newfoundland and Labrador 53 H3 46 57N 55 32W
Lawrencetown Nova Scotia 53 L11 44 54N 65 10W
Lax Kw'aiaams British Columbia 38 E4 54 32N 130 25W
Leader Saskatchewan 42 C2 50 55N 109 31W
Leading Tickles Newfoundland and Labrador 53 H4 49 30N 55 28W
Leaf Rapids *tn.* Manitoba 43 B5 56 30N 100 00W
Leamington Ontario 46 D2 42 03N 83 36W
Leaside Ontario 49 C1 43 44N 79 15W
Lebel-sur-Quévillon Québec 51 B3 49 05N 77 08W
Leduc Alberta 41 F3 53 17N 113 30W
Leeds and Grenville *admin.* Ontario 47 K4/L4 44 35N 76 00W
Le Havre River Nova Scotia 53 M11 44 30N 64 30W
Leitrim Ontario 57 K2 45 20N 75 35W
Lemieux Islands Nunavut 55 T3 63 40N 64 20W
Lennox and Addington *admin.* Ontario 47 J4 44 30N 77 00W
Lenore Lake Saskatchewan 42 E3 52 50N 104 40W
Leoville Saskatchewan 42 D3 53 39N 107 33W
Lesser Slave Lake Alberta 41 E4 55 25N 115 25W
Lethbridge Alberta 41 F1 49 43N 112 48W
Level Mountain British Columbia 38 E6 58 33N 131 25W
Lévis Québec 47 Q6 46 47N 71 12W
Lewis Hill *mt.* Newfoundland and Labrador 53 F4 49 48N 58 30W
Lewisporte Newfoundland and Labrador 53 H4 49 15N 55 03W
Liard River Northwest Territories 54 F3 60 00N 120 00W
Liard River *tn.* British Columbia 39 G6 59 28N 126 18W
Liard River Corridor Provincial Park British Columbia 39 H6 59 20N 125 30W
Liddon Gulf Northwest Territories 54 H6 75 03N 113 00W
L'Île-Perrot *i.* Québec 56 M4 45 24N 73 55W
Lillooet British Columbia 39 K2 50 41N 121 59W
Lillooet Lake British Columbia 38 H5 50 15N 122 38W
Lillooet River British Columbia 38 H4 49 59N 122 25W
Limbour Québec 57 K2 45 29N 75 44W
Lindsay Ontario 48 D3 44 21N 78 44W
Linzee, Cape Nova Scotia 53 M12 46 00N 61 30W
Lions Bay *tn.* British Columbia 38 H4 49 28N 123 13W
Lions Head *tn.* Ontario 48 A3 44 59N 81 16W
Lipton Saskatchewan 42 F2 50 55N 103 49W
Liscomb Game Sanctuary Nova Scotia 53 M12 45 10N 62 40W
L'Islet *admin.* Québec 47 R7 47 00N 70 20W
L'Isle-Verte Québec 47 S8 48 00N 69 21W
Lismore Nova Scotia 53 M12 45 42N 62 16W
Listowel Ontario 48 B2 43 44N 80 57W
Little Abitibi River Provincial Park Ontario 45 L5 49 45N 81 00W
Little Bow River Alberta 41 F2 50 20N 113 40W
Little Buffalo Alberta 41 D5 56 25N 116 15W
Little Buffalo River Alberta 41 F6 59 45N 113 30W
Little Churchill River Manitoba 43 E5 56 40N 96 00W
Little Current *tn.* Ontario 46 E5 45 58N 81 56W
Little Current River Provincial Park Ontario 44 H6 50 45N 86 15W
Little Dover Nova Scotia 53 M12 45 20N 61 05W
Little Grand Rapids *tn.* Manitoba 43 E3 52 10N 95 30W
Little Maitland River Ontario 48 A2 43 48N 81 10W
Little Mecatina River Newfoundland and Labrador 52 E6 52 40N 61 30W
Little Narrows *tn.* Nova Scotia 53 M12 45 59N 61 00W
Little River *tn.* British Columbia 38 H4 49 45N 124 56W
Little Rouge Creek Ontario 49 D2 43 54N 79 14W
Little Sachigo Lake Ontario 44 E8 54 09N 92 11W
Little Smoky River Alberta 41 D4 54 05N 117 45W
Liverpool Nova Scotia 53 M11 44 03N 64 43W
Liverpool Bay Northwest Territories 54 D4 69 45N 130 00W
Livingstone Cove *tn.* Nova Scotia 53 M12 45 52N 61 58W
Lloyd George, Mount British Columbia 39 H5 57 50N 124 58W
Lloyd Lake Alberta 40 A1 50 52N 114 10W
Lloyd Lake Saskatchewan 42 C5 57 20N 108 40W
Lloydminster Saskatchewan 42 C3 53 18N 110 00W
Lobstick Lake Newfoundland and Labrador 52 C7 54 00N 65 00W
Lockeport Nova Scotia 53 E6 43 40N 65 10W
Lockport Manitoba 43 D2 50 04N 97 00W
Lodge Creek Alberta/Saskatchewan 41 G1 49 15N 110 05W
Logan Lake *tn.* British Columbia 39 K2 50 28N 120 50W
Logan, Mount Yukon Territory 54 B3 60 34N 140 25W
Logan Mountains Yukon Territory 54 E3 60 30N 128 30W
London Ontario 48 A1 42 58N 81 15W
Long Beach *tn.* Ontario 48 C1 42 51N 79 23W
Long Cove *tn.* Newfoundland and Labrador 53 J3 47 34N 53 40W
Long Creek Saskatchewan 42 F1 49 20N 103 55W
Long Harbour *tn.* Newfoundland and Labrador 53 J3 47 26N 53 48W
Long Island Nova Scotia 53 L11 44 20N 66 15W
Longlac Ontario 45 H5 49 47N 86 34W
Long Lake New Brunswick 53 B3 47 00N 66 50W
Long Lake Nova Scotia 57 Q6 44 37N 63 37W
Long Lake Ontario 45 H5 49 00N 87 00W
Long Lake *I.R.* Ontario 45 H5 49 45N 86 32W
Long Point Manitoba 43 C3 52 50N 98 20W
Long Point Ontario 48 B1 42 33N 80 04W
Long Point *tn.* Ontario 48 B1 42 34N 80 15W
Long Point Bay Ontario 48 B1 42 40N 80 14W
Long Point Provincial Park Ontario 48 B1 42 40N 80 15W

Long Pond Newfoundland and Labrador	53	H4	48 00N	55 52W
Long Range Mountains Newfoundland and Labrador	53	F3	50 00N	57 00W
Long Sault Ontario	47	M5	45 02N	74 53W
Longueuil Québec	47	N5	45 32N	73 31W
Lookout, Cape Ontario	44	K8	55 18N	83 56W
Loon Lake Nova Scotia	57	Q6	44 42N	63 30W
Loon Lake *tn.* Saskatchewan	42	C4	54 00N	109 10W
Loon River Alberta	41	E5	56 40N	115 20W
L'Original Ontario	47	M5	45 37N	74 42W
Loring Ontario	46	F5	45 56N	80 00W
Lorne Park *tn.* Ontario	48	C2	43 31N	79 36W
Lorraine Québec	56	M5	45 38N	73 47W
Lotbinière *admin.* Québec	47	Q6	46 20N	71 65W
Lougheed Island Nunavut	55	J6	77 26N	105 06W
Louisbourg Nova Scotia	53	N12	45 56N	59 58W
Louisbourg National Historic Site Nova Scotia	53	N12	45 55N	60 00W
Louise Island British Columbia	38	E3	52 59N	131 50W
Louiseville Québec	47	P6	46 16N	72 56W
Lourdes Newfoundland and Labrador	53	F4	48 39N	59 00W
Low, Cape Nunavut	55	N3	63 07N	85 18W
Lower Arrow Lake British Columbia	39	L1	49 40N	118 09W
Lower Foster Lake Saskatchewan	42	E5	56 30N	105 10W
Lower Manitou Lake Ontario	44	E5	49 15N	93 00W
Lower Post British Columbia	39	F6	59 56N	128 09W
Lower Sackville Nova Scotia	53	M11	44 40N	63 40W
Lubicon Lake Alberta	41	E5	56 23N	115 56W
Lucan Ontario	48	A2	43 11N	81 24W
Lucknow Ontario	48	A2	43 58N	81 31W
Lucky Lake *tn.* Saskatchewan	42	D2	50 59N	107 10W
Lulu Island British Columbia	40	F3	49 09N	123 09W
Lumby British Columbia	39	L2	50 15N	118 58W
Lumsden Saskatchewan	42	E2	50 39N	104 52W
Lund British Columbia	38	H4	49 59N	124 46W
Lundar Manitoba	43	C2	50 41N	98 01W
Lunenburg Nova Scotia	53	M11	44 23N	64 21W
Lunenburg *admin.* Nova Scotia	53	M11	44 35N	64 30W
Luseland Saskatchewan	42	C3	52 06N	109 24W
Luther Lake Ontario	48	B2	43 52N	80 26W
Łutselk'e *(Snowdrift)* Northwest Territories	54	H3	62 24N	110 44W
Lyall, Mount Alberta/British Columbia	41	E2	50 05N	114 42W
Lyell Islands British Columbia	38	E3	52 00N	131 00W
Lynn Lake *tn.* Manitoba	43	B5	56 51N	101 01W
Lynx Lake Northwest Territories	54	J3	62 25N	106 15W
Lytton British Columbia	39	K2	50 12N	121 34W

M

Maaset British Columbia	38	D4	54 00N	132 01W
Mabel Lake British Columbia	39	L2	50 35N	118 40W
Mabou Nova Scotia	53	M12	46 04N	61 22W
McAdam New Brunswick	53	B2	45 34N	67 20W
MacAlpine Lake Nunavut	55	K4	66 45N	130 00W
Macamic Québec	51	A3	48 46N	79 02W
McBride British Columbia	39	K3	53 21N	120 19W
McCabe Lake Nova Scotia	57	Q7	44 47N	63 43W
Maccan Nova Scotia	53	M12	45 43N	64 16W
McClintock Manitoba	43	E5	57 50N	94 10W
McConnell River Bird Sanctuary Nunavut	55	M3	60 30N	94 00W
McCreary Manitoba	43	C2	50 45N	99 30W
Macdiarmid Ontario	45	G5	49 23N	88 08W
MacDowell Ontario	44	E7	52 10N	92 40W
MacDowell Lake Ontario	44	E7	52 15N	92 42W
McFarlane River Saskatchewan	42	D5	57 50N	107 55W
McGivney New Brunswick	53	B3	46 22N	66 34W
MacGregor Manitoba	43	C1	49 57N	98 48W
McGregor Lake Alberta	41	F2	50 25N	112 52W
Macgregor Point Provincial Park Ontario	48	A3	44 25N	81 27W
McGregor River British Columbia	39	K4	54 10N	121 20W
McKay Lake Newfoundland and Labrador	52	C6	53 44N	65 37W
Mackay Lake Northwest Territories	54	H3	63 55N	110 25W
McKeller Ontario	46	G5	45 30N	79 00W
Mackenzie British Columbia	39	J4	55 18N	123 10W
Mackenzie Bay Yukon Territory	54	C4	69 00N	137 30W
Mackenzie Bison Sanctuary Northwest Territories	54	G3	61 30N	116 30W
McKenzie Creek Ontario	48	B2	43 02N	80 17W
Mackenzie Highway Alberta	41	D5	57 55N	117 40W
Mackenzie King Island Northwest Territories/Nunavut	54	H6	77 45N	111 00W
Mackenzie Mountains Yukon Territory/Northwest Territories	54	E3	66 00N	132 00W
Mackenzie River Northwest Territories	54	E4	66 20N	125 55W
Mackey Ontario	46	J6	46 10N	77 49W
Macklin Saskatchewan	42	C3	52 20N	109 58W
Maclean Strait Nunavut	55	K6	77 30N	102 30W
McLeese Lake *tn.* British Columbia	39	J3	52 25N	122 20W
McLennan Alberta	41	D4	55 42N	116 54W
McLeod Lake *tn.* British Columbia	39	J4	55 00N	123 00W
McLeod River Alberta	41	E3	53 40N	116 20W
M'Clintock Channel Nunavut	55	K5	72 00N	102 00W
M'Clure, Cape Northwest Territories	54	F4	74 32N	121 19W
M'Clure Strait Northwest Territories	54	G5	74 59N	120 10W
Macmillan Pass Yukon Territory	54	D3	63 25N	130 00W
Macmillan River Yukon Territory	54	D3	63 00N	134 00W
McNabs Island Nova Scotia	57	Q6	44 37N	63 31W
McNutt Island Nova Scotia	53	L11	43 40N	65 20W
Macoun Lake Saskatchewan	42	F5	56 30N	103 40W
Macrae Point Provincial Park Ontario	48	C3	44 30N	79 10W
McTavish Arm *b.* Northwest Territories	54	G4	66 06N	118 04W
MacTier Ontario	46	G5	45 08N	79 47W
McVicar Arm *b.* Northwest Territories	54	F3	65 20N	120 10W
Madawaska Ontario	46	J5	45 30N	77 59W
Madawaska *admin.* New Brunswick	53	A3/B3	47 30N	68 00W
Madawaska River Ontario	45	N3	45 10N	77 30W
Madoc Ontario	47	J4	44 30N	77 29W
Mad River Ontario	48	B3	44 18N	80 02W
Madsen Ontario	44	E6	50 58N	93 55W
Maelpaeg Réservoir Newfoundland and Labrador	53	G4	48 20N	56 40W
Magnetawan Ontario	46	G5	45 40N	79 39W
Magnetawan River Ontario	46	F5	45 46N	80 37W
Magog Québec	47	P5	45 16N	72 09W
Magpie River Ontario	45	J5	48 00N	84 50W
Magrath Alberta	41	F1	49 27N	112 52W
Maguse Lake Nunavut	55	M3	61 40N	95 10W
Mahone Bay Nova Scotia	53	M11	44 25N	64 15W
Mahone Bay *tn.* Nova Scotia	53	M11	44 27N	64 24W
Mahood Creek British Columbia	40	G3	49 09N	122 50W
Maidstone Saskatchewan	42	C3	53 06N	109 18W
Main Brook *tn.* Newfoundland and Labrador	52	G5	51 11N	56 01W
Main Channel Ontario	46	E5	45 00N	82 00W
Maitland River Ontario	48	A2	43 50N	81 28W
Major, Lake Nova Scotia	57	R6	44 45N	63 30W
Makkovik Newfoundland and Labrador	52	F7	55 05N	59 11W
Makoop Lake Ontario	44	F7	53 24N	90 50W
Malartic Québec	51	A3	48 09N	78 09W
Malaspina Strait British Columbia	38	H4	49 47N	124 30W
Mallet River Ontario	48	B2	43 51N	80 42W
Malpeque Bay Prince Edward Island	53	M12	46 35N	63 50W
Malton Ontario	48	C2	43 42N	79 38W
Manicouagan Québec	51	F4	50 40N	68 46W
Manigotagan Manitoba	43	D2	51 00N	96 10W
Manigotagan River Manitoba	43	E2	51 00N	96 10W
Manitoba *province*	43			
Manitoba, Lake Manitoba	43	C2	50 30N	98 15W
Manito Lake Saskatchewan	42	C3	52 40N	109 20W
Manitou Manitoba	43	C1	49 15N	98 32W
Manitou Lake Ontario	46	E5	45 48N	82 00W
Manitoulin *admin.* Ontario	46	C5/D5	45 45N	82 30W
Manitoulin Island Ontario	46	D5	45 50N	82 20W
Manitouwadge Ontario	45	J5	49 10N	85 55W
Maniwaki Québec	47	L6	46 22N	75 58W
Manning Alberta	41	D5	56 55N	117 37W
Manning Provincial Park British Columbia	38	H4	49 09N	120 50W
Manotick Ontario	57	K1	45 14N	75 43W
Mansel Island Nunavut	55	Q3	62 00N	80 00W
Manson Creek *tn.* British Columbia	39	H4	55 40N	124 32W
Maple Ontario	48	C2	43 50N	79 30W
Maple Creek *tn.* Saskatchewan	42	B1	49 55N	109 28W
Maple Ridge British Columbia	38	H4	49 13N	122 36W
Mara Provincial Park Ontario	48	C3	44 30N	79 15W
Marathon Ontario	45	H5	48 44N	86 23W
Margaree Forks Nova Scotia	53	M12	46 20N	61 10W
Margaree Harbour *tn.* Nova Scotia	53	M12	46 26N	61 08W
Margaret Lake Alberta	41	E6	58 56N	115 25W
Margaretville Nova Scotia	53	L12	45 05N	65 05W
Marieville Québec	47	N5	45 27N	73 08W
Markdale Ontario	48	B3	44 19N	80 39W
Markham Ontario	48	C2	43 53N	79 14W
Markham Bay Nunavut	55	R3	63 02N	72 00W
Marmora Ontario	46	J4	44 29N	77 41W
Marten Falls *I.R.* Ontario	44	J6	51 40N	85 55W
Martensville Saskatchewan	42	D3	52 10N	106 30W
Mary's Harbour *tn.* Newfoundland and Labrador	52	H6	52 19N	55 50W
Marystown Newfoundland and Labrador	53	H3	47 10N	55 09W
Marysville New Brunswick	53	B2	45 58N	66 35W
Mascouche Québec	47	N5	45 47N	73 49W
Maskinongé *admin.* Québec	47	M7	47 40N	74 50W
Massasauga Provincial Park Ontario	46	F5	45 12N	80 02W
Massey Ontario	46	D6	46 12N	82 05W
Massey Sound Nunavut	55	L6	78 00N	95 00W
Matachewan Ontario	45	L4	47 56N	80 39W
Matagami Québec	51	B3	49 40N	77 40W
Matane Québec	51	G3	48 50N	67 31W
Matapédia Québec	51	G2	47 59N	66 58W
Matheson Ontario	45	L5	48 32N	80 28W
Matsqui British Columbia	38	H4	49 05N	122 22W
Mattagami Lake Ontario	45	L4	47 54N	81 35W
Mattagami River Ontario	45	L5	49 00N	81 50W
Mattawa Ontario	46	H6	46 19N	78 42W
Mattice Ontario	45	K5	49 36N	83 16W
Maurelle Island British Columbia	38	G5	50 16N	125 11W
Mayerthorpe Alberta	41	E3	53 57N	115 08W
Mayne Island British Columbia	38	H4	48 50N	123 18W
Maynooth Ontario	46	J5	45 14N	77 57W
Mayo Yukon Territory	54	C3	63 34N	135 52W
Mayo Lake Yukon Territory	54	C3	135 00N	63 50W
Mayson Lake Saskatchewan	42	D5	57 50N	107 30W
Meadow Lake *tn.* Saskatchewan	42	C4	54 09N	108 26W
Meadow Lake Provincial Park Saskatchewan	42	C4	54 30N	108 00W
Meadowvale West Ontario	48	C2	43 35N	79 45W
Meaford Ontario	48	B3	44 36N	80 35W
Meaghers Grant Nova Scotia	53	M11	44 57N	63 15W
Mealy Mountains Newfoundland and Labrador	52	F6	53 10N	60 00W
Meander River *tn.* Alberta	41	D6	59 02N	117 42W
Meath Park *tn.* Saskatchewan	42	E3	53 27N	105 22W
Medicine Hat Alberta	41	G2	50 03N	110 41W
Medley Alberta	41	G4	54 25N	110 16W
Meductic New Brunswick	53	B2	45 55N	67 30W
Medway Creek Ontario	48	A2	43 07N	81 18W
Medway River Nova Scotia	53	M11	44 15N	64 50W
Mégantic *admin.* Québec	47	Q6	46 10N	71 40W
Meighen Island Nunavut	55	L7	80 00N	99 30W
Melbourne Island Nunavut	54	J4	68 30N	104 45W
Meldrum Bay *tn.* Ontario	46	C5	45 56N	83 06W
Melfort Saskatchewan	42	E3	52 52N	104 38W
Melita Manitoba	43	B1	49 16N	101 00W
Melville Saskatchewan	42	F2	50 57N	102 49W
Melville Hills Northwest Territories/Nunavut	54	F4	69 00N	121 00W
Melville Island Northwest Territories/Nunavut	54	H6	75 30N	112 00W
Melville, Lake Newfoundland and Labrador	52	F6	53 45N	59 00W
Melville Peninsula Nunavut	55	P4	68 00N	84 00W
Melville Sound Nunavut	54	J4	68 05N	107 30W
Melville Sound Ontario	48	A3	43 00N	81 04W
Menihek Lakes Newfoundland and Labrador	52	B6	53 50N	66 50W
Menihek Siding Newfoundland and Labrador	52	B7	54 28N	66 36W
Mercier Québec	47	N5	45 20N	73 45W
Mercy Bay Northwest Territories	54	G5	74 05N	119 00W
Merigomish Nova Scotia	53	M12	45 37N	62 25W
Merrickville Ontario	47	L4	44 55N	75 50W
Merritt British Columbia	39	K2	50 09N	120 49W
Mersey River Nova Scotia	53	M11	44 10N	65 00W
Metabetchouane Québec	47	Q8	48 26N	71 52W
Meta Incognita Peninsula Nunavut	55	S3	63 30N	70 00W
Metcalfe Ontario	57	L1	45 14N	75 29W
Metchosin British Columbia	38	H4	48 22N	123 32W
Meteghan Nova Scotia	53	L11	44 12N	66 10W
Meziadin Junction British Columbia	39	F5	56 10N	129 15W
Mica Creek *tn.* British Columbia	39	L3	52 00N	118 28W
Mica Dam British Columbia	39	L3	52 04N	118 28W
Michaud Point Nova Scotia	53	M12	45 35N	60 40W
Michel Peak British Columbia	39	G3	53 30N	126 25W
Michikamats Lake Newfoundland and Labrador	52	C7	54 38N	64 19W
Michikamau Lake Newfoundland and Labrador	52	D6	54 00N	64 00W
Michipicoten Island Ontario	45	J4	47 45N	85 45W
Michipicoten River *tn.* Ontario	45	J4	47 56N	84 52W
Micmac, Lake Nova Scotia	57	Q6	44 41N	63 32W
Midale Saskatchewan	42	F1	49 23N	103 21W
Middle Arm Newfoundland and Labrador	53	G4	49 42N	56 06W
Middle Maitland River Ontario	48	A2	43 43N	81 11W
Middle Ridge Newfoundland and Labrador	53	H4	48 20N	55 15W
Middle Ridge Wildlife Reserve Newfoundland and Labrador	53	H4	48 30N	55 15W
Middle Sackville Nova Scotia	53	M11	44 47N	63 41W
Middlesex *admin.* Ontario	48	A2	42 46N	81 46W
Middleton Nova Scotia	53	L11	44 56N	65 04W
Midhurst Ontario	48	C3	44 26N	79 45W
Midland Ontario	46	G4	44 45N	79 53W
Midnapore Alberta	40	A1	50 55N	114 05W
Midway British Columbia	39	L1	49 02N	118 45W
Midway Mountains British Columbia	39	L1	49 25N	118 45W
Mikkwa River Alberta	41	E5	57 40N	114 08W
Mildmay Ontario	48	A3	44 03N	81 08W
Milestone Saskatchewan	42	E1	49 59N	104 31W
Milk River Alberta	41	G1	49 10N	110 05W
Milk River *tn.* Alberta	41	F1	49 09N	112 05W
Millbrook Ontario	46	H4	44 09N	78 28W
Miller Lake Nova Scotia	57	Q7	44 49N	63 35W
Millet Alberta	41	F3	53 06N	113 28W
Mill Island Nunavut	55	Q3	64 00N	78 00W
Milltown Newfoundland and Labrador	53	H3	47 54N	55 46W
Mill Village Nova Scotia	53	M11	44 10N	64 40W
Millville New Brunswick	53	B3	46 08N	67 12W
Milo Alberta	41	F2	50 34N	112 53W
Milton Nova Scotia	53	M11	44 04N	64 44W
Milton Ontario	48	C2	43 31N	79 53W
Milton Prince Edward Island	53	M12	46 20N	63 10W
Milverton Ontario	48	B2	43 34N	80 55W
Miminegash Prince Edward Island	53	M12	46 54N	64 15W
Minaki Ontario	44	D5	50 00N	94 40W
Minas Basin Nova Scotia	53	M12	45 15N	64 15W
Minas Channel Nova Scotia	53	M12	45 10N	64 50W
Minden Ontario	46	H4	44 56N	78 44W
Minipi Lake Newfoundland and Labrador	52	E6	52 25N	60 45W
Miniss Lake Ontario	44	F6	50 48N	90 50W
Minitonas Manitoba	43	B3	52 04N	101 02W
Minnedosa Manitoba	43	C2	50 14N	99 50W
Minnitaki Lake Ontario	44	F5	49 58N	92 00W
Minonipi Lake Newfoundland and Labrador	52	E6	52 50N	60 50W
Minto New Brunswick	53	B3	46 05N	66 05W
Minto Yukon Territory	54	C3	62 34N	136 50W
Minto Inlet Northwest Territories	54	G5	71 20N	117 00W
Mira Bay Nova Scotia	53	N12	46 05N	59 50W
Mirabel Québec	47	M5	45 41N	74 20W
Miramichi New Brunswick	53	C3	46 55N	65 35W
Miramichi Bay New Brunswick	53	C3	47 05N	65 00W
Mira River Nova Scotia	53	M12	46 00N	60 10W
Miscouche Prince Edward Island	53	M12	46 26N	63 52W
Miscou Island New Brunswick	53	C3	47 50N	64 30W
Misery Point Newfoundland and Labrador	52	H6	52 01N	55 18W
Missanabie Ontario	45	J5	48 19N	84 05W
Missinaibi Lake Ontario	45	K5	48 23N	83 40W
Missinaibi River Ontario	45	K5	49 30N	83 20W
Missinaibi River Provincial Park Ontario	45	K6	50 00N	83 15W
Mission British Columbia	38	H4	49 08N	122 20W
Missisa Lake Ontario	44	J7	52 18N	85 12W
Mississagi River Ontario	45	K4	46 10N	83 01W
Mississagi River Provincial Park Ontario	45	K4	47 10N	82 35W
Mississauga Ontario	48	C2	43 38N	79 36W
Missouri Coteau *hills* Saskatchewan	42	D2	50 40N	106 30W
Mistassini Québec	51	D3	48 54N	72 13W
Mistastin Lake Newfoundland and Labrador	52	D7	55 50N	63 00W
Mistissini Québec	51	D4	50 25N	73 50W
Mitchell Ontario	48	A2	43 27N	81 13W
Mitchells Brook *tn.* Newfoundland and Labrador	53	J3	47 08N	53 31W
Mobert *I.R.* Ontario	45	J5	48 40N	85 40W
Moisie Québec	51	G4	50 12N	66 06W
Molson Lake Manitoba	43	D4	54 20N	96 50W
Monarch Mountain British Columbia	39	H2	51 55N	125 57W
Monashee Mountains British Columbia	39	L2	51 30N	118 50W
Moncton New Brunswick	53	M12	46 04N	64 50W
Monkman Pass British Columbia	39	K4	54 30N	121 10W
Monkman Provincial Park British Columbia	39	K4	54 00N	121 10W
Mono Cliffs Provincial Park Ontario	48	B3	44 02N	80 03W
Mono Mills Ontario	48	C2	43 55N	79 57W
Montague Prince Edward Island	53	M12	46 10N	62 39W
Montcalm *admin.* Québec	47	L7	47 40N	76 15W
Mont D'Iberville *mt.* Québec/Newfoundland	52	D9	58 50N	64 40W
Mont Jacques-Cartier *mt.* Québec	51	H3	49 00N	66 00W
Mont-Joli *tn.* Québec	51	F3	48 36N	68 14W
Mont-Laurier *tn.* Québec	47	L6	46 33N	75 31W
Montmagny Québec	47	R6	46 58N	70 34W
Montmagny *admin.* Québec	47	R6	46 50N	70 20W
Montmorency *admin.* Québec	47	Q7	47 34N	71 20W
Montréal Québec	47	N5	45 32N	73 36W
Montreal Lake Saskatchewan	42	E4	54 15N	105 30W
Montreal Lake *tn.* Saskatchewan	42	E4	54 03N	105 49W
Montreal River Ontario	45	J4	47 20N	84 20W
Montreal River Saskatchewan	42	E4	54 50N	105 30W
Montreal River *tn.* Ontario	45	J4	47 14N	84 39W
Montrose British Columbia	39	M1	49 06N	117 30W
Monts Chic-Chocs *mts.* Québec	51	G3	49 00N	66 40W
Monts Notre Dame *mts.* Québec	51	F3	48 00N	69 00W
Monts Otish *mts.* Québec	51	E5	52 30N	70 20W
Monts Povungnituk *mts.* Québec	50	C9	61 30N	75 59W
Monts Torngat *mts.* Québec/Newfoundland	50	H8	59 00N	64 15W
Moose Creek Provincial Forest Manitoba	43	D2	51 30N	96 45W
Moose Factory Ontario	45	L6	51 16N	80 37W
Moose Jaw Saskatchewan	42	E2	50 23N	105 35W
Moosejaw River Saskatchewan	42	E2	50 15N	105 10W
Moose Lake *tn.* Manitoba	43	B3	53 43N	100 20W
Moose Mountain Creek Saskatchewan	42	F2	50 15N	103 25W
Moose Mountain Provincial Park Saskatchewan	42	F1	49 50N	102 20W
Moose River *tn.* Ontario	45	L6	50 48N	81 18W
Moosomin Saskatchewan	42	G2	50 09N	101 41W
Moosonee Ontario	45	L6	51 18N	80 39W
Morden Manitoba	43	C1	49 12N	98 05W
Morell Prince Edward Island	53	M12	46 25N	62 42W
Moresby Camp British Columbia	38	D3	53 05N	132 04W
Moresby Island British Columbia	38	D3	53 00N	132 00W

Morice Lake British Columbia 39 G3/G4 53 55N 127 30W
Moricetown British Columbia 39 G4 55 02N 127 20W
Morinville Alberta 41 F3 53 48N 113 39W
Morris Manitoba 43 D1 49 22N 97 21W
Morrisburg Ontario 47 L4 44 54N 75 11W
Morse Saskatchewan 42 D2 50 24N 107 00W
Morson Ontario 44 D5 49 03N 94 19W
Moser River *tn.* Nova Scotia 53 M11 44 58N 62 18W
Mostoos Hills Saskatchewan 42 C4 55 20N 109 30W
Mould Bay *m.s.* Northwest Territories 54 G6 76 14N 119 20W
Mountain Lake Ontario 48 A3 44 42N 81 02W
Mount Albert *tn.* Ontario 48 C3 44 07N 79 18W
Mount Burke British Columbia 40 H4 49 18N 122 42W
Mount Carleton Provincial Park New Brunswick 53 B3 47 20N 66 30W
Mount Edziza Provincial Park British Columbia 38 E5 57 40N 131 40W
Mount Forest *tn.* Ontario 48 B2 43 58N 80 44W
Mount Hope *tn.* Ontario 48 C2 43 09N 79 54W
Mount Pearl *tn.* Newfoundland and Labrador 53 J3 47 31N 52 47W
Mount Revelstoke National Park British Columbia 39 L2/M2 50 40N 118 00W
Mount Robson Provincial Park British Columbia 39 L3 52 50N 118 40W
Mount Brydges *tn.* Ontario 48 A1 42 54N 81 30W
Mount Seymour Provincial Park British Columbia 38 G4 49 22N 122 56W
Mount Stewart *tn.* Prince Edward Island 53 M12 46 22N 62 52W
Mount Uniacke *tn.* Nova Scotia 53 M11 44 54N 63 50W
Mud Bay British Columbia 40 G3 49 04N 122 53W
Mudjatik River Saskatchewan 42 D5 56 40N 107 10W
Mud Lake *tn.* Newfoundland and Labrador 52 E6 53 19N 60 10W
Mukutawa River Manitoba 43 D3 53 10N 97 10W
Mulgrave Nova Scotia 53 M12 45 36N 61 25W
Muncho Lake British Columbia 39 H6 59 05N 125 47W
Muncho Lake *tn.* British Columbia 39 H6 59 00N 125 46W
Muncho Lake Provincial Park British Columbia 39 H6 58 50N 125 40W
Mundare Alberta 41 F3 53 36N 112 20W
Murdochville Québec 51 H3 48 57N 65 30W
Murray Harbour *tn.* Prince Edward Island 53 M12 46 00N 62 32W
Murray River *tn.* Prince Edward Island 53 M12 46 00N 62 38W
Murtle Lake British Columbia 39 L3 52 09N 119 40W
Musgrave Harbour Newfoundland and Labrador 53 J4 49 27N 53 58W
Musgravetown Newfoundland and Labrador 53 J4 48 24N 53 53W
Muskoka Falls *tn.* Ontario 46 G4 44 59N 79 16W
Musktrat Dam Lake Ontario 44 F7 53 25N 91 40W
Muskwa River British Columbia 39 J6 58 30N 123 20W
Musquodoboit Harbour Nova Scotia 53 M11 44 48N 63 10W
Muzon, Cape British Columbia 38 D4 54 41N 132 40W
Myles Bay Ontario 48 A3 44 56N 81 23W
Myrnam Alberta 41 G3 53 40N 111 14W

N

Nachvak Fiord *in.* Newfoundland and Labrador 52 D9 59 03N 63 45W
Nackawic New Brunswick 53 B2 46 00N 67 15W
Nagagami Lake Ontario 45 J5 49 25N 85 01W
Nagagami River Ontario 45 J5 49 30N 84 50W
Nahanni Butte *(Tthenáágóo) tn.* Northwest Territories 54 F3 61 30N 123 20W
Nahanni National Park Reserve Northwest Territories 54 E3 61 30N 126 00W
Nahatlatch River British Columbia 38 H4 49 55N 121 59W
Nahlin River British Columbia 38 E6 58 58N 131 30W
Naicam Saskatchewan 42 E3 52 26N 104 31W
Naikoon Provincial Park British Columbia 38 E3 53 59N 131 35W
Nain Newfoundland and Labrador 52 E8 56 32N 61 41W
Nakina Ontario 44 H6 50 11N 86 43W
Nakina River British Columbia 38 D6 59 07N 132 59W
Nakusp British Columbia 39 M2 50 15N 117 45W
Nanaimo British Columbia 38 H4 49 08N 123 58W
Nanaimo River British Columbia 38 H4 49 08N 123 54W
Nanisivik Nunavut 55 P5 73 00N 79 58W
Nansen Sound Nunavut 55 M7 81 00N 90 35W
Nanticoke Ontario 48 B1 42 48N 80 04W
Nanticoke Creek Ontario 48 B1 42 56N 80 16W
Nanton Alberta 41 F2 50 21N 113 46W
Napaktokh (Black Duck) Bay Newfoundland and Labrador 52 D9 58 01N 62 19W
Napaktulik Lake Nunavut 54 H4 66 30N 112 50W
Napanee Ontario 47 K4 44 15N 76 57W
Nares Strait 55 R6 78 30N 72 30W
Narrow Hills Provincial Park Saskatchewan 42 E4 54 10N 103 30W
Narrows, The *sd.* Nova Scotia 57 Q6 44 40N 63 35W
Naskaupi River Newfoundland and Labrador 52 D7 54 20N 62 40W
Nass River British Columbia 38 F4 55 10N 129 20W
Nastapoka Islands Nunavut 50 B7 56 50N 76 50W
Natashquan Québec 51 K4 50 10N 61 50W
Natashquan River Newfoundland and Labrador 52 D6 52 30N 62 50W
Nation Lakes British Columbia 39 H4 55 08N 125 15W
Nation River British Columbia 39 H4 55 11N 124 25W
Natuashish Newfoundland and Labrador 52 E7 55 51N 62 04W
Nauwigewauk New Brunswick 53 L12 45 28W 65 53W
Nazko British Columbia 39 J3 53 00N 123 37W
Nechako Plateau British Columbia 39 H4/J4 54 40N 124 40W
Nechako River British Columbia 39 H3 53 35N 124 50W
Neeb Saskatchewan 42 D4 54 00N 107 50W
Neepawa Manitoba 43 C2 50 14N 99 29W
Neguac New Brunswick 53 C3 47 14N 65 03W
Nejanilini Lake Manitoba 43 D6 59 50N 97 20W
Nelson British Columbia 39 M1 49 29N 117 17W
Nelson Forks *tn.* British Columbia 39 H6 59 30N 124 00W
Nelson House *tn.* Manitoba 43 C4 55 49N 98 51W
Nelson Island British Columbia 38 H4 49 43N 124 03W
Nelson River Manitoba 43 F5 56 50N 93 40W
Némiscau Québec 51 B4 51 20N 77 01W
Nepean Ontario 47 L5 45 16N 75 48W
Nepewassi Lake Ontario 46 F6 46 22N 80 38W
Nepisiguit River New Brunswick 53 B3 47 20N 66 30W
Nesselrode, Mount British Columbia 38 C6 58 55N 134 20W
Nestor Falls *tn.* Ontario 44 E5 49 05N 93 55W
Nettilling Lake Nunavut 55 R4 66 30N 71 10W
Neustadt Ontario 48 A3 44 04N 81 00W
New Aiyansh British Columbia 39 F4 55 15N 129 02W
Newboro' Ontario 47 K4 44 39N 76 19W
New Brunswick *province* 53 B3/C3
Newburgh Ontario 47 K4 44 19N 76 52W
New Carlisle Québec 51 H3 48 00N 65 22W
New Denver British Columbia 39 M1 49 59N 117 22W
Newell, Lake Alberta 41 G2 50 26N 111 55W
Newfoundland *i.* Newfoundland and Labrador 53 G4 53 51N 56 56W
Newfoundland and Labrador *province* 52/53
New Germany Nova Scotia 53 M11 44 34N 64 44W
New Glasgow Nova Scotia 53 M12 45 36N 62 38W
New Hazelton British Columbia 39 G4 55 15N 127 30W
New Liskeard Ontario 45 M4 47 31N 79 41W
Newmarket Ontario 48 C3 44 03N 79 27W
New Minas Nova Scotia 53 M12 45 00N 64 30W
New Osnaburgh Ontario 44 F6 51 16N 90 15W
New Richmond Québec 51 H3 48 12N 65 52W
New Ross Nova Scotia 53 M11 44 44N 64 27W
Newton British Columbia 40 G3 49 07N 122 50W
Newtown Newfoundland and Labrador 53 J4 49 12N 53 31W
New Waterford Nova Scotia 53 M12 46 17N 60 05W
New Westminster British Columbia 38 H4 49 10N 122 58W
Niagara *admin.* Ontario 48 C2 43 02N 79 34W
Niagara Escarpment Ontario 48 B3 44 30N 80 45W
Niagara Falls *tn.* Ontario 48 C2 43 05N 79 06W
Niagara-on-the-Lake Ontario 48 C2 43 14N 79 16W
Nicolet Québec 47 P6 46 14N 72 36W
Nicolet *admin.* Québec 47 P6 46 00N 72 30W
Nicomekl *r.* British Columbia 40 H3 49 05N 122 43W
Nictau New Brunswick 53 B3 47 16N 67 11W
Night Hawk Lake Ontario 45 L5 48 28N 80 58W
Nipawin Saskatchewan 42 E3 53 23N 104 01W
Nipigon Ontario 45 G5 49 02N 88 26W
Nipigon Bay Ontario 45 G5 48 50N 88 10W
Nipigon, Lake Ontario 44 G5 49 50N 88 30W
Nipishish Lake Newfoundland and Labrador 52 E7 54 10N 60 30W
Nipissing Ontario 46 G6 46 05N 79 31W
Nipissing *admin.* Ontario 46 G6/H6 46 00N 79 00W
Nipissing, Lake Ontario 46 G6 46 17N 80 00W
Nirjutiqavvik National Wildlife Area Nunavut 55 Q6 76 00N 79 55W
Nisgara Memorial Lava Bed Park British Columbia 39 F4 55 15N 128 55W
Nisling Range *mts.* Yukon Territory 54 C3 62 00N 138 40W
Nitchequon Québec 51 E5 53 10N 70 58W
Nith River Ontario 48 B2 43 12N 80 22W
Nitinat Lake British Columbia 38 H4 48 45N 124 42W
Nitinat River British Columbia 38 H4 49 06N 124 35W
Niverville Manitoba 43 D1 49 39N 97 03W
Nobleton Ontario 48 C2 43 53N 79 39W
Nokomis Saskatchewan 42 E2 51 30N 105 00W
Nokomis Lake Saskatchewan 42 F5 56 55N 103 00W
Nootka Island British Columbia 39 G1 49 45N 126 50W
Nootka Sound British Columbia 39 G1 49 34N 126 39W
Nopiming Provincial Park Manitoba 43 E2 50 40N 95 10W
Noralee British Columbia 39 G3 53 59N 126 26W
Norman Bay *tn.* Newfoundland and Labrador 52 G6 52 55N 56 10W
Norman, Cape Newfoundland and Labrador 52 H5 51 38N 55 54W
Normandale Ontario 48 B1 42 41N 80 19W
Normansland Point Ontario 44 L7 52 00N 81 00W
Norman Wells *(Tłegǫ́hłı̨) tn.* Northwest Territories 54 E4 65 19N 126 46W
Normétal Québec 51 A3 48 59N 79 53W
Norquay Saskatchewan 42 F2 51 52N 102 00W
Norris Arm *tn.* Newfoundland and Labrador 53 H4 49 05N 55 15W
Norris Point *tn.* Newfoundland and Labrador 53 G4 49 31N 57 53W
North Arm *b.* Northwest Territories 54 G3 62 05N 114 40W
North Arm *r.* British Columbia 40 F3 49 12N 123 05W
North Aulatsivik Island Newfoundland and Labrador 52 C9 59 46N 64 05W
North Baffin National Park Nunavut 55 P5 73 30N 82 30W
North Battleford Saskatchewan 42 C3 52 47N 108 19W
North Bay *tn.* Ontario 46 G6 46 20N 79 28W
North, Cape Nova Scotia 53 M12 47 10N 60 00W
North Cape Prince Edward Island 53 M12 47 10N 64 00W
North Caribou Lake Ontario 44 F7 52 50N 90 40W
North Castor *r.* Ontario 57 K2 45 18N 75 31W
North Channel Ontario 46 C6/D6 46 00N 83 00W
Northern Indian Lake Manitoba 43 D5 57 30N 97 30W
Northern Peninsula Newfoundland and Labrador 52 G5 50 30N 57 00W
Northern Rocky Mountains Provincial Park British Columbia 39 H6 58 00N 124 00W
Northern Woods and Water Route Canada 42 D4 54 10N 107 20W
North French River Ontario 45 L6 50 20N 81 00W
North Head *tn.* New Brunswick 53 L11 44 46N 66 45W
North Kent Island Nunavut 55 M6 76 40N 90 14W
North Knife Lake Manitoba 43 D6 58 10N 96 40W
North Knife River Manitoba 43 E6 58 40N 95 50W
North Moose Lake Manitoba 43 B4 54 00N 100 10W
North Pender Island British Columbia 38 H4 48 49N 123 17W
North River Newfoundland and Labrador 52 D8 57 30N 63 20W
North River *tn.* Manitoba 43 E6 58 55N 94 30W
North River *tn.* Newfoundland and Labrador 52 F7 53 49N 57 05W
North River Bridge *tn.* Nova Scotia 53 M12 46 19N 60 40W
North Rustico Prince Edward Island 53 M12 46 26N 63 20W
North Saskatchewan River Alberta/Saskatchewan 42 D3 52 40N 106 40W
North Saugeen River Ontario 48 A3 44 18N 81 10W
North Seal River Manitoba 43 B6 59 00N 100 30W
North Spirit Lake Ontario 44 E7 52 31N 92 55W
North Spirit Lake *tn.* Ontario 44 E7 52 31N 93 01W
North Sydney Nova Scotia 53 M12 46 13N 60 15W
North Thames River Ontario 48 A2 43 02N 81 14W
North Thompson River British Columbia 39 L2 51 32N 120 00W
North Tweedsmuir Provincial Park British Columbia 39 G3 53 30N 126 30W
North Twin Island Northwest Territories 44 M7 53 20N 80 00W
Northumberland *admin.* New Brunswick 53 B3 47 10N 66 30W
Northumberland Strait Atlantic Provinces 53 M12 46 30N 64 30W
North Vancouver British Columbia 38 H4 49 21N 123 05W
North Wabasca Lake Alberta 41 F5 56 10N 113 55W
Northwest Angle Provincial Park Manitoba 43 E1 49 20N 95 30W
Northwest Bay *tn.* Ontario 44 E5 48 50N 93 38W
Northwest Gander River Newfoundland and Labrador 53 H4 48 30N 55 40W
North West River *tn.* Newfoundland and Labrador 52 E6 53 32N 60 08W
Northwest Territories *territory* 54
North York *bor.* Metropolitan Toronto Ontario 49 C2 43 46N 79 26W
Norton New Brunswick 53 L12 45 38N 65 43W
Norway House *tn.* Manitoba 43 D3 53 59N 97 50W
Norwich Ontario 48 B1 42 59N 80 36W
Nose Creek Alberta 40 A2 51 08N 114 02W
Nose Hill Alberta 40 A2 51 06N 114 07W
Notekwin River Alberta 41 C5 56 55N 118 20W
Notre Dame Bay Newfoundland and Labrador 53 H4 49 45N 55 00W
Notre-Dame-des-Champs Ontario 57 L2 45 25N 75 28W
Nottawasaga Bay Ontario 48 B3 44 40N 80 30W
Nottawasaga River Ontario 48 C3 43 27N 79 53W
Nottingham Island Nunavut 55 Q3 63 05N 7800W
Nova Scotia *province* 53 C1/E3
Nueltin Lake Manitoba/Nunavut 43 C6 60 00N 99 55W
Numaykoos Lake Provincial Park Manitoba 43 D5 57 55N 96 00W
Nunaksaluk Island Newfoundland and Labrador 52 E7 55 49N 60 20W
Nunavut *territory* 54/55
Nutak Newfoundland and Labrador 52 E8 57 28N 61 52W
Nut Mountain Saskatchewan 42 F3 52 20N 102 50W
Nut Mountain *tn.* Saskatchewan 42 F3 52 08N 103 21W

O

Oakbank Manitoba 43 D1 49 57N 96 54W
Oak Bay British Columbia 38 H4 48 27N 123 18W
Oak Island Nova Scotia 53 M11 44 30N 63 55W
Oak Lake *tn.* Manitoba 43 B1 49 40N 100 45W
Oak Ridges Ontario 48 C2 44 55N 79 27W
Oakville Manitoba 43 C1 49 56N 98 00W
Oakville Ontario 48 C2 43 27N 79 41W
Oakwood Ontario 48 D3 44 20N 78 52W
Obabika River Provincial Park Ontario 45 L4 47 00N 80 30W
Oban Saskatchewan 42 C3 52 09N 108 09W
Obaska Québec 47 J8 48 12N 77 20W
Observatory Inlet British Columbia 38 F4 55 05N 129 59W
Ocean Falls *tn.* British Columbia 39 G3 52 24N 127 42W
Odei River Manitoba 43 C4 55 50N 98 00W
Ogden Alberta 40 A1 50 59N 114 00W
Ogidaki Mountain Ontario 45 K4 46 57N 83 59W
Ogilvie Mountains Yukon Territory 54 C4 65 05N 139 00W
Ogoki Ontario 44 J6 51 38N 85 57W
Ogoki Lake Ontario 44 H6 50 50N 87 10W
Ogoki Reservoir Ontario 44 G6 50 48N 88 18W
Ogoki River Ontario 44 H6 51 10N 86 30W
Oil Springs *tn.* Ontario 46 D2 42 47N 82 07W
Okak Bay Newfoundland and Labrador 52 D8 57 28N 62 20W
Okak Islands Newfoundland and Labrador 52 E8 57 30N 61 50W
Okanagan Lake British Columbia 39 L2 49 45N 119 32W
Okotoks Alberta 41 F2 50 44N 113 59W
Old Crow Yukon Territory 54 C4 67 34N 139 43W
Old Crow River Yukon Territory 54 C4 68 00N 140 00W
Oldman River Alberta 41 G1 49 50N 112 00W
Old Perlican Newfoundland and Labrador 53 J4 48 05N 53 01W
Olds Alberta 41 E2 51 50N 114 06W
Old Wives Lake Saskatchewan 42 D2 50 15N 106 40W
O'Leary Prince Edward Island 53 M12 46 43N 64 15W
Oliphant Ontario 48 A3 44 44N 81 16W
Oliver British Columbia 39 L1 49 10N 119 37W
Omemee Ontario 46 H4 44 19N 78 33W
Omineca Mountains British Columbia 39 G5/H4 57 15N 127 50W
Omineca River British Columbia 39 H4 56 02N 126 00W
Onaman Lake Ontario 44 H6 50 00N 87 26W
Onaping Lake Ontario 45 L4 46 57N 81 30W
Ontario *province* 44
Ontario, Lake Ontario/USA 46/47 H3/K3
Ootsa Lake British Columbia 39 G3 53 40N 126 30W
Ootsa Lake *tn.* British Columbia 39 H3 53 42N 125 56W
Opasatika Ontario 45 K5 49 32N 82 52W
Opasquia Provincial Park Ontario 44 E7 53 30N 93 10W
Opeongo Lake Ontario 45 M3 45 42N 78 23W
Opinnagau River Ontario 44 K8 54 20N 83 50W
Orangeville Ontario 48 B2 43 55N 80 06W
Orillia Ontario 48 C3 44 36N 79 26W
Orleans Ontario 57 K2 45 28N 75 34W
Ormatown Québec 47 M5 45 08N 74 02W
Oromocto New Brunswick 53 B2 45 50N 66 28W
Orono Ontario 48 D2 43 59N 78 36W
Oshawa Ontario 48 D2 43 53N 78 51W
Oskélanéo Québec 47 L8 48 07N 75 14W
Osoyoos British Columbia 39 L1 49 00N 119 29W
Ospika River British Columbia 39 J5 56 55N 124 10W
Ossokmanuan Reservoir Newfoundland and Labrador 52 C6 53 25N 65 00W
Otoskwin-Attawapiskat Provincial Park Ontario 44 G6 52 15N 88 00W
Otoskwin River Ontario 44 G6 51 50N 89 40W
Ottawa Ontario 47 L5 45 24N 75 38W
Ottawa-Carleton *admin.* Ontario 47 L5 45 31N 75 22W
Ottawa Islands Nunavut 55 P2 59 10N 80 25W
Ottawa River Ontario/Québec 47 K5 45 34N 76 30W
Otter Lake Saskatchewan 42 E4 55 35N 104 30W
Otter Rapids *tn.* Ontario 45 L6 50 12N 81 40W
Outer Harbour East Headland Ontario 49 C1 43 38N 79 19W
Outlook Saskatchewan 42 D2 51 30N 107 03W
Owen Sound Ontario 48 B3 44 38N 80 56W
Owen Sound *tn.* Ontario 48 B3 44 34N 80 56W
Owl River Manitoba 43 F5 57 50N 93 20W
Oxbow Saskatchewan 42 F1 49 16N 102 12W
Oxford Nova Scotia 53 M12 45 43N 63 52W
Oxford *admin.* Ontario 48 B2 43 06N 80 59W
Oxford House *tn.* Manitoba 43 E4 54 58N 95 17W
Oxford Lake Manitoba 43 E4 54 40N 95 50W
Oyen Alberta 41 G2 51 22N 110 28W
Oyster River British Columbia 38 G4 49 50N 125 42W
Ozhiski Lake Ontario 44 G7 52 01N 88 30W

P

Pacific Rim National Park British Columbia 38 G4 48 52N 125 35W
Packs Harbour *tn.* Newfoundland and Labrador 52 G6 53 51N 56 59W
Pacquet Newfoundland and Labrador 53 H4 49 59N 55 53W

Paddle Prairie *tn.* Alberta 41 D5 57 57N 117 29W
Paint Lake Provincial Park Manitoba 43 D4 55 30N 97 40W
Paisley Ontario 48 A3 44 17N 81 16W
Pakashkan Lake Ontario 44 F5 49 21N 90 15W
Pakowki Lake Alberta 41 G1 49 20N 111 55W
Pakwash Lake Ontario 44 E6 50 45N 93 30W
Palmerston Ontario 48 B2 43 50N 80 50W
Panache Lake Ontario 46 E6 46 15N 81 20W
Pangnirtung *(Panniqtuuq)* Nunavut 55 S4 66 05N 65 45W
Panmure Island Prince Edward Island 53 M12 46 10N 62 30W
Papineau *admin.* Québec 47 L5 45 40N 75 30W
Paradise Hill *tn.* Saskatchewan 42 C3 53 32N 109 26W
Paradise River Newfoundland and Labrador 52 G6 52 50N 57 50W
Paradise River *tn.* Newfoundland and Labrador 52 G6 53 27N 57 17W
Parc de Conservation d'Aiguebelle Québec 51 A3 48 30N 78 50W
Parc de Conservation de la Jacques-Cartier Québec 47 Q7 47 23N 71 30W
Parc de Conservation des Grands-Jardins Québec 47 R7 47 47N 70 59W
Parc de Conservation de la Gaspésie Québec 51 G3 48 52N 65 57W
Parc de Conservation du Saguenay Québec 47 R8 48 15N 70 45W
Parc de la Gatineau Québec 47 K5 45 31N 75 53W
Parc de Récréation de Frontenac Québec 47 Q5 45 52N 71 17W
Parc de Récréation des Îles-de-Boucherville Québec 56 P5 45 36N 73 27W
Parc de Récréation du Mont-Tremblant Québec 47 M6 46 20N 74 43W
Parc National de Forillon Québec 51 H3 49 00N 64 00W
Parc National de la Mauricie Québec 47 N6/P6 46 50N 73 05W
Parc québecois d'Oka Québec 56 M4 45 24N 73 58W
Parent Québec 47 M7 47 55N 74 36W
Paris Ontario 48 B2 43 12N 80 25W
Parke Lake Newfoundland and Labrador 52 F6 53 10N 58 50W
Parkhill Ontario 48 A2 43 10N 81 41W
Parksville British Columbia 38 H4 49 20N 124 19W
Parrsboro Nova Scotia 53 M12 45 25N 64 21W
Parry Island Ontario 46 F5 45 17N 80 11W
Parry Islands Northwest Territories/Nunavut 54 H6 75 30N 110 00W
Parry Sound *admin.* Ontario 46 F5/G5 45 22N 80 08W
Parry Sound *tn.* Ontario 46 F5 45 21N 80 03W
Parson's Pond *tn.* Newfoundland and Labrador 53 G5 50 02N 57 43W
Pasadena Newfoundland and Labrador 53 G4 49 01N 57 36W
Pasfield Lake Saskatchewan 42 E6 58 20N 105 45W
Pasqui Hills Saskatchewan 42 F3 53 10N 103 00W
Pass Lake Ontario 45 G5 48 34N 88 44W
Pattullo, Mount British Columbia 38 F5 56 15N 129 43W
Patuanak Saskatchewan 42 D4 55 53N 107 38W
Paudash Ontario 46 J4 44 56N 78 04W
Paulatuk *(Paulatuuq)* Northwest Territories 54 F4 69 49N 123 59W
Paul Island Newfoundland and Labrador 52 E8 56 30N 61 25W
Payne Bay Québec 50 F8 60 00N 70 01W
Peace Point *tn.* Alberta 41 F6 59 07N 112 27W
Peace River Alberta 41 E6 58 40N 114 30W
Peace River *tn.* Alberta 41 D5 56 15N 117 18W
Peachland British Columbia 39 L1 49 49N 119 48W
Peary Channel Nunavut 55 K6 79 40N 101 30W
Peawanuk Ontario 44 J8 55 00N 85 30W
Peel *admin.* Ontario 48 C2 43 49N 79 57W
Peel River Yukon Territory 54 C4 66 05N 136 00W
Peel River Game Reserve Northwest Territories 54 D4 66 30N 134 00W
Peel Sound Northwest Territories 55 L5 73 15N 96 30W
Peerless Lake Alberta 41 E5 56 40N 114 35W
Pefferlaw Ontario 48 C3 44 18N 79 14W
Pefferlaw Brook Ontario 48 C3 44 10N 79 15W
Peggys Cove *tn.* Nova Scotia 53 M11 44 30N 63 50W
Pelee Island Ontario 46 D1 41 47N 82 40W
Pelee Island *tn.* Ontario 46 D1 41 45N 82 40W
Pelee Point Ontario 46 D1 41 45N 82 39W
Pelham Ontario 48 C2 43 02N 79 19W
Pelican Bay Manitoba 43 B3 52 40N 100 30W
Pelican Lake Manitoba 43 B3 52 30N 100 30W
Pelican Mountains Alberta 41 E4 55 35N 114 00W
Pelican Narrows *tn.* Saskatchewan 42 F4 55 12N 102 55W
Pelly Bay Nunavut 55 N4 68 53N 89 51W
Pelly Crossing Yukon Territory 54 C3 62 48N 136 30W
Pelly Mountains Yukon Territory 54 D3 62 10N 134 10W
Pelly Point British Columbia 40 F3 49 06N 123 13W
Pelly River Yukon Territory 54 D3 62 30N 134 50W
Pemberton British Columbia 38 H5 50 19N 122 49W
Pembina Alberta 41 E3 53 08N 115 09W
Pembina River Alberta 41 E3 53 15N 116 05W
Pembina River Manitoba 43 C1 49 10N 99 10W
Pembroke Ontario 47 J5 45 49N 77 08W
Penetanguishene Ontario 46 G4 44 47N 79 56W
Penhold Alberta 41 F3 52 08N 113 52W
Péninsule de la Gaspésie *p.* Québec 51 H3 48 30N 65 30W
Péninsule d'Ungava *p.* Québec 50 C8/C9 60 50N 76 00W
Penticton British Columbia 39 L1 49 30N 119 38W
Percé Québec 51 H3 48 32N 64 14W
Percé, Cape Nova Scotia 53 N12 46 10N 59 40W
Perdue Saskatchewan 42 D3 52 05N 107 33W
Perrault Falls *tn.* Ontario 44 E6 50 20N 93 08W
Perry Island *tn.* Nunavut 55 K4 67 48N 102 33W
Perth Ontario 47 K4 44 54N 76 15W
Perth *admin.* Ontario 48 A2 43 22N 81 10W
Perth Andover New Brunswick 53 B3 46 45N 67 42W
Petawawa Ontario 47 J5 45 54N 77 17W
Peterborough Ontario 46 H4 44 19N 78 20W
Peterborough *admin.* Ontario 46 H4 44 40N 78 30W
Peter Pond Lake Saskatchewan 42 C5 56 00N 108 50W
Petitcodiac New Brunswick 53 L12 45 57N 65 11W
Petite Rivière *tn.* Nova Scotia 53 M11 44 15N 64 25W
Petite Rivière de la Baleine *r.* Québec 50 C6 55 55N 75 58W
Petit Étang Nova Scotia 53 M12 46 39N 61 00W
Petit Lac de Loups Marins *l.* Québec 50 D7 56 30N 73 30W
Petit Lac Manicouagan *l.* Québec 51 G4 52 10N 67 40W
Petitot River British Columbia 39 K6 59 55N 122 15W
Petitsikapau Lake Newfoundland and Labrador 52 B7 54 37N 66 25W
Petre, Point Ontario 47 J3 43 50N 77 09W
Petrolia Ontario 46 D2 42 52N 82 09W
Phelps Lake Saskatchewan 42 F6 59 20N 102 55W
Philpots Island Nunavut 55 Q5 74 57N 79 58W
Pickerel Lake Ontario 45 F5 48 37N 91 19W
Pickering Ontario 48 C2 43 48N 79 11W
Pickering Village Ontario 48 C2 43 51N 79 02W
Pickle Lake *tn.* Ontario 44 F6 51 28N 90 12W
Pic River Ontario 45 H5 48 50N 86 20W
Picton Ontario 47 J4 44 00N 77 07W
Pictou Nova Scotia 53 M12 45 41N 62 42W
Pictou *admin.* Nova Scotia 53 M12 45 30N 62 40W
Pictou Island Nova Scotia 53 M12 45 41N 62 42W
Picture Butte *tn.* Alberta 41 F1 49 53N 112 47W
Pie Island Ontario 45 G5 48 15N 89 06W
Pierceland Saskatchewan 42 C4 54 20N 109 40W
Pigeon Lake Alberta 41 E3 53 01N 114 02W
Pigeon River Manitoba 43 D3 52 10N 96 50W
Pigeon River Ontario 48 D3 44 13N 78 42W
Pikangikum *I.R.* Ontario 44 E6 51 48N 93 59W
Pikangikum Lake Ontario 44 E6 51 48N 94 00W
Pikwitonei Manitoba 43 D4 55 35N 97 11W
Pilot Butte *tn.* Saskatchewan 42 E2 50 29N 104 29W
Pilot Mound *tn.* Manitoba 43 C1 49 13N 98 52W
Pinawa Manitoba 43 E2 50 13N 95 56W
Pincher Creek *tn.* Alberta 41 F1 49 29N 113 57W
Pinchi Lake British Columbia 39 H4 54 36N 124 25W
Pine, Cape Newfoundland and Labrador 53 J3 46 38N 53 35W
Pinecone Burke Provincial Park British Columbia 38 H4 49 30N 122 40W
Pine Falls *tn.* Manitoba 43 D2 50 33N 96 14W
Pinehouse Lake Saskatchewan 42 D4 55 35N 106 50W
Pineimuta River Ontario 44 F7 52 10N 90 40W
Pine Pass British Columbia 39 J4 55 30N 122 25W
Pine River British Columbia 39 K4 55 50N 121 50W
Pine River Ontario 48 B3 44 18N 80 06W
Pinery Provincial Park Ontario 46 E3 43 16N 81 50W
Pinto Butte *mt.* Saskatchewan 42 B1 49 21N 107 25W
Pinware Newfoundland and Labrador 52 G5 51 37N 56 42W
Pipestone River Ontario 44 F7 52 20N 90 10W
Pipestone River Provincial Park Ontario 44 G7 52 55N 90 00W
Pistolet Bay Newfoundland and Labrador 52 H5 51 35N 55 45W
Pitman River British Columbia 39 G6 58 00N 128 15W
Pitt Island British Columbia 38 F3 53 38N 129 59W
Pitt Lake British Columbia 38 H4 49 25N 122 33W
Pitt Meadows *tn.* British Columbia 38 H4 49 13N 122 42W
Pitt River British Columbia 38 H4 49 42N 122 40W
Placentia Newfoundland and Labrador 53 J3 47 14N 53 58W
Placentia Bay Newfoundland and Labrador 53 H3 47 00N 54 30W
Plantagenet Ontario 47 L5 45 32N 75 00W
Plaster Rock *tn.* New Brunswick 53 B3 46 55N 67 24W
Playgreen Lake Manitoba 43 C3 53 50N 98 10W
Pleasant Bay *tn.* Nova Scotia 53 M12 46 50N 60 48W
Pledger Lake Ontario 45 K6 50 53N 83 42W
Plessisville Québec 47 Q6 46 14N 71 46W
Plum Coulee Manitoba 43 D1 49 12N 97 45W
Plum Point *tn.* Newfoundland and Labrador 52 G5 51 04N 56 53W
Pohénégamook Québec 47 S7 47 28N 69 17W
Pointe au Baril Station *tn.* Ontario 46 F5 45 36N 80 22W
Pointe aux Pins Ontario 46 E2 42 29N 84 28W
Pointe de l'Est *c.* Québec 51 K3 49 00N 64 00W
Pointe-Gatineau *tn.* Québec 57 K2 45 27N 75 42W
Pointe Louis-XIV *c.* Québec 55 P1 54 38N 79 45W
Point Farms Provincial Park Ontario 48 A2 43 48N 81 42W
Point Lake Northwest Territories 54 H4 65 15N 113 04W
Point Pelee National Park Ontario 46 D1 41 57N 82 31W
Points North Landing Saskatchewan 42 E6 58 20N 104 10W
Polar Bear Provincial Park Ontario 44 J8 54 50N 84 30W
Pomquet Nova Scotia 53 M12 45 34N 61 50W
Pond Inlet Nunavut 55 Q5 72 41N 78 00W
Pond Inlet *(Mittimatalik) tn.* Nunavut 55 Q5 72 40N 77 59W
Ponhook Lake Nova Scotia 53 M11 44 50N 64 10W
Ponoka Alberta 41 F3 52 42N 113 33W
Ponteix Saskatchewan 42 D1 49 45N 107 20W
Pontiac *admin.* Québec 46 K6 46 28N 77 40W
Pont Rouge Québec 47 Q5 46 45N 71 43W
Pont-Viau Québec 56 N5 45 33N 73 41W
Poplar Hill *tn.* Ontario 44 D7 52 05N 94 18W
Poplar/Nanowin Rivers Park Reserve Manitoba 43 D3 53 00N 96 50W
Poplar River Manitoba 43 D3 52 50N 97 00W
Porcher Island British Columbia 38 E3 54 00N 130 30W
Porcupine, Cape Newfoundland and Labrador 52 G6 53 56N 57 08W
Porcupine Hills Manitoba/Saskatchewan 42 G3 52 30N 101 40W
Porcupine Plain *tn.* Saskatchewan 42 F3 52 36N 103 15W
Porcupine Provincial Forest Manitoba 43 B3 52 30N 101 20W
Portabello Nova Scotia 57 Q6 44 44N 63 32W
Portage Prince Edward Island 53 M12 46 42N 64 08W
Portage la Prairie Manitoba 43 C1 49 58N 98 20W
Port Alberni British Columbia 38 H4 49 11N 124 49W
Port Alice British Columbia 39 G2 50 23N 127 24W
Port au Choix Newfoundland and Labrador 53 G5 50 43N 57 22W
Port au Port Peninsula Newfoundland and Labrador 53 F4 48 35N 59 00W
Port Bickerton *tn.* Nova Scotia 53 M12 45 10N 61 40W
Port Blandford *tn.* Newfoundland and Labrador 53 H4 48 21N 54 10W
Port Bruce Ontario 48 A1 42 40N 81 00W
Port Bruce Provincial Park Ontario 48 A1 42 40N 81 00W
Port Burwell Ontario 48 B1 42 39N 80 47W
Port Burwell Provincial Park Ontario 48 B1 42 40N 80 45W
Port Carling Ontario 46 G5 45 07N 79 35W
Port Cartier Québec 51 G4 50 02N 66 58W
Port Clements British Columbia 38 D3 53 41N 132 11W
Port Colborne Ontario 48 C1 42 53N 79 16W
Port Coquitlam British Columbia 38 H4 49 16N 122 45W
Port Credit Ontario 48 C2 43 33N 79 36W
Port Dover Ontario 48 B1 42 47N 80 12W
Port Edward British Columbia 38 E4 54 11N 130 16W
Port Elgin New Brunswick 53 M12 46 03N 64 08W
Port Elgin Ontario 48 A3 44 25N 81 23W
Porter Lake Saskatchewan 42 D5 56 20N 107 10W
Port Essington British Columbia 38 F4 54 08N 129 58W
Port Hammond British Columbia 40 H3 49 12N 122 40W
Port Hardy British Columbia 39 G2 50 37N 127 15W
Port Hawkesbury Nova Scotia 53 M12 45 36N 61 22W
Port Hood Nova Scotia 53 M12 46 00N 61 32W
Port Hope Ontario 45 M2 43 58N 78 18W
Port Hope Simpson Newfoundland and Labrador 52 G6 52 33N 56 18W
Port Kells British Columbia 40 H3 49 09N 122 43W
Portland Inlet British Columbia 38 E4 54 40N 130 30W
Port Lorne Nova Scotia 53 L11 44 50N 65 20W
Port McNeill British Columbia 39 G2 50 30N 127 01W
Port Maitland Nova Scotia 53 L11 43 59N 66 04W
Port Maitland Ontario 48 C1 42 51N 79 33W
Port Mellon British Columbia 38 H4 49 31N 123 30W
Port Menier Québec 51 H3 49 50N 64 20W
Port Moody British Columbia 38 H4 49 13N 122 57W
Port Mouton Nova Scotia 53 M11 43 58N 64 50W
Port Nelson Manitoba 43 F5 57 10N 92 35W
Portneuf *admin.* Québec 47 P7 46 50N 72 20W
Port Perry Ontario 48 D3 44 06N 78 58W
Port Renfrew British Columbia 38 H4 48 00N 124 00W
Port Rowan Ontario 48 B1 42 38N 80 27W
Port Royal Nova Scotia 53 L11 44 45N 65 40W
Port Saunders Newfoundland and Labrador 53 G5 50 39N 57 18W
Port Stanley Ontario 48 A1 42 40N 81 14W
Postville Newfoundland and Labrador 52 F7 54 54N 59 47W
Pouce Coupé British Columbia 39 K4 55 40N 120 08W
Pouch Cove *tn.* Newfoundland and Labrador 53 J3 47 46N 52 46W
Powassan Ontario 46 G6 46 05N 79 22W
Powell Lake British Columbia 38 H5 50 08N 124 26W
Powell River *tn.* British Columbia 38 H4 49 54N 124 34W
Powerview Manitoba 43 D2 50 30N 96 10W
Preeceville Saskatchewan 42 F2 51 58N 102 40W
Prelate Saskatchewan 42 C2 50 52N 109 22W
Prescott Ontario 47 L4 44 43N 75 33W
Prescott and Russell *admin.* Ontario 47 M5 45 30N 74 45W
Preston Nova Scotia 57 R6 44 41N 63 26W
Preston Ontario 48 B2 43 23N 80 21W
Price Island British Columbia 39 F3 52 25N 128 40W
Prim, Point Prince Edward Island 53 M12 46 10N 63 00W
Primrose Lake Saskatchewan 42 C4 54 50N 109 30W
Primrose Lake Air Weapons Range Saskatchewan 42 C4 55 00N 109 00W
Prince *admin.* Prince Edward Island 53 M12 46 30N 64 00W
Prince Albert Saskatchewan 42 E3 53 13N 105 45W
Prince Albert National Park Saskatchewan 42 D3/D4 54 00N 106 00W
Prince Albert Peninsula Northwest Territories 54 H5 72 30N 117 00W
Prince Albert Sound Northwest Territories 54 G5 70 15N 117 30W
Prince Alfred, Cape Northwest Territories 54 F5 74 20N 124 46W
Prince Charles Island Nunavut 55 Q4 67 40N 77 00W
Prince Edward Island *province* 53 M12
Prince Edward Island National Park Prince Edward Island 53 M12 46 10N 63 10W
Prince George British Columbia 39 J3 53 55N 122 49W
Prince Gustaf Adolf Sea Nunavut 55 J6 78 30N 107 00W
Prince of Wales Icefield Nunavut 55 Q6 78 00N 80 00W
Prince of Wales Island Nunavut 55 L5 73 00N 98 00W
Prince of Wales Strait Northwest Territories 54 G5 71 00N 119 50W
Prince Patrick Island Northwest Territories 54 G6 77 00N 120 00W
Prince Regent Inlet Nunavut 55 M5 72 40N 91 00W
Prince Rupert British Columbia 38 E4 54 09N 130 20W
Princess Margaret Range *mts.* Nunavut 55 M6 81 00N 92 30W
Princess Royal Island British Columbia 39 F3 53 04N 129 00W
Princeton British Columbia 39 K1 49 25N 120 35W
Princeville Québec 47 Q6 46 10N 71 52W
Prophet River British Columbia 39 J6 58 20N 123 00W
Prophet River *tn.* British Columbia 39 J6 58 20N 122 50W
Provost Alberta 41 G3 52 21N 110 16W
Pubnico Nova Scotia 53 L11 43 42N 65 48W
Pugwash Nova Scotia 53 M12 45 52N 63 40W
Pukaskwa Provincial Park Ontario 45 J5 48 20N 85 40W
Pukatawagan Manitoba 43 B4 55 46N 101 14W
Pukeashun Mountain British Columbia 39 L2 51 12N 119 14W
Purcell Mountains British Columbia 39 M2 50 58N 116 59W
Purcell's Cove *tn.* Nova Scotia 57 Q6 44 35N 63 33W
Purcell Wilderness Conservancy British Columbia 39 M2 50 00N 116 00W
Purtuniq Québec 50 D9 61 52N 74 00W
Puvirnituq Québec 50 B9 59 45N 77 20W

Q

Qikiqtarjuaq *(Broughton Island)* Nunavut 55 T4 67 40N 63 50W
Quadra Island British Columbia 38 G5 50 11N 125 20W
Qualicum Beach *tn.* British Columbia 38 H4 49 21N 124 27W
Qu'Appelle Saskatchewan 42 F2 50 33N 103 54W
Qu'Appelle Dam Saskatchewan 42 D2 50 55N 106 20W
Qu'Appelle River Saskatchewan 42 F2 50 30N 102 20W
Quaqtaq Québec 50 F9 61 00N 69 40W
Quathiaski Cove *tn.* British Columbia 38 G5 50 03N 125 11W
Quatsino Sound British Columbia 39 G2 50 25N 128 55W
Québec Québec 47 Q6 46 49N 71 13W
Québec *admin.* Québec 47 P7/Q7 47 50N 72 30W
Québec *province* 50/51
Queen Bess, Mount British Columbia 39 H2 51 13N 124 35W
Queen Charlotte British Columbia 38 D3 53 18N 132 04W
Queen Charlotte Islands British Columbia 38 D3/E3 53 30N 131 50W
Queen Charlotte Sound British Columbia 39 F2 51 48N 129 25W
Queen Charlotte Strait British Columbia 39 G2 51 00N 127 55W
Queen Elizabeth Foreland Nunavut 55 T3 62 23N 64 28W
Queen Elizabeth Islands Northwest Territories 54 G6 77 30N 120 00W
Queen Maud Gulf Nunavut 55 K4 68 00N 101 00W
Queen Maud Gulf Migratory Bird Sanctuary Nunavut 55 K4 67 30N 103 20W
Queens *admin.* New Brunswick 53 C3 45 50N 65 50W
Queens *admin.* Nova Scotia 53 L11 44 10N 65 10W
Queens *admin.* Prince Edward Island 53 M12 46 20N 63 10W
Queenston Ontario 48 C2 43 09N 79 03W
Queenswood Heights Ontario 57 L2 45 28N 75 29W
Quesnel British Columbia 39 J3 53 03N 122 31W
Quesnel Lake British Columbia 39 K3 52 30N 121 20W

Quesnel River British Columbia 39 J3 52 58N 122 29W
Quetico Provincial Park Ontario 45 F5 48 30N 91 30W
Quill Lake *tn.* Saskatchewan 42 E3 52 03N 104 12W
Quill Lakes Saskatchewan 42 E2 52 03N 104 12W
Quince, Bay of Ontario 47 J4 44 07N 77 32W
Quirke Lake Ontario 45 K4 46 28N 82 33W
Quispamsis New Brunswick 53 L12 45 25N 65 55W
Quoich River Nunavut 55 M3 64 50N 94 40W
Quttinirpaaq National Park Nunavut 55 R7 82 00N 72 30W

R

Raanes Peninsula Nunavut 55 N6 78 30N 85 45W
Rabbit Lake Mine Saskatchewan 42 F2 58 10N 103 42W
Rabbit River British Columbia 39 G6 59 20N 127 20W
Radisson Québec 51 B5 53 43N 77 46W
Radisson Saskatchewan 42 D3 52 27N 107 24W
Radium Hot Springs British Columbia 39 L2 50 39N 116 09W
Radville Saskatchewan 42 E1 49 28N 104 19W
Rae *(Mbehchoko)* Northwest Territories 54 G3 62 50N 116 03W
Rae Lakes *(Gahmiti) tn.* Northwest Territories 54 G3 64 10N 117 20W
Rae River Nunavut 54 G4 68 10N 116 50W
Rae Strait Nunavut 55 L4 68 50N 95 00W
Ragged Lake Nova Scotia 57 Q6 44 37N 63 39W
Rainbow Lake Alberta 41 C6 58 17N 119 16W
Rainbow Lake *tn.* Alberta 41 C6 58 30N 119 23W
Rainy Lake Ontario 44 E5 48 00N 93 00W
Rainy River Ontario 44 D5 48 40N 94 10W
Rainy River *tn.* Ontario 44 D5 48 44N 94 33W
Ralston Alberta 41 G2 50 15N 111 10W
Ralz, Mount British Columbia 38 D5 57 24N 132 19W
Ramah Newfoundland and Labrador 52 D9 58 50N 63 12W
Ramea Newfoundland and Labrador 53 G3 47 31N 57 23W
Ramea Islands Newfoundland and Labrador 53 G3 47 31N 57 22W
Ramsey Lake Ontario 45 K4 47 13N 82 15W
Rankin Inlet Nunavut 55 M3 62 45N 92 05W
Rankin Inlet *(Kangiqtinq) tn.* Nunavut 55 M3 62 49N 92 05W
Rapide-Blanc-Station Québec 47 N7 47 00N 73 00W
Rapide-des-Cèdres Québec 51 B3 49 00N 77 09W
Rapides de Lachine Québec 56 N4 45 26N 73 39W
Rat Lake Manitoba 43 C5 56 10N 99 40W
Rat River Manitoba 43 C5 56 10N 99 20W
Ray, Cape Newfoundland and Labrador 53 F3 47 37N 59 19W
Raymond Alberta 41 F1 49 27N 112 39W
Raymore Saskatchewan 42 E2 51 24N 104 32W
Razorback *mt.* British Columbia 39 H2 51 28N 124 35W
Read Island British Columbia 38 G5 50 11N 125 05W
Red Bay *tn.* Newfoundland and Labrador 52 G5 51 44N 56 25W
Red Bay *tn.* Ontario 48 A3 44 47N 81 19W
Redberry Lake Saskatchewan 42 D3 52 45N 107 20W
Redcliff Alberta 41 G2 50 05N 110 47W
Red Deer Alberta 41 F3 52 15N 113 48W
Red Deer Lake Manitoba 43 B3 52 50N 101 30W
Red Deer River Alberta 41 F2 51 20N 112 35W
Red Deer River Saskatchewan 42 F3 52 50N 103 05W
Redfern-Keily Creek Provincial Park British Columbia 39 J5 57 25N 124 00W
Red Indian Lake Newfoundland and Labrador 53 G4 48 40N 57 10W
Red Lake Ontario 44 E6 51 10N 93 50W
Red Lake *tn.* Ontario 44 E6 51 01N 93 50W
Red Lake Road *tn.* Ontario 44 E5 49 59N 93 22W
Redonda Island British Columbia 38 H5 50 15N 124 50W
Red River British Columbia 39 F6 59 23N 128 14W
Red River Manitoba 43 D1 49 30N 97 20W
Red Rock Ontario 45 G5 48 55N 88 15W
Redstone River Northwest Territories 54 E3 63 47N 128 00W
Red Sucker Lake Manitoba 43 G4 54 10N 94 10W
Redvers Saskatchewan 42 G1 49 34N 101 42W
Redwater Alberta 41 F3 53 57N 113 06W
Red Wine River Newfoundland and Labrador 52 E7 54 10N 62 00W
Reed Lake Manitoba 43 B4 54 30N 100 10W
Refuge Cove *tn.* British Columbia 38 H5 50 07N 124 51W
Regina Saskatchewan 42 E2 50 30N 104 38W
Regina Beach *tn.* Saskatchewan 42 E2 50 49N 105 00W
Reindeer Grazing Reserve Northwest Territories 54 D4 69 00N 132 00W
Reindeer Island Manitoba 43 D3 52 30N 97 20W
Reindeer Lake Saskatchewan/Manitoba 42 F5 57 30N 102 30W
Reindeer River Saskatchewan 42 F5 56 10N 103 10W
Reliance Northwest Territories 54 J3 62 42N 109 08W
Renews Newfoundland and Labrador 53 J3 46 56N 52 56W
Renfrew Ontario 47 K5 45 28N 76 44W
Renfrew *admin.* Ontario 47 J5/K5 45 28N 76 41W
Rennie Lake Northwest Territories 54 J3 61 32N 105 35W
Repentigny Québec 47 N5 45 29N 73 46W
Repulse Bay *(Naujat) tn.* Nunavut 55 N4 66 32N 86 15W
Réserve de la Rivière Matamec Québec 51 H4 50 30N 65 30W
Réserve Duchénier Québec 51 F3 48 08N 68 40W
Réserve du Parc National de l'Archipelago de Mingan Québec 51 J4 50 10N 62 30W
Réserve Faunique Ashuapmushuan Québec 51 D3 49 00N 73 30W
Réserve Faunique Assinica Québec 51 C4 50 48N 75 40W
Réserve Faunique de Dunière Québec 51 G3 48 30N 66 40W
Réserve Faunique de l'Île d'Anticosti Québec 51 H3/J3 49 25N 62 58W
Réserve Faunique de Matane Québec 51 G3 48 45N 67 00W
Réserve Faunique de Papineau-Labelle Québec 47 L6 46 20N 75 21W
Réserve Faunique de Portneuf Québec 47 P7 47 10N 72 20W
Réserve Faunique de Port-Daniel Québec 51 H3 48 13N 65 00W
Réserve Faunique de Rimouski Québec 51 F3 48 00N 68 20W
Réserve Faunique des Chic-Chocs Québec 51 H3 49 10N 65 10W
Réserve Faunique de Sept-Îles-Port-Cartier Québec 51 G4 50 30N 67 30W
Réserve Faunique des Laurentides Québec 47 Q7 47 50N 71 47W
Réserve Faunique des Lacs-Albanel-Mistassini-et-Waconichi Québec 51 C4 50 10N 74 20W
Réserve Faunique du Saint-Maurice Québec 47 N7 47 08N 73 18W
Réserve Faunique la Vérendrye Québec 47 J7/K7 47 08N 73 18W
Réserve Faunique Mastigouche Québec 47 N6 46 35N 73 47W
Réserve Faunique Rouge-Matawin Québec 47 M6 46 52N 74 35W
Réservoir Baskatong *res.* Québec 47 L6 47 00N 76 00W
Réservoir Blanc *res.* Québec 47 N7 47 49N 73 06W
Réservoir Cabonga *res.* Québec 47 K7 47 31N 76 45W
Réservoir Caniapiscau *res.* Québec 50 F6 54 10N 69 10W
Réservoir de La Grande 2 *res.* Québec 51 B5 53 38N 78 40W
Réservoir de La Grande 3 *res.* Québec 50 C5 54 10N 72 30W
Réservoir de La Grande 4 *res.* Québec 50 D5 53 59N 72 50W
Réservoir Dozois *res.* Québec 47 J7 47 30N 77 26W
Réservoir du Poisson Blanc *res.* Québec 47 L6 46 05N 75 50W
Réservoir Evans *res.* Québec 51 B4 50 45N 76 50W
Réservoir Gouin *res.* Québec 51 C3 48 30N 74 00W
Réservoir Kiamika *res.* Québec 47 L6 46 40N 75 05W
Réservoir Laforge 1 *res.* Québec 50 E6 54 20N 71 50W
Réservoir Laforge 2 *res.* Québec 50 E6 54 30N 71 20W
Réservoir Manic 2 *res.* Québec 51 F3 49 30N 68 25W
Réservoir Manic 3 *res.* Québec 51 F4 50 00N 68 40W
Réservoir Manicouagan *res.* Québec 51 F4 51 00N 58 00W
Réservoir Opinaca *res.* Québec 51 B5 52 30N 75 30W
Réservoir Outardes 4 *res.* Québec 51 F4 50 20N 69 20W
Réservoir Pipmuacan *res.* Québec 51 E3 49 30N 70 10W
Réservoir Soscumica-Matagami *res.* Québec 51 B4 50 10N 77 32W
Réservoir Taureau *res.* Québec 47 N6 46 47N 73 47W
Resolute *(Qausuittuq)* Nunavut 55 M5 74 40N 95 00W
Resolution Island Nunavut 55 T3 61 18N 64 53W
Restigouche *admin.* New Brunswick 53 B3 47 40N 67 10W
Restigouche River New Brunswick 53 B3 47 35N 67 30W
Reston Manitoba 43 B1 49 33N 101 05W
Revelstoke British Columbia 39 L2 51 02N 118 12W
Revelstoke, Lake British Columbia 39 L2 51 32N 118 40W
Rexton New Brunswick 53 C3 46 41N 64 56W
Ribstone Creek Alberta 41 G3 52 10N 111 55W
Rice Lake Ontario 46 H4 44 12N 78 10W
Richard Collinson Inlet Northwest Territories 54 H5 72 45N 113 55W
Richards Island Northwest Territories 54 C4 69 20N 134 30W
Richardson Mountains Yukon Territory/Northwest Territories 54 C4 67 50N 137 00W
Richardson River Alberta 41 G6 58 15N 110 55W
Rich, Cape Ontario 48 B3 44 43N 80 39W
Richibucto New Brunswick 53 C3 46 42N 64 54W
Richmond British Columbia 38 H4 49 09N 123 09W
Richmond Québec 47 P5 45 40N 72 10W
Richmond *admin.* Nova Scotia 53 M12 45 40N 60 40W
Richmond *admin.* Québec 47 P5 45 30N 72 10W
Richmond Hill *tn.* Ontario 48 C2 43 53N 79 26W
Rideau River Ontario 45 P3 44 50N 76 00W
Rideau River and Canal Ontario 57 K2 45 16N 75 43W
Ridgetown Ontario 46 E2 42 26N 81 54W
Riding Mountain Manitoba 43 B2 50 40N 100 40W
Riding Mountain National Park Manitoba 43 B2 50 50N 100 30W
Rigolet Newfoundland and Labrador 52 F7 54 11N 58 26W
Rimbey Alberta 41 E3 52 38N 114 41W
Rimouski Québec 51 F3 48 27N 68 32W
Riondel British Columbia 39 M1 49 46N 116 51W
Riou Lake Saskatchewan 42 D6 59 00N 106 30W
Ripley Ontario 48 A3 44 04N 81 34W
River Herbert *tn.* Nova Scotia 53 M12 45 42N 64 25W
River John *tn.* Nova Scotia 53 M12 45 44N 63 03W
Rivers *tn.* Manitoba 43 B2 50 02N 100 14W
Riverside-Albert New Brunswick 53 M12 45 40N 64 40W
Rivers Inlet British Columbia 39 G2 51 30N 127 30W
Riverton Manitoba 43 D2 51 00N 97 00W
Riverview New Brunswick 53 M12 46 06N 64 51W
Rivière Aguanus *r.* Québec 51 J4 51 15N 62 05W
Rivière à la Baleine *r.* Québec 50 G7 57 00N 67 40W
Rivière à l'Argent *r.* Québec 51 F4 50 30N 69 40W
Rivière Arnaud *r.* Québec 50 D8 59 37N 72 55W
Rivière Ashuapmushuan *r.* Québec 51 D3 49 22N 73 25W
Rivière aux Feuilles *r.* Québec 50 D8 57 45N 73 00W
Rivière aux Mélèzes *r.* Québec 50 D7 56 50N 72 15W
Rivière aux Outardes *r.* Québec 51 F4 51 38N 69 55W
Rivière-aux-Rats *tn.* Québec 47 P7 47 11N 72 52W
Rivière Bécancour *r.* Québec 47 P6/Q6 46 15N 72 20W
Rivière Bell *r.* Québec 51 B3 49 30N 77 30W
Rivière Betsiamites *r.* Québec 51 F3 49 27N 69 30W
Rivière Blanche *r.* Québec 57 K3 45 32N 75 38W
Rivière Broadback *r.* Québec 51 A4 51 15N 78 42W
Rivière Caniapiscau *r.* Québec 50 F7 56 38N 69 15W
Rivière Capitachouane *r.* Québec 47 K7 47 42N 76 49W
Rivière Casapédia *r.* Québec 51 G3 48 45N 66 20W
Rivière Chaudière *r.* Québec 47 Q6 46 30N 71 10W
Rivière Chicoutimi *r.* Québec 47 Q8 48 11N 71 29W
Rivière Chukotat *r.* Québec 50 B9 61 02N 77 15W
Rivière Coats *r.* Québec 50 B6 55 30N 76 50W
Rivière Coulonge *r.* Québec 47 J6 46 44N 77 10W
Rivière d'Argent *r.* Québec 47 L7 46 59N 75 00W
Rivière Delay *r.* Québec 50 E7 56 50N 71 10W
Rivière de Pas *r.* Québec 50 H6 55 12N 65 35W
Rivière de Rupert *r.* Québec 51 A4 51 22N 78 10W
Rivière des Mille Îles *r.* Québec 56 M5 45 37N 73 47W
Rivière des Outaouais *r.* Ontario/Québec 46 H6 45 35N 76 30W
Rivière des Prairies *r.* Québec 56 N5 45 36N 73 37W
Rivière du Chène *r.* Québec 56 M5 45 34N 73 59W
Rivière du Gué *r.* Québec 50 E7 56 48N 72 00W
Rivière du Lièvre *r.* Québec 47 L5 45 50N 75 39W
Rivière-du-Loup *admin.* Québec 47 S7 47 50N 69 20W
Rivière-du-Loup *tn.* Québec 47 S7 47 49N 69 32W
Rivière Dumoine *r.* Québec 46 J6 46 20N 77 52W
Rivière du Petit Mécatina *r.* Québec 51 K4 51 50N 60 10W
Rivière du Sable *r.* Québec 50 F6 55 28N 68 20W
Rivière du Vieux Comptoir *r.* Québec 51 A5 52 33N 78 40W
Rivière Eastmain *r.* Québec 51 D5 52 20N 73 00W
Rivière False *r.* Québec 50 F7 57 40N 68 30W
Rivière Ford *r.* Québec 50 H8 58 20N 65 30W
Rivière Gatineau *r.* Québec 47 L5 45 58N 75 52W
Rivière George *r.* Québec 50 H7 57 50N 65 30W
Rivière Harricana *r.* Québec 51 A4 50 40N 79 20W
Rivière Innuksuac *r.* Québec 50 B8 58 40N 77 30W
Rivière Kanaaupscow *r.* Québec 50 C6 54 40N 75 00W
Rivière Kitchigama *r.* Québec 51 A4 50 50N 78 10W
Rivière Kogaluc *r.* Québec 50 B8 59 33N 76 18W
Rivière Koksoak *r.* Québec 50 F7 57 50N 69 10W
Rivière Koroc *r.* Québec 50 H8 58 40N 65 20W
Rivière Kovik *r.* Québec 50 B9 61 50N 77 20W
Rivière Magpie *r.* Québec 51 H4 50 42N 64 25W
Rivière Malbaie *r.* Québec 47 R7 48 01N 70 40W
Rivière Manicouagan *r.* Québec 51 F4 50 51N 68 55W
Rivière Manitou *r.* Québec 51 H4 51 08N 65 20W
Rivière Manouane *r.* Québec 51 E4 50 05N 70 59W
Rivière Maquatua *r.* Québec 51 A5 53 05N 78 40W
Rivière Mariet *r.* Québec 50 B8 59 05N 77 30W
Rivière Matapédia *r.* Québec 51 G3 48 30N 67 30W
Rivière Matawin *r.* Québec 47 N6 46 55N 73 39W
Rivière-Matawin *tn.* Québec 47 P6 46 54N 72 55W
Rivière Mégiscane *r.* Québec 51 B3 48 17N 76 50W
Rivière Métabetchouane *r.* Québec 47 P7 47 59N 72 05W
Rivière Mistanipiscou *r.* Québec 51 J4 51 50N 62 25W
Rivière Mistassibi *r.* Québec 51 D4 50 20N 72 15W
Rivière Mistassibi Nord-Est *r.* Québec 51 E4 50 01N 71 59W
Rivière Mistassini *r.* Québec 51 D4 50 20N 72 40W
Rivière Moisie *r.* Québec 51 G4 50 52N 66 33W
Rivière Montmorency *r.* Québec 47 Q7 47 19N 71 12W
Rivière Mucaliq *r.* Québec 50 G8 58 15N 67 30W
Rivière Nabisipi *r.* Québec 51 J4 50 59N 62 32W
Rivière Nastapoca *r.* Québec 50 C7 56 52N 75 30W
Rivière Natashquan *r.* Québec 51 K4 51 00N 61 35W
Rivière Nicolet *r.* Québec 47 P6 46 14N 72 35W
Rivière Nipissis *r.* Québec 51 H4 50 30N 66 00W
Rivière Noire *r.* Québec 47 J6 46 40N 77 23W
Rivière Nottaway *r.* Québec 51 A4 51 05N 78 20W
Rivière Olomane *r.* Québec 51 K4 50 58N 60 35W
Rivière Opinaca *r.* Québec 51 A5 52 20N 78 00W
Rivière Pentecôte *r.* Québec 51 G4 50 18N 67 35W
Rivière Peribonka *r.* Québec 51 E3 48 58N 71 30W
Rivière Pons *r.* Québec 50 F6 55 50N 69 50W
Rivière Pontax *r.* Québec 51 B4 51 50N 77 05W
Rivière Racine de Bouleau *r.* Québec 51 F5 52 00N 68 40W
Rivière Richelieu *r.* Québec 47 N5 45 03N 73 25W
Rivière Romaine *r.* Québec 51 J4 51 10N 63 40W
Rivière Saguenay *r.* Québec 51 E3 48 20N 70 43W
Rivière Saint-Augustin *r.* Québec 50 L4 51 58N 60 10W
Rivière Sainte-Anne *r.* Québec 47 P6 46 40N 72 11W
Rivière Sainte-Marguerite *r.* Québec 51 G4 51 20N 66 59W
Rivière Saint-François *r.* Québec 47 Q5 45 40N 71 30W
Rivière Saint-Jean *r.* Québec 51 H4 50 50N 64 03W
Rivière Saint-Maurice *r.* Québec 47 N7 47 55N 73 46W
Rivière Saint-Paul *r.* Québec 50 M4 51 55N 57 59W
Rivière Sakami *r.* Québec 51 D5 53 05N 73 15W
Rivière Sérigny *r.* Québec 50 F6 55 30N 69 59W
Rivière Témiscamie *r.* Québec 51 D4 51 15N 72 40W
Rivière Vachon *r.* Québec 50 D9 60 40N 72 25W
Rivière Vermillion *r.* Québec 47 N7 47 19N 73 22W
Rivière-Verte *tn.* New Brunswick 53 A3 47 19N 68 09W
Rivière Wacouna *r.* Québec 51 H4 50 57N 65 40W
Rivière Wheeler *r.* Québec 50 G7 56 25N 67 35W
Rivière Yamaska *r.* Québec 47 P5 45 40N 73 00W
Robert's Arm *tn.* Newfoundland and Labrador 53 H4 49 29N 55 49W
Roberts Creek *tn.* British Columbia 38 H4 49 25N 123 37W
Roberval Québec 51 D3 48 31N 72 16W
Roblin Manitoba 43 B2 51 15N 101 20W
Robson, Mount British Columbia 39 L3 53 08N 118 18W
Rock Bay *tn.* British Columbia 38 G5 50 18N 125 31W
Rockcliffe Park Ontario 47 L5 45 27N 75 39W
Rockglen Saskatchewan 42 E1 49 11N 105 57W
Rockland Ontario 47 L5 45 33N 75 18W
Rock Point Provincial Park Ontario 48 C1 42 50N 79 30W
Rockwood Ontario 48 B2 43 37N 80 10W
Rocky Bay *I.R.* Ontario 45 G5 49 26N 88 08W
Rocky Harbour *tn.* Newfoundland and Labrador 53 G4 49 39N 57 55W
Rocky Island Lake Ontario 45 K4 46 55N 83 04W
Rocky Lake Nova Scotia 57 Q7 44 45N 63 36W
Rocky Mountain House Alberta 41 E3 52 22N 114 55W
Rocky Mountains Forest Reserve Alberta 41 D3/E2 52 30N 116 30W
Rocky Mountain Trench British Columbia 39 H5 57 50N 126 00W
Rocky Saugeen River Ontario 48 B3 44 13N 80 52W
Roddickton Newfoundland and Labrador 52 G5 50 52N 56 08W
Rodney Ontario 46 E2 42 34N 81 41W
Roes Welcome Sound Nunavut 55 N3 63 30N 87 30W
Rogers Pass British Columbia 39 M2 51 23N 117 23W
Rogersville New Brunswick 53 C3 46 44N 65 28W
Romaine River Newfoundland and Labrador 52 D6 52 30N 64 00W
Rondeau Provincial Park Ontario 46 E2 42 17N 81 51W
Root River Ontario 44 F6 50 50N 91 40W
Rorketon Manitoba 43 C2 51 24N 99 35W
Roseau River Manitoba 43 D1 49 10N 96 50W
Rose Blanche Newfoundland and Labrador 53 F3 47 37N 58 41W
Rosedale Ontario 48 D3 44 34N 78 47W
Rosemère Québec 56 M5 45 38N 73 49W
Rose Point British Columbia 38 E4 54 11N 131 39W
Rosetown Saskatchewan 42 D2 51 34N 107 59W
Rose Valley *tn.* Saskatchewan 42 F3 52 19N 103 49W
Ross Bay Junction *tn.* Newfoundland and Labrador 52 B6 53 03N 66 12W
Rossburn Manitoba 43 B2 50 40N 100 49W
Rosseau Ontario 46 G5 45 16N 79 39W
Rosseau, Lake Ontario 46 G5 45 10N 79 35W
Rossignol, Lake Nova Scotia 53 L11 44 10N 65 20W
Ross Island Manitoba 43 D4 54 20N 97 50W
Rossland British Columbia 39 M1 49 05N 117 48W
Rossport Ontario 45 H5 48 50N 87 31W
Ross River *tn.* Yukon Territory 54 D3 62 02N 132 28W
Rosswood British Columbia 39 F4 54 49N 128 42W
Rosthern Saskatchewan 42 D3 52 40N 106 20W
Rothesay New Brunswick 53 L12 45 23N 66 00W
Rouge River Ontario 48 C2 43 52N 79 15W
Rouleau Saskatchewan 42 E2 50 12N 104 56W
Round Pond Newfoundland and Labrador 53 H4 48 10N 55 50W
Route Jacques-Cartier Québec 51 H4 50 20N 66 00W
Rouyn-Noranda Québec 51 A3 48 15N 79 00W
Rowley Island Nunavut 55 Q4 69 06N 77 52W
Russell Manitoba 43 B2 50 47N 101 17W

Russell, Cape Northwest Territories 54 G6 75 15N 117 35W

Russell Point *c.* Northwest Territories 54 H5 73 30N 115 00W

S

Saanich British Columbia 38 H4 48 28N 123 22W

Sabine Peninsula Nunavut 54 J6 76 20N 109 30W

Sable, Cape Nova Scotia 53 C1 43 23N 65 37W

Sable Island Nova Scotia 13 Z2 43 57N 60 00W

Sable River *tn.* Nova Scotia 53 L11 43 50N 65 05W

Sachigo *I.R.* Ontario 44 E7 53 50N 92 10W

Sachigo Lake Ontario 44 E7 53 49N 92 08W

Sachigo River Ontario 44 F8 54 50N 90 50W

Sachs Harbour *(Ikaahuk) tn.* Northwest Territories 54 E5 71 59N 125 13W

Sackville New Brunswick 53 M12 45 54N 64 23W

Sacré-Coeur Québec 47 S8 48 26N 68 35WE

Saglek Bay Newfoundland and Labrador 52 D9 58 30N 63 00W

Saglek Fiord Newfoundland and Labrador 52 D9 58 29N 63 15W

Saguenay Québec 47 R8 48 25N 71 04W

Saguenay *admin.* Québec 47 S8 48 20N 70 00W

Saint-Agapit Québec 47 Q6 46 34N 71 26W

St. Albans Newfoundland and Labrador 53 H3 47 52N 55 51W

St. Albert Alberta 41 F3 53 38N 113 38W

Saint-Ambroise Québec 51 E3 48 33N 71 20W

St. Andrews New Brunswick 53 B2 45 05N 67 04W

St. Anthony Newfoundland and Labrador 52 H5 51 22N 55 35W

Saint-Antoine New Brunswick 53 M12 46 22N 64 50W

St. Antoine Québec 47 M5 45 47N 74 01W

St. Barbe Newfoundland and Labrador 52 G5 51 13N 56 45W

St. Bernard's Newfoundland and Labrador 53 H3 47 32N 54 47W

St. Bride's Newfoundland and Labrador 53 H3 46 55N 54 10W

St. Catharines Ontario 48 C2 43 10N 79 15W

St. Clair, Lake Ontario/USA 46 D2 42 28N 82 40W

St. Croix River New Brunswick 53 B2 45 30N 67 40W

Saint-Donat Québec 47 M6 46 19N 74 15W

Sainte-Agathe-des-Monts Québec 47 M6 46 03N 74 19W

Ste. Anne Manitoba 43 D1 49 40N 96 40W

Ste. Anne de Beaupré Québec 47 R7 47 02N 70 58W

Sainte-Anne-des-Monts Québec 51 G3 49 07N 66 29W

Sainte-Anne-du-Lac Québec 47 L6 46 54N 75 20W

Sainte-Catherine Québec 56 N4 45 25N 73 35W

Sainte-Claire Québec 47 R6 46 37N 70 51W

Sainte-Croix Québec 47 Q6 46 38N 71 43W

Sainte-Dorothée Québec 56 M5 45 32N 73 49W

Sainte-Eustache Québec 56 M5 45 33N 73 54W

Sainte-Hyacinthe Québec 47 P5 45 38N 72 57W

St. Eleanors Prince Edward Island 53 M12 46 30N 63 50W

Saint Elias Mountains Yukon Territory 54 C3 60 12N 140 57W

Sainte-Marie Québec 47 Q6 46 26N 71 00W

Sainte-Marthe-sur-le-Lac Québec 56 M5 45 31N 73 55W

Sainte-Rose Québec 56 M5 45 36N 73 47W

Ste. Rose du Lac Manitoba 43 C2 51 04N 99 31W

Sainte-Thérèse Québec 47 N5 45 38N 73 50W

Saint-Félicien Québec 51 D3 48 38N 72 29W

St. Francis Harbour *tn.* Nova Scotia 53 M12 45 30N 61 20W

St. Francis, Lake Québec 47 M5 45 05N 74 30W

Saint-François Québec 56 N5 45 38N 73 35W

St. George New Brunswick 53 B2 45 08N 66 50W

St. George's Newfoundland and Labrador 53 F4 48 26N 58 29W

Saint-Georges Québec 47 P6 46 38N 72 35W

Saint-Georges Québec 47 R6 46 08N 70 40W

St. George's Bay Newfoundland and Labrador 53 F4 48 28N 59 16W

St. Georges Bay Nova Scotia 53 M12 45 40N 61 40W

St. Ignace Island Ontario 45 H5 48 45N 87 55W

St. Jacobs Ontario 48 B2 43 32N 80 33W

Saint-Jacques New Brunswick 53 A3 47 20N 68 28W

St. James, Cape British Columbia 38 E2 51 58N 131 00W

St. Jean Baptiste Manitoba 43 D1 49 15N 97 20W

Saint-Jean-Port-Joili Québec 47 R7 47 13N 70 16W

Saint-Jean-sur-Richelieu Québec 47 N5 45 18N 73 18W

St.-Jerôme Québec 47 M5 45 47N 74 01W

Saint John New Brunswick 53 L12 45 16N 66 03W

Saint John *admin.* New Brunswick 53 L12 45 20N 65 50W

St. John Bay Newfoundland and Labrador 52 G5 50 55N 57 09W

St. John, Cape Newfoundland and Labrador 53 H4 50 00N 55 32W

St. John, Lake Ontario 48 C3 44 38N 79 19W

St. John's Newfoundland and Labrador 53 J3 47 34N 52 43W

St. Joseph New Brunswick 53 M12 45 59N 64 30W

St. Joseph Island Ontario 46 C6 46 13N 83 57W

St. Joseph, Lake Ontario 44 F6 51 05N 90 35W

St. Lawrence Newfoundland and Labrador 53 H3 46 55N 55 24W

St. Lawrence, Cape Nova Scotia 53 M12 47 10N 60 40W

St. Lawrence, Gulf of Québec 51 J3 48 40N 63 20W

St. Lawrence River Québec 51 C1 45 00N 75 00W

St. Lawrence Seaway Ontario/Québec/USA 47 L4 44 38N 78 34W

Saint Léonard New Brunswick 53 B3 47 10N 67 55W

St. Lewis Newfoundland and Labrador 52 H6 52 22N 55 41W

St. Lewis River Newfoundland and Labrador 52 G6 52 20N 56 50W

Saint-Louis de-Kent New Brunswick 53 C3 46 50N 65 00W

St. Lunaire Newfoundland and Labrador 52 H5 51 30N 55 29W

St. Malo Manitoba 43 D1 49 20N 96 55W

St. Margarets Bay Nova Scotia 53 M11 44 30N 64 50W

St. Martin, Lake Manitoba 43 C2 51 40N 98 20W

St. Martins New Brunswick 53 L12 45 20N 65 30W

St. Mary, Cape Nova Scotia 53 L11 44 10N 66 10W

St. Mary's Newfoundland and Labrador 53 J3 46 55N 53 34W

St. Marys Ontario 48 A2 43 15N 81 09W

St. Mary's Bay Newfoundland and Labrador 53 J3 46 50N 53 45W

St. Mary's Bay Nova Scotia 53 L11 44 20N 66 10W

St. Mary's River Nova Scotia 53 M12 45 20N 62 30W

St.-Maurice *admin.* Québec 47 M7 47 40N 74 30W

Saint-Michel-des-Saints Québec 47 N6 46 40N 73 55W

Saint-Pacôme Québec 47 S7 47 24N 69 58W

St.-Pamphile Québec 47 S6 46 58N 69 48W

Saint-Pascal Québec 47 S7 47 32N 69 48W

St. Paul Alberta 41 G4 53 59N 111 17W

St. Peters Nova Scotia 53 M12 45 40N 60 53W

St. Peters Prince Edward Island 53 M12 46 26N 62 35W

St. Pierre-Jolys Manitoba 43 D1 49 28N 96 58W

Saint-Prosper Québec 47 R6 46 12N 70 29W

Saint-Quentin New Brunswick 53 B3 47 30N 67 20W

Saint-Raymond Québec 47 Q6 46 54N 71 50W

St. Romauld Québec 47 Q6 46 52N 71 49W

Saint-Siméon Québec 47 S7 47 50N 69 55W

St. Stephen New Brunswick 53 B2 45 12N 67 18W

St. Stephens Newfoundland and Labrador 53 J3 46 47N 53 37W

St. Theresa Point *tn.* Manitoba 43 E3 53 45N 94 50W

St. Thomas Ontario 48 A1 42 46N 81 12W

Saint-Tite Québec 47 P6 46 44N 72 34W

Saint-Vincent-de-Paul Québec 56 N5 45 38N 73 39W

St. Walburg Saskatchewan 42 C3 53 38N 109 12W

Sakami Québec 51 B5 53 50N 76 10W

Salaberry-de-Valleyfield Québec 47 M5 45 16N 74 11W

Salisbury New Brunswick 53 L12 46 02N 65 03W

Salisbury Island Nunavut 55 Q3 63 10N 77 20W

Salluit Québec 50 C10 62 20N 75 40W

Salmo British Columbia 39 M1 49 11N 117 16W

Salmon Arm *tn.* British Columbia 39 L2 50 41N 119 18W

Salmon Inlet British Columbia 38 H4 49 39N 123 47W

Salmon River New Brunswick 53 C3 46 10N 65 50W

Salmon River *tn.* Nova Scotia 53 L11 44 10N 66 10W

Saltcoats Saskatchewan 42 F2 51 03N 102 12W

Saltery Bay *tn.* British Columbia 38 H4 49 47N 124 10W

Saltspring Island British Columbia 38 H4 48 50N 123 30W

Sambro, Cape Nova Scotia 53 M11 44 30N 63 30W

San Cristoval Mountains British Columbia 38 E3 52 30N 131 30W

Sandilands Provincial Forest Manitoba 43 D1/E1 49 30N 96 00W

Sand Lakes Provincial Park Manitoba 43 C5 58 00N 98 30W

Sandspit British Columbia 38 E3 53 14N 131 50W

Sandy Bay *tn.* Saskatchewan 42 F4 55 30N 102 10W

Sandy Lake Newfoundland and Labrador 53 G4 49 20N 56 50W

Sandy Lake Nova Scotia 57 Q6 44 44N 63 40W

Sandy Lake Ontario 44 E7 53 02N 93 00W

Sandy Lake *I.R.* Ontario 44 E7 53 04N 93 20W

Sanikiluaq *(Sanikilluaq)* Nunavut 55 Q2 56 32N 79 14W

San Juan River British Columbia 38 H4 48 37N 124 20W

Sardis British Columbia 38 H4 49 07N 121 57W

Sarnia Ontario 46 D2 42 58N 82 23W

Sasaginnigak Lake Manitoba 43 E2 51 30N 95 30W

Sasamat Lake British Columbia 40 G4 49 19N 122 52W

Saskatchewan *province* 42

Saskatchewan River Manitoba/Saskatchewan 42 F3 53 50N 103 10W

Saskatoon Saskatchewan 42 D3 52 10N 106 40W

Saturna Island British Columbia 38 H4 48 47N 123 07W

Sauble Beach *tn.* Ontario 48 A3 44 38N 81 17W

Sauble Falls Provincial Park Ontario 48 A3 44 40N 81 15W

Sauble River Ontario 48 A3 44 36N 81 09W

Saugeen River Ontario 48 A3 44 23N 81 18W

Sault Ste. Marie Ontario 45 J4 46 31N 84 20W

Savant Lake Ontario 44 F6 50 30N 90 25W

Savant Lake *tn.* Ontario 44 F6 50 14N 90 43W

Sawbill Newfoundland and Labrador 52 B6 53 37N 66 21W

Sayabec Québec 51 G3 48 35N 67 41W

Sayward British Columbia 39 H2 50 19N 125 58W

Scarborough *bor.* Metropolitan Toronto Ontario 49 D2 43 46N 79 14W

Scarborough Bluffs *tn.* Ontario 49 D1 43 42N 79 15W

Scaterie Island Nova Scotia 53 N12 46 00N 59 40W

Schreiber Ontario 45 H5 48 48N 87 17W

Schultz Lake Nunavut 55 L3 64 45N 97 30W

Scotsburn Nova Scotia 53 M12 45 40N 62 51W

Scott Islands British Columbia 39 F2 50 48N 128 38W

Scott Lake Saskatchewan 42 D6 59 50N 106 30W

Scudder Ontario 46 D1 41 47N 82 39W

Scugog Island Ontario 48 D3 44 10N 78 52W

Scugog, Lake Ontario 48 D3 44 10N 78 51W

Scugog River Ontario 48 D3 44 16N 78 46W

Seaforth Ontario 48 A2 43 03N 81 24W

Sea Island British Columbia 40 F3 49 11N 123 11W

Seal Cove *tn.* Newfoundland and Labrador 53 G3 47 30N 56 00W

Seal Cove *tn.* Newfoundland and Labrador 53 G4 49 56N 56 23W

Seal Cove *tn.* Nova Scotia 53 L11 44 38N 66 52W

Seal Harbour *tn.* New Brunswick 53 M12 45 10N 61 30W

Seal Lake Newfoundland and Labrador 52 E7 54 20N 61 40W

Seal River Manitoba 43 D6 58 50N 97 00W

Sechelt British Columbia 38 H4 49 28N 123 46W

Sechelt Peninsula British Columbia 38 H4 49 45N 123 58W

Selkirk Manitoba 43 D2 50 10N 96 52W

Selkirk Ontario 48 C1 42 50N 79 55W

Selkirk Mountains British Columbia 39 M2 51 40N 118 20W

Selkirk Provincial Park Ontario 48 C1 42 50N 80 00W

Selwyn Lake Northwest Territories 54 K3 60 05N 104 25W

Selwyn Mountains Yukon Territory 54 D3 64 30N 134 50W

Semchuck Trail Saskatchewan 42 C5 57 35N 109 20W

Senneterre Québec 47 J8 48 24N 77 16W

Sentinel Peak British Columbia 39 K4 54 56N 121 59W

Serpentine River British Columbia 40 G3 49 06N 122 46W

Seseganaga Lake Ontario 44 F6 50 00N 90 28W

Setting Lake Manitoba 43 C4 55 10N 98 50W

Seven Sisters Bay Newfoundland and Labrador 52 D9 59 25N 63 45W

70 Mile House British Columbia 39 K2 51 21N 121 25W

Severn Lake Ontario 44 F7 53 54N 90 48W

Severn River Ontario 44 H8 55 30N 88 30W

Severn River Provincial Park Ontario 44 F8 54 15N 90 30W

Sexsmith Alberta 41 C4 55 21N 118 47W

Seymour Creek British Columbia 40 F4 49 18N 123 01W

Seymour Inlet British Columbia 39 G2 51 03N 127 05W

Shabaqua Ontario 45 G5 48 35N 89 54W

Shabo Newfoundland and Labrador 52 B6 53 19N 66 12W

Shabogamo Lake Newfoundland and Labrador 52 B6 53 15N 66 30W

Shag Harbour *tn.* Nova Scotia 53 L11 43 30N 65 40W

Shakespeare Ontario 48 B2 43 22N 80 50W

Shaler Mountains Northwest Territories 54 H5 72 10N 111 00W

Shallow Lake *tn.* Ontario 48 A3 44 38N 81 06W

Shamattawa Manitoba 43 F4 55 51N 92 05W

Shamattawa River Ontario 44 J8 54 05N 85 50W

Shapio Lake Newfoundland and Labrador 52 E7 55 00N 61 18W

Sharon Ontario 48 C3 44 06N 79 26W

Shaunavon Saskatchewan 42 C1 49 40N 108 25W

Shawinigan Québec 47 P6 46 34N 72 45W

Shawnigan Lake *tn.* British Columbia 38 H4 48 38N 123 39W

Shawville Québec 47 K5 45 36N 76 30W

Shebandowan Ontario 45 F5 48 38N 90 04W

Shediac New Brunswick 53 M12 46 13N 64 35W

Sheet Harbour *tn.* Nova Scotia 53 M11 44 56N 62 31W

Shefford *admin.* Québec 47 P5 45 30N 72 45W

Shelburne Nova Scotia 53 M11 43 37N 65 20W

Shelburne Ontario 48 B3 44 05N 80 13W

Shelburne *admin.* Nova Scotia 53 L11 43 50N 65 30W

Sheldon Creek Ontario 48 B3 44 05N 80 06W

Shellbrook Saskatchewan 42 D3 53 14N 106 24W

Shelsey River British Columbia 38 E6 58 33N 132 02W

Shelter Bay *tn.* British Columbia 39 M2 50 38N 117 59W

Shepherd Bay Nunavut 55 M4 65 00N 90 00W

Sherbrooke Nova Scotia 53 M12 45 10N 61 58W

Sherbrooke Québec 47 Q5 45 24N 71 54W

Sherbrooke *admin.* Québec 47 P5 45 20N 72 10W

Sherbrooke Lake Nova Scotia 53 M11 44 40N 64 40W

Sherridon Manitoba 43 B4 55 07N 101 05W

Sherwood Park *tn.* Alberta 41 F3 53 31N 113 19W

Sheshatsheits Newfoundland and Labrador 52 E6 53 30N 60 10W

Shibogama Lake Ontario 44 G7 53 35N 88 15W

Shipiskan Lake Newfoundland and Labrador 52 D7 54 39N 62 19W

Shippagan New Brunswick 53 C3 47 45N 64 44W

Shirleys Bay Ontario 57 J2 45 22N 75 54W

Shoal Bay *tn.* Newfoundland and Labrador 53 H4 49 41N 54 12W

Shoal Harbour *tn.* Newfoundland and Labrador 53 J4 48 11N 53 59W

Shoal Lake Ontario/Manitoba 44 D5 49 33N 95 01W

Shoal Lake *tn.* Manitoba 43 B2 50 28N 100 35W

Shoal Lakes Manitoba 43 D2 50 25N 97 35W

Shubenacadie Nova Scotia 53 M12 45 05N 63 25W

Shubenacadie Grand Lake Nova Scotia 57 Q7 44 53N 63 37W

Shubenacadie River Nova Scotia 53 M12 45 20N 63 30W

Shunacadie Nova Scotia 53 M12 46 00N 60 40W

Shuswap Lake British Columbia 39 L2 51 00N 119 00W

Sibbald Point Provincial Park Ontario 48 C3 44 15N 79 20W

Sicamous British Columbia 39 L2 50 50N 119 00W

Sidney British Columbia 38 H4 48 39N 123 25W

Sidney Bay Ontario 48 A3 44 55N 81 04W

Sifton Manitoba 43 B2 51 21N 100 09W

Sifton Pass British Columbia 39 G5 57 51N 126 17W

Sikanni Chief British Columbia 39 J5 57 11N 122 43W

Sikanni Chief River British Columbia 39 J5 57 16N 125 25W

Silver Dollar Ontario 44 F5 49 50N 91 15W

Silverthrone Mountain British Columbia 39 G2 51 30N 126 03W

Silvertip Mountain British Columbia 38 H4 49 09N 121 12W

Simcoe Ontario 48 B1 42 50N 80 19W

Simcoe *admin.* Ontario 48 C3 44 32N 79 54W

Simcoe, Lake Ontario 48 C3 44 23N 79 18W

Simonette River Alberta 41 C4 54 25N 118 20W

Simpson Bay Nunavut 54 H4 69 00N 113 40W

Simpson Peninsula Nunavut 55 N4 68 34N 88 45W

Simpson Strait Nunavut 55 L4 68 27N 97 45W

Sioux Lookout Ontario 44 F6 50 07N 91 54W

Sioux Narrows Ontario 44 D5 49 23N 94 08W

Sipiwesk Manitoba 43 D4 55 27N 97 24W

Sipiwesk Lake Manitoba 43 D4 55 10N 97 50W

Sir Alexander, Mount British Columbia 39 K3 53 52N 120 25W

Sir James McBrien, Mount Yukon Territory 54 E3 62 15N 128 01W

Sir Wilfred Laurier, Mount British Columbia 39 L3 52 45N 119 40W

Sisipuk Lake Manitoba 43 B4 55 30N 101 40W

Skagit Valley Recreation Area British Columbia 38 H4 49 06N 121 09W

Skeena Mountains British Columbia 38/39 F5 57 30N 129 59W

Skeena River British Columbia 39 F4 54 15N 129 15W

Skidegate British Columbia 38 E3 53 13N 132 02W

Skihist Mountain British Columbia 39 K2 50 12N 122 53W

Skownan Manitoba 43 C2 51 58N 99 35W

Slave Lake *tn.* Alberta 41 E4 55 17N 114 43W

Slave River Alberta/Northwest Territories 54 H3 60 30N 112 50W

Sleeping Giant (Sibley) Provincial Park Ontario 45 G5 48 10N 88 50W

Slocan British Columbia 39 M1 49 46N 117 28W

Slocan Lake British Columbia 39 M1 49 50N 117 20W

Smallwood Reservoir Newfoundland and Labrador 52 C7 54 10N 64 00W

Smeaton Saskatchewan 42 E3 53 30N 104 50W

Smith Alberta 41 E4 55 10N 114 02W

Smith Arm *b.* Northwest Territories 54 F4 66 15N 124 00W

Smith Bay Nunavut 55 Q6 77 12N 78 50W

Smithers British Columbia 39 G4 54 45N 127 10W

Smith Island Nunavut 50 A9 60 44N 78 30W

Smith Point Nova Scotia 53 M12 45 52N 63 25W

Smith River British Columbia 39 G6 59 56N 126 28W

Smiths Falls *tn.* Ontario 47 K4 44 45N 76 01W

Smithville Ontario 48 C2 43 06N 79 32W

Smokey Newfoundland and Labrador 52 G7 54 28N 57 14W

Smoky, Cape Nova Scotia 53 M12 46 40N 60 20W

Smoky Lake *tn.* Alberta 41 F4 54 07N 112 28W

Smoky River Alberta 41 C4 55 30N 118 00W

Smooth Rock Falls *tn.* Ontario 45 L5 49 17N 81 38W

Smoothrock Lake Ontario 44 G6 50 30N 89 30W

Smoothstone Lake Saskatchewan 42 D4 54 40N 106 30W

Snake Creek Ontario 48 A3 44 23N 81 16W

Snake River Yukon Territory 54 D4 65 20N 133 30W

Snegamook Lake Newfoundland and Labrador 52 E7 54 33N 61 27W

Snowbird Lake Northwest Territories 55 K3 60 41N 102 56W

Snow Lake *tn.* Manitoba 43 B4 54 56N 100 00W

Snug Harbour *tn.* Newfoundland and Labrador 52 H6 52 53N 55 52W

Soldier Lake Nova Scotia 57 Q7 44 49N 63 33W

Somerset Manitoba 43 C1 49 26N 98 39W

Somerset Island Nunavut 55 M5 73 15N 93 30W

Sonora Island British Columbia 38 G5 50 21N 125 13W

Sooke British Columbia 38 H4 48 20N 123 42W

Sorel Québec 47 N6 46 03N 73 06W

Soulanges *admin.* Québec 47 M5 45 15N 74 20W

Sounding Creek Alberta 41 G2 51 40N 111 05W

Sounding Lake Alberta 41 G3 52 08N 110 29W

Souris Manitoba 43 B1 49 38N 100 17W

Souris Prince Edward Islan 53 M12 46 22N 62 16W

Souris River Manitoba/US 43 B1 49 30N 100 50W

Southampton Ontario 48 A3 44 29N 81 22W

Southampton Island Nunavut 55 P3 64 50N 85 00W
South Aulatsivik Island Newfoundland and Labrador 52 E8 56 46N 61 30W
South Bay *tn.* Ontario 44 E6 51 03N 92 45W
South Brookfield Nova Scotia 53 M11 44 23N 64 58W
Southend Saskatchewan 42 F5 56 20N 103 14W
Southern Indian Lake Manitoba 43 C5 57 00N 98 00W
Southey Saskatchewan 42 E2 50 57N 104 33W
South Gloucester Ontario 57 K2 45 17N 75 34W
South Hazelton British Columbia 39 G4 55 12N 127 42W
South Henik Lake Nunavut 55 L3 61 30N 97 30W
South Indian Lake *tn.* Manitoba 43 C5 56 48N 98 55W
South Knife River Manitoba 43 D6 58 20N 96 10W
South Maitland River Ontario 48 A2 43 39N 81 27W
South Moose Lake Manitoba 43 B3 53 40N 100 10W
South Nahanni River Northwest Territories 54 E3 61 30N 123 22W
South Porcupine Ontario 45 L5 48 28N 81 13W
South River *tn.* Ontario 46 G5 45 50N 79 23W
South Saskatchewan River Saskatchewan 42 C2 50 50N 110 00W
South Saugeen River Ontario 48 B3 44 00N 80 45W
South Seal River Manitoba 43 C5 58 00N 99 10W
South Tweedsmuir Provincial Park British Columbia 39 H3 52 30N 126 00W
South Twin Island Northwest Territories 44 M7 53 10N 79 50W
Southwest Miramichi River New Brunswick 53 B3 46 30N 66 50W
Spallumcheen British Columbia 39 L2 50 24N 119 14W
Spanish Ontario 46 D6 46 12N 82 12W
Spanish River Ontario 46 E6 46 32N 81 57W
Sparwood British Columbia 39 N1 49 55N 114 53W
Spatsizi Plateau Wilderness Park British Columbia 39 F5/G5 57 30N 128 30W
Spear Harbour *tn.* Newfoundland and Labrador 52 H6 52 25N 55 42W
Speed River Ontario 48 B2 43 29N 80 17W
Speers Saskatchewan 42 D3 52 43N 107 32W
Spicer Islands Nunavut 55 Q4 63 19N 71 52W
Spirit River *tn.* Alberta 41 C4 55 46N 118 51W
Spiritwood Saskatchewan 42 D3 53 24N 107 33W
Split, Cape Nova Scotia 53 M12 45 20N 64 30W
Split Lake Manitoba 43 E5 56 10N 95 50W
Split Lake *tn.* Manitoba 43 D5 56 16N 96 08W
Spotted Island Newfoundland and Labrador 52 H6 53 31N 55 47W
Sprague Manitoba 43 E1 49 02N 95 36W
Springdale Newfoundland and Labrador 53 G4 49 30N 56 04W
Springfield Nova Scotia 53 M11 44 37N 64 52W
Springfield Ontario 48 B1 42 49N 80 57W
Springhill Nova Scotia 53 M12 45 40N 64 04W
Spring Water Provincial Park Ontario 48 C3 44 30N 79 45W
Sproat Lake British Columbia 38 G4 49 16N 125 05W
Spruce Grove Alberta 41 F3 53 32N 113 55W
Spruce Woods Provincial Forest Manitoba 43 C1 49 40N 99 40W
Spruce Woods Provincial Park Manitoba 43 C1 49 40N 99 10W
Spryfield Ontario 57 L3 44 36N 63 40W
Spry Harbour *tn.* Nova Scotia 53 M11 44 50N 62 45W
Spuzzum British Columbia 39 K1 49 40N 121 25W
Squamish British Columbia 38 H4 49 41N 123 11W
Squamish River British Columbia 38 H5 49 42N 123 11W
Square Islands Newfoundland and Labrador 52 H6 52 45N 55 52W
Stanley New Brunswick 53 B3 46 17N 66 45W
Stanstead *admin.* Québec 47 P5 45 10N 72 10W
Starbuck Manitoba 43 D1 49 47N 97 38W
Star City Saskatchewan 42 E3 52 52N 104 20W
Stave Lake British Columbia 38 H4 49 21N 122 19W
Stayner Ontario 48 B3 44 25N 80 06W
Steele River Provincial Park Ontario 45 H5 49 25N 86 40W
Stefansson Island Nunavut 55 K5 73 20N 105 00W
Steinbach Manitoba 43 D1 49 32N 96 40W
Stein Valley Provincial Park British Columbia 39 J2 50 10N 122 10W
Stellarton Nova Scotia 53 M12 45 34N 62 40W
Stephens Lake Manitoba 43 E5 56 30N 95 00W
Stephenville Newfoundland and Labrador 53 F4 48 33N 57 32W
Stephenville Crossing Newfoundland and Labrador 53 F4 48 30N 58 26W
Stettler Alberta 41 F3 52 19N 112 43W
Stevenson Lake Manitoba 43 E3 53 50N 95 50W
Steveston British Columbia 40 F3 49 07N 123 10W
Stewart British Columbia 38 F4 55 07N 129 58W
Stewart Yukon Territory 54 C3 63 15N 139 15W
Stewart Crossing Yukon Territory 54 C3 60 37N 128 37W
Stewart River Yukon Territory 54 C3 63 40N 138 20W
Stewiacke Nova Scotia 53 M12 45 09N 63 22W
Stikine British Columbia 38 E5 56 42N 131 45W
Stikine Range *mts.* British Columbia 38 E6/F6 57 00N 127 20W
Stikine River British Columbia 38 E5 58 00N 131 20W
Stikine River Recreation Area British Columbia 39 F5 58 07N 129 35W
Stirling Alberta 41 F1 49 34N 112 30W
Stirling Ontario 47 J4 44 18N 77 33W
Stittsville Ontario 57 J2 45 16N 75 54W
Stokes Bay Ontario 48 A3 45 00N 81 23W
Stone Mountain Provincial Park British Columbia 39 H6 58 35N 124 40W
Stonewall Manitoba 43 D2 50 08N 97 20W
Stoney Creek *tn.* Ontario 48 C2 43 13N 79 46W
Stony Lake Manitoba 43 C6 58 50N 98 30W
Stony Lake Ontario 46 H4 44 33N 78 06W
Stony Plain *tn.* Alberta 41 E3 53 32N 114 00W
Stony Rapids *tn.* Saskatchewan 42 E6 59 14N 105 48W
Storkerson Peninsula Nunavut 54 J5 72 30N 106 30W
Stormont, Dundas and Glengarry *admin.* Ontario 47 M5 45 10N 75 00W
Stormy Lake Ontario 44 E5 49 23N 92 18W
Stouffville Ontario 48 C2 43 59N 79 15W
Stoughton Saskatchewan 42 F1 49 40N 103 00W
Stout Lake Ontario 44 D7 52 08N 94 35W
Strasbourg Saskatchewan 42 E2 51 05N 104 58W
Stratford Ontario 48 B2 43 07N 81 00W
Strathcona Provincial Park British Columbia 38 G4 49 40N 125 30W
Strathmore Alberta 41 F2 51 03N 113 23W
Strathnaver British Columbia 39 J3 53 21N 112 32W
Strathroy Ontario 48 A1 42 57N 81 40W
Streetsville Ontario 48 C2 43 25N 79 44W
Stuart Island *tn.* British Columbia 38 G5 50 22N 125 09W
Stuart Lake British Columbia 39 H4 54 35N 124 40W
Stuart River British Columbia 39 J4 54 10N 124 05W
Stupart River Manitoba 43 E4 55 30N 94 30W
Sturgeon Bay Manitoba 43 D3 51 50N 98 00W
Sturgeon Falls *tn.* Ontario 46 G6 46 22N 79 57W
Sturgeon Lake Alberta 41 D4 55 06N 117 32W
Sturgeon Lake Ontario 44 F5 50 00N 91 00W
Sturgeon Lake Ontario 48 D3 44 30N 78 43W
Sturgeon Landing Saskatchewan 42 G4 54 18N 101 49W
Sturgeon Point *tn.* Ontario 48 D3 44 28N 78 42W
Sturgeon River Ontario 45 L4 47 00N 80 30W
Sturgeon River Saskatchewan 42 D3 53 30N 106 20W
Sturgeon River Provincial Park Ontario 45 L4 47 00N 80 50W
Sturgis Saskatchewan 42 F2 51 58N 102 32W
Styx River Ontario 48 B3 44 15N 80 58W
Sudbury Ontario 46 E6 46 30N 81 01W
Sudbury *admin.* Ontario 46 E6 47 10N 82 00W
Sudbury, Regional Municipality of Ontario 46 E6 46 32N 81 00W
Suggi Lake Saskatchewan 42 F4 54 20N 103 10W
Sullivan Bay *tn.* British Columbia 39 G2 50 55N 126 52W
Sullivan Lake Alberta 41 F3 52 00N 112 00W
Sultan Ontario 45 K4 47 36N 82 45W
Summer Beaver Ontario 44 G7 52 50N 88 30W
Summerford Newfoundland and Labrador 53 H4 49 29N 54 47W
Summerland British Columbia 39 L1 49 35N 119 41W
Summerside Prince Edward Island 53 M12 46 24N 63 46W
Summerville Newfoundland and Labrador 53 J4 48 27N 53 33W
Sunbury *admin.* New Brunswick 53 B2 45 50N 66 40W
Sundre Alberta 41 E2 51 48N 114 38W
Sundridge Ontario 46 G5 45 46N 79 24W
Sunnyside Newfoundland and Labrador 53 J3 47 51N 53 55W
Superb Saskatchewan 42 C2 51 56N 109 25W
Superior, Lake Ontario/USA 45 G4/H4 48 00N 88 00W
Surrey British Columbia 38 H4 49 08N 122 50W
Sussex New Brunswick 53 L12 45 43N 65 32W
Sussex Corner New Brunswick 53 L12 45 40N 65 30W
Sutton Ontario 48 C3 44 18N 79 22W
Sutton Québec 47 P5 45 05N 72 36W
Sutton Lake Ontario 44 J8 54 15N 84 44W
Sutton River Ontario 44 J8 54 50N 84 30W
Svendsen Peninsula Nunavut 55 P6 77 45N 84 00W
Sverdrup Islands Nunavut 55 L6 79 00N 96 00W
Swan Hills Alberta 41 E4 54 45N 115 45W
Swan Hills *tn.* Alberta 41 E4 54 43N 115 24W
Swan Lake Manitoba 43 B3 52 20N 100 50W
Swan Lake/Kispoix River Provincial Park British Columbia 39 F4 55 55N 128 25W
Swannell Range British Columbia 39 H5 56 38N 126 10W
Swan Pelican Provincial Forest Manitoba 43 B3 52 30N 100 30W
Swan River *tn.* Manitoba 43 B3 52 06N 101 17W
Swift Current *tn.* Saskatchewan 42 D2 50 17N 107 49W
Swift Current Creek Saskatchewan 42 C1 49 40N 108 30W
Swift River *tn.* Yukon Territory 54 D3 60 02N 131 10W
Swinburne, Cape Nunavut 55 L5 71 13N 98 33W
Swindle Island British Columbia 39 F3 52 33N 128 25W
Sydenham River Ontario 46 D2 42 40N 82 20W
Sydenham River Ontario 48 B3 44 32N 80 57W
Sydney Nova Scotia 53 M12 46 10N 60 10W
Sydney Mines *tn.* Nova Scotia 53 M12 46 16N 60 15W
Sylvan Lake *tn.* Alberta 41 E3 52 19N 114 05W

T

Taber Alberta 41 F1 49 48N 112 09W
Table Bay Newfoundland and Labrador 52 G6 53 40N 56 25W
Tadoule Lake Manitoba 43 C6 58 30N 98 50W
Tadoussac Québec 47 S8 48 09N 69 43W
Tagish Yukon Territory 54 D3 60 18N 134 16W
Tagish Lake British Columbia 38 C6 59 50N 134 33W
Tahiryuak Lake Northwest Territories 54 H5 70 56N 112 15W
Tahoe Lake Nunavut 54 J4 70 15N 108 45W
Tahsis British Columbia 39 G1 49 50N 126 39W
Tahtsa Lake British Columbia 39 G3 53 41N 127 30W
Takla Lake British Columbia 39 H4 55 12N 125 45W
Takla Landing British Columbia 39 H4 55 27N 125 59W
Taku Arm *l.* British Columbia 38 C6 60 10N 134 05W
Taku River British Columbia 38 D6 58 43N 133 20W
Talbot Lake Manitoba 43 C4 54 00N 99 40W
Taloyoak *(Spence Bay)* Nunavut 55 M4 69 30N 93 20W
Taltson River Northwest Territories 54 H3 60 40N 111 30W
Tantalus Provincial Park British Columbia 38 H4 49 50N 123 16W
Tara Ontario 48 A3 44 29N 81 09W
Taseko Mountain British Columbia 39 J2 51 12N 123 07W
Taseko River British Columbia 39 J2 51 35N 123 40W
Tasisuak Lake Newfoundland and Labrador 52 D8 56 45N 62 46W
Tasiujaq Québec 50 F8 58 40N 70 00W
Tasu Sound British Columbia 38 D3 52 40N 132 03W
Tatamagouche Nova Scotia 53 M12 45 43N 63 19W
Tatamagouche Bay Nova Scotia 53 M12 45 45N 63 15W
Tathlina Lake Northwest Territories 54 G3 60 33N 117 39W
Tatla Lake British Columbia 39 H3 51 59N 124 25W
Tatlatui Provincial Park British Columbia 39 G5 57 00N 127 20W
Tatlayoko Lake British Columbia 39 H2 51 39N 124 23W
Tatnam, Cape Manitoba 43 G5 57 25N 91 00W
Tatshenshini River British Columbia 38 B6 59 30N 137 30W
Tavistock Ontario 48 B2 43 19N 80 50W
Taylor British Columbia 39 K5 56 09N 120 40W
Taylor Head *p.* Nova Scotia 53 M11 44 40N 62 30W
Tazin Lake Saskatchewan 42 C6 59 50N 109 10W
Tazin River Saskatchewan 42 D6 59 50N 108 00W
Tecumseh Ontario 46 D2 42 18N 82 49W
Teeswater Ontario 48 A2 43 59N 81 18W
Teeswater River Ontario 48 A3 44 07N 81 22W
Tehek Lake Nunavut 55 L3 64 55N 95 38W
Telegraph Creek *tn.* British Columbia 38 E5 57 56N 131 11W
Telkwa British Columbia 39 G4 54 44N 127 05W
Temagami Ontario 45 M4 47 04N 79 47W
Temagami, Lake Ontario 45 L4 47 00N 80 05W
Témiscamingue *admin.* Québec 46 H6 46 44N 79 06W
Templeton Québec 57 K2 45 29N 75 36W
Terence Bay Nova Scotia 53 M11 44 20N 63 40W
Terrace British Columbia 39 F4 54 31N 128 32W
Terrace Bay *tn.* Ontario 45 H5 48 47N 87 06W
Terra Cotta Ontario 48 C2 43 42N 79 55W
Terra Nova National Park Newfoundland and Labrador 53 H4 48 40N 54 20W
Terrebonne Québec 47 N5 45 42N 73 37W
Terrebonne *admin.* Québec 47 M6 46 00N 74 30W
Terrenceville Newfoundland and Labrador 53 H3 47 40N 54 44W
Teslin Yukon Territory 54 D3 60 10N 132 42W
Teslin Lake British Columbia/Yukon Territory 54 D3 59 50N 132 25W
Teslin River British Columbia 38 E6 59 20N 131 50W
Tetachuk Lake British Columbia 39 H3 53 38N 127 40W
Teulon Manitoba 43 D2 50 26N 97 18W
Texada Island British Columbia 38 H4 49 30N 124 30W
Thamesford Ontario 48 A2 43 03N 81 00W
Thames River Ontario 46 E2 42 19N 82 27W
Thelon River Northwest Territories 54 K3 64 40N 102 30W
Thelon Wildlife Sanctuary Northwest Territories/Nunavut 55 K3 64 30N 103 00W
The Pas Manitoba 43 B3 53 49N 101 14W
Thesiger Bay Northwest Territories 54 E5 71 30N 124 05W
Thessalon Ontario 46 C6 46 15N 83 34W
Thetford Mines *tn.* Québec 47 Q6 46 06N 71 18W
Thicket Portage Manitoba 43 D4 55 20N 97 42W
Thirty Thousand Islands Ontario 46 F5 45 56N 80 57W
Thlewiaza River Nunavut 55 L3 60 50N 98 00W
Thomas Hubbard, Cape Nunavut 55 M6 81 45N 90 10W
Thomlinson, Mount British Columbia 39 G4 55 30N 127 30W
Thompson Manitoba 43 D4 55 45N 97 54W
Thompson River British Columbia 39 K2 50 12N 121 30W
Thomsen River Northwest Territories 54 G5 73 00N 119 50W
Thorah Island Ontario 48 C3 44 27N 79 13W
Thorhild Alberta 41 F4 54 10N 113 07W
Thornbury Ontario 48 B3 44 34N 80 27W
Thornhill *tn.* Ontario 48 C2 43 49N 79 26W
Thornloe Ontario 45 M4 47 42N 79 41W
Thorold Ontario 48 C2 43 08N 79 14W
Thorsby Alberta 41 E3 53 14N 114 03W
Thousand Islands Ontario 47 K4/L4 44 22N 75 55W
Three Hills *tn.* Alberta 41 F2 51 42N 113 16W
Three Mile Plains *tn.* Nova Scotia 53 M11 44 55N 64 10W
Thunder Bay *tn.* Ontario 45 G5 48 27N 89 12W
Thurso Québec 47 L5 45 38N 75 19W
Thutade Lake British Columbia 39 G5 56 59N 126 40W
Tide Head *tn.* New Brunswick 53 B3 47 58N 66 49W
Tignish Prince Edward Island 53 M12 46 58N 64 03W
Tikkoatokak Bay Newfoundland and Labrador 52 D8 56 42N 62 12W
Tilbury Ontario 46 D2 42 16N 82 26W
Tilbury Island British Columbia 40 F3 49 08N 123 02W
Tilden Lake *tn.* Ontario 46 G6 46 37N 79 39W
Tillsonburg Ontario 48 B1 42 53N 80 44W
Timberlea Nova Scotia 53 M11 44 40N 63 45W
Timiskaming Québec 45 M4 46 44N 79 05W
Timiskaming, Lake Ontario 45 M4 46 52N 79 15W
Timmins Ontario 45 L5 48 30N 81 20W
Tinniswood, Mount British Columbia 38 H5 50 19N 123 47W
Tip Top Mountain Ontario 45 J5 48 16N 85 59W
Tirya River British Columbia 38 E6 58 46N 130 50W
Tisdale Saskatchewan 42 E3 52 51N 104 01W
Tiverton Ontario 48 A3 44 15N 81 33W
Toad River *tn.* British Columbia 39 H6 58 50N 125 12W
Toba Inlet British Columbia 38 H5 50 25N 124 30W
Toba River British Columbia 38 H5 50 31N 124 18W
Tobeatic Wildlife Management Area Nova Scotia 53 L11 44 12N 65 25W
Tobermory Ontario 48 A4 45 15N 81 39W
Tobin Lake Saskatchewan 42 F3 53 30N 103 30W
Tofield Saskatchewan 41 F3 53 22N 112 40W
Tofino British Columbia 39 H1 49 05N 125 51W
Torbay Newfoundland and Labrador 53 J3 47 40N 52 44W
Tor Bay Nova Scotia 53 M12 45 15N 61 15W
Torch River Saskatchewan 42 F3 53 40N 103 50W
Tornado Mountain Alberta/British Columbia 39 N1 49 57N 114 35W
Torngat Mountains Newfoundland and Labrador 52 C9 59 00N 63 40W
Toronto Ontario 48 C2 43 42N 79 46W
Toronto Islands Ontario 48 C2 43 42N 79 25W
Tottenham Ontario 48 C3 44 02N 79 48W
Touraine Québec 57 K2 45 29N 75 42W
Tracadie Nova Scotia 53 M12 45 38N 61 40W
Tracadie-Sheila New Brunswick 53 C3 47 32N 64 57W
Tracy New Brunswick 53 B2 45 41N 66 42W
Tracy Québec 47 N5 45 59N 73 04W
Trail British Columbia 39 M1 49 04N 117 39W
Trans-Canada Highway Canada 42 C2 50 10N 108 30W
Treherne Manitoba 43 C1 49 39N 98 41W
Trembleur Lake British Columbia 39 H4 54 50N 124 55W
Trenton Nova Scotia 53 M12 45 37N 62 38W
Trenton Ontario 46 J4 44 07N 77 34W
Trent-Severn Waterway Ontario 48 C3 44 20N 79 23W
Trepassey Newfoundland and Labrador 53 J3 46 45N 53 20W
Trinity Bay Newfoundland and Labrador 53 J3 47 50N 53 40W
Trinity East Newfoundland and Labrador 53 J4 48 23N 53 20W
Triton Newfoundland and Labrador 53 H4 49 30N 55 30W
Trochu Alberta 41 F2 51 50N 113 13W
Trois-Pistoles Québec 47 S8 48 08N 69 10W
Trois-Rivières *tn.* Québec 47 P6 46 21N 72 34W
Trout Creek *tn.* Ontario 46 G5 45 59N 79 22W
Trout Lake Ontario 44 E6 51 20N 93 20W
Trout Lake *tn.* Alberta 41 E5 56 30N 114 32W
Trout Lake *(Saamba Tu) tn.* Northwest Territories 54 F3 61 00N 121 30W
Trout River *tn.* Newfoundland and Labrador 53 H4 49 29N 58 08W
Troy Nova Scotia 53 M12 45 40N 61 30W
Truro Nova Scotia 53 M12 45 24N 63 18W
Tsawwassen British Columbia 38 H4 49 03N 123 06W
Tsiigehtchic *(Arctic Red River)* Northwest Territories 54 D4 67 27N 133 46W
Ts'yl-os Provincial Park British Columbia 39 H2 51 10N 123 50W
Tuchitua Yukon Territory 54 E3 61 20N 129 00W
Tuktoyaktuk *(Tuktuujaqrtuuq)* Northwest Territories 54 D4 69 24N 133 01W
Tuktut Nogait National Park Northwest Territories 54 F4 69 00N 121 50W
Tulemalu Lake Nunavut 55 L3 62 58N 99 25W
Tulit'a *(Fort Norman)* Northwest Territories 54 E3 64 55N 125 29W
Tumbler Ridge *tn.* British Columbia 39 K4 55 10N 121 01W
Tungsten Northwest Territories 54 E3 61 59N 128 09W
Tunungayualok Island Newfoundland and Labrador 52 E8 56 05N 61 05W
Turkey Point Ontario 48 B1 42 37N 80 20W
Turkey Point *tn.* Ontario 48 B1 43 41N 80 20W
Turkey Point Provincial Park Ontario 48 B1 42 45N 80 20W
Turnagain River British Columbia 39 F6 58 25N 129 08W
Turnavik Island Newfoundland and Labrador 52 F7 55 18N 59 21W
Turner Valley *tn.* Alberta 41 E2 50 40N 114 17W
Turnor Lake Saskatchewan 42 C5 56 35N 109 10W

A

Aachen Germany	78	J9	50 46N	6 06E
Aalst Belgium	78	H9	50 57N	4 03E
Aba Nigeria	100	F9	5 06N	7 21E
Abādān Iran	89	E5	30 20N	48 15E
Abadla Algeria	100	D14	31 01N	2 45W
Abaetetuba Brazil	72	H13	1 45S	48 54W
Abaiang *is.* Kiribati	103	P11	1 51N	172 58E
Abakan Russia	87	M7	53 43N	91 25E
Abakan *r.* Russia	87	L7	52 00N	90 00E
Abancay Peru	72	C11	13 37S	72 52W
Abashiri Japan	94	D3	44 02N	144 17E
Abbe, Lake Ethiopia	100	N10	11 00N	44 00E
Abbeville Fr.	78	F9	50 06N	1 51E
'Abd al Kūrī *i.* Yemen	89	F1	11 55N	52 20E
Abéché Chad	100	J10	13 49N	20 49E
Abemama *is.* Kiribati	103	P11	0 21N	173 51E
Abeokuta Nigeria	100	E9	7 10N	3 26E
Aberdeen UK	78	D12	57 10N	2 04W
Aberdeen HK China	92	B1	22 14N	114 09E
Aberdeen Maryland USA	65	B1	39 31N	76 10N
Aberdeen South Dakota USA	63	G6	45 28N	98 30W
Aberdeen Washington USA	62	B6	46 58N	123 49W
Aberystwyth UK	78	C10	52 25N	4 05W
Abhā Saudi Arabia	88	D2	18 14N	42 31E
Abidjan Côte d'Ivoire	100	D9	5 19N	4 01W
Abilene Texas USA	62	G3	32 27N	99 45W
Absaroka Range *mts.* USA	62	D6/E5	45 00N	110 00W
Abu Dhabi UAE	89	F3	24 28N	54 25E
Abu Hamed Sudan	100	L11	19 32N	33 20E
Abuja Nigeria	100	F9	9 10N	7 11E
Āl Bū Kamāl Syria	88	D5	34 29N	40 56E
Abu Kebîr Egypt	101	R3	30 44N	31 48E
Abunã Brazil	72	D12	9 41S	65 20W
Acambaro Mexico	66	D3	20 00N	100 42W
Acaponeta Mexico	66	C4	22 30N	102 25W
Acapulco Mexico	66	E3	16 51N	99 56W
Acarigua Venezuela	72	D15	9 35N	69 12W
Acatlán Mexico	66	E3	18 12N	98 02W
Acayucán Mexico	66	E3	17 59N	94 58W
Accra Ghana	100	D9	5 33N	0 15W
Achacachi Bolivia	72	D10	16 01S	68 44W
Achinsk Russia	87	M8	56 20N	90 33E
Acklins Island Bahamas	67	K4	22 30N	74 30W
Aconcagua *mt.* Argentina	73	C7	32 40S	70 02W
Acre Israel	88	N11	32 55N	35 04E
Acre *admin.* Brazil	72	C12	8 30S	71 30W
Ada Oklahoma USA	63	G3	34 47N	96 41W
Adaga *r.* Sp.	79	C4	40 45N	4 45W
Adams New York USA	47	K3	43 49N	76 01W
Adana Turkey	88	C6	37 00N	35 19E
Ad Dakhla Western Sahara	100	A12	23 50N	15 58W
Ad Dammām Saudi Arabia	89	F4	26 25N	50 06E
Ad Dilam Saudi Arabia	89	E3	23 59N	47 06E
Ad Dir'īyah Saudi Arabia	89	E3	24 45N	46 32E
Addis Ababa Ethiopia	100	M9	9 03N	38 42E
Addison New York USA	47	J2	42 06N	77 14W
Ad Dīwānīyah Iraq	88	D5	32 00N	44 57E
Adelaide Aust.	103	G4	34 56S	138 36E
Adelanto California USA	64	E2	34 35N	117 24W
Adelie Land *geog. reg.* Antarctica	109		70 00S	135 00E
Aden Yemen	88	E1	12 50N	45 03E
Aden, Gulf of Indian Ocean	89	E1	12 30N	47 30E
Adirondack Mountains New York USA	63	M5	43 15N	74 40W
Admiralty Island Alaska USA	38	C5	57 45N	134 30W
Admiralty Island National Monument Alaska USA	38	C6	58 05N	134 00W
Admiralty Islands PNG	103	J10	2 30S	147 00E
Adoni India	90	D3	15 38N	77 16E
Adra Sp.	79	D2	36 45N	3 01W
Adrar Algeria	100	D13	27 51N	0 19W
Adrian Michigan USA	45	J1	41 54N	84 02W
Adriatic Sea Mediterranean Sea	81	E5	43 00N	15 00E
Ādwa Ethiopia	100	M10	14 12N	38 56E
Aegean Sea Mediterranean Sea	81	K3	39 00N	24 00E
AFGHANISTAN	89	H5/K6		
Afyon Turkey	88	B6	38 46N	30 32E
Agadez Niger	100	F11	17 00N	7 56E
Agadir Morocco	100	C14	30 30N	9 40W
Agano *r.* Japan	94	C2	37 50N	139 30E
Agartala India	91	G4	23 49N	91 15E
Agen Fr.	79	F6	44 12N	0 38E
Āgios Nikólaos Greece	81	K1	35 11N	25 43E
Agout *r.* Fr.	79	G5	43 50N	1 50E
Agra India	90	D5	27 09N	78 00E
Agri *r.* Italy	81	F4	40 00N	16 00E
Ağri Daği *mt.* Turkey	88	D6	39 44N	44 15E
Agrigento Italy	81	D2	37 19N	13 35E
Agrínio Greece	81	H3	38 38N	21 25E
Aguadas Col.	72	B15	5 36N	75 30W
Aguadilla Puerto Rico	67	L3	18 27N	67 08W
Agua Prieta Mexico	66	C6	31 20N	109 32W
Aguascalientes Mexico	66	D4	21 51N	102 18W
Agueda *r.* Sp.	79	B4	40 50N	6 50W
Aguilas Sp.	79	E2	37 25N	1 35W
Aguiles Serdan Mexico	66	C5	28 40N	105 57W
Agulhas Basin Indian Ocean	105	A2	45 00S	20 00E
Agulhas, Cape RSA	101	J1	34 50S	20 00E
Ahmadabad India	90	C4	23 03N	72 40E
Ahmadnagar India	90	C3	19 08N	74 48E
Ahuachapán El Salvador	66	G2	13 57N	89 49W
Ahvāz Iran	89	E5	31 17N	48 43E
Ain *r.* Fr.	79	H7	46 30N	5 30E
Aïn Sefra Algeria	100	D14	32 45N	0 35W
Aïr *mts.* Niger	100	F11	19 10N	8 20E
Aire-sur-l'Adour Fr.	79	E5	43 42N	0 15W
Aix-en-Provence Fr.	79	H5	43 31N	5 27E
Aizawl India	91	M9	23 43N	92 47E
Aizu-wakamatsu Japan	94	C2	37 30N	139 58E
Ajaccio France	79	K4	41 55N	8 43E
Ajay *r.* India	91	J9	23 50N	88 00E
Ajdabiya Libya	100	J14	30 46N	20 14E
'Ajlūn Jordan	88	N11	32 20N	35 35E
Ajmer India	90	C5	26 29N	74 40E
Ajo Arizona USA	62	D3	32 24N	112 51W
Akabira Japan	94	D3	43 40N	141 55E
Akashi Japan	94	B1	34 39N	135 00E
Aketi CDR	100	J8	2 42N	23 51E
Akita Japan	94	D2	39 44N	140 05E
Akobo Sudan	100	L9	7 50N	33 05E
Akola India	90	D4	20 49N	77 05E
Ákra Akrítas *c.* Greece	81	H2	36 43N	21 52E
Ákra Kafiréas *c.* Greece	81	K3	38 10N	24 35E
Ákra Maléas *c.* Greece	81	J2	36 27N	23 12E
Ákra Taínaro *c.* Greece	81	J2	36 23N	22 29E
Akron Ohio USA	63	K5	41 04N	81 31W
Aktau Kazakhstan	86	H5	43 37N	51 11E
Aktyubinsk Kazakhstan	86	H7	50 16N	57 13E
Alabama *r.* Alabama USA	63	J3	31 00N	88 00W
Alabama *state* USA	63	J3	32 00N	87 00W
Alagoas *admin.* Brazil	72	K12	9 30S	37 00W
Alagoinhas Brazil	72	K11	12 09S	38 21W
Alagón *r.* Sp.	79	B3	40 00N	6 30W
Alajuela Costa Rica	67	H2	10 00N	84 12W
Al 'Amārah Iraq	89	E5	31 51N	47 10E
Alamo Nevada USA	64	F3	37 23N	115 10W
Alamosa Colorado USA	62	E4	37 28N	105 54W
Åland *is.* Finland	80	G14	60 15N	20 00E
Alanya Turkey	88	B6	36 32N	32 02E
Al Artāwīyah Saudi Arabia	88	E4	26 31N	45 21E
Ala Shan *mts.* China	93	J6/J7	40 00N	102 30E
Alaska *state* USA	38	C5	58 00N	135 00W
Alaska, Gulf of Alaska USA	107	M13	58 00N	147 00W
Alaska Range *mts.* Alaska USA	54	A3/B3	62 30N	145 00W
Al 'Ayn UAE	89	G3	24 10N	55 43E
Alay Range *mts.* Asia	86	K4	39 00N	70 00E
Albacete Sp.	79	E3	39 00N	1 52W
Alba Iulia Romania	81	J7	46 04N	23 33E
ALBANIA	81	G4/H4		
Albany Aust.	102	C4	34 57S	117 54E
Albany Georgia USA	63	K3	31 37N	84 10W
Albany New York USA	63	M5	42 40N	73 49W
Albany Oregon USA	62	B5	44 38N	123 07W
Al Başrah Iraq	89	E5	30 30N	47 50E
Al Bayda Libya	100	J14	32 00N	21 30E
Albert, Lake Uganda/CDR	100	L8	2 00N	31 00E
Albert Lea Minnesota USA	63	H5	43 38N	93 16W
Albi Fr.	79	G5	43 56N	2 08E
Albion Michigan USA	46	B2	42 14N	84 45W
Albion New York USA	46	H3	43 14N	78 11W
Al Bi'r Saudi Arabia	88	C4	28 50N	36 16E
Ålborg Denmark	80	B12	57 05N	9 50E
Albuquerque New Mexico USA	62	E4	35 05N	106 38W
Al Buraymī Oman	89	G3	24 16N	55 48E
Alcalá de Henares Sp.	79	D4	40 28N	3 22W
Alcamo Italy	81	D2	37 58N	12 58E
Alcañiz Sp.	79	E4	41 03N	0 09W
Alcázar de San Juan Sp.	79	D3	39 24N	3 12W
Alcira Sp.	79	E3	39 10N	0 27W
Alcoy Sp.	79	E3	38 42N	0 29W
Aldabra Islands Indian Ocean	105	D6	9 00S	46 00E
Aldama Mexico	66	E4	22 54N	98 05W
Aldan Russia	87	Q8	58 44N	124 22E
Aldan *r.* Russia	87	R8	59 00N	132 30E
Alderney *i.* British Isles	78	D8	49 43N	2 12W
Alegrete Brazil	73	F8	29 45S	55 40W
Aleksandrovsk-Sakhalinskiy Russia	87	S7	50 55N	142 12E
Alençon Fr.	78	F8	48 25N	0 05E
Alenuihaha Channel *sd.* Hawaiian Islands	107	Y18	20 20N	156 20W
Aleppo Syria	88	C6	36 14N	37 10E
Alès Fr.	79	H6	44 08N	4 05E
Alessándria Italy	81	B6	44 55N	8 37E
Aleutian Basin Pacific Ocean	106	J13	54 00N	178 00W
Aleutian Islands Pacific Ocean	106	H13	52 00N	178 00W
Aleutian Ridge Pacific Ocean	106	H13	53 55N	178 00W
Aleutian Trench Pacific Ocean	106	H13	50 55N	178 00W
Alexander Archipelago *is.* Alaska USA	38	B5/D4	57 00N	137 30W
Alexander Bay *tn.* RSA	101	H2	28 40S	16 30E
Alexander Island Antarctica	109		71 00S	70 00W
Alexandria Egypt	100	K14	31 13N	29 55E
Alexandria Romania	81	K5	43 59N	25 19E
Alexandria Louisiana USA	63	H3	31 19N	92 29W
Alexandria Bay *tn.* New York USA	45	P3	44 20N	75 55W
Alexandroúpoli Greece	81	K4	40 51N	25 53E
Alfambra *r.* Sp.	79	E4	40 40N	1 00W
Alfeiós *r.* Greece	81	H2	37 30N	21 45E
Al Fuḩayḩīl Kuwait	89	E4	29 07N	47 02E
Algeciras Sp.	79	C2	36 08N	5 27W
ALGERIA	100	C13		
Alghero Italy	81	B4	40 34N	8 19E
Algiers Algeria	100	E15	36 50N	3 00E
Al Ḩadīthah Iraq	88	D5	34 06N	42 25E
Al Ḩarīq Saudi Arabia	89	E3	23 34N	46 35E
Al Ḩasakah Syria	88	D6	36 32N	40 44E
Al Ḩillah Iraq	88	D5	32 28N	44 29E
Al Hufūf Saudi Arabia	89	E4	25 20N	49 34E
Aliákmanas *r.* Greece	81	J4	40 00N	22 00E
Alicante Sp.	79	E3	38 21N	0 29W
Alice Texas USA	63	G2	27 45N	98 06W
Alice Springs *tn.* Aust.	102	F6	23 42S	133 52E
Aligarh India	90	D5	27 54N	78 04E
Aling Kangri *mt.* China	92	E5	32 51N	81 03E
Alipur Duar India	91	K11	26 27N	89 38E
Al Jahrah Kuwait	89	E4	29 22N	47 40E
Al Jawf Libya	100	J12	24 12N	23 18E
Al Jawf Saudi Arabia	88	C4	29 49N	39 52E
Al Jubayl Saudi Arabia	89	E4	26 59N	49 40E
Aljustrel Port.	79	A2	37 52N	8 10W
Al Karāmah Jordan	88	N10	31 58N	35 34E
Al Khums Libya	100	G14	32 39N	14 16E
Al Kufrah Oasis Libya	100	J12	24 10N	23 15E
Al Kūt Iraq	88	E5	32 30N	45 51E
Allagash River Maine USA	47	S6	46 45N	69 20W
Allahabad India	90	E5	25 27N	81 50E
Allegheny River Pennsylvania USA	46	G1	41 40N	79 30W
Allegheny Mountains Pennsylvania USA	65	A2	40 30N	78 25W
Allegheny Reservoir Pennsylvania/New York USA	45	M1	41 52N	79 00W
Allende Mexico	66	D5	28 22N	100 50W
Allentown Pennsylvania USA	63	L5	40 37N	75 30W
Alleppey India	90	D1	9 30N	76 22E
Alliance Nebraska USA	62	F5	42 08N	102 54W
Allier *r.* Fr.	79	G7	46 40N	3 00E
Al Līth Saudi Arabia	88	D3	20 10N	40 20E
Alma Michigan USA	46	B3	43 23N	84 40W
Almada Port.	79	A3	38 40N	9 09W
Almadén Sp.	79	C3	38 47N	4 50W
Almansa Sp.	79	E3	38 52N	1 06W
Almanzora *r.* Sp.	79	D2	37 15N	2 10W
Almaty Kazakhstan	86	K5	43 19N	76 55E
Almería Sp.	79	D2	36 50N	2 26W
Älmhult Sweden	80	E12	56 32N	14 10E
Almodôvar Port.	79	A2	37 31N	8 03W
Al Mubarraz Saudi Arabia	89	E4	25 26N	49 37E
Al Mukhā Yemen	88	D1	13 20N	43 16E
Al Muqdādīyah Iraq	88	D5	33 58N	44 58E
Alor *i.* Indonesia	95	G2	8 15S	124 30E
Alor Setar Malaysia	95	C5	6 07N	100 21E
Alpena Michigan USA	45	K3	45 03N	83 27W
Alpes Maritimes *mts.* Fr./Italy	79	J5/J6	44 15N	6 45E
Alpi Carniche *mts.* Europe	81	D7	46 00N	13 00E
Alpi Cozie *mts.* Europe	79	J6	45 00N	8 00E
Alpi Dolomitiche *mts.* Italy	81	C7	46 00N	12 00E
Alpi Graie *mts.* Europe	81	A6	45 00N	7 00E
Alpi Lepontine *mts.* Switz.	79	K7	46 26N	8 30E
Alpine Texas USA	62	F3	30 22N	103 40W
Alpi Pennine *mts.* Italy/Switz.	79	J7	45 55N	7 30E
Alpi Retiche *mts.* Switz.	79	K7/L7	46 25N	9 45E
Alps *mts.* Europe	79	J6/L7	46 00N	7 30E
Al Qāmishlī Syria	88	D6	37 03N	41 15E
Al Qunayţirah Syria	88	N11	33 08N	35 49E
Al Qunfudhah Saudi Arabia	88	D2	19 09N	41 07E
Alsek River Alaska USA	38	A6	59 15N	138 40W
Alta Gracia Argentina	73	E7	31 42S	64 25W
Altai *mts.* Mongolia	92	G8	47 00N	92 30E
Altamaha *r.* Georgia USA	63	K3	32 00N	82 00W
Altamira Brazil	72	G13	3 13S	52 15W
Altamura Italy	81	F4	40 49N	16 34E
Altay China	92	F8	47 48N	88 07E
Altay *mts.* Russia	87	L7	51 00N	89 00E
Alto Molocue Mozambique	101	M4	15 38S	37 42E
Altoona Pennsylvania USA	63	L5	40 32N	78 32W
Alto Purus *r.* Peru	72	C11	10 30S	72 00W
Altun Shan *mts.* China	92	E6/F6	37 30N	86 00E
Altus Oklahoma USA	62	G3	34 39N	99 21W
Alva Oklahoma USA	63	G4	36 48N	98 40W
Al Wajh Saudi Arabia	88	C4	26 16N	32 28E
Alwar India	90	D5	27 32N	76 35E
Amadeus, Lake Aust.	102	F6	24 00S	132 30E
Amadi Sudan	100	L9	5 32N	30 20E
Amagasaki Japan	94	C1	34 42N	135 23E
Amakusa-shotō *is.* Japan	94	B1	32 50N	130 05E
Amapá Brazil	72	G14	2 00N	50 50W
Amapá *admin.* Brazil	72	G14	2 00N	52 30W
Amargosa Desert Nevada USA	64	E3	36 45N	116 37W
Amargosa Valley *tn.* Nevada USA	64	E3	36 40N	116 22W
Amarillo Texas USA	62	F4	35 14N	101 50W
Amazonas *admin.* Brazil	72	D13	4 30S	65 00W
Amazonas *r.* Brazil	72	G13	2 00S	53 00W
Amazon, Mouths of the *est.* Brazil	72	G14	1 00N	51 00W
Ambala India	90	D6	30 19N	76 49E
Ambarchik Russia	87	U10	69 39N	162 37E
Ambato Ecuador	72	B13	1 18S	78 39W
Ambon Indonesia	95	H3	3 41S	128 10E
Ambovombe Madagascar	101	P2	25 10S	46 06E
Amboy California USA	64	F2	34 33N	115 44W
Amderma Russia	86	J10	66 44N	61 35E
Amdo China	92	G5	32 22N	91 07E
Ameca Mexico	66	D4	20 34N	104 03W
American Falls *tn.* Idaho USA	62	D5	42 47N	112 50W
American Samoa Pacific Ocean	107	K6	15 00S	170 00W
Amery Ice Shelf Antarctica	109		70 00S	70 00E
Amfípoli Greece	81	J4	40 48N	23 52E
Amga Russia	87	R9	61 51N	131 59E
Amga *r.* Russia	87	R9	60 30N	130 00E
Amgun' *r.* Russia	87	R7	52 00N	137 00E
Amiens Fr.	78	G8	49 54N	2 18E
Amindivi Islands India	90	C2	11 23N	72 23E
Amirante Islands Seychelles	105	E6	5 00S	55 00E
Amman Jordan	88	C5	31 04N	46 17E
Amorgós *i.* Greece	81	K2	36 50N	25 55E
Ampana Indonesia	95	G3	0 54S	121 35E
Amravati India	90	D4	20 58N	77 50E
Amritsar India	90	C6	31 35N	74 56E
Amsterdam Neths.	78	H10	52 22N	4 54E
Amsterdam New York USA	65	C3	42 57N	74 11W
Amstetten Austria	80	E8	48 08N	14 52E
Am Timan Chad	100	J10	10 59N	20 18E
Amudar'ya *r.* Asia	86	J4/J5	40 00N	64 00E
Amundsen Sea Southern Ocean	109		72 00S	130 00W
Amur *r.* Asia	93	P9	52 30N	126 30E
Amursk Russia	87	R7	50 16N	136 55E
Anabar *r.* Russia	87	P11	71 30N	113 00E
Anacapa Islands California USA	64	D2	34 01N	119 23W
Anaconda Montana USA	62	D6	46 09N	112 56W
Anacortes Washington USA	38	H4	48 29N	122 35W
Anadolu Dağlari *mts.* Turkey	88	C7/D7	40 30N	38 30E
Anadyr' Russia	87	V9	64 50N	178 00E
Anadyr' *r.* Russia	87	V10	65 00N	175 00E
Anadyr', Gulf of Russia	87	W9	65 00N	178 00W
Anáfi *i.* Greece	81	K2	36 20N	25 45E
Anaheim California USA	64	E1	33 50N	117 54W
Anai Mudi *mt.* India	90	D2	10 20N	77 15E
Anan Japan	94	B1	33 54N	134 40E
Ananindeua Brazil	72	H13	1 22S	48 20W
Anantapur India	90	D2	14 42N	77 05E
Anápolis Brazil	72	H10	16 19S	48 58W
Anatom *i.* Vanuatu	103	N6	20 10S	169 50E
Ancona Italy	81	D5	43 37N	13 31E
Andaman and Nicobar *admin.* India	91	G1	12 30N	92 45E
Andaman Islands India	91	G2	12 00N	94 00E
Anderson South Carolina USA	63	K3	34 30N	82 39W
Anderson Indiana USA	63	J5	40 05N	85 41W
Andes *mts.* South America	72/73	B14	10 00S	77 00W
Andhra Pradesh *admin.* India	90	D3	16 00N	79 00E
Andizhan Uzbekistan	86	K5	40 40N	72 12E
Andkhvoy Afghanistan	89	J6	36 59N	65 08E
ANDORRA	79	F5		
Andorra la Vella Andorra	79	F5	42 30N	1 30E
Andros *i.* Bahamas	67	J4	24 00N	78 00W
Ándros *i.* Greece	81	K2	37 49N	24 54E
Androscoggin River Maine USA	51	E1	44 27N	70 50W
Andújar Sp.	79	C3	38 02N	4 03W
Andulo Angola	101	H5	11 29S	16 43E
Angara *r.* Russia	87	M8	58 00N	97 30E
Angarsk Russia	87	N7	52 31N	103 55E
Angel de la Guarda *i.* Mexico	66	B5	29 00N	113 30W
Angelholm Sweden	80	D12	56 15N	12 50E
Angels Camp California USA	64	C4	38 04N	120 34W
Angers Fr.	79	E7	47 29N	0 32W
Anglesey *i.* UK	78	C10	53 18N	4 25W
ANGOLA	101	H5		
Angola Indiana USA	45	J1	41 38N	84 59W
Angola New York USA	46	G2	42 39N	79 02W
Angola Basin Atlantic Ocean	108	J5	15 00S	3 00E
Angoon Alaska USA	38	C5	57 30N	133 35W
Angoulême Fr.	79	F6	45 40N	0 10E
Anguilla *i.* Leeward Islands	66	P10	18 14N	63 05W
Anjō Japan	94	C1	34 56N	137 05E
Ankara Turkey	88	B6	39 55N	32 50E
Ankaratra *mt.* Madagascar	101	P4	19 25S	47 12E
'Annaba Algeria	100	F15	36 55N	7 47E
An Nabk Saudi Arabia	88	C5	31 21N	37 20E
An Nabk Syria	88	C5	34 02N	36 43E
An Nafud *d.* Saudi Arabia	88	D4	28 20N	40 30E
An Najaf Iraq	88	D5	31 59N	44 19E
Annapolis Maryland USA	63	L4	38 59N	76 30W
Annapurna *mt.* Nepal	90	E5	28 34N	83 50E
Ann Arbor Michigan USA	45	K2	42 17N	83 45W
An Nāsirīyah Iraq	88	E5	31 04N	46 17E
Annecy Fr.	79	J6	45 54N	6 07E
Annette Island Alaska USA	38	E4	55 10N	131 30W
Anniston Alabama USA	63	J3	33 38N	85 50W
Annotto Bay *tn.* Jamaica	67	U14	18 16N	76 47W
Anqing China	93	M5	30 46N	119 40E
Ansbach Germany	80	C8	49 18N	10 36E
Anshan China	93	N7	41 05N	122 58E
Anshun China	93	K4	26 15N	105 51E
Antakya Turkey	88	C6	36 12N	36 10E
Antalya Turkey	88	B6	36 53N	30 42E
Antananarivo Madagascar	101	P4	18 52S	47 30E
Antarctica	109			
Antarctic Peninsula Antarctica	109		68 00S	65 00W
Antequera Sp.	79	C2	37 01N	4 34W
Antibes Fr.	79	J5	43 35N	7 07E
Antigua Guatemala	66	F2	14 33N	90 42W
Antigua *i.* Antigua & Barbuda	66	Q9	17 09N	61 49W
ANTIGUA AND BARBUDA	66	Q9		
Antioch California USA	64	C4	38 00N	121 49W
Antipodes Islands Southern Ocean	106	H3	49 42S	178 50E
Antofagasta Chile	72	C9	23 40S	70 23W
Antsiranana Madagascar	101	P5	12 19S	49 17E

Antwerp New York USA	**47**	L4	44 13N	75 38W
Antwerpen Belgium	**78**	H9	51 13N	4 25W
Anuradhapura Sri Lanka	**90**	E1	8 20N	80 25E
Anxi China	**92**	H7	40 32N	95 57E
Anyang China	**93**	L6	36 04N	114 20E
Anza California USA	**64**	E1	33 33N	116 41W
Anzhero-Sudzhensk Russia	**87**	L8	56 10N	86 01E
Aomori Japan	**94**	D3	40 50N	140 43E
Aosta Italy	**81**	A6	45 43N	7 19E
Aozou Strip Chad	**100**	H12	23 00N	17 00E
Apaporis *r.* Col.	**72**	C14	1 00N	72 30W
Aparri Philippines	**95**	G7	18 22N	121 40E
Apatity Russia	**86**	F10	67 32N	33 21E
Apatzingán Mexico	**66**	D3	19 05N	102 20W
Apostle Islands Wisconsin USA	**45**	F4	47 02N	90 30W
Appalachian Mountains USA	**63**	K4	37 00N	82 00W
Appennini *mts.* Italy	**81**	B6/E4	43 00N	12 30E
Appennino Abruzzese *mts.* Italy	**81**	D5/E4	42 00N	14 00E
Appennino Ligure *mts.* Italy	**81**	B6	44 00N	9 00E
Appennino Lucano *mts.* Italy	**81**	E4	40 30N	15 30E
Appennino Tosco-Emiliano *mts.* Italy	**81**	C6/D5	44 00N	12 00E
Appleton Wisconsin USA	**63**	J5	44 17N	88 24W
Apure *r.* Venezuela	**72**	D15	7 40N	68 00W
'Aqaba Jordan	**88**	C5	29 32N	35 00E
Aqaba, Gulf of Middle East	**88**	N9	28 40N	34 40E
Aquidauana Brazil	**72**	F9	20 27S	55 45W
Aquidauana *r.* Brazil	**72**	F10	20 00S	56 00W
Arabian Basin Indian Ocean	**105**	F7/F8	10 00N	65 00E
Arabian Sea Indian Ocean	**105**	F8	17 00N	60 00E
Aracaju Brazil	**72**	K11	10 54S	37 07W
Aracati Brazil	**72**	K13	4 32S	37 45W
Arad Romania	**81**	H7	46 10N	21 19E
Arafura Sea Indonesia	**95**	J2	8 00S	132 00E
Aragón *r.* Sp.	**79**	E5	42 15N	1 40W
Araguaia *r.* Brazil	**72**	H12	7 20S	49 00W
Araguaína Brazil	**72**	H12	7 16S	48 18W
Araguari Brazil	**72**	H10	18 38S	48 13W
Arāk Iran	**89**	E5	34 05N	49 42E
Aral Sea *l.* Asia	**86**	H5/J6	45 00N	60 00E
Aral'sk Kazakhstan	**86**	J6	46 56N	61 43E
Arambag India	**91**	K9	22 50N	87 59E
Aranda de Duero Sp.	**79**	D4	41 40N	3 41W
Aran Islands RoI	**78**	A10	53 10N	9 50W
Aranjuez Sp.	**79**	D4	40 02N	3 37W
Aranuka *is.* Kiribati	**103**	P10	0 11N	173 36E
Arapiraca Brazil	**72**	K12	9 45S	36 40W
Ar'ar Saudi Arabia	**88**	D5	30 58N	41 03E
Araraquara Brazil	**72**	H9	21 46S	48 08W
Ararat, Mount Turkey	**88**	D6	39 44N	44 15E
Aras *r.* Turkey	**88**	D7	40 00N	43 30E
Arauca Col.	**72**	C15	7 04N	70 41W
Arauca *r.* Venezuela	**72**	D15	7 10N	68 30W
Araxá Brazil	**72**	H10	19 37S	46 50W
Araz *r.* Iran	**88**	E6	38 40N	46 30E
Arbil Iraq	**88**	D6	36 12N	44 01E
Arcachon Fr.	**79**	E6	44 40N	1 11W
Arcade New York USA	**46**	H2	42 32N	78 25W
Arctic National Wildlife Refuge Alaska USA	**54**	A4/B4	68 30N	144 30W
Arctic Ocean	**109**			
Arda *r.* Bulgaria	**81**	K4	41 30N	26 00E
Ardabīl Iran	**89**	E6	38 15N	48 18E
Ardennes *mts.* Belgium	**78**	H9/J9	50 10N	5 45E
Ardila *r.* Sp.	**79**	B3	38 15N	6 50W
Ardmore Oklahoma USA	**63**	G3	34 11N	97 08W
Arendal Norway	**78**	K13	58 27N	8 56E
Arequipa Peru	**72**	C10	16 25S	71 32W
Arezzo Italy	**81**	C5	43 28N	11 53E
Argentan Fr.	**78**	E8	48 45N	0 01W
ARGENTINA	**73**	D6		
Argentine Basin Atlantic Ocean	**108**	J3	42 00S	45 00W
Argeș *r.* Romania	**81**	K6	44 00N	26 00E
Argun *r.* Asia	**93**	M9	51 30N	120 00E
Argyle, Lake Aust.	**102**	E7	17 00S	128 30E
Århus Denmark	**80**	C12	56 15N	10 10E
Arica Chile	**72**	C10	18 30S	70 20W
Arima Trinidad and Tobago	**67**	V15	10 38N	61 17W
Aripuanã *r.* Brazil	**72**	E12	7 00S	60 30W
Ariquemes Brazil	**72**	E12	9 55S	63 06W
Arizona *state* USA	**62**	D3	34 00N	112 00W
Arizpe Mexico	**66**	B6	30 20N	110 11W
Arjona Col.	**72**	B16	10 14N	75 22W
Arkalyk Kazakhstan	**86**	J7	50 17N	66 51E
Arkansas *r.* USA	**62**	G4	36 00N	99 00W
Arkansas *state* USA	**63**	H3	34 00N	93 00W
Arkansas City Kansas USA	**63**	G4	37 03N	97 02W
Arkhangel'sk Russia	**86**	G9	64 32N	40 40E
Arklow RoI	**78**	B10	52 48N	6 09W
Arlanza *r.* Sp.	**79**	D5	42 00N	3 30W
Arlanzón *r.* Sp.	**79**	D5	42 00N	4 00W
Arles Fr.	**79**	H5	43 41N	4 38E
Arlington Washington USA	**38**	H4	48 08N	122 15W
Arlit Niger	**100**	F11	18 50N	7 00E
Arlon Belgium	**78**	H8	49 41N	5 49E
Armagh UK	**78**	B11	54 21N	6 39W
Armavir Russia	**86**	G5	44 59N	41 40E
ARMENIA	**86**	G5		
Armenia Col.	**72**	B14	4 32N	75 40W
Armenia Mountain Pennsylvania USA	**47**	K1	41 45N	76 55W
Armidale Aust.	**103**	K4	30 32S	151 40E
Arnhem Neths.	**78**	H9	52 00N	5 53E
Arnhem Land *geog. reg.* Aust.	**102**	F8	13 00S	133 00E
Arno *r.* Italy	**81**	C5	43 00N	10 00E
Arnold California USA	**64**	C4	38 15N	120 20W
Aroostook River Maine USA	**51**	F2	46 48N	68 30W
Arorae *i.* Kiribati	**103**	Q10	2 38S	176 49E
Arquipélago dos Bijagós *is.* Guinea-Bissau	**100**	A10	11 20N	16 40W
Ar Ramādī Iraq	**88**	D5	33 27N	43 19E
Ar Ramlah Jordan	**88**	N9	29 28N	25 58E
Arran *i.* UK	**78**	C11	55 35N	5 15W
Ar Raqqah Syria	**88**	C6	35 57N	39 03E
Arroyo Grande California USA	**64**	C2	35 08N	120 34W
Árta Greece	**81**	H3	39 10N	20 59E
Artigas Uruguay	**73**	F7	30 25S	56 28W
Arua Uganda	**100**	L8	3 02N	30 56E
Aruba *i.* Neths.	**72**	C16	12 30N	70 00W
Arunachal Pradesh *admin.* India	**91**	G5/H5	28 00N	95 00E
Arusha Tanzania	**100**	M7	3 23S	36 40E
Aruwimi *r.* CDR	**100**	K8	2 00N	25 00E
Arvika Sweden	**80**	D13	59 41N	12 38E
Arvin California USA	**64**	D2	35 11N	118 50W
Asahi-dake *mt.* Japan	**94**	D3	43 42N	142 54E
Asahikawa Japan	**94**	D3	43 46N	142 23E
Asamankese Ghana	**100**	D9	5 45N	0 45W
Asansol India	**91**	F4	23 40N	86 59E
Asbury Park *tn.* New Jersey USA	**65**	C2	40 14N	74 00W
Ascension Island Atlantic Ocean	**108**	G6	7 57S	14 22W
Ascoli Piceno Italy	**81**	D5	42 52N	13 35E
Assab Eritrea	**100**	N10	13 01N	42 47E
Asenovgrad Bulgaria	**81**	K4	42 00N	24 53E
Ashburton *r.* Aust.	**102**	C6	22 30S	116 00E
Ashdod Israel	**88**	N10	31 48N	34 48E
Asheville North Carolina USA	**63**	K4	35 35N	82 35W
Ash Fork Arizona USA	**62**	D4	35 13N	112 29W
Ashgabat Turkmenistan	**86**	H4	37 58N	58 24E
Ashikaga Japan	**94**	C2	36 21N	139 26E
Ashizuri-misaki *c.* Japan	**94**	B1	32 42N	133 00E
Ashland Kentucky USA	**63**	K4	38 28N	82 40W
Ashland Oregon USA	**62**	B5	42 14N	122 44W
Ashland Wisconsin USA	**45**	F4	46 35N	90 53W
Ashqelon Israel	**88**	N10	31 40N	34 35E
Ash Springs *tn.* Nevada USA	**64**	F3	37 32N	115 12W
Ashtabula Ohio USA	**45**	L1	41 52N	80 48W
Askim Norway	**78**	L13	59 15N	11 10E
Asmara Eritrea	**100**	M11	15 20N	38 58E
Assam *admin.* India	**91**	G5	26 20N	92 00E
As Samāwah Iraq	**88**	E5	31 18N	45 18E
Assis Brazil	**72**	G9	22 37S	50 25W
Assisi Italy	**81**	D5	43 04N	12 37E
As Sulaymaniyah Iraq	**88**	E6	35 32N	45 27E
As Sūq Saudi Arabia	**88**	D3	21 55N	42 02E
As Suwaydā' Syria	**88**	P11	32 43N	36 33E
Astana Kazakhstan	**86**	K7	51 10N	71 28E
Asti Italy	**81**	B6	44 54N	8 13E
Astoria Oregon USA	**62**	B6	46 12N	123 50W
Astrakhan' Russia	**86**	G6	46 22N	48 04E
Astypálaia *i.* Greece	**81**	L2	36 30N	26 20E
Asunción Paraguay	**72**	F8	25 15S	57 40W
Aswa *r.* Uganda	**100**	L8	3 30N	32 30E
Aswân Egypt	**100**	L12	24 05N	32 56E
Aswân Dam Egypt	**100**	L12	23 40N	31 50E
Asyût Egypt	**100**	L13	27 14N	31 07E
Atar Mauritania	**100**	B12	20 32N	13 08W
Atascadero California USA	**64**	C2	35 30N	120 40W
Atbara Sudan	**100**	L11	17 42N	34 00E
Atbara *r.* Sudan	**100**	M11	17 28N	34 30E
Atbasar Kazakhstan	**86**	J7	51 49N	68 18E
Atchison Kansas USA	**63**	G4	39 33N	95 09W
Athens Greece	**81**	J2	38 00N	23 44E
Athens Georgia USA	**63**	K3	33 57N	83 24W
Athens Pennsylvania USA	**47**	K1	41 57N	76 31W
Athlone RoI	**78**	B10	53 25N	7 56W
Athol Springs *tn.* New York USA	**48**	D1	42 45N	78 49W
Áthos *mt.* Greece	**81**	K4	40 10N	24 19E
Ati Chad	**100**	H10	13 11N	18 20E
Atlanta Georgia USA	**63**	K3	33 45N	84 23W
Atlanta Michigan USA	**45**	J3	45 00N	84 08W
Atlantic City New Jersey USA	**63**	M4	39 23N	74 27W
Atlantic-Indian Ridge Atlantic Ocean	**108**	H1/K1	53 00S	3 00E
Atlantic Ocean	**108**			
Atlas Saharien *mts.* Algeria	**100**	D14	33 30N	1 00E
Atrai *r.* India/Bangladesh	**91**	K10	25 10N	88 50E
At Tā'if Saudi Arabia	**88**	D3	21 15N	40 21E
Attica New York USA	**46**	H2	42 52N	78 17W
Atyrau Kazakhstan	**86**	H6	47 08N	51 59E
Aubagne Fr.	**79**	H5	43 17N	5 35E
Aubenas Fr.	**79**	H6	44 37N	4 24E
Auburn Indiana USA	**46**	A1	41 22N	85 02W
Auburn Maine USA	**63**	M5	44 04N	70 27W
Auburn Massachusetts USA	**65**	E3	42 11N	71 51W
Auburn New York USA	**63**	L5	42 57N	76 34W
Auburn Reservoir California USA	**64**	C4	39 05N	120 55W
Auch Fr.	**79**	F5	43 40N	0 36E
Auckland NZ	**103**	P3	36 51S	174 46E
Auckland Islands Southern Ocean	**106**	G2	50 35S	116 00E
Aude *r.* Fr.	**79**	G5	43 00N	2 00E
Au Gres Michigan USA	**46**	C3	44 03N	83 40W
Augsburg Germany	**80**	C8	48 21N	10 54E
Augusta Aust.	**102**	C4	34 19S	115 09E
Augusta Georgia USA	**63**	K3	33 29N	82 00W
Augusta Maine USA	**63**	N5	44 17N	69 50W
Aulne *r.* Fr.	**78**	D8	48 10N	4 00W
Aurangābād India	**90**	D3	19 52N	75 22E
Aurillac Fr.	**79**	G6	44 56N	2 26E
Au Sable Michigan USA	**45**	K3	44 23N	83 20W
Au Sable *r.* Michigan USA	**45**	J3	44 39N	84 08W
Austin Nevada USA	**64**	E4	39 30N	117 05W
Austin Texas USA	**63**	G3	30 18N	97 47W
AUSTRALIA	**102**			
Australian Capital Territory *admin.* Aust.	**103**	J3	35 00S	144 00E
AUSTRIA	**80/81**	D7/E7		
Autlán Mexico	**66**	D3	19 48N	104 20W
Autun Fr.	**79**	H7	46 58N	4 18E
Auxerre Fr.	**78**	G7	47 48N	3 35E
Avallon Fr.	**79**	G7	47 30N	3 54E
Avalon California USA	**64**	D1	33 21N	118 19W
Avawatz Mountains California USA	**64**	E2	35 32N	116 30W
Aveiro Port.	**79**	A4	40 38N	8 40W
Avellaneda Argentina	**73**	F7	34 40S	58 20W
Avenal California USA	**64**	C3	36 00N	120 10W
Avesta Sweden	**80**	F14	60 09N	16 10E
Aveyron *r.* Fr.	**79**	G6	44 30N	2 05E
Avezzano Italy	**81**	D5	42 02N	13 26E
Avila Sp.	**79**	C4	40 39N	4 42W
Avilés Sp.	**79**	C5	43 33N	5 55W
Avon Lake *tn.* Ohio USA	**46**	D1	41 31N	82 01W
Avranches Fr.	**78**	E8	48 42N	1 21W
Awali *r.* Lebanon	**88**	N11	33 35N	35 32E
Awash Ethiopia	**100**	N9	9 01N	41 10E
Awash *r.* Ethiopia	**100**	N9	10 00N	40 00E
Awa-shima *i.* Japan	**94**	C2	38 40N	139 15E
Awbāri Libya	**100**	G13	26 35N	12 46E
Ayacucho Peru	**72**	C11	13 10S	74 15W
Ayaguz Kazakhstan	**86**	L6	47 59N	80 27E
Ayamonte Sp.	**79**	B2	37 13N	7 24W
Ayan Russia	**87**	R8	56 29N	138 07E
Ayaviri Peru	**72**	C11	14 53S	70 35W
Ayers Rock *mt.* Aust.	**102**	F5	25 18S	131 18E
'Aynūnah Saudi Arabia	**88**	C4	28 06N	35 08E
Ayod Sudan	**100**	L9	8 08N	31 24E
Ayon *i.* Russia	**87**	U10	69 55N	169 10E
Ayr UK	**78**	C11	55 28N	4 38W
Ayutthaya Thailand	**95**	C6	14 20N	100 35E
AZERBAIJAN	**86**	G4		
Aziscohos Lake Maine USA	**47**	R5	45 08N	70 59W
Azogues Ecuador	**72**	B13	2 46S	78 56W
Azores *is.* Atlantic Ocean	**108**	F10	38 30N	28 00W
Azoum *r.* Chad	**100**	J10	12 00N	21 00E
Azuero, Peninsula de Panama	**67**	H1	7 40N	81 00W
Azul Argentina	**73**	F6	36 46S	59 50W
Azurduy Bolivia	**72**	E10	20 00S	64 29W
Az Zabadānī Syria	**88**	P11	33 42N	36 03E

B

Ba'albek Lebanon	**88**	P12	34 00N	36 12E
Babahoyo Ecuador	**72**	B13	1 53S	79 31W
Bab el Mandab *sd.* Red Sea	**100**	N10	12 30N	47 00E
Babylon *hist. site* Iraq	**88**	D5	32 33N	44 25E
Bacabal Brazil	**72**	J13	4 15S	44 45W
Bacău Romania	**81**	L7	46 33N	26 58E
Bacolod Philippines	**95**	G6	10 38N	122 58E
Badajoz Sp.	**79**	B3	38 53N	6 58W
Badalona Sp.	**79**	G4	41 27N	2 15E
Bad Axe Michigan USA	**45**	K2	43 48N	82 59W
Baden Austria	**80**	F7	48 01N	16 14E
Badulla Sri Lanka	**90**	E1	6 59N	81 03E
Bafoussam Cameroon	**100**	G9	5 31N	10 25E
Bāfq Iran	**89**	G5	31 35N	55 21E
Bagé Brazil	**73**	G7	31 22S	54 06W
Baghdad Iraq	**88**	D5	33 20N	44 26E
Baghlān Afghanistan	**89**	J6	36 11N	68 44E
BAHAMAS, THE	**67**	J4		
Baharampur India	**91**	K10	24 06N	88 15E
Bahawalpur Pakistan	**90**	C5	29 24N	71 47E
Bahia *admin.* Brazil	**72**	J11	12 00S	42 30W
Bahía Blanca Argentina	**73**	E6	38 45S	62 15W
Bahía Blanca *b.* Argentina	**73**	E6	39 00S	61 00W
Bahía de Campeche *b.* Mexico	**66**	E4/F4	20 00N	95 00W
Bahía Grande *b.* Argentina	**73**	D3	51 30S	68 00W
Bahra el Manzala Lake Egypt	**101**	R4	31 18N	31 54E
Bahraich India	**90**	E5	27 35N	81 36E
BAHRAIN	**89**	F4		
Bahrain, Gulf of The Gulf	**89**	F4	25 55N	50 30E
Bahr el Abiad *r.* Sudan	**100**	L10	14 00N	32 20E
Bahr el Arab *r.* Sudan	**100**	K9	10 00N	27 30E
Bahr el Azraq *r.* Sudan	**100**	L10	13 30N	33 45E
Bahr el Baqar *r.* Egypt	**101**	S3	30 54N	32 02E
Bahr el Ghazal *r.* Chad	**100**	H10	14 00N	16 00E
Bahr Faqus *r.* Egypt	**101**	R3	30 42N	31 42E
Bahr Hadus *r.* Egypt	**101**	R4	31 01N	31 43E
Bahr Saft *r.* Egypt	**101**	R3	30 57N	31 48E
Baia Mare Romania	**80**	J7	47 39N	23 36E
Baicheng China	**93**	N8	45 37N	122 48E
Baie de la Seine *b.* Fr.	**78**	E8	49 40N	0 30W
Baja Hungary	**81**	G7	46 11N	18 58E
Baja California *p.* Mexico	**66**	A6/C4	27 30N	113 00W
Baker California USA	**64**	E2	35 16N	116 06W
Baker Oregon USA	**62**	C5	44 46N	117 50W
Baker Island Alaska USA	**38**	D4	55 30N	133 30W
Baker Islands Pacific Ocean	**106**	J8	0 30N	173 00W
Baker, Mount Washington USA	**38**	H4	48 48N	121 50W
Baker River Washington USA	**38**	H4	48 40N	121 30W
Bakersfield California USA	**62**	C4	35 25N	119 00W
Balaghat India	**90**	E4	21 48N	80 16E
Balaghat Range *mts.* India	**90**	D3	18 45N	77 00E
Balakovo Russia	**86**	G7	52 04N	47 46E
Balama Mozambique	**101**	M5	13 19S	38 35E
Bala Morghab Afghanistan	**89**	H6	35 35N	63 21E
Balassagyarmat Hungary	**80**	G7	48 06N	19 17E
Balaton *l.* Hungary	**81**	F7	47 00N	17 30E
Balboa Panama	**67**	J1	8 57N	79 33W
Spain Mediterranean Sea	**79**	F3/H3	40 00N	2 00E
Bali *i.* Indonesia	**95**	E2/F2	8 30S	115 00E
Balikesir Turkey	**88**	A6	39 37N	27 51E
Balikpapan Indonesia	**95**	F3	1 15S	116 50E
Balipar India	**91**	M11	27 00N	92 30E
Balkhash Kazakhstan	**86**	K6	46 50N	74 57E
Ballarat Aust.	**103**	H3	37 36S	143 58E
Balleny Islands Southern Ocean	**106**	G1	66 30S	164 00E
Ballymena UK	**78**	B11	54 52N	6 17W
Balsas Mexico	**66**	E3	18 00N	99 44W
Balta Ukraine	**80**	M7	47 58N	29 39E
Bălţi Moldova	**80**	L7	47 44N	28 41E
Baltic Sea Europe	**80**	G12	55 15N	17 00E
Baltimore Maryland USA	**63**	L4	39 18N	76 38W
Baluchistan *geog. reg.* Pakistan	**90**	A5	27 30N	65 00E
Balurghat India	**91**	K10	25 12N	88 50E
Bam Iran	**89**	G4	29 07N	58 20E
Bamako Mali	**100**	C10	12 40N	7 59W
Bambari CAR	**100**	J9	5 40N	20 37E
Bamberg Germany	**80**	C8	49 54N	10 54E
Bamenda Cameroon	**100**	G9	5 55N	10 09E
Banaba *i.* Kiribati	**103**	N10	0 52S	169 35E
Banas *r.* India	**90**	D5	26 00N	75 00E
Banda Aceh Indonesia	**95**	B5	5 30N	95 20E
Bandama Blanc *r.* Côte d'Ivoire	**100**	C9	8 00N	5 45W
Bandar-e 'Abbās Iran	**89**	G4	27 12N	56 15E
Bandar-e Lengeh Iran	**89**	F4	26 34N	54 52E
Bandar-e Torkeman Iran	**89**	F6	36 55N	54 01E
Bandar Khomeynī Iran	**89**	E5	30 40N	49 08E
Bandar Seri Begawan Brunei	**95**	F4	4 53N	115 00E
Banda Sea Indonesia	**95**	H2	5 50S	126 00E
Bandirma Turkey	**88**	A7	40 21N	27 58E
Bandundu CDR	**100**	H7	3 20S	17 24E
Bandung Indonesia	**95**	D2	6 57S	107 34E
Banfora Burkina	**100**	D10	10 36N	4 45W
Bangalore India	**90**	D2	12 58N	77 35E
Bangassou CAR	**100**	J8	4 41N	22 48E
Bangkok Thailand	**95**	C6	13 44N	100 30E
BANGLADESH	**91**	F4/G4		
Bangor Wales UK	**78**	C10	53 13N	4 08W
Bangor Northern Ireland UK	**78**	C11	54 40N	5 40W
Bangor Maine USA	**63**	N5	44 49N	68 47W
Bangui CAR	**100**	H8	4 23N	18 37E
Bangweulu, Lake Zambia	**101**	K5	11 15S	29 45E
Banja Luka Bosnia-Herzegovina	**81**	F6	44 47N	17 11E
Banjarmasin Indonesia	**95**	E3	3 22S	114 33E
Banjul The Gambia	**100**	A10	13 28N	16 39W
Banks Islands Vanuatu	**103**	N8	13 40S	167 30E
Banmi Pakistan	**90**	C6	33 00N	70 30E
Banning California USA	**64**	E1	33 55N	116 52W
Banská Bystrica Slovakia	**80**	G8	48 44N	19 10E
Banyuwangi Indonesia	**95**	E2	8 12S	114 22E
Baoding China	**93**	M6	38 54N	115 26E
Baoji China	**93**	K5	34 23N	107 16E
Baotou China	**93**	K7	40 38N	109 59E
Ba'qūbah Iraq	**88**	D5	33 45N	44 40E
Baracaldo Sp.	**79**	D5	43 17N	2 59W
Barahona Dom. Rep.	**67**	K3	18 13N	71 07W
Barakpur India	**91**	K9	22 45N	88 23E
Baral *r.* Bangladesh	**91**	K10	24 20N	89 05E
Baranof Alaska USA	**38**	C5	57 05N	134 50W
Baranof Island Alaska USA	**38**	C5	57 30N	135 00W
Barbacena Brazil	**72**	J9	21 13S	43 47W
BARBADOS	**66**	S11		
Barbastro Sp.	**79**	F5	42 02N	0 07E
Barbuda *i.* Antigua & Barbuda	**66**	Q9	17 41N	61 48W
Barcaldine Aust.	**103**	J6	23 31S	145 15E
Barcellona Italy	**81**	E3	38 10N	15 15E
Barcelona Sp.	**79**	G4	41 25N	2 10E
Barcelona Venezuela	**72**	E16	10 08N	64 43W
Barcelonnette Fr.	**79**	J6	44 24N	6 40E
Barcelos Brazil	**72**	E13	0 59S	62 58W
Barcoo *r.* Aust.	**103**	H6	24 00S	144 00E
Barcs Hungary	**81**	F6	45 58N	17 30E
Barddhaman India	**91**	F4	23 20N	88 00E
Bareilly India	**90**	D5	28 20N	79 24E
Barents Sea Arctic Ocean	**109**		75 00N	40 00E
Barge Canal New York USA	**46**	H3	43 14N	78 23W
Barharwa India	**91**	J10	24 51N	87 49E
Bari Italy	**81**	F4	41 07N	16 52E
Barinas Venezuela	**72**	C15	8 36N	70 15W
Barisal Bangladesh	**91**	L9	22 41N	90 20E
Barkly Tableland *geog. reg.* Aust.	**102**	G7	17 30S	137 00E
Bârlad Romania	**81**	L7	46 14N	27 40E
Bar-le-Duc Fr.	**78**	H8	48 46N	5 10E
Barlee, Lake Aust.	**102**	C5	28 30S	120 00E
Barletta Italy	**81**	F4	41 20N	16 17E
Barnaul Russia	**87**	L7	53 21N	83 45E
Barnstaple UK	**78**	C9	51 05N	4 04W
Barpeta Road *tn.* India	**91**	L11	26 27N	90 56E
Barquisimeto Venezuela	**72**	D16	10 03N	69 18W
Barra do Corba Brazil	**72**	H12	5 30S	45 12W
Barrancabermeja Col.	**72**	C15	7 06N	73 54W
Barrancas Venezuela	**72**	E15	8 45N	62 13W
Barranquilla Col.	**72**	C16	11 10N	74 50W
Barre Vermont USA	**63**	M5	44 12N	72 31W
Barreiras Brazil	**72**	J11	12 09S	44 58W
Barreiro Port.	**79**	A3	38 40N	9 05W
Barron Wisconsin USA	**45**	F3	45 24N	91 50W
Barrow *r.* RoI	**78**	B10	52 38N	6 58W

Barrow-in-Furness UK	**78**	D11	54 07N	3 14W
Barrow Island Aust.	**102**	C6	21 00S	115 00E
Barry UK	**78**	D9	51 24N	3 18W
Barstow California USA	**62**	C3	34 55N	117 01W
Bartlesville Oklahoma USA	**63**	G4	36 44N	95 59W
Bartolome, Cape Alaska USA	**38**	D4	55 15N	133 39W
Basalt Nevada USA	**64**	D3	38 02N	118 18W
Basalt Island HK China	**92**	D1	22 18N	114 21E
Basel Switz.	**79**	J7	47 33N	7 36E
Basingstoke UK	**78**	E9	51 16N	1 05W
Basirhat India	**91**	K9	22 39N	88 52E
Bassas da India *i.* Mozambique Channel	**101**	M3	22 00S	40 00E
Bassein Myanmar	**95**	A7	16 46N	94 45E
Basse Terre Lesser Antilles	**66**	Q9	16 00N	61 20W
Basseterre St. Kitts and Nevis	**66**	P9	17 18N	62 43W
Basse Terre *i.* Lesser Antilles	**66**	Q9	16 10N	61 40W
Bass Strait Aust.	**103**	J2/J3	40 00S	145 00E
Basswood Lake Minnesota USA	**45**	F5	48 00N	91 50W
Bastia Fr.	**79**	K5	42 14N	9 26E
Bastogne Belgium	**78**	H8	50 00N	5 43E
Bastrop Louisiana USA	**63**	H3	32 49N	91 54W
Bata Eq. Guinea	**100**	F8	1 51N	9 49E
Batakan Indonesia	**95**	E3	4 03S	114 39E
Batala India	**90**	D6	31 48N	75 17E
Batang China	**93**	H5	30 02N	99 01E
Batangafo CAR	**100**	H9	7 27N	18 11E
Batangas Philippines	**95**	G6	13 46N	121 01E
Batavia New York USA	**45**	M2	42 59N	78 10W
Batdâmbâng Cambodia	**95**	C6	13 06N	103 13E
Bath UK	**78**	D9	51 23N	2 22W
Bath New York USA	**47**	J2	42 20N	77 18W
Batha *r.* Chad	**100**	H10	13 00N	19 00E
Bathinda India	**90**	C6	30 10N	74 58E
Bathurst Aust.	**103**	J4	33 27S	149 35E
Bathurst Island Aust.	**102**	F8	12 00S	130 00E
Batna Algeria	**100**	F15	35 34N	6 10E
Baton Rouge Louisiana USA	**63**	H3	30 30N	91 10W
Batroûn Lebanon	**88**	N12	36 16N	35 40E
Batticaloa Sri Lanka	**90**	E1	7 43N	81 42E
Battle Creek *tn.* Michigan USA	**63**	J5	42 20N	85 21W
Bat Yam Israel	**88**	N10	31 59N	34 45E
Baubau Indonesia	**95**	G2	5 30S	122 37E
Bauchi Nigeria	**100**	F10	10 16N	9 50E
Baudette Minnesota USA	**43**	E1	48 42N	94 34W
Bauru Brazil	**72**	H9	22 19S	49 07W
Bautzen Germany	**80**	E9	51 11N	14 29E
Bayamo Cuba	**67**	J4	20 23N	76 39W
Bay City Michigan USA	**63**	K5	43 35N	83 52W
Bay City Texas USA	**63**	G2	28 59N	96 00W
Baydhabo Somalia	**100**	N8	3 08N	43 34E
Bayerische Alpen *mts.* Germany	**81**	C7	47 00N	11 00E
Bayeux Fr.	**78**	E8	49 16N	0 42W
Baykonur Kazakhstan	**86**	J6	47 50N	66 03E
Bayonne Fr.	**79**	E5	43 30N	1 28W
Bayonne New Jersey USA	**65**	H1	40 39N	74 07W
Bayreuth Germany	**80**	C8	49 27N	11 35E
Bay Ridge *tn.* New York USA	**65**	H1	40 37N	74 02W
Baytown Texas USA	**63**	H2	29 43N	94 59W
Baza Sp.	**79**	D2	37 30N	2 45W
Bcharre Lebanon	**88**	P12	34 15N	36 00E
Bear Lake USA	**62**	D5	42 00N	111 20W
Beatrice Nebraska USA	**63**	G5	40 17N	96 45W
Beatty Nevada USA	**62**	C4	36 54N	116 45W
Beaufort South Carolina USA	**63**	K3	32 26N	80 40W
Beaufort Island HK China	**92**	C1	22 11N	114 15E
Beaumont Texas USA	**63**	H3	30 04N	94 06W
Beaune Fr.	**79**	H7	47 02N	4 50E
Beauvais Fr.	**78**	G8	49 26N	2 05E
Beaver Island Michigan USA	**45**	J3	45 39N	85 30W
Béchar Algeria	**100**	D14	31 35N	2 17W
Beckley West Virginia USA	**63**	K4	37 46N	81 12W
Bedford UK	**78**	E10	52 08N	0 29W
Bedford Pennsylvania USA	**65**	A2	40 01N	78 31W
Beersheba Israel	**88**	N10	31 15N	34 47E
Beeville Texas USA	**63**	G2	28 25N	97 47W
Behbehān Iran	**89**	F5	30 34N	50 18E
Behm Canal *sd.* Alaska USA	**38**	D4/E5	56 00N	131 00W
Bei'an China	**93**	P8	48 16N	126 36E
Beihai China	**93**	K3	21 29N	109 10E
Beijing China	**93**	M6	39 55N	116 26E
Beira Mozambique	**101**	L4	19 49S	34 52E
Beirut Lebanon	**88**	N11	33 52N	35 30E
Beja Port.	**79**	B3	38 01N	7 52W
Bejaïa Algeria	**100**	F15	36 49N	5 03E
Béjar Sp.	**79**	C4	40 24N	5 45W
Békescsaba Hungary	**81**	H7	46 45N	21 09E
Bela Pakistan	**90**	B5	26 12N	66 20E
BELARUS	**86**	E7		
Belém Brazil	**72**	H13	1 27S	48 29W
Belfast UK	**78**	C11	54 35N	5 55W
Belfast Maine USA	**51**	F1	44 26N	69 01W
Belfort Fr.	**79**	J7	47 38N	6 52E
Belgaum India	**90**	C3	15 54N	74 36E
BELGIUM	**78**	G9/H9		
Belgorod Russia	**86**	F7	50 38N	36 36E
Belgrade SM	**81**	H6	44 50N	20 30E
BELIZE	**66**	G3		
Belize Belize	**66**	G3	17 29N	88 10W
Bellac Fr.	**79**	F7	46 07N	1 04E
Bellaire Michigan USA	**46**	A4	44 59N	85 12W
Bellary India	**90**	D3	15 11N	76 54E
Bella Vista Argentina	**73**	F8	28 31S	59 00W
Belle-Île *i.* Fr.	**79**	D7	47 20N	3 10W
Bellingham Washington USA	**62**	B6	48 45N	122 29W
Bellingshausen Sea Southern Ocean	**109**		71 00S	85 00W
Bello Col.	**72**	B15	6 20N	75 41W
Belluno Italy	**81**	D7	46 08N	12 13E
Belmopan Belize	**66**	G3	17 13N	88 48W
Belogorsk Russia	**87**	Q7	50 55N	128 26E
Belo Horizonte Brazil	**72**	J10	19 54S	43 54W
Belted Range *mts.* Nevada USA	**64**	E3	37 28N	116 05W
Belyy *i.* Russia	**86**	K11	73 00N	70 00E
Belyy Yar Russia	**87**	L8	58 28N	85 03E
Bembézar *r.* Sp.	**79**	C2/C3	38 00N	5 15W
Bemidji Minnesota USA	**63**	H6	47 29N	94 52W
Benavente Sp.	**79**	C4	42 00N	5 40W
Bend Oregon USA	**62**	B5	44 04N	121 20W
Bender-Bayla Somalia	**100**	Q9	9 30N	50 50E
Bendigo Aust.	**103**	H3	36 48S	144 21E
Benevento Italy	**81**	E4	41 08N	14 46E
Bengal, Bay of Indian Ocean	**91**	F3	17 00N	88 00E
Bengbu China	**93**	M5	32 56N	117 27E
Benghazi Libya	**100**	J14	32 07N	20 04E
Bengkulu Indonesia	**95**	C3	3 46S	102 16E
Benguela Angola	**101**	G5	12 34S	13 24E
Beni *r.* Bolivia	**72**	D11	13 00S	67 30W
Beni Abbès Algeria	**100**	D14	30 11N	2 14W
Benicarló Sp.	**79**	F4	40 25N	0 25E
Beni Mellal Morocco	**100**	C14	32 22N	6 29W
BENIN	**100**	E10		
Benin, Bight of *b.* West Africa	**100**	E9	5 50N	2 30E
Benin City Nigeria	**100**	F9	6 19N	5 41E
Beni Suef Egypt	**100**	L13	29 05N	31 05E
Benjamin Constant Brazil	**72**	C13	4 23S	69 59W
Ben Macdui *mt.* UK	**78**	D12	57 04N	3 40W
Ben Nevis *mt.* UK	**78**	C12	56 40N	5 00W
Bennington Vermont USA	**65**	D3	42 53N	73 12W
Benson Arizona USA	**62**	D3	31 58N	110 19W
Benton Harbor *tn.* Michigan USA	**63**	J5	42 07N	86 27W
Benue *r.* Nigeria/Cameroon	**100**	F9	8 00N	7 40E
Benxi China	**93**	N7	41 21N	123 45E
Beppu Japan	**94**	B1	33 18N	131 30E
Bequia *i.* Lesser Antilles	**66**	R11	13 01	61 13W
Berat Albania	**81**	H4	40 43N	19 46E
Berber Sudan	**100**	L11	18 01N	34 00E
Berbera Somalia	**100**	P10	10 28N	45 02E
Berbérati CAR	**100**	H8	4 19N	15 51E
Berck Fr.	**78**	F9	50 24N	1 35E
Berdychiv Ukraine	**80**	M8	49 54N	28 39E
Beregovo Ukraine	**80**	J8	48 13N	22 39E
Berezniki Russia	**86**	H8	59 26N	56 49E
Berezovo Russia	**86**	J9	63 58N	65 00E
Bérgamo Italy	**81**	B6	45 42N	9 40E
Bergerac Fr.	**79**	F6	44 50N	0 29E
Ber Harbor *tn.* Maine USA	**51**	F1	44 24N	68 10W
Bering Sea Pacific Ocean	**106/107**	H13	60 00N	175 00W
Berkakit Russia	**87**	Q8	56 36N	124 49E
Berkeley California USA	**64**	B3	37 53N	122 17W
Berkner Island Antarctica	**109**		80 00S	45 00W
Berlin Germany	**80**	D10	52 32N	13 25E
Berlin New Hampshire USA	**63**	M5	44 27N	71 13W
Bermejo *r.* Argentina	**72**	E8	25 00S	61 00W
Bermuda *i.* Atlantic Ocean	**108**	B10	32 50N	64 20W
Bern Switz.	**79**	J7	46 57N	7 26E
Berner Alpen *mts.* Switz.	**79**	J7/K7	46 25N	7 30E
Berryessa, Lake California USA	**64**	B4	38 37N	122 15W
Bertoua Cameroon	**100**	G8	4 34N	13 42E
Beru *i.* Kiribati	**103**	Q10	1 20S	176 00E
Berwick Pennsylvania USA	**65**	B2	41 04N	76 15W
Berwick-upon-Tweed UK	**78**	E11	55 46N	2 00W
Besançon Fr.	**79**	H7	47 14N	6 02E
Beskidy Zachodnie *mts.* Poland	**80**	H8	50 00N	20 00E
Bethesde Maryland USA	**65**	B1	38 58N	77 06W
Bethlehem Middle East	**88**	N10	31 42N	35 12E
Bethlehem Pennsylvania USA	**65**	C2	40 37N	75 23W
Béthune Fr.	**78**	G9	50 32N	2 38E
Betsiboka *r.* Madagascar	**101**	P4	17 00S	46 30E
Beyla Guinea	**100**	C9	8 42N	8 39W
Beyşehir Gölü *l.* Turkey	**88**	B6	37 40N	31 43E
Béziers Fr.	**79**	G5	43 21N	3 13E
Bhadravati India	**90**	D2	13 54N	75 38E
Bhagalpur India	**91**	F5	25 14N	86 59E
Bhairab Bazar Bangladesh	**91**	L10	24 04N	91 00E
Bhandara India	**90**	D4	21 10N	79 41E
Bhanga Bangladesh	**91**	L9	23 24N	89 58E
Bharatpur India	**90**	D5	27 14N	77 29E
Bharuch India	**90**	C4	21 40N	73 02E
Bhatpara India	**91**	K9	22 51N	88 24E
Bhavnagar India	**90**	C4	21 46N	72 14E
Bhilwara India	**90**	C5	25 23N	74 39E
Bhima *r.* India	**90**	D3	17 00N	76 00E
Bhopal India	**90**	D4	23 17N	77 28E
Bhubaneshwar India	**91**	F4	20 13N	85 50E
Bhuj India	**90**	B4	23 12N	69 54E
Bhusawal India	**90**	D4	21 01N	75 50E
BHUTAN	**91**	G5		
Biała Podlaska Poland	**80**	J9	52 03N	23 05E
Białystok Poland	**80**	J10	53 09N	23 10E
Biarritz Fr.	**79**	E5	43 29N	1 33W
Bibai Japan	**94**	D3	43 21N	141 53E
Bida Nigeria	**100**	F9	9 06N	5 59E
Biddeford Maine USA	**63**	M5	43 29N	70 27W
Biebrza *r.* Poland	**80**	J10	53 00N	22 00E
Biel Switz.	**79**	J7	46 27N	8 13E
Bielefeld Germany	**80**	B10	52 02N	8 32E
Biella Italy	**81**	B6	45 34N	8 04E
Bielsko-Biała Poland	**80**	G8	49 50N	19 00E
Bielsk Podlaski Poland	**80**	J10	52 47N	23 11E
Biferno *r.* Italy	**81**	E4	41 00N	14 00E
Big Bay De Noc *b.* Michigan USA	**45**	H3	45 55N	86 50W
Big Black *r.* Mississippi USA	**63**	H3	33 00N	90 00W
Bigelow Mountain Maine USA	**47**	R5	45 10N	70 18W
Bighorn *r.* USA	**62**	E6	45 00N	108 00W
Bighorn Mountains USA	**62**	E5	44 00N	108 00W
Big Lake Maine USA	**51**	G1	44 10N	67 45W
Big Muddy Creek *r.* Montana USA	**42**	E1	48 50N	105 20W
Big Pine California USA	**64**	D3	37 10N	118 18W
Big Rapids *tn.* Michigan USA	**45**	J2	43 42N	85 29W
Big Sioux *r.* Minnesota/South Dakota USA	**63**	G5	44 00N	96 00W
Big Smokey Valley Nevada USA	**64**	E4	38 52N	117 08W
Big Spring *tn.* Texas USA	**62**	F3	32 15N	101 30W
Big Sur California USA	**64**	C3	36 15N	121 47W
Bihać Bosnia-Herzegovina	**81**	E6	44 49N	15 53E
Bihar *admin.* India	**91**	F5	24 40N	86 00E
Biharamulo Tanzania	**100**	L7	2 37S	31 20E
Bijapur India	**90**	D3	16 47N	75 48E
Bījār Iran	**89**	E6	35 52N	47 39E
Bikaner India	**90**	C5	28 01N	73 22E
Bilaspur India	**90**	E4	27 51N	82 00E
Bila Tserkva Ukraine	**80**	N8	49 49N	30 10E
Bilbao Sp.	**79**	D5	43 15N	2 56W
Bilibino Russia	**87**	U10	68 00N	166 15E
Billings Montana USA	**62**	E6	45 47N	108 30W
Biloxi Mississippi USA	**63**	J3	30 24N	88 55W
Binghampton New York USA	**63**	L5	42 06N	75 55W
Bintulu Malaysia	**95**	E4	3 10N	113 02E
Bioko *i.* Eq. Guinea	**100**	F8	3 00N	8 20E
Birao CAR	**100**	J10	10 11N	22 49E
Biratnagar Nepal	**91**	F5	26 27N	87 17E
Birch Lake Minnesota USA	**45**	F4	47 35N	91 55W
Birdsville Aust.	**103**	G5	25 50S	139 20E
Bīrjand Iran	**89**	G5	32 55N	59 10E
Birkenhead UK	**78**	D10	53 24N	3 02W
Birmingham UK	**78**	E10	52 30N	1 50W
Birmingham Alabama USA	**63**	J3	33 30N	86 55W
Birnin Kebbi Nigeria	**100**	E10	12 30N	4 11E
Birobidzhan Russia	**87**	R6	48 49N	132 54E
Birzai Lithuania	**80**	K12	56 12N	24 48E
Biscay, Bay of Atlantic Ocean	**79**	D6	45 30N	2 50W
Bishkek Kyrgyzstan	**86**	K5	42 53N	74 46E
Bismarck North Dakota USA	**62**	F6	46 50N	100 48W
Bismarck Archipelago *is.* PNG	**103**	J10	2 00S	146 00E
Bismarck Sea PNG	**103**	J10	3 30S	148 00E
Bissau Guinea-Bissau	**100**	A10	11 52N	15 39W
Bistrița Romania	**81**	K7	47 08N	24 30E
Bistrița *r.* Romania	**81**	K7	47 00N	25 00E
Bitola FYROM	**81**	H4	41 01N	21 21E
Bitterroot Range *mts.* USA	**62**	D6	46 00N	114 00W
Biwa-ko *l.* Japan	**94**	C2	35 20N	135 20E
Biysk Russia	**87**	L7	52 35N	85 16E
Bizerte Tunisia	**100**	F15	37 18N	9 52E
Blackall Aust.	**103**	J6	24 23S	145 27E
Blackburn UK	**78**	D10	53 45N	2 29W
Black Lake Michigan USA	**46**	B5	45 30N	84 20W
Black Lake New York USA	**47**	L4	44 30N	75 30W
Black Point *c.* HK China	**92**	A2	22 25N	113 54E
Blackpool UK	**78**	D10	53 50N	3 03W
Black River Michigan USA	**46**	D3	43 25N	82 35W
Black River New York USA	**47**	L3	43 47N	75 30W
Black River *tn.* Jamaica	**67**	U14	18 02N	77 52W
Black Volta *r.* Africa	**100**	D9	9 00N	2 40W
Blackwell Oklahoma USA	**63**	G4	36 47N	97 18W
Blagoevgrad Bulgaria	**81**	J5	42 01N	23 05E
Blagoveshchensk Russia	**87**	Q7	50 19N	127 30E
Blaine Washington USA	**38**	H4	49 00N	122 44W
Blantyre Malawi	**101**	L4	15 46S	35 00E
Blida Algeria	**100**	E15	36 30N	2 50E
Bligh Water *sd.* Fiji	**106**	T16	17 00S	178 00E
Bloemfontein RSA	**101**	K2	29 07S	26 14E
Bloomfield New Jersey USA	**65**	H2	40 37N	74 10W
Bloomington Illinois USA	**63**	J5	40 29N	89 00W
Bloomington Indiana USA	**63**	J4	39 10N	86 31W
Bloomsburg Pennsylvania USA	**65**	B2	41 00N	76 27W
Bluefield West Virginia USA	**63**	K4	37 14N	81 17W
Bluefields Nicaragua	**67**	H2	12 00N	83 49W
Blue Mountains Jamaica	**67**	U14	18 00N	76 30W
Bluff Island HK China	**92**	D1	22 19N	114 21E
Blumenau Brazil	**72**	H8	26 55S	49 07W
Blyth UK	**78**	E11	55 07N	1 30W
Blythe California USA	**62**	D3	33 38N	114 35W
Bo Sierra Leone	**100**	B9	7 58N	11 45W
Boa Vista Brazil	**72**	E14	2 49N	60 40W
Bobo Dioulasso Burkina	**100**	D10	11 11N	4 18W
Bocholt Germany	**80**	A9	51 49N	6 37E
Bodega Head *c.* California USA	**64**	B4	38 18N	123 06W
Bodélé *dep.* Chad	**100**	H11	17 00N	17 50E
Bodensee *l.* Switz.	**79**	K7	47 40N	9 30E
Bogalusa Louisiana USA	**63**	J3	30 56N	89 53W
Bogor Indonesia	**95**	D2	6 34S	106 45E
Bogotá Col.	**72**	C14	4 38N	74 05W
Bo Hai *b.* China	**93**	M6	38 30N	118 30E
Böhmer Wald *mts.* Germany	**80**	D8	49 00N	13 00E
Bohol *i.* Philippines	**95**	G5	10 00N	124 00E
Bois Blanc Island Michigan USA	**46**	B5	45 45N	84 30W
Boise Idaho USA	**62**	C5	43 38N	116 12W
Boise City Oklahoma USA	**62**	F4	36 44N	102 31W
Bokaro India	**91**	F4	23 46N	85 55E
Boké Guinea	**100**	B10	10 57N	14 13W
Bolesławiec Poland	**80**	E9	51 16N	15 34E
Bolgatanga Ghana	**100**	D10	10 44N	0 53W
Bolhrad Ukraine	**81**	M6	45 42N	28 35E
BOLIVIA	**72**	D10		
Bolmen *l.* Sweden	**80**	D12	57 00N	13 30E
Bologna Italy	**81**	C6	44 30N	11 20E
Bolzano Italy	**81**	C7	46 30N	11 22E
Boma CDR	**101**	G6	5 50S	13 03E
Bom Jesus da Lapa Brazil	**72**	J11	13 16S	43 23W
Bomu *r.* Central Africa	**100**	J8	4 50N	24 00E
Bonaire *i.* Lesser Antilles	**67**	L2	12 15N	68 27W
Bonaparte Archipelago *is.* Aust.	**102**	E8	19 00S	126 00E
Bondo CDR	**100**	J8	1 22N	23 54E
Bongor Chad	**100**	H10	10 18N	15 20E
Bonifacio Fr.	**79**	K4	41 23N	9 10E
Bonifacio, Strait of Fr./Sp.	**79**	K4	41 20N	8 45E
Bonn Germany	**80**	A9	50 44N	7 06E
Bonners Ferry *tn.* Idaho USA	**39**	M1	48 41N	116 20W
Bonny, Bight of *b.* West Africa	**100**	F8	2 10N	7 30E
Bonthe Sierra Leone	**100**	B9	7 32N	12 30W
Boosaaso Somalia	**100**	P10	11 18N	49 10E
Bor Sudan	**100**	L9	6 18N	31 34E
Borås Sweden	**80**	D12	57 44N	12 55E
Bordeaux Fr.	**79**	E6	44 50N	0 34W
Borgholm Sweden	**80**	F12	56 51N	16 40E
Borislav Ukraine	**80**	J8	49 18N	23 28E
Borneo *i.* Indonesia/Malaysia	**95**	D3/F5	1 00N	113 00E
Bornholm *i.* Denmark	**80**	E11	55 02N	15 00E
Borūjerd Iran	**89**	E5	33 55N	48 48E
Borzya Russia	**87**	P7	50 24N	116 35E
Bosna *r.* Bosnia-Herzegovina	**81**	G6	45 00N	18 00E
BOSNIA-HERZEGOVINA	**81**	F6/H6		
Bossangoa CAR	**100**	H9	6 27N	17 21E
Bosso Niger	**100**	G10	13 43N	13 19E
Boston Massachusetts USA	**63**	M5	42 20N	71 05W
Boston Mountains Arkansas USA	**63**	H4	36 00N	94 00W
Botoşani Romania	**80**	L7	47 44N	26 41E
BOTSWANA	**101**	J3/K3		
Bottineau North Dakota USA	**43**	B1	48 48N	100 28W
Bouaké Côte d'Ivoire	**100**	D9	7 42N	5 00W
Bouar CAR	**100**	H9	5 58N	15 35E
Bouârfa Morocco	**100**	D14	32 30N	1 59W
Bougainville Island PNG	**103**	K9/L9	6 15S	155 00E
Bougouni Mali	**100**	C10	11 25N	7 28W
Boulder Colorado USA	**62**	E5	40 02N	105 16W
Boulevard California USA	**64**	E1	32 39N	116 15W
Boulogne-sur-Mer Fr.	**78**	F9	50 43N	1 37E
Boundary Bald Mountain Maine USA	**47**	R5	45 45N	70 14W
Bourem Mali	**100**	D11	16 59N	0 20W
Bourges Fr.	**79**	G7	47 05N	2 23E
Bourke Aust.	**103**	J4	30 09S	145 59E
Bournemouth UK	**78**	E9	50 43N	1 54W
Bou Saâda Algeria	**100**	F15	35 10N	4 09E
Bousso Chad	**100**	H10	10 32N	16 45E
Bouvet Island Atlantic Ocean	**108**	J1	54 26S	3 24E
Bowbells North Dakota USA	**42**	F1	48 53N	102 15W
Bowen Aust.	**103**	J6	20 00S	148 10E
Bowling Green Kentucky USA	**63**	J4	37 00N	86 29W
Bowling Green Missouri USA	**63**	H4	39 21N	91 11W
Bowling Green Ohio USA	**45**	K1	41 22N	83 39W
Bowman North Dakota USA	**62**	F6	46 11N	103 26W
Boyne City Michigan USA	**46**	B5	45 13N	85 00W
Boyoma Falls CDR	**100**	J8	0 18N	25 30E
Bozeman Montana USA	**62**	D6	45 40N	111 00W
Bozoum CAR	**100**	H9	6 16N	16 22E
Brač *i.* Croatia	**81**	F5	43 00N	16 00E
Bradenton Florida USA	**63**	K2	27 29N	82 33W
Bradford UK	**78**	D10	53 48N	1 45W
Bradford Pennsylvania USA	**46**	H1	41 57N	78 38W
Brady Texas USA	**62**	G3	31 08N	99 22W
Braemar UK	**78**	D12	57 01N	3 23W
Braga Port.	**79**	A4	41 32N	8 26W
Bragança Brazil	**72**	H13	1 02S	46 46W
Bragança Port.	**79**	B4	41 47N	6 46W
Brahman Baria Bangladesh	**91**	L9	23 58N	91 04E
Brahmaputra *r.* India/Bangladesh	**91**	G5	26 40N	93 00E
Brăila Romania	**81**	L6	45 17N	27 58E
Brainerd Minnesota USA	**63**	H6	46 20N	94 10W
Branco *r.* Brazil	**72**	E14	0 00	62 00W
Brandenburg Germany	**80**	D10	52 25N	12 34E
Brasileia Brazil	**72**	D11	10 59S	68 45W
Brásília Brazil	**72**	H10	15 45S	47 57W
Braşov Romania	**81**	K6	45 39N	25 35E
Bratislava Slovakia	**80**	F8	48 10N	17 10E
Bratsk Russia	**87**	N8	56 20N	101 50E
Bratsk Vodokhrahnilishche *res.* Russia	**87**	N8	56 00N	102 00E
Brattleboro Vermont USA	**65**	D3	42 51N	72 34W
Braunschweig Germany	**80**	C10	52 15N	10 30E
Brawley California USA	**62**	C3	32 59N	115 30W
BRAZIL	**72**	F11		

Brazil Basin Atlantic Ocean 108 F5/F6 10 00S 26 00W
Brazos *r.* Texas USA 63 G3 32 00N 97 00W
Brazzaville Congo 100 H7 4 14S 15 14E
Breda Neths. 78 H9 51 35N 4 46E
Bremen Germany 80 B10 53 05N 8 48E
Bremerhaven Germany 80 B10 53 33N 8 35E
Bremerton Washington USA 62 B6 47 34N 122 40W
Brenham Texas USA 63 G3 30 09N 96 24W
Brenner Pass Austria/Italy 81 C7 47 02N 11 32E
Brescia Italy 81 C6 45 33N 10 13E
Brest Belarus 80 J10 52 08N 23 40E
Brest Fr. 78 C8 48 23N 4 30W
Brewer Maine USA 51 F1 44 52N 68 01W
Brewerton New York USA 45 N2 43 14N 76 08W
Bria CAR 100 J9 6 32N 22 00E
Briançon Fr. 79 J6 44 53N 6 39E
Bridgeport California USA 64 D4 38 14N 119 15W
Bridgeport Connecticut USA 63 M5 41 12N 73 12W
Bridgeton New Jersey USA 65 C1 39 26N 75 14W
Bridgetown Barbados 66 S11 13 06N 59 37W
Bridgwater UK 78 D9 51 08N 3 00W
Briey Fr. 78 H8 49 15N 5 57E
Brigham City Utah USA 62 D5 41 30N 112 02W
Brighton UK 78 E9 50 50N 0 10W
Brighton Beach *tn.* New York USA 65 J1 40 34N 73 58W
Brindisi Italy 81 F4 40 37N 17 57E
Brisbane Aust. 103 K5 27 30S 153 00E
Bristol UK 78 D9 51 27N 2 35W
Bristol Channel UK 78 C9/D9 51 20N 3 50W
Bristol Lake California USA 64 F2 34 30N 115 40W
Brive-la-Gaillarde Fr. 79 F6 45 09N 1 32E
Brno Czech Rep. 80 F8 49 13N 16 40E
Brockport New York USA 46 J3 43 13N 77 56W
Brockton Massachusetts USA 63 M5 42 06N 71 01W
Brody Ukraine 80 K9 50 05N 25 08E
Broken Hill *tn.* Aust. 103 H4 31 57S 141 30E
Broken Ridge Indian Ocean 105 J3 30 00S 93 00E
Bronx *admin.* New York USA 65 D2 40 48N 73 50W
Brookings South Dakota USA 63 G5 44 19N 96 47W
Brooklyn *admin.* New York USA 65 D2 40 41N 73 57W
Broome Aust. 102 D7 17 58S 122 15E
Browning Montana USA 62 D6 48 33N 113 00W
Brownsville Texas USA 63 G2 25 54N 97 30W
Brownwood Texas USA 62 G3 31 42N 98 59W
Bruay-en-Artois Fr. 78 G9 50 29N 2 33E
Brugge Belgium 78 G9 51 13N 3 14E
BRUNEI 95 E4/F4
Brunswick Georgia USA 63 K3 31 09N 81 30W
Brussels Belgium 78 H9 50 50N 4 21E
Bryan Ohio USA 46 B1 41 30N 84 34W
Bryan Texas USA 63 G3 30 41N 96 24W
Bryansk Russia 86 F7 53 15N 34 09E
Brzeg Poland 80 F9 50 52N 17 27E
Bucaramanga Col. 72 C15 7 08N 73 10W
Bucharest Romania 81 L6 44 25N 26 07E
Buchanan Liberia 100 B9 5 57N 10 02W
Budapest Hungary 81 G7 47 30N 19 03E
Budjala CAR 100 H8 2 38N 19 48E
Buellton California USA 64 C2 34 37N 120 11W
Buenaventura Col. 72 B14 3 54N 77 02W
Buenaventura Mexico 66 C5 29 50N 107 30W
Buena Vista Lake California USA 64 D2 35 13N 119 18W
Buenos Aires Argentina 73 F7 34 40S 58 30W
Buenos Aires, Lake Argentina/Chile 73 C4 47 00S 72 00W
Buffalo New York USA 63 L5 42 52N 78 55W
Buffalo Wyoming USA 62 E5 44 21N 106 40W
Buhusi Romania 81 L7 46 44N 26 41E
Bujumbura Burundi 100 K7 3 22S 29 19E
Bukachacha Russia 87 P7 53 00N 116 58E
Bukama CDR 101 K6 9 13S 25 52E
Bukavu CDR 100 K7 2 30S 28 50E
Bukhara Uzbekistan 86 J4 39 47N 64 26E
Bukittinggi Indonesia 95 C3 0 18S 100 20E
Bukoba Tanzania 100 L7 1 19S 31 49E
Bula Indonesia 95 J3 3 07S 130 27E
Bulawayo Zimbabwe 101 K3 20 10S 28 43E
BULGARIA 81 J5/K5
Bullion Mountains California USA 64 E2 34 30N 116 15W
Bull Shoals Lake USA 63 H4 36 00N 93 00W
Bulun Russia 87 Q11 70 45N 127 20E
Bumba CDR 100 J8 2 10N 22 30E
Bunbury Aust. 102 C4 33 20S 115 34E
Bundaberg Aust. 103 K6 24 50S 152 21E
Bungo-suidō *sd.* Japan 94 B1 33 00N 132 30E
Bunia CDR 100 L8 1 33N 30 13E
Buôn Mê Thuôt Vietnam 95 D6 12 41N 108 02E
Bura Kenya 100 M7 1 06S 39 58E
Buraydah Saudi Arabia 88 D4 26 20N 43 59E
Burbank California USA 64 D2 34 10N 118 17W
Burdur Turkey 88 B6 37 44N 30 17E
Bureya *r.* Russia 87 R7 52 00N 133 00E
Bûr Fu'ad Egypt 101 S4 31 50N 32 19E
Burgas Bulgaria 81 L5 42 30N 27 29E
Burgos Sp. 79 D5 42 21N 3 41W
Burgsvik Sweden 80 G12 57 03N 18 19E
Burhanpur India 90 D4 21 18N 76 08E
BURKINA 100 D10
Burlington Colorado USA 62 F4 39 17N 102 17W
Burlington Iowa USA 63 H5 40 50N 91 07W
Burlington Vermont USA 63 M5 44 28N 73 14W
Burlington Washington USA 38 H4 48 26N 122 20W
Burnie Aust. 103 J2 41 03S 145 55E
Bursa Turkey 88 A7 40 12N 29 04E
Bûr Safâga Egypt 100 L13 25 43N 33 55E
Bûr Taufiq Egypt 101 T1 29 57N 32 34E
Burt Lake Michigan USA 46 B5 45 30N 84 40W
Buru *i.* Indonesia 95 H3 3 30S 126 30E
BURUNDI 100 K7/L7
Burwell Nebraska USA 62 G5 41 48N 99 09W
Būshehr Iran 89 F4 28 57N 50 52E
Busira *r.* CDR 100 H7/J7 1 00S 20 00E
Busto Arsizio Italy 81 B6 45 37N 8 51E
Buta CDR 100 J8 2 49N 24 50E
Butare Rwanda 100 K7 2 35S 29 44E
Butaritari *is.* Kiribati 103 P11 3 03N 172 49E
Buthidaung Myanmar 91 M8 20 49N 92 34E
Buton *i.* Indonesia 95 G2/G3 5 00S 122 45E
Butte Montana USA 62 D6 46 00N 112 31W
Butuan Philippines 95 H5 8 56N 125 31E
Buulobarde Somalia 100 P8 3 50N 45 33E
Buzău Romania 81 L6 45 09N 26 49E
Bydgoszcz Poland 80 F10 53 16N 18 00E
Bygland Norway 78 J13 58 50N 7 49E
Byrranga Mountains Russia 87 M11 75 00N 100 00E
Bytom Poland 80 G9 50 21N 18 51E

C

Cabanatuan Philippines 95 G7 15 30N 120 58E
Cabimas Venezuela 72 C16 10 26N 71 27W
Cabinda *admin.* Angola 100 G6 5 30S 12 20E
Cabinet Mountains Montana USA 39 N1 48 15N 115 45W
Cabo Brazil 72 K12 8 16S 35 00W
Cabo Blanco *c.* Costa Rica 67 G1 9 36N 85 06W
Cabo Catoche *c.* Mexico 67 G4 21 38N 87 08W
Cabo Corrientes *c.* Col. 72 B15 5 29N 77 36W
Cabo Corrientes *c.* Mexico 66 C4 20 25N 105 42W
Cabo de Gata *c.* Sp. 79 D2 36 44N 2 10W
Cabo de Hornos *c.* Chile 73 D2 56 00S 67 15W
Cabo de la Nao *c.* Sp. 79 F3 38 44N 0 14E
Cabo Delgado *c.* Mozambique 101 N5 10 45S 40 45E
Cabo de Palos *c.* Sp. 79 E2 37 38N 0 40W
Cabo de Peñas *c.* Sp. 79 C5 43 39N 5 50W
Cabo de São Vicente *c.* Port. 79 A2 37 01N 8 59W
Cabo de Tortosa *c.* Sp. 79 F4 40 44N 0 54E
Cabo Dos Bahías *c.* Argentina 73 D5 45 00S 65 30W
Cabo Espichel *c.* Port. 79 A3 38 24N 9 13W
Cabo Falso *c.* Mexico 66 B4 22 50N 110 00W
Cabo Finisterre *c.* Sp. 79 A5 42 52N 9 16W
Cabo Gracias á Dios *c.* Nicaragua 67 H3 15 00N 83 10W
Cabo Orange *c.* Brazil 72 G14 4 25N 51 32W
Cabo Ortegal *c.* Sp. 79 B5 43 46N 7 54W
Cabora Bassa Dam Mozambique 101 L4 16 00S 33 00E
Caborca Mexico 66 B6 30 42N 112 10W
Cabo San Juan *c.* Argentina 73 E3 54 45S 63 46W
Cabo Santa Elena *c.* Costa Rica 67 G2 10 54N 85 56W
Cabo Vírgenes *c.* Argentina 73 D3 52 20S 68 00W
Cabrera *i.* Sp. 79 G3 39 00N 2 59E
Cabriel *r.* Sp. 79 E3 39 20N 1 15W
Čačak SM 81 H5 43 54N 20 22E
Cáceres Brazil 72 F10 16 05S 57 40W
Cáceres Sp. 79 B3 39 29N 6 23W
Cachoeira Brazil 72 K11 12 35S 38 59W
Cachoeira do Sol Brazil 73 G7 30 03S 52 52W
Cachoeiro de Itapemirim Brazil 72 J9 20 51S 41 07W
Cadillac Michigan USA 45 J3 44 14N 85 23W
Cadiz Philippines 95 G6 10 57N 123 18E
Cádiz Sp. 79 B2 36 32N 6 18W
Cádiz, Gulf of Sp. 79 B2 36 30N 7 15W
Cadiz Lake California USA 64 F2 34 17N 115 23W
Caen Fr. 78 E8 49 11N 0 22W
Caernarfon UK 78 C10 53 08N 4 16W
Cagayan de Oro Philippines 95 G5 8 29N 124 40E
Cágliari Italy 81 B3 39 13N 9 08E
Caguas Puerto Rico 67 L3 18 41N 66 04W
Cahors Fr. 79 F6 44 28N 0 26E
Caicos Passage *sd.* W. Indies 67 K4 22 20N 72 30W
Cairns Aust. 103 J7 16 51S 145 43E
Cairo Egypt 100 L13 30 00N 31 15E
Cairo Illinois USA 63 J4 37 01N 89 09W
Cajamarca Peru 72 B12 7 09S 78 32W
Cajàzeiras Brazil 72 K12 6 52S 38 31W
Cakovec Croatia 81 F7 46 24N 16 26E
Calabar Nigeria 100 F8 4 56N 8 22E
Calahorra Sp. 79 E5 46 19N 1 58W
Calais Fr. 78 F9 50 57N 1 52E
Calais Maine USA 51 G1 44 11N 67 16W
Calama Chile 72 D9 22 30S 68 55W
Calamar Col. 72 C16 10 16N 74 55W
Calamian Group *is.* Philippines 95 F6/G6 12 00N 120 00E
Calamocha Sp. 79 E4 40 54N 1 18W
Calapan Philippines 95 G6 13 23N 121 10E
Calatayud Sp. 79 E4 41 21N 1 39W
Calçoene Brazil 72 G14 2 30N 50 55W
Caldas da Rainha Port. 79 A3 39 24N 9 08W
Caldwell Idaho USA 62 C5 43 39N 116 40W
Caledonia New York USA 46 J2 42 58N 77 51W
Calexico California USA 64 F1 32 40N 115 30W
Cali Col. 72 B14 3 24N 76 30W
Calicut India 90 D2 11 15N 75 45E
Caliente Nevada USA 62 D4 37 36N 114 31W
California *state* USA 62 C4 35 00N 119 00W
Calistoga California USA 64 B4 38 36N 122 35W
Callao Peru 72 B11 12 05S 77 08W
Caltanissetta Italy 81 E2 37 29N 14 04E
Calvi Fr. 79 K5 42 34N 8 44E
Calvinia RSA 101 H1 31 25S 19 47E
Camaçari Brazil 72 K11 12 44S 38 16W
Camacupa Angola 101 H5 12 03S 17 50E
Camagüey Cuba 67 J4 21 25N 77 55W
CAMBODIA 95 C6/D6
Cambria California USA 64 C2 35 34N 121 05W
Cambrian Mountains UK 78 D10 52 15N 3 45W
Cambridge UK 78 F10 52 12N 0 07E
Cambridge Maryland USA 63 L4 38 34N 76 04W
Camden New Jersey USA 65 C1 39 57N 75 07W
CAMEROON 100 G9
Cametá Brazil 72 H13 2 12S 49 30W
Camiri Bolivia 72 E9 20 08S 63 33W
Camocim Brazil 72 J13 2 55S 40 50W
Camorta Island Nicobar Islands 91 G1 7 30N 93 30E
Campbell Island Southern Ocean 106 G2 52 30S 169 10E
Campbeltown UK 78 C11 55 26N 5 36W
Campeche Mexico 66 F3 19 50N 90 30W
Câmpina Romania 81 K6 45 08N 25 44E
Campina Grande Brazil 72 K12 7 15S 35 50W
Campinas Brazil 72 H9 22 54S 47 06W
Campoalegre Col. 72 B14 2 49N 75 19W
Campobasso Italy 81 E4 41 33N 14 39E
Campo Grande Brazil 72 G9 20 24S 54 35W
Campo Maior Brazil 72 J13 4 50S 42 12W
Campo Mourão Brazil 72 G9 24 01S 52 24W
Campos Brazil 72 J9 21 46S 41 21W
Camptonville California USA 64 C4 39 28N 121 01W
Cam Rahn Vietnam 95 D6 11 54N 109 14E
Canadian *r.* USA 62 F4 35 00N 104 00W
Canajoharie New York USA 65 C3 42 55N 74 46W
Canakkale Turkey 88 A7 40 09N 26 25E
Canal du Midi Fr. 79 G5 43 20N 2 00E
Canandaigua New York USA 47 J2 42 53N 77 17W
Canandaigua Lake New York USA 47 J2 42 50N 77 17W
Cananea Mexico 66 B6 30 59N 110 20W
Canary Basin Atlantic Ocean 108 E9/F9 26 20N 30 00W
Canary Islands Sp. 100 A13 28 30N 15 10W
Canaveral, Cape Florida USA 63 K2 28 28N 80 28W
Canberra Aust. 103 J3 35 18S 149 08E
Cancún Mexico 67 G4 21 09N 86 45W
Cangamba Angola 101 H5 13 40S 19 47E
Cangzhou China 93 M6 38 19N 116 54E
Canisteo New York USA 46 J2 42 16N 77 37W
Cannanore India 90 D2 11 53N 75 23E
Cannanore Islands India 90 C2 10 05N 72 10E
Cannes Fr. 79 J5 43 33N 7 00E
Cannonsville Reservoir New York USA 47 L2 42 05N 75 20W
Canõas Brazil 73 G8 28 55S 51 10W
Canouan *i.* Lesser Antilles 66 R11 12 43N 61 20W
Canterbury UK 78 F9 51 17N 1 05E
Can Tho Vietnam 95 D6 10 03N 105 46E
Canton New York USA 45 P3 44 36N 75 10W
Canton Ohio USA 63 K5 40 48N 81 23W
Canton East Pennsylvania USA 47 K1 41 38N 76 50W
Cap Corse *c.* Fr. 79 K5 43 00N 9 21E
Cap d'Ambre *c.* Madagascar 101 P5 12 00S 49 15E
Cap de Creus *c.* Sp. 79 G5 42 19N 3 19E
Cap de la Hague *c.* Fr. 78 E8 49 44N 1 56W
Cape Basin Atlantic Ocean 108 J3 36 00S 6 00E
Cape Coast *tn.* Ghana 100 D9 5 10N 1 13W
Cape Cod Bay Massachusetts USA 65 E2 41 00N 70 00W
Cape Girardeau *tn.* Missouri USA 63 J4 37 19N 89 31W
Cape May *tn.* New Jersey USA 65 C1 38 56N 74 54W
Cape Rise Atlantic Ocean 108 K2 42 00S 11 00E
Cape Town RSA 101 H1 33 56S 18 28E
CAPE VERDE 108 E8
Cape Verde Basin Atlantic Ocean 108 E8 11 00N 35 00W
Cape York Peninsula Aust. 103 H8 12 30S 142 30E
Cap-Haïtien Haiti 67 K3 19 47N 72 17W
Capo Carbonara *c.* Italy 81 B3 39 07N 9 33E
Capo Passero *c.* Italy 81 E2 36 42N 15 09E
Capo Santa Maria di Leuca *c.* Italy 81 G3 39 47N 18 22E
Capo San Vito *c.* Italy 81 D3 38 12N 12 43E
Capri *i.* Italy 81 E4 40 33N 14 15E
Capricorn Channel Aust. 103 K6 23 00S 152 30E
Caprivi Strip *geog. reg.* Namibia 101 J4 17 30S 27 50E
Cap Ste. Marie *c.* Madagascar 101 P2 25 34S 45 10E
Cap Vert *c.* Senegal 100 A10 14 43N 17 33W
Caqueta *r.* Col. 72 C13 0 05S 72 30W
Caracal Romania 81 K6 44 07N 24 18E
Caracas Venezuela 72 D16 10 35N 66 56W
Caratinga Brazil 72 J10 19 50S 42 06W
Caravelas Brazil 72 K10 17 45S 39 15W
Carbondale Pennsylvania USA 47 L1 41 35N 75 31W
Carcassonne Fr. 79 G5 43 13N 2 21E
Cardamom Hills India 90 D1 9 50N 77 00E
Cárdenas Mexico 66 E4 22 00N 99 41W
Cardiff UK 78 D9 51 30N 3 13W
Cardigan Bay UK 78 C10 52 30N 4 30W
Carei Romania 80 J7 47 40N 22 28E
Cargados Carajos Shoals Indian Ocean 105 E5 16 00S 60 00E
Cariacica Brazil 72 J10 20 15S 40 23W
Caribbean Sea Central America 67 J3/L3 15 00N 75 00W
Caribou Maine USA 51 F2 46 52N 68 01W
Caripito Venezuela 72 E16 10 07N 63 07W
Carlisle UK 78 D11 54 54N 2 55W
Carlsbad California USA 64 E1 33 09N 117 20W
Carlsbad New Mexico USA 62 F3 32 25N 104 14W
Carlsberg Ridge Indian Ocean 105 F7 5 00N 65 00E
Carmarthen UK 78 C9 51 51N 4 20W
Carmen Col. 72 B15 9 46N 75 06W
Carmichael California USA 64 C4 38 36N 121 20W
Carnarvon Aust. 102 B6 24 51S 113 45E
Carnegie, Lake Aust. 102 D5 27 00S 124 00E
Carnegie Ridge Pacific Ocean 107 T7 1 30S 95 00W
Car Nicobar Island Nicobar Islands 91 G1 9 00N 93 00E
Carnot CAR 100 H8 4 59N 15 56E
Caro *r.* Michigan USA 46 C3 43 29N 83 24W
Carolina Brazil 72 H12 7 20S 47 25W
Caroline Island Kiribati 107 M7 10 00S 150 00W
Caroline Islands Pacific Ocean 106 E8 8 00N 148 00E
Caroni *r.* Venezuela 72 E15 7 00N 62 30W
Carpathians *mts.* Europe 80/81 G8/K7 49 00N 22 00E
Carpatii Meridionali *mts.* Romania 81 J6/K6 45 00N 24 00E
Carpentaria, Gulf of Aust. 102 G7 13 30S 138 00E
Carpentras Fr. 79 H6 44 03N 5 03E
Carriacou *i.* Lesser Antilles 66 R11 12 30N 61 27W
Carrion *r.* Sp. 79 C5 42 30N 4 45W
Carson *r.* Nevada USA 64 D4 39 15N 119 36W
Carson City Nevada USA 62 C4 39 10N 119 46W
Cartagena Col. 72 B16 10 24N 75 33W
Cartagena Sp. 79 E2 37 36N 0 59W
Cartago Costa Rica 67 H1 9 50N 83 52W
Carteret New Jersey USA 65 H1 40 34N 74 13W
Caruarú Brazil 72 K12 8 15S 35 55W
Carúpano Venezuela 72 E16 10 39N 63 14W
Casablanca Morocco 100 C14 33 39N 7 35W
Casa Grande Arizona USA 62 D3 32 52N 111 46W
Cascade Range *mts.* North America 62 B5/B6 48 00N 121 00W
Cascais Port. 79 A3 38 41N 9 25W
Cascavel Brazil 72 K13 4 10S 38 15W
Caserta Italy 81 E4 41 04N 14 20E
Casper Wyoming USA 62 E5 42 50N 106 20W
Cassino Italy 81 D4 41 29N 13 50E
Cass River Michigan USA 46 C3 43 30N 83 30W
Castellane Fr. 79 J5 43 50N 6 30E
Castellón de la Plana Sp. 79 E3 39 59N 0 03W
Castelo Branco Port. 79 B3 39 50N 7 30W
Castlebar RoI 78 A10 53 52N 9 17W
Castle Peak HK China 92 A2 22 23N 113 57E
Castres Fr. 79 G5 43 36N 2 14E
Castries St. Lucia 66 R12 14 02N 60 59W
Castrovillari Italy 81 F3 39 48N 16 12E
Catamarca Argentina 73 D8 28 28S 65 46W
Catánia Italy 81 E2 37 31N 15 06E
Catanzaro Italy 81 F3 38 54N 16 36E
Cataract, 1st Egypt 100 L12 24 00N 32 45E
Cataract, 2nd Sudan 100 L12 21 40N 31 12E
Cataract, 3rd Sudan 100 L11 19 45N 30 25E
Cataract, 4th Sudan 100 L11 18 40N 32 10E
Cataract, 5th Sudan 100 L11 18 25N 33 52E
Cathedral Provincial Park Washington USA 39 K1/L1 48 55N 120 00W
Cat Island Bahamas 67 J4 24 30N 75 30W
Catskill Mountains New York USA 63 L5 42 10N 74 20W
Cattaraugus New York USA 46 H2 42 20N 78 50W
Cattaraugus Creek New York USA 46 H2 42 28N 78 30W
Caucaia Brazil 72 K13 3 44S 38 45W
Caura *r.* Venezuela 72 E15 6 00N 64 00W
Cauvery *r.* India 90 D2 11 05N 78 15E
Cavalier North Dakota USA 43 D1 48 47N 97 38W
Caxias Brazil 72 J13 4 53S 43 20W
Caxias do Sul Brazil 73 G8 29 14S 51 10W
Cayenne French Guiana 72 G14 4 55N 52 18W
Cayman Trench Caribbean Sea 108 A8 15 00N 80 00W
Cayuga Lake New York USA 45 N2 42 40N 76 50W
Ceará *admin.* Brazil 72 J12 5 30S 40 00W
Cebu Philippines 95 G6 10 17N 123 56E
Cedar *r.* Iowa USA 63 H5 42 00N 92 00W
Cedar City Utah USA 62 D4 37 40N 113 04W
Cedar Creek *r.* North Dakota USA 62 F6 46 00N 102 00W
Cedar Grove New Jersey USA 65 H2 40 51N 74 14W
Cedar Rapids *tn.* Iowa USA 63 H5 41 59N 91 39W
Cedros *i.* Mexico 66 A5 28 00N 115 00W
Ceduna Aust. 102 F4 32 07S 133 42E
Ceerigaabo Somalia 100 P10 10 40N 47 20E
Cegléd Hungary 81 G7 47 10N 19 47E
Celaya Mexico 66 D4 20 32N 100 48W
Celebes Sea Indonesia 95 G4 3 00N 122 00E
Celje Slovenia 81 E7 46 15N 15 16E
Celle Germany 80 C10 52 37N 10 05E
CENTRAL AFRICAN REPUBLIC 100 H9/J9
Central District HK China 92 C1 22 17N 114 10E

Central Pacific Basin Pacific Ocean 106 J8 10 00N 177 00W
Central Siberian Plateau Russia 87 N10 65 00N 110 00E
Cerro de Pasco Peru 72 B11 10 43S 76 15W
Cesis Latvia 80 K12 57 18N 25 18E
České Budějovice Czech Rep. 80 E8 48 58N 14 29E
Ceuta *territory* Sp. 79 C1 35 53N 5 19W
Ceva-i-Ra *is.* Fiji 103 P6 21 45S 174 35E
Cévennes *mts.* Fr. 79 G6 44 20N 3 30E
Ceyhan *r.* Turkey 88 C6 37 45N 36 45E
Cèze *r.* Fr. 79 H6 44 30N 4 00E
Chachapoyas Peru 72 B12 6 13S 77 54W
CHAD 100 H10
Chad, Lake West Africa 100 G10 13 50N 14 00E
Chagai Hills Afghanistan/Pakistan 90 A5 29 30N 63 00E
Chaghcharan Afghanistan 89 J5 34 28N 65 03E
Chagos Archipelago Indian Ocean 105 G6 6 00S 73 00E
Chagos-Laccadive Ridge Indian Ocean 105 G6 0 00 75 00E
Chāh Bahār Iran 89 H4 25 16N 60 41E
Chaine des Mitumba *mts.* CDR 101 K6 7 30S 27 30E
Chai Wan HK China 92 C1 22 16N 114 14E
Chalkída Greece 81 J3 38 28N 23 36E
Chalkidikí *p.* Greece 81 J4 40 30N 23 00E
Chalkyitsik Alaska USA 54 B4 66 38N 143 49W
Challenger Fracture Zone Pacific Ocean 107 R4/T4 33 30S 100 00W
Châlons-sur-Marne Fr. 78 H8 48 58N 4 22E
Chalon-sur-Saône Fr. 79 H7 46 47N 4 51E
Chaman Pakistan 90 B6 30 55N 66 27E
Chambal *r.* India 90 D5 26 00N 77 00E
Chamberlain Lake Maine USA 47 S6 46 15N 69 20W
Chambersburg Pennsylvania USA 65 B1 39 56N 77 39W
Chambéry Fr. 79 H6 45 34N 5 55E
Chamo, Lake Ethiopia 100 M9 5 55N 37 35E
Champaign Illinois USA 63 J5 40 07N 88 14W
Champlain New York USA 47 N4 44 59N 73 29W
Champlain, Lake Vermont USA 47 N4 44 53N 73 10W
Champotón Mexico 66 F3 19 20N 90 43W
Chānaral Chile 72 C8 26 23S 70 40W
Chandigarh India 90 D6 30 44N 76 54E
Chandigarh *admin.* India 90 D6 30 44N 76 54E
Chandpur Bangladesh 91 L9 23 15N 90 40E
Chandrapur India 90 D3 19 58N 79 21E
Changara Mozambique 101 L4 16 50S 33 17E
Changchun China 93 P7 43 53N 125 20E
Changde China 93 L4 29 03N 111 35E
Chang Jiang *r.* China 93 K5 31 00N 110 00E
Changsha China 93 L4 28 10N 113 00E
Changzhi China 93 L6 36 05N 113 12E
Changzhou China 93 N5 31 39N 120 45E
Chaniá Greece 81 K1 35 31N 24 01E
Channel Island National Park California USA 64 C2 34 04N 120 00W
Channel Islands British Isles 78 D8 49 30N 2 30W
Chaoyang China 93 N7 41 36N 120 25E
Chaozhou China 93 M3 23 42N 116 36E
Chapada Diamantina *mts.* Brazil 72 J11 12 30S 42 30W
Chapecó Brazil 72 G8 27 14S 52 41W
Chardzhev Turkmenistan 86 J4 39 09N 63 34E
Chari *r.* Chad/Sudan 100 H10 11 00N 16 00E
Charikar Afghanistan 89 J5 35 01N 69 11E
Charleroi Belgium 78 H9 50 25N 4 27E
Charleston South Carolina USA 63 L3 32 48N 79 58W
Charleston West Virginia USA 63 K4 38 23N 81 40W
Charleston Peak *mt.* Nevada USA 64 F3 36 16N 115 41W
Charlestown Rhode Island USA 65 E2 41 23N 71 39W
Charleville-Mézières Fr. 78 H8 49 46N 4 43E
Charlevoix Michigan USA 45 J3 45 18N 85 15W
Charlotte North Carolina USA 63 K4 35 03N 80 50W
Charlottesville Virginia USA 63 L4 38 02N 78 29W
Charlotteville Trinidad and Tobago 67 V15 11 16N 60 36W
Charters Towers Aust. 103 J6 20 02S 146 20E
Chartres Fr. 78 F8 48 27N 1 30E
Chateaubelair St. Vincent and the Grenadines 66 R11 13 17N 61 15W
Châteaubriant Fr. 78 E7 47 43N 1 22W
Chateaugay New York USA 47 M4 44 55N 74 06W
Châteauroux Fr. 79 F7 46 49N 1 41E
Château-Thierry Fr. 78 G8 49 03N 3 24E
Châtellerault Fr. 79 F7 46 49N 0 33E
Chatham Alaska USA 38 C5 57 30N 135 00W
Chatham Massachusetts USA 65 F2 41 41N 69 58W
Chatham Islands Pacific Ocean 103 R2 44 00S 176 30W
Chatham Rise Pacific Ocean 106 H3 45 00S 175 00E
Chatham Strait *sd.* Alaska USA 38 C5 57 45N 134 50W
Châtillon-sur-Seine Fr. 78 H7 47 52N 4 35E
Chattanooga Tennessee USA 63 J4 35 02N 85 18W
Chattisgarh *admin.* India 90 E4 22 30N 82 30E
Chaumont Fr. 78 H8 48 07N 5 08E
Chautauqua Lake New York USA 46 G2 42 12N 79 30W
Chazy New York USA 47 N4 44 53N 73 29W
Cheb Czech Rep. 80 D9 50 08N 12 28E
Cheboksary Russia 86 G8 56 08N 47 12E
Cheboygan Michigan USA 45 J3 45 39N 84 28W
Cheju do *i.* South Korea 93 P5 33 00N 126 30E
Chek Lap Kok *i.* HK China 92 A1 22 18N 113 56E
Chelan, Lake Washington USA 38 H4 48 06N 120 20W
Chelan National Recreation Area Washington USA 38 H4 48 25N 120 30W
Chełm Poland 80 J9 51 08N 23 29E
Chelmsford UK 78 F9 51 44N 0 28E
Chelsea Michigan USA 46 B2 42 19N 84 01W
Cheltenham UK 78 D9 51 54N 2 04W
Chelyabinsk Russia 86 J8 55 12N 61 25E
Chemnitz Germany 80 D9 50 50N 12 55E
Chemung River New York USA 47 K2 42 02N 76 50W
Chenab *r.* Pakistan 90 C6 32 30N 74 00E
Chenango River New York USA 47 L2 42 28N 75 40W
Chengde China 93 M7 40 59N 117 52E
Chengdu China 93 J5 30 37N 104 06E
Chennai India 90 E2 13 05N 80 18E
Cher *r.* Fr. 79 F7 47 17N 0 50E
Cherbourg Fr. 78 E8 49 38N 1 37W
Cheremkhovo Russia 87 N7 53 08N 103 01E
Cherepovets Russia 86 F8 59 09N 37 50E
Chernihiv Ukraine 80 N9 51 30N 31 18E
Chernivtsi Ukraine 80 K8 48 19N 25 52E
Chernyakhovsk Russia 80 H11 54 36N 21 48E
Cherokee Iowa USA 63 G5 42 45N 95 32W
Cherry *i.* Solomon Islands 103 N8 11 00S 169 50E
Cherskogo Range *mts.* Russia 87 R10/S9 66 30N 140 00E
Chervonograd Ukraine 80 K9 50 25N 24 10E
Chesaning Michigan USA 46 B3 43 12N 84 08W
Chesapeake Virginia USA 63 L4 36 45N 76 15W
Chesapeake Bay Maryland USA 63 L4 39 00N 76 20W
Chester UK 78 D10 53 12N 2 54W
Chester Maryland USA 65 B1 38 59N 76 17W
Chesuncook Lake Maine USA 47 S6 46 00N 69 22W
Chetumal Mexico 66 G3 18 30N 88 17W
Cheung Chau *i.* HK China 92 B1 22 10N 114 02E
Cheung Sha HK China 92 A1 22 14N 113 57E
Chewack River Washington USA 38 H4 48 45N 120 10W
Chewelah Washington USA 39 M1 48 17N 117 44W
Cheyenne Wyoming USA 62 F5 41 08N 104 50W
Cheyenne *r.* USA 62 F5 44 00N 102 00W
Chhatak Bangladesh 91 L10 25 02N 91 38E
Chhukha Bhutan 91 K11 27 01N 89 35E
Chiai Taiwan 93 N3 23 09N 120 11E
Chiang Mai Thailand 95 B7 18 48N 98 59E
Chiba Japan 94 D2 35 38N 140 07E
Chicago Illinois USA 63 J5 41 50N 87 45W
Chicapa *r.* Angola/CDR 101 J6 8 00S 20 30E
Chichagof Island Alaska USA 38 C5 57 40N 136 00W
Chickasha Oklahoma USA 63 G4 35 03N 97 57W
Chicken Alaska USA 54 B3 64 04N 142 00W
Chiclayo Peru 72 B12 6 47S 79 47W
Chico California USA 62 B4 39 46N 121 50W
Chico *r.* Argentina 73 D4 49 00S 70 00W
Chico *r.* Argentina 73 D5 45 00S 67 30W
Chienti *r.* Italy 81 D5 43 00N 14 00E
Chieti Italy 81 E5 42 21N 14 10E
Chihuahua Mexico 66 C5 28 40N 106 06W
CHILE 72/73 C5/C8
Chile Basin Pacific Ocean 107 T4 36 00S 84 00W
Chile Chico Chile 73 C4 46 34S 71 44W
Chile Rise Pacific Ocean 107 S4 40 00S 92 00W
Chillán Chile 73 C6 36 37S 72 10W
Chilpancingo Mexico 66 E3 17 33N 99 30W
Chilumba Malawi 101 L5 10 25S 34 18E
Chilung Taiwan 93 N4 25 10N 121 43E
Chi Ma Wan Peninsula HK China 92 A1 22 14N 113 58E
Chimborazo *mt.* Ecuador 72 B13 1 29S 78 52W
Chimbote Peru 72 B12 9 04S 78 34W
CHINA 92/93
China Lake California USA 64 E2 35 45N 117 36W
Chinandega Nicaragua 66 G2 12 35N 87 10W
Chincha Alta Peru 72 B11 13 25S 76 07W
Chinchilla Aust. 103 K5 26 42S 150 35E
Chinde Mozambique 101 M4 18 35S 36 28E
Chinese Turkestan *geog. reg.* China 92 D6 40 00N 80 00E
Chingola Zambia 101 K5 12 31S 27 53E
Chinju South Korea 93 P6 35 10N 128 06E
Chinko *r.* CAR 100 J9 5 00N 24 00E
Chinook Montana USA 42 C1 48 36N 109 14W
Chíos Greece 81 L3 38 23N 26 07E
Chíos *i.* Greece 81 K3/L3 38 00N 26 00E
Chippewa Falls *tn.* Wisconsin USA 45 F3 44 56N 91 23W
Chippewa River Michigan USA 46 B3 43 36N 84 45W
Chiquimula Guatemala 66 G2 14 48N 89 32W
Chirchik Uzbekistan 86 J5 41 28N 69 31E
Chişinău Moldova 81 M7 47 00N 28 50E
Chita Russia 87 P7 52 03N 113 35E
Chitembo Angola 101 H5 13 33S 16 47E
Chitral Pakistan 90 C7 35 52N 71 58E
Chittagong Bangladesh 91 L9 22 20N 91 48E
Chittoor India 90 D2 13 13N 79 06E
Chocolate Mountains California USA 64 F1 33 30N 115 30W
Choiseul *i.* Solomon Islands 103 L9 7 00S 157 00E
Chojnice Poland 80 F10 53 42N 17 32E
Cholet Fr. 79 E7 47 04N 0 53W
Choluteca Honduras 66 G2 13 15N 87 10W
Chone Ecuador 72 A13 0 44S 80 04W
Chongjin North Korea 93 P7 41 50N 129 55E
Chongju South Korea 93 P6 36 39N 127 27E
Chongqing China 93 K4 29 30N 106 35E
Chonju South Korea 93 P6 35 50N 127 50E
Chornobyl Ukraine 80 N9 51 17N 30 15E
Chott El Jerid *salt l.* Tunisia 100 F14 30 00N 9 00E
Chott Melrhir *salt l.* Algeria 100 F14 33 30N 6 10E
Chowchilla California USA 64 C3 37 07N 120 14W
Choybalsan Mongolia 93 L8 48 02N 114 32E
Christchurch NZ 103 P2 43 32S 172 38E
Christmas Island Aust. 102 A8 10 15S 106 00E
Chu *r.* Asia 86 K5 45 00N 72 30E
Chubut *r.* Argentina 73 D5 43 30S 67 30W
Chūgoku-sanchi *mts.* Japan 94 B1 35 00N 133 00E
Chukchi Sea Arctic Ocean 109 70 00N 170 00W
Chuk Kok HK China 92 C2 22 21N 114 15E
Chukotsk Peninsula Russia 87 W10 66 00N 175 00W
Chukotsk Range *mts.* Russia 87 V10 68 00N 175 00E
Chulucanas Peru 72 A12 5 08S 80 10W
Chulym *r.* Russia 87 L8 57 30N 87 30E
Chumphon Thailand 95 B6 10 30N 99 11E
Chuna *r.* Russia 87 M8 57 30N 98 00E
Chunchon South Korea 93 P6 37 56N 127 40E
Chunchura India 91 K9 22 55N 88 15E
Ch'ungju South Korea 93 P6 36 59N 127 53E
Chunya *r.* Russia 87 N9 62 00N 101 00E
Chur Switz. 79 K7 46 52N 9 32E
Ciego de Avila Cuba 67 J4 21 51N 78 47W
Ciénaga Col. 72 C16 11 01N 74 15W
Cienfuegos Cuba 67 H4 22 10N 80 27W
Cimarron *r.* USA 62 F4 37 00N 103 00W
Cimislia Moldova 81 M7 46 30N 28 50E
Cinca *r.* Sp. 79 F4 41 45N 0 15E
Cincinnati Ohio USA 63 K4 39 10N 83 30W
Circle Alaska USA 54 B4 65 50N 144 11W
Cirebon Indonesia 95 D2 6 46S 108 33E
Cisco Texas USA 62 G3 32 23N 98 59W
Cisneros Col. 72 B15 6 32N 75 04W
Citlaltépetl *mt.* Mexico 66 E3 19 00N 97 18W
City Island New York USA 65 J2 40 51N 73 48W
Ciucea Romania 81 J7 46 58N 22 50E
Ciudad Acuna Mexico 66 D5 29 20N 100 58W
Ciudad Bolívar Venezuela 72 E15 8 06N 63 36W
Ciudad Camargo Mexico 66 C5 27 41N 105 10W
Ciudad del Carmen Mexico 66 F3 18 38N 91 50W
Ciudad del Este Paraguay 72 G8 25 32S 54 34W
Ciudadela Sp. 79 G3 40 00N 3 50E
Ciudad Guayana Venezuela 72 E15 8 22N 62 37W
Ciudad Juárez Mexico 66 C6 31 42N 106 29W
Ciudad Lerdo Mexico 66 D5 25 34N 103 30W
Ciudad Madero Mexico 66 E4 22 19N 97 50W
Ciudad Manté Mexico 66 E4 22 44N 98 59W
Ciudad Obregón Mexico 66 C5 27 28N 109 59W
Ciudad Real Sp. 79 D3 38 59N 3 55W
Ciudad Rodrigo Sp. 79 B4 40 36N 6 33W
Ciudad Victoria Mexico 66 E4 23 43N 99 10W
Civitavecchia Italy 81 C5 42 05N 11 47E
Cizre Turkey 88 D6 37 21N 42 11E
Clan Alpine Mountains Nevada USA 64 E4 39 34N 117 53W
Clare Michigan USA 46 B3 43 49N 84 47W
Claremont New Hampshire USA 65 D3 43 22N 72 20W
Clarence Island South Shetland Islands 73 G1 61 10S 54 00W
Clarence Strait *sd.* Alaska USA 38 D4 56 00N 133 30W
Clarendon Pennsylvania USA 46 G1 41 46N 79 06W
Clarion Fracture Zone Pacific Ocean 107 N9 18 00N 130 00W
Clark Fork *r.* Montana USA 39 N1 48 00N 115 55W
Clark Hill Lake South Carolina USA 63 K3 33 00N 82 00W
Clarksburg West Virginia USA 63 K4 39 16N 80 22W
Clarks Ferry *tn.* Pennsylvania USA 65 B2 40 25N 77 56W
Clarksville Tennessee USA 63 J4 36 31N 87 21W
Clayton New York USA 47 K4 44 15N 76 06W
Clearfield Pennsylvania USA 65 A2 41 01N 78 26W
Clear Lake California USA 64 B4 39 04N 122 48W
Clearwater Florida USA 63 K2 27 57N 82 48W
Clearwater *r.* Idaho USA 62 C6 46 00N 116 00W
Clermont-Ferrand Fr. 79 G6 45 47N 3 05E
Cleveland New York USA 63 K5 43 15N 75 50W
Cleveland Peninsula Alaska USA 38 D4 55 30N 132 00W
Clinton Iowa USA 63 H5 41 51N 90 12W
Clinton Oklahoma USA 62 G4 35 32N 98 59W
Clipperton Fracture Zone Pacific Ocean 107 P8/Q9 10 00N 120 00W
Clipperton Island Pacific Ocean 107 R9 10 20N 109 13W
Cloncurry Aust. 103 H6 20 41S 140 30E
Clonmel RoI 78 B10 52 21N 7 42W
Cloppenburg Germany 80 B10 52 52N 8 02E
Cloquet Minnesota USA 45 E4 46 43N 92 27W
Cloverdale California USA 64 B4 38 47N 123 01W
Clovis California USA 64 D3 36 47N 119 43W
Clovis New Mexico USA 62 F3 34 14N 103 13W
Cluj-Napoca Romania 81 J7 46 47N 23 37E
Clyde Ohio USA 46 D1 41 17N 82 58W
Clydebank UK 78 C11 55 54N 4 24W
Coaldale Nevada USA 64 E4 38 02N 117 52W
Coalinga California USA 64 C3 36 08N 120 22W
Coari Brazil 72 E13 4 08S 63 07W
Coast Ranges *mts.* California USA 62 B4/B6 41 00N 123 00W
Coatepec Mexico 66 E3 19 29N 96 59W
Coats Land *geog. reg.* Antarctica 109 77 00S 25 00W
Coatzacoalcos Mexico 66 F3 18 10N 94 25W
Cobán Guatemala 66 F3 15 28N 90 20W
Cobar Aust. 103 J4 31 32S 145 51E
Cobija Bolivia 72 D11 11 01S 68 45W
Coburg Germany 80 C9 50 15N 10 58E
Cochabamba Bolivia 72 D10 17 26S 66 10W
Cochin India 90 D1 9 56N 76 15E
Cochraine Chile 73 C4 47 16S 72 33W
Cochranton Pennsylvania USA 46 F1 41 32N 80 03W
Cocos Basin Indian Ocean 105 J6 5 00S 96 00E
Cocos Islands Indian Ocean 105 J5 12 30S 97 00E
Cocos Ridge Pacific Ocean 107 S8 4 00N 90 00W
Codajás Brazil 72 E13 3 55S 62 00W
Cod, Cape Massachusetts USA 63 N5 42 05N 70 12W
Codó Brazil 72 J13 4 28S 43 51W
Codrington Antigua and Barbuda 66 Q9 17 43N 61 49W
Coeur d'Alene Idaho USA 62 C6 47 40N 116 46W
Cognac Fr. 79 E6 45 42N 0 19W
Coihaique Chile 73 C4 45 35S 72 08W
Coimbatore India 90 D2 11 00N 76 57E
Coimbra Port. 79 A4 40 12N 8 25W
Colchester UK 78 F9 51 54N 0 54E
Cold Springs *tn.* Nevada USA 64 E4 39 22N 117 53W
Coldwater Michigan USA 45 J1 41 56N 84 59W
Coleen River Alaska USA 54 B4 67 30N 142 30W
Coleraine UK 78 B11 55 08N 6 40W
Colima Mexico 66 D3 19 14N 103 41W
College Alaska USA 54 A3 64 54N 147 55W
Collie Aust. 102 C4 33 20S 116 06E
Colmar Fr. 78 J8 48 05N 7 21E
Cologne Germany 80 A9 50 56N 6 57E
COLOMBIA 72 C14
Colombo Sri Lanka 90 D1 6 55N 79 52E
Colón Panama 67 J1 9 21N 79 54W
Colorado *r.* Argentina 73 D6 37 30S 69 00W
Colorado *r.* North America 62 D3 33 00N 114 00W
Colorado *r.* Texas USA 63 G2 29 00N 96 00W
Colorado *state* USA 62 E4/F4 39 00N 106 00W
Colorado Desert California USA 64 E1/F1 33 18N 116 00W
Colorado Plateau Arizona USA 62 D4 36 00N 111 00W
Colorado River Aqueduct California USA 64 E1 34 00N 116 30W
Colorado Springs *tn.* Colorado USA 62 F4 38 50N 104 50W
Columbia Missouri USA 63 H4 38 58N 92 20W
Columbia South Carolina USA 63 K3 34 00N 81 00W
Columbia *r.* North America 62 B6 46 00N 120 00W
Columbus Georgia USA 63 K3 32 28N 84 59W
Columbus Indiana USA 63 J4 39 12N 85 57W
Columbus Mississippi USA 63 J3 33 30N 88 27W
Columbus Nebraska USA 63 G5 41 27N 97 21W
Columbus Ohio USA 63 K5 39 59N 83 03W
Columbus Salt Marsh Nevada USA 64 E4 38 06N 117 57W
Colville Washington USA 39 M1 48 33N 117 55W
Colvocoresses Bay Antarctica 109 66 00S 120 00E
Comilla Bangladesh 91 L9 23 28N 91 10E
Comitán Mexico 66 F3 16 18N 92 09W
Como Italy 81 B6 45 48N 9 05E
Comodoro Rivadavia Argentina 73 D4 45 50S 67 30W
COMOROS 101 N5
Compiègne Fr. 78 G8 49 25N 2 50E
Comrat Moldova 81 M7 46 18N 28 40E
Conakry Guinea 100 B9 9 30N 13 43W
Concepción Chile 73 C5 36 50S 73 03W
Concepción Mexico 66 D4 24 38N 101 25W
Concepción Paraguay 72 F9 23 22S 57 26W
Concepción del Uruguay Argentina 73 F7 32 30S 58 15W
Conchos *r.* Mexico 66 C5 27 30N 107 00W
Concord California USA 64 B3 37 59N 122 03W
Concord New Hampshire USA 63 M5 43 13N 71 34W
Concordia Argentina 73 F7 31 25S 58 00W
Concordia Kansas USA 63 G4 39 35N 97 39W
Concrete Washington USA 38 H4 48 30N 121 45W
Condom Fr. 79 F5 43 58N 0 23E
Conduit *r.* Israel 88 N11 32 25N 35 00E
Conecuh *r.* Alabama USA 63 J3 31 00N 87 00W
Conesus Lake New York USA 46 J2 42 48N 77 44W
Coney Island New York USA 65 J1 40 34N 74 00W
CONGO 100 H7
Congo *r.* Congo/CDR 100 H7 2 00S 17 00E
CONGO DEMOCRATIC REPUBLIC 100 H7
Conneaut Ohio USA 46 F1 41 58N 80 34W
Connecticut *r.* North America 63 M5 43 00N 72 00W
Connecticut *state* USA 63 M5 41 00N 73 00W
Constanța Romania 81 M6 44 12N 28 40E
Constantine Algeria 100 F15 36 22N 6 40E
Constitución Chile 73 C6 31 05S 57 51W
Contamana Peru 72 B12 7 19S 75 04W

Place	Page	Grid	Latitude	Longitude
Cook Islands Pacific Ocean	107	L6	19 30S	159 50W
Cook, Mount NZ	103	P2	43 36S	170 09E
Cook Strait NZ	103	P2	41 24S	174 36E
Cooktown Aust.	103	J7	15 29S	145 15E
Coolgardie Aust.	102	D4	31 01S	121 12E
Cooper Creek Aust.	102/103	G5	28 00S	138 00E
Coosa *r.* Alabama USA	63	J3	33 00N	86 00W
Coos Bay *tn.* Oregon USA	62	B5	43 23N	124 12W
Copenhagen Denmark	80	D11	55 43N	12 34E
Copiapó Chile	72	C8	27 20S	70 23W
Copper Harbor Michigan USA	63	J6	47 28N	87 54W
Coquimbo Chile	73	C8	29 57S	71 25W
Coral Sea Pacific Ocean	103	K8	15 00S	154 00E
Coral Sea Islands Territory *admin.* Aust.	103	K7	17 00S	150 00E
Corantijn *r.* Suriname	72	F14	4 30N	57 30W
Cordillera Cantabrica *mts.* Sp.	79	B5/C5	43 00N	5 30W
Córdoba Argentina	73	E7	31 25S	64 11W
Córdoba Mexico	66	E3	18 55N	96 55W
Córdoba Sp.	79	C2	37 53N	4 46W
Corfu Greece	81	G3	39 38N	19 55E
Corinth Mississippi USA	63	J3	34 58N	88 30W
Cork RoI	78	A9	51 54N	8 28W
Corning New York USA	47	J2	42 09N	77 05W
Cornwall Bridge *tn.* Connecticut USA	65	D2	41 49N	73 22W
Coro Venezuela	72	D16	11 20N	70 00W
Coroico Bolivia	72	D10	16 19S	67 45W
Coromandel Coast India	90	E2	12 30N	81 30E
Corona California USA	64	E1	33 52N	117 34W
Coronado California USA	64	E1	32 40N	117 07W
Coronation Island South Orkney Islands	73	H1	61 00S	46 00W
Coronation Island Alaska USA	38	C4	55 50N	134 15N
Coronel Pringles Argentina	73	E6	37 56S	61 25W
Corpus Christi Texas USA	63	G2	27 47N	97 26W
Corrientes Argentina	72	F8	27 30S	58 48W
Corrientes *r.* Peru	72	B13	2 30S	76 30W
Corriverton Guyana	72	F15	5 53N	57 10W
Corry Pennsylvania USA	46	G1	41 56N	79 39W
Corsica *i.* Fr.	79	K4/K5	42 00N	9 00E
Corte Fr.	79	K5	41 18N	9 08E
Cortland New York USA	45	N2	42 36N	76 11W
Çoruh *r.* Turkey	88	D7	40 45N	40 45E
Corumbá Brazil	72	F10	19 00S	57 35W
Corunna Michigan USA	46	B2	42 58N	84 05W
Corvallis Oregon USA	62	B5	44 34N	123 16W
Cosenza Italy	81	F3	39 17N	16 16E
Costa Blanca *geog. reg.* Sp.	79	E3	38 15N	0 20W
Costa Brava *geog. reg.* Sp.	79	G4	41 40N	3 50E
Costa del Sol *geog. reg.* Sp.	79	C2	36 40N	4 40W
COSTA RICA	67	H1		
Cotagaita Bolivia	72	D9	20 47S	65 40W
Côte D'Azur *geog. reg.* Fr.	79	J5	43 00N	7 00E
CÔTE D'IVOIRE	100	C9		
Cotonou Benin	100	E9	6 24N	2 31E
Cotopaxi *mt.* Ecuador	72	B13	0 40S	78 28W
Cottbus Germany	80	E9	51 43N	14 21E
Coudersport Pennsylvania USA	46	H1	41 47N	78 00W
Council Bluffs Iowa USA	63	G5	41 14N	95 54W
Coupeville Washington USA	38	H4	48 08N	122 38W
Coventry UK	78	E10	52 25N	1 30W
Covilhã Port.	79	B4	40 17N	7 30W
Covington Kentucky USA	63	K4	39 04N	84 30W
Cox's Bazar Bangladesh	91	L8	21 25N	91 59E
Coyote Lake California USA	64	E2	35 05N	116 45W
Craig Alaska USA	38	D4	55 29N	133 06W
Craiova Romania	81	J6	44 18N	23 47E
Crandon Wisconsin USA	45	G3	45 34N	88 54W
Cremona Italy	81	C6	45 08N	10 01E
Cres *i.* Croatia	81	E6	45 00N	14 00E
Crescent City California USA	62	B5	41 46N	124 13W
Crescent Island HK China	92	C3	22 32N	114 19E
Creston Iowa USA	63	H5	41 04N	94 20W
Crestview Florida USA	63	J3	30 44N	86 34W
Crete, Sea of Mediterranean Sea	81	K2/L2	36 00N	25 00E
Crewe UK	78	D10	53 05N	2 27W
Criciúma Brazil	73	H8	28 45S	49 25W
CROATIA	81	F6		
Crooked Island Bahamas	67	K4	22 45N	74 10W
Crooked Island HK China	92	C3	22 33N	114 18E
Crookston Minnesota USA	63	G6	47 47N	96 36W
Crosby North Dakota USA	42	F1	48 59N	103 20W
Cross Sound Alaska USA	38	B6	58 00N	137 00W
Crotone Italy	81	F3	39 05N	17 08E
Crow Peak *mt.* Montana USA	62	D6	46 19N	111 56W
Croydon Aust.	103	H7	18 10S	142 15E
Crozet Basin Indian Ocean	105	E3/F2	40 00S	55 00E
Cruzeiro do Sul Brazil	72	C12	7 40S	72 39W
Crystal Falls *tn.* Michigan USA	45	G4	46 06N	89 20W
Cuando *r.* Southern Africa	101	J4	16 00S	21 30E
Cuango *r.* Angola	101	H6	9 00S	18 30E
Cuanza *r.* Angola	101	H6	9 40S	15 00E
CUBA	67	H4		
Cubango *r.* Southern Africa	101	H4	17 00S	18 00E
Cúcuta Col.	72	C15	7 55N	73 31W
Cuddalore India	90	D2	11 43N	79 46E
Cuddapah India	90	D2	14 30N	78 50E
Cuddeback Lake California USA	64	E2	35 17N	117 29W
Cuenca Ecuador	72	B13	2 54S	79 00W
Cuenca Sp.	79	D4	40 04N	2 07W
Cuernavaca Mexico	66	E3	18 57N	99 15W
Cuiabá Brazil	72	F10	15 32S	56 05W
Cuito *r.* Angola	101	H4	17 30S	19 30E
Culiacán Mexico	66	C4	24 50N	107 23W
Cumaná Venezuela	72	E16	10 29N	64 12W
Cumberland Maryland USA	63	L4	39 40N	78 47W
Cumberland *r.* North America	63	J4	37 00N	86 00W
Cumberland Plateau USA	63	J4/K4	36 00N	85 00W
Cumbernauld UK	78	D11	55 57N	4 00W
Cumbrian Mountains UK	78	D11	54 30N	3 00W
Cunene *r.* Angola/Namibia	101	G4	17 00S	13 30E
Cuneo Italy	81	A6	44 24N	7 33E
Cunnamula Aust.	103	J5	28 04S	145 40E
Curaçao *i.* Lesser Antilles	67	L2	12 20N	68 20W
Curacautín Chile	73	C6	38 28S	71 52W
Curicó Chile	73	C6	35 00S	71 15W
Curitiba Brazil	72	H8	25 25S	49 25W
Curvelo Brazil	72	J10	18 45S	44 27W
Cut Bank Montana USA	41	F1	48 37N	112 18W
Cut Bank Creek *r.* Montana USA	41	F1	48 40N	112 50W
Cuttack India	91	F4	20 26N	85 56E
Cuxhaven Germany	80	B10	53 52N	8 42E
Cuzco Peru	72	C11	13 32S	71 59W
CYPRUS	88	B5		
CZECH REPUBLIC	80	D8		
Częstochowa Poland	80	G9	50 49N	19 07E

D

Place	Page	Grid	Latitude	Longitude
Dabgram India	91	K9	23 50N	88 17E
Dabola Guinea	100	B10	10 48N	11 02W
Dadra and Nagar Haveli *admin.* India	90	C4	20 00N	73 00E
Da Hinggan Ling *mts.* China	93	M8	50 00N	122 00E
Dahūk Iraq	88	D6	36 52N	43 00E
Daiō-zaki *c.* Japan	94	C1	34 16N	136 55E
Daisen *mt.* Japan	94	B2	35 23N	133 34E
Dakar Senegal	100	A10	14 38N	17 27W
Dakhin Shahbazpur Island Bangladesh	91	L9	22 30N	90 45E
Dakhla Oasis Egypt	100	K13	26 00N	28 00E
Dalälven *r.* Sweden	80	F14	60 30N	17 00E
Da Lat Vietnam	95	D6	11 56N	108 25E
Dalbandin Pakistan	90	A5	28 56N	64 30E
Dalby Aust.	103	K5	27 11S	151 12E
Dalhart Texas USA	62	F4	36 05N	102 32W
Dali China	93	J4	25 33N	100 09E
Dalian China	93	N6	38 53N	121 37E
Dalkhola India	91	J10	25 57N	87 51E
Dallas Texas USA	63	G3	32 47N	96 48W
Dall Island Alaska USA	38	D4	55 00N	133 00W
Daloa Côte d'Ivoire	100	C9	6 56N	6 28W
Dalton Georgia USA	63	K3	34 46N	84 59W
Daly *r.* Aust.	102	F8	14 00S	132 00E
Daly Waters *tn.* Aust.	102	F7	16 13S	133 20E
Daman India	90	C4	20 15N	72 58E
Damascus Syria	88	C5	33 30N	36 19E
Damāvand Iran	89	F6	35 47N	52 04E
Damāvand *mt.* Iran	89	F6	35 56N	52 08E
Damba Angola	101	H6	6 44S	15 20E
Damietta Egypt	101	R4	31 26N	31 48E
Damman and Diu *admin.* India	90	C4	15 00N	74 00E
Damodar *r.* India	91	K9	22 30N	88 00E
Dampier Aust.	102	C6	20 45S	116 48E
Da Năng Vietnam	95	D7	16 04N	108 14E
Danau Toba *l.* Indonesia	95	B4	2 30N	98 30E
Danbury Connecticut USA	63	M5	41 24N	73 26W
Dandong China	93	N7	40 08N	124 24E
Danforth Maine USA	51	G1	45 42N	67 50W
Danielson Connecticut USA	65	E2	41 48N	71 53W
Danli Honduras	67	G2	14 02N	86 30W
Danville Illinois USA	63	J5	40 09N	87 37W
Danville Pennsylvania USA	65	B2	40 58N	76 37W
Danville Virginia USA	63	L4	36 34N	79 25W
Daqing China	93	P8	46 28N	125 01E
Dar'ā Syria	88	P11	32 37N	36 06E
Darbhanga India	91	F5	26 10N	85 54E
Dardanelles *sd.* Turkey	88	A7	40 08N	26 10E
Dar es Salaam Tanzania	101	M6	6 51S	39 18E
Dargaville NZ	103	P3	35 56S	173 52E
Darjiling India	91	F5	27 02N	88 20E
Darling *r.* Aust.	103	H4	30 30S	144 00E
Darling Downs *mts.* Aust.	103	J5	28 00S	148 30E
Darlington UK	78	E11	54 31N	1 34W
Darmstadt Germany	80	B8	49 52N	8 39E
Darnah Libya	100	J14	32 46N	22 39E
Daroca Sp.	79	E4	41 07N	1 25W
Darrington Washington USA	38	H4	48 15N	121 37W
Dartmoor *hills* UK	78	C9	50 35N	3 50W
Daru PNG	103	H9	9 05S	143 10E
Darwin Aust.	102	F8	12 23S	130 44E
Darwin California USA	64	E3	36 17N	117 36W
Daryācheh-ye Orūmīyeh *l.* Iran	88	E6	37 20N	45 55E
Dashkhovuz Turkmenistan	86	H5	41 49N	59 58E
Dasht-e-Kavir *geog. reg.* Iran	89	F5/G5	34 30N	54 30E
Dasht-e-Lut *geog. reg.* Iran	89	G5	32 00N	57 00E
Dasht-i-Margo *d.* Afghanistan	89	H5	30 30N	62 30E
Datong China	93	L7	40 02N	113 33E
Datong Shan *mts.* China	93	H6/J6	38 00N	99 00E
Datong He *r.* China	93	J6	37 30N	102 00E
Datu Piang Philippines	95	G5	7 02N	124 30E
Dauki India	91	L10	25 10N	92 00E
Davangere India	90	D2	14 30N	75 52E
Davao Philippines	95	H5	7 05N	125 38E
Davenport California USA	64	B3	37 02N	122 14W
Davenport Iowa USA	63	H5	41 32N	90 36W
David Panama	67	H1	8 26N	82 26W
Davidson Mountains Alaska USA	54	B4	68 30N	143 30W
Davis California USA	64	C4	38 33N	121 46W
Davison Michigan USA	46	C3	43 02N	83 30W
Davos Switz.	79	K7	46 47N	9 50E
Dawna Range *mts.* Myanmar/Thailand	95	B7	17 10N	98 00E
Dax Fr.	79	E5	43 43N	1 03W
Dayr az Zawr Syria	88	D6	35 20N	40 02E
Dayton Ohio USA	63	K4	39 45N	84 10W
Daytona Beach *tn.* Florida USA	63	K2	29 11N	81 01W
De Aar RSA	101	J1	30 40S	24 01E
Dead Sea Israel/Jordan	88	N10	31 35N	35 30E
Deán Funes Argentina	73	E7	30 25S	64 22W
Dearborn Michigan USA	45	K2	42 18N	83 16W
Death Valley California USA	62	C4	36 00N	117 00W
Death Valley Junction *tn.* California USA	64	E3	36 18N	116 25W
Death Valley National Monument California USA	64	E3	36 30N	117 00W
Debrecen Hungary	81	H7	47 30N	21 37E
Debre Mark'os Ethiopia	100	M10	10 19N	37 41E
Debre Tabor Ethiopia	100	M10	11 50N	38 06E
Decatur Alabama USA	63	J3	34 36N	87 00W
Decatur Illinois USA	63	J4	39 51N	88 57W
Deccan *plat.* India	90	D3	18 00N	78 00E
Dee *r.* UK	78	D10	53 15N	3 10W
Deep Bay HK China	92	A3	22 30N	113 58E
Defiance Ohio USA	45	J1	41 17N	84 22W
Degeh Bur Ethiopia	100	N9	8 11N	43 31E
Dehra Dun India	90	D6	30 19N	78 03E
Dej Romania	81	J7	47 08N	23 55E
Dekese CDR	100	J7	3 28S	21 24E
Delano California USA	64	D2	35 46N	119 15W
Delaware *state* USA	63	L4	39 00N	75 00W
Delaware Bay Delaware/New Jersey USA	63	L4	39 10N	75 10W
Delaware River Delaware USA	65	C1	39 40N	75 30W
Delhi India	90	D5	28 40N	77 14E
Delhi *admin.* India	90	D5	28 40N	77 14E
Del Rio Texas USA	62	F2	29 23N	100 56W
Delta Colorado USA	62	E4	38 42N	108 04W
Delta Junction Alaska USA	54	A3	63 30N	146 00W
Dembi Dolo Ethiopia	100	L9	8 34N	34 50E
Deming New Mexico USA	62	E3	32 17N	107 46W
Deming Washington USA	38	H4	48 50N	122 17W
Den Helder Neths.	78	H10	52 58N	4 46E
Denison Texas USA	63	G3	33 47N	96 34W
Denizli Turkey	88	A6	37 46N	29 05E
DENMARK	80	B11		
Denmark Strait Atlantic Ocean	108	F13	66 30N	25 00W
Denpasar Indonesia	95	F2	8 40S	115 14E
Denton Texas USA	63	G3	33 14N	97 18W
D'Entrecasteaux Islands PNG	103	K8	9 15S	150 45E
Denver Colorado USA	62	E4	39 45N	105 00W
Dépression du Mourdi *dep.* Chad	100	J11	17 00N	22 41E
Deputatskiy Russia	87	R10	69 15N	139 59E
Dera Ghazi Khan Pakistan	90	C6	30 05N	70 44E
Dera Ismail Khan Pakistan	90	C6	31 51N	70 56E
Derby Aust.	102	D7	17 19S	123 38E
Derby UK	78	E10	52 55N	1 30W
Derby Connecticut USA	65	D2	41 20N	73 06W
Dese Ethiopia	100	M10	11 05N	39 40E
Deseado Argentina	73	D4	47 44S	65 56W
Deseado *r.* Argentina	73	D4	47 00S	68 00W
Desert Center California USA	64	F1	33 44N	115 23W
Desierto de Atacama *d.* Chile	72	C9	22 30S	70 00W
Des Moines Iowa USA	63	H5	41 35N	93 35W
Des Moines *r.* Iowa USA	63	H5	41 00N	92 00W
Desna *r.* Russia/Ukraine	80	N9	52 00N	32 30E
Dessau Germany	80	D9	51 51N	12 15E
Detroit Michigan USA	63	K5	42 23N	83 05W
Deva Romania	81	J6	45 53N	22 55E
Deveron *r.* UK	78	D12	57 35N	2 35W
Devil's Lake *tn.* North Dakota USA	63	G6	48 03N	98 57W
Devonport Aust.	103	J2	41 09S	146 16E
Dexter Maine USA	51	F1	45 01N	69 19W
Dezfūl Iran	89	E5	32 23N	48 28E
Dezhou China	93	M6	37 29N	116 11E
Dhahran Saudi Arabia	89	F4	26 13N	50 02E
Dhaka Bangladesh	91	L9	23 42N	90 22E
Dhamār Yemen	88	D1	14 33N	44 30E
Dhanbad India	91	F4	23 47N	86 32E
Dharoor *r.* Somalia	100	P10	10 00N	54 00E
Dharwad India	90	D3	15 30N	75 04E
Dhaulagiri *mt.* Nepal	90	E5	28 40N	83 28E
Dhule India	90	C4	20 52N	74 50E
Diablo Lake Washington USA	38	H4	48 45N	121 05W
Diablo, Mount California USA	64	C3	37 50N	121 47W
Diamantina Brazil	72	J10	18 17S	43 37W
Diamantina *r.* Aust.	103	H6	24 00S	143 00E
Diamantina Fracture Zone Indian Ocean	105	K3	38 00S	110 00E
Diamond Harbour *tn.* India	91	K9	22 10N	88 13E
Dibrugarh India	91	G5	27 29N	95 00E
Dickinson North Dakota USA	62	F6	46 54N	102 48W
Diepholz Germany	80	B10	52 37N	8 22E
Dieppe Fr.	78	F8	49 55N	1 05E
Digne-les-Bains Fr.	79	J6	44 05N	6 14E
Dijon Fr.	79	H7	47 20N	5 02E
Dikson Russia	87	L11	73 32N	80 39E
Dikwa Nigeria	100	G10	12 01N	13 55E
Dili East Timor	95	H2	8 33S	125 34E
Dimitrovgrad Bulgaria	81	K5	42 03N	25 34E
Dinajpur Bangladesh	91	K10	25 38N	88 44E
Dinan Fr.	78	D8	48 27N	2 02W
Dinant Belgium	78	H9	50 16N	4 55E
Dinara Planina *mts.* Europe	81	F5	44 00N	17 00E
Dindigul India	90	D2	10 23N	78 00E
Dingwall UK	78	C12	57 35N	4 29W
Dipolog Philippines	95	G5	8 34N	123 23E
Dire Dawa Ethiopia	100	N9	9 35N	41 50E
Disappointment, Lake Aust.	102	D6	23 00S	123 00E
Discovery Bay *tn.* HK China	92	B1	22 18N	114 01E
Dispur India	91	G5	26 07N	91 48E
Diu India	90	C4	20 41N	71 03E
Divinópolis Brazil	72	J9	20 08S	44 55W
Divriği Turkey	88	C6	39 23N	38 06E
Dixie Valley *tn.* Nevada USA	64	D4	39 41N	118 04W
Dixon California USA	64	C4	38 26N	121 53W
Diyarbakir Turkey	88	D6	37 55N	40 14E
Djambala Congo	100	G7	2 32S	14 43E
Djanet Algeria	100	F12	24 27N	9 32E
Djelfa Algeria	100	E14	34 43N	3 14E
DJIBOUTI	100	N10		
Djibouti Djibouti	100	N10	11 35N	43 11E
Djougou Benin	100	E9	9 40N	1 47E
Dnestr *r.* Ukraine	80	K8	48 00N	27 30E
Doboj Bosnia-Herzegovina	81	G6	44 44N	18 05E
Dobrich Bulgaria	81	L5	43 34N	27 51E
Dobrogea *geog. reg.* Romania	81	M6	44 00N	29 00E
Dodekánisos *is.* Greece	81	L2	37 00N	26 00E
Dodge City Kansas USA	62	F4	37 45N	100 02W
Dōgo *i.* Japan	94	B2	36 20N	133 15E
Doha Qatar	89	F4	25 15N	51 36E
Dolina Ukraine	80	J8	49 00N	23 59E
Dolo Odo Ethiopia	100	N8	4 11N	42 03E
Domar Bangladesh	91	K11	26 08N	88 57E
DOMINICA	66	Q8		
DOMINICAN REPUBLIC	67	L3		
Dominica Passage *sd.* Caribbean Sea	66	Q8	15 10N	61 15W
Don *r.* Russia	86	G7	50 00N	41 00E
Donau *r.* Germany/Austria	80	C8	48 00N	16 00E
Don Benito Sp.	79	C3	38 57N	5 52W
Doncaster UK	78	E10	53 32N	1 07W
Donegal RoI	78	A11	54 39N	8 07W
Donegal Bay RoI	78	A11	54 30N	8 30W
Dongchuan China	93	J4	26 07N	103 05E
Dông Hôi Vietnam	95	D7	17 32N	106 35E
Dongola Sudan	100	L11	19 10N	30 27E
Dongou Congo	100	H8	2 02N	18 02E
Don Pedro Reservoir California USA	64	C3	37 45N	120 23W
Donting Hu *l.* China	93	L4	29 00N	112 30E
Door Peninsula Wisconsin USA	63	J5	45 00N	87 00W
Dora Báltea *r.* Italy	81	A6	45 45N	8 00E
Dordogne *r.* Fr.	79	F6	44 55N	0 30E
Dordrecht Neths.	78	H9	51 48N	4 40E
Dori *r.* Afghanistan	89	H5/J5	31 20N	65 00E
Dornbirn Austria	79	K7	47 25N	9 46E
Dortmund Germany	80	A9	51 32N	7 27E
Dos Palos California USA	64	C3	36 59N	120 39W
Dosso Niger	100	E10	13 03N	3 10E
Dothan Alabama USA	63	J3	31 12N	85 25W
Douai Fr.	78	G9	50 22N	3 05E
Douala Cameroon	100	F8	4 04N	9 43E
Douarnenez Fr.	78	C8	48 05N	4 20W
Double Island HK China	92	C3	22 31N	114 19E
Doubs *r.* Fr.	79	J7	47 20N	6 25E
Douglas Alaska USA	38	C6	58 15N	134 24W
Douglas Arizona USA	62	E3	31 21N	109 34W
Dourados Brazil	72	G9	22 09S	54 52W
Douro *r.* Port./Sp.	79	B4	41 00N	8 30W
Dover UK	78	F9	51 08N	1 19E
Dover Delaware USA	63	L4	39 10N	75 32W
Dover New Hampshire USA	65	E3	43 12N	70 53W
Dover, Strait of *sd.* English Channel	78	F9	51 00N	1 20W
Dōzen *is.* Japan	94	B2	36 05N	133 00E
Dragon's Mouths Trinidad and Tobago	67	V15	10 37N	61 50W
Draguignan Fr.	79	J5	43 32N	6 28E
Drakensberg *mts.* RSA	101	K1/L2	30 00S	28 00E
Drake Passage *sd.* Southern Ocean	73	C2/E2	58 00S	66 00W
Dráma Greece	81	K4	41 10N	24 11E
Drammen Norway	80	L13	59 45N	10 15E
Drau *r.* Austria	81	E7	46 00N	14 00E
Drava *r.* Europe	81	F7	46 00N	18 00E
Dresden Germany	80	D9	51 03N	13 45E
Dreux Fr.	78	F8	48 44N	1 23E
Drin *r.* Albania	81	G5	42 00N	20 00E
Drina *r.* Europe	81	G6	44 00N	19 30E
Drobeta-Turnu-Severin Romania	81	J6	44 36N	22 39E
Drohobyč Ukraine	80	J8	49 22N	23 33E
Drôme *r.* Fr.	79	H6	44 50N	5 00E
Dronning Maud Land *geog. reg.* Antarctica	109		73 00S	10 00E
Drummond Island Michigan USA	45	K3	46 00N	83 50W

Dubai UAE 89 G4 25 14N 55 17E
Dubbo Aust. 103 J4 32 16S 148 41E
Dublin RoI 78 B10 53 20N 6 15W
Dublin Georgia USA 63 K3 32 31N 82 54W
Dubno Ukraine 80 K9 50 28N 25 40E
Du Bois Pennsylvania USA 65 A2 41 07N 78 48W
Dubrovnik Croatia 81 G5 42 40N 18 07E
Dubuque Iowa USA 63 H5 42 31N 90 41W
Dudhanai India 91 L10 25 57N 90 47E
Dudinka Russia 87 L10 69 27N 86 13E
Duero *r.* Sp./Port. 79 B4 41 25N 6 30W
Dugi Otok *i.* Croatia 81 E5/E6 44 00N 15 00E
Duisburg Germany 80 A9 51 26N 6 45E
Duke Island Alaska USA 38 E4 54 50N 131 30W
Dulce *r.* Argentina 73 E8 29 00S 63 00W
Duluth Minnesota USA 63 H6 46 45N 92 10W
Dumfries UK 78 D11 55 04N 3 37W
Duna *r.* Hungary 81 G6/G7 46 00N 19 00E
Dunaújváros Hungary 81 G7 47 00N 18 55E
Dunav *r.* SM/Bulgaria 81 J5 45 00N 20 00E
Duncan Oklahoma USA 63 G3 34 30N 97 57W
Dundalk RoI 78 B11 54 01N 6 25W
Dundee UK 78 D12 56 28N 3 00W
Dunedin NZ 103 P1 45 53S 170 30E
Dunfermline UK 78 D12 56 04N 3 29W
Dungeness Washington USA 38 H4 48 07N 123 06W
Dunkerque Fr. 78 G9 51 02N 2 23E
Dunkirk New York USA 63 L5 42 29N 79 21W
Dún Laoghaire RoI 78 B10 53 17N 6 08W
Dunnigan California USA 64 C4 38 53N 121 57W
Duque de Caxias Brazil 72 J9 22 46S 43 18W
Durand Michigan USA 46 C2 42 55N 83 58W
Durango Mexico 66 D4 24 01N 104 40W
Durango Colorado USA 62 E4 37 16N 107 53W
Durant Oklahoma USA 63 G3 33 59N 96 24W
Durazno Uruguay 73 F7 33 22S 56 31W
Durban RSA 101 L2 29 53S 31 00E
Durgapur India 91 F4 24 47N 87 44E
Durg-Bhilai India 90 E4 21 12N 81 20E
Durham UK 78 E11 54 47N 1 34W
Durham North Carolina USA 63 L4 36 00N 78 54W
Durrës Albania 81 G4 41 18N 19 28E
Dushanbe Tajikistan 86 J4 38 38N 68 51E
Düsseldorf Germany 80 A9 51 13N 6 47E
Duyun China 93 K4 26 16N 107 29E
Dzhetygara Kazakhstan 86 J7 52 14N 61 10E
Dzhugdzhur Range *mts.* Russia 87 R8 57 00N 137 00E

E

Eagle Alaska USA 54 B3 64 46N 141 20W
Eagle Crags *mt.* California USA 64 E2 35 25N 117 04W
Eagle Lake Maine USA 47 S6 46 25N 69 20W
Eagle Mountain Minnesota USA 45 F4 47 54N 90 31W
Eagle Pass *tn.* Texas USA 62 F2 28 44N 100 31W
Eagle River *tn.* Wisconsin USA 45 G3 45 55N 89 14W
East Aurora New York USA 46 H2 42 46N 78 37W
Eastbourne UK 78 F9 50 46N 0 17E
East Cape NZ 103 Q3 37 41S 178 33E
East Caroline Basin Pacific Ocean 106 E8 4 00N 148 00E
East China Sea China/Japan 93 N5/N6 32 00N 126 00E
Easter Island Pacific Ocean 107 R5 27 05S 109 20W
Easter Island Fracture Zone Pacific Ocean 107 R5 24 00S 100 00W
Eastern Ghats *mts.* India 90 D2/E3 15 00N 80 00E
Eastern Group *is.* Fiji 106 V16 17 40S 178 30W
Eastern Sayan *mts.* Russia 87 M7 53 00N 97 30E
East Falkland *i.* Falkland Islands 73 F3 52 00S 58 50W
East Glacier Park *tn.* Montana USA 41 F1 48 27N 113 13W
East Lamma Channel HK China 92 B1 22 14N 114 09E
East Lansing Michigan USA 45 J2 42 44N 84 29W
East London RSA 101 K1 33 00S 27 54E
East Marianas Basin Pacific Ocean 106 F9 13 00N 153 00E
East Pacific Basin Pacific Ocean 107 L9 16 00N 153 00E
East Pacific Ridge Pacific Ocean 107 Q4/R7 20 00S 113 00W
East Pacific Rise Pacific Ocean 107 R9 13 00N 103 00W
Eastport Maine USA 51 G1 44 55N 67 01W
East Rift Valley East Africa 100 M8 6 00N 37 00E
East River New York USA 65 J2 40 48N 73 55W
East Siberian Sea Arctic Ocean 109 72 00N 165 00E
Eastsound Washington USA 38 H4 48 43N 123 05W
EAST TIMOR 95 H2
East Walker *r.* Nevada USA 64 D4 38 48N 119 03W
Eaton Rapids *tn.* Michigan USA 46 B2 42 30N 84 40W
Eau Claire *tn.* Wisconsin USA 63 H5 44 50N 91 30W
Eauripik-New Guinea Rise Pacific Ocean 106 E8 2 00N 142 00E
Ebensburg Pennsylvania USA 65 A2 40 29N 78 44W
Eberswalde-Finow Germany 80 D10 52 50N 13 53E
Ebinur Hu *l.* China 92 E7 45 00N 83 00E
Ebolowa Cameroon 100 G8 2 56N 11 11E
Ebro *r.* Sp. 79 F4 43 00N 4 30W
Ech Chellif Algeria 100 E15 36 05N 1 15E
Ecija Sp. 79 C2 37 33N 5 04W
ECUADOR 72 B13
Ed Damer Sudan 100 L11 17 37N 33 59E
Ed Debba Sudan 100 L11 18 02N 30 56E
Edéa Cameroon 100 G8 3 47N 10 13E
Eden New York USA 48 D1 42 39N 78 55W
Eden North Carolina USA 63 L4 36 30N 79 46W
Eder *r.* Germany 80 B9 51 00N 9 00E
Edessa Greece 81 J4 40 48N 22 03E
Edgecombe, Cape Alaska USA 38 C5 57 00N 135 45W
Edgewood Maryland USA 65 B1 39 25N 76 18W
Edinboro Pennsylvania USA 45 L1 41 52N 80 08W
Edinburgh UK 78 D11 55 57N 3 13W
Edward, Lake CDR/Uganda 100 K7 0 30S 29 00E
Edwards Plateau Texas USA 62 F3 31 00N 100 00W
Éfaté *i.* Vanuatu 103 N7 17 30S 168 00E
Eger Hungary 80 H7 47 53N 20 28E
Eğirdir Gölü *l.* Turkey 88 B6 37 52N 30 51E
EGYPT 100 K13
Eifel *plat.* Germany 80 A9 50 00N 7 00E
Eight Degree Channel Indian Ocean 90 C1 8 00N 73 30E
Eighty Mile Beach Aust. 102 D7 19 00S 121 00E
Eindhoven Neths. 78 H9 51 26N 5 30E
Eisenach Germany 80 C9 50 59N 10 19E
Ekibastuz Kazakhstan 86 K7 51 50N 75 10E
Eksjö Sweden 80 E12 57 40N 15 00E
El Arco Mexico 66 B5 28 00N 113 25W
Elat Israel 88 B4 29 33N 34 57E
Elâzığ Turkey 88 C6 38 41N 39 14E
El Bahr el Saghir Egypt 101 R4 31 38N 31 39E
El Ballâh Egypt 101 S3 30 47N 32 19E
El Banco Col. 72 C15 9 04N 73 59W
Elbasan Albania 81 H4 41 07N 20 05E
El Bayadh Algeria 100 E14 33 40N 1 00E
Elbe *est.* Europe 80 B10 54 00N 9 00E
Elbert, Mount Colorado USA 62 E4 39 05N 106 27W
Elbląg Poland 80 G11 54 10N 19 25E
Elburz Mountains Iran 89 F6 36 15N 51 00E
El Cajon California USA 64 E1 32 48N 116 58W
El Callao Venezuela 72 E15 7 18N 61 50W
El Cap Egypt 101 S3 30 55N 32 23E
El Centro California USA 62 C3 32 47N 115 33W
Elche Sp. 79 E3 38 16N 0 41W
Elda Sp. 79 E3 38 29N 0 47W
El Dorado Arkansas USA 63 H3 33 12N 92 40W
El Dorado Kansas USA 63 G4 37 51N 96 52W
Eldoret Kenya 100 M8 0 31N 35 17E
Elephant Island South Shetland Islands 73 F1 62 00S 55 00W
El Faiyûm Egypt 100 L13 29 19N 30 50E
El Fasher Sudan 100 K10 13 37N 25 22E
El Ferrol del Caudillo Sp. 79 A5 43 29N 8 14W
El Firdân Egypt 101 S3 30 42N 32 20E
El Fuerte Mexico 66 C5 26 28N 108 35W
Elgin UK 78 D12 57 39N 3 20W
El Gîza Egypt 100 L13 30 01N 31 12E
El Golea Algeria 100 E14 30 35N 2 51E
Elgon, Mount Uganda/Kenya 100 L8 1 07N 34 35E
Elista Russia 86 G6 46 18N 44 14E
Elizabeth Aust. 103 G4 34 45S 138 39E
Elizabeth New Jersey USA 65 H1 40 39N 74 13W
Elizabeth City North Carolina USA 63 L4 36 18N 76 16W
El Jadida Morocco 100 C14 33 19N 8 35W
El Jafr Jordan 88 P10 30 16N 36 11E
Ełk Poland 80 J10 53 51N 22 20E
Elk California USA 64 B4 39 08N 123 43W
Elk City Oklahoma USA 62 G4 34 25N 99 26W
Elk Creek *tn.* California USA 64 B4 39 36N 122 34W
Elk Grove California USA 64 C4 38 26N 121 26W
El Khârga Egypt 100 L13 25 27N 30 32E
Elkhart Indiana USA 63 J5 41 52N 85 56W
Elkhorn *r.* Nebraska USA 63 G5 42 00N 98 00W
Elkland Pennsylvania USA 47 J1 42 00N 77 20W
Elko Nevada USA 62 C5 40 50N 115 46W
Ellis Island New Jersey USA 65 H1 40 42N 74 02W
Ellsworth Maine USA 51 F1 44 34N 68 24W
Ellsworth Land *geog. reg.* Antarctica 109 75 00S 80 00W
El Mahalla El Kubra Egypt 100 L14 30 59N 31 10E
El Manzala Egypt 101 R4 31 09N 31 57E
El Matarîya Egypt 101 S4 31 10N 32 02E
El Médano Mexico 66 B4 24 35N 111 29W
Elmhurst Pennsylvania USA 65 C2 41 20N 75 32W
el Milk *r.* Sudan 100 K11 17 00N 29 00E
El Minya Egypt 100 L13 28 06N 30 45E
Elmira New York USA 63 L5 42 06N 76 50W
El Muglad Sudan 100 K10 11 01N 27 50E
El Obeid Sudan 100 L10 13 11N 30 10E
El Paso Texas USA 62 E3 31 45N 106 30W
El Porvenir Mexico 66 C6 31 15N 105 48W
El Progreso Honduras 66 G3 15 20N 87 50W
El Puerto de Santa Maria Sp. 79 B2 36 36N 6 14W
El Qantara Egypt 101 S3 30 53N 32 20E
El Reno Oklahoma USA 63 G4 35 32N 97 57W
El Sâlhîya Egypt 101 R3 30 47N 31 59E
El Salto Mexico 66 C4 23 47N 105 22W
EL SALVADOR 66 G2
El Shallûfa Egypt 101 T2 30 06N 32 33E
El Sueco Mexico 66 C5 29 54N 106 22W
Eltanin Fracture Zone Pacific Ocean 107 M3 52 00S 135 00W
El Tigre Venezuela 72 E15 8 44N 64 18W
El Tina Egypt 101 S4 31 03N 32 19E
El Toro California USA 64 E1 33 36N 117 40W
Eluru India 90 E3 16 45N 81 10E
Elvas Port. 79 B3 38 53N 7 10W
Ely Nevada USA 62 D4 39 15N 114 53W
Elyria Ohio USA 63 K5 41 22N 82 06W
Emāmrūd Iran 89 F6 36 15N 54 59E
Emba Kazakhstan 86 H6 48 47N 58 05E
Emba *r.* Kazakhstan 86 H6 47 30N 56 00E
Embalse de Guri *l.* Venezuela 72 E15 7 30N 62 30W
Emden Germany 80 A10 53 23N 7 13E
Emerald Aust. 103 J6 23 30S 148 08E
Emi Koussi *mt.* Chad 100 H11 19 52N 18 31E
Empalme Mexico 66 B5 28 00N 110 49W
Emperor Seamounts Pacific Ocean 106 G12 42 00N 169 00E
Emporia Kansas USA 63 G4 38 24N 96 10W
Emporium Pennsylvania USA 46 H1 41 30N 78 14W
Ems *r.* Germany 80 A10 53 00N 7 00E
Encarnación Paraguay 72 F8 27 20S 55 50W
Encinitas California USA 64 E1 33 04N 117 17W
Endeh Indonesia 95 G2 8 51S 121 40E
Enderby Land *geog. reg.* Antarctica 109 65 00S 45 00E
Endicott New York USA 47 K2 42 06N 76 00W
Engel's Russia 86 G7 51 30N 46 07E
England *admin.* UK 78 D11 53 00N 2 00W
Enid Oklahoma USA 63 G4 36 24N 97 54W
Enna Italy 81 E2 37 34N 14 16E
En Nahud Sudan 100 K10 12 41N 28 28E
Enniskillen UK 78 B11 54 21N 7 38W
Enns *r.* Austria 80 E7 48 00N 14 40E
Enosburg Falls *tn.* Vermont USA 47 P4 44 55N 72 49W
Enschede Neths. 78 J10 52 13N 6 55E
Ensenada Mexico 66 A6 31 53N 116 38W
Entebbe Uganda 100 L8 0 04N 32 27E
Enugu Nigeria 100 F9 6 20N 7 29E
Épernay Fr. 78 G8 49 02N 3 58E
Épinal Fr. 78 J8 48 10N 6 28E
EQUATORIAL GUINEA 100 F8
Erechim Brazil 72 G8 27 35S 52 15W
Erenhot China 93 L7 43 50N 112 00E
Erfurt Germany 80 C9 50 58N 11 02E
Erg Chech *geog. reg.* Algeria 100 D12 24 30N 3 00W
Erg Iguidi *geog. reg.* Algeria 100 C13 26 00N 6 00W
Erie Pennsylvania USA 63 K5 42 07N 80 05W
Erimo-misaki *c.* Japan 94 D3 41 55N 143 13E
ERITREA 100 N10
Erode India 90 D2 11 21N 77 43E
Erris Head *c.* RoI 78 A11 54 20N 10 00W
Erromango *i.* Vanuatu 103 N7 19 00S 169 00E
Er Roseires Sudan 100 L10 11 52N 34 23E
Erzgebirge *mts.* Europe 80 D9 50 00N 13 00E
Erzincan Turkey 88 C6 39 44N 39 30E
Erzurum Turkey 88 D6 39 57N 41 17E
Esashi Japan 94 D3 41 54N 140 09E
Esbjerg Denmark 80 B11 55 20N 8 20E
Escanaba Michigan USA 63 J6 45 47N 87 04W
Escobal Panama 67 Y2 9 11N 79 59W
Escondido California USA 62 C3 33 07N 117 05W
Eşfahān Iran 89 F5 32 41N 51 41E
Eskilstuna Sweden 80 F13 59 22N 16 31E
Eskişehir Turkey 88 B6 39 46N 30 30E
Esmeraldas Ecuador 72 B14 0 56N 79 40W
Esparto California USA 64 B4 38 42N 122 00W
Esperance Aust. 102 D3 33 49S 121 52E
Espírito Santo *admin.* Brazil 72 J10 18 40S 40 00W
Espiritu Santo *i.* Vanuatu 103 N7 15 10S 167 00E
Espoo Finland 80 K14 60 10N 24 40E
Esquel Argentina 73 C5 42 55S 71 20W
Es Semara Western Sahara 100 B13 26 25N 11 30W
Essen Germany 80 A9 51 27N 6 57E
Essequibo *r.* Guyana 72 F14 2 30N 58 00W
Essex California USA 64 F2 34 45N 115 15W
Estância Brazil 72 K11 11 15S 37 28W
ESTONIA 80 J13
Estrecho de Magallanes *sd.* Chile 73 C3 53 00S 71 00W
Etawah India 90 D5 26 46N 79 01E
ETHIOPIA 100 M9
Etna, Mount Italy 81 E2 37 45N 15 00E
Etolin Island Alaska USA 38 D5 56 10N 132 30W
Etosha Pan *salt l.* Namibia 101 H4 18 30S 16 30E
Eucla Aust. 102 E4 31 40S 128 51E
Euclid Ohio USA 45 L1 41 34N 81 32W
Eugene Oregon USA 62 B5 44 03N 123 04W
Euphrates *r.* Iraq/Syria/Turkey 88 D5 34 40N 42 00E
Eureka California USA 62 B5 40 49N 124 10W
Eureka Montana USA 39 N1 48 56N 115 05W
Eureka Nevada USA 64 F4 39 49N 115 58W
Evansville Indiana USA 63 J4 38 00N 87 33W
Eveleth Minnesota USA 45 E4 47 28N 92 32W
Everest, Mount China/Nepal 91 F5 27 59N 86 56E
Everett Washington USA 62 B6 47 59N 122 14W
Evora Port. 79 B3 38 46N 7 41W
Evreux Fr. 78 F8 49 03N 1 11E
Evvoia *i.* Greece 81 K3 38 00N 24 00E
Excelsior Mountains Nevada USA 64 D4 38 15N 118 30W
Exeter UK 78 D9 50 43N 3 31W
Exeter California USA 64 D3 36 18N 119 08W
Exmoor *hills* UK 78 D9 51 08N 3 40W
Exmouth Aust. 102 B6 21 54S 114 10E
Eyasi, Lake Tanzania 100 M7 4 00S 35 00E
Eyre Creek Aust. 102 G5 26 00S 138 00E
Eyre, Lake Aust. 102 G5 28 00S 136 00E
Eyre Peninsula Aust. 102 G4 34 00S 136 00E

F

Fada Chad 100 J11 17 14N 21 32E
Faeroes *i.* Atlantic Ocean 108 H13 62 00N 7 00W
Fafan *r.* Ethiopia 100 N9 7 30N 44 00E
Fagersta Sweden 80 E13 59 59N 15 49E
Fairbanks Alaska USA 54 A3 64 50N 147 50W
Fairfield California USA 64 B4 38 14N 122 03W
Fair Isle *i.* UK 78 E13 59 32N 1 38W
Fairmont West Virginia USA 63 K4 39 28N 80 08W
Fairview Park HK China 92 B2 22 29N 114 03E
Faisalabad Pakistan 90 C6 31 25N 73 09E
Faizabad India 90 E5 26 46N 82 08E
Fakfak Indonesia 95 J3 2 55S 132 17E
Falam Myanmar 92 G3 22 58N 93 45E
Falfurrias Texas USA 63 G2 27 17N 98 10W
Falkenburg Sweden 80 D12 56 55N 12 30E
Falkirk UK 78 D11 55 59N 3 48W
Falkland Islands South Atlantic Ocean 73 E3/F3 52 30S 60 00W
Falköping Sweden 80 D13 58 10N 13 32E
Fallon Nevada USA 64 D4 39 29N 118 46W
Fall River *tn.* Massachusetts USA 63 M5 41 41N 71 08W
Falmouth Antigua and Barbuda 66 Q9 17 01N 61 46W
Falmouth Jamaica 67 U14 18 29N 77 39W
Falmouth Massachusetts USA 65 E2 41 34N 70 37W
Famagusta Cyprus 88 B6 35 07N 33 57E
Fan Lau HK China 92 A1 22 12N 113 51E
Fanling HK China 92 B2 22 29N 114 07E
Fâqûs Egypt 101 R3 30 44N 31 48E
Farafangana Madagascar 101 P3 22 50S 47 50E
Farāh Afghanistan 89 H5 32 22N 62 07E
Farah Rud *r.* Afghanistan 89 H5 32 00N 62 00E
Fargo North Dakota USA 63 G6 46 52N 96 49W
Faridabad India 90 D5 28 24N 77 18E
Faridpur Bangladesh 91 K9 23 29N 89 31E
Farmington Maine USA 47 R4 44 41N 70 11W
Farmington New Mexico USA 62 E4 36 43N 108 12W
Farnham New York USA 48 C1 42 36N 79 05W
Faro Port. 79 B2 37 01N 7 56W
Farquhar Islands Seychelles 101 Q6 9 00N 50 00E
Fastov Ukraine 80 M9 50 08N 29 59E
Fatehgarh India 90 D5 27 22N 79 38E
Faya-Largeau Chad 100 H11 17 58N 19 06E
Fayetteville Arkansas USA 63 H4 36 03N 94 10W
Fayetteville North Carolina USA 63 L4 35 03N 78 53W
Fâyid Egypt 101 S2 30 18N 31 19E
Fderik Mauritania 100 B12 22 30N 12 30W
Fécamp Fr. 78 F8 49 45N 0 23E
FEDERATED STATES OF MICRONESIA 106 E8/F8
Feira de Santana Brazil 72 K11 12 17S 38 53W
Feni Bangladesh 91 L9 23 00N 91 24E
Fenton Michigan USA 46 C2 42 48N 83 42W
Fergana Uzbekistan 86 K5 40 23N 71 19E
Fergus Falls *tn.* Minnesota USA 63 G6 46 18N 96 07W
Ferndale Washington USA 38 H4 48 50N 122 35W
Fernley Nevada USA 64 D4 39 36N 119 17W
Ferrara Italy 81 C6 44 50N 11 38E
Ferreñafe Peru 72 B12 6 42S 79 45W
Fès Morocco 100 C14 34 05N 5 00W
Fethiye Turkey 88 A6 36 37N 29 06E
Feyzābād Afghanistan 89 K6 37 06N 70 34E
Fianarantsoa Madagascar 101 P3 21 27S 47 05E
Fier Albania 81 G4 40 44N 19 33E
Figeac Fr. 79 G6 44 32N 2 01E
Figueira da Foz Port. 79 A4 40 09N 8 51W
Figueres Sp. 79 G5 42 16N 2 57E
FIJI 100 H6
Filchner Ice Shelf Antarctica 109 80 00S 37 00W
Findlay Ohio USA 45 K1 41 01N 83 39W
FINLAND 86 E9
Finland, Gulf of Finland/Russia 80 J13 59 40N 23 30E
Fiordland NZ 103 N1 45 09S 167 18E
Firat *r.* Turkey/Syria/Iraq 88 C6 37 30N 38 00E
Firozabad India 90 D5 27 09N 78 24E
Firth of Clyde *est.* UK 78 C11 55 30N 5 00W
Firth of Forth *est.* UK 78 D12 56 05N 3 00W
Firth of Lorn *est.* UK 78 B12 56 15N 6 00W
Fish *r.* Namibia 101 H2 26 30S 17 30E
Fishguard UK 78 C9 51 59N 4 59W
Fitchburg Massachusetts USA 65 E3 42 35N 71 48W
Fitzroy *r.* Aust. 102 D7 18 00S 124 00E
Flagstaff Arizona USA 62 D4 35 12N 111 38W
Flagstaff Lake Maine USA 47 R5 45 14N 70 20W
Flambeau River Wisconsin USA 45 F3 45 59N 90 30W
Flamborough Head *c.* UK 78 E11 54 06N 0 04W
Flatbush New York USA 65 J1 40 38N 73 56W
Flathead Lake Montana USA 62 D6 47 55N 114 05W
Flathead River Montana USA 41 E1 48 55N 114 30W
Flatlands New York USA 65 J1 40 37N 73 54W
Flattery, Cape Washington USA 62 B6 48 24N 124 43W

Grand Island *tn.* Nebraska USA 63 G5 40 56N 98 21W
Grand Junction *tn.* Colorado USA 62 E4 39 04N 108 33W
Grand Ledge Michigan USA 46 B2 42 45N 84 44W
Grand Marais Minnesota USA 45 F4 47 45N 90 20W
Grand Rapids *tn.* Michigan USA 63 J5 42 57N 86 40W
Grand Rapids *tn.* Minnesota USA 63 H6 47 13N 93 31W
Grand Rapids *tn.* Ohio USA 46 C1 41 23N 83 52W
Grand River Michigan USA 46 A2 42 55N 85 15W
Grand River Ohio USA 46 F1 41 25N 80 57W
Grand Traverse Bay Michigan USA 45 J3 45 00N 85 30W
Grandyle New York USA 48 D2 43 01N 78 57W
Granite Peak Montana USA 62 E6 45 10N 109 50W
Grant, Mount Nevada USA 64 D4 38 34N 118 48W
Grant Range *mts.* Nevada USA 64 F4 38 24N 115 27W
Grants Pass *tn.* Oregon USA 62 B5 42 26N 123 20W
Grasse Fr. 79 J5 43 40N 5 56E
Grass Island HK China 92 D2 22 29N 114 22E
Grass Valley *tn.* California USA 64 C4 39 13N 121 04W
Grassy Hill *mt.* HK China 92 B2 22 25N 114 10E
Gravesend New York USA 65 J1 40 36N 73 58W
Gravina Island Alaska USA 38 E4 55 25N 131 45W
Grayling Michigan USA 45 J3 44 39N 84 43W
Graz Austria 81 E7 47 05N 15 22E
Great Abaco *i.* Bahamas 67 J5 26 40N 77 00W
Great Astrolabe Reef Fiji 106 U15 18 45S 178 50E
Great Australian Bight *b.* Aust. 102 E4/F4 33 00S 130 00E
Great Barrier Reef Aust. 103 H8/J7 15 00S 146 00E
Great Basin *dep.* Nevada USA 62 C4 40 00N 117 00W
Great Bend Kansas USA 63 G4 38 22N 98 47W
Great Bitter Lake Egypt 101 S2 30 22N 32 22E
Great Dividing Range *mts.* Aust. 103 H8/J3 35 00S 148 00E
Greater Antilles *is.* W. Indies 67 H4/L3 19 00N 78 00W
Great Exuma *i.* Bahamas 67 J4 23 30N 76 00W
Great Falls *tn.* Montana USA 62 D6 47 30N 111 16W
Great Inagua *i.* Bahamas 67 K4 21 40N 73 00W
Great Karoo *mts.* RSA 101 J1 32 30S 22 30E
Great Neck New York USA 65 K2 40 48N 72 44W
Great Nicobar *i.* Nicobar Islands 91 G1 6 30N 94 00E
Great Salt Lake Utah USA 62 D5 41 10N 112 40W
Great Sand Sea *d.* Sahara Desert 100 J13 27 00N 25 00E
Great Sandy Desert Aust. 102 D6/E6 21 00S 124 00E
Great Sea Reef Fiji 106 T16 16 30S 178 00E
Great Victoria Desert Aust. 102 E5/F5 28 00S 130 00E
Great Wall China 93 L6 40 00N 111 00E
Great Yarmouth UK 78 F10 52 37N 1 44E
Great Zab *r.* Iraq 88 D6 36 00N 44 00E
GREECE 81 H3/K3
Greeley Colorado USA 62 F5 40 26N 104 43W
Green *r.* USA 62 D5 42 00N 110 00W
Green *r.* USA 62 E4 39 00N 110 00W
Green Bay Wisconsin USA 63 J6 45 00N 87 00W
Green Bay *tn.* Wisconsin USA 63 J5 44 32N 88 00W
Greenbush Minnesota USA 43 D1 48 42N 96 11W
Greenfield Massachusetts USA 65 D3 42 36N 72 36W
Green Islands PNG 103 K10 4 30S 154 15E
GREENLAND 55 U6
Greenland Basin Atlantic Ocean 108 H14 72 00N 0 00
Greenland Sea Arctic Ocean 109 76 00N 5 00W
Green Mountains Vermont USA 63 M5 43 00N 73 00W
Greenock UK 78 C11 55 57N 4 45W
Greensboro North Carolina USA 63 L4 36 03N 79 50W
Greenville Liberia 100 C9 5 01N 9 03W
Greenville Maine USA 47 S5 45 28N 69 36W
Greenville Mississippi USA 63 H3 33 23N 91 03W
Greenville South Carolina USA 63 K3 34 52N 82 25W
Greenville Texas USA 63 G3 33 09N 97 06W
Greenwood Mississippi USA 63 H3 33 31N 90 10W
Grenå Denmark 80 C12 56 25N 10 53E
GRENADA 66 R11
Grenoble Fr. 79 H6 45 11N 5 43E
Greymouth NZ 103 P2 42 27S 171 12E
Grey Range *mts.* Aust. 103 H5 27 00S 144 00E
Gridley California USA 64 C4 39 24N 121 42W
Griffin Georgia USA 63 K3 33 15N 84 17W
Grimsby UK 78 E10 53 35N 0 05W
Grindstone Lake Wisconsin USA 45 F3 45 59N 91 20W
Groningen Neths. 78 J10 53 13N 6 35E
Groom Lake Nevada USA 64 F3 37 18N 115 49W
Groote Eylandt *i.* Aust. 102 G8 14 00S 137 00E
Grootfontein Namibia 101 H4 19 32S 18 05E
Grosseto Italy 81 C5 42 46N 11 07E
Gross Glockner *mt.* Austria 81 D7 47 05N 12 44E
Groveland California USA 64 C3 37 43N 120 56W
Grover City California USA 64 C2 35 08N 120 35W
Groznyy Russia 86 G5 43 21N 45 42E
Grudziądz Poland 80 G10 53 29N 18 45E
Guadalajara Mexico 66 D4 20 40N 103 20W
Guadalajara Sp. 79 D4 40 37N 3 10W
Guadalcanal *i.* Solomon Islands 103 L9 9 30S 160 00E
Guadalope *r.* Sp. 79 E4 40 50N 0 30W
Guadalquivir *r.* Sp. 79 C2 37 45N 5 30W
Guadalupe *i.* Mexico 66 A5 29 00N 118 24W
Guadeloupe *i.* Lesser Antilles 66 Q9 16 30N 61 30W
Guadeloupe Passage *sd.* Caribbean Sea 66 Q9 16 40N 61 50W
Guadiana *r.* Sp./Port. 79 B3 38 30N 7 30W
Guadix Sp. 79 D2 37 19N 3 08W
Guainía *r.* Col./Venezuela 72 D14 2 30N 67 30W
Guajará Mirim Brazil 72 D11 10 50S 65 21W
Gualala California USA 64 B4 38 45N 123 31W
GUAM 106 E9
Guamúchil Mexico 66 C5 25 28N 108 10W
Guangzhou China 93 L3 23 08N 113 20E
Guantánamo Cuba 67 J4 20 09N 75 14W
Guaporé *r.* Brazil/Bolivia 72 E11 13 00S 62 00W
Guaqui Bolivia 72 D10 16 38S 68 50W
Guarapuava Brazil 72 G8 25 22S 51 28W
Guarda Port. 79 B4 40 32N 7 17W
Guardiana *r.* Sp. 79 C3 39 00N 4 00W
Guasdualito Venezuela 72 C15 7 15N 70 40W
GUATEMALA 66 F3
Guatemala Basin Pacific Ocean 107 S9 12 00N 95 00W
Guatemala City Guatemala 66 F2 14 38N 90 22W
Guaviare *r.* Col. 72 C14 3 00N 70 00W
Guayaquil Ecuador 72 A13 2 13S 79 54W
Guaymas Mexico 66 B5 27 59N 110 54W
Guéret Fr. 79 F7 46 10N 1 52E
Guernsey *i.* British Isles 78 D8 46 27N 2 35W
Guildford UK 78 E9 51 14N 0 35W
Guilin China 93 L4 25 21N 110 11E
Guimarães Port. 79 A4 41 26N 8 19W
GUINEA 100 B10
Guinea Basin Atlantic Ocean 108 H7 1 00N 8 00W
GUINEA-BISSAU 100 A10
Güines Cuba 67 H4 22 50N 82 02W
Güiria Venezuela 72 E16 10 37N 62 21W
Guiyang China 93 K4 26 35N 106 40E
Gujarat *admin.* India 90 C4 23 20N 72 00E
Gujranwala Pakistan 90 C6 32 06N 74 11E
Gujrat Pakistan 90 C6 32 35N 74 06E
Gulbarga India 90 D3 17 22N 76 47E
Gulfport Mississippi USA 63 J3 30 21N 80 08W
Gulf, The Middle East 89 F4 27 20N 51 00E
Gulu Uganda 100 L8 2 46N 32 21E
Gunnison *r.* Colorado USA 62 E4 38 00N 107 00W
Guntersville Lake Alabama USA 63 J3 34 00N 86 00W
Guntur India 90 E3 16 20N 80 27E
Gunung Kinabalu *mt.* Malaysia 95 F5 6 03N 116 32E
Gurgueia *r.* Brazil 72 J12 9 00S 44 00W
Gurupi *r.* Brazil 72 H13 4 00S 47 00W
Gusev Russia 80 J11 54 32N 22 12E
Gushgy Turkmenistan 89 H6 36 01N 62 43E
Güstrow Germany 80 D10 53 48N 12 11E
Guthrie Oklahoma USA 63 G4 35 53N 97 26W
Guwahati India 91 G5 26 10N 91 45E
GUYANA 72 F14
Guyana Basin Atlantic Ocean 108 D7 8 00N 50 00W
Gwalior India 90 D5 26 12N 78 09E
Gweru Zimbabwe 101 K4 19 27S 29 49E
Gyda Peninsula Russia 87 K11 70 00N 77 30E
Gympie Aust. 103 K5 26 10S 152 35E
Gyöngyös Hungary 80 G7 47 46N 20 00E
Györ Hungary 81 F7 47 41N 17 40E

H

Haapsalu Estonia 80 J13 58 58N 23 32E
Haarlem Neths. 78 H10 52 23N 4 39E
Hab *r.* Pakistan 90 B5 25 20N 67 00E
Habbān Yemen 89 E1 14 21N 47 04E
Haboro Japan 94 D3 44 23N 141 43E
Hachinohe Japan 94 D3 40 30N 141 30E
Hackensack River New Jersey USA 65 H2 40 47N 74 06W
Hadejia Nigeria 100 G10 12 30N 10 03E
Hadejia *r.* Nigeria 100 F10 4 10N 9 30E
Hadera Israel 88 N11 32 26N 34 55E
Haderslev Denmark 80 B11 55 15N 9 30E
Hadhramaut *geog. reg.* Yemen 89 E2 15 40N 47 30E
Hadiboh Yemen 89 F1 12 36N 53 59E
Hadraibari India 91 L9 23 55N 91 50E
Haeju North Korea 93 P6 38 04N 125 40E
Hagerstown Maryland USA 63 L4 39 39N 77 44W
Ha Giang Vietnam 93 J3 22 50N 105 00E
Haifa Israel 88 N11 32 49N 34 59E
Haikou China 93 L3 20 00N 110 25E
Hā'il Saudi Arabia 88 D4 27 31N 41 45E
Hailar China 93 M8 49 15N 119 41E
Hainan Dao *i.* China 93 K2/L2 18 50N 109 50E
Haines Alaska USA 38 C6 59 11N 135 23W
Hai Phong Vietnam 93 K3 20 50N 106 41E
HAITI 67 K3
Hakodate Japan 94 D3 41 46N 140 44E
Halaib Sudan 100 M12 22 12N 36 35E
Halawa, Cape Hawaiian Islands 107 Y18 21 09N 157 15W
Halba Lebanon 88 P12 34 33N 36 04E
Halden Norway 78 L13 59 08N 11 13E
Haldia India 91 K9 22 02N 88 05E
Halle Germany 80 C9 51 28N 11 58E
Hallock Minnesota USA 43 D1 48 50N 96 59W
Halls Creek *tn.* Aust. 102 E7 18 17S 127 38E
Halmahera *i.* Indonesia 95 H4 0 30S 127 00E
Halmstad Sweden 80 D12 56 41N 12 55E
Hamada Japan 94 B1 34 56N 132 04E
Hamadān Iran 89 E5 34 46N 48 35E
Ḥamāh Syria 88 C6 35 10N 36 45E
Hamamatsu Japan 94 C1 34 42N 137 42E
Hambantota Sri Lanka 90 E1 6 07N 81 07E
Hamburg Germany 80 C10 53 33N 10 00E
Hamburg New York USA 46 H2 42 43N 78 50W
Hamden Connecticut USA 65 D2 41 20N 72 55W
Hamersley Range *mts.* Aust. 102 C6 22 00S 117 00E
Hamhung North Korea 93 P6 39 54N 127 35E
Hami China 92 G7 42 37N 93 32E
Hamilton NZ 103 Q3 37 47S 175 17E
Hamilton Ohio USA 63 K4 39 23N 84 33W
Hamm Germany 80 A9 51 40N 7 49E
Hammond Indiana USA 63 J5 41 36N 87 30W
Hampton Virginia USA 63 L4 37 02N 76 23W
Hancock Maryland USA 65 B1 39 41N 78 10W
Hancock Michigan USA 45 G4 47 08N 88 36W
Hancock New York USA 65 C2 41 58N 75 17W
Handan China 93 L6 36 35N 114 31E
Hanford California USA 64 D3 36 20N 119 38W
Hangzhou China 93 N5 30 18N 120 07E
Hanimadu Island Maldives 90 C1 6 30N 73 00E
Hanko Finland 80 J13 50 50N 23 00E
Hannah North Dakota USA 43 C1 48 58N 98 42W
Hannibal Missouri USA 63 H4 39 41N 91 20W
Hannover Germany 80 B10 52 23N 9 44E
Hanöbukten *b.* Sweden 80 E11 55 50N 14 30E
Hanoi Vietnam 93 K3 21 01N 105 52E
Hanover Pennsylvania USA 65 B1 39 48N 76 59W
Haora India 91 K9 22 35N 88 19E
Ḥaql Saudi Arabia 88 B4 29 14N 34 56E
Ḥaraḍ Saudi Arabia 89 E3 24 12N 49 12E
Harare Zimbabwe 101 L4 17 50S 31 03E
Harbang Bangladesh 91 M8 21 56N 92 05E
Harbin China 93 P8 45 45N 126 41E
Harbor Beach *tn.* Michigan USA 45 K2 43 51N 82 39W
Harbor Springs *tn.* Michigan USA 46 B5 45 25N 84 59W
Harer Ethiopia 100 N9 9 20N 42 10E
Hargeysa Somalia 100 N9 9 31N 44 02E
Harima-nada *sea* Japan 94 B1 34 30N 134 30E
Haringhat *r.* Bangladesh 91 K9 22 10N 89 55E
Hari Rud *r.* Afghanistan 89 H5 34 00N 64 00E
Harlem New York USA 65 J2 40 48N 73 56W
Harlingen Texas USA 63 G2 26 12N 97 43W
Harper Liberia 100 C8 4 25N 7 43W
Harper Lake California USA 64 E2 35 03N 117 15W
Harris *i.* UK 78 B12 57 50N 6 55W
Harrisburg Pennsylvania USA 63 L5 40 17N 76 54W
Harrison Michigan USA 45 J3 44 01N 84 48W
Harrisonburg Virginia USA 63 L4 38 27N 78 54W
Harrisville Michigan USA 45 K3 44 39N 83 19W
Harrisville New York USA 47 L4 44 09N 75 20W
Harrogate UK 78 E11 54 00N 1 33W
Hart Michigan USA 45 H2 43 42N 86 21W
Hartford Connecticut USA 63 M5 41 46N 72 42W
Hartland Point *c.* UK 78 C9 51 02N 4 31W
Hartlepool UK 78 E11 54 41N 1 13W
Haryana *admin.* India 90 D5 29 20N 75 30E
Harz *mts.* Europe 80 C9 52 00N 10 00E
Hasselt Belgium 78 H9 50 56N 5 20E
Hassi Messaoud Algeria 100 F14 31 52N 5 43E
Hastings Michigan USA 46 A2 42 38N 85 17W
Hastings Nebraska USA 63 G5 40 37N 98 22W
Hatteras, Cape North Carolina USA 63 L4 35 14N 75 31W
Hattiesburg Mississippi USA 63 J3 31 20N 89 19W
Hat Yai Thailand 95 C5 7 00N 100 25E
Haud *geog. reg.* Africa 100 N9/P9 8 00N 50 00E
Haugesund Norway 78 H13 59 25N 5 16E
Haut Atlas *mts.* Morocco 100 C14 30 45N 6 50W
Havana Cuba 67 H4 23 07N 82 25W
Haverhill New Hampshire USA 65 E3 42 47N 71 05W
Havre Montana USA 62 E6 48 34N 109 40W
Hawaii *i.* Hawaiian Islands 107 Z17 19 50N 157 50W
Hawaiian Islands Pacific Ocean 100 J10 25 00N 166 00W
Hawaiian Ridge Pacific Ocean 107 K10 23 00N 166 00W
Hawick UK 78 D11 55 25N 2 47W
Hawthorne Nevada USA 64 D4 38 33N 118 37W
Hayward California USA 64 B3 37 40N 122 07W
Hayward Wisconsin USA 45 F4 46 01N 91 29W
Hazaribagh Range *mts.* India 90/91 E4 22 30N 84 00E
Hazleton Pennsylvania USA 65 C2 40 58N 75 59W
Healdsburg California USA 64 B4 38 36N 122 53W
Heard Island Indian Ocean 105 G1 53 07S 73 20E
Heart *r.* North Dakota USA 62 F6 47 00N 102 00W
Hebi China 93 L6 35 57N 114 08E
Hebron Middle East 88 N10 31 32N 35 06E
Heceta Island Alaska USA 38 D4 55 45N 134 40W
Hechuan China 93 K5 30 02N 106 5E
Heerlen Neths. 78 H9 50 53N 5 59E
Hefei China 93 M5 31 55N 117 18E
Hegang China 93 Q8 47 36N 130 30E
Hegura-jima *i.* Japan 94 C2 37 52N 136 56E
Heidelberg Germany 80 B8 49 25N 8 42E
Heilbronn Germany 80 B8 49 08N 9 14E
Hei Ling Chau *i.* HK China 92 B1 22 15N 114 02E
Hekou China 93 J3 22 30N 104 00E
Helan Shan *mts.* China 93 K6 38 00N 106 00E
Helena Montana USA 62 D6 46 35N 112 00W
Helendale California USA 64 E2 34 45N 117 19W
Heligoland Bight *b.* Germany 80 B11 54 00N 8 00E
Hellín Sp. 79 E3 38 31N 1 43W
Helmand *r.* Afghanistan 89 H5 30 00N 62 30E
Helsingborg Sweden 80 D12 56 03N 12 43E
Helsingør Denmark 80 D12 56 03N 12 38E
Helsinki Finland 80 K14 60 08N 25 00E
Hemet California USA 64 E1 33 45N 116 58W
Henares *r.* Sp. 79 D4 40 45N 3 10W
Henderson Nevada USA 62 D4 36 01N 115 00W
Henderson Island Pacific Ocean 107 N5 23 00S 127 00W
Hengelo Neths. 78 J10 52 16N 6 46E
Hengyang China 93 L4 26 58N 112 31E
Henryetta Oklahoma USA 63 G4 35 27N 96 00W
Henzada Myanmar 95 B7 17 36N 95 26E
Herāt Afghanistan 89 H5 34 20N 62 12E
Hérault *r.* Fr. 79 G5 43 50N 3 30E
Hereford UK 78 D10 52 04N 2 43W
Hermel Lebanon 88 P12 34 25N 36 23E
Hermon New York USA 47 L4 44 28N 75 12W
Hermon, Mount Lebanon/Syria 88 N11 33 24N 35 50E
Hermosillo Mexico 66 B5 29 15N 110 59W
Herning Denmark 80 B12 56 08N 8 59E
Hesperia California USA 64 E2 34 25N 117 19W
Hetch Hetchy Aqueduct California USA 64 C3 37 35N 121 45W
Hetch Hetchy Reservoir California USA 64 D3 37 57N 119 45W
Hibbing Minnesota USA 45 E4 47 25N 92 56W
Hickory North Carolina USA 63 K4 35 44N 81 23W
Hicksville Ohio USA 46 B1 41 18N 84 45W
Hidalgo Mexico 66 E4 24 16N 99 28W
Hidalgo del Parral Mexico 66 C5 26 58N 105 40W
High Island HK China 92 D2 22 21N 114 21E
High Island Reservoir HK China 92 D2 22 22N 114 20E
High Point *tn.* North Carolina USA 63 L4 35 58N 80 00W
High Veld *mts.* RSA 101 K2 28 00S 28 00E
Hiiumaa *i.* Estonia 80 J13 58 55N 22 30E
Hiko Nevada USA 64 F3 37 36N 115 14W
Hildesheim Germany 80 B10 52 09N 9 58E
Hillsdale Michigan USA 46 B1 41 56N 84 37W
Hilo Hawaiian Islands 107 Z17 19 42N 155 04W
Hilton New York USA 46 J3 43 17N 77 47W
Hilversum Neths. 78 H10 52 14N 5 10E
Himachal Pradesh *admin.* India 90 D6 32 00N 77 30E
Himalaya *mts.* Asia 90/91 D6 28 00N 85 00E
Himeji Japan 94 B1 34 50N 134 40E
Hinckley Lake New York USA 47 L3 43 20N 75 10W
Hindu Kush *mts.* Afghanistan 89 J5/K6 35 00N 70 00E
Hirakud Reservoir India 90 E4 21 40N 83 40E
Hirosaki Japan 94 D3 40 34N 140 28E
Hiroshima Japan 94 B1 34 23N 132 27E
Hisar India 90 D5 29 10N 75 45E
Hispaniola *i.* W. Indies 67 K3/L3 18 00N 70 00W
Hitachi Japan 94 D2 36 35N 140 40E
Hjørring Denmark 80 B12 57 28N 9 59E
Ho Ghana 100 E9 6 38N 0 38E
Hobart Aust. 103 J2 42 54S 147 18E
Hoboken New Jersey USA 65 H1 40 44N 74 02W
Hobyo Somalia 100 P9 5 20N 48 30E
Hô Chi Minh Vietnam 95 D6 10 46N 106 43E
Ho Chung HK China 92 C2 22 22N 114 14E
Hodeida Yemen 88 D1 14 50N 42 58E
Hódmezovásárhely Hungary 81 H7 46 26N 20 21E
Hof Germany 80 C9 50 19N 11 56E
Hofu Japan 94 B1 34 02N 131 34E
Hogeland Montana USA 42 C1 48 51N 108 39W
Hoggar *mts.* Algeria 100 F12 23 45N 6 00E
Hohhot China 93 L7 40 49N 117 37E
Hoi Ha HK China 92 C2 22 28N 114 20E
Hokkaidō *i.* Japan 94 D3 43 30N 143 00E
Holbaek Denmark 80 C11 56 33N 10 19E
Holguín Cuba 67 J4 20 54N 76 15W
Hollister California USA 64 C3 36 47N 121 25W
Holly Michigan USA 46 C2 42 48N 83 37W
Holstebro Denmark 80 B12 56 22N 8 38E
Holston *r.* USA 63 K4 37 00N 82 00W
Holyoke Massachusetts USA 65 D3 42 13N 72 38N
Homestead Florida USA 63 K2 25 29N 80 29W
Homs Syria 88 C5 34 42N 36 40E
Honda Col. 72 C15 5 15N 74 50W
HONDURAS 66 G2
Hønefoss Norway 78 L14 60 10N 10 16E
Honesdale Pennsylvania USA 47 L1 41 34N 75 15W
Hong Kong *admin.* China 93 L3 23 00N 114 00E
Hong Kong Island HK China 92 B1/C1 22 15N 114 12E
Hong Lok Yuen HK China 92 B2 22 27N 114 09E
Honiara Solomon Islands 103 L9 9 28S 159 57E
Honokaa Hawaiian Islands 107 Z18 20 04N 155 27W
Honolulu Hawaiian Islands 107 Y18 21 19N 157 50W
Honshū *i.* Japan 94 C2 37 15N 139 00E
Hood, Mount Oregon USA 62 B6 45 24N 121 41W
Hoolehua Hawaiian Islands 107 Y18 21 11N 157 06W
Hoonah Alaska USA 38 C6 58 06N 135 25W
Hopkinsville Kentucky USA 63 J4 36 50N 87 30W

Name	Page	Grid	Latitude	Longitude
Ho Pui HK China	92	B2	22 24N	114 04E
Ho Pui Reservoir HK China	92	B2	22 25N	114 05E
Hormuz, Strait of The Gulf	89	G4	26 35N	56 30E
Hornell New York USA	46	J2	42 20N	77 40W
Horsens Denmark	80	B11	55 53N	9 53E
Horsham Aust.	103	H3	36 45S	142 15E
Hospet India	90	D3	15 16N	76 20E
Hospitalet Sp.	79	G4	41 21N	2 06E
Hotan China	92	D6	37 07N	79 57E
Hotan He *r.* China	92	E6	39 00N	80 30E
Hot Springs *tn.* Arkansas USA	63	H3	34 30N	93 02W
Houghton Michigan USA	45	G4	47 07N	88 35W
Houghton Lake Michigan USA	46	B4	44 20N	84 45W
Houghton Lake *tn.* Michigan USA	46	B4	44 17N	84 45W
Houlton Maine USA	51	G2	46 09N	67 50W
Houma China	93	L6	35 36N	111 15E
Houma Louisiana USA	63	H2	29 35N	90 44W
Houston Texas USA	63	G2	29 45N	95 25W
Hovd Mongolia	92	G8	48 00N	91 43E
Hövsgöl Nuur *l.* Mongolia	93	J9	51 00N	100 30E
Howar *r.* Sudan	100	K11	17 00N	25 00E
Howard City Michigan USA	45	J2	43 23N	85 28W
Howe, Cape Aust.	103	J3	37 20S	149 59E
Howland Islands Pacific Ocean	106	J8	2 00N	177 00W
Hoy *i.* UK	78	D13	58 48N	3 20W
Hradec Králové Czech Rep.	80	E9	50 13N	15 50E
Hrodna Belarus	80	J10	53 40N	23 50E
Hron *r.* Slovakia	80	G8	48 00N	18 00E
Hsinchu Taiwan	93	N3	24 48N	120 59E
Huacho Peru	72	B11	11 05S	77 36W
Huaide China	93	N7	43 30N	124 48E
Huainan China	93	M5	32 41N	117 06E
Huajuápan de León Mexico	66	E3	17 50N	97 48W
Huambo Angola	101	H5	12 44S	15 47E
Huancayo Peru	72	B11	12 05S	75 12W
Huang He *r.* China	93	L6	38 00N	111 00E
Huangshi China	93	M5	30 13N	115 05E
Huanuco Peru	72	B12	9 55S	76 11W
Huaráz Peru	72	B12	9 33S	77 31W
Huascaran *mt.* Peru	72	B12	9 08S	77 36W
Huashixia China	93	H6	35 13N	99 12E
Hubbard Lake Michigan USA	46	C4	44 50N	83 30W
Huddersfield UK	78	E10	53 39N	1 47W
Hudson River New York USA	65	D2/D3	42 00N	73 55W
Huê Vietnam	95	D7	16 28N	107 35E
Huelva Sp.	79	B2	37 15N	6 56W
Huelva *r.* Sp.	79	B2	37 50N	6 30W
Huesca Sp.	79	E5	42 08N	0 25W
Hughenden Aust.	103	H6	20 50S	144 10E
Hugli *r.* India	91	K8	22 00N	88 00E
Hugo Oklahoma USA	63	G3	34 01N	95 31W
Huixtla Mexico	66	F3	15 09N	92 30W
Huizhou China	93	L3	23 08N	114 28E
Humaitá Brazil	72	E12	7 33S	63 01W
Humboldt *r.* Nevada USA	62	C5	41 00N	118 00W
HUNGARY	80/81	F7		
Hungnam North Korea	93	P6	39 49N	127 40E
Hung Shui Kiu HK China	92	A2	22 25N	113 59E
Hunjiang China	93	P7	41 54N	126 23E
Hunsrück *mts.* Germany	80	J8/J9	50 00N	7 00E
Hunter *i.* New Caledonia	103	P6	22 24S	172 03E
Hunter Trench Pacific Ocean	106	H5	23 00S	175 00E
Huntington West Virginia USA	63	K4	38 24N	82 26W
Huntington Beach *tn.* California USA	64	D1	33 40N	118 00W
Huntsville Alabama USA	63	J3	34 44N	86 35W
Huntsville Texas USA	63	G3	30 43N	95 34W
Hurghada Egypt	100	L13	27 17N	33 47E
Hurley Wisconsin USA	45	F4	46 26N	90 10W
Huron River Michigan USA	46	C2	42 10N	83 15W
Huskvarna Sweden	80	E12	57 47N	14 15E
Husn Jordan	88	N11	32 29N	35 53E
Hutchinson Kansas USA	63	G4	38 03N	97 56W
Huzhou China	93	N5	30 56N	120 04E
Hvar *i.* Croatia	81	F5	43 00N	17 00E
Hwange Zimbabwe	101	K4	18 22S	26 29E
Hyder Alaska USA	38	E4	55 45N	130 10W
Hyderabad India	90	D3	17 22N	78 26E
Hyderabad Pakistan	90	B5	25 23N	68 24E
I				
Ialomiţa *r.* Romania	81	L6	44 00N	27 00E
Iaşi Romania	81	L7	47 09N	27 38E
Ibadan Nigeria	100	E9	7 23N	3 56E
Ibagué Col.	72	B14	4 25N	75 20W
Ibarra Ecuador	72	B14	0 23N	78 05W
Ibb Yemen	88	D1	14 03N	44 10E
Ibi Nigeria	100	F9	8 11N	9 44E
Ibiza Sp.	79	F3	38 54N	1 26E
Ibiza *i.* Sp.	79	F3	39 00N	1 20E
Ibotirama Brazil	72	J11	12 13S	43 12W
Ibrī Oman	89	G3	23 15N	56 35E
Ica Peru	72	B11	14 02S	75 48W
Icacos Point Trinidad and Tobago	67	V15	10 41N	61 42W
ICELAND	108	F13		
Ichalkaranji India	90	C3	16 40N	74 33E
Ichinomiya Japan	94	C2	35 18N	136 48E
Icy Strait *sd.* Alaska USA	38	C6	58 20N	135 45W
Idaho *state* USA	62	D5	44 00N	115 00W
Idaho Falls *tn.* Idaho USA	62	D5	43 30N	112 01W
Idfu Egypt	100	L12	24 58N	32 50E
Igarka Russia	87	L10	67 31N	86 33E
Iglesias Italy	81	B3	39 19N	8 32E
Iguaçu *r.* Brazil	72	G8	26 00S	51 00W
Iguala Mexico	66	E3	18 21N	99 31W
Iguape Brazil	72	H9	24 37S	47 30W
Iguatu Brazil	72	K12	6 22S	39 20W
Ihavandiffulu Atoll *i.* Maldives	90	C1	7 00N	72 55E
Ihosy Madagascar	101	P3	22 23S	46 09E
Iida Japan	94	C2	35 32N	137 48E
IJsselmeer *l.* Neths.	78	H10	52 50N	5 15E
Ikaría *i.* Greece	81	L2	37 35N	26 10E
Ikela CDR	100	J7	1 06S	23 06E
Iki *i.* Japan	94	A1	33 50N	129 40E
Ilagan Philippines	95	G7	17 07N	121 53E
Île Amsterdam *i.* Indian Ocean	105	G3	37 56S	77 40E
Ilebo CDR	100	J7	4 20S	20 35E
Ile de Jerba *i.* Tunisia	100	G14	33 40N	11 00E
Île de l'Europe *i.* Mozambique Channel	101	N3	22 20S	40 20E
Île de Ré *i.* Fr.	79	E7	46 10N	1 26W
Île d'Oléron *i.* Fr.	79	E6	45 55N	1 16W
Île d'Ouessant *i.* Fr.	78	C8	48 28N	5 05W
Île d'Yeu *i.* Fr.	79	D7	46 43N	2 20W
Ilesa Nigeria	100	E9	7 39N	4 38E
Île St. Paul *i.* Indian Ocean	105	G3	38 44S	77 30E
Îles Chesterfield *is.* Pacific Ocean	103	L7	19 00S	153 30E
Îles Crozet *is.* Indian Ocean	105	E2	46 27S	52 00E
Îles d'Hyères *is.* Fr.	79	J5	43 10N	6 25E
Îles Kerguelen *is.* Indian Ocean	105	F2	49 30S	69 30E
Îles Loyauté *is.* Pacific Ocean	103	N6	21 00S	167 00E
Ilha Bazaruto *i.* Mozambique	101	M3	21 40S	35 30E
Ilha de Marajó *i.* Brazil	72	G13	1 30S	50 00W
Ilha Fernando de Noronha *i.* Brazil	72	L13	3 50S	32 25W
Ilhéus Brazil	72	K11	14 50S	39 06W
Ili *r.* Asia	86	K5	44 00N	78 00E
Iligan Philippines	95	G5	8 12N	124 13W
Illapel Chile	73	C7	31 40S	71 13W
Illinois *state* USA	63	J5	40 00N	89 00W
Illizi Algeria	100	F13	26 45N	8 30E
Iloilo Philippines	95	G6	10 41N	122 33E
Ilorin Nigeria	100	E9	8 32N	4 34E
Imabari Japan	94	B1	34 04N	132 59E
Imi Ethiopia	100	N9	6 28N	42 10E
Imperatriz Brazil	72	H12	5 32S	47 28W
Imperia Italy	81	B5	43 53N	8 03E
Impfondo Congo	100	H8	1 36N	18 00E
Imphal India	91	G4	24 47N	93 55E
Inca Sp.	79	G3	39 43N	2 54E
Inchon South Korea	93	P6	37 30N	126 38E
Independence California USA	64	D3	36 48N	118 14W
Independence Kansas USA	63	G4	37 13N	95 43W
INDIA	90/91	B4/F4		
Indiana *state* USA	63	J5	40 00N	86 00W
Indian Antarctic Basin Southern Ocean	106	A2	57 00S	113 00E
Indian-Antarctic Ridge Southern Ocean	106	A3	51 00S	124 00E
Indianapolis Indiana USA	63	J4	39 45N	86 10W
Indian Ocean	105			
Indian Springs *tn.* Nevada USA	64	F3	36 33N	115 40W
Indigirka *r.* Russia	87	S10	70 00N	147 30E
Indio California USA	64	E1	33 44N	116 14W
Indispensable Reefs Vanuatu	103	M8	12 40S	160 25E
INDONESIA	95	C3/H3		
Indravati *r.* India	90	E3	19 00N	81 30E
Indre *r.* Fr.	79	F7	46 50N	1 25E
Indus *r.* Pakistan	90	B5	28 00N	69 00E
Indus, Mouths of the *est.* Pakistan	90	B4	24 00N	67 00E
Ingham Aust.	103	J7	18 35S	146 12E
Inglewood California USA	64	D1	33 58N	118 22W
Ingolstadt Germany	80	C8	48 46N	11 27E
Ingraj Bazar India	91	K10	24 59N	88 10E
Inhambane Mozambique	101	M3	23 51S	35 29E
Inírida *r.* Col.	72	D14	2 30N	70 00W
Inn *r.* Europe	81	C7	48 00N	12 00E
Innisfail Aust.	103	J7	17 30S	146 00E
Innsbruck Austria	81	C7	47 17N	11 25E
Inongo CDR	100	H7	1 55S	18 20E
Inowrocław Poland	80	G10	52 49N	18 12E
In Salah Algeria	100	E13	27 20N	2 03E
Insein Myanmar	95	B7	16 54N	96 08E
Inta Russia	86	J10	66 04N	60 01E
Inubō-zaki *c.* Japan	94	D2	35 41N	140 52E
Invercargill NZ	103	N1	46 25S	168 22E
Inverness UK	78	C12	57 27N	4 15W
Inyo Range *mts.* California USA	64	D3	36 37N	117 52W
Ioánnina Greece	81	H3	39 40N	20 51E
Ione Washington USA	39	M1	48 45N	117 25W
Ionia Michigan USA	46	A2	42 58N	85 06W
Iónia Nisiá Greece	81	G3	39 00N	20 00E
Ionian Sea Mediterranean Sea	81	F2/G2	38 00N	27 00E
Íos *i.* Greece	81	K2	36 00N	25 00E
Iowa *state* USA	63	H5	42 00N	94 00W
Iowa City Iowa USA	63	H5	41 39N	91 31W
Ipatinga Brazil	72	J10	19 32S	42 30W
Ipiales Col.	72	B14	0 52N	77 38W
Ipoh Malaysia	95	C4	4 36N	101 05E
Ipswich UK	78	F10	52 04N	1 10E
Ipu Brazil	72	J13	4 32S	40 44W
Iquique Chile	72	C9	20 15S	70 08W
Iquitos Peru	72	C13	3 51S	73 13W
Irákleio Greece	81	K1	35 20N	25 08E
IRAN	89	F5/G5		
Irānshahr Iran	89	H4	27 15N	60 41E
Irapuato Mexico	66	D4	20 40N	101 30W
IRAQ	88	D5		
Irbid Jordan	88	C5	32 33N	35 51E
Irecê Brazil	72	J11	11 22S	41 51W
Irian Jaya *admin.* Indonesia	95	J3	3 00S	133 00E
Iriri *r.* Brazil	72	G13	5 00S	54 50W
Irkutsk Russia	87	N7	52 18N	104 15E
Iron Knob *tn.* Aust.	102	G4	32 44S	137 08E
Iron Mountain *tn.* Michigan USA	45	G3	45 49N	88 04W
Ironwood Michigan USA	63	H6	46 25N	90 08W
Irrawaddy *r.* Myanmar	95	A8	20 00N	95 00E
Irtysh *r.* Asia	86	K8	57 30N	72 30E
Irún Sp.	79	E5	43 20N	1 48W
Irving Texas USA	63	G3	32 49N	96 57W
Irvington New Jersey USA	65	H1	40 44N	74 15W
Isabella Reservoir California USA	64	D2	35 41N	118 28W
Ise Japan	94	C1	34 29N	136 41E
Isère *r.* Fr.	79	H6	45 17N	5 47E
Ishikari *r.* Japan	94	D3	43 20N	141 45E
Ishikari-wan *b.* Japan	94	D3	43 30N	141 00E
Ishim *r.* Russia	86	J8	56 00N	69 00E
Ishinomaki Japan	94	D2	38 25N	141 18E
Isiro CDR	100	K8	2 50N	27 40E
Iskenderun Turkey	88	C6	36 37N	36 08E
Iskŭr *r.* Bulgaria	81	K5	43 30N	24 00E
Isla Asinara *i.* Italy	81	B4	41 00N	8 00E
Isla de Chiloé *i.* Chile	73	C5	42 30S	74 00W
Isla de Coco *i.* Costa Rica	107	S8	4 00N	85 00W
Isla de Coiba *i.* Panama	67	H1	7 40N	82 00W
Isla de Cozumel *i.* Mexico	67	G4	20 30N	87 00W
Isla de la Juventud *i.* Cuba	67	H4	22 00N	82 30W
Isla d'Elba *i.* Italy	81	C5	42 00N	10 00E
Isla de los Estados *i.* Argentina	73	E3	55 00S	64 00W
Isla Grande de Tierra del Fuego *i.* Chile/Argentina	73	D3	54 00S	67 30W
Islamabad Pakistan	90	C6	33 40N	73 08E
Isla Margarita *i.* Venezuela	72	E16	11 30N	64 00W
Islampur India	91	K11	26 16N	88 11E
Island Beach New Jersey USA	65	C1	39 55N	74 05W
Isla San Felix *i.* Chile	107	U5	26 23S	80 05W
Islas de la Bahia *is.* Honduras	67	G3	16 40N	86 00W
Islas Galápagos *i.* Ecuador	107	S7	0 05S	90 00W
Islas Juan Fernández *is.* Chile	107	T4	33 30S	80 00W
Islas Marias *is.* Mexico	66	C4	22 00N	107 00W
Islas Revillagigedo *is.* Pacific Ocean	66	B3	19 00N	112 30W
Isla Wellington *i.* Chile	107	U3	48 50S	79 00W
Islay *i.* UK	78	B11	55 48N	6 12W
Isle of Man British Isles	78	C11	54 15N	4 15W
Isle of Wight *i.* UK	78	E9	50 40N	1 20W
Isle Royale *i.* Michigan USA	45	G4	48 00N	89 0W
Isle Royale National Park Michigan USA	45	G4	48 00N	89 0W
Ismâ'ilîya Egypt	101	S3	30 36N	32 16E
Isoka Zambia	101	L5	10 09S	32 39E
Isola Lipari *is.* Italy	81	E3	38 00N	14 00E
ISRAEL	88	N9		
Istanbul Turkey	88	A7	41 02N	28 57E
Istmo de Tehuantepec *ist.* Mexico	66	F3	17 20N	93 10W
Istres Fr.	79	H5	43 30N	4 59E
Itabaiana Brazil	72	K11	10 42S	37 37W
Itabuna Brazil	72	K11	14 48S	39 18W
Itacoatiara Brazil	72	F13	3 06S	58 22W
Itagüi Col.	72	B15	6 13N	75 40W
Itaituba Brazil	72	F13	4 15S	55 56W
Itajaí Brazil	72	H8	26 50S	48 39W
ITALY	81	C5/D5		
Itapipoca Brazil	72	K13	3 29S	39 35W
Itaqui Brazil	73	F8	29 10S	56 30W
Ithaca New York USA	47	K2	42 27N	76 30W
Ituí *r.* Brazil	72	C12	5 30S	71 00W
Ivano-Frankivs'k Ukraine	80	K8	48 40N	24 40E
Ivanovo Russia	86	G8	57 00N	41 00E
Ivdel' Russia	86	J9	60 45N	60 30E
Iwaki Japan	94	D2	37 03N	140 58E
Iwakuni Japan	94	B1	34 10N	132 09E
Iwamizawa Japan	94	D3	43 12N	141 47E
Iwanai Japan	94	D3	43 01N	140 32E
Iwo Nigeria	100	E9	7 38N	4 11E
Ixtaccihuati *mt.* Mexico	66	E3	19 11N	98 38W
Ixtepec Mexico	66	E3	16 32N	95 10W
Iyo-nada *b.* Japan	94	B1	33 50N	132 00E
Izhevsk Russia	86	H8	56 49N	53 11E
Izhma *r.* Russia	86	H9	64 00N	54 00E
Izmayil Ukraine	81	M6	45 20N	28 48E
Izmir Turkey	88	A6	38 25N	27 10E
Izra' Syria	88	P11	32 52N	36 15E
Izu-shotō *is.* Japan	94	C1	34 20N	139 20E
J				
Jabal Akhdar *mt.* Oman	89	G3	24 00N	56 30E
Jabal al Akhdar *mts.* Libya	100	J14	33 00N	22 00E
Jabal as Sawdā' *mts.* Libya	100	G13	29 00N	15 00E
Jabalpur India	90	D4	23 10N	79 59E
Jablonec Czech Rep.	80	E9	50 44N	15 10E
Jaboatão Brazil	72	K12	8 05S	35 00W
Jackman Maine USA	47	R5	45 37N	70 16W
Jack Mountain Washington USA	38	H4	48 45N	120 55W
Jackson California USA	64	C4	38 19N	120 47W
Jackson Michigan USA	63	K5	42 15N	84 24W
Jackson Mississippi USA	63	H3	32 20N	90 11W
Jackson Tennessee USA	63	J4	35 37N	88 50W
Jackson Wyoming USA	62	D5	43 28N	110 45W
Jackson Heights New York USA	65	J2	40 45N	73 52W
Jacksonville Florida USA	63	K3	30 20N	81 40W
Jacksonville North Carolina USA	63	L3	34 45N	77 26W
Jacksonville Beach *tn.* Florida USA	63	K3	30 18N	81 24W
Jack Wade Alaska USA	54	B3	64 05N	141 35W
Jacmel Haiti	67	K3	18 18N	72 32W
Jacobabad Pakistan	90	B5	28 16N	68 30E
Jacobina Brazil	72	J11	11 13S	40 30W
Jaén Sp.	79	D2	37 46N	3 48W
Jaffna Sri Lanka	90	E1	9 40N	80 01E
Jagdalpur India	90	E3	19 04N	82 05E
Jahrom Iran	89	F4	28 29N	53 32E
Jaintiapur Bangladesh	91	M10	25 06N	92 08E
Jaipur India	90	D5	26 53N	75 50E
Jakarta Indonesia	95	D2	6 08S	106 45E
Jalālābād Afghanistan	89	C6	34 26N	70 25E
Jalandhar India	90	D6	31 18N	75 40E
Jalapa Enriquez Mexico	66	E3	19 32N	96 56W
Jalgaon India	90	D4	21 01N	75 39E
Jalón *r.* Sp.	79	E4	41 30N	1 35W
Jalpaiguri India	91	K11	26 29N	88 47E
Jālū Libya	100	J13	29 02N	21 33E
JAMAICA	67	J3		
Jamaica New York USA	65	J1	40 42N	73 48W
Jamaica Bay New York USA	65	J1	40 37N	73 50W
Jambi Indonesia	95	C3	1 34S	103 37E
James *r.* South Dakota USA	63	G5	44 00N	98 00W
James *r.* Virginia USA	63	L4	37 00N	77 00W
Jamestown New York USA	63	L5	42 05N	79 15W
Jamestown North Dakota USA	63	G6	46 54N	98 42W
Jamiltepec Mexico	66	E3	16 18N	97 51W
Jammu India	90	C6	32 43N	74 54E
Jammu and Kashmir *state* Southern Asia	90	D6	29 40N	76 30E
Jamnagar India	90	C4	22 28N	70 06E
Jamshedpur India	91	F4	22 47N	86 12E
Jamuna *r.* Bangladesh	91	K10	25 00N	89 40E
Janesville Wisconsin USA	63	J5	42 42N	89 02W
Jangipur India	91	K10	24 27N	88 04E
Jan Mayen *i.* Arctic Ocean	109		71 00N	9 00W
Januária Brazil	72	J10	15 28S	44 23W
JAPAN	94			
Japan, Sea of Pacific Ocean	94	C2	39 00N	137 00E
Japan Trench Pacific Ocean	106	E11	35 00N	143 00E
Japurá *r.* Brazil	72	D13	2 00S	67 30W
Jari *r.* Brazil	72	G14	2 00N	54 00W
Jarú Brazil	72	E11	10 24S	62 45W
Jarvis Islands Pacific Ocean	107	K8	0 00	163 00W
Jāsk Iran	89	G4	25 40N	57 46E
Jasło Poland	80	H8	49 45N	21 28E
Jastrowie Poland	80	F10	53 25N	16 50E
Jaunpur India	90	E5	25 44N	82 41E
Java Sea Indonesia	95	E2	5 00S	112 00E
Java Trench Indian Ocean	105	L5	10 00S	110 00E
Jawa *i.* Indonesia	95	D2/E2	7 00S	110 00E
Jayapura Indonesia	103	H10	2 37S	140 39E
Jaynagar Manzilpur India	91	K9	22 10N	88 24E
Jaza'ir Farasān *is.* Saudi Arabia	88	D2	16 45N	42 10E
Jean Nevada USA	64	F2	35 46N	115 20W
Jebel Abyad Plateau Sudan	100	K11	18 00N	28 00E
Jebel Marra *mts.* Sudan	100	J10	13 00N	24 00E
Jedda Saudi Arabia	88	C3	21 30N	39 10E
Jefferson Ohio USA	46	F1	41 44N	80 46W
Jefferson City Missouri USA	63	H4	38 33N	92 10W
Jefferson, Mount Nevada USA	64	E4	38 47N	116 58W
Jelenia Góra Poland	80	E9	50 55N	15 45E
Jelgava Latvia	80	J12	56 39N	23 40E
Jena Germany	80	C9	50 56N	11 35E
Jenin Jordan	88	N11	32 28N	35 18E
Jequié Brazil	72	J11	13 52S	40 06W
Jequitinhonha *r.* Brazil	72	J10	16 00S	41 00W
Jérémie Haiti	67	K3	18 40N	74 09W
Jerez de la Frontera Sp.	79	B2	36 41N	6 08W
Jerez de los Caballeros Sp.	79	B3	38 20N	6 45W
Jericho Middle East	88	N10	31 51N	35 27E
Jersey *i.* British Isles	78	D8	49 13N	2 07W
Jersey City New Jersey USA	65	C2	40 43N	74 06W
Jerusalem Israel/Jordan	88	N10	31 47N	35 13E
Jessore Bangladesh	91	K9	23 10N	89 12E
Jezioro Sniardwy *.* Poland	80	H10	53 00N	21 00E
Jhang Maghiana Pakistan	90	C6	31 19N	72 22E
Jhansi India	90	D5	25 27N	78 34E
Jharkhand *admin.* India	91	E4/F4	23 50N	85 00E
Jhelum *r.* Pakistan	90	C6	32 30N	72 30E
Jhenida Bangladesh	91	K9	23 32N	89 09E
Jiamusi China	93	Q8	46 59N	130 29E
Ji'an China	93	M4	27 08N	115 00E
Jiangmen China	93	L3	22 40N	113 05E
Jiaxing China	93	N5	30 15N	120 52E
Jiayuguan China	93	H6	39 47N	98 14E
Jihlavá Czech Rep.	80	E8	49 24N	15 34E
Jilin China	93	P7	43 53N	126 35E
Jiloca *r.* Sp.	79	E4	41 08N	1 45W
Jima Ethiopia	100	M9	7 39N	36 47E
Jinan China	93	M6	36 41N	117 00E
Jingdezhen China	93	M4	29 17N	117 12E

Jinhua China	93	M4	29 06N	119 40E
Jining China	93	L7	40 58N	113 01E
Jining China	93	M6	35 25N	116 40E
Jinja Uganda	100	L8	0 27N	33 14E
Jinsha Jiang *r.* China	93	J4	27 30N	103 00E
Jinxi China	93	N7	40 46N	120 47E
Jinzhou China	93	N7	41 07N	121 06E
Jiparaná *r.* Brazil	72	E12	8 00S	62 30W
Jiu *r.* Romania	81	J6	44 00N	24 00E
Jiujiang China	93	M4	29 41N	116 03E
Jixi China	93	Q8	45 17N	131 00E
Jīzān Saudi Arabia	88	D2	16 56N	42 33E
João Pessoa Brazil	72	K12	7 06S	34 53W
Jodhpur India	90	C5	26 18N	73 08E
Jōetsu Japan	94	C2	37 06N	138 15E
Jogighopa India	91	L11	26 12N	90 34E
Johannesburg RSA	101	K2	26 10S	28 02E
John Day *r.* Oregon USA	62	B5/C5	45 00N	120 00W
John H. Kerr Reservoir USA	63	L4	37 00N	78 00W
Johnson City Tennessee USA	63	K4	36 20N	82 23W
Johnston Atoll *is.* Pacific Ocean	107	K9	17 00N	168 00W
Johnstown Pennsylvania USA	63	L5	40 20N	78 56W
Johor Bahru Malaysia	95	C4	1 27N	103 45E
Joinville Brazil	72	H8	26 20S	48 55W
Jonesboro Arkansas USA	63	H4	35 50N	90 41W
Jonesville Michigan USA	46	B1	41 59N	84 39W
Jönköping Sweden	80	E12	57 45N	14 10E
Joplin Missouri USA	63	H4	37 04N	94 31W
JORDAN	88	C5		
Jordan *r.* Middle East	88	N11	32 15N	32 10E
Jos Nigeria	100	F9	9 54N	8 53E
Joseph Bonaparte Gulf Aust.	102	E8	14 00S	128 30E
Joshua Tree *tn.* California USA	64	E2	34 09N	116 20W
Joshua Tree National Monument California USA	64	F1	33 54N	116 00W
Jos Plateau Nigeria	100	F9	9 30N	8 55E
Joûnié Lebanon	88	N11	33 58N	35 38E
Jowai India	91	M10	25 26N	92 16E
Juan de Fuca Strait North America	62	B6	48 00N	124 00W
Juàzeiro Brazil	72	J12	9 25S	40 30W
Juàzeiro do Norte Brazil	72	K12	7 10S	39 18W
Juba Sudan	100	L8	4 50N	31 35E
Jubba *r.* Somalia	100	N8	3 00N	42 30E
Jubilee Reservoir HK China	92	B2	22 23N	114 09E
Júcar *r.* Sp.	79	E3	39 08N	1 50W
Juchitán Mexico	66	E3	16 27N	95 05W
Juiz de Fora Brazil	72	J9	21 47S	43 23W
Juliaca Peru	72	C10	15 29S	70 09W
Julijske Alpe *mts.* Europe	81	D7	46 00N	13 00E
Junagadh India	90	C4	21 32N	70 32E
Junction City Kansas USA	63	G4	39 02N	96 51W
Jundiaí Brazil	72	H9	23 10S	46 54W
Juneau Alaska USA	38	C6	58 20N	134 20W
Jungfrau *mt.* Switz.	79	J7	46 33N	7 58E
Junggar Pendi China	92	E7/G7	44 00N	87 30E
Junipero Serra Peak *mt.* California USA	64	C3	36 09N	121 26W
Junk Bay HK China	92	C1	22 18N	114 15E
Jur *r.* Sudan	100	K9	8 00N	28 00E
Jura *i.* UK	78	C11/C12	55 55N	6 00W
Jura *mts.* Fr./Switz.	79	H7/J7	46 30N	6 00E
Jura Krakowska *mts.* Poland	80	G9/H9	50 00N	20 00E
Jurmala Latvia	80	J12	56 59N	23 35E
Juruá *r.* Brazil	72	C12	9 30S	73 00W
Juruá *r.* Brazil	72	D13	4 30S	67 00W
Juruena *r.* Brazil	72	F11	10 00S	57 40W

K

K2 *mt.* China/India	92	D6	35 47N	76 30E
Kabrit Egypt	101	S2	30 16N	32 29E
Kābul Afghanistan	89	J5	34 30N	69 10E
Kabwe Zambia	101	K5	14 29S	28 25E
Kachchh, Gulf of India	90	B4	22 40N	69 30E
Kadoma Zimbabwe	101	K4	18 21N	29 55E
Kaduna Nigeria	100	F10	10 28N	7 25E
Kaduna *r.* Nigeria	100	F10	10 00N	6 30E
Kaédi Mauritania	100	B11	16 12N	13 32W
Kaesong South Korea	93	P6	37 59N	126 30E
Kafue Zambia	101	K4	15 44S	28 10E
Kafue *r.* Zambia	101	K5	16 00S	27 00E
Kagoshima Japan	94	B1	31 37N	130 32E
Kahoolawe *i.* Hawaiian Islands	107	Y18	20 30N	156 40W
Kahuku Point *c.* Hawaiian Islands	107	Y18	21 42N	158 00W
Kaifeng China	93	L5	34 47N	114 20E
Kailua Hawaiian Islands	107	Z17	19 43N	155 59W
Kaimana Indonesia	95	J3	3 39S	133 44E
Kainji Reservoir Nigeria	100	E10	10 25N	4 56E
Kairouan Tunisia	100	G14	35 42N	10 01E
Kaiserslautern Germany	80	A8	49 27N	7 47E
Kaitaia NZ	103	P3	35 07S	173 16E
Kaiwi Channel *sd.* Hawaiian Islands	107	Y18	21 20N	157 30W
Kākināda India	90	E3	16 59N	82 20E
Kalae *c.* Hawaiian Islands	107	Z17	18 58N	155 24W
Kalahari Desert Southern Africa	101	J3	23 30S	23 00E
Kalamáta Greece	81	J2	37 02N	22 07E
Kalamazoo Michigan USA	63	J5	42 17N	85 36W
Kalambo Falls Tanzania/Zambia	101	L6	8 35S	31 13E
Kalat Pakistan	90	B5	29 01N	66 38E
Kalémié CDR	101	K6	5 57S	29 10E
Kalgoorlie Aust.	102	D4	30 49S	121 29E
Kalimantan *admin.* Indonesia	95	E3	0 00	115 00E
Kalindri *r.* India	91	J10	25 30N	88 00E
Kaliningrad Russia	80	H11	54 40N	20 30E
Kaliningrad *admin.* Russia	80	H11	54 40N	21 00E
Kalispell Montana USA	62	D6	48 12N	114 19W
Kalisz Poland	80	G9	51 46N	18 02E
Kalmar Sweden	80	F12	56 39N	16 20E
Kalni *r.* Bangladesh	91	L10	24 45N	91 15E
Kalomo Zambia	101	K4	17 02S	26 29E
Kaluga Russia	86	F7	54 31N	36 16E
Kalundborg Denmark	80	C11	55 42N	11 06E
Kama *r.* Russia	86	H8	57 00N	55 00E
Kamaishi Japan	94	D2	39 18N	141 52E
Kamarān *i.* Yemen	88	D2	15 21N	42 40E
Kambara *i.* Fiji	106	V15	18 57S	178 58W
Kamchatka *p.* Russia	87	T7	57 30N	160 00E
Kamchatka Bay Russia	87	U7	55 00N	164 00E
Kamchiya *r.* Bulgaria	81	L5	43 00N	27 00E
Kamensk-Ural'skiy Russia	86	J8	56 29N	61 49E
Kamet *mt.* India	90	D6	30 55N	79 36E
Kamina CDR	101	K6	8 46S	25 00E
Kampala Uganda	100	L8	0 19N	32 35E
Kâmpóng Cham Cambodia	95	D6	11 59N	105 26E
Kâmpóng Chhnăng Cambodia	95	C6	12 16N	104 39E
Kam Tin HK China	92	B2	22 26N	114 04E
Kam'yanets'-Podil's'kyy Ukraine	80	L8	48 40N	26 36E
Kamyshin Russia	86	G7	50 05N	45 24E
Kananga CDR	101	J6	5 53S	22 26E
Kanazawa Japan	94	C2	36 35N	136 38E
Kanbe Myanmar	95	B7	16 45N	96 04E
Kandahār Afghanistan	89	J5	31 35N	65 45E
Kandalaksha Russia	86	F10	67 09N	32 31E
Kandavu *i.* Fiji	106	U15	19 10S	178 30E
Kandavu Passage *sd.* Fiji	106	T15	18 50S	178 00E
Kandi Benin	100	E10	11 05N	2 59E
Kandla India	90	C4	23 03N	70 11E
Kandy Sri Lanka	90	E1	7 17N	80 40E
Kane Pennsylvania USA	46	H1	41 41N	78 49W
Kaneohe Hawaiian Islands	107	Y18	21 25N	157 48W
Kangan Iran	89	F4	27 51N	52 07E
Kangar Malaysia	95	C5	6 27N	100 11E
Kangaroo Island Aust.	102	G3	35 50S	137 50E
Kangnung South Korea	93	P6	37 48N	127 52E
Kaniet Islands PNG	103	J10	0 53S	145 30E
Kanin Peninsula Russia	86	G10	68 00N	45 00E
Kankakee Illinois USA	63	J5	41 08N	87 52W
Kankan Guinea	100	C10	10 22N	9 11W
Kannapolis North Carolina USA	63	K4	35 30N	80 36W
Kano Nigeria	100	F10	12 00N	8 31E
Kanoya Japan	94	B1	31 22N	130 50E
Kanpur India	90	E5	26 27N	80 14E
Kansas *state* USA	62/63	G4	38 00N	98 00W
Kansas City Missouri USA	63	H4	39 02N	94 33W
Kansk Russia	87	M8	56 11N	95 48E
Kanye Botswana	101	J3	24 59S	25 19E
Kaohsiung Taiwan	93	N3	22 36N	120 17E
Kaolack Senegal	100	A10	14 09N	16 08W
Kapaa Hawaiian Islands	107	X19	22 04N	159 20W
Kapfenberg Austria	81	E7	47 27N	15 18E
Kapingamarangi Rise Pacific Ocean	106	F8	3 00N	154 00E
Kaposvár Hungary	81	F7	46 21N	17 49E
Kara Bogaz Gol *b.* Turkmenistan	86	H5	42 00N	53 00E
Karabük Turkey	88	B7	41 12N	32 36E
Karachi Pakistan	90	B4	24 51N	67 02E
Karaganda Kazakhstan	86	K6	49 53N	73 07E
Karaginskiy *i.* Russia	87	U8	58 00N	164 00E
Karaj Iran	89	F6	35 48N	50 58E
Karak Jordan	88	N10	31 11N	35 42E
Karakoram Pass China/Kashmir	90	D7	35 33N	77 51E
Kara Kum *geog. reg.* Turkmenistan	86	H4/J4	40 00N	60 00E
Karasburg Namibia	101	H2	28 00S	18 43E
Kara Sea Russia	87	K11	75 00N	70 00E
Karatoya *r.* Bangladesh	91	K10	25 15N	89 15E
Karbalā' Iraq	88	D5	32 37N	44 03E
Karcag Hungary	81	H7	47 19N	20 53E
Kariba Dam Zambia/Zimbabwe	101	K4	16 31S	28 50E
Kariba, Lake Zambia/Zimbabwe	101	K4	17 00S	28 00E
Karibib Namibia	101	H3	21 59S	15 51E
Karimganj India	91	M10	24 50N	92 21E
Karisimbi, Mount Rwanda/CDR	100	K7	1 32S	29 27E
Karlino Poland	80	E11	54 02N	15 52E
Karlovac Croatia	81	E6	45 30N	15 34E
Karlovy Vary Czech Rep.	80	D9	50 13N	12 52E
Karlshamn Sweden	80	E12	56 10N	14 50E
Karlskoga Sweden	80	E13	59 19N	14 33E
Karlskrona Sweden	80	E12	56 10N	15 35E
Karlsruhe Germany	80	B8	49 00N	8 24E
Karlstad Sweden	80	D13	59 24N	13 32E
Karnafuli Reservoir Bangladesh	91	M9	22 30N	92 20E
Karnataka *admin.* India	90	D2	14 40N	75 30E
Kárpathos *i.* Greece	81	L1	35 30N	27 12E
Karpenísi Greece	81	H3	38 55N	21 47E
Kars Turkey	88	D7	40 35N	43 05E
Karsakpay Kazakhstan	86	J6	47 47N	66 43E
Karwar India	90	C2	14 50N	74 09E
Kasai *r.* Angola/CDR	100	H7	4 00S	19 00E
Kasama Zambia	101	L5	10 10S	31 11E
Kasaragod India	90	C2	12 30N	74 59E
Kasempa Zambia	101	K5	13 28S	25 48E
Kasese Uganda	100	L8	0 10N	30 06E
Kāshān Iran	89	F5	33 59N	51 35E
Kashi China	92	D6	39 29N	76 02E
Kashinatpur Bangladesh	91	K9	23 58N	89 37E
Kashiwazaki Japan	94	C2	37 22N	138 33E
Kásos *i.* Greece	81	L1	35 20N	26 55E
Kassala Sudan	100	M11	15 24N	36 30E
Kassel Germany	80	B9	51 18N	9 30E
Kastamonu Turkey	88	B7	41 22N	33 47E
Kastoriá Greece	81	H4	40 33N	21 15E
Kasur Pakistan	90	C6	31 07N	74 30E
Kataba Zambia	101	K4	16 02S	25 03E
Katchall Island India	91	G1	7 57N	93 22E
Kateríni Greece	81	J4	40 15N	22 30E
Katha Myanmar	92	H3	24 11N	96 20E
Katherine Aust.	102	F8	14 29S	132 20E
Kathiawar *p.* India	90	C4	21 10N	71 00E
Kathmandu Nepal	91	F5	27 42N	85 19E
Katowice Poland	80	G9	50 15N	18 59E
Katrineholm Sweden	80	F13	58 59N	16 15E
Katsina Nigeria	100	F10	13 00N	7 32E
Katsina Ala Nigeria	100	F9	7 10N	9 30E
Kattegat *sd.* Denmark/Sweden	80	C12	57 00N	11 00E
Kauai *i.* Hawaiian Islands	107	X18	22 00N	159 30W
Kauai Channel *sd.* Hawaiian Islands	107	X18	21 45N	158 50W
Kaula *i.* Hawaiian Islands	107	W18	21 35N	160 40W
Kaulakahi Channel *sd.* Hawaiian Islands	107	X18	21 58N	159 50W
Kaunas Lithuania	80	J11	54 52N	23 55E
Kaura Namoda Nigeria	100	F10	12 39N	6 38E
Kau Sai Chau *i.* HK China	92	C2	22 22N	114 19E
Kau Yi Chau *i.* HK China	92	B1	22 17N	114 04E
Kavajë Albania	81	G4	41 11N	19 33E
Kavála Greece	81	K4	40 56N	24 25E
Kavaratti India	90	C2	10 33N	72 39E
Kawagoe Japan	94	C2	35 55N	139 30E
Kawaihae Hawaiian Islands	107	Z18	20 02N	155 05W
Kawasaki Japan	94	C2	35 30N	139 45E
Kaya Burkina	100	D10	13 04N	1 09W
Kayes Mali	100	B10	14 26N	11 28W
Kayseri Turkey	88	C6	38 42N	35 28E
Kazach'ye Russia	87	R11	70 46N	136 15E
KAZAKHSTAN	86	H6/J6		
Kazakh Upland Kazakhstan	86	K6	47 00N	75 00E
Kazan' Russia	86	G8	55 45N	49 10E
Kazanlŭk Bulgaria	81	K5	42 37N	25 23E
Kazatin Ukraine	80	M8	49 41N	28 49E
Kāzerūn Iran	89	F4	29 35N	51 40E
Kazym *r.* Russia	86	J9	63 00N	67 30E
Kéa *i.* Greece	81	K2	37 00N	24 00E
Kearney Nebraska USA	62	G5	40 42N	99 04W
Kearny New Jersey USA	65	H2	40 45N	74 07W
Kecskemét Hungary	81	G7	46 56N	19 43E
Kediri Indonesia	95	E2	7 45S	112 01E
Keene New Hampshire USA	65	D3	42 56N	72 17W
Keetmanshoop Namibia	101	H2	26 36S	18 08E
Kefallonia *i.* Greece	81	H3	38 00N	20 00E
Kei Ling Ha Hoi *b.* HK China	92	C2	22 26N	114 17E
K'elafo Ethiopia	100	N9	5 37N	44 10E
Kelkit *r.* Turkey	88	C7	40 20N	37 40E
Kelseyville California USA	64	B4	38 58N	122 50W
Kelso California USA	64	F2	35 01N	115 39W
Kemerovo Russia	87	L8	55 25N	86 05E
Kemp Land *geog. reg.* Antarctica	109		65 00S	60 00E
Kempten Germany	80	C7	47 44N	10 19E
Kendal UK	78	D11	54 20N	2 45W
Kendari Indonesia	95	G3	3 57S	122 36E
Kenema Sierra Leone	100	B9	7 57N	11 11W
Kengtung Myanmar	93	H3	21 15N	99 40E
Keningau Malaysia	95	F5	5 21N	116 11E
Kénitra Morocco	100	C14	34 20N	6 34W
Kenmare North Dakota USA	42	F1	48 40N	101 59W
Kennebec River Maine USA	47	S5	45 10N	69 42W
Kennebunk Maine USA	65	E3	43 24N	70 31W
Kennedy Town HK China	92	B1	22 17N	114 07E
Kenosha Wisconsin USA	63	J5	42 34N	87 50W
Kentucky *state* USA	63	J4	37 00N	85 00W
Kentwood Michigan USA	45	J2	42 54N	85 35W
KENYA	100	M7		
Kenya, Mount Kenya	100	L13	0 10S	37 19E
Kepulauan Anambas *is.* Indonesia	95	D4	3 00N	106 20E
Kepulauan Aru *is.* Indonesia	95	J2	6 00S	134 30E
Kepulauan Babar *is.* Indonesia	95	H2	7 50S	129 30E
Kepulauan Batu *is.* Indonesia	95	B3	0 18S	98 29E
Kepulauan Kai *is.* Indonesia	95	J2	5 30S	132 30E
Kepulauan Lingga *is.* Indonesia	95	C3	0 10S	104 30E
Kepulauan Mentawai *is.* Indonesia	95	B3	2 00S	99 00E
Kepulauan Obi *is.* Indonesia	95	H3	1 30S	127 30E
Kepulauan Riau *is.* Indonesia	95	C4	0 30N	104 30E
Kepulauan Sangir *is.* Indonesia	95	H4	3 00N	125 30E
Kepulauan Sula *is.* Indonesia	95	G3	1 50S	124 50E
Kepulauan Tanimbar *is.* Indonesia	95	J2	7 30S	131 30E
Kerala *admin.* India	90	D1/D2	10 10N	76 30E
Kerema PNG	103	J9	7 59S	145 46E
Keren Eritrea	100	M11	15 46N	38 30E
Kerguelen Plateau Indian Ocean	105	G1	55 00S	80 00E
Kérkyra *i.* Greece	81	G3	39 00N	19 00E
Kermadec Islands Pacific Ocean	103	R4/R5	30 00S	178 30W
Kermadec Trench Pacific Ocean	106	J4	33 00S	177 00W
Kermān Iran	89	G5	30 18N	57 05E
Kermānshāh Iran	89	E5	34 19N	47 04E
Kern *r.* California USA	64	D2	36 00N	118 28W
Kerrville Texas USA	62	G3	30 03N	99 09W
Kerulen *r.* Mongolia	93	L8	47 30N	112 30E
Ket' *r.* Russia	87	L8	58 30N	87 00E
Ketapang Indonesia	95	E3	1 50S	110 00E
Ketchikan Alaska USA	38	E4	55 25N	131 40W
Ketrzyn Poland	80	H10	54 05N	21 24E
Kettle Creek *r.* Pennsylvania USA	46	J1	41 30N	77 40W
Keuka Lake New York USA	47	J2	42 30N	77 10W
Kevin Montana USA	41	G1	48 45N	111 57W
Keweenaw Bay Michigan USA	45	G4	47 05N	88 15W
Keweenaw Peninsula Michigan USA	63	J6	47 00N	88 00W
Key West Florida USA	63	K1	24 34N	81 48W
Khabarovsk Russia	87	R6	48 32N	135 08E
Khalîg el Tîna Egypt	101	T4	31 08N	32 36E
Khambhat India	90	C4	22 19N	72 39E
Khambhat, Gulf of India	90	C4	20 30N	72 00E
Khammam India	90	E3	17 15N	80 11E
Khānābād Afghanistan	89	J6	36 42N	69 08E
Khānaqīn Iraq	88	E5	34 22N	45 22E
Khandwa India	90	D4	21 49N	76 23E
Khanty-Mansiysk Russia	86	J9	61 01N	69 00E
Khān Yūnis Middle East	88	N10	31 21N	34 18E
Kharagpur India	91	F4	22 23N	87 22E
Kharan Pakistan	90	B5	28 32N	65 26E
Khārg *i.* Iran	89	F4	29 14N	50 20E
Khartoum Sudan	100	L11	15 33N	32 35E
Khāsh Iran	89	H4	28 14N	61 15E
Khash *r.* Afghanistan	89	H5	31 30N	62 30E
Khasi Hills *mts.* India	91	L10	25 34N	91 30E
Khaskovo Bulgaria	81	K4	41 57N	25 32E
Khatanga Russia	87	N11	71 59N	102 31E
Khatanga *r.* Russia	87	N11	72 30N	102 30E
Khaybar Saudi Arabia	88	C4	25 50N	39 00E
Khemisset Morocco	100	C14	33 50N	6 03W
Kheta *r.* Russia	87	M11	71 30N	95 00E
Khilok *r.* Russia	87	N7	51 00N	107 30E
Khiva Uzbekistan	86	J5	41 25N	60 49E
Khmel'nyts'kyy Ukraine	80	L8	49 25N	26 59E
Kholmsk Russia	87	S6	47 02N	142 03E
Khorog Tajikistan	86	K4	37 22N	71 32E
Khorramābād Iran	89	E5	33 29N	48 21E
Khorramshahr Iran	89	E5	30 25N	48 09E
Khotin Ukraine	80	L8	48 30N	26 31E
Khouribga Morocco	100	C14	32 54N	6 57W
Khowai India	91	L10	24 05N	91 36E
Khulna Bangladesh	91	K9	22 49N	89 34E
Khyber Pass Afghanistan/Pakistan	90	C6	34 06N	71 05E
Kibombo CDR	100	K7	3 58S	25 54E
Kiel Germany	80	C11	54 20N	10 08E
Kielce Poland	80	H9	50 51N	20 39E
Kieta PNG	103	L9	6 15S	155 37E
Kiev Ukraine	80	N9	50 25N	30 30E
Kigali Rwanda	100	L7	1 56S	30 04E
Kigoma Tanzania	100	K7	4 52S	29 36E
Kii-suidō *sd.* Japan	94	B1	34 00N	134 45E
Kikinda SM	81	H6	45 50N	20 30E
Kikori PNG	103	H9	7 25S	144 13E
Kikwit CDR	100	H6	5 02S	18 51E
Kilanea Hawaiian Islands	107	X19	22 05N	159 35W
Kilimanjaro *mt.* Tanzania	100	M7	3 04S	37 22E
Kilkenny RoI	78	B10	52 39N	7 15W
Kilkís Greece	81	J4	40 59N	22 52E
Killarney RoI	78	A10	52 03N	9 30W
Killeen Texas USA	63	G3	31 08N	97 44W
Kilmarnock UK	78	C11	55 36N	4 30W
Kilwa Masoko Tanzania	101	M6	8 55S	39 31E
Kimberley RSA	101	J2	28 45S	24 46E
Kimberley Plateau Aust.	102	E7	17 30S	126 00E
Kimchaek North Korea	93	P7	40 41N	129 12E
Kindia Guinea	100	B10	10 03N	12 49W
Kindu CDR	100	K7	3 00S	25 56E
King City California USA	64	C3	36 13N	121 09W
King George Island South Shetland Islands	73	F1	62 00S	58 00W
King Island Aust.	103	H3	40 00S	144 00E
Kingman Arizona USA	62	D4	35 12N	114 02W
Kings *r.* California USA	64	D3	36 32N	119 30W
Kings Canyon National Park California USA	64	D3	36 45N	118 30W
King's Lynn UK	78	F10	52 45N	0 24E
King Sound Aust.	102	D7	16 00S	123 00E
Kings Point *tn.* New York USA	65	J2	40 49N	73 45W
Kingsport Tennessee USA	63	K4	36 33N	82 34W
Kingston Jamaica	67	U13	17 58N	76 48W
Kingston New York USA	65	C2	41 56N	74 00W
Kingston upon Hull UK	78	E10	53 45N	0 20W
Kingstown St. Vincent and The Grenadines	66	R11	13 12N	61 14W
Kingsville Texas USA	63	G2	27 32N	97 53W
Kinkala Congo	100	G7	4 18S	14 49E
Kinshasa CDR	100	H7	4 18S	15 18E
Kipili Tanzania	101	L6	7 30S	30 39E
Kirensk Russia	87	N8	57 45N	108 02E
KIRIBATI	106/107	H8/L7		
Kirikkale Turkey	88	B6	39 51N	33 32E
Kiritimati Island Kiribati	107	L8	2 10N	157 00W
Kirkcaldy UK	78	D12	56 07N	3 10W
Kirkcudbright UK	78	C11	54 50N	4 03W

Kirksville Missouri USA	63	H5	40 12N	92 35W
Kirkūk Iraq	88	D6	35 28N	44 26E
Kirkwall UK	78	D13	58 59N	2 58W
Kirov Russia	86	G8	58 00N	49 38E
Kiryū Japan	94	C2	36 26N	139 18E
Kisangani CDR	100	K8	0 33N	25 14E
Kishiwada Japan	94	C1	34 28N	135 22E
Kiskunfélegyháza Hungary	81	G7	46 42N	19 52E
Kiskunhalas Hungary	81	G7	46 26N	19 29E
Kismaayo Somalia	100	N7	0 25S	42 31E
Kisumu Kenya	100	L7	0 08S	34 47E
Kita-Kyūshu Japan	94	B1	33 52N	130 49E
Kitami Japan	94	D3	43 51N	143 54E
Kittery Maine USA	65	E3	43 06N	70 46W
Kitwe Zambia	101	K5	0 08S	30 30E
Kivu, Lake CDR/Rwanda	100	K7	2 00S	29 00E
Kızıl Irmak *r.* Turkey	88	B7	40 30N	34 00E
Kykládes *is.* Greece	81	K2	37 00N	25 00E
Kladno Czech Rep.	80	E9	50 10N	14 07E
Klagenfurt Austria	81	E7	46 38N	14 20E
Klaipėda Lithuania	80	H11	55 43N	21 07E
Klamath *r.* USA	62	B5	42 00N	123 00W
Klamath Falls *tn.* Oregon USA	62	B5	42 14N	121 47W
Klatovy Czech Rep.	80	D8	49 24N	13 17E
Klerksdorp RSA	101	K2	26 52S	26 39E
Klintehamn Sweden	80	G12	57 24N	18 14E
Kłodzko Poland	80	F9	50 28N	16 40E
Klukwan Alaska USA	38	C6	59 25N	135 55W
Klyuchevskaya Sopka *mt.* Russia	87	U8	56 03N	160 38E
Knokke-Heist Belgium	78	G9	51 21N	3 19E
Knoxville Tennessee USA	63	K4	36 00N	83 57W
Kōbe Japan	94	C1	34 40N	135 12E
Koblenz Germany	80	A9	50 21N	7 36E
Kobryn Belarus	80	K10	52 16N	24 22E
Kocaeli Turkey	88	A7	40 47N	29 55E
Koch Bihar India	91	F5	26 18N	89 32E
Kōchi Japan	94	B1	33 33N	133 32E
Kodiak Island Alaska USA	107	L13	57 20N	153 40W
Kodok Sudan	100	L9	9 51N	32 07E
Koforidua Ghana	100	D9	6 01N	0 12W
Kōfu Japan	94	C2	35 42N	138 34E
Kohat Pakistan	90	C6	33 37N	71 30E
Kohima India	91	G5	25 40N	94 08E
Koh-i-Mazar *mt.* Afghanistan	89	J5	32 30N	66 23E
Kokand Uzbekistan	86	K5	40 33N	70 55E
Kokomo Indiana USA	63	J5	40 30N	86 09W
Kokshetau Kazakhstan	86	J7	53 18N	69 25E
Kola Peninsula Russia	86	F10	67 30N	37 30E
Kolar Gold Fields *tn.* India	90	D2	12 54N	78 16E
Kolding Denmark	80	B11	55 29N	9 30E
Kolguyev *i.* Russia	86	G10	69 00N	49 30E
Kolhapur India	90	C3	16 40N	74 20E
Kolín Czech Rep.	80	E9	50 02N	15 11E
Kolka Latvia	80	J12	57 44N	22 27E
Kolkata India	91	F4	22 30N	88 20E
Kołobrzeg Poland	80	E11	54 10N	15 35E
Kolomyya Ukraine	80	K8	48 31N	25 00E
Kolosib India	91	M10	24 05N	92 50E
Kolpashevo Russia	87	L8	58 21N	82 59E
Kolwezi CDR	101	K5	10 45S	25 25E
Kolyma *r.* Russia	87	T10	66 30N	152 00E
Kolyma Lowland Russia	87	T10	69 00N	155 00E
Kolyma Range *mts.* Russia	87	T9	63 00N	160 00E
Komandorskiye Ostrova *is.* Russia	106	G13	60 00N	175 00W
Komárno Slovakia	80	G7	47 46N	18 05E
Komatsu Japan	94	C2	36 25N	136 27E
Komotiní Greece	81	K4	41 06N	25 25E
Kâmpóng Saôm Cambodia	95	C6	10 38N	103 28E
Komsomol'sk-na-Amure Russia	87	R7	50 32N	136 59E
Kondūz Afghanistan	89	J6	36 45N	68 51E
Kongolo CDR	100	K6	5 20S	27 00E
Kongsvinger Norway	80	C14	60 12N	12 01E
Konin Poland	80	G10	52 12N	18 12E
Konosha Russia	86	G9	60 58N	40 08E
Konstanz Germany	80	B7	47 40N	9 10E
Konya Turkey	88	B6	37 51N	32 30E
Koocanusa, Lake Montana USA	39	N1	48 55N	115 10W
Koper Slovenia	81	D6	45 31N	13 44E
Kopychintsy Ukraine	80	K8	49 10N	25 58E
Korçë Albania	81	H4	40 38N	20 44E
Korčula *i.* Croatia	81	F5	43 00N	17 00E
Korea Bay China/North Korea	93	N6	39 00N	124 00E
Korea Strait Japan/South Korea	93	P5/Q6	33 00N	129 00E
Korhogo Côte d'Ivoire	100	C9	9 22N	5 31W
Korinthiakós Kólpos *g.* Greece	81	J3	38 00N	22 00E
Kórinthos Greece	81	J2	37 56N	22 55E
Kōriyama Japan	94	D2	37 23N	140 22E
Korla China	92	F7	41 48N	86 10E
Koro *i.* Fiji	106	U16	17 20S	179 25E
Koro Sea Fiji	106	U16	17 35S	180 00
Korosten' Ukraine	80	M9	51 00N	28 30E
Korsakov Russia	87	S6	46 36N	142 50E
Kortrijk Belgium	78	G9	50 50N	3 17E
Koryak Range *mts.* Russia	87	V9	62 00N	170 00E
Kós *i.* Greece	81	L2	36 45N	27 10E
Kosciusko Island Alaska USA	38	D4	56 00N	133 45W
Kosciusko, Mount Aust.	103	J3	36 28S	148 17E
Košice Slovakia	80	H8	48 44N	21 15E
Kosovska Mitrovica SM	81	H5	42 54N	20 52E
Kosti Sudan	100	L10	13 11N	32 28E
Kostroma Russia	86	G8	57 46N	40 59E
Koszalin Poland	80	F11	54 10N	16 10E
Kota India	90	D5	25 11N	75 58E
Kota Bharu Malaysia	95	C5	6 08N	102 14E
Kota Kinabalu Malaysia	95	F5	5 59N	116 04E
Kotlas Russia	86	G9	61 15N	46 35E
Kotri Pakistan	90	B5	25 22N	68 18E
Kotto *r.* CAR	100	J9	7 00N	22 30E
Kotuy *r.* Russia	87	N10	67 30N	102 00E
Koudougou Burkina	100	D10	12 15N	2 23W
Koulamoutou Gabon	100	G7	1 12S	12 29E
Koulikoro Mali	100	C10	12 55N	7 31W
Koumra Chad	100	H9	8 56N	17 32E
Kourou French Guiana	72	G15	5 08N	52 37W
Kovel' Ukraine	80	K9	51 12N	24 48E
Kowloon HK China	92	C1	22 19N	114 11E
Kowloon Peak *mt.* HK China	92	C2	22 20N	114 14E
Kowloon Reservoirs HK China	92	B2	22 21N	114 09E
Kowloon Tong HK China	92	C2	22 20N	114 11E
Kozáni Greece	81	H4	40 18N	21 48E
Kpalimé Togo	100	E9	6 55N	0 44E
Kragujevac SM	81	H5	44 01N	20 55E
Kraków Poland	80	G9	50 03N	19 55E
Kraljevo SM	81	H5	43 44N	20 41E
Kranj Slovenia	81	E7	46 15N	14 20E
Krasnodar Russia	86	F6	45 02N	39 00E
Krasnovodsk Turkmenistan	86	H5	40 01N	53 00E
Krasnoyarsk Russia	87	M8	56 05N	92 46E
Krefeld Germany	80	A9	51 20N	6 32E
Krementes Ukraine	80	K9	50 05N	25 48E
Krems Austria	80	E8	48 25N	15 36E
Kribi Cameroon	100	F8	2 56N	9 56E
Krishna *r.* India	90	D3	16 00N	77 30E
Krishnanagar India	91	K9	23 25N	88 30E
Kristiansand Norway	78	J13	58 08N	8 01E
Kristianstad Sweden	80	E12	56 02N	14 10E
Kristinehamn Sweden	80	E13	59 17N	14 09E
Kríti *i.* Greece	81	K1	35 00N	25 00E
Krk *i.* Croatia	81	E6	45 00N	14 00E
Krosno Poland	80	J8	49 40N	21 46E
Kruševac SM	81	H5	43 34N	21 20E
Kruzof Island Alaska USA	38	C5	57 15N	135 40W
Kuala Lumpur Malaysia	95	C4	3 09N	101 42E
Kuala Terengganu Malaysia	95	C5	5 20N	103 09E
Kuantan Malaysia	95	C4	3 48N	103 19E
Kuching Malaysia	95	E4	1 35N	110 21E
Kuito Angola	101	H5	12 25S	16 56E
Kuiu Island Alaska USA	38	C5/D5	56 45N	134 00W
Kujū-san *mt.* Japan	94	B1	33 07N	131 14E
Kukës Albania	81	H5	42 05N	20 24E
Kuldiga Latvia	80	H12	56 58N	21 58E
Kuma *r.* Russia	86	G5	45 00N	45 00E
Kumagaya Japan	94	C2	36 09N	139 22E
Kumamoto Japan	94	B1	32 50N	130 42E
Kumanovo FYROM	81	H5	42 07N	21 40E
Kumasi Ghana	100	D9	6 45N	1 35W
Kumba Cameroon	100	F8	4 39N	9 26E
Kumbakonam India	90	D2	10 59N	79 24E
Kunar *r.* Afghanistan/Pakistan	89	K6	34 50N	71 05E
Kunashir *i.* Russia	94	E3	44 30N	146 20E
Kundat Malaysia	95	F5	6 54N	116 50E
Kungrad Uzbekistan	86	H5	43 06N	58 54E
Kunlun Shan *mts.* China	92	E6/F6	36 30N	85 00E
Kunming China	93	J4	25 04N	102 41E
Kunsan South Korea	93	P6	35 57N	126 42E
Kununurra Aust.	102	E7	15 42S	128 50E
Kupa *r.* Croatia	81	E6	45 30N	15 00E
Kupang Indonesia	95	G1	10 13S	123 38E
Kupreanof Island Alaska USA	38	D5	56 50N	133 30W
Kurashiki Japan	94	B1	34 36N	133 43E
Kure Japan	94	B1	34 14N	132 32E
Kuressaare Estonia	80	J13	58 22N	28 40E
Kureyka *r.* Russia	87	M10	67 30N	91 00E
Kurgan Russia	86	J8	55 30N	65 20E
Kuria Muria Islands Oman	89	G2	17 30N	56 00E
Kurigram Bangladesh	91	K10	25 49N	89 39E
Kuril Islands Russia	87	T6	50 00N	155 00E
Kuril Ridge Pacific Ocean	106	F12	47 50N	152 00E
Kuril Trench Pacific Ocean	106	F12	45 40N	154 00E
Kurnool India	90	D3	15 51N	78 01E
Kursk Russia	86	F7	51 45N	36 14E
Kurskiy Zaliv *g.* Russia	80	H11	55 00N	21 00E
Kurtalan Turkey	88	D6	37 55N	41 44E
Kurume Japan	94	B1	33 20N	130 29E
Kushiro Japan	94	D3	42 58N	144 24E
Kustanay Kazakhstan	86	J7	53 15N	63 40E
Kütahya Turkey	88	A6	39 25N	29 56E
Kutno Poland	80	G10	52 13N	19 20E
Kutubdia Island Bangladesh	91	L8	21 50N	91 52E
Kuvango Angola	101	H5	14 27S	16 20E
KUWAIT	89	E4		
Kuwait Kuwait	89	E4	29 20N	48 00E
Kuytun China	92	E7	44 30N	85 00E
Kwai Chung HK China	92	B2	22 22N	114 07E
Kwangju South Korea	93	P6	35 07N	126 52E
Kwango *r.* CDR	101	H6	6 00S	17 00E
Kwekwe Zimbabwe	101	K4	18 55S	29 49E
Kwilu *r.* CDR	101	H6	6 00S	19 00E
Kwun Tong HK China	92	C1	22 18N	114 13E
Kwu Tung HK China	92	B3	22 31N	114 06E
Kyburz California USA	64	C4	38 47N	120 19W
Kyle of Lochalsh UK	78	C12	57 17N	5 43W
Kyoga, Lake Uganda	100	L8	2 00N	34 00E
Kyōga-misaki *c.* Japan	94	C2	35 48N	135 12E
Kyōto Japan	94	C2	35 02N	135 45E
Kyparissiakós Kólpos *g.* Greece	81	H2	37 00N	21 00E
KYRGYZSTAN	86	K5		
Kythira *i.* Greece	81	J2	36 00N	23 00E
Kýthnos *i.* Greece	81	K2	37 25N	24 25E
Kyūshū *i.* Japan	94	B1	32 20N	131 00E
Kyushu-Palau Ridge Pacific Ocean	106	D9	15 00N	135 00E
Kyustendil Bulgaria	81	J5	42 26N	22 40E
Kyzyl Russia	87	M7	51 45N	94 28E
Kyzyl Kum *d.* Asia	86	J5	43 00N	65 00E
Kzylorda Kazakhstan	86	J5	44 25N	65 28E
L				
Laascaanood Somalia	100	P9	8 35N	46 55E
Laâyoune Western Sahara	100	B13	27 10N	13 11W
la Baule-Escoublac Fr.	79	D7	47 18N	2 22W
Labé Guinea	100	B10	11 17N	12 11W
Labrador Basin Atlantic Ocean	108	C12	58 00N	50 00W
Lábrea Brazil	72	E12	7 20S	64 46W
La Brea Trinidad and Tobago	67	V15	10 14N	61 37W
Labytnangi Russia	86	J10	66 43N	66 28E
Lac Alaotra *l.* Madagascar	101	P4	17 30S	54 00E
Laccadive Islands India	90	C1/C2	11 00N	72 00E
La Ceiba Honduras	67	G3	15 45N	86 45W
Lac Fitri *l.* Chad	100	H10	13 00N	17 30E
Lachlan *r.* Aust.	103	J4	34 00S	145 00E
La Chorrera Panama	67	Y1	8 51N	79 46W
Lackawanna New York USA	48	D1	42 49N	78 49W
Lac Léman *l.* Switz.	79	J7	46 20N	6 20E
Lac Mai-Ndombe *l.* CDR	100	H7	2 00S	18 20E
La Coruña Sp.	79	A5	43 22N	8 24W
La Crosse Wisconsin USA	63	H5	43 48N	91 04W
Lacul Razim *l.* Romania	81	M6	45 00N	29 00E
Ladakh Range *mts.* Kashmir	90	D6	34 30N	78 30E
Ladozhskoye Ozero *l.* Russia	86	F9	61 00N	30 00E
Ladysmith RSA	101	K2	28 34S	29 47E
Ladysmith Wisconsin USA	45	F3	45 28N	91 06W
Lae PNG	103	J9	6 43S	147 01E
La Esmeralda Venezuela	72	D14	3 11N	65 33W
Lafayette Indiana USA	63	J5	40 25N	86 54W
Lafayette Louisiana USA	63	H3	30 12N	92 18W
La Fé Cuba	67	H4	22 02N	84 15W
Laghouat Algeria	100	E14	33 49N	2 55E
Lago Argentino *l.* Argentina	73	C3	50 10S	72 30W
Lago de Chapala *l.* Mexico	66	D4	20 05N	103 00W
Lago de Maracaibo *l.* Venezuela	72	C15	9 50N	71 30W
Lago de Nicaragua *l.* Nicaragua	67	G2	11 50N	86 00W
Lago de Poopó *l.* Bolivia	72	D10	18 30S	67 20W
Lago di Bolsena *l.* Italy	81	C5	42 00N	12 00E
Lago di Como *l.* Italy	81	B6	46 00N	9 00E
Lago di Garda *l.* Italy	81	C6	45 00N	10 00E
Lago Maggiore *l.* Italy	81	B6	46 00N	8 00E
Lagos Nigeria	100	E9	6 27N	3 28E
Lagos Port.	79	A2	37 05N	8 40W
Lago Titicaca *l.* Peru/Bolivia	72	C10	16 00S	69 30W
La Grande Oregon USA	62	C6	45 21N	118 05W
La Grange Georgia USA	63	J3	33 02N	85 02W
La Guaira Venezuela	72	D16	10 38N	66 55W
Laguna Caratasca *l.* Honduras	67	H3	15 05N	84 00W
Laguna de Perlas *l.* Nicaragua	67	H2	12 30N	83 30W
Laguna Madre *l.* Mexico	66	E4	25 00N	98 00W
Laguna Mar Chiquita *l.* Argentina	73	E7	30 30S	62 30W
Lagunillas Venezuela	72	C16	10 07N	71 16W
Lahaina Hawaiian Islands	107	Y18	20 23N	156 40W
Lahontan Reservoir Nevada USA	64	D4	39 22N	119 08W
Lahore Pakistan	90	C6	31 34N	74 22E
Lai Chi Wo HK China	92	C3	22 32N	114 15E
Lajes Brazil	73	G8	27 48S	50 20W
La Junta Colorado USA	62	F4	37 59N	103 34W
Lake Alpine *tn.* California USA	64	D4	38 30N	120 00W
Lake Charles *tn.* Louisiana USA	63	H3	30 13N	93 13W
Lake City *tn.* Michigan USA	45	J3	44 19N	85 13W
Lake Gogebic Michigan USA	45	G4	46 30N	89 30W
Lake Isabella *tn.* California USA	64	D2	35 37N	118 28W
Lakeland Florida USA	63	K2	28 02N	81 59W
Lakemba Passage *sd.* Fiji	106	V16	18 10S	179 00W
Lake Orion *tn.* Michigan USA	46	C2	42 47N	83 13W
Lakeport California USA	62	B4	39 04N	122 56W
Lake Success California USA	64	D3	36 07N	118 55W
Lake Timsâh Egypt	101	S3	30 34N	32 18E
Lakeview Oregon USA	62	B5	42 13N	120 21W
Lake View *tn.* New York USA	48	D1	42 43N	78 56W
Lakshadweep *admin.* India	90	C1/C2	9 30N	73 00E
La Línea de la Concepción Sp.	79	C2	36 10N	5 21W
Lalitpur India	90	D4	24 42N	78 24E
Lalmanir Hat Bangladesh	91	K10	25 51N	89 34E
La Maddalena Italy	81	B4	41 13N	9 25E
La Mancha *admin.* Sp.	79	D3	39 10N	2 45W
Lamar Colorado USA	62	F4	38 04N	102 37W
Lambaréné Gabon	100	G7	0 41S	10 13E
Lambasa Fiji	106	U16	16 25S	179 24E
Lambert Glacier Antarctica	109		73 00S	70 00E
Lambertville New Jersey USA	65	C2	40 22N	74 57W
Lamego Port.	79	B4	41 05N	7 49W
La Mesa California USA	64	E1	32 45N	117 00W
Lamía Greece	81	J3	38 55N	22 26E
Lamma Island HK China	92	B1	22 12N	114 08E
Lampazos Mexico	66	D5	27 00N	100 30W
Lam Tei Hong Kong China	92	A2	22 25N	113 59E
Lamu Kenya	100	N7	2 17S	40 54E
Lanai *i.* Hawaiian Islands	107	Y18	20 50N	156 55W
Lanai City Hawaiian Islands	107	Y18	20 50N	156 56W
Lancang Jiang *r.* China	93	H4/H5	30 00N	98 00E
Lancaster UK	78	D11	54 03N	2 48W
Lancaster California USA	62	C3	34 42N	118 09W
Lancaster Ohio USA	63	K4	39 43N	82 37W
Lancaster Pennsylvania USA	63	L5	40 01N	76 19W
Land's End *c.* UK	78	C9	50 03N	5 44W
Landshut Germany	80	D8	48 31N	12 10E
Landskrona Sweden	80	D12	55 53N	12 50E
Langdon North Dakota USA	43	C1	48 50N	98 25W
Langon Fr.	79	E6	44 33N	0 14W
Langres Fr.	78	H7	47 53N	5 20E
Lannion Fr.	78	D8	48 44N	3 27W
L'Anse Michigan USA	45	G4	46 45N	88 26W
Lansing Michigan USA	63	K5	42 44N	85 34W
Lantau Channel HK China	92	A1	22 11N	113 52E
Lantau Island HK China	92	A1	22 15N	113 56E
Lantau Peak *mt.* HK China	92	A1	22 15N	113 55E
Lanzarote *i.* Canary Islands	100	B13	29 00N	13 38W
Lanzhou China	93	J6	36 01N	103 45E
Laoag Philippines	95	G7	18 14N	120 36E
Lao Cai Vietnam	93	J3	22 30N	103 57E
Laon Fr.	78	G8	49 34N	3 37E
La Oroya Peru	72	B11	11 36S	75 54W
LAOS	95	C7/D7		
La Paz Bolivia	72	D10	16 30S	68 10W
La Paz Mexico	66	B4	24 10N	110 17W
Lapeer Michigan USA	45	K2	43 03N	83 19W
La Pesca Mexico	66	E4	23 46N	97 47W
La Plata Argentina	73	F6	34 52S	57 55W
Laptev Sea Arctic Ocean	109		76 00N	125 00E
Laptev Strait Russia	87	S11	73 00N	141 00E
L'Aquila Italy	81	D5	42 22N	13 24E
Lār Iran	89	F4	27 42N	54 19E
Larache Morocco	100	C15	35 12N	6 10W
Laramie Wyoming USA	62	E5	41 20N	105 38W
Lärbro Sweden	80	G12	57 47N	18 50E
Laredo Texas USA	62	G2	27 32N	99 22W
La Rioja Argentina	73	D8	29 26S	66 50W
Lárisa Greece	81	J3	39 38N	22 25E
Larkana Pakistan	90	B5	27 32N	68 18E
Larnaca Cyprus	88	B5	34 54N	33 29E
Larne UK	78	C11	54 51N	5 49W
la Rochelle Fr.	79	E7	46 10N	1 10W
la Roche-sur-Yon Fr.	79	E7	46 40N	1 25W
La Romana Dom. Rep.	67	L3	18 27N	68 57W
Larsen Ice Shelf Antarctica	109		67 00S	62 00W
Las Cruces New Mexico USA	62	E3	32 18N	106 47W
La Serena Chile	73	C8	29 54S	71 18W
la Seyne-sur-Mer Fr.	79	H5	43 06N	5 53E
Lashio Myanmar	93	H3	22 58N	97 48E
Las Marismas *geog. reg.* Sp.	79	B2/C2	36 55N	6 00W
Las Palmas Canary Islands	100	A13	28 08N	15 27W
La Spézia Italy	81	B6	44 07N	9 48E
Las Vegas Nevada USA	62	C4	36 10N	115 10W
Las Vegas New Mexico USA	62	E4	35 36N	105 15W
Latacunga Ecuador	72	B13	0 58S	78 36W
Latakia Syria	88	C6	35 31N	35 47E
Latina Italy	81	D4	41 28N	12 53E
Latur India	90	D3	18 24N	76 34E
LATVIA	80	J12		
Lau Fau Shan HK China	92	A2	22 28N	113 59E
Launceston Aust.	103	J2	41 25S	147 07E
Laurel Mississippi USA	63	J3	31 41N	89 09W
Laurie Island South Orkney Islands	73	J1	61 30S	46 00W
Lausanne Switz.	79	J7	46 32N	6 39E
Laut *i.* Indonesia	95	F3	4 40S	116 00E
Lautoka Fiji	106	T16	17 36S	177 28E
Laval Fr.	78	E8	48 04N	0 45W
La Vega Dom. Rep.	67	K3	19 15N	70 33W
Laverton Aust.	102	D5	28 49S	122 25E
La Victoria Venezuela	72	D16	10 16N	67 21W
Lawrence Kansas USA	63	G4	38 58N	95 15W
Lawrence Massachusetts USA	65	E3	42 41N	71 11W
Lawrence Park *tn.* Pennsylvania USA	46	F2	42 08N	80 02W
Lawton Oklahoma USA	63	G3	34 36N	98 25W
Laylá Saudi Arabia	89	E3	22 16N	46 45E
Laysan *i.* Hawaiian Islands	106	J10	25 46N	171 44W
Laytonville California USA	64	B4	39 41N	123 29W
LEBANON	88	N11/P12		
Lebanon Missouri USA	63	H4	37 40N	92 40W
Lebanon Pennsylvania USA	65	B2	40 23N	76 20W
Lebu Chile	73	C6	37 38S	73 43W
Lecce Italy	81	G4	40 21N	18 11E
Leeds UK	78	E10	53 50N	1 35W
Leeuwarden Neths.	78	H10	53 12N	5 48E
Leeuwin, Cape Aust.	102	C4	34 24S	115 09E
Lee Vining California USA	64	D3	37 58N	119 09W
Leeward Islands Lesser Antilles	67	M3	17 30N	64 00W
Lefkáda *i.* Greece	81	H3	38 45N	20 40E
Le François Martinique	66	R12	14 37N	60 54W
Leganés Sp.	79	D4	40 20N	3 46WE

Legnica Poland	80	F9	51 12N	16 10E
le Havre Fr.	78	F8	49 30N	0 06E
Leicester UK	78	E10	52 38N	1 05W
Leiden Neths.	78	H10	52 10N	4 30E
Leipzig Germany	80	D9	51 20N	12 25E
Leiria Port.	79	A3	39 45N	8 49W
Leivadiá Greece	81	J3	38 26N	22 53E
Leizhou Bandao *p.* China	93	L3	21 00N	110 00E
Lek *r.* Neths.	78	H9	51 48N	4 47E
le Mans Fr.	78	F7	48 00N	0 12E
Lemoore California USA	64	D3	36 18N	119 47W
Lena *r.* Russia	87	Q10	70 00N	125 00E
Leninogorsk Kazakhstan	87	L7	50 23N	83 32E
Leninsk-Kuznetskiy Russia	87	L7	54 44N	86 13E
Lens Fr.	78	G9	50 26N	2 50E
Lensk Russia	87	P9	60 48N	114 55E
Leoben Austria	81	E7	47 23N	15 06E
León Mexico	66	D4	21 10N	101 42W
León Nicaragua	66	G2	12 24N	86 52W
León Sp.	79	C5	42 35N	5 34W
Leon *r.* Texas USA	63	G3	32 00N	98 00W
Leonora Aust.	102	D5	28 54S	121 20E
le Puy Fr.	79	G6	45 03N	3 53E
Léré Chad	100	G9	9 41N	14 17E
Le Roy New York USA	46	J2	42 59N	77 59W
Lerwick UK	78	E14	60 09N	1 09W
Les Abymes Guadeloupe	66	Q9	16 15N	61 31W
Les Cayes Haiti	67	K3	18 15N	73 46W
Leskovac SM	81	J5	43 00N	21 57E
LESOTHO	101	K2		
les Sables-d'Olonne Fr.	79	E7	46 30N	1 47W
Lesser Antilles *is.* W. Indies	67	L2	18 00N	65 00W
Lésvos *i.* Greece	81	L3	39 00N	26 00E
Leszno Poland	80	F9	51 51N	16 35E
Leticia Col.	72	C13	4 09S	69 57W
le Tréport Fr.	78	F9	50 04N	1 22E
Leuven Belgium	78	H9	50 53N	4 42E
Lévêque, Cape Aust.	102	D7	16 25S	122 55E
Levice Slovakia	80	G8	48 14N	18 35E
Levuka Fiji	106	U16	17 42N	178 50E
Lewis *i.* UK	78	B12	58 15N	6 30W
Lewiston Idaho USA	62	C6	46 25N	117 00W
Lewiston Maine USA	63	M5	44 08N	70 14W
Lewiston New York USA	45	M2	43 10N	79 02W
Lewistown Montana USA	62	E6	47 04N	109 26W
Lewistown Pennsylvania USA	65	B2	40 36N	77 34W
Lexington Kentucky USA	63	K4	38 03N	84 30W
Lexington Heights *tn.* Michigan USA	46	D3	43 15N	82 32W
Leyte *i.* Philippines	95	G6/H6	11 00N	125 00E
Lezhë Albania	81	G4	41 47N	19 39E
Lhasa China	92	G4	29 41N	91 10E
Lhaze China	92	F4	29 08N	87 43E
Lianyungang China	93	M5	34 37N	119 10E
Liaoyang China	93	N7	41 16N	123 12E
Liaoyuan China	93	P7	42 53N	125 10E
Libby Montana USA	39	N1	48 25N	115 33W
Libenge CDR	100	H8	3 39N	18 39E
Liberal Kansas USA	62	F4	37 03N	100 56W
Liberec Czech Rep.	80	E9	50 48N	15 05E
LIBERIA	100	B9/C9		
Liberty New York USA	65	C2	41 48N	74 44W
Libourne Fr.	79	E6	44 55N	0 14W
Libreville Gabon	100	F8	0 30N	9 25E
LIBYA	100	G13		
Libyan Desert North Africa	100	J13	25 00N	25 00E
Libyan Plateau Egypt	100	K14	31 00N	26 00E
Licata Italy	81	D2	37 07N	13 57E
Lichinga Mozambique	101	M5	13 19S	35 13E
Lidköping Sweden	80	D13	58 30N	13 10E
LIECHTENSTEIN	79	K7		
Liège Belgium	78	H9	50 38N	5 35E
Lienz Austria	81	D7	46 51N	12 50E
Liepaja Latvia	80	H12	56 30N	21 00E
Lifou *i.* Pacific Ocean	103	N6	21 00S	167 00E
Ligurian Sea Mediterranean Sea	81	B5	44 00N	9 00E
Lihue Hawaiian Islands	107	X18	21 59N	159 23W
Likasi CDR	101	K5	10 58S	26 47E
Lille Fr.	78	G9	50 39N	3 05E
Lilongwe Malawi	101	L5	13 58S	33 49E
Lim *r.* Europe	81	G5	43 00N	19 00E
Lima Peru	72	B11	12 04S	77 03W
Lima Ohio USA	63	K5	40 43N	84 06W
Lima *r.* Port.	79	A4	42 00N	8 30W
Limassol Cyprus	88	B5	34 04N	33 03E
Limay *r.* Argentina	73	D6	39 30S	69 30W
Limbe Cameroon	100	F8	3 58N	9 10E
Limerick RoI	78	A10	52 04N	8 38W
Limfjorden *sd.* Denmark	80	B12	57 00N	8 50E
Límnos *i.* Greece	81	K3	39 00N	25 00E
Limoges Fr.	79	F6	45 50N	1 15E
Limón Costa Rica	67	H2	10 00N	83 01W
Limoux Fr.	79	G5	43 03N	2 13E
Limpopo *r.* Southern Africa	101	L3	22 30S	32 00E
Linares Mexico	66	E4	24 54N	99 38W
Linares Sp.	79	D3	38 05N	3 38W
Lincoln UK	78	E10	53 14N	0 33W
Lincoln Nebraska USA	63	G5	40 49N	96 41W
Linden Guyana	72	F15	5 59N	58 19W
Linden New Jersey USA	65	H1	40 37N	74 13W
Line Islands Kiribati	107	L7	0 00	155 00W
Linhares Brazil	72	K10	19 22S	40 04W
Linköping Sweden	80	E13	58 25N	15 35E
Linton North Dakota USA	62	F6	46 17N	100 14W
Lin Tong Mei HK China	92	B2	22 29N	114 06E
Linxia China	93	J6	35 31N	103 08E
Linz Austria	80	E8	48 19N	14 18E
Lipetsk Russia	86	F7	52 37N	39 36E
Lisbon Port.	79	A3	38 44N	9 08W
Lisburn UK	78	B11	54 31N	6 03W
Lisianski *i.* Hawaiian Islands	106	J10	26 04N	173 58W
Lisieux Fr.	78	F8	49 09N	0 14E
Lismore Aust.	103	K5	28 48S	153 17E
Lītāni *r.* Lebanon	88	N11	33 35N	35 40E
Lithgow Aust.	103	K4	33 30S	150 09E
LITHUANIA	80	J11		
Little Aden Yemen	88	D1	12 47N	44 55E
Little Andaman *i.* Andaman Islands	91	G2	10 30N	92 40E
Little Bitter Lake Egypt	101	T2	30 14N	32 33E
Little Colorado *r.* Arizona USA	62	D4	36 00N	111 00W
Little Falls *tn.* Minnesota USA	63	H6	45 58N	94 20W
Little Missouri *r.* USA	62	F6	46 00N	104 00W
Little Nicobar *i.* Nicobar Islands	91	G1	7 00N	94 00E
Little Rock Kansas USA	63	H3	34 42N	92 17W
Little Sioux *r.* USA	63	G5	42 00N	96 00W
Little Snake *r.* USA	62	E5	41 00N	108 00W
Little Traverse Bay Michigan USA	46	A5	45 25N	85 00W
Liuzhou China	93	K3	24 17N	109 15E
Livermore California USA	64	C3	37 40N	121 46W
Liverpool UK	78	D10	53 25N	2 55W
Livingston Montana USA	62	D6	45 40N	110 33W
Livingstone Zambia	101	K4	17 50S	25 53E
Livingston Island South Shetland Islands	73	E1	62 38S	60 30W
Livorno Italy	81	C5	43 33N	10 18E
Liwale Tanzania	101	M6	9 47S	38 00E
Lizard Point UK	78	C8	49 56N	5 13W
Ljubljana Slovenia	81	E7	46 04N	14 30E
Ljungby Sweden	80	D12	56 49N	13 55E
Llanelli UK	78	C9	51 42N	4 10W
Llanos *geog. reg.* Venezuela	72	D15	7 30N	67 30W
Lleida Sp.	79	F4	41 37N	0 38E
Lobatse Botswana	101	K2	25 11S	25 40E
Lobito Angola	101	G5	12 20S	13 34E
Loch Ness *l.* UK	78	C12	57 02N	4 30W
Loch Tay *l.* UK	78	D12	56 31N	4 10W
Lockhart Texas USA	63	G2	29 54N	97 14W
Lock Haven *tn.* Pennsylvania USA	65	B2	41 09N	77 28W
Lockport New York USA	45	M2	43 10N	78 42W
Lod Israel	88	N10	31 57N	34 54E
Lodi California USA	64	C4	38 07N	121 18W
Łodz Poland	80	G9	51 49N	19 28E
Lo Fu Tau *mt.* HK China	92	A1	22 18N	114 00E
Logan Utah USA	62	D5	41 45N	111 50W
Logan, Mount Washington USA	38	H4	48 30N	121 00W
Logone *r.* Chad	100	G10	11 00N	15 00E
Logroño Sp.	79	D5	42 28N	2 26W
Loir *r.* Fr.	79	F7	47 30N	0 35E
Loire *r.* Fr.	79	E7	47 20N	1 20W
Loja Ecuador	72	B13	3 59S	79 16W
Loja Sp.	79	C2	37 10N	4 09W
Lok Ma Chau HK China	92	B3	22 31N	114 05E
Lokoja Nigeria	100	F9	7 49N	6 44E
Lol *r.* Sudan	100	K9	9 00N	28 00E
Lolland *i.* Denmark	80	C11	54 45N	12 20E
Lomami *r.* CDR	100	K6	5 30S	25 30E
Lomblen *i.* Indonesia	95	G2	8 30S	123 30E
Lombok *i.* Indonesia	95	F2	8 30S	116 30E
Lomé Togo	100	E9	6 10N	1 21E
Lomela CDR	100	J7	2 19S	23 15E
Lomela *r.* CDR	100	J7	3 00S	23 00E
Lompoc California USA	64	C2	34 39N	120 27W
Łomza Poland	80	J10	53 11N	22 04E
London UK	78	E9	51 30N	0 10W
Londonderry UK	78	B11	54 59N	7 19W
Londrina Brazil	72	G9	23 18S	51 13W
Lone Pine California USA	64	D3	36 35N	118 04W
Long Beach *tn.* California USA	62	C3	33 47N	118 15W
Long Beach Island New Jersey USA	65	C1	39 40N	74 15W
Long Branch New Jersey USA	63	M5	40 17N	73 59W
Longfellow Mountains Maine USA	47	R5/S5	45 10N	70 00W
Longford RoI	78	B10	53 44N	7 47W
Long Island Bahamas	67	J4/K4	23 20N	75 00W
Long Island New York USA	65	D2	40 43N	73 05W
Long Island City New York USA	65	J2	40 46N	73 55W
Long Island Sound New York USA	65	D2	40 50N	73 05W
Long Lake Maine USA	51	F2	47 14N	68 18W
Longreach Aust.	103	H6	23 30S	144 15E
Longview Texas USA	63	H3	32 20N	94 45W
Longview Washington USA	62	B6	46 08N	122 56W
Longwy Fr.	78	H8	49 32N	5 46E
Lopez, Cape Gabon	100	F7	0 36S	8 45E
Lopez Island Washington USA	38	H4	48 25N	123 05W
Lop Nur *l.* China	92	G7	40 15N	90 20E
Lorain Ohio USA	63	K5	41 28N	82 11W
Lorca Sp.	79	E2	37 40N	1 41W
Lord Howe Rise Pacific Ocean	106	F5	27 30S	162 00E
Lorient Fr.	78	D7	47 45N	3 21W
Los Alamos Mexico USA	62	E4	35 52N	106 19W
Los Angeles Chile	73	C6	37 28S	72 23W
Los Angeles California USA	62	C3	34 00N	118 15W
Los Angeles Aqueduct California USA	64	D2	35 12N	118 08W
Los Banos California USA	64	C3	37 03N	120 53W
Los Gatos California USA	64	C3	37 13N	121 57W
Los Mochis Mexico	66	C5	25 48N	109 00W
Los Teques Venezuela	72	D16	10 25N	67 01W
Lot *r.* Fr.	79	F6	44 35N	1 10E
Louangphrabang Laos	95	C7	19 53N	102 10E
Loubomo Congo	100	G7	4 09S	12 47E
Loudéac Fr.	78	D8	48 11N	2 45W
Lough Corrib *l.* RoI	78	A10	53 10N	9 10W
Lough Derg *l.* RoI	78	A10	52 55N	8 15W
Lough Mask *l.* RoI	78	A10	53 40N	9 30W
Lough Neagh *l.* UK	78	B11	54 35N	6 30W
Lough Ree *l.* RoI	78	B10	53 35N	8 00W
Louisade Archipelago *is.* PNG	103	K8	12 00S	153 00E
Louisiana *state* USA	63	H3	32 00N	92 00W
Louis Trichardt RSA	101	K3	23 01S	29 43E
Louisville Kentucky USA	63	J4	38 13N	85 48W
Lourdes Fr.	79	E5	43 06N	0 02W
Lowell Massachusetts USA	63	M5	42 38N	71 19W
Lower Bay New York USA	65	H1	40 32N	74 04W
Lower Hutt NZ	103	P2	41 13S	174 55E
Lower Lake *tn.* California USA	64	B4	38 55N	122 37W
Lower Lough Erne *l.* UK	78	B11	54 30N	7 45W
Lower Red Lake Minnesota USA	63	H6	48 00N	95 00W
Lowestoft UK	78	F10	52 29N	1 45E
Łowicz Poland	80	G10	52 06N	19 55E
Lo Wu HK China	92	B3	22 32N	114 07E
Lowville New York USA	45	P2	43 47N	75 29W
Loznica SM	81	G6	44 31N	19 14E
Lualaba *r.* CDR	100	K7	4 00S	26 30E
Luanda Angola	101	G6	8 50S	13 15E
Luangwa *r.* Zambia	101	L5	12 00S	32 30E
Luanshya Zambia	101	K5	13 09S	28 24E
Luarca Sp.	79	B5	43 33N	6 31W
Luau Angola	101	J5	10 42S	22 12E
Lubango Angola	101	G5	14 55S	13 30E
Lubbock Texas USA	62	F3	33 35N	101 53W
Lübeck Germany	80	C10	53 52N	10 40E
Lubilash *r.* CDR	101	J6	4 00S	24 00E
Lublin Poland	80	J9	51 18N	22 31E
Lubumbashi CDR	101	K5	11 41S	27 29E
Lucena Sp.	79	C2	37 25N	4 29W
Luckenwalde Germany	80	D10	52 05N	13 11E
Lucknow India	90	E5	26 50N	80 54E
Lucusse Angola	101	J5	12 38S	20 52E
Lüderitz Namibia	101	H2	26 38S	15 10E
Ludhiana India	90	D6	30 56N	75 52E
Ludington Michigan USA	45	H2	43 57N	86 26W
Luena Angola	101	H5	11 47S	19 52E
Lufkin Texas USA	63	H3	31 21N	94 47W
Lugo Sp.	79	B5	43 00N	7 33W
Lugoj Romania	81	H6	45 41N	21 57E
Luiana *r.* Angola	101	J4	17 00S	21 00E
Luk Keng HK China	92	C3	22 32N	114 13E
Łuków Poland	80	J9	51 57N	22 21E
Lulua *r.* CDR	101	J6	9 00S	22 00E
Lumberton North Carolina USA	63	L3	34 37N	79 03W
Lummi Island Washington USA	38	H4	48 40N	122 36W
Lund Sweden	80	D12	55 42N	13 10E
Lund Nevada USA	64	F4	38 53N	115 01W
Lüneburg Germany	80	C10	53 15N	10 24E
Lunéville Fr.	78	J8	48 35N	6 30E
Lung Kwu Chau *i.* HK China	92	A2	22 23N	113 53E
Lunglei India	91	M9	22 54N	92 49E
Lungue Bungo *r.* Angola/Zambia	101	J5	13 00S	22 00E
Luni *r.* India	90	C5	26 00N	73 00E
Luoshan China	93	L5	31 12N	114 30E
Luoyang China	93	L5	34 47N	112 26E
Lurgan UK	78	B11	54 28N	6 20W
Lurio *r.* Mozambique	101	M5	14 00S	39 00E
Lusaka Zambia	101	K4	15 26S	28 20E
Lusambo CDR	100	J7	4 59S	23 26E
Lüshun China	93	N6	38 46N	121 15E
Luton UK	78	E9	51 53N	0 25W
Luts'k Ukraine	80	K9	50 42N	25 15E
Luuq Somalia	100	N8	2 52N	42 34E
LUXEMBOURG	78	H8		
Luxembourg Luxembourg	78	J8	49 37N	6 08E
Luxor Egypt	100	L13	25 41N	32 24E
Luzern Switz.	79	K7	47 03N	8 17E
Luzhou China	93	K4	28 55N	105 25E
Luziânia Brazil	72	H10	16 16S	47 57W
Luzon *i.* Philippines	95	G7	15 00N	122 00E
Luzon Strait China/Philippines	95	G8	20 00N	121 30E
L'viv Ukraine	80	K8	49 50N	24 00E
Lyna *r.* Poland	80	H11	54 00N	20 00E
Lynchburg Virginia USA	63	L4	37 24N	79 09W
Lynden Washington USA	38	H4	48 56N	122 28W
Lynn Massachusetts USA	65	E3	42 28N	70 58W
Lynn Canal *sd.* Alaska USA	38	C6	58 50N	135 05W
Lyons Fr.	79	H6	45 46N	4 50E
Lyons New York USA	45	N2	43 04N	76 59W

M

Ma'ān Jordan	88	C5	30 11N	35 43E
Ma'anshan China	93	M5	31 49N	118 32E
Maastricht Neths.	78	H9	50 51N	5 42E
Mabalane Mozambique	101	L3	23 51S	32 38E
McAlester Oklahoma USA	63	G3	34 56N	95 46W
McAllen Texas USA	63	G2	26 13N	98 15W
Macao China	93	L3	22 10N	113 40E
Macapá Brazil	72	G14	0 04N	51 04W
Macarata Italy	81	D5	43 18N	13 27E
McClure, Lake California USA	64	C3	37 38N	120 16W
McComb Mississippi USA	63	H3	31 13N	90 29W
McCook Nebraska USA	62	F5	40 13N	100 35W
McDonald, Lake Montana USA	41	E1/F1	48 50N	114 00W
Macdonnell Ranges *mts.* Aust.	102	F6	24 00S	132 30E
Maceió Brazil	72	K12	9 40S	35 44W
Machala Ecuador	72	B13	3 20S	79 57W
Machanga Mozambique	101	L3	20 58N	35 01E
Machias Maine USA	51	G1	44 50N	67 20W
Machiques Venezuela	72	C16	10 04N	72 37W
Mackay Aust.	103	J6	21 10S	149 10E
Mackay, Lake Aust.	102	E6	22 30S	128 00E
Mackinac, Straits of *sd.* Michigan USA	46	B5	45 48N	84 43W
Mackinaw City Michigan USA	63	K6	45 47N	84 43W
McKinney Texas USA	63	G3	33 14N	96 37W
Macleod, Lake Aust.	102	B6	24 00S	113 30E
Mâcon Fr.	79	H7	46 18N	4 50E
Macon Georgia USA	63	K3	32 49N	83 37W
McPherson Kansas USA	63	G4	38 22N	97 41W
Macquarie Island Southern Ocean	106	F2	54 29S	158 58E
Macquarie Ridge Southern Ocean	106	F2	55 00S	160 00E
Mādabā Jordan	88	N10	31 44N	35 48E
MADAGASCAR	101	P2/P5		
Madagascar Basin Indian Ocean	105	E4	25 00S	55 00E
Madagascar Ridge Indian Ocean	105	D3	30 00S	45 00E
Madang PNG	103	J9	5 14S	145 45E
Madaripur Bangladesh	91	L9	23 09N	90 11E
Madden Lake Panama	67	Y2	9 15N	79 35W
Madeira *r.* Brazil	72	E12	6 00S	61 30W
Madeira Islands Atlantic Ocean	100	A14	32 45N	17 00W
Madera California USA	64	C3	36 59N	120 12W
Madhya Pradesh *admin.* India	90	D4/E4	23 00N	78 30E
Madīnat ash Sha'b Yemen	88	D1	12 50N	44 56E
Madison Maine USA	47	S4	44 48N	69 53W
Madison Wisconsin USA	63	J5	43 04N	89 22W
Madiun Indonesia	95	E2	7 37S	111 33E
Mado Gashi Kenya	100	M8	0 45N	39 11E
Madre de Dios *r.* Bolivia	72	D11	12 00S	68 00W
Madrid Sp.	79	D4	40 25N	3 43W
Madura *i.* Indonesia	95	E2	7 00S	113 00E
Madurai India	90	D1	9 55N	78 07E
Maebashi Japan	94	C2	36 24N	139 04E
Maevantanana Madagascar	101	P4	16 57S	46 50E
Mafia Island Tanzania	101	M6	7 00S	39 00E
Mafikeng RSA	101	K2	25 53S	25 39E
Mafraq Jordan	88	C5	32 20N	36 12E
Magadan Russia	87	T8	59 38N	150 50E
Magangué Col.	72	C15	9 14N	74 47W
Magdalena Mexico	66	B6	30 38N	110 59W
Magdalena *r.* Col.	72	C15	8 00N	73 30W
Magdeburg Germany	80	C10	52 08N	11 37E
Magelang Indonesia	95	E2	7 28S	110 11E
Magnitogorsk Russia	86	H7	53 28N	59 06E
Mahadeo Hills India	90	D4	22 30N	78 30E
Mahajanga Madagascar	101	P4	15 40S	46 20E
Mahanadi *r.* India	91	E4	21 00N	85 00E
Maharashtra *admin.* India	90	C3	19 30N	75 00E
Mahón Sp.	79	H3	39 54N	4 15E
Maiduguri Nigeria	100	G10	11 53N	13 16E
Main *r.* Germany	80	B8	50 00N	8 00E
Maine *state* USA	63	N6	45 00N	70 00W
Mainland *i.* Orkney Islands UK	78	D13	59 00N	3 15W
Mainland *i.* Shetland Islands UK	78	E14	60 15N	1 20W
Maintirano Madagascar	101	N4	18 01S	44 03E
Mainz Germany	80	B8	50 00N	8 16E
Mai Po Hong Kong China	92	B2	22 29N	114 03E
Maiquetía Venezuela	72	D16	10 38N	66 59W
Maiskhal Island Bangladesh	91	L8	21 36N	91 53E
Maitland Aust.	103	K4	32 33S	151 33E
Maizuru Japan	94	C2	35 30N	135 20E
Majene Indonesia	95	F3	3 33S	118 59E
Maji Ethiopia	100	M9	6 12N	35 32E
Makassar Strait *sd.* Indonesia	95	F3/F4	0 00	119 00E
Makeni Sierra Leone	100	B9	8 57N	12 02W
Makgadikgadi Salt Pan Botswana	101	K3	21 00S	26 00E
Makhachkala Russia	86	G5	42 59N	47 30E
Makó Hungary	81	H7	46 11N	20 30E
Makokou Gabon	100	G8	0 38N	12 47E
Makurdi Nigeria	100	F9	7 44N	8 35E
Malabar Coast India	90	C2/D1	12 00N	74 00E
Malabo Eq. Guinea	100	F8	3 45N	8 48E
Malacca, Strait of Indonesia	95	B5/C4	4 00N	100 00E
Málaga Sp.	79	C2	36 43N	4 25W
Malaga New Jersey USA	65	C1	39 34N	75 03W
Malaita *i.* Solomon Islands	103	M9	9 00S	161 00E
Malakal Sudan	100	L9	9 31N	31 40E
Malang Indonesia	95	E2	7 59S	112 45E
Malanje Angola	101	H6	9 32S	16 20E
Mälaren *l.* Sweden	80	F13	59 30N	17 00E
Malaspina Glacier Alaska USA	54	B2	59 50N	140 40W
Malatya Turkey	88	C6	38 22N	38 18E
MALAWI	101	L5		
MALAYSIA	95	C5/E5		
Malbork Poland	80	G11	54 02N	19 01E
MALDIVES	105	G7		
Maldonado Uruguay	73	G7	34 57S	54 59W

Malegaon India	90	C4	20 32N	74 38E
Malekula *i.* Vanuatu	103	N7	16 30S	167 20E
Malema Mozambique	101	M5	14 57S	37 25E
MALI	100	C10		
Malin Head *c.* RoI	78	B11	55 30N	7 20W
Ma Liu Shui HK China	92	C2	22 25N	114 12E
Mallaig UK	78	C12	57 00N	5 50W
Mallorca *i.* Sp.	79	G3	39 50N	2 30E
Malmédy Belgium	78	J9	50 26N	6 02E
Malmesbury RSA	101	H1	33 28S	18 43E
Malmö Sweden	80	D12	55 35N	13 00E
Malone New York USA	45	P3	44 51N	74 18W
Malonga CDR	101	J5	10 26S	23 10E
Malpelo *i.* Col.	72	A14	4 00N	81 35W
MALTA	81	E1		
Malta Montana USA	62	E6	48 22N	107 51W
Malta *i.* Mediterranean Sea	81	E1	35 00N	14 00E
Maluku *is.* Indonesia	95	H3	4 00S	127 00E
Mamanutha Group *is.* Fiji	106	T16	17 40S	177 00E
Mambasa CDR	100	K8	1 20N	29 05E
Mammoth Lakes *tn.* California USA	64	D3	37 38N	118 58W
Mamoré *r.* Bolivia	72	E10	15 00S	65 00W
Man Côte d'Ivoire	100	C9	7 31N	7 37W
Manacapuru Brazil	72	E13	3 16S	60 37W
Manacor Sp.	79	G3	39 35N	3 12E
Manado Indonesia	95	G4	1 32N	124 55E
Managua Nicaragua	67	G2	12 06N	86 18W
Manali India	90	D6	32 12N	77 06E
Manama Bahrain	89	F4	26 12N	50 38E
Manas *r.* India/Bhutan	91	L11	27 00N	91 00E
Manaus Brazil	72	F13	3 06S	60 00W
Manchester UK	78	D10	53 30N	2 15W
Manchester California USA	64	B4	38 58N	123 42W
Manchester Connecticut USA	65	D2	41 47N	72 32W
Manchester Michigan USA	46	B2	42 10N	84 01W
Manchester New Hampshire USA	63	M5	42 59N	71 28W
Manchester Tennessee USA	63	J4	35 29N	86 04W
Mandal Norway	78	J13	58 02N	7 30E
Mandalay Myanmar	92	H3	21 57N	96 04E
Mandeville Jamaica	67	U14	18 02N	77 31W
Manfredonia Italy	81	E4	41 37N	15 55E
Mangalore India	90	C2	12 54N	74 51E
Mango *i.* Fiji	106	V16	17 20S	179 20W
Mangoky *r.* Madagascar	101	N3	22 00S	45 00E
Mangui China	93	N9	52 05N	122 17E
Manhattan Kansas USA	63	G4	39 11N	96 35W
Manhattan Nevada USA	64	E4	38 31N	117 05W
Manhattan New York USA	65	J2	40 48N	73 58W
Mania *r.* Madagascar	101	P4	19 30S	50 30E
Manica Mozambique	101	L4	18 56S	32 52E
Manicoré Brazil	72	E12	5 48S	61 16W
Manila Philippines	95	G6	14 37N	120 58E
Manipur *admin.* India	91	G4	24 30N	94 00E
Manipur *r.* India/Myanmar	91	G4	24 00N	93 00E
Manistee Michigan USA	45	H3	44 14N	86 19W
Manistee River Michigan USA	45	J3	44 20N	85 30W
Manistique Michigan USA	45	H3	45 57N	86 14W
Manistique Lake Michigan USA	46	A6	46 25N	85 45W
Manitowoc Wisconsin USA	63	J5	44 04N	87 40W
Manizales Col.	72	B15	5 03N	75 32W
Manjra *r.* India	90	D3	18 30N	77 30E
Man Kam To HK China	92	B3	22 32N	114 08E
Mankato Minnesota USA	63	H5	44 10N	94 00W
Mannar Sri Lanka	90	D1	8 58N	79 54E
Mannar, Gulf of India/Sri Lanka	90	D1	8 30N	79 00E
Mannheim Germany	80	B8	49 30N	8 28E
Manokwari Indonesia	95	J3	0 53S	134 05E
Manresa Sp.	79	F4	41 43N	1 50E
Mansa Zambia	101	K5	11 10S	28 52E
Mansfield Ohio USA	63	K5	40 46N	82 31W
Mansfield Pennsylvania USA	47	J1	41 47N	77 05W
Manta Ecuador	72	A13	0 59S	80 44W
Manteca California USA	64	C3	37 50N	121 16W
Mantes-la-Jolie Fr.	78	F8	48 59N	1 43E
Manuta Italy	81	C6	45 10N	10 47E
Manyoni Tanzania	100	L6	5 46S	34 50E
Manzanares Sp.	79	D3	39 00N	3 23W
Manzanillo Cuba	67	J4	20 21N	77 21W
Manzanillo Mexico	66	D3	19 00N	104 20W
Manzhouli China	93	M8	46 36N	117 28E
Maoming China	93	L3	21 50N	110 56E
Ma On Shan HK China	92	C2	22 26N	114 13E
Ma On Shan *mt.* HK China	92	C2	22 24N	114 16E
Maple Heights *tn.* Ohio USA	46	E1	41 24N	81 35W
Maputo Mozambique	101	L2	25 58S	32 35E
Marabá Brazil	72	H12	5 23S	49 10W
Maracaibo Venezuela	72	C16	10 44N	71 37W
Maracay Venezuela	72	D16	10 20N	67 28W
Maradi Niger	100	F10	13 29N	7 10E
Maranhão *admin.* Brazil	72	H12	5 20S	46 00W
Marañón *r.* Peru	72	B13	4 50S	77 30W
Marbella Sp.	79	C2	36 31N	4 53W
Marble Bar *tn.* Aust.	102	C6	21 16S	119 45E
Marble Canyon *tn.* Arizona USA	62	D4	36 50N	111 38W
Marburg Germany	80	B9	50 49N	8 36E
Marcus Island Pacific Ocean	106	F10	24 30N	157 30E
Mardan Pakistan	90	C6	34 14N	72 05E
Mar del Plata Argentina	73	F6	38 00S	57 32W
Mardin Turkey	88	D6	37 19N	40 43E
Mare *i.* Pacific Ocean	103	N6	22 00S	167 30E
Maria Elena Chile	72	D9	22 18S	69 40W
Marianas Trench Pacific Ocean	106	E9	16 00N	147 30E
Maribor Slovenia	81	E7	46 34N	15 38E
Maricopa California USA	64	D2	34 04N	119 25W
Marie Byrd Land *geog. reg.* Antarctica	109		77 00S	130 00W
Marie Galente *i.* Lesser Antilles	66	Q8	15 56N	61 16W
Mariehamn Finland	80	G14	60 05N	19 55E
Mariental Namibia	101	H3	24 36S	17 59E
Mariestad Sweden	80	D13	58 44N	13 50E
Marigot Dominica	66	Q8	15 32N	61 18W
Marijampole Lithuania	80	J11	54 31N	23 20E
Marília Brazil	72	G9	22 13S	49 58W
Maringá Brazil	72	G9	23 26S	52 02W
Marion Ohio USA	63	K5	40 35N	83 08W
Marion, Lake South Carolina USA	63	K3	33 00N	80 00W
Mariposa California USA	64	D3	37 30N	119 59W
Mariscal Estigarribia Paraguay	72	E9	22 03S	60 35W
Marjayoûn Lebanon	88	N11	33 22N	35 34E
Marka Somalia	100	N8	1 42N	44 47E
Markha *r.* Russia	87	P9	64 00N	12 30E
Markovo Russia	87	V9	64 40N	170 24E
Marlette Michigan USA	46	C3	43 20N	83 04W
Marmara, Sea of Turkey	88	A7	15 40N	28 10E
Maroantsetra Madagascar	101	P4	15 23S	49 44E
Maroni *r.* Suriname	72	G14	4 00N	54 30W
Maroua Cameroon	100	G10	10 35N	14 20E
Marquesas Islands Pacific Ocean	107	N7	10 00S	137 00W
Marquette Michigan USA	63	J6	46 33N	87 23W
Marrakesh Morocco	100	C14	31 49N	8 00W
Marsabit Kenya	100	M8	2 20N	37 59E
Marsala Italy	81	D2	37 48N	12 27E
Marseilles Fr.	79	H5	43 18N	5 22E
MARSHALL ISLANDS	106	G9		
Marshfield Wisconsin USA	45	F3	44 40N	90 10W
Martaban, Gulf of Myanmar	95	B7	15 30N	92 30E
Martha's Vineyard *is.* Massachusetts USA	65	E2	41 18N	70 37W
Martinique *i.* Lesser Antilles	66	R12	14 30N	61 00W
Martin Lake Alabama USA	63	J3	33 00N	86 00W
Martinsburg West Virginia USA	65	B1	39 26N	77 58W
Martinsville Virginia USA	63	L4	36 43N	79 53W
Martin Vaz *i.* Atlantic Ocean	108	F4	21 00S	27 30W
Mary Turkmenistan	86	J4	37 42N	61 54E
Maryborough Aust.	103	K5	25 32S	152 36E
Maryland *state* USA	63	L4	39 00N	77 00W
Marysville California USA	62	B4	39 10N	121 34W
Masada *hist. site* Israel	88	N10	31 17N	35 20E
Masan South Korea	93	P6	35 10N	128 35E
Masaya Nicaragua	67	G2	11 59N	86 03W
Masbate *i.* Philippines	95	G6	12 21N	123 36E
Mascarene Basin Indian Ocean	105	E5	15 00S	55 00E
Maseru Lesotho	101	K2	29 19S	27 29E
Mashhad Iran	89	G6	36 16N	59 34E
Masindi Uganda	100	L8	1 41N	31 45E
Maṣīrah *i.* Oman	89	G3	20 25N	58 40E
Mason Michigan USA	46	B2	42 34N	84 27W
Mason City Iowa USA	63	H5	43 10N	93 10W
Massachusetts *state* USA	63	M5	42 00N	72 00W
Massachusetts Bay Massachusetts USA	65	E3	42 00N	70 00W
Massawa Eritrea	100	M11	15 42N	39 25E
Massena New York USA	63	M5	44 56N	74 57W
Massif Central *mts.* Fr.	79	G6	45 00N	3 30E
Massif de L'Isola *mts.* Madagascar	101	N3/P3	23 00S	45 00E
Massif des Bongos *mts.* CAR	100	J9	9 00N	23 00E
Massif de Tsaratanana *mts.* Madagascar	101	P5	14 00S	49 00E
Masuda Japan	94	B1	34 42N	131 51E
Masuku Gabon	100	G7	1 40S	13 31E
Masvingo Zimbabwe	101	L3	20 05S	30 50E
Matachel *r.* Sp.	79	B3	38 40N	6 00W
Matadi CDR	101	G6	5 50S	13 32E
Matagalpa Nicaragua	67	G2	12 52N	85 58W
Matale Sri Lanka	90	E1	7 28N	80 37E
Matamoros Mexico	66	D5	25 33N	103 51W
Matamoros Mexico	66	E5	25 50N	97 31W
Matanzas Cuba	67	H4	23 04N	81 35W
Matara Sri Lanka	90	E1	5 57N	80 32E
Mataram Indonesia	95	F2	8 36S	116 07E
Mataró Sp.	79	G4	41 32N	2 27E
Matehuala Mexico	66	D4	23 40N	100 40W
Matera Italy	81	F4	40 40N	16 37E
Mathura India	90	D5	27 30N	77 42E
Matla *r.* India	91	K8/K9	22 00N	88 35E
Mato Grosso *admin.* Brazil	72	F11	14 00S	56 00W
Mato Grosso *tn.* Brazil	72	F10	15 05S	59 57W
Mato Grosso do Sul *admin.* Brazil	72	G9	20 00S	55 00W
Matopo Hills Zimbabwe	101	K3	21 00S	28 30E
Matosinhos Port.	79	A4	41 08N	8 45W
Maṭraḥ Oman	89	G3	23 31N	58 18E
Matsudo Japan	94	C2	35 46N	139 54E
Matsue Japan	94	B2	35 29N	133 04E
Matsumoto Japan	94	C2	36 18N	137 58E
Matsuyama Japan	94	B1	33 50N	132 47E
Matterhorn *mt.* Switz.	79	J6	45 59N	7 39E
Matthew *i.* New Caledonia	103	P6	22 20S	171 20E
Matuku *i.* Fiji	106	U15	19 11S	179 45E
Maturín Venezuela	72	E15	9 45N	63 10W
Maubeuge Fr.	78	G9	50 17N	3 58E
Maués Brazil	72	F13	3 22S	57 38W
Maui *i.* Hawaiian Islands	107	Y18	21 00N	156 30W
Maulvi Bazar Bangladesh	91	L10	24 30N	91 48E
Maumee Ohio USA	45	K1	41 34N	83 40W
Maumee River Ohio USA	45	K1	41 34N	83 40W
Maumere Indonesia	95	G2	8 35S	122 13E
Mauna Kea *mt.* Hawaiian Islands	107	Z17	19 50N	155 25W
Mauna Loa *vol.* Hawaiian Islands	107	Z17	19 28N	155 35W
Maungdaw Myanmar	91	M8	20 47N	92 26E
MAURITANIA	100	B11		
MAURITIUS	105	E4		
Ma Wan *i.* HK China	92	B2	22 21N	114 03E
Ma Wan Chung HK China	92	A1	22 17N	113 56E
Mawlaik Myanmar	92	G3	23 40N	94 26E
Mayādīn Syria	88	D6	35 01N	40 28E
Mayaguana *i.* Bahamas	67	K4	22 30N	72 40W
Mayagüez Puerto Rico	67	L3	18 13N	67 09W
Mayenne *r.* Fr.	78	E7	47 45N	0 50W
Maykop Russia	86	G5	44 37N	40 48E
Mayotte *i.* Indian Ocean	101	P5	13 00S	45 00E
May Pen Jamaica	67	U13	17 58N	77 15W
Mayumba Gabon	100	G7	3 23S	10 38E
Mayville New York USA	46	G2	42 15N	79 32W
Mazabuka Zambia	101	K4	15 50S	27 47E
Mazama Washington USA	38	H4	48 40N	120 15W
Mazār-e Sharīf Afghanistan	89	J6	36 42N	67 06E
Mazatenango Guatemala	66	F2	14 31N	91 30W
Mazatlán Mexico	66	C4	23 11N	106 25W
Mazeikiai Lithuania	80	J12	56 20N	22 22E
Mazirbe Latvia	80	J12	57 40N	22 21E
Mbabane Swaziland	101	L2	26 20S	31 08E
Mbaiki CAR	100	H8	3 53N	18 01E
Mbala Zambia	101	L6	8 50S	31 24E
Mbalmayo Cameroon	100	G8	3 30N	11 31E
Mbandaka CDR	100	H8	0 03N	18 28E
Mbengga *i.* Fiji	106	U15	18 24S	178 09E
Mbeya Tanzania	101	L6	8 54S	33 29E
Mbuji-Mayi CDR	101	J6	6 10S	23 39E
Mead, Lake USA	62	D4	36 10N	114 25W
Meadville Pennsylvania USA	63	K5	41 38N	80 10W
Meaux Fr.	78	G8	48 58N	2 54E
Mecca Saudi Arabia	88	C3	21 26N	39 49E
Mechelen Belgium	78	H9	51 02N	4 29E
Mecheria Algeria	100	D14	33 31N	0 20W
Mecklenburg Bay Europe	80	C11	54 00N	12 00E
Medan Indonesia	95	B4	3 35N	98 39E
Medellín Col.	72	B15	6 15N	75 36W
Medenine Tunisia	100	G14	33 24N	10 25E
Medford Oregon USA	62	B5	42 20N	122 52W
Medford Wisconsin USA	45	F3	45 08N	90 21W
Medina Saudi Arabia	88	C3	24 30N	39 35E
Medina New York USA	46	H3	43 13N	78 23W
Medina del Campo Sp.	79	C4	41 18N	4 55W
Medinipur India	91	F4	22 25N	87 24E
Mediterranean Sea Africa/Europe	79	D1/K3	35 00N	15 00E
Medvezh'yegorsk Russia	86	F9	62 56N	34 28E
Meekatharra Aust.	102	C5	26 30S	118 30E
Meerut India	90	D5	29 00N	77 42E
Mega Ethiopia	100	M8	4 02N	38 19E
Meghalaya *admin.* India	91	G5	25 30N	91 00E
Meizhou China	93	M3	24 19N	116 13E
Mekele Ethiopia	100	M10	13 32N	39 33E
Meknès Morocco	100	C14	33 53N	5 37W
Mekong *r.* Asia	95	C8	16 00N	105 00E
Mekong, Mouths of the *est.* Vietnam	95	D5	9 30N	106 45E
Melaka Malaysia	95	C4	2 11N	102 14E
Melanesia *geog. reg.* Pacific Ocean	106	E8	0 00	150 00E
Melbourne Aust.	103	H3	37 45S	144 58E
Melbourne Florida USA	63	K2	28 04N	80 38W
Melilla *territory* Sp.	79	D1	35 17N	2 57W
Melo Uruguay	73	G7	32 22S	54 10W
Melun Fr.	78	G8	48 32N	2 40E
Melville, Cape Aust.	103	H8	14 08S	144 31E
Melville Island Aust.	102	F8	11 30S	131 00E
Memmingen Germany	80	C7	47 59N	10 11E
Memphis Tennessee USA	63	J4	35 10N	90 00W
Mende Fr.	79	G6	44 32N	3 30E
Menderes *r.* Turkey	88	A6	37 50N	28 10E
Mendi PNG	103	H9	6 13S	143 39E
Mendocino California USA	64	B4	39 20N	123 47W
Mendocino Seascarp Pacific Ocean	107	M12	41 00N	145 00W
Mendota California USA	64	C3	36 44N	120 24W
Mendoza Argentina	73	D7	32 48S	68 52W
Mengdingjie China	93	H3	23 03N	99 03E
Menongue Angola	101	H5	14 36S	17 48E
Menorca *i.* Sp.	79	G4	39 45N	4 15E
Mentawai Islands Indonesia	105	J7	2 00N	99 00E
Mentor Ohio USA	63	K5	41 42N	81 22W
Merauke Indonesia	103	H9	8 30S	140 22E
Merced California USA	62	B4	37 17N	120 29W
Mercedes Argentina	73	D7	33 41S	65 28W
Mercedes Uruguay	73	F7	34 15S	58 02W
Mergui Myanmar	95	B6	12 26N	98 34E
Mergui Archipelago *is.* Myanmar	95	B6	11 00N	97 40E
Mérida Mexico	66	G4	20 59N	89 39W
Mérida Sp.	79	B3	38 55N	6 20W
Mérida Venezuela	72	C15	8 24N	71 08W
Meriden Connecticut USA	65	D2	41 32N	72 49W
Meridian Mississippi USA	63	J3	32 21N	88 42W
Merowe Sudan	100	L11	18 30N	31 49E
Mersin Turkey	88	B6	36 47N	34 37E
Merthyr Tydfil UK	78	D9	51 46N	3 23W
Mesa Arizona USA	62	D3	33 25N	111 50W
Mesabi Range *mts.* Minnesota USA	45	E4	47 30N	92 56W
Mesolóngi Greece	81	H3	38 21N	21 26E
Mesopotamia *geog. reg.* Middle East	88	D6	35 00N	42 00E
Mesquite Lake California USA	64	F2	35 43N	115 36W
Messina Italy	81	E3	38 13N	15 33E
Messina RSA	101	K3	22 23S	30 00E
Meta *r.* Col.	72	C15	6 00N	71 00W
Methow River Washington USA	38	H4	48 40N	120 15W
Metlakatla Alaska USA	38	E4	55 09N	131 35W
Metz Fr.	78	J8	49 07N	6 11E
Meuse *r.* Belgium/Fr.	78	H9	50 03N	4 40E
Mexicali Mexico	66	A6	32 36N	115 30W
MEXICO	66	C5/E3		
Mexico New York USA	47	K3	43 28N	76 14W
Mexico City Mexico	66	E3	19 25N	99 10W
Mexico, Gulf of Mexico	66	F4/G4	25 00N	90 00W
Meymaneh Afghanistan	89	H6	35 55N	64 47E
Mezen' Russia	86	G10	65 50N	44 20E
Miami Florida USA	63	K2	25 45N	80 15W
Miami Oklahoma USA	63	H4	36 53N	94 54W
Mīāneh Iran	89	E6	37 23N	47 45E
Mianwali Pakistan	90	C6	32 32N	71 33E
Miass Russia	86	J7	55 00N	60 08E
Michelson, Mount Alaska USA	54	B4	69 19N	144 20W
Michigan *state* USA	63	J5/K5	45 00N	85 00W
Michigan, Lake Canada/USA	63	J5/J6	45 00N	87 00W
Micronesia *geog. reg.* Pacific Ocean	106	G8	10 00N	160 00E
Mid-Atlantic Ridge Atlantic Ocean	108	F11	15 00S	13 00W
Middle America Trench Pacific Ocean	107	R9/T9	16 30N	99 00W
Middle Andaman *i.* Andaman Islands	91	G2	12 30N	93 00E
Middleburg RSA	101	K2	31 28S	25 01E
Middle Loup *r.* Nebraska USA	62	F5	42 00N	101 00W
Middlesbrough UK	78	E11	54 35N	1 14W
Middletown Connecticut USA	65	D2	41 33N	72 39W
Mid-Indian Basin Indian Ocean	105	H5/H6	10 00S	80 00E
Mid-Indian Ridge Indian Ocean	105	F5/G3	27 00S	70 00E
Midland Michigan USA	63	K5	43 38N	84 14W
Midland Texas USA	62	F3	32 00N	102 09W
Midland Beach New York USA	65	H1	40 33N	74 07W
Mid-Pacific Mountains Pacific Ocean	106	F10	21 00N	160 00E
Midway Islands Pacific Ocean	106	J10	28 15N	177 25W
Mieres Sp.	79	C5	43 15N	5 46W
Mijares *r.* Sp.	79	E4	40 03N	0 30W
Milagro Ecuador	72	B13	2 11S	79 36W
Milan Italy	81	B6	45 28N	9 12E
Mildura Aust.	103	H4	34 14S	142 13E
Miles City Montana USA	62	E6	46 24N	105 48W
Milford Pennsylvania USA	65	C2	41 19N	74 48W
Milford Utah USA	62	D4	38 22N	113 00W
Milford Haven UK	78	C9	51 44N	5 02W
Milk *r.* Canada/USA	62	D6	49 00N	112 00W
Millau Fr.	79	G6	44 06N	3 05E
Mill Creek *r.* Michigan USA	46	C3	43 10N	83 00W
Millerton New York USA	65	D2	41 57N	73 31W
Millinocket Maine USA	51	F1	45 42N	68 43W
Millville New Jersey USA	65	C1	39 24N	75 02W
Milos *i.* Greece	81	K2	36 00N	24 00E
Milton Keynes UK	78	E10	52 02N	0 42W
Milwaukee Wisconsin USA	63	J5	43 03N	87 56W
Mimizan Fr.	79	E6	44 12N	1 14W
Minahassa Peninsula Indonesia	95	G4	0 30N	123 00E
Minamata Japan	94	B1	32 13N	130 23E
Minas Uruguay	73	F7	34 20S	55 15W
Minas Gerais *admin.* Brazil	72	H10	17 30S	45 00W
Minatitlán Mexico	66	F3	17 59N	94 32W
Mindanao *i.* Philippines	95	G5	8 00N	125 00E
Minden Germany	80	B10	52 18N	8 54E
Minden Louisiana USA	63	H3	32 26N	93 17W
Mindoro *i.* Philippines	95	G6	13 00N	121 00E
Minerva Reefs Pacific Ocean	103	R6	23 50S	179 00W
Minicoy Island India	90	C1	8 29N	73 01E
Minneapolis Minnesota USA	63	H5	45 00N	93 15W
Minnesota *r.* Minnesota USA	63	G5	44 00N	95 00W
Minnesota *state* USA	63	H6	47 00N	95 00W
Miño *r.* Sp./Port.	79	A5	42 00N	8 40W
Minot North Dakota USA	62	F6	48 16N	101 19W
Mio Michigan USA	45	J3	44 39N	84 08W
Miram Shah Pakistan	90	B6	32 59N	70 07E
Miranda de Ebro Sp.	79	D5	42 41N	2 57W
Miri Malaysia	95	E4	4 23N	114 00E
Mirnyy Russia	87	P9	62 30N	113 58E
Mirpur Khas Pakistan	90	B5	25 33N	69 05E
Mirs Bay HK China	92	D3	22 31N	114 25E
Mirtoan Sea Greece	81	J2	37 00N	23 00E
Mirzapur India	90	E5	25 09N	82 34E
Misawa Japan	94	D3	40 42N	141 26E
Miskolc Hungary	80	H8	48 07N	20 47E
Misoöl *i.* Indonesia	95	J3	1 50S	129 55E
Misratah Libya	100	G14	32 23N	15 00E
Mississippi *r.* USA	63	H3	35 00N	90 00W
Mississippi *state* USA	63	H3/J3	32 00N	90 00W
Mississippi Delta Louisiana USA	63	J2	30 00N	90 00W
Missoula Montana USA	62	D6	46 52N	114 00W

Missouri *r.* USA	**63**	H4	39 00N	93 00W
Missouri *state* USA	**63**	H4	38 00N	93 00W
Mitchell South Dakota USA	**63**	G5	43 40N	98 01W
Mitchell *r.* Aust.	**103**	H7	16 00S	142 30E
Mitkof Island Alaska USA	**38**	D5	56 40N	132 45W
Mito Japan	**94**	D2	36 22N	140 29E
Mitre *i.* Solomon Islands	**103**	P8	11 30S	170 10E
Mitú Col.	**72**	C14	1 07N	70 05W
Miyako Japan	**94**	D2	39 38N	141 59E
Miyakonojō Japan	**94**	B1	31 43N	131 02E
Miyazaki Japan	**94**	B1	31 56N	131 27E
Mizen Head *c.* RoI	**78**	A9	51 30N	9 50W
Mizoram *admin.* India	**91**	G4	23 40N	93 30E
Mjölby Sweden	**80**	E13	58 19N	15 10E
Mladá Boleslav Czech Rep.	**80**	E9	50 26N	14 55E
Mława Poland	**80**	H10	53 08N	20 20E
Moala *i.* Fiji	**106**	U15	18 34S	179 56E
Mobaye CAR	**100**	J8	4 19N	21 11E
Mobile Alabama USA	**63**	J3	30 40N	88 05W
Moçambique Mozambique	**101**	N4	15 03S	40 45E
Mocuba Mozambique	**101**	M4	16 52S	36 57E
Módena Italy	**81**	C6	44 39N	10 55E
Modesto California USA	**62**	B4	37 37N	121 00W
Moe Aust.	**103**	J3	38 09S	146 22E
Mogadishu Somalia	**100**	P8	2 02N	45 21E
Mogocha Russia	**87**	P7	53 44N	119 45E
Mogollon Rim *plat.* Arizona USA	**62**	D3	34 00N	111 00W
Mohall North Dakota USA	**42**	G1	48 50N	101 34W
Mohe China	**93**	N9	52 55N	122 20E
Mohyliv-Podil's'kyy Ukraine	**80**	L8	48 29N	27 49E
Mojave California USA	**62**	C4	35 02N	118 11W
Mojave *r.* California USA	**64**	E2	34 47N	117 15W
Mojave Desert California USA	**64**	E2	35 08N	117 21W
Mokelumne *r.* California USA	**64**	C4	38 13N	121 05W
Mokolo Cameroon	**100**	G10	10 49N	13 54E
Mokp'o South Korea	**93**	P5	34 50N	126 25E
Molango Mexico	**66**	E4	20 48N	98 44W
MOLDOVA	**80/81**	M7		
Moldova *r.* Romania	**81**	L7	47 00N	26 00E
Molepolole Botswana	**101**	K3	24 25S	25 30E
Mollendo Peru	**72**	C10	17 00S	72 00W
Molokai *i.* Hawaiian Islands	**107**	Y18	21 40N	155 55W
Molopo *r.* Southern Africa	**101**	J2	26 30S	22 30E
Molucca Sea Indonesia	**95**	G3	0 30S	125 30E
Mombasa Kenya	**100**	M7	4 04S	39 40E
MONACO	**79**	J5		
Monahans Texas USA	**62**	F3	31 35N	102 54W
Monbetsu Japan	**94**	D3	42 28N	142 10E
Monbetsu Japan	**94**	D3	44 23N	143 22E
Monçaõ Brazil	**72**	H13	3 30S	45 15W
Mönchengladbach Germany	**80**	A9	51 12N	6 25E
Monclova Mexico	**66**	D5	26 55N	101 25W
Mondego *r.* Port.	**79**	A4	40 30N	8 15W
Mondovi Italy	**81**	A6	44 23N	7 49E
Monemvasia Greece	**81**	J2	36 41N	23 03E
Mong Kok HK China	**92**	B1	22 19N	114 09E
MONGOLIA	**92/93**	F8		
Mongu Zambia	**101**	J4	15 13S	23 09E
Mono Lake California USA	**64**	D4	38 00N	119 00W
Monopoli Italy	**81**	F4	40 57N	17 18E
Monroe Louisiana USA	**63**	H3	32 31N	92 06W
Monroe Michigan USA	**45**	K1	41 54N	83 24W
Monrovia Liberia	**100**	B9	6 20N	10 46W
Montana Bulgaria	**81**	J5	43 25N	23 11E
Montana *state* USA	**62**	E6	47 00N	111 00W
Montañas de León *mts.* Sp.	**79**	B5	42 30N	6 15E
Montargis Fr.	**78**	G7	48 00N	2 44E
Montauban Fr.	**79**	F6	44 01N	1 20E
Montauk Point New York USA	**65**	E2	41 05N	71 55W
Montbéliard Fr.	**79**	J7	47 31N	6 48E
Mont Blanc *mt.* Fr./Italy	**79**	J6	45 50N	6 52E
Mont Cameroun *mt.* Cameroon	**100**	F8	4 13N	9 10E
Montclair New Jersey USA	**65**	H2	40 48N	74 12W
Mont-de-Marsan Fr.	**79**	E5	43 54N	0 30W
Monte Cinto *mt.* Fr.	**79**	K5	42 23N	8 57E
Montego Bay *tn.* Jamaica	**67**	U14	18 27N	77 56W
Montélimar Fr.	**79**	H6	44 33N	4 45E
Monterey California USA	**62**	B4	36 35N	121 55W
Monterey Bay California USA	**64**	C3	36 46N	121 51W
Montería Col.	**72**	B15	8 45N	75 54W
Montero Bolivia	**72**	E10	17 20S	63 15W
Monte Roraima *mt.* Guyana	**72**	E15	5 14N	60 44W
Monterrey Mexico	**66**	D5	25 40N	100 20W
Montes Claros *tn.* Brazil	**72**	J10	16 45S	43 52W
Montes de Toledo *mts.* Sp.	**79**	C3	39 35N	4 30W
Montevideo Uruguay	**73**	F7	34 55S	56 10W
Montgomery Alabama USA	**63**	J3	32 22N	86 20W
Monti del Gennargentu *mts.* Italy	**81**	B3/B4	40 00N	9 30E
Monti Nebrodi *mts.* Italy	**81**	E2	37 00N	14 00E
Montluçon Fr.	**79**	G7	46 20N	2 36E
Montmorillon Fr.	**79**	F7	46 26N	0 52E
Monto Aust.	**103**	K6	24 53S	151 06E
Montpelier Ohio USA	**46**	B1	41 35N	84 35W
Montpellier Fr.	**79**	G5	43 36N	3 53E
Montreux Switz.	**79**	J7	46 27N	6 55E
Montrose UK	**78**	D12	56 43N	2 29W
Montrose Colorado USA	**62**	E4	38 29N	107 53W
Monts d'Auvergne *mts.* Fr.	**79**	G6	45 30N	2 50E
Montserrat *i.* Lesser Antilles	**66**	P9	16 45N	62 14W
Monts Nimba *mts.* Guinea/Liberia	**100**	C9	7 39N	8 30W
Monywa Myanmar	**92**	H3	22 05N	95 12E
Monza Italy	**81**	B6	45 35N	9 16E
Moora Aust.	**102**	C4	30 40S	116 01E
Moore, Lake Aust.	**102**	C5	30 00S	117 30E
Moorhead Minnesota USA	**63**	G6	46 51N	96 44W
Moosehead Lake Maine USA	**47**	S5	45 40N	69 40W
Mooselookmeguntic Lake Maine USA	**51**	E1	44 56N	71 00W
Mopti Mali	**100**	D10	14 29N	4 10W
Moradabad India	**90**	D5	28 50N	78 45E
Morant Point Jamaica	**67**	U13	17 55N	76 12W
Moratuwa Sri Lanka	**90**	D1	6 47N	79 53E
Morava *r.* Europe	**80**	F8	48 00N	17 00E
Moray Firth *est.* UK	**78**	D12	57 45N	3 45W
Moreau *r.* South Dakota USA	**62**	F6	45 00N	102 00W
Moree Aust.	**103**	J5	29 29S	149 53E
Morelia Mexico	**66**	D3	19 40N	101 11W
Morenci Arizona USA	**62**	E3	33 05N	109 22W
Morgan Hill California USA	**64**	C3	37 05N	121 48W
Morgantown West Virginia USA	**63**	L4	39 38N	79 57W
Mori Japan	**94**	D3	42 07N	140 33E
Morioka Japan	**94**	D2	39 43N	141 08E
Morlaix Fr.	**78**	D8	48 35N	3 50W
Morne Diablotins *mt.* Dominica	**66**	Q8	15 30N	61 24W
MOROCCO	**100**	C14		
Morogoro Tanzania	**101**	M6	6 49S	37 40E
Moro Gulf Philippines	**95**	G5	7 00N	123 00E
Morón Cuba	**67**	J4	22 08N	78 39W
Morondava Madagascar	**101**	N3	20 19S	44 17E
Moroni Comoros	**101**	N5	11 40S	43 16E
Morotai *i.* Indonesia	**95**	H4	2 30N	128 30E
Moroto Uganda	**100**	L8	2 32N	34 41E
Morristown New Jersey USA	**65**	C2	40 49N	74 29W
Morro Bay *tn.* California USA	**64**	C2	35 22N	120 50W
Moscow Russia	**86**	F8	55 45N	37 42E
Moscow Idaho USA	**62**	C6	46 44N	117 00W
Mosel *r.* Germany/Fr.	**80**	A8	50 00N	7 00E
Moses Lake *tn.* Washington USA	**62**	C6	47 09N	119 20W
Moshi Tanzania	**100**	M7	3 21S	37 19E
Mosquito Creek Lake *res.* Ohio USA	**46**	F1	41 20N	80 45W
Moss Norway	**78**	L13	59 26N	10 41E
Mossoró Brazil	**72**	K12	5 10S	37 18W
Most Czech Rep.	**80**	D9	50 31N	13 39E
Mostar Bosnia-Herzegovina	**81**	F5	43 20N	17 50E
Móstoles Sp.	**79**	D4	40 19N	3 53W
Mosul Iraq	**88**	D6	36 21N	43 08E
Motala Sweden	**80**	E13	58 34N	15 05E
Mothe *i.* Fiji	**106**	V15	18 39S	178 32W
Motherwell UK	**78**	D11	55 48N	3 59W
Motril Sp.	**79**	D2	36 45N	3 31W
Mouila Gabon	**100**	B7	1 50S	11 02E
Moulins Fr.	**79**	G7	47 00N	3 48E
Moulmein Myanmar	**95**	B7	16 30N	97 39E
Moundou Chad	**100**	H9	8 35N	16 01E
Mount Darwin *tn.* Zimbabwe	**101**	L4	16 45S	31 39E
Mount Desert Island Maine USA	**51**	F1	44 22N	68 15W
Mount Gambier *tn.* Aust.	**103**	H3	37 51S	140 50E
Mount Hagen *tn.* PNG	**103**	H9	5 54S	144 13E
Mount Isa *tn.* Aust.	**103**	G6	20 50S	139 29E
Mount Magnet *tn.* Aust.	**102**	C5	28 06S	117 50E
Mount Morgan *tn.* Aust.	**103**	K6	23 40S	150 25E
Mount Pleasant *tn.* Michigan USA	**45**	J2	43 36N	84 46W
Mount Union *tn.* Pennsylvania USA	**65**	B2	40 22N	77 52W
Mount Vernon *tn.* Illinois USA	**63**	J4	38 19N	88 52W
Mount Vernon *tn.* Washington USA	**38**	H4	48 25N	122 20W
Moyale Kenya	**100**	M8	3 31N	39 04E
Moyobamba Peru	**72**	B12	6 04S	76 56W
MOZAMBIQUE	**101**	L3/M5		
Mozambique Basin Indian Ocean	**105**	C3	35 00S	40 00E
Mozambique Channel Mozambique/Madagascar	**101**	N4	18 00S	42 00E
Mpanda Tanzania	**101**	L6	6 21S	31 01E
Mtwara Tanzania	**101**	N5	10 17S	40 11E
Muang Chiang Rai Thailand	**95**	B7	19 56N	99 51E
Muang Khon Kaen Thailand	**95**	C7	16 25N	102 50E
Muang Lampang Thailand	**95**	B7	18 16N	99 30E
Muang Nakhon Sawan Thailand	**95**	B7	15 42N	100 10E
Muang Phitsanulok Thailand	**95**	C7	16 49N	100 18E
Muchinga Mountains Zambia	**101**	L5	12 30S	32 30E
Mudanjiang China	**93**	P7	44 36N	129 42E
Mufulira Zambia	**101**	K5	12 30S	28 12E
Muğla Turkey	**88**	A6	37 13N	28 22E
Muir Woods National Monument California USA	**64**	B3	37 54N	122 32W
Mui Wo HK China	**92**	A1	22 16N	113 59E
Mukachevo Ukraine	**80**	J8	48 26N	22 45E
Mukalla Yemen	**89**	E1	14 34N	49 09E
Mulegé Mexico	**66**	B5	26 54N	112 00W
Mulhacén *mt.* Sp.	**79**	D2	37 04N	3 19W
Mulhouse Fr.	**78**	J7	47 45N	7 21E
Mull *i.* UK	**78**	B12	56 25N	6 00W
Mullett Lake Michigan USA	**46**	B5	45 30N	84 30W
Mullingar RoI	**78**	B10	53 32N	7 20W
Multan Pakistan	**90**	C6	30 10N	71 36E
Mumbai India	**90**	C3	18 56N	72 51E
Muna *i.* Indonesia	**95**	G2/G3	5 00S	122 20E
Muncie Indiana USA	**63**	J5	40 11N	85 22W
Muncy Pennsylvania USA	**65**	B2	41 12N	76 48W
Mundo *r.* Sp.	**79**	D3/E3	38 30N	2 00W
Mungbere CDR	**100**	K8	2 40N	28 25E
Mungla Bangladesh	**91**	K9	22 18N	89 34E
Munich Germany	**80**	C8	48 08N	11 35E
Munising Michigan USA	**45**	H4	46 24N	86 39W
Münster Germany	**80**	A9	51 58N	7 37E
Mur *r.* Europe	**81**	E7	48 00N	14 40E
Murat *r.* Turkey	**88**	D6	38 50N	40 20E
Murchison *r.* Aust.	**102**	C5	26 00S	117 00E
Murcia Sp.	**79**	E2	37 59N	1 08W
Mureş *r.* Romania	**81**	J6	46 00N	22 00E
Murfreesboro Tennessee USA	**63**	J4	35 50N	86 25W
Müritz *l.* Germany	**80**	D10	53 00N	12 00E
Murmansk Russia	**86**	F10	68 59N	33 08E
Murom Russia	**86**	G8	55 34N	42 04E
Muroran Japan	**94**	D3	42 21N	140 59E
Muroto Japan	**94**	B1	33 13N	134 11E
Muroto-zaki *c.* Japan	**94**	B1	33 13N	134 11E
Murray *r.* Aust.	**103**	H3	35 30S	144 00E
Murray Bridge *tn.* Aust.	**103**	G3	35 10S	139 17E
Murray Seascarp Pacific Ocean	**107**	N11	32 00N	138 00W
Murrumbidgee *r.* Aust.	**103**	J4	34 30S	146 30E
Murwara India	**90**	E4	23 49N	80 28E
Murzuq Libya	**100**	G13	25 55N	13 55E
Muş Turkey	**88**	D6	38 45N	41 30E
Muscat Oman	**89**	G3	23 37N	58 38E
Musgrave Ranges Aust.	**102**	F5	26 00S	132 00E
Mushin Nigeria	**100**	E9	6 30N	3 15E
Muskegon Michigan USA	**63**	J5	43 13N	86 15W
Muskegon River Michigan USA	**46**	A3	44 00N	85 05W
Muskogee Oklahoma USA	**63**	G4	35 35N	95 21W
Musselshell *r.* Montana USA	**62**	E6	47 00N	108 00W
Mustique *i.* Lesser Antilles	**66**	R11	12 39N	61 15W
Mutarara Mozambique	**101**	M4	17 30S	35 06E
Mutare Zimbabwe	**101**	L4	18 58N	32 40E
Mutsu Japan	**94**	D3	41 18N	141 15E
Mutsu-wan *b.* Japan	**94**	D3	41 05N	140 40E
Muyun Kum *d.* Kazakhstan	**86**	J5/K5	44 00N	70 00E
Muzaffarnagar India	**90**	D5	29 28N	77 42E
Muzaffarpur India	**91**	F5	26 07N	85 23E
Muzon, Cape Alaska USA	**38**	D4	54 41N	132 40W
Mwanza Tanzania	**100**	L7	2 31S	32 56E
Mweru, Lake CDR/Zambia	**101**	K6	8 30S	28 30E
MYANMAR	**95**	B7		
Myitkyina Myanmar	**93**	H4	25 24N	97 25E
Mymensingh Bangladesh	**91**	L10	24 45N	90 23E
Mys Chelyuskin *c.* Russia	**87**	N12	77 44N	103 55E
Mys Kanin Nos *c.* Russia	**86**	G10	68 38N	43 20E
Mys Navarin *c.* Russia	**87**	V9	62 17N	179 13E
Mys Olyutorskiy *c.* Russia	**87**	V9	59 58N	170 25E
Mysore India	**90**	D2	12 18N	76 37E
Mys Tolstoy *c.* Russia	**87**	T8	59 00N	155 00E
My Tho Vietnam	**95**	D6	10 21N	106 21E
Mytilíni Greece	**81**	L3	39 06N	26 34E
Mzuzu Malawi	**101**	L5	11 31S	34 00E

N

Naas RoI	**78**	B10	53 13N	6 39W
Naberezhnyye Chelny Russia	**86**	H8	55 42N	52 19E
Nablus Jordan	**88**	N11	32 13N	35 16E
Nacimiento Reservoir California USA	**64**	C2	34 45N	121 00W
Nacogdoches Texas USA	**63**	H3	31 36N	94 40W
Nadiad India	**90**	C4	22 42N	72 55E
Nador Morocco	**100**	D15	35 10N	3 00W
Nadym Russia	**86**	K10	65 25N	72 40E
Naestved Denmark	**80**	C11	55 14N	11 47E
Náfplio Greece	**81**	J2	37 34N	22 48E
Naga Philippines	**95**	G6	13 36N	123 12E
Nagaland *admin.* India	**91**	G5	26 00N	94 30E
Nagano Japan	**94**	C2	36 39N	138 10E
Nagaoka Japan	**94**	C2	37 27N	138 50E
Nagaon India	**91**	G5	26 20N	92 41E
Nagasaki Japan	**94**	A1	32 45N	129 52E
Nagato Japan	**94**	B1	34 22N	131 11E
Nagercoil India	**90**	D1	8 11N	77 30E
Nagornyy Russia	**87**	Q8	55 57N	124 54E
Nagoya Japan	**94**	C2	35 08N	136 53E
Nagpur India	**90**	D4	21 10N	79 12E
Nagykanizsa Hungary	**81**	F7	46 27N	17 00E
Nahariyya Israel	**88**	N11	33 01N	35 05E
Nairobi Kenya	**100**	M7	1 17S	36 50E
Najd *geog. reg.* Saudi Arabia	**88**	D4	25 40N	42 30E
Najrān Saudi Arabia	**88**	D2	17 37N	44 40E
Nakamura Japan	**94**	B1	33 02N	132 58E
Nakatsu Japan	**94**	B1	33 37N	131 11E
Nakhodka Russia	**87**	R5	42 53N	132 54E
Nakhon Ratchasima Thailand	**95**	C6	14 59N	102 06E
Nakhon Si Thammarat Thailand	**95**	B5	8 24N	99 58E
Nakuru Kenya	**100**	M7	0 16S	36 05E
Nal *r.* Pakistan	**90**	B5	26 10N	65 30E
Nal'chik Russia	**86**	G5	43 31N	43 38E
Namangan Uzbekistan	**86**	K5	40 59N	71 41E
Nam Dinh Vietnam	**93**	K3	20 25N	106 12E
Namib Desert Namibia	**101**	G3/H2	22 00S	14 00E
Namibe Angola	**101**	G4	15 10S	12 09E
NAMIBIA	**101**	H3		
Nampa Idaho USA	**62**	C5	43 35N	116 34W
Nampo North Korea	**93**	P6	38 51N	125 10E
Nampula Mozambique	**101**	M4	15 09S	39 14E
Namtu Myanmar	**93**	H3	23 04N	97 26E
Namur Belgium	**78**	H9	50 28N	4 52E
Nam Wan HK China	**92**	B2	22 20N	114 05E
Nanao Japan	**94**	C2	37 03N	136 58E
Nanchang China	**93**	M4	28 33N	115 58E
Nanchong China	**93**	K5	30 54N	106 06E
Nancowry Island India	**91**	G1	7 59N	93 32E
Nancy Fr.	**78**	J8	48 42N	6 12E
Nanda Devi *mt.* India	**90**	D6	30 21N	79 58E
Nānded India	**90**	D3	19 11N	77 21E
Nanduri Fiji	**106**	U16	16 26S	179 08E
Nanjing China	**93**	M5	32 03N	118 47E
Nan Ling *mts.* China	**93**	L3	25 00N	112 00E
Nanning China	**93**	K3	22 50N	108 19E
Nanpan Jiang *r.* China	**93**	K3	25 00N	106 00E
Nanping China	**93**	M4	26 40N	118 07E
Nantes Fr.	**79**	E7	47 14N	1 35W
Nantong China	**93**	N5	32 06N	121 04E
Nantucket Island Massachusetts USA	**63**	M5	41 15N	70 05W
Nantucket Sound Massachusetts USA	**65**	E2	41 20N	70 08W
Nanuku Passage *sd.* Fiji	**106**	V15	16 40S	179 25W
Nanumanga *i.* Tuvalu	**103**	Q9	6 18S	176 20E
Nanumea *is.* Tuvalu	**103**	Q9	5 43S	176 00E
Nanyang China	**93**	L5	33 06N	112 31E
Nanyuki Kenya	**100**	M8	0 01N	37 05E
Naogaon Bangladesh	**91**	K10	24 49N	88 59E
Napa California USA	**64**	B4	38 18N	122 17W
Napier NZ	**103**	Q3	39 30S	176 54E
Naples Italy	**81**	E4	40 50N	14 15E
Naples Florida USA	**63**	K2	26 09N	81 48W
Napo *r.* Peru	**72**	C13	2 30S	73 30W
Napolean Ohio USA	**46**	B1	41 24N	84 09W
Napoopoo Hawaiian Islands	**107**	Z17	19 29N	155 55W
Nara Japan	**94**	C1	34 41N	135 49E
Narail Bangladesh	**91**	K9	23 18N	89 45E
Narayanganj Bangladesh	**91**	L9	23 36N	90 28E
Narbonne Fr.	**79**	G5	43 11N	3 00E
Narcondam Island India	**91**	G2	13 15N	94 30E
Nares Deep Atlantic Ocean	**108**	B9	26 00N	61 10W
Narew *r.* Europe	**80**	H10	53 00N	21 00E
Narmada *r.* India	**90**	C4	22 00N	75 00E
Narrogin Aust.	**102**	C4	32 57S	117 07E
Nar'yan Mar Russia	**86**	H10	67 37N	53 02E
Nasca Ridge Pacific Ocean	**107**	T5	20 00S	81 00W
Nashik India	**90**	C3	20 00N	73 52E
Nashua New Hampshire USA	**63**	M5	42 44N	71 28W
Nashville Tennessee USA	**63**	J4	36 10N	86 50W
Nassau Bahamas	**67**	J5	25 05N	77 20W
Nasser, Lake Egypt	**100**	L12	22 35N	31 40E
Nässjö Sweden	**80**	E12	57 40N	14 40E
Natal Brazil	**72**	K12	5 46S	35 15W
Natchez Mississippi USA	**63**	H3	31 32N	91 24W
Natewa Peninsula Fiji	**106**	U15	16 40S	180 00
National City California USA	**64**	E1	32 39N	117 05W
Natron, Lake Tanzania	**100**	M7	2 00S	36 00E
Natuna Besar *i.* Indonesia	**95**	D4	3 40N	108 00E
Naturaliste, Cape Aust.	**102**	C4	33 32S	115 01E
NAURU	**103**	N10		
Nausori Fiji	**106**	U15	18 01S	178 31E
Navadwip India	**91**	K9	23 25N	88 22E
Navia *r.* Sp.	**79**	B5	43 10N	7 05W
Naviti *i.* Fiji	**106**	T16	17 08S	177 15E
Navoi Uzbekistan	**86**	J5	40 04N	65 20E
Navojoa Mexico	**66**	C5	27 04N	109 28W
Navsari India	**90**	C4	20 58N	73 01E
Nawabganj Bangladesh	**91**	K10	24 35N	88 21E
Náxos *i.* Greece	**81**	K2	37 00N	25 00E
Nayoro Japan	**94**	D3	44 21N	142 30E
Nazareth Israel	**88**	N11	32 41N	35 16E
Nazca Peru	**72**	C11	14 53S	74 54W
Nazwá Oman	**89**	G3	22 56N	57 33E
Ndélé CAR	**100**	J9	8 25N	20 38E
Ndjamena Chad	**100**	H10	12 10N	14 59E
Ndola Zambia	**101**	K5	13 00S	28 39E
Neah Bay *tn.* Washington USA	**38**	H4	48 20N	124 38W
Néapoli Greece	**81**	J2	36 31N	23 03E
Nebitdag Turkmenistan	**86**	H4	39 31N	54 24E
Nebraska *state* USA	**62**	F5	42 00N	102 00W
Neche North Dakota USA	**43**	D1	48 59N	97 33W
Neckei *i.* Hawaiian Islands	**107**	K10	23 25N	164 42W
Necochea Argentina	**73**	F6	38 31S	58 46W
Needles California USA	**62**	D3	34 51N	114 36W
Negele Ethiopia	**100**	M9	5 20N	39 35E
Negev *d.* Israel	**88**	N10	30 50N	30 45E
Negombo Sri Lanka	**90**	D1	7 13N	79 51E
Negritos Peru	**72**	A13	4 42S	81 18W
Negro *r.* Argentina	**73**	E6	40 00S	65 00W
Negro *r.* Brazil	**72**	D13	0 05S	67 00W
Negro *r.* Uruguay	**73**	F7	33 00S	57 30W
Negros *i.* Philippines	**95**	G5	10 00N	123 00E
Neijiang China	**93**	K4	29 32N	105 03E
Nei Mongol Zizhiqu *admin.* China	**93**	K7	42 30N	112 30E
Neiva Col.	**72**	B14	2 58N	75 15W
Nek'emte Ethiopia	**100**	M9	9 04N	36 30E
Nellore India	**90**	D2	14 29N	80 00E
Nelson *admin.* NZ	**103**	P2	41 30S	172 30E
Neman *r.* Lithuania/Russia	**80**	J11	55 00N	22 00E
Nemuro Japan	**94**	E3	43 22N	145 36E
Nemuro-kaikyō *sd.* Japan	**94**	E3	44 00N	146 00E
Nenjiang China	**93**	P8	49 10N	125 15E
Nen Jiang *r.* China	**93**	P9	50 00N	125 00E

Omo *r.* Ethiopia	**100**	M9	7 00N	37 00E
Omolon *r.* Russia	**87**	U10	65 00N	160 00E
Omoloy *r.* Russia	**87**	R10	70 00N	132 00E
Omsk Russia	**86**	K8	55 00N	73 22E
Ōmuta Japan	**94**	B1	33 02N	130 26E
Onaway Michigan USA	**46**	B5	45 23N	84 14W
Oneida New York USA	**45**	P2	43 05N	75 39W
Oneida Lake New York USA	**45**	P2	43 14N	76 00W
Oneonta New York USA	**47**	L2	42 30N	75 04W
Oneşti Romania	**81**	L7	46 15N	26 45E
Onezhskoye Ozero *l.* Russia	**86**	F9	62 00N	40 00E
Ongea Levu *i.* Fiji	**106**	V15	19 11S	178 28W
Onitsha Nigeria	**100**	F9	6 10N	6 47E
Onomichi Japan	**94**	B1	34 25N	133 11E
Onon *r.* Russia/Mongolia	**93**	L9	51 00N	114 00E
Onotoa *i.* Kiribati	**103**	Q10	1 52S	175 34E
Onslow Aust.	**102**	C6	21 41S	115 12E
Ontario California USA	**62**	C3	34 04N	117 38W
Ontonagon Michigan USA	**63**	J6	46 52N	89 18W
Oostende Belgium	**78**	G9	51 13N	2 55E
Opala CDR	**100**	J7	0 40S	24 20E
Opava Czech Rep.	**80**	F8	49 58N	17 55E
Opheim Montana USA	**42**	D1	48 56N	106 25W
Opole Poland	**80**	F9	50 40N	17 56E
Oporto Port.	**79**	A4	41 09N	8 37W
Oradea Romania	**81**	H7	47 03N	21 55E
Orai India	**90**	D5	26 00N	79 26E
Oran Algeria	**100**	D15	35 45N	0 38W
Orán Argentina	**72**	E9	23 07S	64 16W
Orange Aust.	**103**	J4	33 19S	149 10E
Orange Fr.	**79**	H6	44 08N	4 48E
Orange New Jersey USA	**65**	H2	40 45N	74 14W
Orange Texas USA	**63**	H3	30 05N	93 43W
Orange *r.* Southern Africa	**101**	H2	28 30S	17 30E
Orangeburg South Carolina USA	**63**	K3	33 28N	80 53W
Oraviţa Romania	**81**	H6	45 02N	21 43E
Orbigo *r.* Sp.	**79**	C5	42 15N	5 45W
Orcas Island Washington USA	**38**	H4	48 40N	123 05W
Orchard Park *tn.* New York USA	**46**	H2	42 46N	78 45W
Orcia *r.* Italy	**81**	C5	42 00N	11 00E
Ord Mountain California USA	**64**	E2	34 42N	116 50W
Ordu Turkey	**88**	C7	41 00N	37 52E
Örebro Sweden	**80**	E13	59 17N	15 13E
Oregon *state* USA	**62**	B5/C5	44 00N	120 00W
Oregon City Oregon USA	**62**	B6	45 21N	122 36W
Orël Russia	**86**	F7	52 58N	36 04E
Orem Utah USA	**62**	D5	40 20N	111 45W
Orenburg Russia	**86**	H7	51 50N	55 00E
Orense Sp.	**79**	B5	42 20N	7 52W
Orient New York USA	**65**	D2	41 09N	72 18W
Orihuela Sp.	**79**	E3	38 05N	0 56W
Orinoco *r.* Venezuela	**72**	E15	8 00N	64 00W
Orissa *admin.* India	**91**	E4	20 20N	83 00E
Oristano Italy	**81**	B3	39 54N	8 36E
Orizaba Mexico	**66**	E3	18 51N	97 08W
Orkney Islands UK	**78**	D13	59 00N	3 00W
Orlando Florida USA	**63**	K2	28 33N	81 21W
Orléans Fr.	**78**	F7	47 54N	1 54E
Oroville California USA	**64**	C4	39 32N	121 34W
Oroville Washington USA	**39**	L1	48 57N	119 27W
Orsk Russia	**86**	H7	51 13N	58 35E
Ortigueira Sp.	**79**	B5	43 43N	8 13W
Orūmīyeh Iran	**88**	D6	37 40N	45 00E
Oruro Bolivia	**72**	D10	17 59S	67 08W
Ōsaka Japan	**94**	C1	34 40N	135 30E
Ō-shima *i.* Japan	**94**	C1	34 45N	139 25E
Oshkosh Wisconsin USA	**63**	J5	44 01N	88 32W
Oshogbo Nigeria	**100**	E9	7 50N	4 35E
Osijek Croatia	**81**	G6	45 33N	18 41E
Oskarshamn Sweden	**80**	F12	57 16N	16 25E
Oslo Norway	**78**	L13	59 56N	10 45E
Oslofjorden *fj.* Norway	**78**	L13	59 20N	10 37E
Osmaniye Turkey	**88**	C6	37 04N	36 15E
Osnabrück Germany	**80**	B10	52 17N	8 03E
Osorno Chile	**73**	C5	40 35S	73 14W
Ossa, Mount Aust.	**103**	J2	41 52S	146 04E
Osseo Wisconsin USA	**45**	F3	44 35N	91 13W
Ostfriesische Inseln *is.* Germany	**80**	A10	53 00N	7 00E
Ostrava Czech Rep.	**80**	G8	49 50N	18 15E
Ostróda Poland	**80**	G10	53 42N	19 59E
Ostrołęka Poland	**80**	H10	53 05N	21 32E
Ostrowiec Swietokrzyski Poland	**80**	H9	50 58N	21 22E
Ostrów Mazowiecka Poland	**80**	H10	52 50N	21 51E
Ostrów Wielkopolski Poland	**80**	F9	51 39N	17 50E
Osumi-kaikyo *sd.* Japan	**94**	B1	30 50N	131 00E
Oswego New York USA	**63**	L5	43 27N	76 31W
Otaru Japan	**94**	D3	43 14N	140 59E
Otavalo Ecuador	**72**	B14	0 13N	78 15W
Otra *r.* Norway	**78**	J13	56 17N	7 30E
Otranto Italy	**81**	G4	40 08N	18 30E
Otranto, Strait of Adriatic Sea	**81**	G3/G4	40 00N	19 00E
Ōtsu Japan	**94**	C2	35 00N	135 50E
Ottawa Kansas USA	**63**	G4	38 35N	95 16W
Ottumwa Iowa USA	**63**	H5	41 02N	92 26W
Ouachita *r.* USA	**63**	H3	34 00N	93 00W
Ouachita Mountains USA	**63**	G3/H3	34 00N	95 00W
Ouadda CAR	**100**	J9	8 09N	22 20E
Ouagadougou Burkina	**100**	D10	12 20N	1 40W
Ouahigouya Burkina	**100**	D10	13 31N	2 20W
Ouargla Algeria	**100**	F14	32 00N	5 16E
Oubangui *r.* Central Africa	**100**	H8	0 00	17 30E
Oudtshoorn RSA	**101**	J1	33 35S	22 12E
Oued Dra *r.* Morocco	**100**	B13	28 10N	11 00W
Ouesso Congo	**100**	H8	1 38N	16 03E
Ouham *r.* CAR	**100**	H9	7 00N	17 30E
Oujda Morocco	**100**	D14	34 41N	1 45W
Ōu-sanmyaku *mts.* Japan	**94**	D2	39 20N	141 00E
Oust *r.* Fr.	**78**	D7	47 50N	2 30W
Outer Hebrides *is.* UK	**78**	B12	58 00N	7 00W
Ovalau *i.* Fiji	**106**	U16	17 40S	178 47E
Ovalle Chile	**73**	C7	30 33S	71 16W
Oviedo Sp.	**79**	C5	43 21N	7 18W
Owando Congo	**100**	H7	0 27S	15 44E
Owego New York USA	**47**	K2	42 07N	76 16W
Owen Falls Dam Uganda	**100**	L8	0 29N	33 11E
Owen Fracture Zone Indian Ocean	**105**	E7	10 00N	55 00E
Owensboro Kentucky USA	**63**	J4	37 45N	87 05W
Owens Lake California USA	**62**	C4	36 25N	117 56W
Owen Stanley Range *mts.* PNG	**103**	J9	9 15S	148 30E
Owosso Michigan USA	**45**	J2	42 59N	84 10W
Owyhee *r.* USA	**62**	C5	43 00N	117 00W
Oxford UK	**78**	E9	51 46N	1 15W
Oxnard California USA	**62**	C3	34 11N	119 10W
Oyama Japan	**94**	C2	36 18N	139 48E
Oyapock *r.* Brazil	**72**	G14	3 00N	52 30W
Oyem Gabon	**100**	G8	1 34N	11 31E
Ozark Plateau Missouri USA	**63**	H4	37 00N	93 00W
Ozarks, Lake of the Missouri USA	**63**	H4	38 00N	93 00W
Ozero Alakol' *salt l.* Kazakhstan	**86**	L6	46 00N	82 00E
Ozero Balkhash *l.* Kazakhstan	**86**	K6	46 00N	75 00E
Ozero Baykal *l.* Russia	**87**	N7	54 00N	109 00E
Ozero Chany *salt l.* Russia	**86**	K7	55 00N	77 30E
Ozero Il'men' *l.* Russia	**86**	F8	58 00N	31 30E
Ozero Issyk-Kul' *salt l.* Kyrgyzstan	**86**	K5	42 30N	77 30E
Ozero Khanka *l.* Asia	**87**	R6	45 00N	132 30E
Ozero Taymyr *l.* Russia	**87**	N11	74 00N	102 30E
Ozero Tengiz *salt l.* Kazakhstan	**86**	J7	51 00N	69 00E
Ozero Zaysan *l.* Kazakhstan	**87**	L6	48 00N	84 00E
Ozieri Italy	**81**	B4	40 35N	9 01E

P

Pabianice Poland	**80**	G9	51 40N	19 20E
Pabna Bangladesh	**91**	K10	24 00N	89 15E
Pacasmayo Peru	**72**	B12	7 27S	79 33W
Pachuca Mexico	**66**	E4	20 10N	98 44W
Pacific-Antarctic Ridge Pacific Ocean	**107**	M1	55 00S	135 00W
Pacific Grove California USA	**62**	B4	36 36N	121 56W
Pacific Ocean	**106/107**			
Padang Indonesia	**95**	C3	1 00S	100 21E
Paderborn Germany	**80**	B9	51 43N	8 44E
Padilla Bolivia	**72**	E10	19 18S	64 20W
Padma *r.* Bangladesh	**91**	L9	23 25N	90 10E
Padua Italy	**81**	C6	45 24N	11 53E
Paducah Kentucky USA	**63**	J4	37 03N	88 36W
Pag *i.* Croatia	**81**	E6	44 00N	15 00E
Pagadian Philippines	**95**	G5	7 50N	123 30E
Pahala Hawaiian Islands	**107**	Z17	19 12N	155 28W
Pahute Mesa *mts.* Nevada USA	**64**	E3	37 15N	116 20W
Painesville Ohio USA	**45**	L1	41 43N	81 15W
Paisley UK	**78**	C11	55 50N	4 26W
Paita Peru	**72**	A12	5 11S	81 09W
Pakanbaru Indonesia	**95**	C4	0 33N	101 30E
PAKISTAN	**90**	B5/C5		
Pak Mong HK China	**92**	A1	22 18N	113 57E
Pakokku Myanmar	**92**	H3	21 20N	95 05E
Pak Tam Chung HK China	**92**	C2	22 24N	114 19E
Pakxé Laos	**95**	D6	15 00N	105 55E
Palana Russia	**87**	T8	59 05N	159 59E
Palangkaraya Indonesia	**95**	E3	2 16S	113 55E
PALAU	**106**	D8		
Palawan *i.* Philippines	**95**	F5/F6	10 00N	119 00E
Palembang Indonesia	**95**	C3	2 59S	104 45E
Palencia Sp.	**79**	C5	41 01N	4 32W
Palermo Italy	**81**	D3	38 08N	13 23E
Palestine Texas USA	**63**	G3	31 45N	95 39W
Palghat India	**90**	D2	10 46N	76 42E
Palk Strait India	**90**	D1	10 00N	80 00E
Palma de Mallorca Sp.	**79**	G3	39 35N	2 39E
Palmar Sur Costa Rica	**67**	H1	8 57N	83 28W
Palmas, Cape Liberia	**100**	C8	4 25N	7 50W
Palmdale California USA	**64**	D2	34 35N	118 07W
Palmer Land *geog. reg.* Antarctica	**109**		72 00S	62 00W
Palmerston Atoll *i.* Pacific Ocean	**107**	K6	18 04S	163 10W
Palmerston North NZ	**103**	Q2	40 22S	175 37E
Palmira Col.	**72**	B14	3 33N	76 17W
Palm Springs *tn.* California USA	**64**	E1	33 49N	116 33W
Palmyra Syria	**88**	C5	34 40N	38 10E
Palmyra New York USA	**47**	J3	43 04N	77 14W
Palmyra Pennsylvania USA	**65**	C2	40 19N	76 36W
Palmyra Atoll *i.* Pacific Ocean	**107**	L8	5 52N	162 05W
Palo Alto California USA	**64**	B3	37 26N	122 10W
Palomares Mexico	**66**	E3	17 10N	95 04W
Palopo Indonesia	**95**	G3	3 01S	120 12E
Palu Indonesia	**95**	F3	0 54S	119 52E
Pamiers Fr.	**79**	F5	43 07N	1 36E
Pampas *geog. reg.* Argentina	**73**	E6	36 00S	63 00W
Pamplona Col.	**72**	C15	7 24N	72 38W
Pamplona Sp.	**79**	E5	42 49N	1 39W
PANAMA	**67**	H1/J1		
Panama Canal Panama	**67**	J1	9 00N	80 00W
Panama City Panama	**67**	J1	8 57N	19 30W
Panama City Florida USA	**63**	J3	30 10N	85 41W
Panay *i.* Philippines	**95**	G6	11 00N	122 00E
Pancake Range *mts.* Nevada USA	**64**	F4	38 45N	115 55W
Pančevo SM	**81**	H5	44 52N	20 40E
Panevezys Lithuania	**80**	K11	55 44N	24 24E
Pangkalpinang Indonesia	**95**	D3	2 05S	106 09E
Panipat India	**90**	D5	29 24N	76 58E
Pantar *i.* Indonesia	**95**	G2	8 30S	124 00E
Pantelleria *i.* Italy	**81**	D2	36 00N	12 00E
Papa Hawaiian Islands	**107**	Z17	19 12N	155 53W
Pápa Hungary	**81**	F7	47 20N	17 29E
Papantla Mexico	**66**	E4	20 30N	97 21W
Papoose Lake Nevada USA	**64**	F3	37 08N	115 52W
Papua, Gulf of PNG	**103**	H9	8 15S	144 45E
PAPUA NEW GUINEA	**103**	H9		
Pará *admin.* Brazil	**72**	G13	4 30S	52 30W
Paraburdoo Aust.	**102**	C6	23 15S	117 45E
Paracel Islands South China Sea	**95**	E7	16 00N	113 30E
Paragua *r.* Bolivia	**72**	E11	14 00S	61 30W
Paragua *r.* Venezuela	**72**	E15	6 00N	63 30W
PARAGUAY	**72**	F9		
Paraguay *r.* Paraguay/Argentina	**72**	F8/F9	26 30S	58 00W
Paraiba *admin.* Brazil	**72**	K12	7 20S	37 10W
Parakou Benin	**100**	E9	9 23N	2 40E
Paramaribo Suriname	**72**	F15	5 52N	55 14W
Paramonga Peru	**72**	B11	10 42S	77 50W
Paraná Argentina	**73**	E7	31 45S	60 30W
Paraná *admin.* Brazil	**72**	G9	24 30S	53 00W
Paraná *r.* Paraguay/Argentina	**72**	F8	27 00S	56 00W
Paranaíba *r.* Brazil	**72**	H10	18 00S	49 00W
Parana Panema *r.* Brazil	**72**	G9	22 30S	52 00W
Paranguá Brazil	**72**	H8	25 32S	48 36W
Pardo *r.* Brazil	**72**	K10	15 10S	40 00W
Pardubice Czech Rep.	**80**	E9	50 03N	15 45E
Parepare Indonesia	**95**	F3	4 00S	119 40E
Parintins Brazil	**72**	F13	2 38S	56 45W
Paris Fr.	**78**	G8	48 52N	2 20E
Paris Texas USA	**63**	G3	33 41N	95 33W
Parish New York USA	**45**	N2	43 24N	76 08W
Parkersburg West Virginia USA	**63**	K4	39 17N	81 33W
Parma Italy	**81**	C6	44 48N	10 19E
Parma Ohio USA	**45**	L1	41 22N	81 44W
Parnaíba Brazil	**72**	J13	2 58S	41 46W
Parnaíba *r.* Brazil	**72**	J12	7 30S	45 00W
Parnassós *mt.* Greece	**81**	J3	38 30N	22 37E
Pärnu *r.* Estonia	**80**	K13	58 30N	24 30E
Paroo *r.* Aust.	**103**	H5	29 00S	144 30E
Páros Greece	**81**	K2	37 04N	25 06E
Parras Mexico	**66**	D5	25 30N	102 11W
Pasadena California USA	**64**	D2	34 10N	118 08W
Pasadena Texas USA	**63**	G2	29 42N	95 14W
Pascagoula Mississippi USA	**63**	J3	30 21N	88 32W
Pasco Washington USA	**62**	C6	46 15N	119 07W
Paso Robles California USA	**64**	C2	35 38N	120 42W
Passaic New Jersey USA	**65**	H2	40 50N	74 08W
Passaic River New Jersey USA	**65**	H2	40 46N	74 09W
Passau Germany	**80**	D8	48 35N	13 28E
Passo Fundo Brazil	**73**	G8	28 16S	52 20W
Pastaza *r.* Peru	**72**	B13	2 30S	77 00W
Pasto Col.	**72**	B14	1 12N	77 17W
Patagonia *geog. reg.* Argentina	**73**	C3	48 00S	70 00W
Patan India	**90**	C4	23 51N	72 11E
Patan Nepal	**91**	F5	27 40N	85 20E
Patchogue New York USA	**65**	D2	40 46N	73 01W
Pate Island Kenya	**100**	N7	2 05S	41 05E
Paterson New Jersey USA	**63**	M5	40 55N	74 08W
Pathankot India	**90**	D6	32 16N	75 43E
Patiala India	**90**	D6	30 21N	76 27E
Patna India	**91**	F5	25 37N	85 12E
Patos Brazil	**72**	K12	6 55S	37 15W
Patras Greece	**81**	H3	38 14N	21 44E
Patterson California USA	**64**	C3	37 29N	121 09W
Pau Fr.	**79**	E5	43 18N	0 22W
Pavia Italy	**81**	B6	45 12N	9 09E
Pavlodar Kazakhstan	**86**	K7	52 21N	76 59E
Pawtucket Rhode Island USA	**65**	E2	41 53N	71 23W
Paysandu Uruguay	**73**	F7	32 21S	58 05W
Pazardzhik Bulgaria	**81**	K5	42 10N	24 20E
Peake Deep Atlantic Ocean	**108**	G11	43 00N	20 05W
Pearl *r.* Mississippi USA	**63**	H3	32 00N	90 00W
Pearl Harbor Hawaiian Islands	**107**	X18	21 22N	158 00W
Peč SM	**81**	H5	42 40N	20 19E
Pechora Russia	**86**	H10	65 14N	57 18E
Pechora *r.* Russia	**86**	H10	66 00N	52 00E
Pecos Texas USA	**62**	F3	30 00N	102 00W
Pecos *r.* USA	**62**	F3	30 00N	102 00W
Pécs Hungary	**81**	G7	46 04N	18 15E
Pedreiras Brazil	**72**	J13	4 32S	44 40W
Pedro Juan Caballero Paraguay	**72**	F9	22 30S	55 44W
Peekskill New York USA	**65**	D2	41 18N	73 50W
Pegu Myanmar	**95**	B7	17 18N	96 31E
Pegunungan Barisan *mts.* Indonesia	**95**	C3	2 30S	102 30E
Pegunungan Maoke *mts.* Indonesia	**102/103**	G10	4 00S	137 00E
Pegunungan Muller *mts.* Indonesia	**95**	E4	0 00	113 00E
Pegunungan Schwaner *mts.* Indonesia	**95**	E3	1 00S	111 00E
Pegunungan Van Rees *mts.* Indonesia	**102**	G10	2 45S	138 30E
Pekalongan Indonesia	**95**	D2	6 54S	109 37E
Pelée, Mount Martinique	**66**	R12	14 47N	61 04W
Pelican Point Namibia	**101**	G3	22 54S	14 25E
Pelješac *i.* Croatia	**81**	F5	43 00N	17 00E
Pelopónnisos *geog. reg.* Greece	**81**	H2/J2	37 00N	22 00E
Pelotas Brazil	**73**	G7	31 45S	52 20W
Pematangsiantar Indonesia	**95**	B4	2 59N	99 01E
Pemba Mozambique	**101**	N5	13 00S	40 30E
Pembina Minnesota USA	**43**	D1	48 59N	97 20W
Peñarroya-Pueblonuevo Sp.	**79**	C3	38 19N	5 16W
Pendleton Oregon USA	**62**	C6	45 40N	118 46W
Pend Oreille Lake Idaho USA	**39**	M1	48 10N	116 20W
Pend Oreille River Washington USA	**39**	M1	48 50N	117 25W
Penedo Brazil	**72**	K11	10 16S	36 33W
Peng Chau *i.* HK China	**92**	B1	22 17N	114 02E
Peninsula de Taitao Chile	**73**	B4	46 30S	75 00W
Peninsular Malaysia *admin.* Malaysia	**95**	C4	5 00N	102 00E
Penner *r.* India	**90**	D2	14 30N	79 30E
Pennines *hills* UK	**78**	C11	54 30N	2 10W
Pennsylvania *state* USA	**63**	L5	41 00N	78 00W
Penn Yan New York USA	**47**	J2	42 40N	77 03W
Penobscot River Maine USA	**51**	F1	44 15N	68 30W
Penonomé Panama	**67**	H1	8 30N	80 20W
Penrith UK	**78**	D11	54 40N	2 44W
Pensacola Florida USA	**63**	J3	30 26N	87 12W
Pentland Firth *sd.* UK	**78**	D13	58 45N	3 10W
Penza Russia	**86**	G7	53 11N	45 00E
Penzance UK	**78**	C9	50 07N	5 33W
Peoria Illinois USA	**63**	J5	40 43N	89 38W
Pereira Col.	**72**	B14	4 47N	75 46W
Périgeuex Fr.	**79**	F6	45 12N	0 44E
Perm' Russia	**86**	H8	58 01N	56 10E
Pernambuco *admin.* Brazil	**72**	K12	8 00S	37 30W
Pernik Bulgaria	**81**	J5	42 36N	23 03E
Perpignan Fr.	**79**	G5	42 42N	2 54E
Perris California USA	**64**	E1	33 47N	117 14W
Perrysburg Ohio USA	**46**	C1	41 33N	83 39W
Perth Aust.	**102**	C4	31 58S	115 49E
Perth UK	**78**	D12	56 42N	3 28W
Perth Amboy New Jersey USA	**65**	C2	40 31N	74 16W
PERU	**72**	B11		
Peru Basin Pacific Ocean	**107**	S6	18 00S	95 00W
Peru-Chile Trench Pacific Ocean	**107**	T7	13 00S	77 00W
Perugia Italy	**81**	D5	43 07N	12 23E
Pesaro Italy	**81**	D5	43 54N	12 54E
Pescadero California USA	**64**	B3	37 15N	122 24W
Pescara Italy	**81**	E5	42 27N	14 13E
Peshawar Pakistan	**90**	C6	34 01N	71 40E
Petah Tiqwa Israel	**88**	N11	32 05N	34 53E
Petaluma California USA	**62**	B4	38 13N	12 39W
Petare Venezuela	**72**	D16	10 31N	66 50W
Petauke Zambia	**101**	L5	14 15S	31 20E
Peterborough Aust.	**103**	G4	33 00S	138 51E
Peterborough UK	**78**	E10	52 35N	0 15W
Peterhead UK	**78**	E12	57 30N	1 46W
Petersburg Alaska USA	**38**	D5	56 49N	132 58W
Petersburg Virginia USA	**63**	L4	37 14N	77 24W
Petoskey Michigan USA	**45**	J3	45 22N	84 58W
Petra *hist. site* Jordan	**88**	N10	30 19N	35 26E
Petrolina Brazil	**72**	J12	9 22S	40 30W
Petropavlovsk Kazakhstan	**86**	J7	54 53N	69 13E
Petropavlovsk-Kamchatskiy Russia	**87**	T7	53 03N	158 43E
Petroşani Romania	**81**	J6	45 25N	23 22E
Petrozavodsk Russia	**86**	F9	61 46N	34 19E
Pevek Russia	**87**	V10	64 41N	170 19E
Phenix City Alabama USA	**63**	J3	32 28N	85 01W
Philadelphia Pennsylvania USA	**63**	L4	40 00N	75 10W
Philippine Sea Pacific Ocean	**106**	C10	21 00N	130 00E
PHILIPPINES, THE	**95**	G7		
Philippine Trench Pacific Ocean	**106**	C8/C9	12 00N	127 00E
Phillipsburg New Jersey USA	**65**	C2	40 42N	75 11W
Phnom Penh Cambodia	**95**	C6	11 35N	104 55E
Phoenix Arizona USA	**62**	D3	33 30N	112 03W
Phoenix Island Kiribati	**106**	J7	3 30S	174 30W
Phoenix Islands Kiribati	**106**	J7	4 40S	177 30W
Phôngsali Laos	**93**	J3	21 40N	102 06E
Phuket Thailand	**95**	B5	7 52N	98 22E
Piacenza Italy	**81**	B6	45 03N	9 41E
Piátra Neamţ Romania	**81**	L7	46 53N	26 23E
Piauí *admin.* Brazil	**72**	J12	7 30S	43 00W
Pico Bolivar *mt.* Venezuela	**72**	C15	8 33N	71 03W
Pico Cristóbal *mt.* Col.	**72**	C16	10 53N	73 48W
Pico de Itambé *mt.* Brazil	**72**	J10	18 23S	43 21W
Picos Brazil	**72**	J12	7 05S	41 24W
Picton NZ	**103**	P2	41 18S	174 00E
Pidurutalagala *mt.* Sri Lanka	**90**	E1	7 01N	80 45E
Piedras Negras Mexico	**66**	D5	28 40N	100 32W
Pierre South Dakota USA	**62**	F5	44 23N	100 20W
Pierreville Trinidad and Tobago	**67**	V15	10 17N	61 01W
Pietermaritzburg RSA	**101**	L2	29 36S	30 24E
Pietersburg RSA	**101**	K3	23 54N	29 23E
Pigeon Michigan USA	**46**	C3	43 50N	83 15W
Pijijiapan Mexico	**66**	F3	15 42N	93 12W
Pikes Peak Colorado USA	**62**	E4	38 50N	105 03W
Pik Pobedy *mt.* Kyrgyzstan	**86**	L5	42 25N	80 15E
Piła Poland	**80**	F10	53 09N	16 44E

Raisin, River Michigan USA 46 C1 41 55N 83 40W
Rajahmundry India 90 E3 17 01N 81 52E
Rajapalaiyam India 90 D1 9 26N 77 36E
Rajasthan *admin.* India 90 C5 26 30N 73 00E
Rajkot India 90 C4 21 18N 70 53E
Rajshahi Bangladesh 91 K10 24 24N 88 40E
Raleigh North Carolina USA 63 L4 35 46N 78 39W
Ralik Chain *is.* Pacific Ocean 106 G8 7 30N 167 30E
Ramat Gan Israel 88 N10 32 04N 34 48E
Ramgarh Bangladesh 91 L9 22 59N 91 43E
Râmnicu Vâlcea Romania 81 K6 45 06N 24 21E
Rampur Himachal Pradesh India 90 D6 31 26N 77 37E
Rampur Uttar Pradesh India 90 D5 28 50N 79 05E
Ramtha Jordan 88 N11 32 34N 36 00E
Rancagua Chile 73 C7 34 10S 70 45W
Ranchi India 91 F4 23 22N 85 20E
Randers Denmark 80 C12 56 28N 10 03E
Rangeley Maine USA 47 R4 44 58N 70 40W
Rangpur Bangladesh 91 K10 25 45N 89 21E
Rann of Kachchh *geog. reg.* India/Pakistan 90 B4/C4 24 00N 69 00E
Rapid City South Dakota USA 62 F5 44 06N 103 14W
Rapid River *tn.* Michigan USA 45 H3 45 56N 86 58W
Ra's al Hadd *c.* Oman 89 G3 22 31N 59 45E
Râs Banâs *c.* Egypt 100 M12 23 58N 35 50E
Ras Dashen Terara *mt.* Ethiopia 100 M10 13 15N 38 27E
Râs el Barr Egypt 101 R5 31 32N 31 42E
Râs el 'Ish Egypt 101 S4 31 07N 32 18E
Ra's Fartak *c.* Yemen 89 F2 15 20N 52 12E
Rasht Iran 89 E6 37 18N 49 38E
Ras Lanuf Libya 100 H14 30 31N 18 34E
Ra's Madrakah *c.* Oman 89 G2 18 58N 57 50E
Ras Nouadhibou *c.* Mauritania 100 A12 20 53N 17 01W
Ratak Chain *is.* Pacific Ocean 106 H9 10 00N 172 30E
Rat Buri Thailand 95 B6 13 30N 99 50E
Ratlam India 90 D4 23 18N 75 06E
Ratno Ukraine 80 K9 51 40N 24 32E
Raton New Mexico USA 62 F4 36 45N 104 27W
Raurkela India 91 E4 22 16N 85 01E
Ravenna Italy 81 D6 44 25N 12 12E
Ravensburg Germany 80 B7 47 47N 9 37E
Ravensthorpe Aust. 102 D4 33 34S 120 01E
Ravi *r.* Pakistan 90 C6 31 00N 73 00E
Rawalpindi Pakistan 90 C6 33 40N 73 08E
Rawlins Wyoming USA 62 E5 41 46N 107 16W
Rawson Argentina 73 E5 43 15S 65 06W
Raymondville Texas USA 63 G2 26 30N 97 48W
Raystown Lake Pennsylvania USA 65 A2 40 10N 78 10W
Razgrad Bulgaria 81 L5 43 31N 26 33E
Reading UK 78 E9 51 28N 0 59W
Reading Pennsylvania USA 63 L5 40 20N 75 55W
Rebun-tō *i.* Japan 94 D4 45 25N 141 04E
Recherche, Archipelago of the *is.* Aust. 102 D4 35 00S 122 50E
Recife Brazil 72 L12 8 06S 34 53W
Reconquista Argentina 73 F8 29 08S 59 38W
Red *r.* USA 63 G3 34 00N 95 00W
Red *r.* USA 63 G6 46 00N 97 00W
Red Bluff California USA 62 B5 40 11N 122 16W
Redding California USA 62 B5 40 35N 122 24W
Redlands California USA 64 E2 34 03N 117 10W
Redon Fr. 78 D7 47 39N 2 05W
Redondo Beach *tn.* California USA 64 D1 33 51N 118 24W
Red Sea Middle East 88 C4/C2 27 00N 35 00E
Red Wing Minnesota USA 63 H5 44 33N 92 31W
Redwood City California USA 64 B3 37 28N 122 15W
Reed City Michigan USA 45 J2 43 53N 85 30W
Reedley California USA 64 D3 36 35N 119 27W
Reedsport Oregon USA 62 B5 43 42N 124 05W
Regensburg Germany 80 D8 49 01N 12 07E
Reggio di Calabria Italy 81 E3 38 06N 15 39E
Reggio nell'Emilia Italy 81 C6 44 42N 10 37E
Rehovot Israel 88 N10 31 54N 34 46E
Reims Fr. 78 H8 49 15N 4 02E
Reinosa Sp. 79 C5 43 01N 4 09W
Rembang Indonesia 95 E2 6 45S 111 22E
Rendsburg Germany 80 B11 54 19N 9 39E
Rennell *i.* Solomon Islands 103 M8 11 45S 160 15E
Rennes Fr. 78 E8 48 06N 1 40W
Reno Nevada USA 62 C4 39 32N 119 49W
Republic Washington USA 39 L1 48 39N 118 45W
REPUBLIC OF IRELAND 78 B10
REPUBLIC OF SOUTH AFRICA 101 J1/J2
Repulse Bay HK China 92 C1 22 14N 114 13E
Resistencia Argentina 72 F8 27 28S 59 00W
Reşiţa Romania 81 H6 45 16N 21 55E
Réthymno Greece 81 K1 35 23N 24 28E
Réunion *i.* Indian Ocean 105 E4 21 00S 55 30E
Reus Sp. 79 F4 41 10N 1 06E
Revillagigedo Island Alaska USA 38 E4 55 30N 131 30W
Rewa India 90 E4 24 32N 81 18E
Reykjanes Ridge Atlantic Ocean 108 E12 57 00N 33 00W
Reynosa Mexico 66 E5 26 05N 98 18W
Rhein *r.* Germany 80 A8 50 30N 8 00E
Rheine Germany 80 A10 52 17N 7 26E
Rhinelander Wisconsin USA 45 G3 45 38N 89 24W
Rhode Island *state* USA 63 M5 41 00N 71 00W
Rhône *r.* Switz./Fr. 79 H6 45 00N 4 50E
Ribe Denmark 80 B11 55 20N 8 47E
Ribeirão Prêto Brazil 72 H9 21 09S 47 48W
Riberalta Bolivia 72 D11 10 59S 66 06W
Richgrove California USA 64 D2 35 46N 119 04W
Richland Washington USA 62 C6 46 17N 119 17W
Richmond Aust. 103 H6 20 45S 143 05E
Richmond California USA 62 B4 37 46N 122 20W
Richmond Indiana USA 63 K4 39 50N 84 51W
Richmond New York USA 65 H1 40 36N 74 10W
Richmond Virginia USA 63 L4 37 34N 77 27W
Richmondville New York USA 65 C3 42 38N 74 34W
Ridgecrest California USA 64 E2 35 37N 117 43W
Ridgeway Pennsylvania USA 46 H1 41 25N 78 40W
Riesa Germany 80 D9 51 18N 13 18E
Rieti Italy 81 D5 42 24N 12 51E
Riga Latvia 80 K12 56 53N 24 08E
Riga, Gulf of Estonia/Latvia 80 J12 57 30N 23 30E
Rijeka Croatia 81 E6 45 20N 14 27E
Rimini Italy 81 D6 44 03N 12 34E
Ringgold Isles *is.* Fiji 106 V16 16 10S 179 50W
Ringkøbing Denmark 80 B12 56 06N 8 15E
Ringkøbing Fjord Denmark 80 B11 56 00N 8 00E
Riobamba Ecuador 72 B13 1 44S 78 40W
Rio Branco *tn.* Brazil 72 D12 9 59S 67 49W
Río Cuarto *tn.* Argentina 73 E7 33 08S 64 20W
Rio de Janeiro *tn.* Brazil 72 I8 22 53S 43 17W
Rio de Janeiro *admin.* Brazil 72 J9 22 00S 42 30W
Río de la Plata *est.* Uruguay/Argentina 73 F6/F7 35 00S 57 00W
Rio de Para *r.* Brazil 72 H13 1 00S 48 00W
Río Gallegos *tn.* Argentina 73 D3 51 35S 68 10W
Río Grande *r.* Mexico/USA 62 E3/F3 30 00N 105 00W
Rio Grande *tn.* Argentina 73 D3 53 45S 67 46W
Rio Grande *tn.* Brazil 73 G7 32 03S 52 08W
Río Grande *tn.* Mexico 66 D4 23 50N 103 02W
Rio Grande do Norte *admin.* Brazil 72 K12 6 00S 37 00W
Río Grande do Sul *admin.* Brazil 73 G8 28 00S 52 30W
Rio Grande Rise Atlantic Ocean 108 E3 32 00S 36 00W
Riohacha Col. 72 C16 11 34N 72 58W
Rio Verde *tn.* Brazil 72 G10 17 50S 50 55W
Río Verde *tn.* Mexico 66 D4 21 58N 100 00W
Rishiri-tō *i.* Japan 94 D4 45 10N 141 20E
Ritter, Mount California USA 62 C4 37 40N 119 15W
Rivera Uruguay 73 F7 30 52S 55 30W
River Cess *tn.* Liberia 100 C9 5 28N 9 32W
Riverside California USA 62 C3 33 59N 117 22W
Rivière-Pilote *tn.* Martinique 66 R12 14 29N 60 54W
Rivne Ukraine 80 L9 50 39N 26 10E
Riyadh Saudi Arabia 89 E3 24 39N 46 46E
Roanne Fr. 79 H7 46 02N 4 05E
Roanoke Virginia USA 63 L4 37 15N 79 58W
Robertsport Liberia 100 B9 6 45N 11 22W
Robin's Nest *mt.* HK China 92 C3 22 33N 114 11E
Roca Alijos *is.* Mexico 107 Q10 24 59N 115 49W
Rochefort Fr. 79 E6 45 57N 0 58W
Roche Harbor *tn.* Washington USA 38 H4 48 38N 123 06W
Rochester Minnesota USA 63 H5 84 01N 92 27W
Rochester New Hampshire USA 65 E3 43 18N 70 59W
Rochester New York USA 63 L5 43 12N 77 37W
Rockall Bank Atlantic Ocean 108 G12 58 00N 15 00W
Rockaway Beach New York USA 65 J1 40 33N 73 55W
Rockaway Inlet New York USA 65 J1 40 34N 73 56W
Rockford Illinois USA 63 J5 42 16N 89 06W
Rockhampton Aust. 103 K6 23 22S 150 32E
Rock Hill *tn.* South Carolina USA 63 K3 34 55N 81 01W
Rockin California USA 64 C4 38 47N 121 18W
Rock Island *tn.* Illinois USA 63 H5 41 30N 90 34W
Rock Lake *tn.* North Dakota USA 43 C1 48 49N 99 13W
Rockport Washington USA 38 H4 48 27N 121 37W
Rock Springs *tn.* Wyoming USA 62 E5 41 35N 109 13W
Rockville Maryland USA 65 B1 39 04N 77 08W
Rocky Mount *tn.* North Carolina USA 63 L4 35 46N 77 48W
Rodez Fr. 79 G6 44 21N 2 34E
Rodopi Planina *mts.* Bulgaria 81 K4 41 00N 25 00E
Rodrigues *i.* Indian Ocean 105 F5 19 43S 63 26E
Rogers City Michigan USA 45 K3 45 25N 83 49W
Rogers Lake California USA 64 E2 34 55N 117 48W
Rolette North Dakota USA 43 C1 48 40N 99 51W
Rolla Missouri USA 63 H4 37 56N 91 55W
Rolla North Dakota USA 43 C1 48 52N 99 37W
Roman Romania 81 L7 46 56N 26 56E
ROMANIA 80 H6
Rome Italy 81 D4 41 53N 12 30E
Rome Georgia USA 63 J3 34 01N 85 02W
Rome New York USA 63 L5 43 13N 75 28W
Ronda Sp. 79 C2 36 45N 5 10W
Rondônia *admin.* Brazil 72 E11 11 30S 63 00W
Rondonópolis Brazil 72 G10 16 29S 54 37W
Ronne Ice Shelf Antarctica 109 77 00S 60 00W
Roosevelt Minnesota USA 43 E1 48 48N 95 06W
Roraima *admin.* Brazil 72 E14 2 30N 62 30W
Rosamond Lake California USA 64 D2 34 50N 118 05W
Rosario Argentina 73 E7 33 00S 60 40W
Rosário Brazil 72 J13 3 0SS 44 15W
Rosario Mexico 66 A6 30 02N 115 46W
Rosario Mexico 66 C4 23 00N 105 51W
Rosario Strait *sd.* Washington USA 38 H4 48 25N 123 00W
Rosarito Mexico 66 B5 28 38N 114 02W
Roscoff Fr. 78 D8 48 43N 3 59W
Roscommon Michigan USA 45 J3 44 30N 84 35W
Roseau Dominica 66 Q8 15 18N 61 23W
Roseau Minnesota USA 43 E1 48 54N 95 43W
Roseburg Oregon USA 62 B5 43 13N 123 21W
Roselle New Jersey USA 65 H1 40 40N 74 16W
Rosenheim Germany 80 D7 47 51N 12 09E
Roseville California USA 64 C4 38 43N 121 20W
Roseville Michigan USA 46 D2 42 29N 82 52W
Rossano Italy 81 F3 39 35N 16 38E
Ross Ice Shelf Antarctica 109 80 00S 180 00
Ross Lake Washington USA 38 H4 48 50N 121 05W
Ross Lake National Recreation Area Washington USA 38 H4 48 50N 121 00W
Rosslare RoI 78 B10 52 15N 6 22W
Rosso Mauritania 100 A11 16 29N 15 53W
Ross Sea Antarctica 109 75 00S 180 00
Rostock Germany 80 D11 54 06N 12 09E
Rostov-na-Donu Russia 86 F6 47 15N 39 45E
Roswell New Mexico USA 62 F3 33 24N 104 33W
Rotorua NZ 103 Q3 38 08S 176 14E
Rotterdam Neths. 78 H9 51 54N 4 28E
Rotuma *i.* Fiji 103 Q8 12 30S 177 08E
Roubaix Fr. 78 G9 50 42N 3 10E
Rouen Fr. 78 F8 49 26N 1 05E
Round Mountain *tn.* Nevada USA 64 E4 38 43N 117 03W
Rovigo Italy 81 C6 45 04N 11 47E
Rowta India 91 M11 26 50N 92 20E
Roxas Philippines 95 G6 11 36N 122 45E
Royal Oak Michigan USA 46 C2 42 29N 83 09W
Royan Fr. 79 E6 45 38N 1 02W
Rub Al Khālī *d.* Saudi Arabia 89 E2 19 30N 48 00E
Rubtsovsk Russia 86 L7 51 43N 81 11E
Rudnyy Kazakhstan 86 J7 53 00N 63 05E
Rudyard Montana USA 41 G1 48 34N 110 33W
Rufiji *r.* Tanzania 101 M6 7 30S 38 40E
Rugao China 93 N5 32 27N 120 35E
Rugby UK 78 E10 52 23N 1 15W
Rügen *i.* Germany 80 D11 54 00N 14 00E
Rukwa, Lake Tanzania 101 L6 8 00S 33 00E
Rumford Maine USA 51 E1 44 33N 70 34W
Rumoi Japan 94 D3 43 57N 141 40E
Ruse Bulgaria 81 L5 43 50N 25 59E
Rusk Texas USA 63 G3 31 49N 95 11W
Russas Brazil 72 K13 4 56S 38 02W
Russell Kansas USA 63 G4 38 54N 98 51W
Russian *r.* California USA 64 B4 38 52N 123 03W
RUSSIAN FEDERATION 86/87
Ruston Louisiana USA 63 H3 32 32N 92 39W
Ruth Nevada USA 62 D4 39 16N 114 59W
Rutland Vermont USA 63 M5 43 37N 72 59W
Rutog China 92 D5 33 27N 79 43E
Ruvuma *r.* Tanzania/Mozambique 101 M5 11 30S 38 00E
Ružomberok Slovakia 80 G8 49 04N 19 15E
RWANDA 100 K7
Ryazan' Russia 86 F7 54 37N 39 43E
Rybinsk Russia 86 F8 58 03N 38 50E
Rybinskoye Vodokhranilische *res.* Russia 86 F8 59 00N 38 00E
Rybnik Poland 80 G9 50 07N 18 30E
Ryukyu Islands Japan 93 N4 27 30N 127 30E
Ryukyu Ridge Pacific Ocean 106 C10 25 50N 128 00E
Rzeszów Poland 80 J9 50 04N 22 00E

S

Saalfeld Germany 80 C9 50 39N 11 22E
Saarbrücken Germany 80 A8 49 15N 6 58E
Saaremaa *i.* Estonia 80 J13 58 20N 22 00E
Šabac SM 81 G6 44 45N 19 41E
Sabadell Sp. 79 G4 41 33N 2 07E
Sabah *admin.* Malaysia 95 F4/F5 5 00N 115 00E
Sabaloka Cataract Sudan 100 L11 16 19N 32 40E
Sabhā Libya 100 G13 27 02N 14 26E
Sabi *r.* Zimbabwe/Mozambique 101 L3 20 30S 33 00E
Sabinas Mexico 66 D5 27 50N 101 09W
Sabinas Hidalgo Mexico 66 D5 26 33N 100 10W
Sabine *r.* USA 63 H3 30 00N 94 00W
Sable, Cape Florida USA 63 K2 25 08N 80 07W
Sabor *r.* Port. 79 B4 41 22N 6 50W
Sabyā Saudi Arabia 88 D2 17 07N 42 39E
Sabzevār Iran 89 G6 36 15N 57 38E
Sacramento California USA 62 B4 38 32N 121 30W
Sacramento *r.* California USA 64 C4 38 05N 121 35W
Sacramento Mountains USA 62 E3 33 00N 105 00W
Sadiya India 91 H5 27 49N 95 38E
Sado *r.* Port. 79 A3 38 15N 8 30W
Sadoga-shima *i.* Japan 94 C2 38 20N 138 30E
Säffle Sweden 80 D13 59 08N 12 55E
Safi Morocco 100 C14 32 20N 9 17W
Saga Japan 94 B1 33 16N 130 18E
Sagamihara Japan 94 C2 35 34N 139 22E
Sagamore Massachusetts USA 65 E2 41 46N 70 31W
Sagar India 90 D4 23 50N 78 44E
Sage Creek *r.* Montana USA 41 G1 48 45N 110 40W
Saginaw Michigan USA 63 K5 43 25N 83 54W
Saginaw Bay Michigan USA 63 K5 44 00N 84 00W
Sagua la Grande Cuba 67 H4 22 48N 80 06W
Sagunto Sp. 79 E3 39 40N 0 17W
Sahara Desert North Africa 100/101 C12
Saharanpur India 90 D5 29 58N 77 33E
Sahiwal Pakistan 90 C6 30 41N 73 11E
Sahuaripa Mexico 66 C5 29 00N 109 13W
Sahuayo Mexico 66 D4 20 05N 102 42W
Saidpur Bangladesh 91 K10 25 48N 89 00E
Saikhoa Ghat India 91 H5 27 40N 95 35E
Sai Kung HK China 92 C2 22 23N 114 16E
St. Albans UK 78 E9 51 46N 0 21W
St. Albans New York USA 65 J1 40 42N 73 45W
St. Albans Vermont USA 51 D1 44 49N 73 07W
St. Andrews UK 78 D12 56 20N 2 48W
St. Ann's Bay *tn.* Jamaica 67 U14 18 26N 77 12W
St. Augustine Florida USA 63 K2 29 54N 81 19W
St. Barthélémy *i.* Lesser Antilles 66 P9 17 55N 62 50W
St-Brieuc Fr. 78 D8 48 31N 2 45W
St. Cloud Minnesota USA 63 H6 45 34N 94 10W
St. Croix *i.* W. Indies 67 M3 22 45N 65 00W
St. Croix *r.* USA 63 H6 46 00N 93 00W
St-Dié Fr. 78 J8 48 17N 6 57E
St-Dizier Fr. 78 H8 48 38N 4 58E
St. Elias, Mount Alaska USA 54 B3 60 12N 140 57W
Ste. Marie Martinique 66 R12 14 47N 61 00W
Saintes Fr. 79 E6 45 44N 0 38W
St-Étienne Fr. 79 H6 45 26N 4 23E
St. Eustatius *i.* Lesser Antilles 66 P9 17 30N 62 55W
St. Francis *r.* USA 63 H4 35 00N 90 00W
St. Gallen Switz. 79 K7 47 25N 9 23E
St-Gaudens Fr. 79 F5 43 07N 0 44E
St. George's Grenada 66 R11 12 04N 61 44W
St. George's Channel British Isles 78 B9 52 00N 6 00W
St. Helena *i.* Atlantic Ocean 108 H5 15 58S 5 43W
St. Helena Bay RSA 101 H1 32 00S 17 30E
St. Ignace Michigan USA 63 K6 45 53N 84 44W
St. John North Dakota USA 43 C1 48 57N 99 43W
St. John *r.* Liberia 100 C9 6 30N 9 40W
Saint John *r.* USA 63 N6 46 00N 69 00W
St. John's Antigua and Barbuda 66 Q9 17 08N 61 50W
St. Johns Michigan USA 46 B3 43 01N 84 31W
St. Joseph Missouri USA 63 H4 39 45N 94 51W
St. Joseph River Indiana/Ohio USA 46 B1 41 12N 84 55W
St. Kitts *i.* St. Kitts and Nevis 66 P9 17 21N 62 48W
ST. KITTS AND NEVIS 66 P9
St. Laurent French Guiana 72 G15 5 29N 54 03W
St. Lawrence Island Alaska USA 107 J14 63 15N 169 50W
St-Lô Fr. 78 E8 49 07N 1 05W
St. Louis Senegal 100 A11 16 01N 16 30W
St. Louis Missouri USA 63 H4 38 40N 90 15W
St. Louis River Minnesota USA 45 E4 47 20N 92 40W
ST. LUCIA 66 R11
St. Lucia Channel *sd.* Caribbean Sea 66 R12 14 09N 60 57W
St. Maarten Lesser Antilles 66 P10 18 04N 63 04W
St-Malo Fr. 78 D8 48 39N 2 00W
St. Martin Lesser Antilles 66 P10 18 04N 63 04W
St. Mary Montana USA 41 F1 48 44N 113 26W
St. Marys Pennsylvania USA 46 H1 41 25N 78 33W
St. Moritz Switz. 79 K7 46 30N 9 51E
St-Nazaire Fr. 79 D7 47 17N 2 12W
St-Omer Fr. 78 G9 50 45N 2 15E
St. Paul Minnesota USA 63 H5 45 00N 93 10W
St. Paul *r.* Liberia 100 B9/C9 7 10N 10 05W
St. Paul Rocks Atlantic Ocean 108 F7 0 23N 29 23W
St. Petersburg Russia 86 F8 59 55N 30 25E
St. Petersburg Florida USA 63 K2 27 45N 82 40W
St. Pölten Austria 80 E8 48 13N 15 37E
St-Quentin Fr. 78 G8 49 51N 3 17E
St. Thomas *i.* W. Indies 67 L3 18 00N 65 30W
St-Tropez Fr. 79 J5 43 16N 6 39E
St. Vincent *i.* St. Vincent and The Grenadines 66 R11 13 15N 61 12W
ST. VINCENT AND THE GRENADINES 66 R11
St. Vincent Passage *sd.* St. Lucia 66 R11 13 30N 61 00W
Sakai Japan 94 C1 34 35N 135 28E
Sakākah Saudi Arabia 88 D4 29 59N 40 12E
Sakakawea, Lake North Dakota USA 62 F6 48 00N 103 00W
Sakarya Turkey 88 B7 40 47N 30 23E
Sakarya *r.* Turkey 88 B7 40 05N 30 15E
Sakata Japan 94 C2 38 55N 139 51E
Sakhalin *i.* Russia 87 S7 50 00N 143 00E
Sakhalin Bay Russia 87 S7 54 00N 141 00E
Saki Nigeria 100 E9 8 39N 3 25E
Sala Sweden 80 F13 59 55N 16 38E
Salado *r.* Argentina 73 D6 35 00S 66 30W
Salado *r.* Argentina 73 E8 28 30S 62 30W
Şalalah Oman 89 F2 17 00N 54 04E
Salamanca Mexico 66 D4 20 34N 101 12W
Salamanca Sp. 79 C4 40 58N 5 40W
Salamanca New York USA 46 H2 42 10N 78 43W
Salay Goméz *i.* Pacific Ocean 107 R5 26 28S 105 28W
Saldus Latvia 80 J12 56 38N 22 30E
Salekhard Russia 86 J10 66 33N 66 35E

Salem India	90	D2	11 38N	78 08E
Salem Massachusetts USA	63	M5	42 32N	70 53W
Salem Oregon USA	62	B5	44 57N	123 01W
Salerno Italy	81	E4	40 40N	14 46E
Salgótarján Hungary	80	G8	49 05N	19 47E
Salgueiro Brazil	72	K12	8 04S	39 05W
Salima Malawi	101	L5	13 45S	34 29E
Salina Kansas USA	63	G4	38 53N	97 36W
Salinas Ecuador	72	A13	2 15S	80 58W
Salinas California USA	62	B4	36 39N	121 40W
Salinas *r.* California USA	64	C3	36 30N	121 40W
Salinas Grandes *l.* Argentina	73	D7/E8	30 00S	65 00W
Saline Michigan USA	46	C2	42 12N	83 46W
Salisbury UK	78	E9	51 05N	1 48W
Salisbury Maryland USA	63	L4	38 22N	75 37W
Salisbury North Carolina USA	63	K4	35 20N	80 30W
Salmon Idaho USA	62	D6	45 11N	113 55W
Salmon *r.* Idaho USA	62	C6	45 00N	116 00W
Salmon Reservoir New York USA	47	L3	43 32N	75 50W
Salmon River Mountains Idaho USA	62	C5	45 00N	115 00W
Salonta Romania	81	H7	46 49N	21 40E
Salt Jordan	88	N11	32 03N	35 44E
Salt *r.* Arizona USA	62	D3	34 00N	110 00W
Salta Argentina	72	D9	24 46S	65 28W
Salt Fork *r.* Texas/Oklahoma USA	62	F3	35 00N	100 00W
Saltillo Mexico	66	D5	25 30N	101 00W
Salt Lake City Utah USA	62	D5	40 45N	111 55W
Salto Uruguay	73	F7	31 27S	57 50W
Salton Sea *l.* California USA	62	C3	33 00N	116 00W
Salvador Brazil	72	K11	12 58S	38 29W
Salween *r.* China/Myanmar	95	B8	20 00N	103 00E
Salzburg Austria	80	D7	47 48N	13 03E
Salzgitter Germany	80	C10	52 13N	10 20E
Samani Japan	94	D3	42 07N	142 57E
Samar *i.* Philippines	95	G6	12 00N	125 00E
Samara Russia	86	H7	53 10N	50 10E
Samarinda Indonesia	95	F3	0 30S	117 09E
Samarkand Uzbekistan	86	J4	39 40N	66 57E
Sāmarrā' Iraq	88	D5	34 13N	43 52E
Sambalpur India	91	E4	21 28N	84 04E
Sambas Indonesia	95	D4	1 22N	109 15E
Sambor Ukraine	80	J8	49 31N	23 10E
SAMOA	106	J6		
Sámos *i.* Greece	81	L2	37 45N	26 45E
Samothráki *i.* Greece	81	K4	40 00N	25 00E
Samsun Turkey	88	C7	41 17N	36 22E
San Mali	100	C10	13 21N	4 57W
Sana Yemen	88	D2	15 23N	44 14E
Sanaga *r.* Cameroon	100	G8	4 30N	12 20E
Sanandaj Iran	89	E6	35 18N	47 01E
San Andrés Tuxtla Mexico	66	E3	18 28N	95 15W
San Angelo Texas USA	62	F3	31 28N	100 28W
San Antonio Chile	73	C7	33 35S	71 39W
San Antonio Texas USA	63	G2	29 25N	98 30W
San Antonio *r.* Texas USA	63	G2	29 00N	97 00W
San Antonio Oeste Argentina	73	E5	40 45S	64 58W
San Benito *r.* California USA	64	C3	36 45N	121 18W
San Bernardino California USA	62	C3	34 07N	117 18W
San Bernardo Chile	73	C7	33 37S	70 45W
San Carlos Venezuela	72	D15	9 39N	68 35W
San Carlos Luzon Philippines	95	G7	15 59N	120 22E
San Carlos Negros Philippines	95	G6	10 30N	123 29E
San Carlos de Bariloche Argentina	73	C5	41 11S	71 23W
San Carlos del Zulia Venezuela	72	C15	9 01N	71 58W
San Clemente California USA	64	E1	33 26N	117 36W
San Clemente Island California USA	62	C3	33 26N	117 36W
San Cristóbal Argentina	73	E7	30 20S	61 14W
San Cristóbal Mexico	66	F3	16 45N	92 40W
San Cristóbal Venezuela	72	C15	7 46N	72 15W
San Cristobal *i.* Solomon Islands	103	M8	11 00S	162 00E
Sancti Spíritus Cuba	67	J4	21 55N	79 28W
Sandakan Malaysia	95	F5	5 52N	118 04E
Sanday *i.* UK	78	D13	59 15N	2 30W
Sandefjord Norway	78	L13	59 00N	10 15E
San Diego California USA	62	C3	32 45N	117 10W
Sandpoint *tn.* Idaho USA	62	C6	48 17N	116 34W
Sandusky Ohio USA	45	K1	41 27N	82 43W
Sandusky Bay Ohio USA	46	D1	41 30N	82 50W
Sandwip Island Bangladesh	91	L9	22 30N	91 25E
Sandy River Maine USA	47	R4	44 45N	70 12W
San Felipe Mexico	66	B6	31 03N	114 52W
San Felipe Venezuela	72	D16	10 25N	68 40W
San Feliú de Guixols Sp.	79	G4	41 47N	3 02E
San Fernando Mexico	66	A5	29 59N	115 10W
San Fernando Sp.	79	B2	36 28N	6 12W
San Fernando Trinidad and Tobago	67	V15	10 16N	61 28W
San Fernando California USA	64	D2	34 17N	118 27W
San Fernando de Apure Venezuela	72	D15	7 53N	67 15W
Sanford Florida USA	63	K2	28 49N	81 17W
San Francisco Argentina	73	E7	31 29S	62 06W
San Francisco Dom. Rep.	67	K3	19 19N	70 15W
San Francisco California USA	62	B4	37 45N	122 27W
San Francisco Bay California USA	64	B3	37 37N	122 15W
San Francisco del Oro Mexico	66	C5	26 52N	105 50W
Sangar Russia	87	Q9	64 02N	127 30E
Sanger California USA	64	D3	36 42N	119 33W
Sangha *r.* Africa	100	H8	2 00N	17 00E
Sangli India	90	C3	16 55N	74 37E
Sangre de Cristo Mountains New Mexico USA	62	E4	37 00N	105 00W
Sangre Grande Trinidad and Tobago	67	V15	10 35N	61 08W
Sangu *r.* Bangladesh	91	M9	22 10N	92 15E
San Jacinto Peak *mt.* California USA	64	E1	33 48N	116 40W
San Javier Bolivia	72	E10	16 22S	62 38W
San Joaquin *r.* California USA	62	B4	37 00N	120 00W
San José Costa Rica	67	H1	9 59N	84 04W
San José Uruguay	73	F7	34 27S	56 40W
San José California USA	62	B4	37 20N	121 55W
San José del Cabo Mexico	66	C4	23 01N	109 40W
San Juan Argentina	73	D7	31 33S	68 31W
San Juan Peru	72	B10	15 22S	75 07W
San Juan Puerto Rico	67	L3	18 29N	66 08W
San Juan *r.* USA	62	D4	37 00N	110 00W
San Juan Islands Washington USA	38	H4	48 30N	123 05W
San Juan Mountains Colorado USA	62	E4	37 50N	107 50W
San Julián Argentina	73	D4	49 17S	67 45W
Sankosh *r.* India/Bhutan	91	K11	26 55N	90 00E
Sankuru *r.* CDR	100	J7	4 00S	23 30E
Sanliurfa Turkey	88	C6	37 08N	38 45E
Sanlúcar de Barrameda Sp.	79	B2	36 46N	6 21W
San Lucas Mexico	66	C4	22 50N	109 52W
San Luis Argentina	73	D7	33 20S	66 23W
San Luis Obispo California USA	62	B4	35 16N	120 40W
San Luis Obispo Bay California USA	64	C2	35 03N	120 39W
San Luis Potosí Mexico	66	D4	22 10N	101 00W
San Marcos Texas USA	63	G2	29 54N	97 57W
SAN MARINO	81	D5	44 00N	12 00E
San Mateo California USA	64	B3	37 33N	122 22W
Sanmenxia China	93	L5	34 46N	111 17E
San Miguel El Salvador	66	G2	13 28N	88 10W
San Miguel *r.* Bolivia	72	E10	15 00S	63 30W
San Miguel de Tucumán Argentina	72	D8	26 47S	65 15W
San Miguel Island California USA	64	C2	34 03N	120 22W
Sanming China	93	M4	26 16N	117 35E
San Nicolas de los Arroyos Argentina	73	E7	33 25S	60 15W
San Nicolas Island California USA	64	D1	33 15N	119 30W
San Pablo Philippines	95	G6	14 03N	121 19E
San Pablo Bay California USA	64	B4	38 00N	122 15W
San Pedro Argentina	72	E9	24 12S	64 55W
San Pedro Côte d'Ivoire	100	C8	4 45N	6 37W
San Pedro Dom. Rep.	67	L3	18 30N	69 18W
San Pedro Channel California USA	64	D1	33 37N	118 30W
San Pedro de las Colonias Mexico	66	D5	25 50N	102 59W
San Pedro Sula Honduras	66	G3	15 26N	88 01W
San Rafael Argentina	73	D7	34 35S	68 24W
San Rafael California USA	62	B4	37 58N	122 30W
San Rafael Mountains California USA	64	D2	34 50N	119 40W
San Remo Italy	81	A5	43 48N	7 46E
San Salvador El Salvador	66	G2	13 40N	89 10W
San Salvador *i.* Bahamas	67	K4	24 00N	74 32W
San Salvador de Jujuy Argentina	72	D9	24 10S	65 48W
San Sebastián Sp.	79	E5	43 19N	1 59W
San Severo Italy	81	E4	41 41N	15 23E
Santa Ana Bolivia	72	D11	13 46S	65 37W
Santa Ana El Salvador	66	G2	14 00N	89 31W
Santa Ana California USA	62	C3	33 44N	117 54W
Santa Barbara Mexico	66	C5	26 48N	105 50W
Santa Barbara California USA	62	C3	33 29N	119 01W
Santa Barbara Channel California USA	64	C2	34 15N	120 00W
Santa Barbara Island California USA	64	D1	33 29N	119 02W
Santa Catalina, Gulf of California USA	64	D1	33 07N	118 00W
Santa Catalina Island California USA	62	C3	33 25N	118 25W
Santa Catarina *admin.* Brazil	72	G8	27 00S	51 00W
Santa Clara Cuba	67	J4	22 25N	79 58W
Santa Clara California USA	64	C3	37 21N	121 57W
Santa Clarita California USA	64	D2	34 23N	118 33W
Santa Cruz Bolivia	72	E10	17 50S	63 10W
Santa Cruz Canary Islands	100	A13	28 28N	16 15W
Santa Cruz California USA	62	B4	36 58N	122 03W
Santa Cruz *r.* Argentina	73	C3	50 00S	70 00W
Santa Cruz Island California USA	62	C3	34 00N	119 40W
Santa Cruz Islands Solomon Islands	103	N8	11 00S	167 00E
Santa Fé Argentina	73	E7	31 35S	60 50W
Santa Fe New Mexico USA	62	E4	35 41N	105 57W
Santa Isabel *i.* Solomon Islands	103	L9	7 30S	158 30E
Santa Maria Brazil	73	G8	29 45S	53 40W
Santa Maria California USA	62	B3	34 56N	120 25W
Santa Marta Col.	72	C16	11 18N	74 10W
Santa Monica California USA	64	D2	34 00N	118 28W
Santana do Livramento Brazil	73	F7	30 52S	55 30W
Santander Col.	72	B14	3 00N	76 25W
Santander Sp.	79	D5	43 28N	3 48W
Sant' Antioco Italy	81	B3	39 04N	8 27E
Santa Paula California USA	64	D2	34 20N	119 04W
Santarém Brazil	72	G13	2 26S	54 41W
Santarém Port.	79	A3	39 14N	8 40W
Santa Rosa Argentina	73	E6	36 37S	64 17W
Santa Rosa Honduras	66	G2	14 48N	88 43W
Santa Rosa California USA	62	B4	38 26N	122 43W
Santa Rosa New Mexico USA	62	F3	34 56N	104 42W
Santa Rosa Island California USA	62	B3	34 00N	120 05W
Santa Rosalia Mexico	66	B5	27 20N	112 20W
Santa Ynez Mountains California USA	64	C2	34 31N	120 00W
Santee California USA	64	E1	32 51N	116 59W
Santiago Chile	73	C7	33 30S	70 40W
Santiago Panama	67	H1	8 08N	80 59W
Santiago de Compostela Sp.	79	A5	42 52N	8 33W
Santiago de Cuba Cuba	67	J4	20 00N	75 49W
Santiago del Estero Argentina	73	E8	27 47S	64 15W
Santiago Ixcuintla Mexico	66	C4	21 50N	105 11W
San Tin HK China	92	B3	22 30N	114 04E
Santipur India	91	K9	23 16N	88 27E
Santo Andre Brazil	72	H9	23 39S	46 29W
Santo Domingo Dom. Rep.	67	L3	18 30N	69 57W
Santo Domingo de los Colorados Ecuador	72	B13	0 13S	79 09W
Santos Brazil	72	H9	23 56S	46 22W
San Vicente El Salvador	66	G2	13 38N	88 42W
San Wai Tsuen HK China	92	B2	22 28N	114 03E
Sanya China	93	K2	18 25N	109 27E
São Bernardo do Campo Brazil	72	H9	23 45S	46 34W
São Borja Brazil	73	F8	28 35S	56 01W
São Francisco *r.* Brazil	72	K12	8 30S	39 00W
São José Brazil	73	H8	27 35S	48 40W
São José do Rio Prêto Brazil	72	H9	20 50S	49 20W
São José dos Campos Brazil	72	H9	23 07S	45 52W
São Luís Brazil	72	J13	2 34S	44 16W
Saône *r.* Fr.	79	H7	46 28N	4 55E
São Paulo Brazil	72	H9	23 33S	46 39W
São Paulo *admin.* Brazil	72	G9	21 30S	50 00W
São Paulo de Olivença Brazil	72	D13	3 34S	68 55W
São Tomé *i.* Gulf of Guinea	100	F8	0 25N	6 35E
SÃO TOMÉ AND PRINCIPE	100	F8		
São Vicente Brazil	72	H9	23 57S	46 23W
Sapporo Japan	94	D3	43 05N	141 21E
Saqqez Iran	88	E6	36 14N	46 15E
Sarajevo Bosnia-Herzegovina	81	G5	43 52N	18 26E
Sarakhs Iran	89	H6	36 32N	61 07E
Saransk Russia	86	G7	54 12N	45 10E
Sarasota Florida USA	63	K2	27 20N	82 32W
Sarata Ukraine	81	M7	46 00N	29 40E
Saratoga Springs *tn.* New York USA	65	D3	43 05N	73 47W
Saratov Russia	86	G7	51 30N	45 55E
Saravan Iran	89	H4	27 25N	62 17E
Sarawak *admin.* Malaysia	95	E4	1 00N	111 00E
Sardindida Plain Kenya	100	M8	2 00N	40 00E
Sardinia *i.* Italy	81	B3/B4	40 00N	9 00E
Sar-e Pol Afghanistan	89	J6	36 15N	65 57E
Sargasso Sea Atlantic Ocean	108	B9	27 00N	66 00W
Sargodha Pakistan	90	C6	32 01N	72 40E
Sarh Chad	100	H9	9 08N	18 22E
Sarīr Calanscio *d.* Libya	100	J13	26 00N	22 00E
Sark *i.* British Isles	78	D8	49 26N	2 22W
Sarles North Dakota USA	43	C1	48 57N	98 59W
Sarmiento Argentina	73	D4	45 38S	69 08W
Sarny Ukraine	80	L9	51 21N	26 31E
Sarpsborg Norway	78	L13	59 17N	11 06E
Sarrebourg Fr.	78	J8	48 43N	7 03E
Sarreguemines Fr.	78	J8	49 06N	6 55E
Sartène France	79	K4	41 37N	8 58E
Sasebo Japan	94	A1	33 10N	129 42E
Sassandra Côte d'Ivoire	100	C8	4 58N	6 08W
Sassandra *r.* Côte d'Ivoire	100	C9	5 50N	6 55W
Sassari Italy	81	B4	40 43N	8 34E
Sassnitz Germany	80	D11	54 32N	13 40E
Satna India	90	E4	24 33N	80 50E
Satpura Range *mts.* India	90	C4/D4	21 40N	75 00E
Sattahip Thailand	95	C6	12 36N	100 56E
Satu Mare Romania	80	J7	47 48N	22 52E
SAUDI ARABIA	88/89	D3/F3		
Sault Ste. Marie Michigan USA	45	J4	46 29N	84 22W
Saumur Fr.	79	E7	47 16N	0 05W
Saurimo Angola	101	J6	9 39S	20 24E
Sava *r.* Europe	81	G6	45 00N	16 00E
Savannah Georgia USA	63	K3	32 04N	81 07W
Savannah *r.* USA	63	K3	33 00N	82 00W
Savannakhet Laos	95	C7	16 34N	104 45E
Savanna la Mar Jamaica	67	T14	18 13N	78 08W
Savona Italy	81	B6	44 18N	8 28E
Sawahlunto Indonesia	95	C3	0 41S	100 52E
Sawu Sea Indonesia	95	G2	9 00S	122 00E
Sayanogorsk Russia	87	M7	53 00N	91 26E
Saylac Somalia	100	N10	11 21N	43 30E
Saynshand Mongolia	93	L8	45 00N	111 10E
Sayre Pennsylvania USA	47	K1	41 58N	76 03W
Say'ūn Yemen	89	E2	15 59N	48 44E
Scarborough Trinidad and Tobago	67	V15	11 11N	60 44W
Scarborough UK	78	E11	54 17N	0 24W
Schenectady New York USA	63	M5	42 48N	73 57W
Schleswig Germany	80	B11	54 32N	9 34E
Schurz Nevada USA	64	D4	38 57N	118 48W
Schwäbisch Alb *mts.* Germany	80	B8	48 00N	9 00E
Schwarzwald *mts.* Germany	80	B8	47 00N	8 00E
Schweinfurt Germany	80	C9	50 03N	10 16E
Schwerin Germany	80	C10	53 38N	11 25E
Scilly, Isles of UK	78	B8	49 56N	6 20W
Scobey Montana USA	42	E1	48 50N	105 29W
Scotia Ridge Atlantic Ocean	108	C1	53 00S	50 00W
Scotia Sea Antarctica	109		55 00S	45 00W
Scotland *admin.* UK	78	C12	56 00N	4 00W
Scott Island Southern Ocean	106	G1	66 35S	180 00
Scottsbluff Nebraska USA	62	F5	41 52N	103 40W
Scranton Pennsylvania USA	63	L5	41 25N	75 40W
Searles Lake California USA	64	E2	35 42N	117 17W
Seaside California USA	64	C3	36 36N	121 51W
Seattle Washington USA	62	B6	47 35N	122 20W
Sebewaing Michigan USA	46	C3	43 44N	83 26W
Seboomook Lake Maine USA	47	S5	45 55N	69 50W
Sedalia Missouri USA	63	H4	38 42N	93 15W
Sedan Fr.	78	H8	49 42N	4 57E
Sedro Woolley Washington USA	38	H4	48 27N	122 18W
Ségou Mali	100	C10	13 28N	6 18W
Segovia Sp.	79	C4	40 57N	4 07W
Segre *r.* Sp.	79	F4	42 00N	1 10E
Segura *r.* Sp.	79	D3	38 00N	1 00W
Seine *r.* Fr.	78	F8	49 15N	1 15E
Sekiu Washington USA	38	H4	48 10N	124 30W
Sekondi Takoradi Ghana	100	D8	4 59N	1 43W
Selat Sunda *sd.* Indonesia	95	D2	5 50S	105 30E
Selemdzha *r.* Russia	87	R7	53 00N	132 00E
Selenge *r.* Mongolia	93	J8	49 00N	102 00E
Selima Oasis Sudan	100	K12	21 22N	29 19E
Selma Alabama USA	63	J3	32 24N	87 01W
Selma California USA	64	D3	36 34N	119 36W
Semarang Indonesia	95	E2	6 58S	110 29E
Seminoe Reservoir Wyoming USA	62	E5	42 00N	106 00W
Seminole Oklahoma USA	63	G4	35 15N	96 40W
Semipalatinsk Kazakhstan	86	L7	50 26N	80 16E
Semnān Iran	89	F6	35 30N	53 25E
Sendai Honshu Japan	94	D2	38 16N	140 52E
Sendai Kyushu Japan	94	B1	31 50N	130 17E
Seneca Falls *tn.* New York USA	47	K2	42 55N	76 48W
Seneca Lake New York USA	45	N2	42 40N	77 01W
SENEGAL	100	A10		
Sénégal *r.* Senegal/Mauritania	100	A11	16 45N	14 45W
Senhor do Bonfim Brazil	72	J11	10 28S	40 11W
Senj Croatia	81	E6	45 00N	14 55E
Sennar Sudan	100	L10	13 31N	33 38E
Sens Fr.	78	G8	48 12N	3 18E
Senyavin Islands Pacific Ocean	106	G8	7 00N	161 30E
Seoul South Korea	93	P6	37 32N	127 00E
Sepik *r.* PNG	103	H10	4 15S	143 00E
Sequoia National Park California USA	64	D3	36 23N	118 38W
Seram *i.* Indonesia	95	H3/J3	3 30S	129 30E
Seram Sea Indonesia	95	H3/J3	2 30S	130 00E
Serang Indonesia	95	D2	6 07S	106 09E
SERBIA AND MONTENEGRO	81	G5/H6		
Seremban Malaysia	95	C4	2 43N	102 57E
Serenje Zambia	101	L5	13 12S	30 15E
Sergino Russia	86	J9	62 30N	65 40E
Sergipe *admin.* Brazil	72	K11	11 00S	38 00W
Sergiyev Posad Russia	86	F8	56 20N	38 10E
Seria Brunei	95	E4	4 39N	114 23E
Serian Malaysia	95	E4	1 10N	110 35E
Sérifos *i.* Greece	81	K2	37 10N	24 25E
Serov Russia	86	J8	59 42N	60 32E
Serpent's Mouth *sd.* Trinidad and Tobago	67	V15	10 10N	61 58W
Serra Brazil	72	J10	20 06S	40 16W
Serra do Mar *mts.* Brazil	72/73	H8	27 30S	49 00W
Serra do Navio Brazil	72	G14	1 00N	52 05W
Serrania de Cuenca *mts.* Sp.	79	D4/E4	40 30N	2 15W
Serra Tumucumaque *mts.* Brazil	72	F14	2 00N	55 00W
Sérres Greece	81	J4	41 03N	23 33E
Sete Lagoas Brazil	72	J10	19 29S	44 15W
Setesdal *geog. reg.* Norway	78	J13	59 30N	7 10E
Sétif Algeria	100	F15	36 11N	5 24E
Setit *r.* Sudan	100	M10	14 20N	36 15E
Seto-naikai *sd.* Japan	94	B1	34 00N	132 30E
Settat Morocco	100	C14	33 04N	7 37W
Setúbal Port.	79	A3	38 31N	8 54W
Severn *r.* UK	78	D10	52 30N	3 15W
Severnaya (North) Dvina *r.* Russia	86	G9	63 00N	43 00E
Severnaya Sos'va *r.* Russia	86	J9	62 30N	62 00E

Severnaya Zemlya *is.* Russia 87 M13 80 00N 95 00E
Severodvinsk Russia 86 F9 64 35N 39 50E
Sevier *r.* Utah USA 62 D4 39 00N 113 00W
Seville Sp. 79 C2 37 24N 5 59W
SEYCHELLES 105 E6
Seychelles Ridge Indian Ocean 105 E6 10 00S 60 00E
Seymchan Russia 87 T9 62 54N 152 26E
Sfântu Gheorghe Romania 81 K6 45 51N 25 48E
Sfax Tunisia 100 G14 34 45N 10 43E
Sha Chau *i.* HK China 92 A2 22 21N 113 53E
Shache China 92 D6 38 27N 77 16E
Shah Alam Malaysia 95 C4 3 02N 101 31E
Shahdol India 90 E4 23 19N 81 26E
Shahjahanpur India 90 D5 27 53N 79 55E
Sha Lo Wan HK China 92 A1 22 17N 113 54E
Sham Chung HK China 92 C2 22 26N 114 17E
Sham Chun River HK China 92 B3 22 30N 114 00E
Shamokin Pennsylvania USA 65 B2 40 47N 76 34W
Sham Shek Tsuen HK China 92 A1 22 17N 113 53E
Sham Shui Po HK China 92 C1 22 20N 114 10E
Shangani *r.* Zimbabwe 101 K4 19 00S 29 00E
Shanghai China 93 N5 31 06N 121 22E
Shangqui China 93 M5 34 27N 115 07E
Shangrao China 93 M4 28 28N 117 54E
Shannon RoI 78 A10 52 41N 8 55W
Shannon *r.* RoI 78 A10 52 45N 8 57W
Shannon, Lake Washington USA 38 H4 48 35N 121 45W
Shantou China 93 M3 23 23N 116 39E
Shaoguan China 93 L3 24 54N 113 33E
Shaoxing China 93 N5 30 02N 120 35E
Shaoyang China 93 L4 27 10N 111 25E
Shaqrā' Saudia Arabia 88 E4 25 18N 45 15E
Sharjah UAE 89 G4 25 20N 55 20E
Sharon Pennsylvania USA 63 K5 41 46N 80 30W
Sharp Island HK China 92 C2 22 22N 114 18E
Sharp Peak HK China 92 D2 22 26N 114 22E
Shashi China 93 L5 30 16N 112 20E
Shasta Lake California USA 62 B5 40 45N 122 20W
Shasta, Mount California USA 62 B5 41 25N 122 12W
Sha Tau Kok HK China 92 C3 22 33N 114 13E
Sha Tin HK China 92 C2 22 23N 114 11E
Shatsky Rise Pacific Ocean 106 G11 34 00N 160 00E
Shebele *r.* Ethiopia/Somalia 100 N9 6 00N 44 00E
Sheberghān Afghanistan 89 J6 36 41N 65 45E
Sheboygan Wisconsin USA 63 J5 43 46N 87 44W
Sheffield UK 78 E10 53 23N 1 30W
Sheffield Pennsylvania USA 46 G1 41 43N 79 02W
Shek Kong HK China 92 B2 22 26N 114 06E
Shek Kwu Chau *i.* HK China 92 A1 22 12N 113 59E
Shek O HK China 92 C1 22 14N 114 15E
Shek Pik HK China 92 A1 22 13N 113 53E
Shek Pik Reservoir HK China 92 A1 22 14N 113 54E
Shek Uk Shan *mt.* HK China 92 C2 22 26N 114 18E
Shek Wu Hui HK China 92 B3 22 30N 114 07E
Shelby Montana USA 62 D6 48 30N 111 52W
Shelekhov Bay Russia 87 T8/T9 60 00N 157 00E
Shell Lake Wisconsin USA 45 F3 45 45N 91 56W
Shelter Island HK China 92 C1 22 19N 114 19E
Shenandoah Iowa USA 63 G5 40 48N 95 22W
Shenandoah Mountains West Virginia USA 65 B1 39 20N 78 45W
Shenandoah National Park West Virginia/Virginia USA 65 B1 39 00N 78 00W
Shenyang China 93 N7 41 50N 123 26E
Shenzhen China 93 L3 22 31N 114 08E
Shepetovka Ukraine 80 L9 50 12N 27 01E
Sherburne New York USA 47 L2 42 41N 75 30W
Sheridan Wyoming USA 62 E5 44 48N 106 57W
's-Hertogenbosch Neths. 78 H9 51 41N 5 19E
Sherwood North Dakota USA 42 G1 48 57N 101 38W
Shetland Islands UK 78 E13/E14 60 00N 1 15W
Sheung Fa Shan HK China 92 B2 22 23N 114 06E
Sham Tseng HK China 92 B2 22 22N 114 03E
Sheung Shui HK China 92 B3 22 31N 114 08E
Shiawassee River Michigan USA 46 B3 43 05N 84 12W
Shihezi China 92 F7 44 19N 86 10E
Shijiazhuang China 93 L6 38 04N 114 28E
Shikarpur Pakistan 90 B5 27 58N 68 42E
Shikoku *i.* Japan 94 B1 33 40N 134 00E
Shikotan *i.* Japan 94 E3 43 47N 148 45E
Shiliguri India 91 F5 26 42N 88 30E
Shilka *r.* Russia 87 P7 52 30N 117 30E
Shillong India 91 G5 25 34N 91 53E
Shimizu Japan 94 C2 35 01N 138 29E
Shimla India 90 D6 31 07N 77 09E
Shimoga India 90 D2 13 56N 75 31E
Shimonoseki Japan 94 B1 33 59N 130 58E
Shinano *r.* Japan 94 C2 37 40N 139 00E
Shīndand Afghanistan 89 H5 33 16N 62 05E
Shingū Japan 94 C1 33 42N 136 00E
Shinjō Japan 94 D2 38 45N 140 18E
Shinyanga Tanzania 100 L7 3 40S 33 25E
Shiono-misaki *c.* Japan 94 C1 33 28N 135 47E
Shirakawa Japan 94 D2 37 07N 140 11E
Shiraoi Japan 94 D3 42 34N 141 19E
Shīrāz Iran 89 F4 29 38N 52 34E
Shiretoko-misaki *c.* Japan 94 E3 44 24N 145 20E
Shizuishan China 93 K6 39 04N 106 22E
Shizuoka Japan 94 C1 34 59N 138 24E
Shkodër Albania 81 G5 42 03N 19 01E
Shoshone California USA 64 E2 35 58N 116 17W
Shreveport Louisiana USA 63 H3 32 30N 93 46W
Shrewsbury UK 78 D10 52 43N 2 45W
Shuangliao China 93 N7 43 30N 123 29E
Shuangyashan China 93 Q8 46 42N 131 20E
Shuen Wan HK China 92 C2 22 28N 114 12E
Shui Tau HK China 92 B2 22 27N 114 04E
Shui Tsiu San Tsuen HK China 92 B2 22 26N 114 02E
Shuksan, Mount Washington USA 38 H4 48 52N 121 30W
Shumen Bulgaria 81 L5 43 17N 26 55E
Shunde China 93 L3 22 50N 113 16E
Shuqrā Yemen 89 E1 13 23N 45 44E
Shymkent Kazakhstan 86 J5 42 16N 69 05E
Sialkot Pakistan 90 C6 32 29N 74 35E
Siauliai Lithuania 80 J11 55 51N 23 20E
Šibenik Croatia 81 E5 43 45N 15 55E
Sibi Pakistan 90 B5 29 31N 67 54E
Sibiti Congo 100 G7 3 40S 13 24E
Sibiu Romania 81 K6 45 46N 24 09E
Sibolga Indonesia 95 B4 1 42N 98 48E
Sibu Malaysia 95 E4 2 19N 111 50E
Sibut CAR 100 H9 5 46N 19 06E
Sichuan Pendi China 93 J5/K5 32 00N 107 00E
Sicilian Channel Mediterranean Sea 81 D2 37 00N 12 00E
Sicily *i.* Italy 81 D2/E2 37 00N 14 00E
Sicuani Peru 72 C11 14 21S 71 13W
Sidi Barrani Egypt 100 K14 31 38N 25 58E
Sidi Bel Abbès Algeria 100 D15 35 15N 0 39W
Sidi Ifni Morocco 100 B13 29 24N 10 12W
Sidney Lanier, Lake Georgia USA 63 K3 34 00N 84 00W
Sidon Lebanon 88 N11 33 32N 35 22E
Siedlce Poland 80 J10 52 10N 22 18E
Siegen Germany 80 B9 50 52N 8 02E
Siena Italy 81 C5 43 19N 11 19E
Sierra Blanca *tn.* Texas USA 62 E3 31 10N 105 22W
Sierra de Maracaju *mts.* Brazil 72 F9 20 00S 55 00W
SIERRA LEONE 100 B9
Sierra Madre del Sur *mts.* Mexico 66 D3/E3 17 30N 100 00W
Sierra Madre Occidental *mts.* Mexico 66 C5/D4 26 00N 107 00W
Sierra Madre Oriental *mts.* Mexico 66 D5/E4 23 30N 100 00W
Sierra Morena *mts.* Sp. 79 B3/C3 38 05N 5 50W
Sierra Nevada *mts.* Sp. 79 D2 37 00N 3 20W
Sierra Nevada *mts.* California USA 62 C4 37 00N 119 00W
Sierras de Córdoba *mts.* Argentina 73 D7/E7 32 30S 65 00W
Sífnos *i.* Greece 81 K2 37 00N 24 40E
Sighetu Marmației Romania 80 J7 47 56N 23 53E
Sighișoara Romania 81 K7 46 12N 24 48E
Sigüenza Sp. 79 D4 41 04N 2 38W
Siguiri Guinea 100 C10 11 28N 9 07W
Sikar India 90 D5 27 33N 75 12E
Sikasso Mali 100 C10 11 18N 5 38W
Sikhote-Alin' *mts.* Russia 87 R6 45 00N 137 00E
Sikkim *admin.* India 91 F5 27 30N 88 30E
Sil *r.* Sp. 79 B5 42 25N 7 05W
Silchar India 91 G4 24 49N 92 47E
Silifke Turkey 88 B6 36 22N 33 57E
Silistra Bulgaria 81 L6 44 06N 27 17E
Silkeborg Denmark 80 B12 56 10N 9 39E
Silute Lithuania 80 H11 55 21N 21 30E
Silver Bay *tn.* Minnesota USA 45 F4 47 18N 91 15W
Silver City New Mexico USA 62 E3 32 47N 108 16W
Silver Creek *tn.* New York USA 46 G2 42 32N 79 10W
Silver Peak Range *mts.* Nevada USA 64 E3 37 30N 117 45W
Silver Springs *tn.* Nevada USA 64 D4 39 25N 119 14W
Silves Port. 79 A2 37 11N 8 26W
Simi Valley *tn.* California USA 64 D2 34 16N 118 47W
Simpson Desert Aust. 102 G6 24 30S 137 30E
Sincelejo Col. 72 B15 9 17N 75 23W
Sind *geog. reg.* Pakistan 90 B5 26 20N 68 40E
Sines Port. 79 A2 37 58N 8 52W
SINGAPORE 95 C4
Singaraja Indonesia 95 F2 8 06S 115 04E
Singatoka Fiji 106 T15 18 10S 177 30E
Sinop Turkey 88 C7 42 02N 35 09E
Sintra Port. 79 A3 38 48N 9 22W
Sinuiju North Korea 93 N7 40 04N 124 25E
Sioux City Iowa USA 63 G5 42 30N 96 28W
Sioux Falls *tn.* South Dakota USA 63 G5 43 34N 96 42W
Siping China 93 N7 43 15N 124 25E
Sira *r.* Norway 78 J13 58 50N 6 40E
Siracusa Italy 81 E2 37 04N 15 19E
Sirajganj Bangladesh 91 K10 24 27N 89 42E
Siret *r.* Romania 80 L7 47 00N 26 00E
Sirte Libya 100 H14 31 13N 16 35E
Sirte Desert Libya 100 H14 30 00N 16 00E
Sirte, Gulf of Libya 100 H14 31 00N 17 00E
Sisak Croatia 81 F6 45 30N 16 22E
Sisophon Cambodia 95 C6 13 37N 102 58E
Sisteron Fr. 79 H6 44 16N 5 56E
Sitka Alaska USA 38 C5 57 05N 135 20W
Sitka Sound Alaska USA 38 C5 57 00N 135 50W
Sittwe Myanmar 92 G3 20 09N 92 55E
Sivas Turkey 88 C6 39 44N 37 01E
Siwa Egypt 100 K13 29 11N 25 31E
Sjaelland *i.* Denmark 80 C11 55 15N 11 30E
Skadarsko ezero *l.* Europe 81 G5 42 00N 19 00E
Skagen Denmark 80 C12 57 44N 10 37E
Skagerrak *sd.* Denmark/Norway 78 K12 57 30N 8 00E
Skagit River Washington USA 38 H4 48 30N 121 20W
Skagway Alaska USA 38 C6 59 23N 135 20W
Skien Norway 78 K13 59 14N 9 37E
Skierniewice Poland 80 H9 51 58N 20 10E
Skikda Algeria 100 F15 36 53N 6 54E
Skive Denmark 80 B12 56 34N 9 02E
Skopje FYROM 81 H4 42 00N 21 28E
Skövde Sweden 80 D13 58 24N 13 52E
Skovorodino Russia 87 Q7 54 00N 123 53E
Skowhegan Maine USA 47 S4 44 46N 69 44W
Skye *i.* UK 78 B12 57 20N 6 15W
Skýros *i.* Greece 81 K3 38 50N 24 35E
Slaney *r.* RoI 78 B10 52 24N 6 33W
Slatina Romania 81 K6 44 26N 24 22E
Slavonski Brod Croatia 81 F6 45 09N 18 02E
Sligo RoI 78 A11 54 17N 8 28W
Sliven Bulgaria 81 L5 42 40N 26 19E
SLOVAKIA 80 F8/H8
SLOVENIA 81 E6
Sluch' *r.* Ukraine 80 L9 50 00N 27 00E
Słupsk Poland 80 F11 54 28N 17 00E
Smederevo SM 81 H6 44 40N 20 56E
Smethport Pennsylvania USA 46 H1 41 48N 78 26W
Smoky Hills Kansas USA 62 G4 39 00N 100 00W
Smolensk Russia 86 F7 54 49N 32 04E
Smolyan Bulgaria 81 K4 41 34N 24 42E
Snake *r.* USA 62 C5 44 00N 118 00W
Snake River Plain USA 62 D5 43 00N 114 00W
Snowdon *mt.* UK 78 C10 53 04N 4 05W
Snowy Mountains Aust. 103 J3 36 50S 147 00E
Snyder Texas USA 62 F3 32 43N 100 54W
Soa-Siu Indonesia 95 H4 0 40N 127 30E
Sobat *r.* Sudan 100 L9 8 00N 33 00E
Sobral Brazil 72 J13 3 45S 40 20W
Sochi Russia 86 F5 43 35N 39 46E
Society Islands Pacific Ocean 107 L6 16 30S 153 00W
Socotra *i.* Yemen 89 F1 12 05N 54 10E
Soda Lake California USA 64 E2 35 09N 116 04W
Soda Springs *tn.* California USA 64 C4 39 19N 120 23W
Södertälje Sweden 80 F13 59 11N 17 39E
Sodo Ethiopia 100 M9 6 49N 37 41E
Sodus New York USA 47 J3 43 14N 77 04W
Sofia Bulgaria 81 J5 42 40N 23 18E
Sogamoso Col. 72 C15 5 43N 72 56W
Sohâg Egypt 100 L13 26 33N 31 42E
Soissons Fr. 78 G8 49 23N 3 20E
Sok Kwu Wan HK China 92 B1 22 13N 114 08E
Sokodé Togo 100 E9 8 59N 1 11E
Soko Islands HK China 92 A1 22 10N 113 54E
Sokoto Nigeria 100 F10 13 02N 5 15E
Sokoto *r.* Nigeria 100 E10 13 02N 4 55E
So Kwun Wat HK China 92 B2 22 23N 114 00E
Solāpur India 90 D3 17 43N 75 56E
Soledad California USA 64 C3 36 25N 121 20W
Solikamsk Russia 86 H8 59 40N 56 45E
Solimões *r.* Brazil 72 D13 3 30S 69 00W
Sóller Spain 79 G3 39 46N 2 42E
Sologne *geog. reg.* Fr. 79 F7 47 35N 1 47E
SOLOMON ISLANDS 103 L9
Solomon Sea PNG 103 K9 7 00S 150 00E
Solothurn Switz. 79 J7 47 13N 7 32E
Soltau Germany 80 B10 52 59N 9 50E
Solway Firth *est.* UK 78 D11 54 45N 3 40W
SOMALIA 100 N8
Somali Basin Indian Ocean 105 E7 5 00N 55 00E
Sombor SM 81 G6 45 46N 19 09E
Sombrerete Mexico 66 D4 23 38N 103 40W
Sombrero Channel *sd.* India 91 G1 7 41N 93 35E
Somerset Michigan USA 45 J2 42 03N 84 22W
Somme *r.* Fr. 78 F8 50 00N 1 45E
Sommen *l.* Sweden 80 E12 58 05N 15 15E
Somoto Nicaragua 67 G2 13 29N 86 36W
Son *r.* India 90 E4 24 00N 84 00E
Sønderborg Denmark 80 B11 54 55N 9 48E
Songea Tanzania 101 M5 10 42S 35 59E
Songhua Jiang *r.* China 93 P8 46 00N 128 00E
Songkhla Thailand 95 C5 7 12N 100 35E
Song-koi *r.* China/Vietnam 93 J3 22 30N 103 00E
Sonoita Mexico 66 B6 31 53N 112 52W
Sonora California USA 64 C3 37 59N 120 21W
Sonsonate El Salvador 66 G2 13 43N 89 44W
Sopot Poland 80 G11 54 27N 18 31E
Soria Sp. 79 D4 41 46N 2 28W
Soroca Moldova 80 M8 48 08N 28 12E
Sorong Indonesia 95 J3 0 50S 131 17E
Soroti Uganda 100 L8 1 42N 33 37E
Sorraia *r.* Port. 79 A3 38 55N 9 30W
Sosnowiec Poland 80 G9 50 16N 19 07E
Soufrière *mt.* Guadeloupe 66 Q9 16 03N 61 40W
Souillac Fr. 79 F6 44 53N 1 29E
Sousse Tunisia 100 G14 35 50N 10 38E
Southampton UK 78 E9 50 55N 1 25W
Southampton New York USA 65 D2 40 53N 72 24W
South Andaman *i.* Andaman Islands 91 G2 11 30N 93 00E
South Australia *state* Aust. 102/103 F4 27 00S 135 00E
South Australian Basin Indian Ocean 105 M3 38 00S 125 00E
South Bend Indiana USA 63 J5 41 40N 86 15W
South Carolina *state* USA 63 K3 34 00N 81 00W
South China Sea Pacific Ocean 95 E6/F7 15 00N 110 00E
South Dakota *state* USA 62 F5 45 00N 102 00W
South East Cape Aust. 103 J2 43 38S 146 48E
Southeast Indian Basin Indian Ocean 105 K3 32 00S 108 00E
Southeast Indian Ridge Indian Ocean 105 H2 45 00S 90 00E
South East Pacific Basin Pacific Ocean 107 S3 53 00S 95 00W
Southend-on-Sea UK 78 F9 51 33N 0 43E
Southern Alps *mts.* NZ 103 N1/P2 43 07S 171 13E
Southern Honshu Ridge Pacific Ocean 106 E10 25 50N 142 30E
Southern Ocean 109
South Fiji Basin Pacific Ocean 106 H5 25 00S 176 50E
South Georgia *i.* Atlantic Ocean 108 E1 54 00S 36 30W
South Hatia Island Bangladesh 91 L9 22 19N 91 07E
South Indian Basin Indian Ocean 105 L1 55 00S 130 00E
South Island NZ 103 N1 42 30S 172 00E
SOUTH KOREA 93 P6
South Lake Tahoe *tn.* California USA 64 D4 38 55N 119 58W
South Loup *r.* Nebraska USA 62 G5 42 00N 99 00W
South Negril Point *c.* Jamaica 67 T14 18 16N 78 22W
South Orkney Islands Southern Ocean 109 60 00S 45 00W
South Platte *r.* USA 62 F5 41 00N 103 00W
South Pole Antarctica 109 90 00S
South Sandwich Trench Atlantic Ocean 108 E2/F1 55 00S 30 00W
South San Francisco California USA 64 B3 37 39N 122 24W
South Shetland Islands Southern Ocean 109 62 00S 60 00W
South Sioux City Nebraska USA 63 G5 42 28N 96 24W
South Uist *i.* UK 78 B12 57 20N 7 15W
Southwest Indian Ridge Indian Ocean 105 C2 40 00S 50 00E
South West Pacific Basin Pacific Ocean 107 L4 35 00S 155 00W
Sovetsk Russia 80 H11 55 02N 21 50E
Sovetskaya Gavan' Russia 87 S6 48 57N 140 16E
SPAIN 79 C3/E3
Spanish Town Jamaica 67 U13 17 59N 76 58W
Sparks Nevada USA 62 B4/C4 39 34N 119 46W
Spartanburg South Carolina USA 63 K3 34 56N 81 57W
Spárti Greece 81 J2 37 05N 22 25E
Spassk-Dal'niy Russia 87 R5 44 37N 132 37E
Speightstown Barbados 66 S11 13 15N 59 39W
Spencer Iowa USA 63 G5 43 08N 95 08W
Spencer Gulf Aust. 102 G3 34 00S 137 00E
Spey *r.* UK 78 D12 57 35N 3 10W
Spitsbergen *i.* Arctic Ocean 86 D12 79 00N 15 00E
Spittal an der Drau Austria 81 D7 46 48N 13 30E
Split Croatia 81 F5 43 31N 16 28E
Spokane Washington USA 62 C6 47 40N 117 25W
Spoleto Italy 81 D5 42 44N 12 44E
Spratly Islands South China Sea 95 E5/F5 8 45N 111 54E
Springbok RSA 101 H2 29 44S 17 56E
Springdale Nevada USA 64 E3 37 02N 116 46W
Springfield Illinois USA 63 J4 39 49N 89 39W
Springfield Massachusetts USA 63 M5 42 07N 72 35W
Springfield Missouri USA 63 H4 37 11N 93 19W
Springfield Ohio USA 63 K4 39 55N 83 48W
Springfield Oregon USA 62 B5 44 03N 123 01W
Springfield Vermont USA 65 D3 43 18N 72 29W
Spring Mountains Nevada USA 64 F3 36 22N 115 52W
Springsure Aust. 103 J6 24 09S 148 04E
Springville New York USA 65 A3 42 30N 78 40W
Spurn Head *c.* UK 78 F10 53 36N 0 07E
Sredinnyy Range *mts.* Russia 87 T7/T8 57 00N 158 00E
Srednekolymsk Russia 87 T10 67 27N 153 35E
Sretensk Russia 87 P7 52 15N 117 52E
Srikakulam India 91 E3 18 19N 84 00E
SRI LANKA 90 E1
Srinagar Kashmir 90 C6 34 08N 74 50E
Stafford UK 78 D10 52 48N 2 07W
Stamford Connecticut USA 65 D2 41 04N 73 33W
Standish Michigan USA 45 K2 43 59N 83 57W
Stanley Falkland Islands 73 F3 51 45S 57 56W
Stanley HK China 92 C1 22 12N 114 12E
Stanovoy Range *mts.* Russia 87 Q8 56 00N 123 00E
Stara Planina *mts.* Europe 81 J5/K5 43 00N 23 00E
Stara Zagora Bulgaria 81 K5 42 25N 25 37E
Stargard Szczeciński Poland 80 E10 53 21N 15 01E
Starogard Gdański Poland 80 G10 53 58N 18 30E
Start Point *c.* UK 78 D9 50 13N 3 38W
Staryy Oskol Russia 86 F7 51 20N 37 50E
State College Pennsylvania USA 63 L5 40 48N 77 52W
Staten Island New York USA 65 H1 40 35N 74 10W
Staunton Virginia USA 63 L4 38 10N 79 05W
Stavanger Norway 78 H13 58 58N 5 45E
Stavropol' Russia 86 G6 45 03N 41 59E

Stehekin Washington USA 38 H4 48 25N 120 30W
Stendal Germany 80 C10 52 36N 11 52E
Stephens Passage *sd.* Alaska USA 38 D5 58 00N 134 00W
Sterling Colorado USA 62 F5 40 37N 103 13W
Sterlitamak Russia 86 H7 53 40N 55 59E
Steubenville Ohio USA 63 K5 40 22N 80 39W
Stewart Island NZ 103 N1 46 55S 167 55E
Stewart Islands Solomon Islands 103 M9 8 20S 162 40E
Steyr Austria 80 E7 48 04N 14 25E
Stillaguamish River Washington USA 38 H4 48 16N 122 00W
Stillwater Nevada USA 64 D4 39 31N 118 33W
Stillwater Reservoir New York USA 47 L3 43 55N 75 00W
Štip FYROM 81 J4 41 44N 22 12E
Stirling UK 78 D12 56 07N 3 57W
Stockbridge Massachusetts USA 65 D3 42 17N 73 19W
Stockholm Sweden 80 G13 59 20N 18 05E
Stockton California USA 62 B4 37 59N 121 20W
Stockton-on-Tees UK 78 E11 54 34N 1 19W
Stœng Trêng Cambodia 95 D6 13 31N 105 59E
Stoke-on-Trent UK 78 D10 53 00N 2 10W
Stonecutters Island HK China 92 B1 22 18N 114 08E
Stonyford California USA 64 B4 39 23N 122 34W
Stornoway UK 78 B13 58 12N 6 23W
Straits of Florida *sd.* Florida USA 63 K1 25 00N 80 00W
Stralsund Germany 80 D11 54 18N 13 06E
Stranraer UK 78 C11 54 55N 5 02W
Strasbourg Fr. 78 J8 48 35N 7 45E
Straubing Germany 80 D8 48 53N 12 35E
Stretto di Messina *sd.* Italy 81 E2 38 00N 15 00E
Strímonas *r.* Greece 81 J4 41 00N 23 00E
Stromboli *mt.* Italy 81 E3 38 48N 15 15E
Stroudsburg Pennsylvania USA 65 C2 40 59N 75 12W
Struma *r.* Bulgaria 81 J4 42 00N 23 00E
Stryy Ukraine 80 J8 49 16N 23 51E
Sturt Creek *r.* Aust. 102 E7 19 00S 127 30E
Stuttgart Germany 80 B8 48 47N 9 12E
Styr' *r.* Ukraine/Belarus 80 K9 51 30N 25 30E
Suakin Sudan 100 M11 19 08N 37 17E
Subotica SM 81 G7 46 04N 19 41E
Suceava Romania 80 L7 47 37N 26 18E
Sucre Bolivia 72 D10 19 05S 65 15W
SUDAN 100 K10
Sudety Reseniky *mts.* Europe 80 E9/F9 50 40N 16 00E
Sue *r.* Sudan 100 K9 7 00N 28 00E
Suez Egypt 101 T1 29 59N 32 33E
Suez Canal Egypt 101 S4 31 30N 32 20E
Suez, Gulf of Egypt 101 T1 29 56N 32 32E
Sugarloaf Mountain Maine USA 47 R5 45 02N 70 18W
Sühbaatar Mongolia 93 K9 50 10N 106 14E
Suiattle River Washington USA 38 H4 48 16N 121 20W
Sukabumi Indonesia 95 D2 6 55S 106 50E
Sukhona *r.* Russia 86 G9 60 00N 45 00E
Sukkur Pakistan 90 B5 27 42N 68 54E
Sulaiman Range *mts.* Pakistan 90 B5/C6 30 00N 70 00E
Sulawesi *i.* Indonesia 95 F3/G3 2 00S 120 00E
Sullana Peru 72 A13 4 52S 80 39W
Sulu Archipelago Philippines 95 G5 6 00N 121 00E
Sulu Sea Philippines/Malaysia 95 F5/G5 8 00N 120 00E
Sumas Washington USA 38 H4 49 00N 122 18W
Sumatera *i.* Indonesia 95 B4/C3 0 00 100 00E
Sumba *i.* Indonesia 95 F2/G1 10 00S 120 00E
Sumbawa *i.* Indonesia 95 F2 8 00S 118 00E
Sumburgh Head *c.* UK 78 E13 59 51N 1 16W
Summer Strait *sd.* Alaska USA 38 D5 56 30N 133 30W
Sunburst Montana USA 41 G1 48 56N 111 58W
Sunbury Pennsylvania USA 65 B2 40 52N 76 47W
Sunchon South Korea 93 P5 34 56N 127 28E
Sundarbans *geog. reg.* India/Bangladesh 91 K8 21 50N 88 50E
Sunderland UK 78 E11 54 55N 1 23W
Sung Kong *i.* HK China 92 C1 22 11N 114 17E
Sunnyvale California USA 64 C3 37 23N 122 00W
Sunset Peak HK China 92 A1 22 15N 113 57E
Sunshine Island HK China 92 B1 22 16N 114 03E
Suntar Russia 87 P9 62 10N 117 35E
Sunyani Ghana 100 D9 7 22N 2 18W
Suō-nada *b.* Japan 94 B1 33 50N 131 30E
Superior Wisconsin USA 63 H6 46 42N 92 05W
Sūr Oman 89 G3 22 34N 59 32E
Surabaya Indonesia 95 E2 7 14S 112 45E
Surakarta Indonesia 95 E2 7 32S 110 50E
Surat India 90 C4 21 10N 72 54E
Surat Thani Thailand 95 B5 9 09N 99 20E
Surgut Russia 86 K9 61 13N 73 20E
SURINAME 72 F14
Susquehanna River Pennsylvania USA 47 K1 41 45N 76 25W
Susuman Russia 87 S9 62 46N 148 08E
Sutlej *r.* Pakistan 90 C6 30 30N 73 00E
Suva Fiji 106 U15 18 08S 178 25E
Suwalki Poland 80 J11 54 06N 22 56E
Suzhou China 93 M5 33 38N 117 02E
Suzhou China 93 N5 31 21N 120 40E
Suzuka Japan 94 C1 34 52N 136 37E
Suzu-misaki *c.* Japan 94 C2 37 30N 137 21E
Svobodnyy Russia 87 Q7 51 24N 128 05E
Swale *r.* UK 78 E11 54 20N 2 00W
Swansea UK 78 D9 51 38N 3 57W
Swanton Ohio USA 46 C1 41 36N 83 54W
Swanton Vermont USA 47 N4 44 56N 73 08W
SWAZILAND 101 L2
SWEDEN 80 D13
Sweetgrass Montana USA 41 G1 48 59N 111 57W
Sweetwater *tn.* Texas USA 62 F3 32 27N 100 25W
Swellendam RSA 101 J1 34 01S 20 26E
Swiebodzin Poland 80 E10 52 15N 15 31E
Swindon UK 78 E9 51 34N 1 47W
Swinoujście Poland 80 E10 53 55N 14 18E
SWITZERLAND 79 J7/K7
Sydney Aust. 103 K4 33 55S 151 10E
Syktyvkar Russia 86 H9 61 42N 50 45E
Sylhet Bangladesh 91 L10 24 53N 91 51E
Sylt Germany 80 B11 54 00N 8 00E
Sylvania Ohio USA 45 K1 41 41N 83 37W
Syracuse New York USA 63 L5 43 03N 76 10W
Syr-Dar'ya *r.* Asia 86 J5 43 30N 66 30E
SYRIA 88 C6
Syrian Desert Middle East 88 C5 32 30N 39 20E
Syzran' Russia 86 G7 53 10N 48 29E
Szczecin Poland 80 E10 53 25N 14 32E
Szczecinek Poland 80 F10 53 42N 16 41E
Szeged Hungary 81 H7 46 15N 20 09E
Székesfehérvár Hungary 81 G7 47 11N 18 22E
Szolnok Hungary 81 H7 47 10N 20 10E
Szombathely Hungary 81 F7 47 14N 16 38E

T

Ţabas Iran 89 G5 33 37N 56 54E
Tabiteuea *is.* Kiribati 103 P10 1 20S 174 50E
Table Rock Lake Missouri USA 63 H4 36 38N 93 17W
Tábor Czech Rep. 80 E8 49 25N 14 39E
Tabora Tanzania 100 L7 5 01S 32 48E
Tabriz Iran 88 E6 38 04N 46 17E
Tabuaaran Island Kiribati 107 L8 4 00N 158 10W
Tabūk Saudi Arabia 88 C4 28 33N 36 36E
Tacloban Philippines 95 G6 11 15N 125 01E
Tacna Peru 72 C10 18 00S 70 15W
Tacoma Washington USA 62 B6 47 16N 122 30W
Taegu South Korea 93 P6 35 52N 128 36E
Taejon South Korea 93 P6 36 20N 127 26E
Tafila Jordan 88 N10 30 52N 35 36E
Taganrog Russia 86 F6 47 14N 38 55E
Tagus *r.* Sp./Port. 79 B3 39 30N 7 00W
Tahat, Mount Algeria 100 F12 23 18N 5 33E
Tahiti *i.* Pacific Ocean 107 M6 17 30S 148 30W
Tahoe, Lake California USA 62 C4 39 00N 120 00W
Tahoua Niger 100 F10 14 57N 5 19E
Tai'an China 93 M6 36 15N 117 10E
Taibei Taiwan 93 N4 25 05N 121 32E
Taichung Taiwan 93 N3 24 09N 124 40E
Tai Lam Chung HK China 92 B2 22 22N 114 01E
Tai Lam Chung Reservoir HK China 92 B2 22 23N 114 01E
Tai Long HK China 92 D2 22 25N 114 22E
Tai Long Wan *b.* HK China 92 D2 22 24N 114 23E
Tai Mei Tuk HK China 92 C2 22 28N 114 14E
Tai Mong Tsai HK China 92 C2 22 23N 114 18E
Tai Mo Shan *mt.* HK China 92 B2 22 25N 114 07E
Tainan Taiwan 93 N3 23 01N 120 14E
Tai O HK China 92 A1 22 15N 113 52E
Tai Po HK China 92 C2 22 27N 114 10E
Tai Shui Hang HK China 92 B1 22 17N 114 01E
Tai Tam Resevoirs HK China 92 C1 22 15N 114 13E
Tai Tam Wan *b.* HK China 92 C1 22 13N 114 13E
Tai Wai HK China 92 C2 22 23N 114 10E
TAIWAN 93 N3
Taiwan Strait China/Taiwan 93 M3 24 00N 119 30E
Tai Wan Tau HK China 92 C1 22 17N 114 17E
Taiyuan China 93 L6 37 50N 112 30E
Ta'izz Yemen 88 D1 13 35N 44 02E
TAJIKISTAN 86 J4/K4
Tajo *r.* Sp./Port. 79 B3 39 00N 7 00W
Tak Thailand 95 B7 16 51N 99 08E
Takamatsu Japan 94 B1 34 20N 134 01E
Takaoka Japan 94 C2 36 47N 137 00E
Takapuna NZ 103 P3 36 48S 174 46E
Takasaki Japan 94 C2 36 20N 139 00E
Takayama Japan 94 C2 36 09N 137 16E
Takefu Japan 94 C2 35 54N 136 10E
Takêv Cambodia 95 C6 11 00N 104 46E
Taki India 91 K9 22 35N 88 56E
Taku Inlet Alaska USA 38 C6 58 30N 134 00W
Talara Peru 72 A13 4 38S 81 18W
Talavera de la Reina Sp. 79 C3 39 58N 4 50W
Talbot, Cape Aust. 102 E8 13 49S 126 42E
Talca Chile 73 C6 35 28S 71 40W
Talcahuano Chile 73 C6 36 40S 73 10W
Taldykorgan Kazakhstan 86 K6 45 02N 78 23E
Tallahassee Florida USA 63 K3 30 26N 84 16W
Tallinn Estonia 80 K13 59 22N 24 48E
Tall Kalakh Syria 88 P12 34 45N 36 17E
Talodi Sudan 100 L10 10 40N 30 25E
Talsi Latvia 80 J12 57 17N 22 37E
Taltal Chile 72 C8 25 26S 70 33W
Tamabo Range Malaysia 95 F4 4 00N 115 30E
Tamale Ghana 100 D9 9 26N 0 49W
Tamana *is.* Kiribati 103 Q10 2 37S 175 40E
Tamanrasset Algeria 100 F12 22 50N 5 28E
Tamazunchale Mexico 66 E4 21 18N 98 46W
Tambov Russia 86 G7 52 44N 41 28E
Tambre *r.* Sp. 79 A5 42 55N 8 50W
Tâmega *r.* Port. 79 B4 41 40N 7 45W
Tamil Nadu *admin.* India 90 D2 12 00N 78 30E
Tampa Florida USA 63 K2 27 58N 82 38W
Tampico Mexico 66 E4 22 18N 97 52W
Tamworth Aust. 103 K4 31 07S 150 57E
Tana *r.* Kenya 100 M7 0 30S 39 00E
Tanabe Japan 94 C1 33 43N 135 22E
Tanahmerah Indonesia 103 H9 6 08S 140 18E
Tana, Lake Ethiopia 100 M10 12 20N 37 20E
Tandil Argentina 73 F6 37 18S 59 10W
Tanega-shima *i.* Japan 94 B1 31 00N 131 00E
Tanezrouft *geog. reg.* Algeria 100 D12 24 00N 0 30W
Tanga Tanzania 100 M6 5 07S 39 05E
Tangail Bangladesh 91 K10 24 15N 89 55E
Tangan *r.* India 91 K10 25 30N 88 20E
Tanganyika, Lake East Africa 101 K6/L6 7 00S 30 00E
Tanggula Shan *mts.* China 92 G5 32 30N 92 30E
Tangier Morocco 100 C15 35 48N 5 45W
Tangshan China 93 M6 39 37N 118 05E
Tanjungkarang-Telukbetung Indonesia 95 D2 5 28S 105 16E
Tanna *i.* Vanuatu 103 N7 19 30S 169 00E
Tannu Ola *mts.* Russia 87 M7 51 00N 92 30E
Tanout Niger 100 F11 15 05N 8 50E
TANZANIA 100/101 L6
Tapachula Mexico 66 F2 14 54N 92 15W
Tapajós *r.* Brazil 72 F12 6 30S 57 00W
Tāpi *r.* India 90 D4 21 30N 76 30E
Tappi-zaki *c.* Japan 94 D3 41 14N 140 21E
Taquari *r.* Brazil 72 F10 18 00S 57 00W
Tarakan Indonesia 95 F4 3 20N 117 38E
Táranto Italy 81 F4 40 28N 17 15E
Tarapoto Peru 72 B12 6 31S 76 23W
Tarauacá Brazil 72 C12 8 06S 70 45W
Tarawa Gilbert Islands 103 P11 1 30N 173 00E
Tarazona Sp. 79 E4 41 54N 1 44W
Tarbes Fr. 79 F5 43 14N 0 05E
Taree Aust. 103 K4 31 54S 152 26E
Tarfaya Morocco 100 B13 27 58N 12 55W
Târgovişte Romania 81 K6 44 56N 25 27E
Târgu-Jiu Romania 81 J6 45 03N 23 18E
Târgu Mureş Romania 81 K7 46 33N 24 34E
Tarija Bolivia 72 D9 21 33S 65 02W
Tarim He *r.* China 92 E7 41 00N 82 00E
Tarim Pendi China 92 E6/F6 39 00N 84 00E
Tarko-Sale Russia 86 K9 64 55N 77 50E
Tarkwa Ghana 100 D9 5 16N 1 59W
Tarn *r.* Fr. 79 G5 44 05N 1 40E
Tarnobrzeg Poland 80 H9 50 35N 21 40E
Tarnów Poland 80 H9 50 01N 20 59E
Tarragona Sp. 79 F4 41 07N 1 15E
Tarrasa Sp. 79 G4 41 34N 2 00E
Tarsus Turkey 88 B6 36 25N 34 52E
Tartary, Gulf of Russia 87 S6/S7 50 00N 141 00E
Tarţūs Syria 88 C5 34 55N 35 52E
Tashkent Uzbekistan 86 J5 41 16N 69 13E
Tasman Basin Southern Ocean 106 F3 48 00S 154 00E
Tasmania *state* Aust. 103 J2 43 00S 147 00E
Tasman Plateau Southern Ocean 106 E3 48 00S 147 00E
Tasman Sea Pacific Ocean 103 L3 40 00S 155 00E
Tassili N'Ajjer *mts.* Algeria 100 F13 26 00N 6 20W
Tatabánya Hungary 81 G7 47 31N 18 25E
Tateyama Japan 94 C1 34 59N 139 50E
Taunggyi Myanmar 93 H3 20 55N 97 02E
Taunton UK 78 D9 51 01N 3 06W
Taunton Massachusetts USA 65 E2 41 54N 71 06W
Tauranga NZ 103 Q3 37 41S 176 10E
Tauu Islands PNG 103 L10 4 45S 157 00E
Tauva Fiji 106 T16 17 31S 177 53E
Tavda *r.* Russia 86 J8 58 00N 64 00E
Taveuni *i.* Fiji 106 U15 16 40S 180 00
Tavira Port. 79 B2 37 07N 7 39W
Tavoy Myanmar 95 B6 14 02N 98 12E
Tawas City Michigan USA 45 K3 44 16N 83 31W
Tawau Malaysia 95 F4 4 16N 117 54E
Taymā' Saudi Arabia 88 C4 27 37N 38 30E
Taymyr Peninsula Russia 87 M12 75 00N 100 00E
Tayshet Russia 87 M8 55 56N 98 01E
Taz *r.* Russia 87 L10 67 00N 82 00E
Taza Morocco 100 D14 34 16N 4 01W
Tchibanga Gabon 100 G7 2 49S 11 00E
Tczew Poland 80 G11 54 05N 18 46E
Tébessa Algeria 100 F15 35 21N 8 06E
Tecopa California USA 64 E2 35 51N 116 13W
Tecuci Romania 81 L6 45 50N 27 27E
Tecumseh Michigan USA 46 C2 42 01N 83 56W
Tees *r.* UK 78 D11 54 40N 1 20W
Tefé Brazil 72 E13 3 24S 64 45W
Tefé *r.* Brazil 72 D12 4 30S 65 30W
Tegal Indonesia 95 D2 6 52S 109 07E
Tegucigalpa Honduras 66 G2 14 05N 87 14W
Tehachapi California USA 64 D2 35 08N 118 27W
Tehachapi Mountains California USA 64 D2 34 52N 118 45W
Tehran Iran 89 F6 35 40N 51 26E
Tehuacán Mexico 66 E3 18 30N 97 26W
Tehuantepec Mexico 66 E3 16 21N 95 13W
Teifi *r.* UK 78 C10 52 03N 4 30W
Tejo *r.* Port. 79 B3 39 30N 8 15W
Tel *r.* India 90 E4 20 30N 84 00E
Tela Honduras 66 G3 15 46N 87 25W
Tel Aviv-Yafo Israel 88 N11 32 05N 34 46E
Telemark *geog. reg.* Norway 78 K13 59 42N 8 00E
Telescope Peak *mt.* California USA 64 E3 36 11N 117 05W
Teles Pires *r.* Brazil 72 F12 8 00S 57 00W
Telford UK 78 D10 52 42N 2 28W
Telsiai Lithuania 80 J12 55 59N 22 17E
Teluk Bone *b.* Indonesia 95 G3 4 00S 121 00E
Teluk Cenderawasih *b.* Indonesia 102 F10 2 15S 135 30E
Teluk Intan Malaysia 95 C4 4 02N 101 01E
Teluk Tomini *b.* Indonesia 95 G3 0 20S 121 00E
Tema Ghana 100 E9 5 41N 0 00
Temecula California USA 64 E1 33 30N 117 08W
Temirtau Kazakhstan 86 K7 50 05N 72 55E
Tempio Pausania Italy 81 B4 40 54N 9 07E
Temple Texas USA 63 G3 31 06N 97 22W
Temuco Chile 73 C6 38 45S 72 40W
Tenali India 90 E3 16 13N 80 36E
Ten Degree Channel Andaman Islands/Nicobar Islands 91 G1 10 00N 93 00E
Tenerife *i.* Canary Islands 100 A13 28 15N 16 35W
Tennant Creek *tn.* Aust. 102 F7 19 31S 134 15E
Tennessee *r.* USA 63 J4 35 00N 88 00W
Tennessee *state* USA 63 J4 35 00N 87 00W
Teófilo Otôni Brazil 72 J10 17 52S 41 31W
Tepatitlán Mexico 66 D4 20 50N 102 46W
Tepic Mexico 66 D4 21 30N 104 51W
Ter *r.* Sp. 79 G4 41 55N 2 30E
Teresina Brazil 72 J12 5 09S 42 46W
Teressa Island India 91 G1 8 15N 93 10E
Termez Uzbekistan 86 J4 37 15N 67 15E
Termim Imerese Italy 81 D2 27 59N 13 42E
Ternate Indonesia 95 H4 0 48N 127 23E
Terni Italy 81 D5 42 34N 12 39E
Ternopil' Ukraine 80 K8 49 35N 25 39E
Terpeniya Bay Russia 87 S6 48 00N 144 0E
Terracina Italy 81 D4 41 17N 13 15E
Terrasini Italy 81 D3 38 09N 13 05E
Terre Haute Indiana USA 63 J4 39 27N 87 24W
Teruel Sp. 79 E4 40 21N 1 06W
Teseney Eritrea 100 M11 15 10N 36 48E
Teshio Japan 94 D3 44 53N 141 46E
Testa del Gargano *c.* Italy 81 F4 41 50N 16 10E
Teteiev *r.* Ukraine 80 M9 50 00N 29 00E
Tétouan Morocco 100 C15 35 34N 5 22W
Tetovo FYROM 81 H5 42 00N 20 59E
Texarkana Arkansas USA 63 H3 33 28N 94 02W
Texas *state* USA 62 G3 31 00N 100 00W
Texel *i.* Neths. 78 H10 53 05N 4 45E
Texoma, Lake Oklahoma/Texas USA 63 G3 34 00N 97 00W
THAILAND 95 B7/C7
Thailand, Gulf of Southern Asia 95 C6 10 50N 101 00E
Thakhek Laos 95 C7 17 22N 104 50E
Thames *r.* UK 78 E9 51 32N 0 50W
Thane India 90 C3 19 14N 73 02E
Thanh Hoa Vietnam 95 D7 19 49N 105 48E
Thanjavur India 90 D2 10 46N 79 09E
Thar Desert India 90 C5 27 30N 72 00E
Thásos *i.* Greece 81 K4 40 00N 24 00E
Thayetmyo Myanmar 95 B7 19 20N 95 10E
The Brothers *is.* HK China 92 A2 22 20N 113 58E
The Dalles *tn.* Oregon USA 62 B6 45 36N 121 10W
The Everglades *swamp* Florida USA 63 K2 26 00N 81 00W
The Hague Neths. 78 H10 52 05N 4 16E
Thermaïkós Kólpos *g.* Greece 81 J3/J4 40 00N 22 50E
Thermopolis Wyoming USA 62 E5 43 39N 108 12W
Thessaloníki Greece 81 J4 40 38N 22 58E
The Valley Anguilla 66 P10 18 03N 63 04W
Thief River Falls *tn.* Minnesota USA 63 G6 48 12N 96 48W
Thiers Fr. 79 G6 45 51N 3 33E
Thiès Senegal 100 A10 14 49N 16 52W
Thimphu Bhutan 91 F5 27 32N 89 43E
Thionville Fr. 78 J8 49 22N 6 11E
Thíra *i.* Greece 81 K2 36 00N 25 00E
Thisted Denmark 80 B12 56 58N 8 42E
Thithia *i.* Fiji 106 V16 17 45S 179 20W
Thíva Greece 81 J3 38 19N 23 19E
Thomasville Georgia USA 63 K3 30 50N 83 59W
Thomson *r.* Aust. 103 H6 24 00S 141 00E
Thornapple River Michigan USA 46 A2/B2 42 38N 85 00W
Thousand Oaks California USA 64 D2 34 10N 118 50W
Three Kings Islands NZ 103 P4 34 10S 172 07E
Three Mile Bay *tn.* New York USA 45 N3 44 05N 76 10W
Three Points, Cape Ghana 100 D8 4 43N 2 06W
Thun Switz. 79 J7 46 46N 7 38E
Thunder Bay Michigan USA 46 C4 45 00N 83 25W
Thüringer Wald *hills* Germany 80 C9 50 00N 10 00E
Thurso UK 78 D13 58 35N 3 32W
Tianjin China 93 M6 39 08N 117 12E
Tianshui China 93 K5 34 25N 105 58E
Tiber *r.* Italy 81 D4 42 00N 12 00E
Tiberias Israel 88 N11 32 48N 35 32E
Tiberias, Lake Israel 88 N11 32 45N 35 30E
Tibesti *mts.* Chad 100 H12 21 00N 17 00E
Tiburón *i.* Mexico 66 B5 28 30N 112 30W
Ticul Mexico 66 G4 20 22N 89 31W
Tierra Blanca Mexico 66 E3 18 28N 96 21W
Tiffin Ohio USA 45 K1 41 07N 83 10W
Tighina Moldova 81 M7 46 50N 29 29E
Tikrit Iraq 88 D5 34 36N 43 42E
Tijuana Mexico 66 A6 32 29N 117 10W
Tiksi Russia 87 Q11 71 40N 128 45E
Tilburg Neths. 78 H9 51 34N 5 05E
Timaru NZ 103 P2 44 24S 171 15E
Timimoun Algeria 100 E13 29 15N 0 14E
Timişoara Romania 81 H6 45 45N 21 15E
Timişul *r.* Romania/SM 81 H6 45 00N 21 00E
Timon Brazil 72 J12 5 08S 42 52W
Timor *i.* Indonesia 95 G1 9 00S 125 00E
Timor Sea Indonesia 95 H1 10 45S 126 00E
Tindouf Algeria 100 C13 27 42N 8 10W
Tinos *i.* Greece 81 K2 37 00N 25 00E
Tin Sam HK China 92 A2 22 26N 113 59E
Tinsukia India 91 H5 27 30N 95 22E

Tionesta Pennsylvania USA	46	G1	41 31N	79 30W
Tionesta Lake Pennsylvania USA	46	G1	41 30N	79 29W
Tiranë Albania	81	G4	41 20N	19 49E
Tir'at el Ismâ'ilîya *can.* Egypt	101	R3	30 32N	31 48E
Tir'at el Mansûrîya *r.* Egypt	101	R4	31 12N	31 38E
Tiraz Mountains Namibia	101	H2	25 30S	16 30E
Tirso *r.* Italy	81	B3	40 00N	9 00E
Tiruchchirappalli India	90	D2	10 50N	78 41E
Tirunelveli India	90	D1	8 45N	77 43E
Tirupati India	90	D2	13 39N	79 25E
Tiruppur India	90	D2	11 05N	77 20E
Tisza *r.* Hungary/SM	81	H7	46 00N	20 00E
Titovo Užice SM	81	G5	43 52N	19 50E
Titov Veles FYROM	81	H4	41 43N	21 49E
Tittabawassee River Michigan USA	46	B3	43 50N	84 25W
Titusville Pennsylvania USA	46	G1	41 37N	79 42W
Tiu Chung Chau *i.* HK China	92	C2	22 20N	114 19E
Tiverton Rhode Island USA	65	E2	41 38N	71 12W
Tivoli Italy	81	D4	41 58N	12 48E
Tizimín Mexico	66	G4	21 10N	88 09W
Tizi Ouzou Algeria	100	E15	36 44N	4 05E
Tiznit Morocco	100	C13	29 43N	9 44W
Tlemcen Algeria	100	D14	34 53N	1 21W
Toamasina Madagascar	101	P4	18 10S	49 23E
Tobago *i.* Trinidad and Tobago	67	V15	11 15N	60 40W
Tobi-shima *i.* Japan	94	C2	39 12N	139 32E
Tobol *r.* Russia	86	J8	57 00N	67 30E
Tobol'sk Russia	86	J8	58 15N	68 12E
Tocantins *admin.* Brazil	72	H11	12 00S	47 00W
Tocantins *r.* Brazil	72	H12	10 00S	49 00W
Toco Trinidad and Tobago	67	V15	10 49N	60 57W
Tocopilla Chile	72	C9	22 05S	70 10W
TOGO	100	E9		
Toi Tan HK China	92	C2	22 26N	114 19E
Toiyabe Range *mts.* Nevada USA	64	E4	39 20N	117 15W
Tok Alaska USA	54	B3	63 20N	142 59W
Tokelau Islands Pacific Ocean	106	J7	9 00S	168 00W
Tokushima Japan	94	B1	34 03N	134 34E
Tokuyama Japan	94	B1	34 03N	131 48E
Tokyo Japan	94	C2	35 40N	139 45E
Tôlanaro Madagascar	101	P2	25 01S	47 00E
Toledo Sp.	79	C3	39 52N	4 02W
Toledo Ohio USA	63	K5	41 40N	83 35W
Toliara Madagascar	101	N3	23 20S	43 41E
Tollhouse California USA	64	D3	37 01N	119 25W
Tolo Channel HK China	92	C2	22 28N	114 17E
Tolo Harbour *b.* HK China	92	C2	22 26N	114 13E
Tolosa Sp.	79	D5	43 09N	2 04W
Toluca Mexico	66	E3	19 20N	99 40W
Tol'yatti Russia	86	G7	53 32N	49 24E
Tomakomai Japan	94	D3	42 39N	141 33E
Tomaniivi *mt.* Fiji	106	U16	17 37S	178 01E
Tomar Port.	79	A3	39 36N	8 25W
Tomatlán Mexico	66	C3	19 54N	105 18W
Tombigbee *r.* USA	63	J3	32 00N	88 00W
Tombouctou Mali	100	D11	16 49N	2 59W
Tombua Angola	101	G4	15 49S	11 53E
Tom Price, Mount Aust.	102	C6	22 49S	117 51E
Tomsk Russia	87	L8	56 30N	85 05E
Tonalá Mexico	66	F3	16 08N	93 41W
Tonasket Washington USA	39	L1	48 42N	119 28W
Tonawanda New York USA	45	M2	43 01N	78 53W
Tonawanda Channel New York USA	48	D2	43 03N	78 55W
Tonawanda Creek *r.* New York USA	46	H3	43 08N	78 35W
TONGA	106	J5		
Tonga Trench Pacific Ocean	106	J5	20 00S	173 00E
Tongchuan China	93	K6	35 05N	109 02E
Tong Fuk HK China	92	A1	22 14N	113 56E
Tonghai China	93	J3	24 07N	104 45E
Tonghua China	93	P7	41 42N	125 45E
Tongking, Gulf of China/Vietnam	93	K2	19 00N	107 00E
Tongling China	93	M5	30 58N	117 48E
Tônlé Sab *l.* Cambodia	95	C6	12 00N	103 50E
Tonopah Nevada USA	62	C4	38 05N	117 15W
Tønsberg Norway	78	L13	59 16N	10 25E
Tooele Utah USA	62	D5	40 32N	112 18W
Toowoomba Aust.	103	K5	27 35S	151 54E
Topeka Kansas USA	63	G4	39 02N	95 41W
Torbay UK	78	D9	50 27N	3 30W
Tordesillas Sp.	79	C4	41 30N	5 00W
Tormes *r.* Sp.	79	C4	41 03N	5 58W
Tororo Uganda	100	L8	0 42N	34 12E
Toros Dağlari *mts.* Turkey	88	B6	37 10N	33 10E
Torre del Greco Italy	81	E4	40 46N	14 22E
Torrelavega Sp.	79	C5	43 21N	4 03W
Torrens, Lake Aust.	102	G4	31 00S	137 50E
Torreón Mexico	66	D5	25 34N	103 25W
Torres Strait Aust.	103	H8	10 00S	142 30E
Torrington Connecticut USA	65	D2	41 48N	73 07W
Tortosa Sp.	79	F4	40 49N	0 31E
Torun Poland	80	G10	53 01N	18 35E
Tosa-wan *b.* Japan	94	B1	33 20N	133 40E
Totoya *i.* Fiji	106	V15	18 56S	179 50W
Tottori Japan	94	B2	35 32N	134 12E
Touggourt Algeria	100	F14	33 08N	6 04E
Toulon Fr.	79	H5	43 07N	5 55E
Toulouse Fr.	79	F5	43 33N	1 24E
Toungoo Myanmar	95	B7	18 57N	96 26E
Tournai Belgium	78	G9	50 36N	3 24E
Tours Fr.	79	F7	47 23N	0 42E
Towanda Pennsylvania USA	47	K1	41 46N	76 27W
Townsville Aust.	103	J7	19 13S	146 48E
Towson Maryland USA	65	B1	39 25N	76 36W
Toyama Japan	94	C2	36 42N	137 14E
Toyohashi Japan	94	C1	34 46N	137 22E
Toyota Japan	94	C2	35 05N	137 09E
Tozeur Tunisia	100	F14	33 55N	8 07E
Trabzon Turkey	88	C7	41 00N	39 43E
Tracy California USA	64	C3	37 39N	121 26W
Tralee RoI	78	A10	52 16N	9 42W
Tranäs Sweden	80	E13	58 03N	15 00E
Transantarctic Mountains Antarctica	109		80 00S	155 00E
Trápani Italy	81	D3	38 02N	12 32E
Traverse City Michigan USA	63	J5	44 46N	85 38W
Treinta-y-Tres Uruguay	73	G7	33 16S	54 17W
Trelew Chile	73	D5	43 13S	65 15W
Trelleborg Sweden	80	D11	55 22N	13 10E
Trenčin Slovakia	80	G8	48 53N	18 00E
Trenque Lauquen Argentina	73	E6	35 56S	62 43W
Trent *r.* UK	78	E10	53 30N	0 50W
Trento Italy	81	C7	46 04N	11 08E
Trenton New Jersey USA	63	M5	40 15N	74 43W
Tres Arroyos Argentina	73	E6	38 26S	60 17W
Três Lagoas Brazil	72	G9	20 46S	51 43W
Treviso Italy	81	D6	45 40N	12 15E
Trichur India	90	D2	10 32N	76 14E
Trieste Italy	81	D6	45 39N	13 47E
Tríkala Greece	81	H3	39 33N	21 46E
Trincomalee Sri Lanka	90	E1	8 34N	81 13E
Trindade *i.* Atlantic Ocean	108	F4	20 30S	29 20W
Trinidad Bolivia	72	E11	14 46S	64 50W
Trinidad Cuba	67	H4	21 48N	80 00W
Trinidad Colorado USA	62	F4	37 11N	104 31W
Trinidad *i.* Trinidad and Tobago	67	V15	11 00N	61 30W
TRINIDAD AND TOBAGO	67	M2		
Trinity *r.* USA	63	G3	32 00N	96 00W
Trípoli Greece	81	J2	37 31N	22 22E
Tripoli Lebanon	88	N12	34 27N	35 50E
Tripoli Libya	100	G14	32 54N	13 11E
Tripura *admin.* India	91	G4	23 40N	92 00E
Tristan da Cunha *i.* Atlantic Ocean	108	G3	37 15S	12 30W
Trivandrum India	90	D1	8 30N	76 57E
Trnava Slovakia	80	F8	48 23N	17 35E
Trollhätten Sweden	80	D13	58 17N	12 20E
Trombetas *r.* Brazil	72	F14	1 30N	57 00W
Trona California USA	64	E2	35 46N	117 24W
Trouville Fr.	78	F8	49 22N	0 05E
Troy Alabama USA	63	J3	31 49N	86 00W
Troy Montana USA	39	N1	48 28N	115 55W
Troy New York USA	63	M5	42 43N	73 43W
Troy *hist. site* Turkey	88	A6	39 55N	26 17E
Troyes Fr.	78	H8	48 18N	4 05E
Trujillo Peru	72	B12	8 06S	79 00W
Trujillo Sp.	79	C3	39 28N	5 53W
Trujillo Venezuela	72	C15	9 20N	70 38W
Truk Islands Pacific Ocean	106	E8	7 30N	152 30E
Truro UK	78	C9	50 16N	5 03W
Tseung Kwan O HK China	92	C1	22 19N	114 14E
Tshane Botswana	101	J3	24 05S	21 54E
Tshuapa *r.* CDR	100	J7	1 00S	23 00E
Tsing Chau Tsai HK China	92	B2	22 20N	114 02E
Tsing Yi HK China	92	B2	22 21N	114 06E
Tsu Japan	94	C1	34 41N	136 30E
Tsuchiura Japan	94	D2	36 05N	140 11E
Tsuen Wan HK China	92	B2	22 22N	114 06E
Tsugaru-kaikyō *sd.* Japan	94	D3	41 30N	140 30E
Tsumeb Namibia	101	H4	19 13S	17 42E
Tsuruga Japan	94	C2	35 40N	136 05E
Tsuruoka Japan	94	C2	38 42N	139 50E
Tsushima *i.* Japan	94	A1	34 30N	129 20E
Tsuyama Japan	94	B2	35 04N	134 01E
Tua *r.* Port.	79	B4	41 20N	7 30W
Tuamotu Archipelago *is.* Pacific Ocean	107	N6	15 00S	145 00W
Tuamotu Ridge Pacific Ocean	107	M6	19 00S	144 00W
Tübingen Germany	80	B8	48 32N	9 04E
Tubruq Libya	100	J14	32 05N	23 59E
Tubuai Islands Pacific Ocean	107	M5	23 23S	149 27W
Tucson Arizona USA	62	D3	32 15N	110 57W
Tucumcari New Mexico USA	62	F4	35 11N	103 44W
Tucupita Venezuela	72	E15	9 02N	62 04W
Tucuruí Brazil	72	H13	3 42S	49 44W
Tudela Sp.	79	E5	42 04N	1 37W
Tuen Mun HK China	92	A2	22 24N	113 58E
Tukums Latvia	80	J12	56 58N	23 10E
Tula Russia	86	F7	54 11N	37 38E
Tula Mexico	66	E4	20 01N	99 21W
Tula Mexico	66	E4	23 00N	99 41W
Tulare California USA	64	D3	36 12N	119 21W
Tulare Lake California USA	64	D3	36 04N	119 45W
Tulcán Ecuador	72	B14	0 50N	77 48W
Tulcea Romania	81	M6	45 10N	28 50E
Tulkarm Jordan	88	N11	32 19N	35 02E
Tulle Fr.	79	F6	45 16N	1 46E
Tulsa Oklahoma USA	63	G4	36 07N	95 58W
Tuluá Col.	72	B14	4 05N	76 12W
Tulun Russia	87	N7	54 32N	100 35E
Tumaco Col.	72	B14	1 51N	78 46W
Tumbes Peru	72	A13	3 37S	80 27W
Tumkur India	90	D2	13 20N	77 06E
Tunduru Tanzania	101	M5	11 08S	37 21E
Tundzha *r.* Bulgaria	81	K5	42 00N	25 00E
Tungabhadra *r.* India	90	D3	15 00N	75 30E
Tung Lung Chau *i.* HK China	92	C1	22 15N	114 17E
Tunis Tunisia	100	G14	36 50N	10 13E
TUNISIA	100	F14		
Tunja Col.	72	C15	5 33N	73 23W
Tunkhannock Pennsylvania USA	47	L1	41 32N	75 46W
Tuolumne *r.* California USA	64	C3	37 53N	120 09W
Tupelo Mississippi USA	63	J3	34 15N	88 43W
Tupiza Bolivia	72	D9	21 27S	65 45W
Túquerres Col.	72	B14	1 06N	77 37W
Tura Russia	87	N9	64 20N	100 17E
Turda Romania	81	J7	46 35N	23 50E
Turgay *r.* Kazakhstan	86	J7	50 00N	64 00E
Turia *r.* Sp.	79	E3	39 45N	0 55W
Turin Italy	81	A6	45 04N	7 40E
Turkana, Lake Ethiopia/Kenya	100	M8	4 00N	36 00E
TURKEY	88	B6		
TURKMENISTAN	86	H4/J4		
Turks and Caicos Islands W. Indies	67	K4	21 30N	72 00W
Turks Island Passage *sd.* W. Indies	67	K4	21 30N	71 30W
Turlock California USA	64	C3	37 30N	120 53W
Turner Montana USA	42	C1	48 51N	108 25W
Turnu Măgurele Romania	81	K5	43 44N	24 53E
Turpan China	92	F7	42 55N	89 06E
Turpan Depression China	92	F7	42 40N	89 30E
Turukhansk Russia	87	L10	65 49N	88 00E
Tuscaloosa Alabama USA	63	J3	33 12N	87 33W
Tuticorin India	90	D1	8 48N	78 10E
Tuttlingen Germany	80	B7	47 59N	8 49E
TUVALU	100	H7		
Tuxpan Mexico	66	C4	21 58N	105 20W
Tuxpan Mexico	66	E4	20 58N	97 23W
Tuxtla Gutierrez Mexico	66	F3	16 45N	93 09W
Túy Sp.	79	A5	42 03N	8 39W
Tuz Gölü *l.* Turkey	88	B6	38 40N	33 35E
Tuzla Bosnia-Herzegovina	81	G6	44 33N	18 41E
Tver' Russia	86	F8	56 49N	35 57E
Tweed *r.* UK	78	D11	55 45N	2 10W
Twentynine Palms California USA	64	E2	34 09N	116 03W
Twin Falls *tn.* Idaho USA	62	D5	42 34N	114 30W
Twisp Washington USA	39	K1	48 22N	120 08W
Twisp River Washington USA	38	H4	48 30N	120 20W
Two Harbors *tn.* Minnesota USA	45	F4	47 02N	91 40W
Two Medicine River Montana USA	41	F1	48 27N	112 50W
Tyan-Shan' Kyrgyzstan	86/87	K5	41 00N	76 00E
Tyler Texas USA	63	G3	32 22N	95 18W
Tym *r.* Russia	87	L8	59 00N	82 30E
Tynda Russia	87	Q8	55 10N	124 35E
Tyne *r.* UK	78	E11	55 58N	2 43W
Tyre Lebanon	88	N11	33 16N	35 12E
Tyrone Pennsylvania USA	65	A2	40 41N	78 14W
Tyrrhenian Sea Europe	81	C4/D4	40 00N	12 00E
Tyumen' Russia	86	J8	57 11N	65 29E
Tyung *r.* Russia	87	P9	65 00N	119 00E
Tywi *r.* UK	78	D9	51 50N	4 25W

U

Uaupés Brazil	72	D13	0 07S	67 05W
Ubangi *r.* CAR	100	H8	4 00N	18 00E
Ube Japan	94	B1	33 57N	131 16E
Uberaba Brazil	72	H10	19 47S	47 57W
Uberlândia Brazil	72	H10	18 57S	48 17W
Ubly Michigan USA	46	D3	43 44N	82 58W
Ubon Ratchathani Thailand	95	C7	15 15N	104 50E
Ubort' *r.* Europe	80	L9	51 00N	27 00E
Ubundu CDR	100	K7	0 24S	25 30E
Ucayali *r.* Peru	72	C12	6 00S	74 00W
Uchiura-wan *b.* Japan	94	D3	42 30N	140 40E
Uda *r.* Russia	87	R7	54 00N	134 00E
Udaipur India	90	C4	24 36N	73 47E
Udaipur India	91	L9	23 32N	91 29E
Uddevalla Sweden	80	C13	58 20N	11 56E
Udine Italy	81	D7	46 04N	13 14E
Udon Thani Thailand	95	C7	17 25N	102 45E
Ueda Japan	94	C2	36 27N	138 13E
Uele *r.* CDR	100	K8	4 00N	27 00E
Uelen Russia	87	W10	66 13N	169 48W
Uelzen Germany	80	C10	52 58N	10 34E
Ufa Russia	86	H7	54 45N	55 58E
Ugab *r.* Namibia	101	H3	21 00S	15 00E
UGANDA	100	L7/L8		
Uinta Mountains Utah USA	62	D5	40 00N	111 00W
Uitenhage RSA	101	K1	33 46S	25 25E
Ujjain India	90	D4	23 11N	75 50E
Ujung Pandang Indonesia	95	F2	5 09S	119 28E
Ukhta Russia	86	H9	63 33N	53 44E
Ukiah California USA	62	B4	39 09N	123 12W
Ukiah California USA	64	B4	39 09N	123 12W
Ukmerge Lithuania	80	K11	55 14N	24 49E
UKRAINE	80	J8/N8		
Ulaangom Mongolia	92	G8	49 59N	92 00E
Ulan Bator Mongolia	93	K8	47 54N	106 52E
Ulan-Ude Russia	87	N7	51 55N	107 40E
Ulhasnagar India	90	C3	19 15N	73 08E
Uliastay Mongolia	93	H8	47 42N	96 52E
Ullapool UK	78	C12	57 54N	5 10W
Ulm Germany	80	C8	48 24N	10 00E
Ulsan South Korea	93	P6	35 32N	129 21E
Ulungur Hu *l.* China	92	F8	47 10N	87 10E
Ul'yanovsk Russia	86	G7	54 19N	48 22E
Uman' Ukraine	80	N8	48 45N	30 10E
Umbagog Lake New Hampshire/Maine USA	47	R4	44 45N	71 00W
Umm as Samīm *geog. reg.* Oman	89	G3	22 10N	56 00E
Umm Ruwaba Sudan	100	L10	12 50N	31 20E
Umtata RSA	101	K1	31 35S	28 47E
Umuarama Brazil	72	G9	23 43S	52 57W
Una *r.* Bosnia-Herzegovina/Croatia	81	F6	45 15N	16 15E
'Unayzah Saudi Arabia	88	D4	26 06N	43 58E
Union New Jersey USA	65	H1	40 42N	74 14W
Union *i.* Lesser Antilles	66	R11	12 36N	61 26W
Union City New Jersey USA	65	H2	40 45N	74 01W
Union City Pennsylvania USA	46	G1	41 56N	79 51W
Union City Reservoir Pennsylvania USA	46	G1	41 58N	79 54W
Uniontown Pennsylvania USA	63	L4	39 54N	79 44W
Unionville Michigan USA	46	C3	43 41N	83 29W
UNITED ARAB EMIRATES	89	F3		
UNITED KINGDOM	78			
UNITED STATES OF AMERICA	62/63			
Unst *i.* UK	78	E14	60 45N	0 55W
Upata Venezuela	72	E15	8 02N	62 25W
Upham North Dakota USA	43	B1	48 35N	100 44W
Upington RSA	101	J2	28 28S	21 14E
Upolu Point *c.* Hawaiian Islands	107	Z18	20 16N	155 52W
Upper Bay New Jersey USA	65	H1	40 40N	74 03W
Upper Lake *tn.* California USA	64	B4	39 10N	122 56W
Upper Lough Erne *l.* UK	78	B11	54 15N	7 30W
Upper Red Lake Minnesota USA	63	H6	48 04N	94 48W
Upper Sandusky Ohio USA	45	K1	40 50N	83 17W
Upplands Vasby Sweden	80	F13	59 30N	18 15E
Uppsala Sweden	80	F13	59 55N	17 38E
Ur *hist. site* Iraq	88	E5	30 56N	46 08E
Urakawa Japan	94	D3	42 10N	142 46E
Ural *r.* Asia	86	H6	48 00N	52 00E
Ural Mountains Russia	86	H7	57 00N	60 00E
Ural'sk Kazakhstan	86	H7	51 19N	51 20E
Uraricuera *r.* Brazil	72	E14	3 00N	62 30W
Urawa Japan	94	C2	35 52N	139 40E
Ure *r.* UK	78	E11	54 20N	1 55W
Urengoy Russia	87	K10	65 59N	78 30E
Urgench Uzbekistan	86	J5	41 35N	60 41E
Urmston Road *sd.* HK China	92	A2	22 23N	113 53E
Uroševac SM	81	H5	42 21N	21 09E
Uruapan Mexico	66	D3	19 26N	102 04W
Urubamba Peru	72	C11	13 20S	72 07W
Uruguaiana Brazil	73	F8	29 45S	57 05W
URUGUAY	73	F7		
Uruguay *r.* Uruguay/Argentina	73	F7	32 00S	57 40W
Ürümqi China	92	F7	43 43N	87 38E
Urziceni Romania	81	L6	44 43N	26 39E
Usa *r.* Russia	86	H10	66 00N	60 00E
Ushuaia Argentina	73	D3	54 48S	68 19W
Usinsk Russia	86	H10	65 57N	57 27E
Üsküdar Turkey	88	A7	41 02N	29 02E
Usol'ye-Sibirskoye Russia	87	N7	52 48N	103 40E
Ussuri *r.* Russia	87	R6	47 00N	134 00E
Ussuriysk Russia	87	R5	43 48N	131 59E
Ustica *i.* Italy	81	D3	38 00N	13 00E
Ust'-Ilimsk Russia	87	N8	58 03N	102 39E
Ustí nad Labem Czech Rep.	80	E9	50 40N	14 02E
Ust'-Kamchatsk Russia	87	U8	56 14N	162 28E
Ust'-Kamenogorsk Kazakhstan	87	L6	49 58N	82 36E
Ust'-Kut Russia	87	N8	56 48N	105 42E
Ust'Maya Russia	87	R9	60 25N	134 28E
Ust'-Nera Russia	87	S9	64 35N	143 14E
Ust'Olenek Russia	87	P11	72 59N	119 57E
Ust Urt Plateau Asia	86	H5	43 30N	55 00E
Usulután Mexico	66	G2	13 20N	88 25W
Utah *state* USA	62	D4	39 00N	112 00W
Utah Lake Utah USA	62	D5	40 10N	111 50W
Utica New York USA	63	L5	43 06N	75 15W
Utrecht Neths.	78	H10	52 05N	5 07E
Utrera Sp.	79	C2	37 10N	5 47W
Utsunomiya Japan	94	C2	36 33N	139 52E
Uttaradit Thailand	95	C7	17 38N	100 05E
Uttaranchal *admin.* India	90	D5/D6	30 00N	78 00E
Uttar Pradesh *admin.* India	90	E5	27 00N	80 00E
Uvalde Texas USA	62	G2	29 14N	99 49W
Uvinza Tanzania	100	L6	5 08S	30 23E
Uvs Nuur *l.* Mongolia	92	G9	50 10N	92 30E
Uwajima Japan	94	B1	33 13N	132 32E
Uyuni Bolivia	72	D9	20 28S	66 47W
Uz *r.* Slovakia	80	H8	48 30N	22 00E
UZBEKISTAN	86	H5/J5		
Uzhgorod Ukraine	80	J8	48 37N	22 22E

V

Vaal *r.* RSA	101	K2	27 30S	25 30E
Vác Hungary	80	G7	47 46N	19 08E
Vacaville California USA	64	C4	38 21N	121 59W
Vadodara India	90	C4	22 19N	73 14E
Vaga *r.* Russia	86	G9	62 00N	43 00E
Váh *r.* Slovakia	80	F8	48 00N	18 00E
Vakh *r.* Russia	87	L9	61 30N	80 30E
Vakhsh *r.* Asia	86	J4	37 00N	68 00E
Valdepeñas Sp.	79	D3	38 46N	3 24W
Valdés, Peninsula Argentina	73	E5	42 30S	63 00W
Valdivia Chile	73	C6	39 46S	73 15W

Valdosta Georgia USA	**63**	K3	30 51N	83 51W
Valença Brazil	**72**	K11	13 22S	39 06W
Valence Fr.	**79**	H6	44 56N	4 54E
Valencia Sp.	**79**	E3	39 29N	0 24W
Valencia Venezuela	**72**	D16	10 14N	67 59W
Valencia, Gulf of Sp.	**79**	F3	39 30N	0 20E
Valenciennes Fr.	**78**	G9	50 22N	3 32E
Valera Venezuela	**72**	C15	9 21N	70 38W
Valjevo SM	**81**	G6	44 16N	19 56E
Valladolid Mexico	**66**	G4	20 40N	88 11W
Valladolid Sp.	**79**	C4	41 39N	4 45W
Valle de la Pascua Venezuela	**72**	D15	9 15N	66 00W
Valledupar Col.	**72**	C16	10 31N	73 16W
Valle Grande Bolivia	**72**	E10	18 30S	64 04W
Vallejo California USA	**62**	B4	38 05N	122 14W
Vallenar Chile	**73**	C8	28 36S	70 45W
Valletta Malta	**81**	E1	35 54N	14 32E
Valley Stream *tn.* New York USA	**65**	K1	40 39N	73 42W
Valmiera Latvia	**80**	K12	57 32N	25 29E
Valparaíso Chile	**73**	C7	33 05S	71 40W
Van Turkey	**88**	D6	38 28N	43 20E
Van Buren Maine USA	**51**	G2	47 10N	67 59W
Vancouver Washington USA	**62**	B6	45 38N	122 40W
Vänern *l.* Sweden	**80**	D13	59 00N	13 30E
Vänersborg Sweden	**80**	D13	58 23N	12 19E
Van Gölü *l.* Turkey	**88**	D6	38 33N	42 46E
Vannes Fr.	**78**	D7	47 40N	2 44W
Vanua Levu *i.* Fiji	**106**	U16	16 20S	179 00E
Vanua Levu Barrier Reef Fiji	**106**	U16	17 10S	179 00E
Vanua Mbalavu *i.* Fiji	**106**	V16	17 15S	178 55W
VANUATU	**103**	N7		
Van Wert Ohio USA	**45**	J1	40 52N	84 35W
Varanasi India	**90**	E5	25 20N	83 00E
Varaždin Croatia	**81**	F7	46 18N	16 21E
Varberg Sweden	**80**	D12	57 07N	12 16E
Varna Bulgaria	**81**	L5	43 12N	27 57E
Värnamo Sweden	**80**	E12	57 11N	14 03E
Várzea Grande Brazil	**72**	J12	6 32S	42 05W
Vaslui Romania	**81**	L7	46 37N	27 46E
Vassar Michigan USA	**46**	C3	43 23N	83 33W
Västerås Sweden	**80**	F13	59 36N	16 32E
Västervik Sweden	**80**	F12	57 45N	16 40E
Vasyugan *r.* Russia	**86**	K8	59 00N	77 30E
Vättern *l.* Sweden	**80**	E13	58 20N	14 20E
Vatulele *i.* Fiji	**106**	T15	18 30S	177 38E
Vaupés *r.* Col.	**72**	C14	1 30N	72 00W
Växjö Sweden	**80**	E12	56 52N	14 50E
Vaygach *i.* Russia	**86**	H11	70 00N	59 00E
Vejle Denmark	**80**	B11	55 43N	9 33E
Velebit *mts.* Croatia	**81**	E6	44 00N	15 00E
Velikiye Luki Russia	**86**	F8	56 19N	30 31E
Veliko Tŭrnovo Bulgaria	**81**	K5	43 04N	25 39E
Vellore India	**90**	D2	12 56N	79 09E
VENEZUELA	**72**	D15		
Venezuelan Basin Caribbean Sea	**108**	B8	14 00N	67 00W
Venice Italy	**81**	D6	45 26N	12 20E
Venta *r.* Latvia/Lithuania	**80**	J12	56 05N	21 50E
Ventspils Latvia	**80**	H12	57 22N	21 31E
Ventura California USA	**62**	C3	34 16N	119 18W
Veracruz Mexico	**66**	E3	19 11N	96 10W
Veraval India	**90**	C4	20 53N	70 28E
Vercelli Italy	**81**	B6	45 19N	8 26E
Verde *r.* Paraguay	**72**	F9	23 20S	60 00W
Verde *r.* Arizona USA	**62**	D3	34 00N	112 00W
Verdun-sur-Meuse Fr.	**78**	H8	49 10N	5 24E
Vereeniging RSA	**101**	K2	26 41S	27 56E
Verin Sp.	**79**	B4	41 55N	7 26W
Verkhoyansk Russia	**87**	R10	67 35N	133 25E
Verkhoyansk Range *mts.* Russia	**87**	Q10	65 00N	130 00E
Vermilion Ohio USA	**46**	D1	41 24N	82 21W
Vermillion Lake Minnesota USA	**45**	E4	47 35N	92 28W
Vermillion Range *mts.* Minnesota USA	**45**	F4	48 00N	91 00W
Vermont *state* USA	**63**	M5	44 00N	73 00W
Vernon Texas USA	**62**	G3	34 10N	99 19W
Véroia Greece	**81**	J4	40 32N	22 11E
Verona Italy	**81**	C6	45 26N	11 00E
Versailles Fr.	**78**	G8	48 48N	2 07E
Verviers Belgium	**78**	H9	50 36N	5 52E
Vesuvio *vol.* Italy	**81**	E4	40 49N	14 26E
Vetlanda Sweden	**80**	E12	57 26N	15 05E
Viano do Castelo Port.	**79**	A4	41 41N	8 50W
Viar *r.* Sp.	**79**	C2	37 45N	5 50W
Viborg Denmark	**80**	B12	56 28N	9 25E
Vicente Guerrero Mexico	**66**	A6	30 48N	116 00W
Vicenza Italy	**81**	C6	45 33N	11 32E
Vichy Fr.	**79**	G7	46 07N	3 25E
Vicksburg Mississippi USA	**63**	H3	32 21N	90 51W
Victoria Chile	**73**	C6	38 20S	72 30W
Victoria Texas USA	**63**	G2	28 49N	97 01W
Victoria *r.* Aust.	**102**	F7	16 00S	131 30E
Victoria *state* Aust.	**103**	H3/J3	37 00S	145 00E
Victoria de las Tunas Cuba	**67**	J4	20 58N	76 59W
Victoria Falls Zambia/Zimbabwe	**101**	K4	17 55S	25 51E
Victoria Harbour HK China	**92**	C1	22 18N	114 10E
Victoria, Lake East Africa	**100**	L7	2 00S	33 00E
Victoria Land *geog. reg.* Antarctica	**109**		75 00S	157 00E
Victoria Peak HK China	**92**	B1	22 17N	114 09E
Victoria West RSA	**101**	J1	31 25S	23 08E
Victorville California USA	**64**	E2	34 31N	117 18W
Vidin Bulgaria	**81**	J5	44 00N	22 50E
Viedma Argentina	**73**	E5	40 45S	63 00W
Vienna Austria	**80**	F8	48 13N	16 22E
Vienne Fr.	**79**	H6	45 32N	4 54E
Vientiane Laos	**95**	C7	17 59N	102 38E
Vierzon Fr.	**79**	G7	47 14N	2 03E
VIETNAM	**95**	D7		
Vieux Fort St. Lucia	**66**	R11	13 44N	60 57W
Vigia Brazil	**72**	H13	0 50S	48 07W
Vigo Sp.	**79**	A5	42 15N	8 44W
Vijayawada India	**90**	E3	16 34N	80 40E
Vijosë *r.* Albania	**81**	H4	40 30N	20 00E
Vila Vanuatu	**103**	N7	17 45S	168 18E
Vila Nova de Gaia Port.	**79**	A4	41 08N	8 37W
Vila Real Port.	**79**	B4	41 17N	7 45W
Vila Velha Brazil	**72**	J9	20 23S	40 18W
Vilhena Brazil	**72**	E11	12 40S	60 08W
Villach Austria	**81**	D7	46 37N	13 51E
Villa Constitución Mexico	**66**	B5	25 05N	111 45W
Villahermosa Mexico	**66**	F3	18 00N	92 53W
Villalba Sp.	**79**	B5	43 17N	7 41W
Villa María Argentina	**73**	E7	32 25S	63 15W
Villa Montes Bolivia	**72**	E9	21 15S	63 30W
Villanueva Mexico	**66**	D4	22 24N	102 53W
Villarrica Chile	**73**	C6	39 15S	72 15W
Villarrobledo Sp.	**79**	D3	39 16N	2 36W
Villa Unión Argentina	**73**	D8	29 27S	62 46W
Villa Unión Mexico	**66**	C4	23 10N	106 12W
Villavicencio Col.	**72**	C14	4 09N	73 38W
Villefranche-sur-Saône Fr.	**79**	H6	46 00N	4 43E
Villeneuve-sur-Lot Fr.	**79**	F6	44 25N	0 43E
Villeurbanne Fr.	**79**	H6	45 46N	4 54E
Vilyuy *r.* Russia	**87**	Q9	64 00N	123 00E
Vilyuysk Russia	**87**	Q9	63 46N	121 35E
Viña del Mar Chile	**73**	C7	33 02S	71 35W
Vinaroz Sp.	**79**	F4	40 29N	0 28E
Vincennes Indiana USA	**63**	J4	38 42N	87 30W
Vindhya Range *mts.* India	**90**	D4	23 00N	75 00E
Vineland New Jersey USA	**63**	L4	39 29N	75 02W
Vinh Vietnam	**95**	D7	18 42N	105 41E
Vinkovci Croatia	**81**	G6	45 16N	18 49E
Vinnytsya Ukraine	**80**	M8	49 11N	28 30E
Vinson Massif *mts.* Antarctica	**109**		78 02S	22 00W
Vipiteno Italy	**81**	C7	46 54N	11 27E
Virgin *r.* USA	**62**	D4	37 00N	114 00W
Virginia Minnesota USA	**63**	H6	47 30N	92 28W
Virginia *state* USA	**63**	L4	38 00N	77 00W
Virginia Beach *tn.* Virginia USA	**63**	L4	36 51N	75 59W
Virgin Islands W. Indies	**67**	M3	18 00N	64 30W
Virovitica Croatia	**81**	F6	45 50N	17 25E
Vis *i.* Croatia	**81**	F5	43 00N	16 00E
Visalia California USA	**62**	C4	36 20N	119 18W
Visby Sweden	**80**	G12	57 32N	18 15E
Vise *i.* Russia	**87**	K12	79 30N	77 00E
Viseu Port.	**79**	B4	40 40N	7 55W
Vishakhapatnam India	**90**	E3	17 42N	83 24E
Vista California USA	**64**	E1	33 12N	117 15W
Viterbo Italy	**81**	D5	42 24N	12 06E
Vitichi Bolivia	**72**	D9	20 14S	65 22W
Viti Levu *i.* Fiji	**106**	T15	18 10S	177 55E
Vitim Russia	**87**	P8	59 28N	112 35E
Vitim *r.* Russia	**87**	P8	58 00N	113 00E
Vitória Brazil	**72**	J9	20 20S	40 18W
Vitória da Conquista Brazil	**72**	J11	14 53S	40 52W
Vitoria Gasteiz Sp.	**79**	D5	42 51N	2 40W
Vitry-le-François Fr.	**78**	H8	48 44N	4 36E
Vityaz Trench Pacific Ocean	**106**	G7	9 30S	170 00E
Vivi *r.* Russia	**87**	M10	61 00N	96 00E
Vizianagaram India	**90**	E3	18 07N	83 30E
Vladikavkaz Russia	**86**	G5	43 02N	44 43E
Vladimir Russia	**86**	G8	56 08N	40 25E
Vladimir Volynskiy Ukraine	**80**	K9	50 51N	24 19E
Vladivostok Russia	**87**	R5	43 09N	131 53E
Vlissingen Neths.	**78**	G9	51 27N	3 35E
Vlorë Albania	**81**	G4	40 29N	19 29E
Vltava *r.* Czech Rep.	**80**	E8	49 00N	14 00E
Voi Kenya	**100**	M7	3 23S	38 35E
Volga *r.* Russia	**86**	G6	50 00N	45 00E
Volgodonsk Russia	**86**	G6	47 35N	42 08E
Volgograd Russia	**86**	G6	48 45N	44 30E
Vologda Russia	**86**	F8	59 10N	39 55E
Vólos Greece	**81**	J3	39 22N	22 57E
Volta, Lake Ghana	**100**	D9	7 30N	0 30W
Volturno *r.* Italy	**81**	E4	41 00N	14 00E
Volzhskiy Russia	**86**	G6	48 48N	44 45E
Vóreioi Sporádes *is.* Greece	**81**	J3/K3	39 00N	24 00E
Vorkuta Russia	**86**	J10	67 27N	64 00E
Voronezh Russia	**86**	F7	51 40N	39 13E
Vørterkaka Nunatak *mt.* Antarctica	**109**		71 45S	32 00E
Vosges *mts.* Fr.	**78**	J8	48 10N	6 50E
Vostochnyy Russia	**87**	R5	42 52N	132 56E
Vouga *r.* Port.	**79**	A4	40 45N	8 15W
Vranje SM	**81**	H5	42 33N	21 54E
Vratsa Bulgaria	**81**	J5	43 12N	23 32E
Vrbas *r.* Bosnia-Herzegovina	**81**	F6	44 00N	17 00E
Vršac SM	**81**	H6	45 07N	21 19E
Vryburg RSA	**101**	J2	26 57S	24 44E
Vukovar Croatia	**81**	G6	45 19N	19 01E
Vung Tau Vietnam	**95**	D6	10 21N	107 04E
Vunisea Fiji	**106**	U15	19 04S	178 09E
Vyatka *r.* Russia	**86**	G8	58 00N	50 00E
Vyborg Russia	**86**	E9	60 45N	28 41E
Vychegda *r.* Russia	**86**	H9	62 00N	52 00E

W

Wa Ghana	**100**	D10	10 07N	2 28W
Wabash *r.* USA	**63**	J4	38 00N	87 30W
Wabuska Nevada USA	**64**	D4	39 09N	119 13W
Waco Texas USA	**63**	G3	31 33N	97 10W
Waddeneilanden Neths.	**78**	H10	53 25N	5 15E
Waddenzee *sea* Neths.	**78**	H10	53 15N	5 15E
Wādī al 'Arabah *r.* Israel	**88**	N10	30 30N	35 10E
Wādī al Masīlah *r.* Yemen	**89**	F2	16 00N	50 00E
Wâdi el Gafra Egypt	**101**	R2	30 16N	31 46E
Wadi Halfa Sudan	**100**	L12	21 55N	31 20E
Wad Medani Sudan	**100**	L10	14 24N	33 30E
Wagga Wagga Aust.	**103**	J3	35 07S	147 24E
Wagin Aust.	**102**	C4	33 20S	117 15E
Waglan Island HK China	**92**	C1	22 11N	114 18E
Wah Pakistan	**90**	C6	33 50N	72 44E
Waha Libya	**100**	H13	28 10N	19 57E
Wahpeton North Dakota USA	**63**	G6	46 16N	96 36W
Waialua Hawaiian Islands	**107**	X18	21 35N	158 08W
Waigeo *i.* Indonesia	**95**	J3	0 15S	130 45E
Wailuku Hawaiian Islands	**107**	Y18	20 54N	156 30W
Wajima Japan	**94**	C2	37 23N	136 53E
Wajir Kenya	**100**	M8	1 46N	40 05E
Wakasa-wan *b.* Japan	**94**	C2	35 40N	135 30E
Wakayama Japan	**94**	C1	34 12N	135 10E
Wakefield Rhode Island USA	**65**	E2	41 26N	71 30W
Wake Islands Pacific Ocean	**106**	G9	19 18N	166 36E
Wakkanai Japan	**94**	D4	45 26N	141 43E
Wałbrzych Poland	**80**	F9	50 48N	16 19E
Wales *admin.* UK	**78**	C10	52 40N	3 30W
Walhalla North Dakota USA	**43**	D1	48 55N	97 55W
Walker *r.* Nevada USA	**64**	D4	39 08N	119 00W
Walker Lake Nevada USA	**62**	C4	38 40N	118 43W
Wallaroo Aust.	**102**	G4	33 57S	137 36E
Walla Walla Washington USA	**62**	C6	46 05N	118 18W
Wallis and Futuna *is.* Pacific Ocean	**106**	J6	13 16S	176 15W
Walsenburg Colorado USA	**62**	F4	37 36N	104 48W
Waltham Massachusetts USA	**65**	E3	42 23N	71 14W
Walvis Bay *tn.* Namibia	**101**	G3	22 59S	14 31E
Walvis Ridge Atlantic Ocean	**108**	J3	30 00S	3 00E
Walyevo Fiji	**106**	V16	17 35S	179 58W
Wamba *r.* CDR	**101**	H6	6 30S	17 30E
Wanganui NZ	**103**	P3	39 56S	175 03E
Wang Chau *i.* HK China	**92**	D1	22 19N	114 22E
Wanxian China	**93**	K5	30 54N	108 20E
Warangal India	**90**	D3	18 00N	79 35E
Wardha *r.* India	**90**	D4	20 30N	79 00E
Warner Springs *tn.* California USA	**64**	E1	33 19N	116 38W
Warren Michigan USA	**45**	K2	42 30N	83 02W
Warren Ohio USA	**63**	K5	41 15N	80 49W
Warren Pennsylvania USA	**46**	G1	41 52N	79 09W
Warrnambool Aust.	**103**	H3	38 23S	142 03E
Warroad Minnesota USA	**43**	E1	48 59N	95 20W
Warsaw Poland	**80**	H10	52 15N	21 00E
Warta *r.* Poland	**80**	F10	52 00N	17 00E
Warwick Aust.	**103**	K5	28 12S	152 00E
Warwick Rhode Island USA	**63**	M5	41 42N	71 23W
Wasco California USA	**64**	D2	35 36N	119 20W
Washburn Wisconsin USA	**45**	F4	46 41N	90 53W
Washington *state* USA	**62**	B6/C6	47 00N	120 00W
Washington Crossing *tn.* New Jersey USA	**65**	C2	40 18N	74 52W
Washington D.C. District of Columbia USA	**63**	L4	38 55N	77 00W
Wash, The *b.* UK	**78**	F10	52 55N	0 10E
Watampone Indonesia	**95**	G3	4 33S	120 20E
Waterbury Connecticut USA	**65**	D2	41 34N	73 02W
Waterford RoI	**78**	B10	52 15N	7 06W
Waterloo Iowa USA	**63**	H5	42 30N	92 20W
Waterloo New York USA	**47**	K2	42 54N	76 53W
Watersmeet Michigan USA	**45**	G4	46 16N	89 10W
Watertown New York USA	**63**	L5	43 57N	75 56W
Watertown South Dakota USA	**63**	G5	44 54N	97 08W
Waterville Maine USA	**63**	N5	44 34N	69 41W
Waterville New York USA	**47**	L2	42 55N	75 24W
Waterville Ohio USA	**46**	C1	41 29N	83 44W
Watkins Glen *tn.* New York USA	**47**	K2	42 23N	76 53W
Watsonville California USA	**64**	C3	36 59N	121 47W
Wau PNG	**103**	J9	7 22S	146 40E
Wau Sudan	**100**	K9	7 40N	28 04E
Waukegan Illinois USA	**63**	J5	42 21N	87 52W
Waukesha Wisconsin USA	**63**	J5	43 01N	88 14W
Wausau Wisconsin USA	**63**	J5	44 58N	89 40W
Wawona California USA	**64**	D3	37 32N	119 39W
Waycross Georgia USA	**63**	K3	31 12N	82 22W
Webster New York USA	**47**	J3	43 13N	77 26W
Weddell Sea Southern Ocean	**109**		71 00S	40 00W
Weiden Germany	**80**	D8	49 40N	12 10E
Weifang China	**93**	M6	36 44N	119 10E
Wei He *r.* China	**93**	K5	34 00N	106 00E
Weipa Aust.	**103**	H8	12 35S	141 56E
Weirton West Virginia USA	**63**	K5	40 24N	80 37W
Wejherowo Poland	**80**	G11	54 36N	18 12E
Wellesley Islands Aust.	**103**	G7	16 30S	139 00E
Wellington NZ	**103**	P2	41 17S	174 46E
Wellington Kansas USA	**63**	G4	37 17N	97 25W
Wellington Nevada USA	**64**	D4	38 45N	119 23W
Wellsboro Pennsylvania USA	**47**	J1	41 45N	77 18W
Wellsville New York USA	**46**	J2	42 07N	77 56W
Wels Austria	**80**	D8	48 10N	14 02E
Wenzhou China	**93**	N4	28 02N	120 40E
Weser *r.* Germany	**80**	B10	53 00N	8 00E
West Australian Basin Indian Ocean	**105**	J4/J5	20 00S	100 00E
West Bank *territory* Israel	**88**	N10	32 00N	35 00E
West Bengal *admin.* India	**91**	F4	22 00N	88 00E
West Branch Michigan USA	**45**	J3	44 17N	84 16W
Westby Montana USA	**42**	E1	48 52N	104 04W
West Caroline Basin Pacific Ocean	**106**	D8	3 00N	136 00E
West Chester Pennsylvania USA	**65**	C1	39 57N	75 36W
Western Australia *state* Aust.	**102**	B6/E6	25 00S	117 00E
Western Ghats *mts.* India	**90**	C3/D2	15 30N	74 00E
WESTERN SAHARA	**100**	A12		
Western Sayan *mts.* Russia	**87**	L7/M7	52 30N	92 30E
Westerwald *geog. reg.* Germany	**80**	A9/B9	50 00N	8 00E
West European Basin Atlantic Ocean	**108**	G11	47 00N	18 00W
West Falkland *i.* Falkland Islands	**73**	E3/F3	51 00S	60 40W
Westfield Massachusetts USA	**65**	D3	42 08N	72 45W
Westfield New York USA	**46**	G2	42 20N	79 34W
West Grand Lake Maine USA	**51**	F1	44 15N	68 00W
Westhope North Dakota USA	**42**	G1	48 57N	101 02W
West Indies *is.* Caribbean Sea	**67**	K4/L4	22 00N	69 00W
Westlake Ohio USA	**46**	E1	41 25N	81 54W
West Lamma Channel HK China	**92**	B1	22 14N	114 05E
West Marianas Basin Pacific Ocean	**106**	D9	16 00N	137 30E
West Memphis Arkansas USA	**63**	H4	35 09N	90 11W
West Palm Beach *tn.* Florida USA	**63**	K2	26 42N	80 05W
West Plains *tn.* Missouri USA	**63**	H4	36 44N	91 51W
Westport RoI	**78**	A10	53 48N	9 32W
Westport California USA	**64**	B4	39 39N	123 47
Westport Connecticut USA	**65**	D2	41 08N	73 21W
West Siberian Lowland Russia	**86**	K8/K9	60 00N	75 00E
West Virginia *state* USA	**63**	K4	39 00N	81 00W
Wetar *i.* Indonesia	**95**	H2	7 15S	126 45E
Wewak PNG	**103**	H10	3 35S	143 35E
Wexford RoI	**78**	B10	52 20N	6 27W
Weymouth UK	**78**	D9	50 37N	2 25W
Weymouth Massachusetts USA	**65**	E3	42 13N	70 59W
Whangarei NZ	**103**	P3	35 43S	174 19E
Wharfe *r.* UK	**78**	E11	54 10N	2 05W
Wharton Pennsylvania USA	**46**	H1	41 31N	78 00W
Wharton Basin Indian Ocean	**105**	J5	15 00S	100 00E
Whatcom, Lake Washington USA	**38**	H4	48 40N	122 26W
Wheeler Lake Alabama USA	**63**	J3	34 00N	87 00W
Wheeling West Virginia USA	**63**	K5	40 05N	80 43W
Whidbey Island Washington USA	**38**	H4	48 20N	122 38W
White *r.* Arkansas USA	**63**	H4	35 00N	92 00W
White *r.* Nevada USA	**64**	F4	38 40N	115 10W
White *r.* South Dakota USA	**62**	F5	43 00N	103 00W
White Nile Dam Sudan	**100**	L11	14 18N	32 20E
White Sea Russia	**86**	F10	66 00N	37 30E
White Volta *r.* Ghana	**100**	D9	9 30N	1 30W
Whitewater Montana USA	**42**	D1	48 46N	107 37W
Whitewater Creek *r.* Montana USA	**42**	D1	48 46N	107 36W
Whitney, Mount California USA	**62**	C4	36 35N	118 17W
Whitney Point *tn.* New York USA	**65**	C3	42 20N	75 58W
Whyalla Aust.	**102**	G4	33 04S	137 34E
Wichita Kansas USA	**63**	G4	37 43N	97 20W
Wichita *r.* Texas USA	**62**	F3	33 00N	100 00W
Wichita Falls *tn.* Texas USA	**63**	G3	33 55N	98 30W
Wick UK	**78**	D13	58 26N	3 06W
Wickliffe Ohio USA	**46**	E1	41 38N	81 25W
Wicklow RoI	**78**	B10	52 59N	6 03W
Wicklow Mountains RoI	**78**	B10	53 00N	6 20W
Wiener Neustadt Austria	**80**	F7	47 49N	16 15E
Wieprz *r.* Poland	**80**	J9	51 00N	23 00E
Wiesbaden Germany	**80**	B9	50 05N	8 15E
Wildrose North Dakota USA	**42**	F1	48 38N	103 11W
Wilhelm II Land *geog. reg.* Antarctica	**109**		70 00S	90 00E
Wilhelmshaven Germany	**80**	B10	53 32N	8 07E
Wilkes-Barre Pennsylvania USA	**63**	L5	41 15N	75 50W
Wilkes Land *geog. reg.* Antarctica	**109**		68 00S	105 00E
Willemstad Curaçao	**67**	L2	12 12N	68 56W
Williams California USA	**64**	B4	39 09N	122 09W
Williams Minnesota USA	**43**	E1	48 45N	94 55W
Williamsport Pennsylvania USA	**63**	L5	41 16N	77 03W
Williston North Dakota USA	**62**	F6	48 09N	103 39W
Willits California USA	**64**	B4	39 23N	123 22W
Willmar Minnesota USA	**63**	G6	45 06N	95 03W
Willoughby Hills *tn.* Ohio USA	**46**	E1	41 35N	81 29W
Willow Creek *r.* Montana USA	**41**	G1	48 40N	111 20W
Willow River Michigan USA	**46**	D3	43 50N	82 58W

Willows California USA	64	B4	39 32N	122 10W
Willow Springs *tn.* Missouri USA	63	H4	36 59N	91 59W
Wilmington Delaware USA	63	L4	39 46N	75 31W
Wilmington North Carolina USA	63	L3	34 14N	77 55W
Wilson New York USA	48	D2	43 15N	78 50W
Wilson North Carolina USA	63	L4	35 43N	77 56W
Wiluna Aust.	102	D5	26 37S	120 12E
Winchendon Massachusetts USA	65	D3	42 41N	72 03W
Winchester UK	78	E9	51 04N	1 19W
Winchester Virginia USA	63	L4	39 11N	78 12W
Windhoek Namibia	101	H3	22 34S	17 06E
Wind River Range *mts.* Wyoming USA	62	E5	43 00N	109 00W
Windsor Locks *tn.* Connecticut USA	65	D2	41 55N	72 37W
Windward Islands Lesser Antilles	67	M2	12 30N	62 00W
Windward Passage *sd.* Cuba/Haiti	67	K3/K4	20 00N	73 00W
Winnemucca Nevada USA	62	C5	40 58N	117 45W
Winona Minnesota USA	63	H5	44 02N	91 37W
Winslow Arizona USA	62	D4	35 01N	110 43W
Winston-Salem North Carolina USA	63	K4	36 05N	80 18W
Winterthur Switz.	79	K7	47 30N	8 45E
Winthrop Washington USA	38	H4	48 35N	120 10W
Winton Aust.	103	H6	22 22S	143 00E
Wisconsin *r.* Wisconsin USA	63	H5	45 00N	90 00W
Wisconsin *state* USA	63	H6/J6	45 00N	90 00W
Wisconsin Rapids *tn.* Wisconsin USA	45	G3	44 23N	89 51W
Wisła *r.* Poland	80	G10	53 00N	19 00E
Wisłok *r.* Poland	80	J9	50 00N	22 00E
Wismar Germany	80	C10	53 54N	11 28E
Wittenberg Germany	80	D9	51 53N	12 39E
Wittenberge Germany	80	C10	52 59N	11 45E
Włocławek Poland	80	G10	52 39N	19 01E
Wolcott New York USA	47	K3	43 13N	76 49W
Wolfsberg Austria	81	E7	46 50N	14 50E
Wolfsburg Germany	80	C10	52 27N	10 49E
Wollongong Aust.	103	K4	34 25S	150 52E
Wolverhampton UK	78	D10	52 36N	2 08W
Wompah Aust.	103	H5	29 04S	142 05E
Wong Chuk Hang HK China	92	C1	22 15N	114 10E
Wonju South Korea	93	P6	37 24N	127 52E
Wonsan North Korea	93	P6	39 07N	127 26E
Woodfords California USA	64	D4	38 47N	119 50W
Woodland California USA	64	C4	38 42N	121 47W
Woodlark Island PNG	103	K9	9 10S	152 50E
Woodward Oklahoma USA	62	G4	36 26N	99 25W
Woonsocket Rhode Island USA	65	E2	42 01N	71 30W
Worcester RSA	101	H1	33 39S	19 26E
Worcester UK	78	D10	52 11N	2 13W
Worcester Massachusetts USA	63	M5	42 17N	71 48W
Workington UK	78	D11	54 39N	3 33W
Worland Wyoming USA	62	E5	44 01N	107 58W
Worthing UK	78	E9	50 48N	0 23W
Worthington Minnesota USA	63	G5	43 37N	95 36W
Wrangel Island Russia	87	V11	61 30N	180 00
Wrangell Alaska USA	38	D5	56 28N	132 23W
Wrangell Island Alaska USA	38	D5	56 25N	132 05W
Wrangell Mountains Alaska USA	54	B3	62 00N	143 00W
Wrangell-St. Elias National Park Alaska USA	54	B3	62 00N	142 30W
Wrexham UK	78	D10	53 03N	3 00W
Wrights Corner New York USA	48	D2	43 10N	78 45W
Wrightsville Pennsylvania USA	65	B2	40 02N	76 32W
Wrocław Poland	80	F9	51 05N	17 00E
Wu Chau Tong HK China	92	C2	22 30N	114 18E
Wuhai China	93	K6	39 40N	106 40E
Wuhan China	93	L5	30 35N	114 19E
Wuhu China	93	M5	31 23N	118 25E
Wukari Nigeria	100	F9	7 49N	9 49E
Wu Kau Tang HK China	92	C3	22 30N	114 15E
Wuppertal Germany	80	A9	51 15N	7 10E
Wurno Nigeria	100	F10	13 18N	5 29E
Wurtsboro New York USA	65	C2	41 35N	74 29W
Würtzburg Germany	80	B8	49 48N	9 57E
Wusul Jiang *r.* China	93	Q8	47 00N	134 00E
Wutongqiao China	93	J2	29 21N	103 48E
Wuxi China	93	N5	31 35N	120 19E
Wuyi Shan *mts.* China	93	M4	26 00N	116 30E
Wuzhou China	93	L3	23 30N	111 21E
Wyandotte Michigan USA	45	K2	42 11N	83 10W
Wye *r.* UK	78	D10	51 50N	2 40W
Wyndham Aust.	102	E7	15 30S	128 09E
Wyoming Michigan USA	45	J2	42 54N	85 44W
Wyoming *state* USA	62	E5	43 00N	108 00W

X

Xaafuun Somalia	100	Q10	10 27N	51 15E
Xam Hua Laos	93	J3	20 28N	104 05E
Xánthi Greece	81	K4	41 07N	24 56E
Xiamen China	93	M3	24 28N	118 05E
Xi'an China	93	K5	34 16N	108 54E
Xiangfan China	93	L5	32 05N	112 03E
Xiangkhoang Laos	95	C7	19 21N	102 23E
Xiangtan China	93	L4	27 48N	112 55E
Xianyang China	93	K5	34 22N	108 42E
Xigaze China	92	F4	29 18N	88 50E
Xi Jiang *r.* China	93	L3	23 30N	111 00E
Xingtai China	93	L6	37 08N	114 29E
Xingu *r.* Brazil	72	G12	5 00S	54 00W
Xining China	93	J6	36 35N	101 55E
Xinjiang Uygur Zizhiqu *admin.* China	92	E7/F7	41 00N	85 00E
Xinjin China	93	N6	39 25N	121 58E
Xiqing Shan *mts.* China	93	J5	34 00N	102 30E
Xizang Zizhiqu *admin.* China	92	E5/G5	33 30N	85 00E
Xochimilco Mexico	66	E3	19 08N	99 09W
Xuanhua China	93	M7	40 36N	115 01E
Xuchang China	93	L5	34 03N	113 48E
Xuwen China	93	L3	20 25N	110 08E
Xuzhou China	93	M5	34 17N	117 18E

Y

Yablonovy Range *mts.* Russia	87	N7/P7	51 30N	110 00E
Yabrūd Syria	88	P11	33 58N	36 39E
Yaizu Japan	94	C1	34 54N	138 20E
Yakima Washington USA	62	B6	46 37N	120 30W
Yakima *r.* Washington USA	62	B6	47 00N	120 00W
Yaku-shima *i.* Japan	94	B1	30 00N	130 30E
Yakutat Alaska USA	38	A6	59 50N	139 49W
Yakutat Bay Alaska USA	38	A6	59 50N	140 00W
Yakutsk Russia	87	Q9	62 10N	129 50E
Yalu *r.* China/North Korea	93	P7	41 00N	126 00E
Yamagata Japan	94	D2	38 16N	140 16E
Yamaguchi Japan	94	B1	34 10N	131 28E
Yamal Peninsula Russia	86	J11	72 00N	70 00E
Yambio Sudan	100	K8	4 34N	28 21E
Yambol Bulgaria	81	L5	42 28N	26 30E
Yamburg Russia	87	K10	68 19N	77 09E
Yamoussoukro Côte d'Ivoire	100	C9	6 50N	5 20W
Yamuna *r.* India	90	E5	26 00N	80 30E
Yamunanagar India	90	D6	30 07N	77 17E
Yana *r.* Russia	87	R10	69 00N	135 00E
Yanbu'al Baḩr Saudi Arabia	88	C3	24 07N	38 04E
Yangcheng China	93	N5	33 23N	120 10E
Yangon Myanmar	95	B7	16 47N	96 10E
Yangquan China	93	L6	37 52N	113 29E
Yanji China	93	P7	42 52N	129 32E
Yanjing China	93	H4	29 01N	98 38E
Yankton South Dakota USA	63	G5	42 53N	97 24W
Yantai China	93	N6	37 30N	121 22E
Yaoundé Cameroon	100	G8	3 51N	11 31E
Yap Islands Pacific Ocean	106	D8	9 30N	138 09E
Yap Trench Pacific Ocean	106	D8	10 00N	139 00E
Yaqui *r.* Mexico	66	C5	28 00N	109 50W
Yarlung Zangbo *r.* China	92	G4	29 00N	92 30E
Yaroslavl' Russia	86	F8	57 34N	39 52E
Yarumal Col.	72	B15	6 59N	75 25W
Yasawa *i.* Fiji	106	T16	16 50S	177 30E
Yasawa Group *is.* Fiji	106	T16	17 00S	177 40E
Yatsushiro Japan	94	B1	32 32N	130 35E
Yau Tong HK China	92	C1	22 18N	114 14E
Yavari *r.* Peru/Brazil	72	C13	5 00S	72 30W
Yawatahama Japan	94	B1	33 27N	132 24E
Yazd Iran	89	F5	31 54N	54 22E
Yazoo *r.* Mississippi USA	63	H3	33 00N	90 00W
Ye Myanmar	95	B7	15 15N	97 50E
Yekaterinburg Russia	86	J8	56 52N	60 35E
Yell *i.* UK	78	E14	60 35N	1 10W
Yellow Sea China	93	N6	35 30N	122 30E
Yellowstone *r.* USA	62	E6	46 00N	108 00W
Yellowstone Lake Wyoming USA	62	D5	44 30N	110 20W
YEMEN REPUBLIC	88/89	D2/E2		
Yenisey *r.* Russia	87	L9	64 00N	87 30E
Yenisey, Gulf of Russia	87	K11	72 30N	80 00E
Yeniseysk Russia	87	M8	58 27N	92 13E
Yeppoon Aust.	103	K6	23 05S	150 42E
Yerington Nevada USA	64	D4	39 00N	119 11W
Yesilirmak *r.* Turkey	88	C7	41 00N	36 25E
Ye Xian China	93	M6	37 10N	119 55E
Yiannitsá Greece	81	J4	40 46N	22 24E
Yibin China	93	J4	28 42N	104 30E
Yichang China	93	L5	30 46N	111 20E
Yinchuan China	93	K6	38 30N	106 19E
Yingkou China	93	N7	40 40N	122 17E
Yining China	92	E7	43 50N	81 28E
Yi Pak HK China	92	B1	22 18N	114 01E
Yirga Alem Ethiopia	100	M9	6 48N	38 22E
Yiyang China	93	L4	28 39N	112 10E
Yoakum Texas USA	63	G2	29 18N	97 20W
Yogyakarta Indonesia	95	E2	7 48S	110 24E
Yoichi Japan	94	D3	43 14N	140 47E
Yokadouma Cameroon	100	H8	3 26N	15 06E
Yokkaichi Japan	94	C1	34 58N	136 38E
Yokohama Japan	94	C2	35 27N	139 38E
Yokosuka Japan	94	C2	35 18N	139 38E
Yokote Japan	94	D2	39 20N	140 31E
Yola Nigeria	100	G9	9 14N	12 32E
Yonago Japan	94	B2	35 27N	133 20E
Yonezawa Japan	94	D2	37 56N	140 06E
Yonkers New York USA	65	D2	40 58N	73 53W
Yonne *r.* Fr.	78	G8	48 00N	3 15E
York UK	78	E10	53 58N	1 05W
York Pennsylvania USA	63	L4	39 57N	76 44W
York, Cape Aust.	103	H8	10 42S	142 32E
Yosemite National Park California USA	64	D3	37 30N	119 00W
Yosu South Korea	93	P5	34 50N	127 30E
Youghal RoI	78	B9	51 51N	7 50W
You Jiang *r.* China	93	K3	23 30N	107 00E
Youngstown New York USA	46	G3	43 14N	79 01W
Youngstown Ohio USA	63	K5	41 05N	80 40W
Youngsville Pennsylvania USA	46	G1	41 52N	79 22W
Ypsilanti Michigan USA	46	C2	42 15N	83 36W
Ystad Sweden	80	D11	55 25N	13 50E
Yuba City California USA	62	B4	39 09N	121 36W
Yūbari Japan	94	D3	43 04N	141 59E
Yucatan *p.* Mexico	66	G3	19 00N	89 00W
Yucatan Basin Caribbean Sea	107	T9	20 00N	85 00W
Yucca Lake Nevada USA	64	F3	37 00N	116 02W
Yuci China	93	L6	37 40N	112 44E
Yuen Long HK China	92	B2	22 26N	114 02E
Yugakir Plateau Russia	87	T10	66 30N	156 00E
Yu Jiang *r.* China	93	K3	23 00N	109 00E
Yukon Flats National Wildlife Refuge Alaska USA	54	A4	66 30N	147 30W
Yuma Arizona USA	62	D3	32 40N	114 39W
Yumen China	93	H6	39 54N	97 43E
Yung Shue Wan *tn.* HK China	92	B1	22 13N	114 06E
Yurimaguas Peru	72	B12	5 54S	76 07W
Yuzhno-Sakhalinsk Russia	87	S6	46 58N	142 45E
Yverdon Switz.	79	J7	46 47N	6 38E
Yvetot Fr.	78	F8	49 37N	0 45E

Z

Zaanstad Neths.	78	H10	52 27N	4 49E
Zābol Iran	89	H5	31 00N	61 32E
Zabrze Poland	80	G9	50 18N	18 47E
Zacapa Guatemala	66	G3	15 00N	89 30E
Zacatecas Mexico	66	D4	22 48N	102 33W
Zacatecoluca El Salvador	66	G2	13 29N	88 51W
Zadar Croatia	81	E6	44 07N	15 14E
Zafra Sp.	79	B3	38 25N	6 25W
Żagań Poland	80	E9	51 37N	15 20E
Zagreb Croatia	81	E6	45 48N	15 58E
Zagros Mountains Iran	89	E5/F5	32 45N	48 50E
Zāhedān Iran	89	H4	29 32N	60 54E
Zahlé Lebanon	88	N11	33 50N	35 55E
Zakopane Poland	80	G8	49 17N	19 54E
Zákynthos *i.* Greece	81	H2	37 45N	20 50E
Zalaegerszeg Hungary	81	F7	46 53N	16 51E
Zalău Romania	81	J7	47 10N	23 04E
Zaltan Libya	100	H13	28 15N	19 52E
Zambeze *r.* Mozambique	101	L4	16 00S	34 00E
Zambezi Zambia	101	J5	13 33S	23 08E
Zambezi *r.* Zambia/Zimbabwe	101	J4	16 00S	23 00E
ZAMBIA	101	J5/L5		
Zamboanga Philippines	95	G5	6 55N	122 05E
Zamora Sp.	79	C4	41 30N	5 45W
Zamość Poland	80	J9	50 43N	23 15E
Zanderij Suriname	72	F15	5 26N	55 14W
Zanesville Ohio USA	63	K4	39 55N	82 02W
Zanjān Iran	89	E6	36 40N	48 30E
Zanthus Aust.	102	D4	31 01S	123 32E
Zanzibar Tanzania	101	M6	6 10S	39 12E
Zanzibar *i.* Tanzania	100/101	M6	6 10S	39 13E
Zaozhuang China	93	M5	34 53N	117 38E
Zaragoza Sp.	79	E4	41 39N	0 54W
Zarand Iran	89	G5	30 50N	56 35E
Zaraza Venezuela	72	D15	9 23N	65 20W
Zarembo Island Alaska USA	38	D5	56 30N	132 50W
Zaria Nigeria	100	F10	11 01N	7 44E
Zarqa Jordan	88	C5	32 04N	36 05E
Zefat Israel	88	N11	32 57N	35 27E
Zell-am-See *tn.* Austria	81	D7	47 19N	12 47E
Zenica Bosnia-Herzegovina	81	F6	44 11N	17 53E
Zephyr Cove *tn.* Nevada USA	64	D4	39 07N	119 57W
Zeya Russia	87	Q7	53 48N	127 14E
Zeya *r.* Russia	87	Q7	53 00N	127 30E
Zêzere *r.* Port.	79	B3	39 50N	8 05W
Zgierz Poland	80	G9	51 52N	19 25E
Zgorzelec Poland	80	E9	51 10N	15 00E
Zhambyl Kazakhstan	86	K5	42 50N	71 25E
Zhangjiakou China	93	L7	40 51N	114 59E
Zhangzhou China	93	M3	24 31N	117 40E
Zhanjiang China	93	L3	21 10N	110 20E
Zhengzhou China	93	L5	34 45N	113 38E
Zhezkazgan Kazakhstan	86	J6	47 44N	67 42E
Zhigansk Russia	87	Q10	66 48N	123 27E
Zhmerynka Ukraine	80	M8	49 00N	28 02E
Zhob Pakistan	90	B6	31 30N	69 30E
Zhob *r.* Pakistan	90	B6	30 55N	68 01E
Zhoukou China	93	L5	33 35N	114 41E
Zhuzhou China	93	L4	27 53N	113 07E
Zhytomyr Ukraine	80	M9	50 18N	28 40E
Zibo China	93	M6	36 51N	118 01E
Zielona Góra Poland	80	E9	51 57N	15 30E
Zigong China	93	J4	29 25N	104 47E
Ziguinchor Senegal	100	A10	12 35N	16 20W
ZIMBABWE	101	K4/L4		
Zinder Niger	100	F10	13 46N	8 58E
Ziqudukou China	92	H5	33 03N	95 51E
Zlatoust Russia	86	H8	55 10N	59 38E
Zlín Czech Rep.	80	F8	49 14N	17 40E
Znojmo Czech Rep.	80	F8	48 52N	16 04E
Zolochev Ukraine	80	K8	49 49N	24 53E
Zomba Malawi	101	M4	15 22S	35 22E
Zonguldak Turkey	88	B7	41 26N	31 47E
Zouar Chad	100	H12	20 30N	16 30E
Zouérate Mauritania	100	B12	22 44N	12 21W
Zrenjanin SM	81	H6	45 22N	20 23E
Zújar *r.* Sp.	79	C3	38 35N	5 30W
Zunyi China	93	K4	27 35N	106 48E
Zürich Switz.	79	K7	47 23N	8 33E
Zvishavane Zimbabwe	101	L3	20 20S	30 02E
Zwickau Germany	80	D9	50 43N	12 30E
Zyrardów Poland	80	H10	52 02N	20 28E
Zyryanka Russia	87	T10	65 42N	150 49E

Glossary

Ákra	cape (Greek)
Älv	river (Swedish)
Bahia	bay (Spanish)
Bahr	stream (Arabic)
Baie	bay (French)
Bugt	bay (Danish)
Cabo	cape (Portugese; Spanish)
Cap	cape (French)
Capo	cape (Italian)
Cerro	hill (Spanish)
Chaîne	mountain range (French)
Chapada	hills (Portugese)
Chott	salt lake (Arabic)
Co	lake (Chinese)
Collines	hills (French)
Cordillera	mountain range (Spanish)
Costa	coast (Spanish)
Côte	coast (French)
-dake	peak (Japanese)
Danau	lake (Indonesian)
Dao	island (Chinese)
Dasht	desert (Persian; Urdu)
Djebel	mountain (Arabic)
Do	island (Korean; Vietnamese)
Embalse	reservoir (Spanish)
Erg	dunes (Arabic)
Estrecho	strait (Spanish)
Estreito	strait (Portugese)
Gebel	mountain (Arabic)
Golfe	gulf; bay (French)
Golfo	gulf; bay (Italian; Spanish)
Gölü	lake (Turkish)
Gora	mountain (Russian)
Gunto	islands (Japanese)
Gunung	mountain (Indonesian; Malay)
Hafen	harbour (German)
Hai	sea (Chinese)
Ho	river (Chinese)
Hu	lake (Chinese)
Île; Isle	island (French)
Ilha	island (Portugese)
Inseln	islands (German)
Isla	island (Spanish)
Istmo	isthmus (Spanish)
Jabal; Jebel	mountain (Arabic)
Jezero	lake (Serb-Croat)
Jezioro	lake (Polish)
Jiang	river (Chinese)
-jima	island (Japanese)
-kaikyō	strait (Japanese)
Kamen'	rock (Russian)
Kap	cape (Danish)
Kepulauan	islands (Indonesian)
-ko	lake (Japanese)
Lac	lake (French)
Lago	lake (Italian; Portugese; Spanish)
Laguna	lagoon (Spanish)
Ling	mountain range (Chinese)
Llyn	lake (Welsh)
-misaki	cape (Japanese)
Mont	mountain (French)
Montagne	mountain (French)
Monts	mountains (French)
Monti	mountains (Italian)
More	sea (Russian)
Muang	city (Thai)
Mys	cape (Russian)
-nada	gulf; sea (Japanese)
-nama	cape (Japanese)
Ostrova	islands (Russian)
Ozero	lake (Russian)
Pergunungan	mountain range (Indonesian)
Pendi	basin (Chinese)
Pic	summit (French; Spanish)
Pico	summit (Spanish)
Pik	summit (Russian)
Planalto	plateau (Portugese)
Planina	mountain range (Bulgarian; Serb-Croat)
Poluostrov	peninsula (Russian)
Puerto	port (Spanish)
Pulau-pulau	islands (Indonesian)
Puncak	mountain (Indonesian)
Punta	cape (Italian; Spanish)
Ras; Râs	cape (Arabic)
Ra's	cape (Persian)
Rio	river (Portugese; Spanish)
Rivière	river (French)
Rubha	cape (Gaelic)
-saki	cape (Japanese)
Salina	salt pan (Spanish)
-san	mountain (Japanese)
-sanchi	mountains (Japanese)
-sanmyaku	mountain range (Japanese)
Sebkra	salt pan (Arabic)
See	lake (German)
Selat	strait (Indonesian)
Seto	strait (Japanese)
Shan	mountains (Chinese)
-shima	island (Japanese)
-shotō	islands (Japanese)
Sierra	mountain range (Spanish)
Song	river (Vietnamese)
-suidō	strait (Japanese)
Tassili	plateau (Berber)
Tau	island (Chinese)
Teluk	bay (Indonesian)
-tō	island (Japanese)
Tonle	lake (Cambodian)
-wan	bay (Japanese)
-zaki	cape (Japanese)
Zaliv	bay (Russian)

OXFORD
UNIVERSITY PRESS

70 Wynford Drive, Don Mills, Ontario M3C 1J9
www.oup.com/ca

Oxford University Press is a department of the University of Oxford.

It furthers the University's objective of excellence in research, scholarship, and education by publishing worldwide in

Oxford New York
Auckland Bangkok Buenos Aires Cape Town Chennai
Dar es Salaam Delhi Hong Kong Istanbul Karachi Kolkata
Kuala Lumpur Madrid Melbourne Mexico City Mumbai Nairobi
São Paulo Shanghai Taipei Tokyo Toronto

Oxford is a registered trademark of Oxford University Press in the UK and in certain other countries

Published in Canada
By Oxford University Press

Copyright © Oxford University Press Canada 2003
The moral rights of the author have been asserted
Database right Oxford University Press (maker)
First published 2003

National Library of Canada Cataloguing in Publication Data

Oxford University Press (Canada)
Canadian Oxford school atlas / Quentin H. Stanford, general editor. — 8th ed.

Includes indexes.
ISBN 0-19-541895-6

1. Atlases, Canadian. 2. Canada–Maps. I. Stanford, Quentin H. II. Title.

G1021.O87 2003   912   C2003-900737-5

National Library of Canada Cataloguing in Publication Data

Oxford University Press (Canada)
Canadian Oxford world atlas / Quentin H. Stanford, general editor. — 5th ed.

ISBN 0-19-541898-0 (bound).—ISBN 0-19-541897-2 (pbk.)

1. Atlases, Canadian. I. Stanford, Quentin H. II. Title.

G1021.O88 2003   912   C2003-901748-6

Printed in Canada

This book is printed on permanent (acid-free) paper ∞

1 2 3 4 — 06 05 04 03

Acquisitions editor: Patti Henderson
Lead editor: Tracey MacDonald
Statistics editor: Heather Kidd
Cover design: Brett Miller
Cartography: Carolyn Anderson, Karen Brittin, Tracey Learoyd, Phoenix Mapping

Credits

Photos

Front cover image Canadian Oxford School Atlas, 8th. ed.: Satellite image of Ottawa, Canada, Digital Vision © 2003

Front cover Canadian Oxford World Atlas, 5th ed.: View from the space shuttle Atlantis of an icy Lake Superior in late march. Lakes Michigan and Huron can also be seen. © 1996 CORBIS; original image courtesy of NASA/CORBIS/MAGMA

p. 7 Satellite image of the area around Winnipeg, MB. Credit: Image ISS004-E-11412 courtesy of Earth Sciences & Image Analysis Laboratory, NASA Johnson Space Center (http://eol.jsc.nasa.gov)
p. 40 Satellite image of Vancouver urban area. Credit: © 1994 Pacific Geomatics Ltd.
p. 40 Satellite image of Calgary urban area. Credit: © 2001 Pacific Geomatics Limited
p. 49 Satellite image of Toronto urban area. Credit: Image STS100-E-5708 courtesy of Earth Sciences & Image Analysis Laboratory, NASA Johnson Space Center (http://eol.jsc.nasa.gov)
p. 49 Satellite image of the Golden Horseshoe. Credit: © AIR-SAT IMAGE MAPS (www.airsatimagemaps.com)
p. 56 Satellite image of Montreal urban area. Credit: © 2001 Pacific Geomatics Limited
p. 57 Satellite image of Halifax urban area. Credit: © 1999 Pacific Geomatics Limited
p. 57 Satellite image of Ottawa. Received by the Canada Centre for Remote Sensing. Processed by RADARSAT International Inc. © CNES 1987
p. 120 Boreal Forest © Jean du Boisberranger/The Image Bank/Getty Images

Maps and Statistics

Every possible effort has been made to trace the original source of material contained in this book. Where the attempt has been unsuccessful, the publisher would be pleased to hear from the copyright holders to rectify any omission.

Statistics Canada information is used with the permission of the Minister of Industry, as Minister responsible for Statistics Canada. Information on the availability of the wide range of data from Statistics Canada can be obtained from Statistics Canada's Regional Offices, World Wide Web site at http://www.statcan.ca, and its toll-free access number 1-800-263-1136.

Page 24 maps were adapted from Natural Resources Canada, Atlas Canada, Natural Hazards maps Web site, http://atlas.gc.ca/site/english/maps/environment/naturalhazards/

Pages 34-35 Statistical information from Census Canada, 2001

Page 36 map was adapted from Natural Resources Canada, Atlas of Canada Web site, http://atlas.gc.ca/site/english/maps/peopleandsociety/aboriginallanguages/bycommunity

World Flags

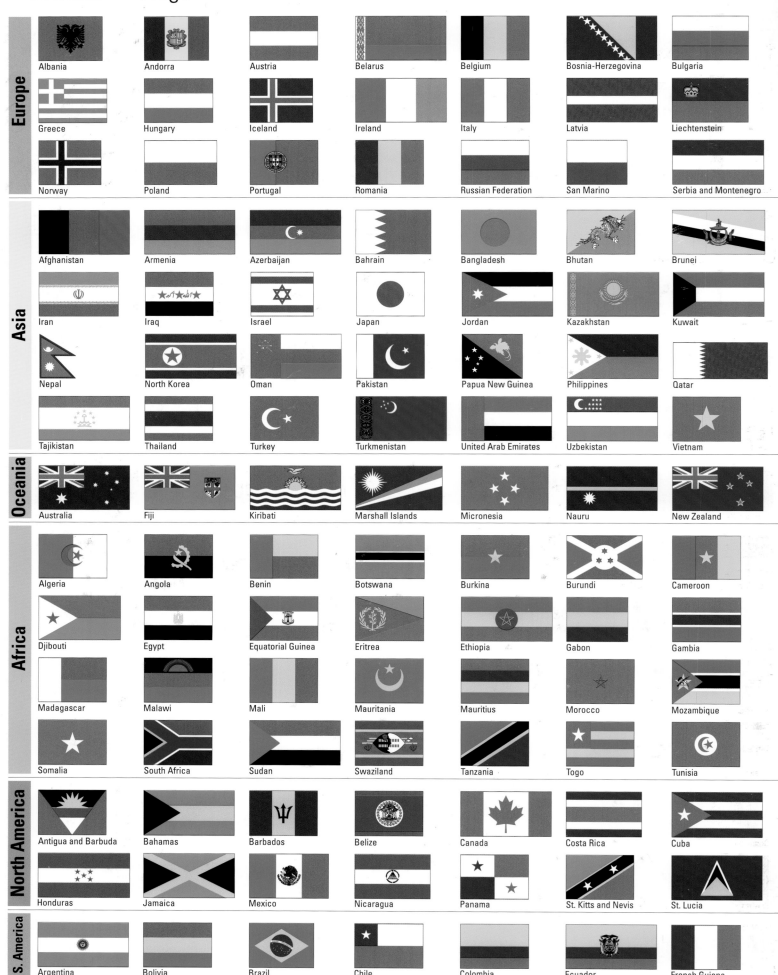

Europe

Albania, Andorra, Austria, Belarus, Belgium, Bosnia-Herzegovina, Bulgaria, Greece, Hungary, Iceland, Ireland, Italy, Latvia, Liechtenstein, Norway, Poland, Portugal, Romania, Russian Federation, San Marino, Serbia and Montenegro

Asia

Afghanistan, Armenia, Azerbaijan, Bahrain, Bangladesh, Bhutan, Brunei, Iran, Iraq, Israel, Japan, Jordan, Kazakhstan, Kuwait, Nepal, North Korea, Oman, Pakistan, Papua New Guinea, Philippines, Qatar, Tajikistan, Thailand, Turkey, Turkmenistan, United Arab Emirates, Uzbekistan, Vietnam

Oceania

Australia, Fiji, Kiribati, Marshall Islands, Micronesia, Nauru, New Zealand

Africa

Algeria, Angola, Benin, Botswana, Burkina, Burundi, Cameroon, Djibouti, Egypt, Equatorial Guinea, Eritrea, Ethiopia, Gabon, Gambia, Madagascar, Malawi, Mali, Mauritania, Mauritius, Morocco, Mozambique, Somalia, South Africa, Sudan, Swaziland, Tanzania, Togo, Tunisia

North America

Antigua and Barbuda, Bahamas, Barbados, Belize, Canada, Costa Rica, Cuba, Honduras, Jamaica, Mexico, Nicaragua, Panama, St. Kitts and Nevis, St. Lucia

S. America

Argentina, Bolivia, Brazil, Chile, Colombia, Ecuador, French Guiana